MW00776036

The Constitutional Bind

The Constitutional Bind

HOW AMERICANS CAME TO IDOLIZE
A DOCUMENT THAT FAILS THEM

Aziz Rana

The University of Chicago Press   Chicago and London

The University of Chicago Press, Chicago 60637
The University of Chicago Press, Ltd., London
© 2024 by The University of Chicago
Published 2024
Printed in the United States of America

33 32 31 30 29 28 27 26 25 24   1 2 3 4 5

ISBN-13: 978-0-226-35072-1 (cloth)
ISBN-13: 978-0-226-35086-8 (e-book)
DOI: https://doi.org/10.7208/chicago/9780226350868.001.0001

Library of Congress Cataloging-in-Publication Data

Names: Rana, Aziz, author.
Title: The constitutional bind : how Americans came to idolize a
    document that fails them / Aziz Rana.
Description: Chicago : The University of Chicago Press, 2024. |
    Includes bibliographical references and index.
Identifiers: LCCN 2023028636 | ISBN 9780226350721 (cloth) |
    ISBN 9780226350868 (ebook)
Subjects: LCSH: Constitutional history—United States. |
    Democracy—United States—History—20th century. | Political
    culture—United States—History—20th century. | Social
    movements—United States—History—20th century. | United
    States—Politics and government—20th century.
Classification: LCC KF4541 .R357 2024 | DDC 342.7302/9—dc23/
    eng/20230710
LC record available at https://lccn.loc.gov/2023028636

♾ This paper meets the requirements of ANSI/NISO Z39.48-1992
(Permanence of Paper).

For Navaz and Taleb

CONTENTS

THREE CENTENNIALS

The year 2087 will mark the third centennial of the drafters' signing of the United States Constitution in Philadelphia, Pennsylvania. What do Americans want to celebrate by that time? What type of society do we want to share, and what kind of world should we make for the future?

In 1887 and in 1987, the US celebrated the first and the second centennials. On the surface, those earlier anniversary events had much in common. They both faced initial funding setbacks but eventually featured patriotic festivities and even speeches by the sitting president. Yet, below the surface, the political climates were radically different, cutting against the idea that Americans' relationship to their Constitution never really changes.

The 1887 centennial faced significant organizing difficulties—problems finding speakers and a general lack of public interest, with events beyond Philadelphia largely faltering. This presaged a broader uncertainty about the Constitution that would define the subsequent decades. The country was still reeling from a brutal civil war, which raised basic questions about whether the existing constitutional system could effectively negotiate deep social cleavages. The consequences of industrialization only intensified these worries, and in the late nineteenth and early twentieth centuries the US suffered the most violent labor conflicts in the world.[1] In the 1920s and 1930s, domestic developments were part of the greatest global capitalist crisis in history.

All the while, legal-political institutions seemed incapable of responding. The constitutional structure's endless veto points made it nearly impossible for those less privileged to use elections to better their lot, while business elites wielded outsized power at virtually every level of government.

Wrestling with these problems, a wide array of early twentieth-century reformers called for basic transformations to the constitutional system. They sought a new governing order in which poor and working people—rather than insulated judges and entrenched corporate and racial elites—could intervene continuously through elections and mass movements to create institutions and programs truly responsive to popular needs.

But by the 1987 bicentennial, virtually all those debates and reform ambitions had been forgotten. Americans were largely swept up in a celebratory wave, one expounding the exceptionalism of the national project and the unique genius of the eighteenth-century framers. Millions of people across the country participated in signing exercises, in which they reaffirmed their constitutional faith by affixing their names to copies of the text.

There were clear reasons for self-congratulation by 1987. The Constitution had proven more durable than many of its earlier critics had imagined. The early- to mid-twentieth-century grafting of a strong president atop the legal-political order eased aspects of the constitutional structure's inflexibility. Greater political respect for civil liberties and civil rights—embodied in Supreme Court decisions like *Brown v. Board of Education*—elevated the status of the judiciary and enhanced the overall legitimacy of governing institutions. And the twilight of the Cold War supercharged these triumphalist sentiments, with impending Soviet collapse offering seemingly undeniable proof of the near perfection of the American model.

By 1987, it appeared, America's romance with its founding document had been set in stone. The Constitution was no longer treated as just one political system among many possibilities. Instead, in the years between the centennials, the document gained a culturally exalted and near-sacrosanct position. Above all, it became fundamentally wrapped up with what Americans viewed as the country's singular characteristics and special global destiny.

Yet, for all the meaningful twentieth-century changes, the mythmaking that took hold around the text obscured how serious defects had never been addressed. And today such flaws have become virtually impossible to ignore. Above all, the Constitution remains deeply undemocratic. Americans have a system that profoundly distorts popular sentiment—through extreme over- and underrepresentation; veto points that allow corporate goals to quietly dictate policy; and unelected judges that, given a dysfunctional Congress, have significant rein to impose their own worldviews, even when they diverge wildly from pervasive national values.

All of this has made it increasingly apparent that—rather than reflecting actual public demands or embodying the principle of one person, one vote—the constitutional order promotes paralysis, at best. At worst, as it did a century ago, it entrenches the interests of a wealthy and largely white minority coalition, which enjoys power well beyond its actual popular support.

But the persistence of a culture of constitutional veneration creates an upside-down world. For decades, Americans have been conditioned to uphold an increasingly dysfunctional system as an ideal-typical embodiment of democratic possibility and to seek to replicate it everywhere. At the same time, the central repositories of constitutional memory and knowledge—in universities and in public life—have, until very recently, spent surprisingly little time questioning the overall narratives or asking where they came from.

It is time, definitively, to turn the page—both on the story of American exceptionalism, and on the continuing romance around a broken legal and political framework. This requires a forthright confrontation with the constitutional culture forged during the American rise to global dominance. It also requires facing the reality that the US is not now and has never been a genuine democracy. The only pathway out of our current malaise is to reconstruct shared state and economic institutions—including the Constitution—on properly democratic terms.

Ours would not be the first generation to aim for such deeper transformation in the United States. This had been the goal of a long line of Americans—significant thinkers who are nonetheless often left out of narratives of the Constitution. Whether Crystal Eastman linking socialist feminism and democracy in the 1910s and 1920s, or W. E. B. Du Bois imagining an anti-colonial world especially from the 1930s to the 1960s, these predecessors argued against the twentieth-century tide of constitutional genuflection. For them and many others, the existing institutional arrangements failed to serve a collective project of equal and effective freedom.

But by the second centennial, these Americans—along with their constitutional politics and their counternarratives of nation and possibility—had been thoroughly marginalized in society. Indeed, they had been so marginalized that their political ideas were, if remembered, effectively treated as foreign and outside the scope of acceptable American argument.

In this book, I aim to remedy—and also explain—that marginalization. I seek to understand how the country moved from open political debates over the basic structures of state and economy—discussions swirling in the years after the first centennial—to the rigid politics of Constitution worship that defined the second. In the process, I hope to demonstrate how long-ignored accounts of constitutional transformation, and even of rupture, provide tools in our own time to reach beyond the impasses of the present.

By 2087, we cannot remain haunted by and beholden to choices made during an increasingly distant past, returning yet again to the same forced reverence for mythic founders. It is long past time to develop new, richer practices of constitutional politics and memory. These practices would move the locus of constitutional politics away from the judges and legal experts that now dominate conversation and toward the more open demands and language that characterized previous movement activism. Perhaps, when the date of the third centennial passes, it will be a marker of all that has changed—of the extent to which Americans have come to build and rebuild institutions that are a genuine home for their own deepening democratic imaginations.

Aziz Fidel Kipngeno Rana

CHAPTER 1

The American Constitutional Romance

If you grew up in the United States around the turn of the twenty-first century, you might well have assumed that the American constitutional system stood at the apex of liberal-democratic ideals. Of course, disagreement marked American political life, and the two dominant political parties fought over reproductive rights, affirmative action, same-sex marriage, the size of the federal government, and many other issues. But on the significant matter of foundational institutions, essentially everyone with a meaningful political voice genuflected before the wisdom of the US Constitution.

The American public witnessed ubiquitous displays of almost religious devotion to the Constitution[1] in schools, on television, and at election time. There were bipartisan readings from the text to usher in new sessions of Congress,[2] ritualistic references to its genius during presidential addresses,[3] and even a national holiday celebrating Constitution Day.[4] Indeed, it seemed that one could not truly be "American," or at least an American patriot, without also being a constitutional believer.

The rise of Donald Trump shifted this conversation. Although veneration of the Constitution remains pervasive, such esteem is hardly unchallenged. In fact, it has become increasingly routine both on the Center-Left and the Left to link Trump's presidency, and the general direction of American politics, to anti-democratic structural flaws in the constitutional system.[5]

These flaws, from a "one person, one vote" perspective, can be almost too numerous to list: presidents elected with a minority of votes, a Senate that gives vastly more power to voters in Wyoming than in California, and a Supreme Court that repudiates abortion protections even as these protections enjoy vast popular support, among others. In fact, commentators have long identified the American system with exaggerated checks on popular authority—from the blockages of the Senate to gerrymandering in the House of Representatives, from an impassable constitutional amendment route to widespread practices of voter disenfranchisement, and of course the high-stakes judicial appointments process and the dramatic power exercised over legal-political life by a tiny group of lifetime federal judges. All of this looks a lot more like the political dysfunctions that Americans typically juxtapose *against* their own idealized constitutional order.

In short, we have seen an increased willingness to distinguish between the *general* benefits of constitutional democracy and the quirks and perversions of *our* specific Constitution. All this highlights a remarkable gulf between the reality of system-wide flaws on the one hand, and the long-dominant culture of constitutional veneration on the other. Indeed, the growing elite and public concern with this disconnect sets our moment apart from any in recent collective memory.

Still, identifying the framework as flawed is not enough. The American constitutional system has always been defective, as critics and activists in decades (and even centuries) past fully recognized. We need to understand *why*, despite these defects, the Constitution has ruled the country for so long. And ruled not just with force but with the approbation and even the devotion of many of its subjects. If the Constitution's placement on a national pedestal undermines efforts at essential democratic reform, we need to ask how it ended up there to begin with—and how the pedestal came to look so appropriate that we lost sight of other alternatives. Otherwise, it will be harder to break the collective spell that has blocked past efforts, and that has deeply impacted American political culture more broadly, with costs that extend well beyond the realm of technical constitutional design alone.

This question—of how constitutional veneration became such a naturalized, unremarked-upon feature of collective life by the late twentieth century—stands at the core of this book. To develop an answer, I offer a large-scale historical reconstruction of the Constitution's role and meaning in American political experience. And through this reconstruction, the book engages with a number of essential and connected questions in contemporary American life: How should we think about the Constitution and its possible revision, and what might earlier generations offer to this discussion? Why has the country failed to enact much-needed reforms in the past, such that eventually those reforms appeared entirely off the table? And what broader elements of American collective life would have to shift to make real constitutional change possible?

This initial chapter lays the foundations for my historical reconstruction, and for the various argumentative strands embedded within it. I begin by briefly detailing the flaws of the constitutional system along with their possible institutional solutions, while pointing out that constitutional veneration itself creates a significant obstacle to improvements. I also suggest that reform is further challenged by a deep ambivalence among liberal voices, many of whom regard the Constitution as the country's salvation, even as they lament its flaws. And I contend that a large part of why Americans rarely raise broader constitutional change is because the text serves not solely as a legal-political system of governance. Instead, the Constitution is invested with an overarching story of national peoplehood, which makes it very difficult culturally to disconnect the document from other deeply embedded commitments.

I argue that this overarching myth of peoplehood—what I call *creedal constitutionalism*—combines commitment to the 1787 document with a conviction that the text manifested redemptive principles already existent at the country's founding. This narrative grounded an American form of constitutional patriotism that became the normative core of what the magazine magnate Henry Luce famously dubbed the "American Century," and a centerpiece of what the country held out to the world.

Received academic wisdom treats constitutional veneration as part of the American fabric since at least the early 1800s.[6] But I argue that this straightforward telling obscures as much as it reveals; that the type of constitutional support prevalent today is really a product of the twentieth century; and that the processes by which the Constitution rose as a dominant political and cultural force displaced alternative traditions of critique that are just as authentically a part of the American constitutional story.

In particular, I suggest that the entrenchment of today's pervasive vision was inextricably bound to the US's emergence as a global power, especially against the backdrop of European imperial collapse and decolonization across Asia and Africa. American elites eventually came to feature the Constitution in developing new national narratives that responded to the contours and conflicts of the shifting global context.

In uncovering this alternative history, the book offers a new cast of characters in American constitutional thought—figures generally ignored in court-centric histories. But the arguments and eventual fates of these constitutional players can help make sense of our current constitutional bind. They also offer insight, and even inspiration, for institutional and ideological alternatives that could be relevant for the present day.

The Constitution as Problem

It would be naïve to argue that the Constitution is all-powerful or fully to blame for the country's social dilemmas. But the way that American party politics intersects with constitutional institutions generates a series of profound political pathologies. And contemporary discussion has pushed these problems into public view, along with a series of potential corresponding solutions.

In particular, the federal Constitution has three clear institutional pathologies that feed off each other. First, the existing order makes it especially difficult for today's multiracial and largely urban majority coalition to implement widely backed policies in response to significant social problems. Given that this majority coalition currently tracks onto the Democratic Party, this means that unless the Democratic Party enjoys massive and historically exceptional supermajorities, it is essentially stymied in governing by legislative means—the central institution of modern mass democracies.

This is because the American state-based system assigns representation to *geography* rather than to actual people, and also because the overarching framework's extensive veto points fundamentally fragment the power of the vote. This fragmentation is achieved through the Electoral College, the Senate, the structure and appointments process of the federal judiciary (especially the Supreme Court), and the capacity of states to gerrymander districts, limit voting rights, or otherwise thwart popular national agendas. In addition, the formal constitutional amendment process is notoriously cumbersome, requiring two-thirds support in both houses of Congress and then ratification by three-fourths of the states—a process that social scientists consider perhaps the most difficult currently existing in the world.[7]

Thus, a second and even more troubling pathology lies in how the existing order, by disempowering majorities, fundamentally empowers rule by a minority coalition. The dependence on state-based decision-making and representation dramatically overrepresents small, rural, and disproportionately white communities when it comes to national politics. These voting blocs, currently tied to the Republican Party, may not reflect the cultural and racial diversity of the American public. But Republicans nonetheless enjoy a basic institutional advantage across all the branches of government—the presidency, the federal courts, and the House and Senate.[8]

The result has been persistent cycles of crisis and popular disaffection. Majorities hold out hope that the political class can resolve key concerns, only to be disappointed, time and again, by gridlock and institutional paralysis. All of this can promote an outsized sense of the Democratic Party as feckless—a sense that can assist the Right in consolidating its base of support and even, on occasion, gaining numerical voting majorities.

With this power, the right-leaning minority can fill the federal judiciary with lifetime appointees, including to the Supreme Court. Even after the Republican Party's coalition effectively loses power, a small number of ideologically aligned judges would serve for decades, promoting broadly rejected political, cultural, and socioeconomic views. In practice, this fact has transformed every Supreme Court opening into a pitched battle over the government's ideological direction. And the extreme obstacles to any mass constitutional amendment process effectively funnel constitutional politics back into the Supreme Court and the federal bench—further emphasizing the importance of who controls the judiciary.

As support for the Right's underlying views slipped from its height during the Richard Nixon and Ronald Reagan years, Republican politicians faced two potential options. They could shift ideologically, responding to a new majority. Or they could invest in anti-democratic constitutional elements to maintain power, even as they lost the claim to represent an actual popular majority. They chose the latter, and the built-in structural advantages only further incentivized a conservative embrace of minority rule itself. In line with a long and very American history of white authoritarianism, exemplified by the defeat of Reconstruction and the segregation-era South, this results in a right-wing political apparatus that treats a true multiracial democracy as an almost existential threat.[9]

Even when conservative efforts at vote suppression descend into open violence, these constitutional incentive structures keep party elites wedded to the politics of minority rule in ways that excuse or even openly condone that violence. This is most recently embodied by both Trump's direct role in and the party's complicity in and later minimization of the January 2021 Capitol attack. Thus, echoing the years after the American

Civil War, white mob actions are both lawless *and* facilitated by the minoritarian tendencies of the constitutional order.

A third, related pathology involves the great twentieth-century
workaround to the legal-political intractability of constitutional design: the rise of the modern presidency. For years, presidents have contended that expanding their power allows them to respond to problems at home and abroad while retaining the benefits of constitutional
checks and balances. But today, presidential power, in the context of
party polarization and a deadlocked Congress, has proven deeply limited for overcoming the anti-democratic flaws of the overall order.

The executive branch certainly excels at housing an expansive, coercive, and insulated security apparatus, capable of unilaterally projecting
violence, whether through overseas strikes or a militarized approach to
the border. Yet, for actually entrenching long-term social policies, executive leadership and lawmaking remain a weak alternative to legislative processes. In effect, the presidential workaround has proven adept
at exercising discretionary authority and overturning civil libertarian
constraints, but poor at implementing necessary and broadly supported
public policies.

If these three overlapping pathologies were once hidden, Trump's ascent made them apparent. Like George W. Bush before him, Trump
gained the presidency despite losing the popular vote. In office, he took
advantage of the coercive tools of the executive to separate families
at the border and crack down on immigrant communities. He intensified anti-democratic fearmongering over "election fraud," including
by seeking to overthrow the 2020 presidential vote and by pursuing a
state-level apparatus to subvert impartial vote counting. Moreover, Supreme Court appointments under Trump mean that, for the foreseeable
future, a small coterie of extreme-right judges—with views well outside
consolidated public opinion—enjoy generational control over central
lawmaking questions, well after their party's minority coalition effectively loses power. And even after Trump the person inevitably exits the
political stage, his example suggests how a virulent and authoritarian
brand of American ethno-nationalism can nonetheless impose its will
in the face of majority opposition.

Today, if these constitutional flaws have become familiar in popular
debate, so too have various proposed solutions. In response to the excessive power of the courts, reformers have called for measures that
reduce the authority of the bench and alleviate its intense politiciza-

tion.[10] For example, many countries have short judicial term limits of nine to twelve years, significantly larger constitutional courts (for instance, thirty-four members in India and sixteen in Germany), and in some cases supermajority rules for decisions. The United States is practically alone in rejecting all these constraints on judicial authority, a fact further underscored by the lack of any ethical oversight of the Supreme Court itself.

As for the blockages to the legislative process, commentators and Democratic lawmakers have circulated ideas that would defuse some of the worst anti-democratic effects of the constitutional structure and electoral system. These include campaign finance reforms, expanded voting rights, ending the Senate filibuster, eliminating the Electoral College, combating gerrymandering and partisan election interference, and adding Washington, DC, as a state. In addition, some in the Democratic Party have expressed interest in moving away from the single-member winner-take-all districts that replicate in the House the same unrepresentative features of the Senate. As the activists Waleed Shahid and Nelini Stamp write, the Fair Representation Act proposed in 2021 would "create large districts spanning urban and rural areas that would elect multiple members of Congress through ranked-choice voting. Such districts would make urban and rural votes count equally, and would reward all parties for competing everywhere."[11]

All of these and more are worthy reforms, and a number might garner strong popular backing. Unfortunately, of course, they are largely off the table because of the very constitutional system they seek to remedy. As long as the Democratic Party cannot wield a supermajority so overwhelming as to overcome the electoral framework's malapportionment, these ideas have a very narrow pathway to implementation.

Yet what remains most striking is the relatively limited nature of the current reform conversation—especially given the debilitating catch-22 that existing institutions impose on even fairly modest changes. To date, the discussion has largely centered on particular, if valuable, procedural adjustments:[12] Should there be an Electoral College? Should federal judges hold their offices for as long as they desire? This has left essential prior questions at the margins of popular discussion: Does the constitutional system as a whole provide an effective instrument for organizing a multiracial and genuinely democratic society? How else might Americans envision their basic institutions and rights—and how would we get from here to there? How can we encourage greater political openness to constitutional change? In a sense, we take our problematic system as a given, and then struggle to patch especially egregious leaks. And even still, the technical procedural suggestions circulating today are met with real trepidation.

Unfortunately, this more limited approach may create its own catch-22. By staying modest, the conversation seems implicitly to yield to the broader inevitability, and perhaps even legitimacy, of the constitutional framework. And this seeming acceptance can undermine the critical energy that would give real reform a serious chance.

The Constitution as Salvation

Of course, pragmatic concerns loom large in shaping public conversation. But deeper constitutional questions also remain suppressed because of a fundamental ambivalence among many liberal voices. For starters, there is a sense that the document's very longevity speaks to the need to hold firm to its text and structures. Depending on scholarly interpretation, either the US or San Marino has the oldest still active national constitution in the world. According to this sentiment, the document is our safety blanket. The fact that it has weathered incredible national storms—the Civil War, the Great Depression—means that we should be deeply hesitant to seek its basic overhaul. Without a shared acceptance of the text, whatever its flaws, perhaps even worse fates could befall us.

Today's divided liberal mind on the Constitution also results from ambivalence on the substance. On the one hand, commentators and politicians decry the anti-democratic features of the Constitution. But many also profess an abiding faith that the very same document and institutions will save Americans from authoritarian entrenchment. After Trump's 2016 election, for example, this tendency emerged in everything from the worshipful invocations of the Constitution when contesting the Muslim Ban to hopes that the Russia investigation and impeachment would provide an off-ramp from the conditions that produced Trump's rise in the first place.

One can see such abiding faith in President Barack Obama's Democratic National Convention speech in 2020, after several years away from a major national spotlight. Tellingly, Obama delivered the speech in Philadelphia, where the Constitution was drafted, in front of an exhibit at the Museum of the American Revolution that included a portrait of James Madison and, in large type, the words, "Writing the Constitution."[13] In a speech that aimed to underscore how "our very democracy is at stake,"[14] Obama acknowledged that the Constitution may not have been a "perfect document," but proclaimed that "embedded in this document was a North Star that would guide future generations; a system of representative government—a democracy—through which we could better realize our highest ideals."[15]

Since that 2020 election, Biden administration officials and various commentators have also returned to the well of Constitution worship. When Trump called for the "termination"[16] of existing election rules, including in the Constitution, many liberal voices decried Trump's authoritarianism by tying their critiques to unstinting devotion to the constitutional system—regardless of its role in perpetuating the dangers they condemned. Andrew Bates, the White House spokesperson, proclaimed that the Constitution as such was a "sacrosanct document" and that "attacking" it was "anathema to the soul of our nation."[17] These defenses implicitly suggest that Americans can only effectively protect their bedrock liberties from demagogues by redoubling their commitment to the text.

But this retreat back into Constitution worship carries with it profound limitations. It ignores how today's pathologies are not simply unintended and contingent consequences. Instead, these effects can be seen, at least in part, as a product of the framers' own hostility toward real democracy. James Madison, Alexander Hamilton, and others riddled the constitutional order with veto points precisely to contain the central political tool that poorer citizens had to pursue their needs: the power of the vote. And, of course, these constitutive and undemocratic features also fit hand in glove with the long history of racial subordination: racial elites have benefited greatly from both state-based representation and the various checks embedded throughout the constitutional system, which create partisan incentives at the national level to avoid meaningful reform. The framers placed this constitutional system largely beyond popular revision through its incredibly elaborate amendment process. The result is a framework that systematically disadvantages those with the fewest resources, while allowing those with power to use a fragmented political system to quietly preserve their interests.

Thus, the call to remain true to Madison amounts to an invitation to hold firm to the very arrangements that have facilitated, both today and in the past, the authoritarian brand of politics that someone like Obama condemns as un-American. And it has the added effect of draining the reform energy that might exist—even around the more specific technical fixes. If the constitutional system protects us from danger, why should politicians and publics engage in serious political struggle to push for revisions?

I will return to these questions about constitutional longevity and the risks and rewards of potential breaks in the book's conclusion. For now, we can note that in recent years—especially in the context of global decolonization in Asia, Africa, and Latin America—many countries around the world have reconstructed their governing documents without collapsing into authoritarian nightmares, and in ways that better fulfill the aspirations of their members.

A Twentieth-Century Story of American Peoplehood

Still, I argue that the ambivalence about reform may come from something even deeper. Many Americans understand the Constitution not simply as a template for legal-political governance, which could be reworked if necessary. Instead, the document has become entangled in a broader account of American peoplehood.[18] This story has developed such a strong hold on the country that its constituent and sometimes conflicting strains have become difficult to unravel, both from each other and from the Constitution itself.

In 1944, the Swedish sociologist Gunnar Myrdal famously asserted that the United States had been committed, from the time of its founding, to the principle emblazoned in the Declaration of Independence: that "all men are created equal, that they are endowed by their Creator with certain unalienable Rights, that among these are Life, Liberty and the pursuit of Happiness."[19] He termed this historical narrative the "American Creed," and argued that the unfolding national experience concretely manifested the narrative, concluding that "the main trend in [American] history is the gradual realization of the American Creed" and thus the fulfillment of the nation's founding promise.[20] Myrdal's phrase captured a way of thinking about the country—simultaneously a historical interpretation and a political ideology—which, since the mid-twentieth century, increasingly became ubiquitous and naturalized.[21]

The Constitution has no necessary relationship to this American creedal vision. Indeed, opinions about the Constitution on the one hand and a creed of equal liberty on the other can be mixed and matched in myriad ways, as demonstrated by the historical figures detailed in the coming chapters. For example, some radical anti-slavery figures in the mid-nineteenth century contended that one could not hold true to the notion that all are created equal and simultaneously remain loyal to the 1787 text—essentially embodying an anti–Constitution creed-alist position. Various white supremacist groups throughout American history have supported the document's legal-political framework but resisted any Myrdallian narrative of unfolding equality, offering an anti-creedal constitutionalist option. And various dissident voices in American history—within labor politics, feminism, the Black radical tradition, and Indigenous movements—have rejected the creed, as well as the Constitution, for actually *failing* to address the ongoing structural consequences of the country's colonial, capitalist, patriarchal, or racist foundations. One could almost make a two-by-two table—views of the Constitution on one axis and attachment to creedal nationalism on the other—to map a broad range of thinkers in the American political and legal tradition.

Given these manifold possibilities, it is striking that mainstream American politics has stayed in one box for so long: the one that combines nationalist faith in the creed with commitment to the Constitution. Throughout the book, I will refer to this fusing of constitutional devotion with the idea of the country as an unfolding project in equal liberty as *creedal constitutionalism*. In the words again of Obama, now from his famed 2008 campaign speech on race, according to this view, the Constitution always "had at its very core the ideal of equal citizenship under the law; a Constitution that promised its people liberty, and justice, and a union that could be and should be perfected over time."[22] Indeed, this belief that the constitutional system is perhaps the defining and concrete instrument for the achievement of creedal ends goes to the center of the contemporary American "ethically constitutive story" of "peoplehood," to use the political scientist Rogers Smith's language.[23]

Although creedal constitutionalism's two core elements are commitment to the document and belief in a national narrative of unfolding equality and liberty, variations on the theme have arisen at different moments, each incorporating additional layers and characteristics. The most important variant historically—and central to the arguments of this book—emerged over the course of the twentieth century. In this version, which solidified with the Cold War, creed and Constitution were further joined to a series of three ideological pillars: an anti-totalitarian account of individual liberty and market capitalism; an embrace of American checks and balances, with the Supreme Court at the forefront; and a commitment to US global leadership and primacy. Together, they provided an official narrative about why the Con-

stitution promoted a just political, economic, and social order and—
eventually—why it should be replicated abroad. This Cold War variant
became a formidable ideological behemoth, lasting largely intact to this
day and providing a bulwark against serious efforts to revise the constitutional framework. When Obama stands before a picture of Madison to champion the Constitution, in many ways it is this interrelated
set of commitments that he defends as the essence of American liberal
nationalism.

This version's merging of additional elements into modern creedal
constitutionalism has meant that the document today has become intertwined not only with narratives of equality but also with three other
claims about the country. First, the Constitution is presented as tangibly distinguishing American political identity from the collectivizing extremes associated with totalitarian states like Nazi Germany and
the Soviet Union. This is because the Constitution is imagined to be
an individual charter of rights—particularly connected to its first ten
amendments, commonly known as the Bill of Rights. These rights link
together essential civil liberties with private property protections, implicitly asserting that free speech and a free market go together. The
Constitution, so the argument goes, preserves the capacity of Americans to think and act—whether in politics or in the market—without
fear of a dominating and all-powerful government.

Second, despite the criticisms today, the Constitution's hardwired
checks and balances are presented as warding off both demagogues and
tyrannical majorities. By limiting the power of any single political actor,
these structures ensure that one does not need a "society of angels" for
democracy to function. They do so both by blocking wild lurches to the
right or left, and by slowing down political decision-making. This forces
politicians and publics to think more seriously about change. If other,
less mature societies engage in revolutionary breaks—with mass politics overwhelming institutional safeguards—or follow populist dicta-
tors, American life proceeds otherwise.

In the US, under this reading, change occurs through multiple and
overlapping institutions, undergirded by a political culture that values
moderation, discursive reflection, and steady improvements over time.
A critical consequence of this focus on the Constitution's liberalizing
discourse is the elevation of the judiciary—and especially the Supreme
Court—as the archetype of such deliberative reason-giving. The Court
may get outcomes wrong, even disastrously so, since it is ultimately

composed of fallible human beings. But, over the centuries, it preserves a shared American language of temperate self-reflection.

Third, all of this speaks to why the US is presumed worthy of a dominant global position. The Constitution offers concrete proof that the country has been grounded, from the very beginning, in universal principles of liberty and equality. This means that its interests are coterminous with the world's interests. Since what it promotes abroad is the same liberal constitutional model it instantiates at home, the US enjoys a legitimate right to serve as the global backstop and to exercise an international police power.

On the face of it, these are disparate ideas and ends—basic creedal nationalism, civil libertarian values, market capitalism, constrained representative government, American primacy—which need not go together and may well be in profound tension. But thanks in part to the story of the country that politicians and commentators have built around the Constitution, these ends have been combined into a unified and driving nationalist faith. This means that the text, with its associated narratives, does more than forge disparate commitments into a coherent whole. This augmented creedal constitutionalism also functions to bind together competing political elites and social constituencies under a shared banner and language of American exceptionalism.

The Reformist Legacy of a National Ideology

At the beginning of the twenty-first century, this consensus linked the Center-Left to the Center-Right in what amounted to a romance about the national project. The eighteenth-century document had evolved beyond merely a set of rules for legal and political decision-making, which could be judged based on its comparative effectiveness and fundamentally changed if found wanting. Instead, for policymakers and academics alike, belief in the Constitution became wrapped up with an alluring set of propositions about the country's unique status: from the genius of its governing institutions to the inherently progressive direction of its unfolding history to the indispensability of its global role.

One great strength of this twentieth-century creedal constitutionalism was its political fluidity, which had important consequences for reform and social cohesion. Activists on both political sides could assert that they were speaking in the true language of the Constitution. And to the extent that governing elites justified their own authority in creedal constitutional terms, more marginal voices could productively reappropriate the dominant framing to push for social change. Thus, during decisive periods of struggle, such as with 1950s and 1960s civil rights protests, many Black American activists—routinely treated as dissidents by state authorities—still claimed the mantle of both the creed and the Constitution. Such movement actors articulated extensive critiques of existing conditions, but they often did so from within the shared national narrative, accentuating particular elements and de-emphasizing others. They thus deployed creedal constitutionalism as a powerful discursive tool for reform.

This very flexibility proved a clear strength in consolidating mid- to late-twentieth-century Cold War politics behind a particular version of American liberal nationalism. As a shared set of claims and arguments, creedal constitutionalism provided a discourse that could incorporate communities long marginalized in American history. It allowed members of many of those communities to see themselves as valued and respected within the dominant, often white, society. Moreover, creedal constitutionalism offered a framework for positing and internalizing the "un-Americanness" of explicit white supremacy, including for white national officials and political elites who built their own political self-conceptions in part around the principle of inclusion.

As highlighted by the civil rights movement's achievements, this fusing of the creed and the Constitution was essential to the great American reform triumphs of the twentieth century. Indeed, generations of political leaders over time came to identify deeply and personally with this story. In a sense, they had worked and suffered for it, and it gave their lives a larger meaning. Despite the contemporary discontent, for periods in the recent past, many saw truth in exceptionalist premises about American life: legal-political institutions appeared to operate smoothly, economic processes generated wealth, excluded groups found a degree of inclusion, and threatening adversaries met with defeat.

Therefore, and not unrelatedly, the very pluralism inherent in twentieth-century creedal constitutionalism played a critical role in cohering Americans around a basic faith in the nation. An individual might have real opposition to specific US policies, at home or abroad, and might even be suspicious of one or more of the country's essential ideological tenets—up to and including market capitalism or belief in the wisdom of the 1787 framers. But, for the most part, the various potential emphases associated with the creedal Constitution provided both elites and popular constituencies with something to hold on to. Individuals could focus on a particular aspect for their personalized vision and simultaneously refuse to see themselves in other practices or ideological commitments that nonetheless exerted significant power under the shared creedal constitutional rubric.

This American ideology, and the social cohesion and reform possibilities it offers, has granted the Constitution significant immunity from challenge. As the lawyer and scholar Laurence Tribe reverentially declared in 2012, "'We the People' cannot simply bracket our Constitution . . . for that very notion presupposes a 'we' that exists outside the Constitution's frame." The Constitution could not possibly be "replaced by a temporary upgrade or substitute" because its "text and invisible structure are part of the nation's beating heart."[24] As a symbolic and institutional center of twentieth-century American nationalist faith, the Constitution was what officials promoted abroad as the basis of global prosperity and defended at home as the engine of the country's exceptional gifts and freedoms. By this account, any serious effort to fundamentally transform the constitutional system would raise profound issues about what it means to be American in the first place.

The Deeper Costs of Creedal Constitutionalism

Still, the reform benefits of creedal constitutionalism come with significant costs that have become more pronounced over time—political-cultural costs that extend beyond procedural, anti-democratic institutional damage alone. For instance, the narrative has rendered largely invisible the country's own colonial infrastructure, and has even provided ideological space for ethno-nationalist politics. In addition, it has bolstered elitist suspicions of mass democracy, and—paradoxically—justified security excess through the language of constitutionalism itself.

To begin with, while many American reformers and activists productively used the creedal discourse to press for significant change, these interactions between reformers and the state nonetheless often operated through a type of bargain: challenges could be made to one feature of the society—for instance, by steadily uprooting formal legal discrimination on the basis of race, gender, or sexual orientation—but not to other elements of the national project, such as American international police power during the Cold War or the basic structural organization of the state and economy.

Indeed, as highlighted in the following chapters, many recent systematic critiques of the constitutional order first emerged as part of radical movements on behalf of workers, women, Black Americans, and Indigenous communities. Yet, over the course of the twentieth century, a combination of state negotiation and governmental violence and suppression resulted in the near disappearance of these appraisals from public consciousness. So while creedal constitutionalist language facilitated national solidarity and promoted change, key reformers also implicitly—and at times explicitly—acceded to a basic rhetorical exchange that refrained from threatening governing accounts about the country's exceptional status. While reformers may have sought to pick and choose among the elements of the broader narrative, at the end of the day it was often very difficult to do so: employing the language of constitutional veneration, especially in the Cold War context, could easily devolve into reproducing the driving logic of the American Century. In this way, alternative visions of constitutional order and meaning slipped away.

Furthermore, the political culture promoted by creedal constitutionalism, especially in its official twentieth-century form, carried additional consequences for collective life and national memory. In particular, it erased mainstream consciousness of the country's foundations as a settler society, in which the freedom, equality, and access to land of in-group members—largely, Anglo-European men of a certain background—depended on the exclusion and subjugation of Black Americans, Indigenous peoples, and women, among others.[25] For all the positives associated with the white national embrace of a vision of the country as free and equal from the founding, a clear problem thus remained: although oppressed groups eventually accessed greater legal protections, these changes ultimately occurred on ideological terms shaped principally by a white majority. Unlike colonized peoples abroad, Black people and Native Americans, among others, were never able to insist on a conscious moment of colonial accounting or, through this moment, a sustained national engagement with the persistent structural hierarchies bound to the country's settler roots.

This failure to confront such settler foundations has meant that, perhaps counterintuitively, creedal constitutionalism has provided cultural space for the development of a modern American ethno-nationalist politics. As the twentieth century progressed, part of the appeal of the ideologically flexible creedal discourse, for some, lay in its openness to racially exclusionary commitments. Critics of a multiracial political identity began to locate the founding's liberal essence and exceptionalism in the distinctive cultural attributes of a Euro-American experience. Figures from Woodrow Wilson in the early twentieth century to backers of Donald Trump more recently have argued that the creed emerged from that special cultural history, and that therefore, unless other communities assimilated into an essentially Euro-American identity, the country's founding ideals would be abandoned.

Thus, the bargain around creedal constitutionalism paired reform with an expectation that historically excluded communities should accept an unconditional attachment to the nation, its central domestic symbols, and its overarching projects abroad. Additionally, and perhaps more troublingly, it promoted a narrative of national innocence in which ethno-nationalist assertions about Euro-American exceptionalism could persist well after explicit defenses of white supremacy became politically unpalatable.

Furthermore, the focus on a specifically "American" mode of change — privileging the mediating institutions and interpretive traditions of the existing constitutional order — proved deeply elitist and sometimes violently coercive. For starters, it promoted a cultural genuflection before the Supreme Court specifically, with speeches and commentary presenting the judiciary as an educational seminar for the public, whatever the record of past court complicity in everything from slavery and segregation to Indigenous expropriation, the violent repression of labor, and the subjugation of women. Those with overweening economic and political power, oftentimes including the individuals sitting on the federal bench, frequently undermined essential rights and democratic values — legitimating exercises of national security and police violence, not to mention voter disenfranchisement and crackdowns on workers. But, under the creedal constitutional narrative, threats to basic liberties almost always came from below; thus, unruly elements had to be contained by a wiser and more mature set of economic, political, and legal elites.

The result was a prevailing tendency to interpret almost any radical political intervention that sought to fundamentally revise the legal-political order and the basic terms of the state and the economy as a danger not just to the existing Constitution, but to constitutionalism *as such*. This sensibility not only evinced real suspicion of the capacity of ordinary Americans to shape collective life; it also operated in practice to transform the dominant brand of creedal constitutionalism into the only possible way Americans could exercise their constitutional imagination and engage in constitutional politics.

Equally concerning, this elevation of the judiciary and other counter-majoritarian spaces obscured the historical conditions under which these institutional actors had gained such exalted status. Past publics did not simply accede to the dramatic narrowing of the boundaries of constitutional politics or to the elevation of federal courts as central articulators of constitutional meaning. As I detail in the following chapters, the first half of the twentieth century involved intense opposition both to a mythologizing of the judiciary and to virtually all the foundational elements of American ideology and statecraft—from the basic legitimacy of the Senate to the US assertion of an expansive and capitalist global authority.

Thus, although late-twentieth-century commentators routinely waxed poetic about the country's liberal self-reflectiveness, such praise systematically ignored the extent to which this self-reflection operated in a dramatically narrowed context—only *after* foundational questions about social ordering and design were largely removed from the table. Moreover, the pervasive and legal discourse-driven conversation around the Constitution effectively sustained that removal, since in practice it offered very little space for broader institutional assessments or competing argumentative languages and tools. All of this underscores how the deliberative practices of the overarching constitutional paradigm significantly circumscribed truly critical self-reflection—whatever the conventional wisdom.

In addition, encomiums to the liberalizing power of the American brand of constitutionalism ignored the extent to which these practices remained bound up with actual and persistent state violence against opponents. They failed to contend with the legitimating role the overall creedal constitutional paradigm played in acts of profound discretionary violence across the globe. Indeed, American governing elites cemented the twentieth-century ties between market capitalism, global primacy, and creedal constitutionalism in ways that often entailed real repression both at home and overseas.

Despite being framed in a constitutional register, then, the American version of liberal nationalism that solidified in the twentieth century shared many commonalities with other more explicitly aggressive and belligerent nationalist projects—projects that US officials were often at pains to distinguish as "un-American." The consequence has been an unavoidably tangled relationship in collective life between the liberal and the "illiberal" dimensions of the governing creedal consensus.

Elements of a Reconstruction

Standing now on the other end of the politics espoused by promoters of the American Century, we can wonder whether the particular compact around creedal constitutionalism too hastily papered over real deficits in the governing order. In recent decades, not only has American political dysfunction become especially apparent; so too have the ways in which national mythologies—including those related to the Constitution—shielded ideological flaws from critical analysis and marginalized political alternatives.

This makes even more pressing the question of *how* we ended up bound by a narrow constitutional narrative, without even realizing how tightly we have been bound. It is not only an issue of identifying institutional problems and proposing appropriate technical solutions—though that analysis and activism are essential. The myths surrounding the Constitution constitute a block to significant reform, and also underpin an American political culture with consequences well beyond constitutional design.

The remainder of this book offers my analysis of how we arrived at the current moment. My historical reconstruction of the Constitution's position in American political life weaves together several central elements. In particular, I emphasize that the Constitution's venerable age hides wild discrepancies in constitutional meaning and support, such that the mythic status of creedal constitutionalism, and especially its twentieth-century variant, becomes a real puzzle that demands explanation. I also argue that any fully successful explanation must incorporate an understanding of America's rise as a global power—and that this frame not only offers a historical corrective to existing explanations, but also sheds light on how American constitutionalism and imperialism may interact in unexpected ways.

THE PUZZLE THAT LONGEVITY HIDES

There is real allure to an ideology of long vintage. And Americans tend to presume the longevity not just of the constitutional text but also of its veneration, roughly along the creedal lines familiar to us today. So one response, again, to the question of modern creedal constitutionalism may be that things have *always* been this way: that reverence for the Constitution, especially as an embodiment of unfolding American ideals of equality, has consistently formed the core of American identity.

As the following chapters make clear, that answer offers an unproductive historical compression. It is certainly true that notables and national elites in the first decades of the republic looked upon the document with real attachment, even treating the text with near-religious devotion. As the historian Jonathan Gienapp has compellingly argued, the decision made at the founding to add amendments to the *end* of an unchanged original text—rather than throughout the document and actually over the objection of James Madison—was critical to jump-starting a politics of veneration. Gienapp describes this choice as "among the most important milestones in the entire sweep of American constitutional history," as it promoted a perception of the pre-amendment Constitution as fixed and "sacred" rather than as "an organic, evolving whole."[26] Furthermore, this "idea of the archival Constitution"[27] fit with the political imagination of national elites in the generations immediately after the founding. It helped them to make sense of their specific relationship to the founding, underscoring their distinctive role as preservers of the great revolutionary generation's central work.[28]

But even if bathed in quasi-religious language, the Constitution's relationship to the broader American social fabric was very different. For most individuals throughout most of the nation's early years, the federal government's Constitution may have engendered general approval as a symbol of the country. But the driving activity of social cohesion in the nineteenth century was territorial settlement—a decentralized process of expansion that focused political and economic life at the local level. This created not a national constitutional culture, but instead what the historian Robert Wiebe famously called a "society of island communities."[29] Unsurprisingly, throughout the nineteenth century, the Constitution was only haphazardly taught at any level of education. More surprisingly, even law schools of the time did not treat it as an important focus of study.[30] Indeed, while today most law scholars with significant public profiles are known for their analysis of the Constitution, this would not have been the case as late as World War II.[31]

In addition, nineteenth-century encomiums to the Constitution often went hand in hand with exclusionary narratives that contemporary creedal constitutionalists would not recognize—a fundamentally different ideology dressed in the same documentary garb. And those initial creedal constitutionalists that we *would* recognize, largely Black and anti-slavery radicals during and after the Civil War, experienced real marginalization. To the vast majority of earlier Americans, the twentieth-century version of creedal constitutionalism—particularly combining racial equality with textual devotion—would have looked like a bizarre ideological jumble.

Thus, what early notables routinely embraced about the federal Constitution and what Americans today venerate is wildly different. As recently as 1900, only a small number of white Americans would have seen their own country in Myrdal's story about the American creed. The far more common national story, promoted by President Theodore Roosevelt and the famed historian Frederick Jackson Turner, revolved around Euro-American continental conquest and settlement, what Roosevelt titled his 1889 work: *The Winning of the West.*[32]

Nineteenth-century politicians presented the Constitution as enabling this ongoing conquest, including through a compromise on the matter of slavery. Northern elites like Massachusetts Senator Daniel Webster, who opposed the evils associated with slavery, nonetheless accepted the *détente* embodied by the document: under the Constitution, slavery should not extend into new territories but also was not, in Webster's words, "to be disturbed or interfered with by the new general government." Such compromise was permissible because it ensured the nation's existence: it embodied the necessary political cost of promoting union and with it the shared goals of prosperity, independence, and appropriate territorial growth—goals vital regardless of region.[33]

To further underscore the point, politicians and notables often defended the Constitution while explicitly *rejecting* universally egalitarian readings of the Declaration. Stephen Douglas, in his victorious 1858 Senate campaign against future president Abraham Lincoln, may have embraced the value of the Constitution. But he made clear that "this government was made on the white basis, by white men, and for the benefit of white men and their posterity forever."[34]

These understandings are entirely antithetical to current visions of the constitutional project and the American story. Even setting aside Douglas's framing, a national narrative built around accommodating slavery in order to facilitate the expropriation of Native lands would be deeply immoral today. But, in the early to mid-nineteenth century, the idea of the Constitution as fostering union and national growth through cross-sectional compromise circulated far more broadly across the parties and within elite Northern politics than something like

Obama's joining of creed and Constitution.[35] Glossing over these im-
mense differences in constitutional meaning requires a real flattening
of historical time and texture. But, of course, such flattening is enabled
and encouraged by today's creedal constitutional ideology itself.

WHY EXISTING EXPLANATIONS ARE INCOMPLETE

Still, what of the Civil War and Reconstruction—a key earlier era that
presages elements of twentieth-century creedal constitutionalism? And
how about the success of the New Deal, including the ultimate acquiescence of the Supreme Court to more extensive regulation, which also
engendered wider acceptance of the constitutional system?

It might be argued that these two major periods, together with internal institutional features, are sufficient to explain the cementing by
the mid-twentieth century of our familiar brand of veneration. Perhaps
these eras' reform achievements reinforced tendencies already embedded in the legal-political system. The very difficulty of formal amendment under Article V, alongside the cultural approach to the document
as an "archival" text (to use Gienapp's phrase), promoted ideas of the
Constitution as both fixed and near perfect to begin with. Thus, a natural response to Reconstruction and New Deal changes may have been
to treat them—including even the amendments added after the Civil
War—as essentially affirming what the Constitution had always stood
for. They could be taken as yet further reason to venerate the system.

Although these explanations are certainly part of the story, I contend that they alone cannot account for the specific process by which
creedal constitutional commitments spread. Internal arguments leave
unexplained how creedal claims declined dramatically in the years after Reconstruction and then consolidated—through clear steps, each
incorporating new features—during very particular moments in the
twentieth century. If we maintain a direct domestic through line from
the Civil War to the New Deal to the present—without considering
international developments—the emergence and timing of these stages
appear deceptively random.

It is true that, to the extent that scholars have explored how and why
the Constitution became joined specifically to basic creedal nationalism, they focus especially on how anti-slavery ideas of equal liberty
gained real political prominence during and after the Civil War.[36] For
example, the journalist and historian Gary Wills points to Lincoln's
1863 Gettysburg Address—with its emphasis on reading American

identity and institutions through a universalistic interpretation of the
Declaration of Independence—as the pivotal moment in the transfor-
mation of American constitutional meaning and the national project.
In Wills's words, the speech "changed the way people thought about
the Constitution" and launched the country on an inclusive enterprise.
"Because of it, we live in a different America."[37]

I agree that creedal commitments emerged out of anti-slavery politics
and enjoyed initial resonance in the context of Civil War experiences—
becoming formally instantiated in the text through Reconstruction-era
amendments. Yet, such histories face a profound problem. By the end
of the nineteenth century, Reconstruction had collapsed. And these
universalist readings of national identity, let alone specific efforts to
fuse them with the Constitution, became associated primarily with the
Black counter-public. They were largely dismissed within white society,
and treated among most Euro-Americans as a threat to the bedrock racial identity of collective life.

In addition, by the 1910s, a driving conversation around the Constitution focused on how ill-equipped the text had become to serve as the
governing framework of the republic—a republic that most Americans
still assumed to be racially restrictive. The Civil War had underscored
the explicit failures of the Constitution's founding compromise. And
the effects of industrialization and resulting class conflict now raised
fundamental issues about the legitimacy of the prevailing order. The
barriers to formal amendment—along with the system's extensive veto
points—hardly promoted reverence for a fixed text. If anything, they
spoke to the sclerotic nature of American legal-political design. Individuals living at that time may well have imagined that the Constitution
might need to be replaced with a new one in the coming years or decades. They likely would have been far more surprised to find a twenty-
first-century America that deifies the very same document, but now as
an embodiment of a universal and equal liberty inherent in the country's founding.

What of the New Deal reforms of the 1930s, achieved without fundamentally rewriting the Constitution? This did create the potential
for a broad settlement in favor of the established legal-political order.
But New Dealers knew full well the difficulty of governing through a
rigid and anti-democratic system. Their success in forcing economic accommodations, after much upheaval and institutional blockage, should
hardly lead them to glorify the constitutional order as near ideal.

Crucially, major turning points in US international engagement help explain the timing of key steps toward modern constitutional veneration — making each of these moments much more cognizable than they would be otherwise. For example, seemingly discarded anti-slavery arguments about creed and Constitution first returned with intensity to official white discourse in the context of overseas expansionism — particularly during the unexpected and brutal Philippine independence fight against US control at the turn of the twentieth century.

Why was this the case? I argue that the imperial setting provided the laboratory in which a new generation of political elites, even avowed white supremacists like Woodrow Wilson, were pressed into framing the American project in response to anti-colonial resistance. To do so, they melded an initially uneasy mix of creedalism, constitutional devotion, and US primacy into a cohesive framework.

Furthermore, it was far from random that Constitution Day was initially popularized as an annual and national day of commemoration in the context of World War I. Pro-war civic figures and politicians spearheaded unprecedented celebrations directly linking constitutional veneration and global assertiveness. At the same time, they also strongly associated in the public imagination socialist anti-Constitution sentiment with disloyalty. In this way, they burnished a pro-business linking of capitalism and the Constitution, giving a previously tarnished position renewed popular vitality.

Similarly, World War II and fears of totalitarian threat served as the explicit backdrop for the rediscovery and rolling celebration of the Bill of Rights between 1939 and 1941. Prior to this time, these amendments had been only haphazardly treated as a unified and defining "charter of individual rights." But now, these amendments became central to wartime accounts of American civil libertarian peoplehood and constitutional meaning.

And again, after the war, the Freedom Train — a joint business-government enterprise that toured the country during the late 1940s, extolling the genius of the American project and the Constitution at its heart — responded directly to Cold War rivalry. In doing so, it was also culturally of a piece with a growing post-war embrace not just of the Constitution in general, but also of the Constitution's institutional intricacy and counter-majoritarianism more particularly, with the Supreme Court at the apex. As the Cold War took shape, such counter-majoritarianism — from the Article V process to judicial review and the Senate — became re-presented: not as a roadblock to democracy, but rather as why the US had avoided the communist and fascist fates of

Europe. It was what separated American *liberal* democracy from a tyrannical Soviet people's democracy.

Perhaps one consequence of today's nationalist narratives of American exceptionalism is that explanations for any major change tend to be sought internally.[38] Again, this is not to say that internal explanations played no role in the consolidation of creed and Constitution. Instead, in order to appreciate *when* and *why* certain domestic legal and institutional features facilitated the entrenchment of creedal constitutionalism, we have to integrate those features with a global explanatory account.

A GLOBAL TAKE: FINDING NARRATIVES FOR A NEW WORLD

I submit that we cannot understand important shifts in the meaning and conversation around the Constitution without reckoning with the rise of the United States from a regional hegemon to the world's preeminent global power—another relatively recent development. This ascent is almost never discussed alongside the story of the Constitution. Perhaps, since the US is so distinctive, it is hard to imagine its evolution as a product of international processes and comparative practices.

To begin, the twentieth century witnessed two devastating world wars and the breakdown of the great European empires. This dissolution resulted in the emergence of formally independent nation-states across the world, and also amplified the US capacity to project global power. As US elites struggled with how to engage on the international arena—in organizing overseas colonies such as the Philippines and then in shaping the terms of Cold War conflict—they eventually converged on today's dominant language of constitutional meaning.

More specifically, as Asian and African independence gained force by the mid-twentieth century, this sustained anti-colonial struggle and non-white political assertiveness permanently transformed international and domestic discussions about inclusion and exclusion across racial and ethnic dimensions. As the great Black American activist, writer, and critic W. E. B. Du Bois declared of the times, "the problem of the twentieth century is the problem of the color-line,—the relation of the darker to the lighter races of men in Asia and Africa, in America and the islands of the sea."[39]

Forced to contend with these changes, European states came to deemphasize racial hegemony and ethno-racial solidarity as the explicit bases of national greatness and ongoing international engagement, even though such visions had underpinned earlier imperial imaginations. Instead, large swathes of Europe steadily shifted toward official stories of civic or liberal nationalism, with political affiliation supposedly grounded on "equal, rights-bearing citizens, united in patriotic attachment to a shared set of political practices and values."[40]

In this way, the United States was no different. The country had long been an outpost of Anglo-European rule in the non-European world. And when reflecting on the national experience, Theodore Roosevelt, for instance, famously viewed the US as most akin to other British ethno-racial colonies of settlement, places like South Africa and Australia. As I detail in a prior book, *The Two Faces of American Freedom*, for long periods of the collective past Roosevelt's characterization of their nation would have made intuitive sense to most Americans.[41]

But for a country whose leaders increasingly sought both meaning in and influence over a decolonizing and largely non-European world, conceiving of the United States as "white man's country"[42]—to use Teddy Roosevelt's evocative phrase—became a non-starter. US officials needed to explain to themselves and to others how the United States actually represented a departure from the racial hegemony that marked the age of European empire. Furthermore, they aimed to explain why the United States should enjoy an essentially imperial right on the global stage—namely, the right to exercise tutelage over foreign, especially non-white, polities, and thus to assert an international police power to reconstruct those societies in keeping with domestic interests.

These interlinked requirements demanded a compelling account of national identity that did not repeat the European imperial racial presumptions. The new account must instead conceive of the country as a break from, rather than a continuation of, such rule. Indeed, these needs were further underscored by the fact that, particularly after World War II, the United States—despite its unparalleled economic and military power—did not stand alone on the world stage. It faced a genuine ideological competitor in the form of the Soviet Union—one with real anti-colonial credentials across Latin America, Asia, and Africa—and this fact drove home the challenge facing American officials hoping to win "hearts and minds."

Against this backdrop, US policymakers and commentators—soul-searching on behalf of the country but also responding to these external realities—steadily embraced creedalism as the core story of American peoplehood over the first half of the twentieth century. Along the Myrdallian lines noted above, this constitutive narrative presented the United States not as principally an extension of European racial empire or as an experiment in settler colonization. Instead, it conceived of the country as committed, from its founding, to the principle that "all men are created equal"—while acknowledging that this unfolding commitment had, at points along its journey, been undercut by racist prejudices and inegalitarian tendencies.

Part of the power of this creedal vision, both at home and abroad, was how the acknowledgment of previous excess was already written into a narrative about an essentially redemptive national project. Officials were able to admit to a racist past while nonetheless rejecting the long-standing and previously acknowledged link between American settlement and Anglo-European empire—indeed, to the point of largely erasing it from collective consciousness.

Such an account allowed political elites in the United States to assert that American civic nationalism was fundamentally distinct from the varieties emerging in mid- to late-twentieth-century Europe. Those countries had been absolutist monarchies and imperial orders, promoting racial hegemony in their overseas colonies. They were latecomers to liberal nationalism, and even worse, their internecine rivalries had left the European continent destroyed and the world in tatters.

By contrast, the United States interpreted itself as an ethically worthy global power because it had never been either a feudal or an imperial society, marked by extensive colonies. Whatever the past sins of slavery and Indigenous mistreatment, the country's core essence, so the narrative went, already fit with the new historical times. According to these arguments, the American nation—like an expanding share of the world's countries—emerged from an anti-imperial fight for independence against the British Empire. And, as the Declaration of Independence highlighted, the US from its genesis was committed to the same universally egalitarian values that increasingly shaped the international system. If anything, the United States stood as nothing less than the first truly universal and liberal nation—and thus a legitimate model for the globe.

THE ALLURE OF CONSTITUTION-WRITING
IN THE INTERNATIONAL IMAGINATION

How did the Constitution come to feature so centrally in this emerging narrative, in which American governing elites fused a liberatory creedal vision with a specific defense of the 1787 document? And how did that document lose its conspicuous association with the country's compromise with slavery—an institutional history so obviously and deeply at odds with the emerging anti-colonial global ethic?

In this brave new world, both formerly colonized peoples and Western governments needed to reconstruct their national stories and positions. Emerging states sought to develop identities and institutions that were domestically politically coherent and also legible at the international level. Similarly, given the global struggle for influence and moral authority, the US and the European imperial powers had to recast their country's narratives in ways that resonated both internally and externally in these unfamiliar times.

In this context, the Constitution gained a central position in both the US's inward-facing self-representations and its outward-facing ideology. In particular, a US claim to constitution-writing itself became central to this transformation. To an important degree, constitution-writing—conceived of as a foundational activity in the initial construction of a self-controlling and self-representing polity—had attained a symbolic status in American life. When the United States adopted its federal Constitution in the late eighteenth century, projects of explicit constitution-writing were historical anomalies. In a global order shaped by European empires, very few polities boasted such formally implemented documents. Of the sovereign states that existed before 1789 (the year the US Constitution went into effect) and that persist today, half would go over three hundred years from their initial founding before eventually writing their own texts.[43]

Even more important than the US Constitution, the process by which American territories acceded to statehood critically involved the drafting and formal adoption of a constitution. The transformation of Indigenous land into a state began with the demographic removal of Native peoples and settlement by Anglo-Europeans, after which settlers would write a new constitution and seek admission to statehood. In this way, constitution-writing became a key marker in the process of westward expansion and the accepted precondition for recognition as equal, self-governing "sister" states. By the mid-nineteenth century, it had spread as a defining political experience in American life.

During the same period, especially in the wake of the European revolutionary upheavals of 1848, constitution-writing also increasingly amounted to an almost automatic political act for new countries.[44] It then proliferated globally precisely through the slow disintegration of the imperial model and with the emergence of newly independent nation-states. Indeed, constitution-writing occurred especially during particular "global waves":[45] those aforementioned 1848 revolutions, the two world wars, mid-twentieth-century decolonization, and then after the fall of the Soviet Union.[46]

Throughout these eras, nationalist elites sought both to establish independence from past imperial rulers and to assert the equal and sovereign status of their polities vis-à-vis other major powers and state formations. Therefore, written constitutions emerged as a key institutional and symbolic mechanism serving multiple related ends: For domestic audiences, the documents codified both political rupture with the old empire and the principles of the new polity. On the international stage, they allowed nationalist leaders, especially in the decolonizing Global South, to assert equal sovereign statehood and to illustrate to European audiences the genuinely "modern" nature of their political projects.

In a world in which the challenges and needs of new polities moved to the forefront of global discussions, American elites came to understand and to position the US as the original constitutional, anti-imperial paradigm—the first among equals, both temporally and substantively. In joining creedal ideals with veneration specifically for the 1787 Constitution, governing elites developed a uniquely American account of liberal nationalism—one attuned to the ideological needs of global primacy in an age of decolonization and rising non-white political power.

In the process, politicians and commentators distinguished the US from Europe generally, but also specifically the legitimacy of twentieth-century American global dominance from the illegitimacy of the old imperial orders. Officials explained their presence on the world stage as a projection of the basic values and ideals of constitutionalism itself, rather than in service of ends such as extraction and conquest. American international police power was justified because the country's organizing principles centered on independence and constitutional democracy, as framed through its governing text.

The US Constitution came to serve as tangible evidence of this fact— as a document that preserved freedoms at home, with principles that could be exported abroad for stable and prosperous development overseas. In this way, whenever the country intervened militarily abroad or asserted its economic and political might, it did so in order to create a stable and self-governing world of liberal constitutional states. Constitutionalism provided both an ideological basis for international arrangements under American supervision and the model for how foreign states should themselves be domestically structured. For this reason, it was inappropriate to compare the US to other empires; instead, its interests were effectively the same as the world's interests.

Of course, many countries have embedded their global projections of power in narratives of singular destiny. The American language of its own exceptionalism vis-à-vis other empires placed US foreign policymakers in a long line of past European imperial officials. European powers had also justified their nations' global authority with claims of special historic destiny and of the unusual gifts that they alone could offer the world.

But the unique American fusion of this narrative with creedal constitutionalism had real resonance globally. It was shaped by the particular international discourses and political contingencies of the early to mid-twentieth century and bolstered by reform successes at home. Thus, the US emphasis on constitutionalism as a hallmark of national identity and national power had ideological strength and significant political ramifications both internally and externally.

None of this is to say that political elites approached their treatment of the Constitution instrumentally, reaching for venerative arguments simply as a veil to justify assertions of power. Rather, policymakers and commentators came to believe deeply and authentically in both a specific vision of US constitutionalism and the necessity of the American Century. This profound emotional investment is a large part of what made the culture that eventually emerged around the Constitution one of romance.

Furthermore, creedal constitutionalism and global primacy, as ideological commitments circulating in American life, had distinct intellectual roots. As becomes clearer in the chapters that follow, one logic did not necessarily cause the other, and the two developed from a variety of cultural and political sources. Nonetheless, as the twentieth century unfolded, they fed off each other and spread in tandem, with creedal constitutionalism and growing assertions of US international authority mutually constituting and reinforcing one another.

The eventual result was a quintessentially American worldview in which it became increasingly difficult to imagine the country without either its Constitution or its global dominance. Therefore, the breakdown in recent years of faith in *both* the existing constitutional system *and* the legitimacy of the country's role abroad (if not much of a reduction in its actual power) should perhaps come as no shock. The legal scholars David Law and Mila Versteeg note a sharp "decline of American constitutional leadership." Outside of the US, societies engaged in drafting and reform exercises have tended to avoid the Constitution's limited rights provisions, let alone its approach to federalism, presidentialism, and judicial review. Simply put, the "content of the U.S. Constitution is becoming increasingly atypical by global standards."[47] In some ways, the effective collapse of the American constitutional system as a model of export may offer one indicator of the intensifying questions about broader American global authority. Just as both were fused together, their mutually entangled limitations now simultaneously face real scrutiny.

IMPERIAL CONSTITUTIONALISM AND AVOIDING CONCEPTUAL PITFALLS

It is not surprising that the conditions that gave birth to the American Century—especially the global backdrop—are rarely explored in work on the country's constitutional culture and politics. I would argue that, in many ways, most American writing about the Constitution has been a product of these same developments. And it can be difficult to recognize the historical contingency and the positionality of one's own analytical framework—a difficulty I struggle with myself.

But the general failure of much of the existing literature to put the Constitution in conversation with key international structural dynamics, and with American global assertiveness, leads to a series of potential political traps. It promotes a conventional treatment of constitutionalism and American primacy as opposed domains, viewing constitutional rights and discourse as principally a constraint on American interventionist excesses or potential geostrategic overreach. In fairness, in some instances the assumed oppositional dynamic holds.

Yet this conceptual framework, which juxtaposes constitutionalism against empire, ignores how the construction and maintenance of American international police power—in service of market dictates and related state security objectives—became invested with moral legitimacy precisely through a constitutional register. Such creedal constitutionalism, therefore, was not antithetical to global dominance. Instead, reverence for the Constitution stood as the ethical core of the modern American imperial imagination. In other words, US global primacy was ideologically grounded in what amounted to a form of imperial constitutionalism.

Focusing too narrowly on domestic explanations can undermine critical distance from that broader twentieth-century mythmaking about US political identity. In assuming creedal constitutionalism's own anti-imperial narrative, it can also implicitly reaffirm, rather than interrogate, the very thing in need of explanation: the genuflection before an eighteenth-century constitutional document often regarded by external observers—and now even by many Americans—as outdated. In this way, bringing to light the international frame not only provides a historical corrective; it also offers one way to contest an exceptionalist—and thus preservationist—approach to American constitutional culture.

An Alternative Historical Approach and a New Cast of Characters

As should be clear from the foregoing arguments, although the following pages proceed through a historical narrative about American constitutional culture, this is not a traditional work of history.[48] Rather, I see this project as a form of social criticism, in which history is presented in service of today's problems as well as tomorrow's latent possibilities. My focus on the historical past is ultimately instrumental; it seeks to illuminate how the American experience itself holds the normative tools for grappling with the current moment and for imagining emancipatory alternatives.[49]

This means that the book does not aim to be comprehensive, despite its length. It does not cover every significant mass political effort related to the Constitution. But it does endeavor to do two related things: First, I try to make sense of how ideas and institutions have fit together over the course of the twentieth century to create durable structures of constitutional meaning and power, with significant ramifications for the organization of state and economy. These structures provided the backdrop against which American activists struggled to reshape their world. Second, and relatedly, I attempt to provide an expansive engagement with the truly wide variety of constitutional experiments pursed by earlier generations of Americans—freedom activists who became constitutional thinkers in their own right.

This book therefore introduces a new cast of characters—largely ignored in mainstream constitutional reflections—who sought to fundamentally transform the constitutional order on grounds of genuine democracy. In part for this reason, the following pages do not primarily focus on the usual substance of constitutional scholarship: discussions oriented toward the courts over how to interpret particular textual clauses. In fact, even what counts in the scholarship as "popular constitutionalism" has tended to study how movement activists participate in court-centered interpretive debates. Critically, however, these debates are largely mediated through the language and assumptions of legal experts and have taken for granted key parameters of the established constitutional order.

This book instead seeks to build an alternative archive of constitutional actors and possibilities—beyond the familiar judges, lawyers, and presidents and what they viewed as worthy of discussion. Thus, it focuses on how this new cast of characters conceived of a very different American institutional landscape. At times this required their engagement with matters of textual interpretation. But frequently it entailed grappling with how to create better institutional and cultural conditions for legal, political, and economic decision-making. So while the following chapters spend time with lawyers and judges and discuss Supreme Court cases, my protagonists often operated well outside the domains of court-centered politics. So too does this book.

These figures though were not simply channels for mass sentiment or public opinion—which is a notoriously tricky thing to capture, even during periods of popular awareness of and interest in the Constitution. Rather, they were elites of a sort.[50] They often formulated and presented culturally salient views—views that tapped into underlying social bases and that enjoyed support from and influence on meaningful stakeholders. But largely because their ideas spilled beyond the consolidated terms of the creedal Constitution, they rarely appear in conventional constitutional writing.

Still, I argue that these characters, familiar and unfamiliar, should be named and understood as important constitutional thinkers—Eugene Debs, Emma Goldman, Crystal Eastman, Hubert Harrison, Laura Cornelius Kellogg, W. E. B. Du Bois, Harry Haywood, Paul Robeson, Norman Thomas, Vito Marcantonio, Martin Luther King Jr., Grace Lee Boggs and James Boggs, Afeni Shakur, Beulah Sanders, Vine Deloria Jr., and Hank Adams, to name just a few. These activists confronted the constraining structures of their times with their own novel and evolving constitutional diagnoses and strategies, many of which remain relevant today.

In important ways, such figures generated deeply American analyses and solutions. This is not to say that they were nationalists. Indeed, many were not, and they were often explicitly *anti*-nationalists. They

refused to elevate solidaristic attachments to fellow citizens above those
to fellow workers, colonized peoples, or women. But they struggled
with how to create new arrangements responsive to the particularities
of the American collective predicament. And they all treated the Constitution as a necessary site of mass-movement intervention in a way
that, in their successes and failures, provides valuable insights as well as
cautionary lessons.

While most accounts of important constitutional actors, and of the
Constitution's role in American life, start at the founding, this book
does not. Indeed, my argument is that the constitutional culture we live
under is a profoundly twentieth-century product. Imagining that the
world of James Madison or Alexander Hamilton will tell us why Americans connect the Constitution to creedal equality or to civil libertarianism engages in the same historical flattening that defined Cold War
American exceptionalism. It reads back into the eighteenth century an
account of American meaning that was the product of later developments, and that only became dominant under twentieth-century international and domestic conditions.

Instead, the story I tell unfolds in four parts, focused especially on
those decisive years between the first and the second centennial, 1887
to 1987. Part I, "Disagreement and Experimentation in the Gilded Age,
1887–1917," returns us to the unfamiliar world before the permanent
fusing of creed and Constitution, and well before their durable connection to global primacy, market capitalism, civil libertarian commitments, and Supreme Court reverence. It engages with the profound
social uncertainty that marked these years as well as the striking experiments, presented especially by socialist and labor reformers, in how to
reimagine the constitutional order. It ultimately concludes by focusing
on how one such experiment—that of American global expansionism—
emerged out of the thicket.

Part II, "The Spread of a New Constitutional Citizenship, 1917–
1945," then explores how America's rising global power and the two
world wars, along with domestic struggles during the Great Depression, disseminated creedal constitutionalism across the American public. These years witnessed the elevation of such claims about peoplehood from a marginal position in white society to the most common
way white Americans spoke to each other about the country. It also explores the last significant moment in which mass publics seriously debated altering the constitutional system root and branch: the mid-1930s

period before eventual conservative Supreme Court capitulation to the New Deal.

Part III, "Consolidating the American Model, 1945–1965," engages with how, against the backdrop of the Cold War, officials began both systematically reconceiving the international system in an American constitutional image and entrenching an increasingly rigid model at home. These chapters also explore the rise of the Supreme Court and of the constitutional lawyer as the definitive guardians of constitutional meaning and possibility. They juxtapose these developments against those remaining sites of domestic dissent, as well as the contesting views of overseas independence leaders engaged in economic and political decolonization.

Part IV, "Alternative Paths and Constitutional Erasure, 1965–1987," concludes the historical narrative by exploring how the war in Vietnam generated the last movement politics of constitutional re-founding, however quixotic. This episode centered around Black radical ideas, especially associated with the Black Panther Party, of a non-imperial and decolonized United States, in keeping with those events in Asia and Africa. It then explores how, after the collapse of Left activism, politicians and commentators increasingly distinguished the "bad" 1960s of Left disintegration and violent excess from the "good" 1960s of a nonviolent civil rights movement grounded in creedal constitutional language. In the process, political figures across the spectrum steadily embraced a return to American origins, one that conservatives in particular transformed into a powerful ideology of restoration. By the second centennial, the result was a mainstream public culture that appeared to imbibe, unquestioningly, Constitution worship.

At the end of this historical arc, Americans have effectively found themselves in a trap of their own making. Our constitutional climate, which looks reverentially over a collective shoulder to the past, certainly enabled supremely important successes, including for the rights of women, racial and ethnic minorities, and LGBTQ+ groups, among others. But such reverence also helped to create ideological space for the emergence of a growing political and legal project wary of, and even hostile to, the very real changes wrought by the preceding decades.

This traditionalist paradigm—originalism—is framed around a return to those eighteenth-century founders and a commitment to implementing their perceived original will across the contemporary social, economic, and political landscape. The official version of creedal con-

stitutionalism, which extols the genius of the founders and proclaims
the country's inherent liberal egalitarianism, set the stage for this interpretive move. Our constitutional culture thus means that legal and
ideological contests already take place on an uneven playing field. It also
pushes certain arguments and proposals off the table, making it harder
for reformers today to access the broader array of political and institutional claims available to activists of previous generations.

Toward a Constitutional Politics of Change

If the process of constitution-writing has been central to US claims
about its exceptional status, the country is no longer at the forefront
of such experiments. Since the 1789 implementation of the US Constitution, 220 countries have appeared on the global stage, and between
them they have produced a remarkable 900 written constitutions, many
marked by genuinely innovative features.[51]

The sheer numbers are telling for another reason as well: for the most
part, societies treat their constitutions instrumentally. Commentators
often conceive of a constitution as embodying the enduring values of a
polity, which suggests a degree of solidity and cultural permanence.[52]
But, at the same time, constitutional texts also establish a governing
structure aimed at resolving collective problems, negotiating internal
conflicts, and securing essential rights. When these legal-political orders break down or social upheaval brings new elites and alliances to
power, old documents may well be jettisoned and new ones written.
Societies rarely treat their written constitutions as being at the core of
national purpose or "peoplehood."

What defines French political identity, for example, has little to do
with the Fifth Republic's 1958 constitution, and far more to do with a
shared republican project rooted in earlier revolutionary traditions. For
most states in modern history, a constitutional document's time horizon is hardly unlimited; its text provides one of many options that may
work well or fail to serve social ends, depending on the circumstances.
Indeed, many outside the US have found deeply puzzling the American
commitment to their clearly dysfunctional document.

The time has come to reconsider the value of US constitutional exceptionalism, including the continued embrace of an order that has proven
ill-suited for a collective American project aimed at equal and effective
freedom. Today's brand of creedal constitutionalism is a real hindrance

to serious discussion of institutional and social change. It promotes a persistent retreat into a politics of constitutional veneration, which has had the effect of naturalizing a fundamentally undemocratic order.

Still, the history of creedal constitutionalism's emergence is also the history of how Americans long thought that things could be otherwise. The following pages aim to present a new, more complete, and more complex national story that brings back the broad-ranging constitutional debates that once circulated among labor leaders, socialists, Black activists, feminists, Indigenous leaders, and immigrants. These debates went to the heart of topics that have become so critical today: which rights to defend; how legal, representative, and economic institutions could be designed otherwise; the extent to which the country should address its colonial and racial foundations; and what all this means for both global power and the structures of the national security state. At a time when Americans are confronting the limits of the path we have taken, revisiting past constitutional alternatives offers a set of guideposts and possibilities for confronting the dilemmas of the present.

Importantly, though, these guideposts should not be understood as applying only to a narrow set of legal-constitutional elites. Truly changing American constitutional culture would require the emergence of a dynamic and coalitional mass movement—one that integrates a constitutional politics within movement efforts aimed at overcoming the vast array of today's hierarchies.

And it would require investing existing movement spaces with a much more expansive understanding of what is, and what has been, constitutionally possible in the United States. Movement activists today certainly organize around specific Supreme Court cases. And policymakers have started to debate procedural corrections to the electoral and judicial structures. But at a deep level, the nature of these engagements highlights the extent to which the Constitution as a whole is more or less treated as a matter for experts, especially lawyers, who serve as intermediaries between publics and governing institutions.

By contrast, our moment requires genuine popular control over the memory, terms, and ambitions of constitutional politics. Ultimately, the Constitution must be removed from its national pedestal. This could begin to unwind some of the more problematic consequences of creedal constitutionalism, even beyond resistance to technical fixes alone. At the very least, it would allow us to start disaggregating the components of today's thick account of creedal constitutionalism, and to ask which of these components are actually worth defending. And it could push us to appreciate how removing the roadblocks imposed by the constitutional system may well require us to challenge other pillars of contemporary American nationalism.

The obstacles to any transformative change are numerous. But a present-day movement culture equipped with a richer constitutional memory could begin to think through these questions in a serious way. Backed by a historically informed understanding of our predicament, and of possible alternatives, we would be positioned to contest the existing apparatus on meaningfully stronger grounds.

PART I

Disagreement and Experimentation in the Gilded Age, 1887–1917

The one hundredth anniversary of American independence. . . . How much happier she would be now if she had England's form of government instead of the miserable delusion of a republic. . . . I venture to say that this republic will never celebrate another centennial as a republic. The English form of government is the only true one.

WOODROW WILSON, SHORTHAND DIARY (JULY 4, 1876)

We can give the Filipinos constitutional government, a government which they can count upon to be just, a government based upon some clear and equitable understanding, intended for their good and not for our aggrandizement; but we must ourselves for the present supply that government. It would, it is true, be an unprecedented operation . . . but America has before this shown the world enlightened processes of politics that were without precedent.

WOODROW WILSON, "THE PLACE OF THE UNITED STATES IN CONSTITUTIONAL DEVELOPMENT" (1907)

CHAPTER 2

Settler Crisis and
Constitutional Uncertainty

Throughout the year of 1887, the privately run Constitutional Centennial Commission labored assiduously to stir up enthusiasm for the document's one hundredth anniversary on September 17.[1] It was an uphill battle for these business and political notables, with the patrician Republican Senator Henry Cabot Lodge serving as vice president. Perhaps surprisingly for modern readers, the Constitution at the time played a relatively tangential role in underpinning political cohesion.

Such civic leaders had in mind events that would mirror the widely celebrated centennial of the Declaration of Independence, just eleven years earlier. The historian Walter Nugent writes that, across the country, the Declaration's anniversary had been marked by "parades, fireworks displays, and speeches—all of monstrous size." And, as the centerpiece of these festivities, nearly ten million people flocked to Philadelphia between May and November to attend the Centennial International Exhibition, despite oppressive summer weather and an ongoing smallpox epidemic.[2] Composed of over two hundred buildings and countless displays, the exhibition—a giant World's Fair— constituted a sprawling city stretching hundreds of acres, drawing spectators from seemingly every corner of the nation.[3] As one Indiana newspaper of the time noted, "the only great question [is] . . . 'Goin' to the Centennial, hey?'"[4]

The Constitution's centennial attracted far less interest, although the Commission's efforts seemed a clear success at first glance. For the weekend of the celebration, hotels in Philadelphia overflowed and flags waved across the city. The *New York Times* noted a massive crowd of some half a million visitors. There were banquets for city dignitaries and a public program entailing a large military parade and patriotic addresses, including from President Grover Cleveland.[5]

But the Commission had set its sights higher. They hoped for exten-sive congressional funding, maybe even along the lines of the one-and-a-half-million-dollar loan extended for the Declaration's anniversary.[6] They sought an official poet and orator, both of great national renown, who would extol the text in verse and prose respectively. They imagined nationwide events on September 17, setting the stage for rolling state-level celebrations over the next two years to commemorate each state's ratification. And they wanted to erect a "permanent memorial" to the Constitution in Philadelphia.[7]

Yet from the very beginning, the celebrations were beset with com-plications. The organizers could not convince Congress to provide funding or support. Major poets declined to participate, and in the end no poet was found. The Commission had limited success in attracting an official orator, and Associate Supreme Court Justice Samuel Miller ultimately agreed only after numerous other figures turned down the request. Many whom the Commission invited to attend the celebration politely declined. And the memorial project was quietly shuttered.[8]

Two local developments eventually saved the constitutional com-memoration from disaster: Pennsylvania elites increasingly saw the impending collapse of the anniversary festivities as a potential embar-rassment for the state and for Philadelphia, leading the state legislature to allocate $75,000 in the summer of 1887. And local business figures, for similar reasons and practically at the last minute, engaged in a con-certed effort to pump large amounts of money, publicity, and logistical support into the September 17 events.[9]

As for countrywide celebrations, very little was done, including by states over the next year to commemorate their ratification of the doc-ument.[10] Numerous cities finally organized mass celebrations in 1889.[11] But, crucially, organizers centered these events around April 30, the day in 1789 that George Washington was sworn in as the country's first president, consciously bootstrapping the Constitution to the greater charismatic appeal of the revolutionary war hero. According to the *Washington Post*, this date—rather than September 17, 1787—entailed "the true beginning of our Constitutional history."[12] Thus, genuine na-tional success entailed shifting the focus away from the text and toward a figure with mass cultural connection.[13]

It was not hard for the Constitutional Centennial Commission to fathom why it was so difficult to promote mass celebratory events. In the words of one key organizer, the problem lay in "the entire absence of any interest or general sentiment in favor of the proposed celebration on the part of the public at large." While all Americans understood that July 4 commemorated the nation's independence, the Commission's secretary noted that "few knew of the 17th of September, or cared to consider its claim to national recognition." And, as the secretary continued, "the proposed demonstration was purely intellectual in its purpose, and appealed neither to passion nor prejudice."[14]

This relative indifference to the Constitution may partly explain why the Commission had such difficulty generating interest outside the state, such as by having other states' governors attend the centennial events. Politicians elsewhere often read the promotion of the Constitution's September signing date in the context of interstate rivalries. They considered it an unwelcome emphasis of Philadelphia's status, rather than a defining national celebration akin to honoring July 4.[15]

This anecdote of the Commission's problems hints at significant—although often overlooked—reasons why the world of 1887 would be so unfamiliar to contemporary Americans. Critically, the activities of territorial settlement and expansion were at the heart of what forged Americans into a distinctive people. These processes provided settler insiders—especially a subset of white Protestant men—access to a particular vision of equal freedom, involving participatory political structures and broad enjoyment of land and property. The federal Constitution, specifically, served as a clear national symbol, but in many ways it was less central to those narratives and experiences.

If anything, at the twilight of the nineteenth century, growing numbers of politically relevant elites began expressing varying degrees of constitutional uncertainty. The central reason had to do with the increasing disconnect between long-standing aspirations to political and economic freedom and lived realities on the ground. The closing of the frontier meant that there were no new Native lands to claim and thus soon no new property to divide among those included as settlers. At the same time, the rise of industrialization and corporate consolidation created a dramatically altered economic landscape—one that regimented work life, heightened class inequalities, and challenged traditional gender relations. And many settler Americans saw a further danger to social order and national identity in the country's increasing heterogeneity, brought on by slavery's demise and then by large-scale migration from southern and eastern Europe, not to mention parts of Asia.

What started to emerge in this context was a view—over time articulated with greater boldness—that the federal Constitution did little to cohere an unraveling American body politic, recently torn apart by civil war and now increasingly undone by industrial strife. Commentators began to wonder if the Constitution had in fact become outmoded—an unwieldy governing structure and the product of a different world altogether. Thus, while business notables were rallying citizens to celebrate the document, questions about the text were creeping closer to the political center: Should the legal-political system be judged responsible for the intensifying conflicts in economic and political life? And to what degree had the Constitution failed as a decision-making framework for this republic, constructed as it was on fundamentally ethno-racial terms?

This chapter explores these profound disagreements swirling through American life by the end of the nineteenth century, including around the basic meaning and legitimacy of the Constitution. Many Americans held firm to a collective identity grounded in a project of Euro-American territorial settlement, which faced increasing pressure as the century closed. Political and legal notables also embraced a cultural tendency of praising the Constitution's genius. But such practices did not signify that the document held the same type of political salience and social cohesion as in the following century, complete with the later rise to a far more exalted status of the Supreme Court. During much of the nineteenth century, there existed hardly any popular education with respect to the Constitution—not to mention strikingly limited memorialization through art and landmarks. Indeed, throughout the country's first hundred years, state constitutions—which routinely rejected the design structures of the federal text—tended to be more central to how ordinary Americans understood their actual constitutional experience and politics.

The chapter also details how creedal ideas about universal racial equality—so integral to current constitutional and national meaning—fit uneasily within these trends. Many Euro-American settlers not only repudiated this vision of national identity, but often saw such commitments as part of the problem. Against the backdrop of collapsing Reconstruction policies and intensifying Jim Crow conditions, Black American leaders kept alive ideas of a creedal and redemptive national constitutional project. But there remained deep Black internal ambivalence about the text and even about political union with the larger white community.

The chapter concludes by detailing the late nineteenth century's systematic dissolution of settler social bonds and institutional conditions—by the Civil War, industrialization and its implications for family structure, the closing of the frontier, and mass European migration. This dissolution intensified broader political conflicts and raised foundational questions about the future of the national project along with the basic legitimacy of the federal Constitution.

The tensions detailed in the chapter as a whole cast doubt on a type of historical compression common in popular and even some scholarly accounts of American constitutional development. Such compression can treat the mid-twentieth-century consolidation of creedal narratives around the Constitution as almost inevitable, a natural development of a much earlier constitutional culture.

But the twentieth-century outcome was far from inevitable. In fact, the American past held remarkable ideological openness—for good and for bad. The years between the 1887 centennial and the 1917 American entry into World War I were defined by extreme discord and by a striking popular willingness to engage in broad-ranging legal-political experimentation. Ignoring this fluidity masks the importance of twentieth-century global and domestic dynamics in eventually reorienting—and melding—American ideas of race, identity, and Constitution.

Settler Freedom in "White Man's Country"

How did early Euro-Americans conceive of social cohesion in their new nation, and how did this vision eventually come apart? Or, alternatively, what collapsing nineteenth-century ideology left a hole large enough for the rise of creedal constitutionalism in the decades that followed?

Most Americans living in 1900 would likely have described their country in ways that mirrored President Theodore Roosevelt's famous phrase. As hinted at in chapter 1, Roosevelt believed that, more than anything else, the US embodied a peopling of North America with European settlers to create a free but ethno-racially defined republic—a project and history shared with Britain's other settler societies.[16] These societies, including South Africa, Australia, New Zealand, and Canada, with the United States at the forefront, embodied the ascendancy of "English speaking peoples over the world's waste spaces." And this political and material transformation of Indigenous land into settled US territory—the actual defining experience of the long nineteenth century—cemented social bonds in the new country.

For Roosevelt, such racial ascendancy brought with it the spread of civilization across the globe and "ha[d] been not only the most striking feature in the world's history, but also the event of all the others most far-reaching in its effect and importance."[17] Indeed, in response to Japan's stunning 1905 military victory over Russia, Roosevelt sent American ships to Australia and New Zealand two years later in a show of white solidarity. As he told his Secretary of the Navy, the tour aimed to reinforce how "those colonies" were "white man's country"[18] — just like the United States.

But the US settlement of North America was not intended to be simply an outgrowth of European political and cultural dominance — a mere transplantation of imperial "civilization" to a presumptively "savage" wilderness. Since well before the founding, it had been typical to imagine the thirteen colonies as both an extension of the Old World and a key corrective to its faults. In particular, territorial expansion and the availability of land made the United States distinctive by allegedly solving those basic problems of class hierarchy and feudalism that had long bedeviled European states. At their most self-congratulatory, Americans throughout the nineteenth century often presented their society as free and equal, in internal class terms, to a degree yet unknown in human history.[19]

In an earlier work, *The Two Faces of American Freedom*, I examined how, as a result, Euro-Americans often presumed that legal and political institutions were meant to do two things simultaneously. First, they were supposed to provide racially defined insiders with an experience of "republican freedom," or the emancipatory conditions for self-government and economic independence. And second, to support this overarching project, these institutions were designed to extract much-needed land and labor from Native and non-settler groups, in the latter case particularly enslaved African workers and their descendants.[20]

I refer to this structuring framework as one of *settler empire* — combining internal freedom for settlers with external subordination and control. The term itself would not have been familiar to early-twentieth-century Americans. But the basic ethical vision and political objectives certainly would have resonated: governmental structures would ensure that settler insiders enjoyed economic and political self-rule, precisely by expanding into Indigenous land and coercing non-settler populations to engage in difficult but economically essential labor.

This framework was *imperial* because many Euro-Americans viewed territorial growth — and thus, necessarily, Indigenous conquest — as the basic engine for their own republican freedom and economic prosper-

ity. Indeed, conquest itself was often embraced as the key social experience cohering disparate European migrants into a single people. For
Frederick Jackson Turner, "movement" was nothing less than the "dominant fact"[21] of the American experience, a point Roosevelt echoed by
describing "winning the West" as "the great epic feat in the history of"
the American "race."[22]

The centrality of expansion to collective life had profound implications for how American ethno-racial identity compared to that in European home countries, particularly in relation to immigration. Even
before US independence, settlers recognized that territorial and economic growth rested on a burgeoning population, beyond what natural
demographic increases and migration by "Anglo-Saxons" alone could
provide. As a result, they created remarkably open immigration policies for Europeans deemed co-ethnics and thus co-participants in the
republican project. This meant that, for the first century of the United
States, the national border was essentially a port of entry for European
migrants, who were quickly incorporated into the political community.
This incorporation included practices that today would be quite surprising, such as noncitizen voting and noncitizen access to federal land
out west.[23] In essence, the territorial need for overseas migrants checked
the most xenophobic tendencies within settler society, by expanding
the ethnic and religious categories for who could count as American.

Indeed, as Turner and Roosevelt both emphasized, conquest and
settlement did more than just promote European inclusiveness or inculcate republican values. It was through this common experience of
building a new social order in a corner of the non-European world that
Europeans of diverse backgrounds became truly *American*. According
to Turner, "the frontier" did nothing less than "promote the formation
of a composite nationality for the American people," offering a "crucible" through which "immigrants were Americanized, liberated, and
fused into a mixed race."[24] As Roosevelt reiterated, this transformative
undertaking, "long before the first Continental Congress assembled,"
forged European migrants "whatever their blood" into "Americans" in
"speech, thought, and character."[25]

Roosevelt clearly understated the reality and circulation of a degree
of anti-immigrant—particularly anti-Catholic—sentiment, especially
in coastal cities like Boston and New York. But despite local electoral
success, nativist parties and organizations during the nineteenth century, such as the 1850s Know-Nothings, ultimately never succeeded in
undermining existing European naturalization or noncitizen suffrage

frameworks. Calls to place quotas on European migration, particularly from Catholic countries like Ireland, or to extend the waiting period before naturalization (for instance, to twenty-one years), were either ignored or rejected.[26]

Over the long term, both Turner and Roosevelt were right to highlight how the country's early focus on territorial and economic expansion relaxed the idea of who counted as a potential insider, and also underscored the ethnically amalgamated nature of American identity. This "strange mixture of blood"—in the words of the French American writer J. Hector St. John de Crèvecoeur—marked American life as separate from Europe, where the nineteenth-century story became one of the growing alignment of territorial boundaries with presumptively closed ethno-racial nations. By contrast, even in 1782, de Crèvecoeur wrote of the degree to which families themselves had become ethnically plural in US colonies: "I could point out to you a family whose grandfather was an Englishman, whose wife was Dutch, whose son married a French woman, and whose present four sons now have four wives of different nations."[27]

Crucially, this did not mean that the "composite nationality" of the United States was remotely universal, or that anyone would be included as a prospective co-participant in activities of settlement and thus a potential American. Race remained essential to navigating a rigid divide between social insiders and subordinated outsiders, precisely because only those seen as culturally assimilable could be included as free republican citizens. And although women were part of settler society, they could not themselves achieve the promise of political and economic freedom that lay at the heart of the settler narrative.

Thus, while many new European migrants may have had immediate access to the conditions necessary for full membership and equal political participation, this was not widely available. Native Americans, Blacks (whether enslaved or nominally free), or Mexicans who had long lived on the land were denied these basic rights. They existed as colonized populations within the territory of the United States. Like the country's settler siblings in the British imperial orbit, "a caste division ... [was] built into the economy, political system, and the law, with particular economic activities and political privileges ... reserved for members of the settler population."[28] As Roosevelt wrote of Chinese migrants, who as the nineteenth century wore on highlighted the limits of migrant inclusiveness, "from the United States and Australia the

Chinaman is kept out because the democracy, with much clearness of vision, has seen that his presence is ruinous to the white race."[29]

Perhaps most noteworthy about this divide between insider and outsider is that it was politically hardwired into the very structure of settler society. Expansion required uprooting Indigenous populations, whose claim to political independence—and therefore formal sovereign equality—had to be systematically rejected. Thus, as its constitutive precondition, the amalgamated Americanism that Turner and Roosevelt both celebrated rested on a basic imperial divide between "civilized" and "savage." Just as important, the early United States was an agricultural society in which most settlers assumed that for some to engage in the dignified "free labor" marked by productive control, there would have to be others that participated in forms of work long perceived to be degraded—such as tenancy, wage labor, and domestic service.

In other words, at the heart of pervasive republican notions of economic independence there existed a basic separation between free and unfree work. And Americans solved this problem by employing subordinated external groups, particularly enslaved Africans, to engage in the most oppressive modes of production. Arguments about ethno-racial superiority were therefore not merely matters of prejudice and xenophobia. They were the essential justifications for bedrock institutional features of the society: the expropriation of Native land and the control of dependent laboring communities. In this way, American political identity was intricately tied to imperial assumptions about the need for both new immigrant settlers and external control over dependent communities.

This structural feature of early American life exposes a basic weakness in how recent scholars have attempted to reconcile the inclusive and exclusive dimensions of the collective project, especially during the nineteenth century. For Rogers Smith, American identity has been permeated by a "multiplicity of traditions"—"liberal, democratic republican, and inegalitarian ascriptive." According to Smith, these "multiple traditions" are best understood as insular and discrete—"none too coherent compromises among distinct mixes."[30] Similarly, the historian Gary Gerstle writes that we can understand American identity through the conflict between "two powerful and contradictory ideals": one an inclusive and egalitarian "civic nationalism" (which he associates with the "hybridity" that Roosevelt often praised), and the other an exclusive and illiberal "racial nationalism."[31] Such arguments implicitly keep the valorized "civic" or "liberal" heritage isolated from and uncontaminated by practices of racial hierarchy; they reject any inherent tie between the two orientations.[32]

Instead of separate currents flowing into the well of American values, frameworks of exclusion and conquest are best seen as ideological and institutional prerequisites for the nineteenth-century growth of Turner's "composite nationality." Rather than contradictory, settler practices and institutions combined both egalitarian ideals *and* ethnoracial modes of subordination into a unified and coherent ideological whole. And it is unsurprising that the closing frontier coupled with industrial hierarchies at the turn of the twentieth century placed both facets of this vision under strain.

The Constitutionalisms That Mattered

The settler foundations of collective life in the first century of the republic highlight another element of profound importance about early American social cohesion. Early notables certainly took to praising the document. Still, constitution-making at the state level had far greater everyday significance than the founding text and institutional machinations of a distant federal government.

THE EARLY FOUNDATIONS OF
REVERENTIAL LANGUAGE

It is true that during the first half of the nineteenth century it became commonplace for politicians and lawyers to praise in speech the genius of the federal Constitution. As the political scientist Simon Gilhooley notes, starting especially with the second generation of Americans— those that came of age in the years after the War of 1812—the dominant relationship of political and economic elites to the revolutionary period was one of "heroic preservation."[33] In this context, extolling the Constitution—the founding era's concrete institutional legacy— became a key means for notables to show loyalty to that first generation's accomplishments. Fourth of July events across the new nation frequently included speeches by local figures on the perfection of the Constitution and the godlike wisdom of its authors.[34] An extensive practice of toasting the text even emerged as part of banquets celebrating independence.[35] In many ways, the eventual 1887 centennial celebration in Philadelphia was a natural extension of these traditions, pressed by business interests and organized around expensive banquets and patriotic speech-making.

More significantly, this period also witnessed a growing language of constitutional sacralization, closely tied to the deep Protestant roots of Anglo-European settlement. Since the seventeenth century, migration to the North American colonies had often involved devout Protestants emigrating in part due to religious persecution. These origins created a long-standing cultural atmosphere in which many settlers combined ideas of republican freedom with those of spiritual independence, viewing the project of colonization as a religious "errand into the wilderness."[36] As the literary scholar Sacvan Bercovitch writes, if the Puritans had once "discovered America in the Bible," this Protestant grounding meant that more and more early-nineteenth-century voices began "discover[ing] the Bible in the Declaration of Independence and the Constitution."[37]

These arguments were promoted by some of the most significant Protestant theologians of the period, such as the Unitarian preacher William Ellery Channing. Channing, for instance, drew parallels between the Bible and the Constitution as two types of holy texts, declaring to church members, "we reason about the Bible precisely as civilians do about the constitution."[38] As mentioned in chapter 1, religious connections were buttressed by the founding-era decision to place amendments after the 1787 document, reinforcing a view of the initial Constitution, according to the historian Jonathan Gienapp, as a "sacred text" or "untouchable historical artifact lodged in the archives."[39] That choice fit naturally with Protestant modes of scriptural reading, which also placed deep emphasis on textual wisdom.

Today, perhaps the best-remembered invocation among this compendium of early federal constitutional faith came from young Abraham Lincoln's 1838 Lyceum address, one of his first published speeches. There he combined the sensibility of "heroic preservation" with a treatment of the document as essentially sacred. Describing the Constitution as exceptional in human history, he presented his generation as "the legal inheritors of these fundamental blessings." The Constitution was part of a "legacy bequeathed to us," and it was his generation's responsibility to "transmit" this "political edifice" "unprofaned," "undecayed," and "untorn" "to the latest generation that fate shall permit the world to know." Given this task, Lincoln exhorted Americans to "pledge [their] life" to the Constitution, with the hope that it would "become the political religion of the nation."[40]

A DIFFERENT CULTURAL PRESENCE

Yet, for all the reverential language that circulated around the document at the time, it is nonetheless worth highlighting how the Constitution's cultural presence then differed from its presence in the late twentieth century. These were years when the document could be both venerated by notables in religious terms and, as the historian Michael Kammen demonstrated,[41] be relatively absent from cultural and educational contexts. Before the Civil War, there was strikingly little organized effort to educate Americans about the Constitution. Lawyers and scholars did write academic treatises about the document, like Justice Joseph Story's 1833 three-volume *Commentaries on the Constitution* (meant to "fix in the minds of the American youth a more devout enthusiasm for the constitution of their country").[42] But during a period when most people had little formal schooling beyond the elementary level, these types of treatises reached a very small segment of the public.

As for the schooling Americans did receive, it offered only the most cursory accounts of the federal Constitution.[43] For instance, at the start of the Civil War in 1861, California was the only state that required schools to teach the document at all.[44] In part, the lack of interest can be explained by the general absence of a "national system of public education."[45] Yet that alone cannot account for the fact that the history textbooks used in the existing schools also paid scant attention to the Constitution, usually only a page or two on the Convention with hardly anything on the first ten amendments (today's sanctified Bill of Rights) or developments since.[46] As one historian concluded of non-college textbooks through the 1850s, "these school histories made little or nothing, either of the Federal Constitution or of the federal government. It was rare indeed to find the text of the document in these books."[47]

This educational deemphasis was of a piece with broader cultural trends. Outside of some banquets, the fiftieth anniversary of the Constitution passed largely unnoticed. The September 17 date came and went with very few Americans engaging in any public commemorations and without Congress making any reference to it at all.[48] As for memorialization of the document, the famed warship USS *Constitution* may have been commissioned in 1797; but it was highly uncommon for cities or streets to be named after the text in the nineteenth century, with 182 locales called Liberty but just one designated Constitution. Indeed, according to Kammen, strikingly little iconography— "objects, paintings, engravings, and lithographs" — of the document or of the Philadelphia

Convention were produced throughout the century, certainly by comparison with the Declaration or, in England, the Magna Carta.[49]

As for the Supreme Court specifically, it did not enjoy the same enduring status that came to define its later place in collective life. The early nineteenth century may have been marked by some of the Court's more famous decisions, such as *Marbury v. Madison* (1803), in which Chief Justice John Marshall asserted the right of judicial review — including the capacity of the federal courts to invalidate those congressional laws federal judges believed were unconstitutional. But as we will explore, the overwhelming identification of the Constitution and constitutional meaning as such with the activities and judgments of the Supreme Court had hardly been cemented.[50] Just as important, the institution competed with other sites, both state and federal, for standing and esteem. These were years in which, as an historian of the Marshall Court declared, "the state courts . . . were more venerable than the federal."[51] The political scientist Justin Crowe writes that during the initial decades of its existence, the Supreme Court had far less institutional "prestige, respect, and power" than one might assume. "It had no building, a small budget, and was largely controlled and handicapped by the other branches of government."[52]

Even where the justices resided speaks to a very different constitutional world. Justices boarded in the same house until 1845, initially because of a lack of adequate accommodations in Washington, DC. Yet this practice continued past when it was necessary, in part because justices preferred to live primarily in their home states, with Marshall remaining in Richmond, Virginia and, as late as 1834, only one justice actually living in DC with his family.[53]

In short, during these decades, the Constitution may have had intense symbolic meaning for individuals like Lincoln or Channing: they were committed to making sense of their own relationship to the founding and their political or spiritual role in preserving the national project. But such real devotion went hand in hand with a perhaps surprising degree of cultural inattention.

STATE CONSTITUTION-WRITING AND TERRITORIAL CONQUEST

Indeed, the greater orientation around the states speaks to the way in which nineteenth-century life was marked by often isolated and disaggregated local communities. This was a direct result of how territorial settlement proceeded: the processes of expansion—and thus resulting institutional authority—were largely decentralized. This meant that driving political and economic debates and concerns were typically located in one's nearby surroundings. The federal policy-making world of Washington, DC, was a distant affair.

Just as significantly, the practical activity of settlement elevated the salience of the writing and construction of constitutions, but it did so most prominently for state efforts. The governing structure of expansion, going all the way back to the process initiated by the 1787 Northwest Ordinance,[54] placed conquered and annexed territories on a path to eventual statehood. This formal presumption that all territory should eventually become a state was ideologically essential for American settler empire. As new land was settled by Anglo-Europeans and fully incorporated into the broader society, economically and culturally, that new land would gain equal legal status. This process, which ensured internal political equality for settler insiders as well as the steady displacement of Native peoples, became crucial for the racialized transformation of the North American land mass.[55]

As part of this transformation, the act by white settlers of writing a state constitution emerged as a defining moment. Just as writing and ratifying the federal Constitution was a key marker of political maturity and sovereignty for the newly independent US polity vis-à-vis the great European empires, state constitution-writing signaled a similar cultural, demographic, and political readiness for full settler self-rule on the expanding territorial frontier. The centrality of written constitutions to political creation and popular sovereignty was no doubt a distinctive feature of American legal-political practice. It perhaps indicates the deeply embedded nature in settler society of a long-standing Protestant focus on text when it came to making sense of both faith and community.

For my purposes, there are two things that are particularly noteworthy about such state constitutionalism. To begin with, it underscored the long-running interconnection in American life between constitutionalism generally and the project of empire. From the earliest days of independence, making land truly "American" went hand in hand with the construction of new constitutions. As we will see, this very much remained the case even in the twentieth century, long after the US abandoned formally annexing new territories. Officials continued to view constitution-writing, overseen now by the US federal state, as central to maturation processes and nation-building efforts in foreign societies. It became closely bound to how American policymakers conceived of themselves as bringing peace and stability to the globe.

Yet, if in later years the US Constitution would become the exclusive "American" model, local settler elites did not mechanistically replicate the design features of the 1787 text. As the political scientist John Dinan details, when it came time to construct governing frameworks throughout the nineteenth century, state constitutional delegates explicitly debated the pluses and minuses of the federal document. And they largely chose not to follow its path, opting instead for far more majoritarian and flexible political systems.[56]

State constitutions tended to be marked by easier amendment processes, greater constraints on executive authority, expanded legislative powers, and an elected rather than an appointed (let alone lifetime-appointed) bench.[57] Indeed, the legal scholars Mila Versteeg and Emily Zackin note that "by 1860, eighteen of the thirty-one existing states had adopted entirely elected, rather than appointed, judiciaries."[58] In Dinan's words, all of this amounted to a basic "rejection of the federal model."[59]

Perhaps counterintuitively, the greater everyday salience of state constitutional politics actually helps to explain why no anti–federal Constitution party emerged in the early nineteenth century. During the 1787–88 ratification process, there had been outspoken opponents of the federal Constitution. Many, like Pennsylvania's Samuel Bryan, viewed the document as simply an effort by coastal and mercantile elites to turn back the small-scale and participatory democratic practices that had taken root during the revolutionary period. Writing under the pseudonym Centinel, Bryan depicted the proposed federal structure as a remote and opaque mechanism that would subvert popular rule and allow the few to wrest power from the many: "The wealthy and ambitious, who in every community think they have a right to lord it over their fellow creatures, have availed themselves, very successfully, of this favorable disposition; for the people thus unsettled in their sentiments, have been prepared to accede to any extreme of government."[60]

But in the post-ratification period, since real political decision-making continued to occur at the state and local levels, what happened at the federal level was often of less immediate concern. And settlers who may have agreed with Samuel Bryan could simply reject the perceived anti-democratic flaws of the federal model and pursue more majoritarian frameworks at the state level. Thus the stakes in continuing to press for a different federal model were limited. As long as settlers wielded decentralized control over the terms of their own property, racial hierarchy, and gender relations—as well as over the ends of territorial expansion—whatever happened in Washington, DC, was of little import.

Indeed, this reality produced a striking duality among many state politicians, especially those associated with President Andrew Jackson and with a particular vision of white producerist democracy. On the one hand, many straightforwardly discarded the 1787 federal model as irrelevant for how to organize self-government within the states where they lived. But on the other hand, there was real utility for Jacksonians in proclaiming a type of fidelity to the Constitution. Such voices would attack national politicians for refusing to abide by a strict construction of the document and for instead giving the federal government authority not explicitly enumerated in the Constitution, thereby inviting an unchecked and oppressive federal power to suppress local popular rule. As a Massachusetts Jacksonian argued against overweening federal legislation, "too many laws and too much government are among the tendencies of the age against which we must guard."[61]

In states and territories with slavery, this suspicion went hand in hand with deeply held anxieties that federal authority—a faraway and discretionary monarchical holdover—always presented the danger of disrupting the racially determined system of local rights and hierarchies. At their extremes, such fears included that the federal government would even emancipate enslaved persons and reduce free white settlers to the status of economically dependent subjects. For many Jacksonian politicians and settlers, defending the Constitution meant highlighting the illegality of such federal intrusion into local matters.

All of this speaks to profound differences with the constitutional life of the late twentieth century. Early notables invoked the genius of the framers, often in near-religious terms. And the idea of constitutions and constitution-writing as a defining and very American legal-political practice certainly took hold. But much more of ordinary constitutional politics was organized around state constitution-making efforts, which very consciously refused to emulate the federal model.[62]

Critically, these state documents gained greater significance on the ground because of their tight connection to the immediate project of territorial expansion, control, and governance. And, as the next section details, to the extent that the federal Constitution did serve a cohesive function, it was routinely cast in fundamentally *anti*-creedal terms—as a text of compromise and nation-building for a racially exclusionary project.

Civil War and the Contested Creed in White Society

While the Civil War and Reconstruction may have banned chattel slavery and entailed genuine steps toward multiracial inclusion, these events ultimately did not break the classic vision of the country as a white republic. If anything, the predominant late-nineteenth-century views about national identity, as well as the Constitution, remained steeped in explicit white supremacy. At the time of the 1887 centennial, the political and academic conventional wisdom took for granted fundamental racial differences in society. And, with respect to Civil War and Reconstruction-era efforts to restructure life on more racially egalitarian lines, this conventional wisdom further viewed such efforts as bound to fail, and as generating an emancipated Black population that may have been formally "free" but was ill-equipped for real membership. For most white Americans, across class lines, Reconstruction's experiment with creedal values was one of the *problems* of the day—a threat to social cohesion and to a settler way of life.

THE EARLY ANTI-SLAVERY ORIGINS OF CREEDAL CONSTITUTIONALISM

A fusing of federal constitutional faith with support for racially inclusive creedal ideals did enjoy a moment of prominence during and after the Civil War, before facing comprehensive pushback in both the North and the South. But in order to make sense of this settler pushback, it is helpful first to chart how a creedal story, as well as accounts linking that story to the Constitution, gained initial relevance.

In the years leading up to the war, abolitionists and Republicans articulated—at first tentatively and then with growing intensity—an egalitarian and redemptive narrative about national promise tied to ending slavery. And during the conflict, Abraham Lincoln's 1863 Gettysburg Address became its most famous expression.[63] For Lincoln, the Declaration was not to be read primarily as a long list of grievances with a distant monarch. Instead, the animating core of the document was a single proposition: the "self-evident truth" that "all men are created equal."[64] Moreover, this proposition expressed the overarching ethical basis of the American project itself, with the Civil War a struggle over whether a nation "conceived in Liberty" and "dedicated to the proposition" of equality "can long endure."[65]

As we have seen, Lincoln had for decades venerated the sacred character of the federal Constitution. Thus, for him, this view of the Declaration also carried with it a specific account of the Constitution's meaning and place in collective life. Lincoln wrote in his own notes, around the time he penned his First Inaugural Address, that the Constitution served as the "picture of silver" that framed the "apple of gold" that was the Declaration.[66] Employing a metaphor from the Bible's Book of Proverbs,[67] Lincoln presented the Constitution as an institutional mechanism for achieving the Declaration's promise of equal liberty: "The picture was made, not to *conceal*, or *destroy* the apple; but to *adorn*, and *preserve* it. The *picture* was made *for* the apple—*not* the apple for the picture."[68]

On the one hand, arguments entwining the Declaration and the Constitution as unified expressions of collective identity were hardly unusual in the first half of the nineteenth century, as highlighted by toasts to the 1787 text delivered as part of July 4 banquets. But on the other hand, Lincoln's account was particularly striking—and foundational for later twentieth-century creedal constitutionalism—because of the implication that the Constitution concretely embodied antislavery goals already grounded in the Declaration.

CREED VERSUS THE CONSTITUTION

As the legal scholar Dorothy Roberts highlights, anti-slavery readings of the Constitution certainly circulated in white abolitionist circles, associated especially with Lysander Spooner and Theodore Dwight Weld.[69] Still, it was far more common before the Civil War to see both the Declaration and the Constitution as joint symbols of a white project of internal freedom, one ultimately accommodating of slavery. Under the era's conventional reading, Thomas Jefferson's famous invocation that "all men were created equal" did not suggest that *all* individuals and groups—regardless of race or gender—were worthy of actual inclusion in political practice. Rather, it used an account of natural liberty to root the collective right of Anglo-European settlers—a free people—to republican self-government. Indeed, someone like Democratic Senator Stephen Douglas, whose 1858 speech was quoted in the first chapter, went even further, deemphasizing any universalist significance in the document or relevance at all to the question of slavery. He focused exclusively on the Declaration as a statement of white settler independence: "The signers of the Declaration of Independence had no reference to the negro whatever when they declared all men to be created equal. They desired to express by that phrase white men, men of European birth and European descent, and had no reference either to the negro, the savage Indians, the Fejee, the Malay, or any other inferior and degraded race, when they spoke of the equality of men."[70]

In the mid-nineteenth century, Lincoln's anti-slavery entwining of the Declaration and the Constitution not only faced intense pushback, but also had obvious conceptual challenges. For starters, the actual list of settler grievances in the Declaration did not necessarily indicate an animating anti-slavery core. Indeed, the final version of the text asserted as reasons for the rebellion fears about enslaved uprisings and Native American land control: "He [King George] has excited domestic insurrections amongst us, and has endeavored to bring on the inhabitants of our frontiers, the merciless Indian Savages, whose known rule of warfare is indistinguished destruction of all ages, sexes and conditions."[71] The conflicts between England and its colonists were not over universalist creedal or anti-slavery ideals. Instead, they often concerned the direction and terms of territorial conquest and land policy, as well as perceived threats to settler social and political supremacy—including with respect to Indigenous peoples, French Catholics in Quebec, and enslaved African workers.[72]

Yet, whatever one might say about the Declaration, the idea of the Constitution as an anti-slavery document faced an even more insurmountable difficulty: it had been the governing law of the land for the better part of a century and had, at the very least, seemingly condoned human bondage. For this reason, in the decades before the Civil War, a competing abolitionist position, vociferously defended by a number of high-profile white activists, argued instead that any creedal and anti-slavery interpretation of both the Declaration and the national story required stridently rejecting the Constitution. Indeed, the famed abolitionist William Lloyd Garrison went so far as to stage his own July 4 protest against the document, in direct opposition to the anniversary's patriotic banquets. On that day in 1854, he declared before a gathered crowd that the Constitution was "the source and parent of all the other atrocities—'a covenant with death, and an agreement with hell,'" and then burned the text.[73]

Although this presentation of the Constitution as an embodiment of political evil was a decidedly minority view within settler society, Garrison's actions highlight that its proponents were vocal and politically present. Wendell Phillips, the abolitionist author of *The Constitution, A Pro-Slavery Compact* (first published in 1844), wrote that it was "undeniable" that the actual history of the Constitution-in-practice "show[s] us the slaves trebling in numbers;—slaveholders monopolizing the offices and dictating the policy of the Government;—prostituting the strength and influence of the Nation to the support of slavery here and elsewhere;—trampling on the rights of the free States, and making the courts of the country their tools."[74] The Three-Fifths Clause, the Fugitive Slave Clause, the Electoral College, the Supreme Court, and state-based representation in the Senate: all these preserved and amplified the power of enslavers. Their dominance—and the grossly unjust social order it produced—emerged because of, rather than in spite of, the Constitution's basic structures, requirements, and effects.

Thus, those in antebellum America arguing for an inherent and natural fit between anything like universalist creedal values and attachment to the US federal Constitution stood on shaky ground. As suggested by Stephen Douglas, such claims ran counter to the dominant white racial understandings of settler identity and constitutional meaning. And, for a not insignificant bloc of abolitionist activists, any link of the Constitution to a redemptive and racially egalitarian promise willfully avoided a basic fact: that actually fulfilling such ends might require truly revolutionary changes to the nation's essential system of government.

Like Spooner, Weld, and Ohio Republican Congressman John Bingham,[75] the future drafter of the Fourteenth Amendment, Lincoln sought to weave around these difficulties by deemphasizing how the Constitution functioned in practice and upholding instead an aspirational text. According to Lincoln, the Constitution's real essence—an extension rather than a repudiation of the Declaration of Independence's presumptively anti-slavery message—was separate from its at times flawed everyday operation. As he argued during his 1854 speech in Peoria, Illinois, the Constitution's relation to slavery was properly seen not as authorization, but instead as "hostility to the PRINCIPLE, and toleration, ONLY BY NECESSITY."[76] This meant that the Constitution, in the historian Gary Wills's language, was best understood as a "provisional embodiment" of the Declaration's "ideal," "to be tested against it, kept in motion toward it."[77] But again, even within anti-slavery circles these views remained hotly contested, with those like Garrison or Phillips considering them a kind of wish fulfillment due to the stranglehold on political power exercised by slaveholding interests.

POSSIBILITIES IN THE CIVIL WAR MOMENT

What ultimately shifted the terms of this debate, and added plausibility to the notion that the Constitution could be made compatible with creedal ideals and thus redeemed, was the Civil War. As Lincoln declared at Gettysburg, the "unfinished work" of slavery's abolition would mark "a new birth for freedom."[78] It would move the Constitution-in-practice closer to a perfected text expressing the Declaration's—and by implication the nation's—inherent commitments. In a sense, victory and Reconstruction—ideally by destroying the slave power—provided the conditions under which aspiration and reality would meet. Under those circumstances, anti-slavery values could infuse the everyday Constitution and, in the process, permanently join creedal and constitutional commitments.

Still, Lincoln himself never articulated a genuinely universal creedal politics; he hesitated to extend his attack on slavery to a defense of a constitutionally required multiracial democracy. In that same 1854 Peoria speech, Lincoln was at pains to argue that although slavery violated basic moral precepts of human equality, this did not mean that the Declaration necessitated treating African Americans as political equals. Just like Stephen Douglas, he too called the Declaration "a white man's charter of freedom."[79] And well into the war, it remained difficult for Lincoln to imagine meaningful Black civic inclusion. As late as 1862, Lincoln continued to view African American removal, through colonization efforts in the Caribbean or Central America, as a potential solution to the problem of race, arguing that since both whites and Blacks "suffer on each side" from the fact of "physical difference," "it is better for us both . . . to be separated."[80]

The closest he came to political equality was in his very last public statement before his assassination. In that statement, Lincoln—who had previously opposed interracial marriage as well as Black jury rights, voting rights, and office-holding[81]—defended limited suffrage for some formerly enslaved persons, given the centrality of Black participation in the war effort. He declared, "I would myself prefer that [voting] were now conferred on the very intelligent, and on those who serve our cause as soldiers."[82]

Nonetheless, the conflict transformed political life, especially in overturning slavery and linking white union soldiers with resisting Black populations in a shared struggle against the Confederacy. This transformation led certain white settlers to assert more full-throated versions of multiracial democracy and to bring together the types of accounts of constitutional faith and creedal inclusion that would become ubiquitous in the twentieth century. Charles Sumner, the abolitionist senator from Massachusetts, famously told a New York City audience, on the 1867 anniversary of Lincoln's Gettysburg Address, that the postwar struggle was to "complete the good work" described by "Lincoln, at Gettysburg, in the most touching speech of all history."

Like Lincoln, Sumner read the Constitution through an anti-slavery interpretation of the Declaration. But for him, this linkage entailed far more than ending chattel slavery or tentative steps to Black civic participation. It conceived of the American project as defined fundamentally by commitments to racial equality: "Liberty is won: Equality must be won also. In England there is Liberty without Equality; in France Equality without Liberty. The two together must be ours."[83] Not to be outdone, Pennsylvania Congressman Thaddeus Stevens imagined this principle of equality as applying to all walks of life and as challenging the pervasive and enforced segregation of settler society. He went so far as to be buried in a Black cemetery in Lancaster, writing as the inscription for his tombstone,

> I repose in this quiet and secluded spot
> Not from any natural preference for solitude
> But, finding other Cemeteries limited as to Race
> by Charter Rules,
> I have chosen this that I might illustrate
> in my death
> The principles which I advocated
> Through a long life
> EQUALITY OF MAN BEFORE HIS CREATOR.[84]

NATIONAL IDENTITY AND EXPLICIT WHITE SUPREMACY IN POST-RECONSTRUCTION AMERICA

At the height of Reconstruction, such creedal arguments temporarily seized the stage, even altering the actual language of the Constitution. The new Thirteenth, Fourteenth, and Fifteenth Amendments—which collectively banned slavery, entrenched Black federal citizenship, asserted the principle of equal protection, and established Black male voting rights—offered an explicit textual basis for creedal claims. But this period lasted only a few years. As Reconstruction receded, racially egalitarian readings of the Declaration and of the Constitution similarly began to fade away from mainstream politics.

Indeed, dominant accounts—across North and South—increasingly viewed those like Thaddeus Stevens as having run Reconstruction into a ditch precisely because of their belief in the possibility of authentic multiracial democracy. As the *New York Times*—a more conservative Republican news organ and articulator of respectable Northern opinion— wrote as early as 1868 (in summarizing Stevens's legacy two days after his death) that his "most extreme views" and refusal to "extend the fraternal hand" to the Southern white planter class made him the "Evil Genius of the Republican Party," a man whose "measures were unjust and impolitic" and "cannot be truthfully said" to have "exercised a happy influence over the Republican policy in the matter of Reconstruction."[85]

The problem facing Radical Republicans like Stevens was simple: most white Americans remained deeply suspicious of creedal egalitarian claims, whether pro- or anti-Constitution. Indeed, an indication of the persistence of exclusionary racial politics can be found in the shift in the editorial tone of the *Nation*, which had been established in July 1865 and which, like the *New York Times*, became a central Republican organ. The magazine initially promoted Congressional Reconstruction along with the new constitutional amendments. Yet, especially as the editors grew increasingly preoccupied with rising industrial tensions in the North, they likewise viewed Reconstruction and federal military presence in the South as counterproductive, dragging the nation back to wartime animosities and undermining white reconciliation.

In fact, like the *New York Times*, the *Nation* came to argue that the problems plaguing Reconstruction were not the result of Southern white subversion, violence, and intransigence. Instead, they often arose from the extremism of Radical Republicans and the perceived incapacities of African Americans. This revival of tropes about Black inability, even among supposed Republican allies, was hardly surprising given the long-standing depth of racial animus across settler politics. In the same 1862 comments arguing for Black colonization, Lincoln himself had defended the need for separation partly on grounds that the majority of African Americans were ill-equipped for republican citizenship. According to him, most Blacks were "very poor material" for self-government; they had "intellects clouded by slavery" and were not "capable of thinking as white men."[86]

A decade and a half later, the *Nation*, in discussing the withdrawal of federal troops from the South, returned to such well-worn claims about

Lincoln - "Address on Colonation" 238

the unfitness of African Americans. Defending the end of Reconstruction, it contended that Black enfranchisement and civic participation in the years since the Civil War countenanced against the very wisdom of democracy or "Majority Government." Although the country may have been premised on notions of majoritarianism and political self-rule, argued the magazine, there were circumstances in which these principles had to fall before common sense and the collective good. Defending what today we would call authoritarianism and reasserting the racially defined nature of the polity, the editorial continued, "the Anglo-Saxon race has owed its political success to the shrewdness which has seen through all attempts to make means more important than ends." This "shrewdness" now required rejecting the necessity of majority rule, and thus accepting a return of white planter control in the South, given that democracy had led to the destructive rule of "a numerical majority of poor, ignorant negroes and their demagogues."[87]

As the century wore on, these views—embracing white authoritarianism and rejecting the rectitude or practicality of civic inclusion—hardened into an oft-repeated conventional wisdom regarding Reconstruction and national identity. Although most white Americans may have accepted the end of slavery, they nonetheless presupposed their own racial superiority as a bedrock feature of constitutional and political life. Prevalent views of race did not differ all that markedly from what Stephen Douglas declared in the 1850s.

Unsurprisingly, it was individuals such as Woodrow Wilson—the son of a Virginia enslaver—who best captured the post-Reconstruction era's prevailing judgments about inclusion and exclusion.[88] In keeping with the widespread presumptions of racial difference, Wilson presented the world as divided into distinct ethno-racial "peoples" at different stages in the process of political evolution. Euro-Americans, especially of Anglo-Saxon descent, stood at the forefront of this evolution, due to their long-standing acculturation in the practices of republican freedom. Black Americans, by contrast, supposedly remained in their political infancy. Reconstruction was so problematic because it inverted this developmental account: it prematurely provided political rights to an ethno-racial people ill-equipped for them while at the same time removing those rights from those long habituated to self-rule. In this way, Reconstruction amounted to a destructive project of racial readjustment, as an effectively foreign power (the Northern army) trampled on the ability of a free white people—the region's "real citizens"[89]—to govern themselves. According to Wilson, "the sudden and absolute emancipation" of enslaved persons, and especially the efforts to impose equal citizenship on whites, embodied "a dark chapter of history."[90]

Such beliefs spanned the political spectrum and dominated academic scholarship. William Dunning, the president of both the American Historical Association and the American Political Science Association, focused—like Wilson—on how Reconstruction inverted a supposedly natural racial hierarchy. He presented the reassertion of white planter rule in the South in heroic terms as "the struggle through which the Southern whites, subjugated by adversaries of their own race, thwarted the scheme which threatened permanent subjugation to another race."[91] Charles Francis Adams, scion of one of the nation's founding families, great-grandson of John Adams, grandson of the anti-slavery John Quincy Adams, and another president of the American Historical Association, similarly concluded that Black limitations required treating the community generally as "a ward and dependent" rather than as a "political equal."[92]

In his magisterial *The American Commonwealth*, among the period's most academically well-respected texts on the US constitutional system,[93] the British jurist, politician, and diplomat James Bryce took for granted judgments about ethno-racial differences. He also accepted the general threat posed to social cohesion and republican institutions by universal inclusion, whether of immigrants from eastern and central Europe (whose status as "white" was indeterminate) or of recently emancipated African Americans. Describing new immigrants as "droves of squalid men" who often bring "no knowledge of the methods of free government," Bryce questioned the wisdom of long-standing practices of easy immigrant access to voting, since these communities were simply "not fit for the suffrage."[94] As for Black civic inclusion, Bryce also concluded, writing of formerly enslaved workers in Louisiana: "Emancipation found them utterly ignorant; and the grant of suffrage found them as unfit for political rights as any population could be."[95] Indeed, to underscore just how widely such views were held, even key voices (as we will see) within the Socialist Party of America (SPA) defended the racially restricted nature of collective membership. For example, Wisconsin Congressman Victor Berger declared "there can be no doubt that Negroes and mulattoes constitute a lower race."[96]

In fact, by the eve of World War I—with President Wilson and Supreme Court Chief Justice Edward White hosting private screenings at the White House and elsewhere of D. W. Griffith's pro-Klan *Birth of a Nation*[97]—creedal arguments had retreated even as an account of the

meaning of Gettysburg. For the fiftieth anniversary of the battle in 1913, white veterans from *both* armies returned to the site. Speakers and organizers emphasized the importance of national healing, but they pointedly refrained from mentioning any claims about the egalitarian and redemptive ethos partially invoked by Lincoln or stated more expansively by Sumner. In the words of the historian David Blight, the Gettysburg remembrances constituted "a Jim Crow reunion, and white supremacy might be said to have been the silent, invisible master of ceremonies."[98] For the *Outlook*, a Progressive journal, Gettysburg—rather than highlighting Lincoln's own language of a biblical contest between freedom and slavery—spoke instead to how North and South had really fought for a common ideal: "But in what other great war has it been true that both sides were loyal to the *same* ideal—the ideal of civil liberty?"[99] In effect, creedal egalitarian claims had become so besieged that they were exiled even from white remembrances of Gettysburg.

More than anything else, that retreat underscored the remarkable continuities across the century in settler judgments about Black exclusion. Racial subordination persisted as a constitutive feature of the collective ethos, despite the end of slavery, a cataclysmic civil war, and the Reconstruction project. And this fact was highlighted by the rise of segregation and the return of coercive and extractive systems of labor for rural freedpeople trapped in the Southern countryside. Some Republican elites, cognizant of Civil War- and Reconstruction-era arguments, no doubt attempted to justify emerging practices as still consistent with new principles of constitutional equality embedded in 1868's Fourteenth Amendment. Perhaps most notoriously, Supreme Court justices in *Plessy v. Ferguson* (1896)—in an opinion authored by a Republican appointee, Henry Billings Brown, and joined by all but one of the other justices involved in the case—constructed a doctrine of "separate but equal" to uphold segregation in public accommodations.[100]

In part, the Court aimed to reframe the rise of Jim Crow as a development that did not entirely repudiate Reconstruction. But whatever the legal gymnastics, the case's outcome exposed an undeniable political fact: large swathes of Northern and Southern society saw the country, as they had during the antebellum period, as an exclusionary republic in which various outsider communities were rightly subject to a complicated structure of political control. And at the dawn of the twentieth century, such control continued to be justified through straightforwardly racist arguments about the relative "fitness" of various communities for self-rule, and thus on terms that flatly rejected equal liberty for all as an overriding value.

If anything, *Plessy* reiterated how, for most Americans, the problem of Reconstruction was with the very idea that formal legal changes either could or should overturn accepted and deeply embedded ethnoracial hierarchies. Explaining why the Supreme Court should not be in the business of uprooting the South's racial order, Brown declared, "legislation is powerless to eradicate racial instincts or to abolish distinctions based upon physical differences, and the attempt to do so can only result in accentuating the difficulties of the present situation."[101]

Creed and Class in the Black Counter-Public

All of this indicated the relative rarity across white society of genuinely creedal readings of the Constitution. Insofar as such interpretations persisted in the late nineteenth and early twentieth centuries, it was primarily within the Black counter-public, such as among recently emancipated African Americans in the urban centers of the South. But Black communities hardly embraced a uniform narrative. Indeed, many Black thinkers after Reconstruction believed that white intransigence and the rise of Jim Crow capitalism rendered creedal constitutionalism quaint or, at least, an uncomfortable fit given the lived African American experience.

FREDERICK DOUGLASS'S VISION OF CREEDAL CONSTITUTIONAL POSSIBILITY

The collapse of the Confederacy facilitated an extensive Black migration to Southern towns and cities in the 1860s, with urban centers offering, as the historian Stephen Hahn writes, "more diverse opportunities for employment, denser concentrations of other black folk, less surveillance from former slaveowners, and the presence of federal troops." These migrations helped to spur a dynamic Black popular discourse, highlighted by the freedmen's conventions which formed across the former Confederate states in late 1865. Local Black leaders of these conventions overwhelmingly read Lincoln's "new birth for freedom" not only as requiring the elimination of slavery but also as necessitating the full inclusion of African Americans as formally equal citizens. As the Virginia Convention declared, Black efforts "to fight [the nation's] battles and to protect the flag that enslaved us" meant "that any attempt to re-construct the states . . . without giving to American citizens of African descent all the rights and immunities accorded to white citizens [was] an act of gross injustice."[102]

Over the ensuing decades, the single Black American figure most identified with this perspective was the great abolitionist Frederick Douglass. In fact, Douglass had been a key pre-war articulator, for both white and Black anti-slavery circles, of a racially egalitarian and redemptive reading of the Constitution.[103] In an 1860 speech before the Scottish Anti-Slavery Society in Glasgow, he underscored how the Constitution was filled with universal rights provisions. Among these was the Fifth Amendment, which to Douglass, as well as to other anti-slavery constitutionalists like Weld and Bingham,[104] highlighted slavery's essential illegality.

That amendment declared, "no person shall be . . . deprived of life, liberty, or property, without due process of law."[105] Given such explicit language, along with the right to trial by jury, the writ of habeas corpus, and the Constitution's guarantee to every state of a "republican form of government,"[106] Douglass contended that one could only maintain slavery's constitutionality "by disregarding the written" words and "by claiming that the Constitution does not mean what it says." As he famously contended, "any one of these provisions in the hands of the ab-olition statesman, and backed up by a right moral sentiment, would put an end to slavery in America."[107]

During and after Reconstruction—even once white opinion shifted dramatically away from egalitarian commitments—Douglass extended these arguments into a broad-ranging account of the Constitution's universally inclusive meaning. Not unlike Frederick Jackson Turner, Douglass too emphasized the idea that the United States should be thought of as a "composite" nation. But his version of hybridity chal-lenged the dominant settler variant. For Turner or Roosevelt, the "com-posite" identity remained racially grounded, with various European communities "Americanized" through a joint project of territorial ex-pansion. Douglass, by contrast, used the term to subvert presumptive settler judgments about inclusion and exclusion. He did so by, once again, arguing for the radical promise embedded from the founding in the nation's constitutive documents, the Declaration and the Consti-tution. As he declared in 1869 of the collective project, "our greatness and grandeur will be found in the faithful application of the principle of perfect civil equality to the people of all races and of all creeds. We are not only bound to this position by our organic structure and by our revolutionary antecedents, but by the genius of our people." For Douglass, different racial communities had "gathered" in the United States "from all quarters of the globe by a common aspiration for national liberty." Their actions, motivated in part by the country's founding tenets, its "organic structure," created the promise of nothing less than the first truly universal polity, a "home . . . not only for the negro, the mulatto and the Latin race," but all groups everywhere.[108]

Douglass was certainly well aware of the centrality of racism to American society. Indeed, in keeping with Black antebellum practices, he had famously delivered his stinging 1852 address, "What to the Slave Is the Fourth of July?" on July 5 to underscore the very absurdity of an enslaved people honoring a national founding that only further entrenched their collective oppression.[109] As the political theorist George Shulman has explored, Douglass fully appreciated that whenever he invoked creedal ideals and his own radicalized version of the United States as a "composite" nation, he in essence sought to call into being a national ethos that did not in reality exist. Douglass's civic rhetoric aimed to redeploy the key texts of the larger society to compel white Americans to reconceive the meaning of their own project.[110]

He also recognized the structural flaws in the constitutional system. Given the role of a Southern president, Andrew Johnson, and later of the Supreme Court in stalling Reconstruction, it became commonplace in the immediate aftermath of the war for Radical Republicans, both white and Black, to call for constitutional reforms to the legal-political process. Against the backdrop of Republican efforts to limit Johnson's ability to fire federal officials, and then to impeach him, Phillips's old framing of the Constitution as a pro-slavery instrument even reemerged in radical circles.

As early as 1867, in the *National Anti-Slavery Standard,* James Redpath, a white friend and ally of Phillips who was also the superintendent of public schools in Charleston, South Carolina in the heady days following Confederate surrender, denounced the document's intricate system of checks and balances as little more than a sustained infrastructure of "oligarchy," one responsible for defeating reforms and preserving white supremacy.[111] As for Thaddeus Stevens, he hesitated publicly to repudiate the Constitution, and his rhetoric tended toward a creedal constitutional posture. But many believed his personal views likely mirrored those of close allies like Phillips and others at the *Standard.* An opponent even accused him of saying behind closed doors that the

Constitution's pro-slavery tendencies and structural failings made it little more than "a worthless bit of old parchment."[112]

Still, Douglass held firm to his constitutional commitment, declaring the document to be "wise and good" and stating, "I concede nothing to those who hold to the inherent weakness of our government." But he too argued for the need for some structural updating, aimed at eliminating those "alien elements . . . antagonistic of republicanism declared by the fathers."[113] He strongly favored efforts to constrain and then impeach Johnson and called for constitutional changes that would curb presidential excess by eliminating the office's veto over legislation and checking its patronage power. Above all, he argued for a federal framework that deemphasized executive and judicial power and strengthened congressional majority rule. This may have paralleled the approach that had come to shape settler constitutional developments at the state level, but it also offered exactly the vision of "majority government" that white racist opponents of Reconstruction condemned.

Ultimately, for Douglass, the Black fate of living as a permanent minority in a majority white country meant that the only plausible method of social transformation must connect to the terms of dominant narratives. This required creatively adapting nationalist sentiment, whether through the language of a "composite" people or through reforms that addressed defects in the constitutional structure. Such adaptation, though, had to remain tethered to both creed and Constitution, as key symbolic resources within white society that could move in more racially inclusive directions. Speaking at the 1893 Chicago World's Fair, Douglass famously declared of rampant racial discrimination—including in the very organization of the Fair—that there was no so-called "Negro problem." Rather, "the true problem . . . is whether the American people have honesty enough, loyalty enough, honor enough, patriotism enough to live up to their own Constitution."[114]

Douglass's words resonated with many African Americans, who with the passage of the Reconstruction Amendments had rallied to the Constitution—and especially to its creedal accounts. Thus, in the wake of the Supreme Court's 1883 decision in the *Civil Rights Cases*—which launched a wave of anger through both urban and rural Black constituencies—the Howard University professor B. K. Sampson called on fellow African Americans to remain "loyal still" to the country and to maintain faith in the Constitution's promise. The decision may have struck down provisions of the 1875 Civil Rights Act as beyond

Congress's authority under the Thirteenth and Fourteenth Amendments. Nonetheless, Sampson declared that the white "public mind is softening as it ripens," and so the judicial outcome, whatever its consequences in the present, should not be read as "a finality."[115]

ANTI-CONSTITUTIONALISM AND SEPARATISM IN THE BLACK COMMUNITY

Still, within the Black counter-public, by the time Frederick Douglass died in 1895, such narratives—linking the Constitution to faith in an unfolding egalitarian project—became an ever more beleaguered position. The steady move of African Americans from bondage to liberty and back again to bondage left growing numbers, especially outside of educated and middle-class circles, embittered by the hypocrisy of white America and the emptiness of constitutional protections.

For instance, the influential African Methodist Episcopal (AME) Reverend Henry McNeal Turner, who after the Civil War had been a Republican politician in Georgia and deeply invested in the Reconstruction project, now grew increasingly skeptical about the capacity of white society to reform itself. According to Turner, Supreme Court decisions such as the *Civil Rights Cases* highlighted the fundamental incompatibility between Black interests and those of the broader white community.[116] Instead of being fellow nationals, previously enslaved persons and their former enslavers had inherently opposed interests. And so long as the polity upheld the power and status of the latter, as with the *Civil Rights Cases*, Blacks owed no allegiance to the republic. In Turner's words, "if the government that freed him cannot protect his freedom, then . . . he does not stand face to face with its laws and institutions, and the negro hereafter who will enlist in the armies of the government, or swear to defend the United States Constitution ought to be hung by the neck."[117]

Motivating Turner's strong condemnation was the ongoing reality of unchecked white violence across the former Confederacy. Throughout the South, white elites were reclaiming political control in part through organized mob actions that subverted elections and, as with 1873's Colfax massacre, brutally murdered Black residents.[118] All the while, the institutions of the federal government—including the Supreme Court—essentially gave legal cover to white practices. Whatever Douglass's creedal constitutional aspirations to multiracial democracy, the actual condition of Black union with white society was an extreme and authoritarian brand of political despotism. The problem did not seem to be "alien elements" incompatible with the spirit of the framers, but precisely the "inherent weakness" of the society and its basic institutional order. Thus, Turner believed that Black emigrationism was the only viable and legitimate response in a context where "the negro is literally driven out of the United States." Under these circumstances, basic Black self-respect required conceiving of oneself as a "rebel to this nation" and treating the Constitution as "a dirty rag, a cheat, a libel," "to be spit upon by every negro in the land."[119]

Turner was hardly alone among Blacks of the era in calling for separation. As the old white planter class reclaimed its property and political authority by force across the former Confederacy, freedpeople—particularly in the rural countryside—saw themselves as exiles again in an oppressive land, and often viewed emigration as the only solution. Due to the prohibitive cost—not to mention white Southern efforts to constrain Black movement and to maintain their labor supply—very few Blacks actually emigrated abroad.[120] But as Henry Adams, a Black activist and founder of the National Colored Colonization Council, reported, by 1879 some 98,000 African Americans had enrolled with the council as potential emigrants. Whether or not Blacks succeeded in escaping the South for Liberia, Haiti, Canada, or even states like Kansas (long associated with John Brown and radical abolitionism), the project of emigration constituted perhaps the largest Black movement organizing of the late nineteenth century.[121] And it set the stage for the Great Migration North starting in the 1910s, in which millions of Black people—often recruited by Northern companies in the context of industrial labor shortages—fled the South and its regime of racial terror in search of economic, social, and political alternatives.[122]

Within educated and middle-class African American circles in the late nineteenth century, separatism and emigrationism were often denounced as the worst brand of political defeatism. Douglass, Sampson, and others saw emigrationism as a rejection of what African Americans had fought and died for during the war and as undermining the unity Blacks needed in the present to achieve real formal equality under the Constitution. However, what allowed emigrationism to tap so deeply into poorer and rural constituencies were growing doubts that Black freedom could ever be achieved in a polity dominated by a white majority, including under any constitutional system such a majority imposed.

CLASS, ECONOMY, AND RUPTURE IN
INTERNAL BLACK DEBATES

To an important degree, the disagreements in Black society reflected both an awareness of white resistance and class divides within the African American community. For starters, many understood just how marginal Douglass's claims were within white American life. If a key rhetorical function of invoking both the Declaration and the Constitution on behalf of creedal values was to shift white public opinion, by the turn of the century this effort seemed to have failed. Across white society, even those segments bathed in constitutional faith, the call for a multiracial democracy was largely treated as revolutionary and destabilizing. Indeed, more and more whites came to view such a project as a "path to anarchy," as the *New York Times* described the ideas of the longtime abolitionist and Radical Republican newspaper, the *National Anti-Slavery Standard*.[123] In a context in which whites in the North and the South now sought to heal old wounds, the fact that abolishing slavery had required intense bloodshed was not lost on many Americans.

This truth had clear implications for any continuing effort at racial transformation. As Douglass had argued during Reconstruction, replacing white control in the South with a new multiracial order necessitated yet more willingness to wield the sword—even a long-term and committed military rule (as those like Thaddeus Stevens too maintained), so as to permanently entrench Black equality. For a white majority with little appetite for such a project, creedal ideas appeared dangerous and socially destructive. Anti-slavery voices had used a high degree of intellectual creativity to join creedalism and constitutional respect, and most white settlers remained suspicious of the fit. Their memory of the war not only emphasized the proximity between constitutional redemption and revolutionary violence, but also underscored the incompatibility of racial egalitarianism with any attempt to restitch the old settler social fabric. Thus, creedal commitment seemed to entail jettisoning the republic as they knew it, along with the Constitution—and doing so by force of arms.

Yet if a redemptive and egalitarian constitutional faith proved too revolutionary for the dominant society, for some Black voices the problem with melding creed and Constitution was not simply the tension between these two elements. For those like Henry McNeal Turner, civic inclusion itself offered limited promise for challenging Black

oppression—certainly under conditions in which the underlying structures of economy and government were not genuinely overturned.

This was especially true given the realities of industrializing Jim
Crow capitalism, as compared to earlier, more small-scale and producer-
driven modes of economic life. During Reconstruction, Douglass, along
with Charles Sumner and Thaddeus Stevens, had called for the confisca-
tion of slave plantations and their division into individual homesteads
for freedpeople and poor whites. But with the reassertion of white rule
and the growing racial backlash in both North and South, Douglass's
aim to connect creedal redemption with sustained federal intervention
into Southern property relations was systematically contained. Douglass always linked the effort to end formal discrimination and to ensure
market access with proactive government interventions that redistrib-
uted land and then protected Black landowners from predatory practices by white economic elites. He viewed these reforms as jointly necessary for fulfilling the Declaration's promise. Yet when Douglass focused
on equality under the law and market opportunities—in a context in
which the federal government left unreconstructed Southern property
relations—the reform vision could ring hollow.

Take, for instance, perhaps Douglass's most popular lecture during
the era, "Self-Made Men" (one he gave "over fifty times"[124] in various
forms, from the late antebellum period to post-Reconstruction). In the
speech, he famously called on whites to "'give the negro fair play and
let him alone.'"[125] Douglass would declare to audiences, "throw open
to him the doors of the schools, the factories, the workshops, and of
all mechanical industries. For his own welfare, give him a chance to do
whatever he can do well. If he fails then, let him fail! I can, however, as-
sure you that he will not fail."[126]

Critically, Douglass's vision of "fair play" required a significant
amount of government intervention to establish Black education and
property holding. As he bluntly continued, "it is not fair play to start
the negro out in life, from nothing and with nothing, while others start
with the advantage of a thousand years behind them."[127] Yet armed with
these essential prerequisites, Douglass imagined a social order in which
Black people would have an equal opportunity to achieve success in
the marketplace and middle-class respectability on the same terms as
whites. In the 1850s, with African Americans enslaved and the Supreme
Court infamously declaring, in *Dred Scott v. Sandford*, Black people "so
far inferior, that they had no rights which the white man was bound to
respect,"[128] Douglass's call for constitutional rights and equal opportu-

nity had an incendiary effect. It offered a powerful statement of Black agency, capacity, and political will in the face of an oppressive and totalizing social order that denied African Americans their very humanity.

Yet by the 1880s, the replacement of chattel slavery with new modes of economic bondage, against the backdrop of rising industrial and corporate power, shifted the implications of Douglass's famous lecture. Douglass continued to embrace Black social mobility and independence through hard work in a small-scale capitalist economy. And the speech remained a galvanizing declaration of Black self-assertiveness. But emerging economic hierarchies raised real challenges for this vision's long-term viability as a broadly accessible goal.[129] In addition, even in 1865, there was a question of whether everyone in the Black community actually wanted marketplace success and middle-class respectability. Tensions existed between that account of uplift and the ideas of community and moral economy among some rural freedpeople, especially on established plantations.

Notably, Douglass's view of economic achievement maintained a careful separation between slavery and other presumptively legitimate modes of individual property.[130] When demanding Black access to land, Douglass tended to promote the Republican Party orthodoxy that linked free citizenship to independent farming and ownership. He thus presented Black inclusion, especially in "Self-Made Men" or when discussing homesteading in the South and on the frontier, as Black participation in an individualized settler way of life.[131]

By contrast, many of the Black poor on what the historian Stephen Hahn describes as the large-scale plantations, "in areas long settled and relatively stable," were less interested in personal advancement or an equal footing within settler society. They had hoped that the end of the Civil War would create a millennial rupture in which biblical deliverance would come through explicit and revolutionary refounding. Indeed, rumors swept through the countryside in the fall of 1865 that Christmastime would bring a "jubilee," in which past wrongs would be made right and the land finally turned over to its legitimate inheritors.[132]

What many in these particular communities—internally organized around bonds of kinship—often sought was Black communal control. They aimed to govern the estates for their shared economic and political benefit. Their hope had been that, through federal action or, barring that, through armed Black insurrection, formerly enslaved workers would gain power, as Hahn says, "not just of any land, but of the estates on which they had lived and labored." For freedmen like the Virginia farmer Bayley Wyat, their suffering and hard labor had built the Southern plantations: "Our wives, our children, our husbands, has been sold over and over again to purchase the lands we now locates on," and for this reason "we has a right to [that] land. . . . [D]idn't we clear the land and raise de crops. . . . And den didn't dem large cities in de North grow up on de cotton and de sugars and de rice dat we made?"[133]

This suggested that the plantations should be "partition[ed]" among Black workers and families in ways that, according to Hahn, "maintain[ed] and reinforce[ed] the networks of kinship, friendship, and customary practice that had sustained them under slavery and informed the sense of right itself."[134] Interest in more individual forms of homesteading tended to be strongest in "non- and small-plantation regions" of the South rather than among African Americans on the great estates. On those estates, the meaning of "jubilee"—truly uprooting slavery—often tied land to Black collective power. It focused less attention on a version of civic inclusion which allowed freedpeople—even if protected, as Douglass argued, by various governmental safeguards—to sink or swim in the marketplace.[135]

Ultimately, many rural freedpeople, especially on such plantations, hoped to maintain existing communal bonds while fundamentally inverting who held sovereign economic and political authority. This outcome challenged any straightforward Black incorporation into settler society, including through individual economic opportunity. It would have meant Black communities as communities exercising control over basic decisions on the plantations—plantations that they themselves had built and to which they had long been connected.

All of this spoke to one reason why, in the 1880s and beyond, continued invocations of constitutional fidelity left some cold. Even in earlier and more hopeful days, the rhetoric and aspirational ends of various middle-class and educated African Americans, including Douglass, could seem insufficient as tools of liberation. And now, especially with Reconstruction contained, a narrow reading of providing African Americans with "fair play" in this new economy offered no meaningful solution to the structural dimensions of racial subordination.

Sharecropping—and Jim Crow conditions more generally—underscored how white material wealth remained tied to the coercion of Black labor and the denial of Black productive control. But even the creedal combination of civic inclusion, individual property rights, and access to competition in the marketplace may not have gone far enough in altering the governing social structure and hierarchies that shaped Black agrarian life. A classic homesteading project would have confronted too the intensifying industrial realities in which laborers, white and Black, found themselves struggling in an economy dominated by expanding corporate wealth and power. Moreover, for some on the great estates, who had sought Black communal authority over the plantation, a striving to be "self-made" did not necessarily speak to their cultural desires—even as they may have to other elements within the Black counter-public.

It was this disconnect between key agrarian sensibilities and the often middle-class agenda of creed and Constitution—especially when emphasizing equal rights and social mobility alongside whites—that helped to build the groundswell of support for emigrationism. In a setting in which even minimal safeguards, let alone real economic transformation, appeared beyond reach, it was hard to take seriously claims by more educated Black elites that white minds were "ripening" or that settler society could be made egalitarian.

In this way, the late nineteenth century entrenched a basic and lasting internal debate within Black politics over the appropriate relationship to the nation and its symbols, including founding documents like the federal Constitution. The Civil War, the experience of emancipation, and the Reconstruction project all bound a substantial bloc of African Americans to the idea of a creedally committed United States. Black freedpeople had fought and died on behalf of the union and now—in a way that had not existed previously—asserted a patriotic attachment to this reborn nation. Before the war, as described in Frederick Douglass's famed July 5 speech, African Americans often "celebrated" Independence Day as an explicit commentary on Black enslavement and exclusion from the body politic.[136] But in the early, heady days of Reconstruction, July 4 emerged as a day of massive Black parades and festivities.[137] As white elites reclaimed power in later years, the hopefulness driving this sentiment waned, but it did not die out entirely.

At the same time, conditions on the ground made it hard for many African Americans to see living in the United States as anything other than internal exile. For such Black voices, their potential post–Civil War language of patriotic attachment—that redemptive story of a creedal Constitution buttressed by the new Reconstruction Amendments—appeared rejected by white society. Just as important, that narrative—even if expressed, as by Douglass, with real self-awareness regarding the larger polity's inherent racism—still seemed to require Blacks to suppress their own deeply felt sense of estrangement and their own accounts of actual emancipation. It compelled African Americans to make political arguments not in their own terms, but instead through the dominant community's available rhetorical language and in ways that highlighted the majority's "better nature." Thus, the call to separation often seemed a more authentic and natural response to a despotic reality—more so than the aspirational hope of somehow persuading those in power.

The result was a politics of ambivalence that dominated Black life, lasting throughout the following century. This ambivalence was marked by creative creedal and constitutional redeployments, but also by genuine hostility to the very enterprise of having to cloak one's own profound alienation.

The Breakdown of the Settler Compact

If, by the end of the nineteenth century, profound ambivalence marked Black politics, such uncertainty was in truth endemic to the age. Society as a whole faced the overarching predicament that—in ways small and large—the bonds that had historically cohered settler life were disintegrating. One obvious cause was the Civil War itself, with its catastrophic human cost and its bitter legacy of post-war hostility.

Indeed, in the years immediately after the conflict, Southern white anger at defeat was so intense that virtually any national symbol, even the Declaration of Independence, became suspect. If Black people celebrated the Declaration during the high tide of Reconstruction, Southern whites often retreated indoors in silent protest. According to one South Carolina diarist, July 4 was a day that African Americans commemorated while "whites stay[ed] at home and work[ed]."[138] This sentiment may well have impacted the response to the 1887 centennial efforts. Kammen writes of the more limited Southern white participation in the Philadelphia festivities, "numerous polite but negative replies from Dixie suggest something less than enthusiasm for a nationalistic celebration of the perdurable Union."[139]

But it was not just the conflict's aftereffects that threatened social cohesion. Deep distrust circulated, but now in an industrializing society increasingly bereft of the classic mechanisms for forging national unity and shared identity—namely, territorial settlement and small-scale producerism. Under these circumstances, the Constitution, for all the surface invocations of its genius, became increasingly a site of disagreement and even disaffection. Such discord highlighted both the general breakdown of social order and the limitations of the document as a source of reconciliation.

INDUSTRIALIZATION, GENDER, AND
THE DECLINE OF FREE LABOR

In his 1859 address at the Wisconsin fair, Lincoln had famously hailed the liberating effects of small-scale capitalism for the ordinary European laborer in the United States. One could start a "prudent, penniless beginner" and through hard work alone earn enough money to become an independent proprietor with a shop of one's own.[140] That same year, Frederick Douglass first delivered the speech "Self-Made Men," which expressed similar sentiments and called for Black access to equal opportunity.

But in the decades following Lincoln's and Douglass's embrace of these free labor ideas, industrialization and the rise of American manufacturing power fundamentally reorganized collective life. Confronted by new national markets and massive business entities, more and more individuals—regardless of racial background or settler status—found themselves dependent on the whims of distant economic actors and subject to expanding modes of bureaucracy and control.[141] These changes were a direct challenge to the classic republican ideals of American settler society, particularly those related to diffuse European property ownership and self-directed work. And, over time, they increasingly raised serious questions about the viability of existing institutions, including the legal-political system itself.

The long-standing national narrative held that the United States had no aristocracies and had solved the problem of class. In the words of Lincoln, easy access to land or financial means, for the purposes of becoming a self-employed artisan, indicated that "if any continue through life in the condition of hired laborer, it is not the fault of the system, but because of either a dependent nature which prefers it, or improvidence, folly, or singular misfortune."[142]

However, by the end of the nineteenth century, economic conditions bore little resemblance to this collective self-image. And being a "hired laborer" increasingly involved a structural reduction to unfree and oppressive work. Many white farmers and laborers, who had once enjoyed some degree of self-sufficiency and productive independence, experienced the country as a place of profound inegalitarianism, not to mention wild cycles of booms and busts. By 1890, 51 percent of all property was held by the top 1 percent, and 88 percent of the population controlled just 14 percent of the wealth.[143] These developments were reinforced by the interpenetration of political decision-making by ever more consolidated corporate interests. At virtually every level of government, giant corporations wielded influence over politicians from both major parties, with railroad companies and industrial magnates enjoying particular access and privilege.[144]

Part of what made these shifts so destabilizing was how they also up-ended classic settler notions of masculinity and male citizenship. Lincoln's artisan or homesteader, whose freedom rested in part on self-directed work, was very clearly understood to be a man. Under the settler account, there existed a division of labor between traditionally "feminine" work at home and "masculine" production at the bench or on the farm. In this family unit, men engaged in productive labor and, through such labor, gained an experience in self-rule and in the type of republican education necessary to participate fully in politics. Women, by contrast, provided the dependent and reproductive work of the household, needed for the maintenance of the family but seen as incompatible with true freedom.

Such a division was justified because of the presumptively natural and complementary differences of the two sexes, and due to the belief that marriage was a contract based on consent: in return for gaining control over the family's political decisions (for instance, through voting and jury service) and its economic decisions (through practices like common-law *coverture*, in which women transferred their property and income—the material prerequisites of independence—to husbands upon marriage), husbands and fathers had responsibilities to support, protect, and represent female interests in public life. Indeed, this vision of female dependency had been central in the early nineteenth century to the disappearance of property rights as a precondition for universal male suffrage. The male status as head of a household offered proof that even poorer white men had sufficient civic attachment and capacity to exercise the vote. Patriarchal authority was thus a key justification for elevating the status of settler men.[145]

But if settler men now became subject to the vagaries of joblessness and harsh industrial work, what did this mean for male citizenship or the classic structure of the family? Far removed from the liberating experience of the artisanal bench or the independently owned farm, male economic life toward the turn of the twentieth century took on variations of the same dependence that long defined women's labor. And heavier financial pressures made sustaining a single, male-earning household increasingly precarious. To the extent that women became part of the "productive" labor force over the course of the nineteenth century, they usually found themselves confined to jobs long viewed as inherently unfree, such as unskilled textile work. But if white men now found themselves filling these positions associated with a gendered incapacity, the economy as a whole seemed to reproduce dependence for everyone.

All of this raised basic questions about the terms of male inclusion, not to mention masculine identity. And, for a growing number of activists in the emerging women's suffrage and labor movements, it also highlighted how the family unit was not a happy division of labor grounded in natural difference. Instead, it now appeared a miniature reproduction of precisely the domination that marked society as a whole. For many settler men—threatened by their own sense of receding patriarchal power and the political assertiveness of a new generation of women activists—it spoke to how tensions generated by the new economy were deeply destructive, reaching even into unquestioned assumptions about hearth and home.

CLASS WAR, THE END OF THE WEST, AND THE TURN AGAINST IMMIGRATION

Underlining this discord, by 1886—just as the Constitutional Centennial Commission started organizing its celebrations—Americans were engulfed in the most sustained industrial conflict the country had ever witnessed. On May 1, between three hundred thousand and half a million workers from small towns and major cities participated in a nationwide general strike, demanding an eight-hour workday. The strike was itself the culmination of a year of rolling labor strife, centered especially around Jay Gould's railway lines in the South and the West. And these events acted as warning shots in an escalating class war—one pitting business conglomerates against their industrial and agricultural workers—that would dominate public life in the decades leading up to World War I.

Extensive academic and popular discussion centered on the worry that the country would devolve again into war.[146] And—given that open violence marked these labor confrontations—the term was treated not simply as a metaphor. Unions found themselves pitted against private

security forces, like the Pinkertons, hired by employers, which "operated in legal grey zones, sometimes with the outright legal sanction
from the courts, and often in cooperation with National Guards or even
Federal troops." In this context, going on strike meant facing the prospect of vigilante retribution or even machine gun fire from the state.[147]

The closing of the frontier only further enflamed class conflict. It
constrained the function of migration and settlement as a concrete
mechanism for achieving independent proprietorship. Just as important, it undermined the frontier narrative as a national salve, a plausible
account—whether or not one actually moved west—of an American
way of life marked by available land, diffuse egalitarianism, and economic possibility. And developments in ever more established frontier communities simply replicated industrial and political hierarchies,
compromising the frontier's role as a safety valve for individuals escaping social tensions in cities back east.

This does not suggest that the formal closing of the frontier meant
that land somehow became scarce, or that available territory could no
longer sustain economic prosperity. Rather, an emergent industrial and
corporate order spread throughout the country in ways that increasingly consigned poor and working-class white settlers to a common set
of economic hierarchies. These hierarchies appeared to drive practical opportunity and life experience everywhere—even when a settler
wanted, in Lincolnian terms, to start a shop of one's own or to pull up
stakes and migrate further west.

This closing coincided with the influx of 22 million new immigrants
from the European continent between the 1890s and the 1920s. These
numbers constituted one of "the largest migrations in human history,"[148] although this movement did not dramatically alter the overall
percentage of foreign-born US residents. Immigrant presence became
so contested during this period, as opposed to earlier eras, in part due
to the ethnic composition of arriving migrants, who often came from
southern and eastern Europe. But above all, the end of frontier settlement shifted the implications of immigrant inclusion and heightened
social tensions.

In particular, without a demographic need to populate new territories, the historic commitment to quick incorporation and de facto open
borders for Europeans waned significantly. Even before the harsh literacy tests and quotas of the 1910s and 1920s, communities gradually
eliminated noncitizen suffrage laws, which had promoted integration

and provided near immediate access to the material and political benefits of free citizenship in earlier periods. In the last quarter of the century, starting in the Idaho Territory in 1874, states and territories began systematically repealing their noncitizen voting laws and rejecting new proposals to enfranchise foreigners.[149]

Many European migrants were no longer considered co-participants in a shared project of territorial expansion, and instead came to be viewed through a racialized lens as threatening economic competitors, and even as a non-white "mud-sill." As the historian Matthew Frye Jacobson details, Slavic immigrants found themselves lumped in with excluded communities as explicit racial outsiders. He writes how US-born Euro-Americans described certain positions in a steel mill as fit only for "Hunkies [Slavs]" and beneath the dignity of a "'white' man" because such work was "too damn dirty and too hot." This sentiment led one Slavic priest to comment, "my people are not in America; they are under it."[150]

Patrician and business elites further reinforced this outsider status by scapegoating European immigrants for the rise of industrial conflict, ignoring of course the inherent structural problems embedded in the new capitalist order. E. L. Godkin, the famed Northern journalist, founder of the *Nation* and editor-in-chief for almost two decades of the *New York Evening Post*, saw in labor activism the nefarious work of foreign and "un-American" influences. Writing of the new immigrant in 1887, Godkin decried how he "declines to take care of himself in the old American fashion. When he is out of work, or does not like his work, he looks about and asks his fellow-citizens sullenly, if not menacingly, what they are going to do about it. He had brought with him, too, what is called 'the labor problem,' probably the most un-American of all the problems which American society has to work over today."[151]

Again, those like Godkin saw a twofold dilemma. First, unlike past waves of migrants, Europeans were supposedly coming from parts of the world culturally ill-suited to understand American values and practices. But to compound the issue, the classic incubator of "Americanization"—the pioneer project—no longer meaningfully existed. Without the mechanism by which Turner's and Roosevelt's version of "composite" nationality could be forged, how could new generations of Americans, whether foreign or native born, be educated into the civic and republican traditions of collective life, let alone imagine themselves as bound to a single, national project?

THE FEDERAL CONSTITUTION: SOLUTION
OR EXACERBATING PROBLEM?

A striking feature of turn-of-the-twentieth-century America is collective uncertainty about the national legal-political system in the face of these challenges. For many, the 1787 Constitution seemed incapable of solving such intransigent problems. And some even considered the text and its associated governmental structures not just insufficient, but an actual and active hindrance to the country's future.

To begin with, the Civil War had spread a double-edged engagement with the federal Constitution's legacy. On the one hand, the war and its aftermath heightened the status of the document as a national symbol. A small but steady drumbeat of states passed new laws requiring school instruction about the Constitution. Since so much of the rhetoric around the war entailed the idea of preserving the union, preserving the Constitution too became connected to this effort in the public imagination. Thus, these new laws, as an historian writing in the 1930s concluded, amounted to an "expression of the nationalism arising from the war."[152]

On the other hand, the very fact of secession and war raised questions about the adequacy of the established constitutional order. The familiar antebellum story about the 1787 text among many Northern political elites—from Whig Party leaders like Daniel Webster to those in the mainstream of the Democratic Party—had long emphasized sectional compromise, including over the matter of slavery.[153] Yet how could the text be thought of as a successful compromise—let alone an institutional mechanism that promoted union and social cohesion—if it had failed to head off such extreme violence? In his best-known academic book, *Congressional Government* (drawn from his dissertation work at Johns Hopkins and published in 1885, just two years before the centennial), Woodrow Wilson noted the extent to which "free, outspoken, unrestrained constitutional criticism" had become commonplace in both the North and the South. And, in his mind, one could trace "this change of attitude towards the Constitution" to "the rude shock of the war," which had left Americans uncertain about whether the text, "whatever the initial wisdom of its design," remained "adapted to serve the purposes for which it was intended."[154]

In the immediate wake of the 1887 centennial celebration in Philadelphia, E. L. Godkin, writing again in the *Nation*, expressed these sentiments about the original document even more pointedly. Although these two men, one a Virginia-born Democrat and the other a long-time voice of the Northern Republican establishment, may have disagreed about many matters, they both expressed a similar ambivalence about the framers' system. According to Godkin, any clear-eyed assessment of the past made it difficult to take seriously the worshipful tone of the recent centennial events. For the "original framers," Godkin remarked, the 1787 text's principal goal had been to address "two great difficulties": "The union of slave and free states under a common government, and the merging of State allegiance and national allegiance in the mind of the citizens of the several States."[155] The Constitution-in-practice, however, had proved incapable of resolving these issues—preserving the durable compromise that men like Daniel Webster had envisioned in the 1840s—and thus avoiding secession and fratricidal violence. For Godkin, one could only conclude that the Constitution had been a "failure," when measured against its founding purpose. This was because the "arrangements by which it sought to" forge unity "broke down one after the other."[156]

Indeed, he went so far as to suggest that he would not be surprised if "those who celebrate the next centennial of the constitution will be disposed to put the date in 1865, rather than in 1787,"[157] in effect no longer marking the work of the original framers at all. Of course, for Southerners like Wilson, that vision of the Constitution as re-founded with the end of the Civil War hardly resolved matters. Did this suggest that Congressional Reconstruction—and in particular the meaning Radical Republicans gave to the new amendments—defined the overall text's meaning?

Key Black voices may have rallied to the Constitution due to how the Reconstruction Amendments appeared to give textual teeth to the creedal vision. Yet, for this very reason, Southern white politicians and notables—including former Confederates—would have been uncomfortable with what the Reconstruction Amendments indicated about the post–Civil War Constitution. Even as the Supreme Court and Northern political elites were moving to defang these provisions, the question persisted for white supremacists: Did the amendments mean that the Constitution now stood for the type of racial equality they fundamentally rejected? In fact, this may have been yet another reason for limited Southern white enthusiasm about the 1887 centennial.

The creeping questions about whether the Constitution could provide the institutional and symbolic means for restitching the collective fabric emerged not only from the Civil War and its seismic effects.

Over time, the very real dysfunctions of Gilded Age politics—which the Constitution seemed ill-equipped to tackle—perhaps played an even greater role. Indeed, by the centennial, extolling the genius of the Constitution had begun to take on a partisan cast. To the extent that the Constitution seemed implicated in ongoing labor struggles, it was most obviously through the extensive weight that a lifetime-appointed federal judiciary—composed overwhelmingly of pro-business lawyers with deep ties to corporate interests—placed on the side of employers in interpreting the document. Rather than a shared instrument of negotiation and compromise, the constitutional framework—with the courts at the forefront—appeared to be a decisive and biased thumb on the scale.

In this way, the emergence of a national industrial order destabilized that balance between state and federal constitutionalism that had been operative in the early part of the nineteenth century. To the extent that settler politics had been primarily local, with the country really a "society of island communities," the federal system was less relevant, for good or bad. Those who opposed the anti-democratic constraints embedded in that system could simply create different state constitutional orders through processes of territorial settlement and governance. But as problems of economy and politics became increasingly national in scope, the nature of the federal system gained heightened importance, as it inevitably shaped the terms of national debate. In this way, the bitter struggles over slavery presaged further events, with increasing pressure placed on the federal system to provide a national resolution to underlying disagreements.

In the context of industrial conflict, emerging labor activists and reformers in particular found the institutions of the federal government similarly wanting. For such activists, even state-level victories over labor and constitutional politics were insufficient in the shadow of a federal judiciary that could halt the implementation of broadly popular laws. Moreover, any genuinely national response to these problems of heightened complexity and scale proved incredibly difficult. At the national level, it was impossible to avoid those structural features of the federal model—like the difficulty of amendment or the checks on legislative power—that had been repudiated in many of the states. Douglass himself during Reconstruction had, for all his constitutional commitment, raised just these institutional concerns as "sources of danger to the republic."[158]

Indeed, during the earlier Jacksonian era, a white settler could proclaim an almost reverential fidelity to the Constitution, in part as a show of nationalism, while sidestepping the deeper implications of perhaps viewing the federal model as not necessarily one to be replicated at the state level. Yet, by the close of the century, the growing everyday relevance and thus effective power of that federal model and its judges cast a spotlight on its perceived defects. As nationally made decisions gained greater salience, a similarly situated American would now have to struggle over the disconnect between the terms of the existing federal Constitution and those of a legal-political system they would actually desire.

Thus, it was not a surprise that commercial and manufacturing notables had swooped in to save Philadelphia's 1887 festivities. If one asked which constituency actually identified wholeheartedly with the Constitution in the late nineteenth century, the single clear group would be legal and business elites—those committed to safeguarding prevailing class relations exactly as they were. During and after the centennial, panegyrics on the Constitution overwhelmingly came from familiar sources: the American Bar Association (ABA), local chambers of commerce, and eventually new entities like the National Civic Federation, the National Association of Manufacturers, and Rotary and Kiwanis clubs.

As a result, the federal Constitution—and especially the courts—eventually became identified with the interests of property. This meant that unabashedly extolling the virtues of the text gained a specific political cast. Henry Cabot Lodge, once the Constitutional Centennial Commission vice president, surveyed with horror the ubiquity of anti-Constitution sentiment by 1911:

> [E]very one who is in distress, or in debt, or discontented, now assails the Constitution, merely because such is the present passion. Every reformer of other people's misdeeds—all of that numerous class which is ever seeking to promote virtue at somebody else's expense—pause in their labors to point out the supposed shortcomings of our national charter. Every raw demagogue, every noisy agitator . . . all such people now lift their hands to tear down or remake the Constitution. In the House and Senate one can hear attacks upon it at any time and listen to men deriding its framers and their work.

Lodge, ever the conservative guardian of the existing order, of course refused to recognize just why the Constitution now left so many cold.

For those like him, this degree of "enmity" to the text was nothing less than "a situation of utmost gravity."[159]

The problem for these defenders was the growing cultural meaning of venerating the Constitution. Given systematic corporate control of the legal and political process, by the beginning of the twentieth century unabashed support appeared to entail throwing one's lot in with the institutionally powerful but numerically beleaguered side in the fight between labor and capital. Even some patrician elites, like Godkin (who wrote his dim assessments of both the 1787 Constitution and new immigrants in the centennial year) or Woodrow Wilson, found it hard to repeat uncritically homilies about the document's eternal wisdom or unifying national power.

Conclusion: The Uncertain Fate of the Constitution in a Time of Social Breakdown

The overall picture of the country in 1900 was one of intense turmoil. And the Constitution, the governing document of a polity under extreme duress, became wrapped up in this larger disarray. As hinted above, uncertainty about the federal Constitution came from a remarkably diverse set of social groups, running the gamut from agrarian and industrial workers to public intellectuals, Southern white supremacists, and newly freed African Americans. Although each group may have been disaffected for competing reasons, such widespread concerns raised real questions about whether the document—or anything else—could cohere a polity wracked by class, racial, gender, and regional divisions.

As chapter 3 explores, these conditions provided sustenance for the emergence of a powerful new class-based counternarrative of the Constitution and the American social order. A strikingly broad array of reformers—from labor activists to Populists, Progressives, and members of the new Socialist Party of America—argued that the United States had never solved the problem of class and that the Constitution embodied, from the founding, a persistent aristocratic impulse. These arguments echoed old abolitionists like Garrison, Redpath, and Phillips, but they struck far deeper roots within white society than Garrison's fiery denunciations of slavery ever had. In fact, such continuities were certainly one reason why men like Redpath and Phillips felt at home in new mass movements, even if white reformers often deemphasized or even rejected the racially egalitarian commitments of the most radical abolitionists.

All of this meant that, in the first two decades of the twentieth century, the idea of drafting a new Constitution to replace the old would hardly have been inconceivable. It appeared to be a plausible pathway to overcome the monarchical and aristocratic elements that riddled an outdated eighteenth-century document. In fact, many individuals living at the time would have considered that outcome far more likely than what eventually emerged: Americans recommitting to Constitution worship, but on grounds that the text was somehow inherently, and from the founding, a universally egalitarian document.

CHAPTER 3

Class Narratives and the High Tide of "Constitution Tinkering"

If business and legal elites struggled to make laborers commemorate the hundredth anniversary of the signing of the federal Constitution in 1887, a far more significant day in the political life of the country's working class that year was the hanging of August Spies and three others for the Chicago Haymarket Square bombing. During a May 1886 rally that was part of the massive nationwide general strike for an eight-hour day, a bomb exploded in the path of the police as they sought to break up the event. Gunfire then ensued from the police and demonstrators, ultimately leaving eight officers and at least four civilians dead. Spies had spoken to those gathered and was still on the stage when the violence erupted. As with the others arrested—all of whom were significant labor radicals in the city—authorities never provided any proof that Spies either carried out the bombing or participated in its planning. Nonetheless, Spies was convicted, as the historian Matthew Frye Jacobson writes, of "'general conspiracy to murder,'" essentially "for his advocacy of worker self-defense" against anti-labor state and private violence.[1]

In effect, government authorities used the Haymarket bombing as an opportunity to crack down on labor activism and especially to target immigrant activists as foreign and "un-American" threats to the nation.[2] In many ways, this response embodied an emerging approach, especially among pro-business elites, for reestablishing social peace in the face of rising industrial strife and dissolving settler bonds: the classic method of propping up a collapsing order by embracing a politics of exclusion—now reaching even new European migrants—and defending racial and economic hierarchies through force.

As the artist Frederic Remington infamously wrote to a former Yale classmate in 1893, "Jews, Injuns, Chinamen, Italians, Huns—the rub-

bish of the earth I hate—I've got some Winchesters and when the mas-
sacring begins . . . I can get my share of 'em."[3] Remington's more sober
interlocutors may have paused at this explicit embrace of frontier logics
and race war as the primary way to manage the multiethnic dynamics of
the industrial city. But many native-born and especially patrician voices
saw the preservation of public order as tied to a reaffirmation of American "Anglo-Saxonism." And, in the context of class conflict, they likewise often embraced anti-labor and anti-immigrant violence.

Yet for many immigrant and native-born Euro-Americans who
found themselves facing the brunt of industrial oppression, this patrician defense of order—apparently for its own sake—seemed no solution at all. Previously, the old settler framework had claimed legitimacy
from a basic set of republican commitments. As Herbert Croly, a co-
founder of the *New Republic* and a key intellectual figure of the time,
commented, "the American pioneer or territorial democrats were, according to their own lights, freemen in both the economic and political sense." The availability of land provided the "promise of ultimate
economic independence": that is, productive control and a daily experience in moral and material autonomy. But Croly concluded—in now
familiar terms—that the end of settlement and the expanding power
and concentration of corporate capital had "converted" Americans
from "freehold[ers]" into regimented and impoverished industrial employees. The nation faced a dilemma that business and governing elites
seemed ill-equipped to address: "How . . . wage-earners [can] obtain an
amount or a degree of economic independence analogous to that upon
which the pioneer democrat could count."[4]

Indeed, for many Americans, Croly included, the only way to restitch collective life would be to make economic and political liberty
somehow compatible with prevailing conditions. Simply asserting the
existence of social mobility through the market and free labor, along
with the supposed greatness of the Constitution—while at the same
time using violence to pacify dissent—was a recipe for continued strife.
Against this backdrop, calls to radically rethink the existing legal-
political system became ubiquitous. Indeed, much to the chagrin of
conservative business and judicial elites, institutional experimentalism
and "Constitution tinkering"[5] were the order of the day, at both state
and federal levels.

In this chapter, I lay out how, in this context, reformers across various
movements embraced a powerful new counternarrative about Amer-

ican founding and constitutionalism. This narrative contended that, while the 1776 revolution unleashed democratic forces, the 1787 Constitution was an aristocratic victory of propertied elites against the mass of ordinary settlers. Therefore, the later text consolidated the institutional and cultural victory of the wealthy few against the many, pushing back democratic ambitions. This meant that the United States, rather than being exceptional in class terms, continued to have far more in common with monarchical Europe than many Americans cared to admit. And these interpretations further reinforced a broad public mood fundamentally open to frank discussions about the value of existing institutions—and also attendant to the countless muckraking exposés of the Constitution that proliferated during the period.

By the late twentieth century, such an account of constitutional meaning receded almost entirely from cultural significance. But at the beginning of the century, it would have been readily familiar and quite compelling to many Americans caught in the vise-grip of industrial conditions. Indeed, I argue that, at the time, class-based readings of the Constitution and of national identity had far deeper resonance within general white society than does our familiar narrative today of the Constitution as fulfilling a racially egalitarian and universally inclusive creed. The ubiquity of this alternative understanding renders even more puzzling the ideological about-face over the subsequent century.

The following pages explore this early class-based narrative in greater depth: how such a narrative developed, as well as how it drove a popular conversation around the need for basic constitutional change. To begin with, especially after the 1890s electoral defeat of the People's (or Populist) Party, public criticism expanded its purview primarily from judges to the system as a whole. This expansion went hand in hand with readings of the 1787 text as a rejection of the revolutionary project and even of the Declaration of Independence. In reflecting this mood, I focus in particular on the early-twentieth-century historian Charles Beard's seminal class-based interpretation of the framers, including the idea of James Madison as offering a more aristocratic theory of politics. The pervasiveness of such arguments during this period speaks to how the framers had lost a considerable part of their sanctified sheen. Indeed, a fair amount of derision might well have met a politician or commentator arguing that all matters of constitutional import should be answered by simply affirming Madison's intentions.

In addition, the chapter considers the two great constitutional developments of the Progressive era: the press for women's suffrage and the focus on American presidentialism. These emerged as a response to the legal-political system's deep disenfranchisement on the one hand, and its institutional paralysis on the other. Today, both developments are usually subsumed within a creedal and venerative account of the Constitution, standing as proof of the American system's unfolding egalitarianism and capacity for institutional renewal and adaptation. Yet, critically, the actual debates over the vote and about grafting presidentialism onto a fractured US system reveal a far more ambiguous political conversation—one driven more by fear of further social breakdown and revolutionary alternatives than by recognition of the deeper wisdom underpinning the American federal model.

Above all, the climate of "Constitution tinkering," complete with a driving counternarrative of the 1787 framing, indicates a cultural reality often deemphasized in scholarship. In the years before World War I, patriotic commitment was often decoupled from support for the Constitution. Indeed, Herbert Croly emerged as a major voice of nationalist sentiment while arguing at the same time for the essential bankruptcy of the 1787 constitutional project. The fact that scholars today tend to paper over this reality means that they also overlook how the last century has witnessed a remarkable reimagining of nationhood—one that re-tied American nationalism to an eighteenth-century document that once seemed far less secure.

Rising Discontent and Experiments with Democratic Alternatives

If the first two decades of the twentieth century were marked by a remarkable openness to institutional experimentalism, these conditions emerged out of a basic structural impasse. Even when earlier mass movements of agrarian farmers, industrial workers, and allied middle-class reformers enjoyed the popular support of a numerical majority, they seemed unable to meaningfully shift the apparatus of corporate and state power. Such realities raised hard questions about the extent to which democratic ends and the federal Constitution actually went together.

Moreover, these questions were being asked during a time that the historian Daniel Rodgers has called a "transatlantic moment."[6] Links between Europe and the US, further deepened by the sheer number of new immigrants, made more Americans wonder why the country remained bound to the governance choices of long departed figures like

James Madison and Alexander Hamilton. Why not learn from and incorporate the various proposals circulating abroad—entailing everything from labor laws and social welfare measures to proportional representation and new structures of mass parliamentary democracy? These conversations and broader shifts, which found practical expression in institutional efforts at the state and federal level, laid the groundwork for a serious reconsideration of the founders and of the country's origin story.

A BACKGROUND OF INSTITUTIONAL EXPERIMENTALISM

It is unsurprising that core national narratives came under attack during a time when legal-institutional experimentation seemed entirely plausible. This context offered an ongoing education in alternative design options, and it may have encouraged greater license to reclaim ownership over the processes of founding and re-founding, in part by emphasizing that such activity was not the purview of mythic national founders alone.

At the state level, this "tinkering" was especially successful. As the historian Noam Maggor notes, settlers out west rejected, just as they had in the decades before the Civil War, the "legal orthodoxy" of the "federal model," choosing instead to write new constitutions that were easy to amend, participatory, and incredibly elaborate. Politicians and activists in these states opposed the federal style of writing "short and elegant constitutions" out of a fear that "any important policy issues left out of the constitution would permit corporations to shape legislation in their best interests."[7]

And when it came to matters of rights, John Dinan notes that "in the late nineteenth and early twentieth centuries," state constitutions also "widely adopted" positive socioeconomic protections in ways that diverged dramatically from the 1787 text. Whereas the federal document had minimal positive guarantees and focused on property protections, the era's state constitutions often included "the right of individuals to enjoy reasonable work hours, a minimum wage, safe work conditions, and compensation for workplace injuries."[8]

Just as significant, in the years preceding World War I, Americans at the national level too seriously debated the formal rewriting of the Constitution—perhaps more so than at any other moment in national history. For a federal text widely understood to be incredibly difficult to alter through the Article V process, four amendments were successfully implemented between 1913 and 1920. These affected some of the most contentious issues of the day—from taxation and the direct election of senators to prohibition and women's suffrage. As the legal scholar Andrea Katz has noted, while there had been some "1,736 amendment proposals initiated on the floor of Congress" between 1789 and 1897, the next thirty years alone saw "an additional 1,370."[9]

In fact, calls for change were so widespread that many reformers across the political spectrum viewed the likelihood of convening an actual second constitutional convention as surprisingly high. Between 1893 and 1911, thirty-one states passed seventy-three petitions demanding a convention to propose an amendment for the direct election of senators.[10] And the Senate finally sent what would become the Seventeenth Amendment (direct senatorial election) "to the states for ratification" after twenty-three states signed one petition demanding a convention to debate a package of five potential revisions.[11] The legal scholars John Kowal and Wilfred Codrington suggest that "the threat of an Article V convention helped to break the Senate's resistance after two decades of obstruction."[12] Just as striking, fifteen states also pursued convention requests from 1899 to 1911 that were not issue-specific or tied to direct election of senators, but that actually called for a general rewriting of the existing text.[13] All this speaks to an underlying discontent in American political life, and a fairly widespread feeling that perhaps another generation could improve upon the 1787 effort.

THE POPULIST ATTACK ON COURTS AND THE LEGAL-POLITICAL IMPLICATIONS OF DEFEAT

General sentiments of discontent in the last decades of the nineteenth century often exploded into anger and forthright opposition. In 1887, the effects of open political struggle extended beyond industrial centers like Chicago. A mood of revolt also swept through the countryside in what remained an overwhelmingly agrarian society.

Faced with a coercive credit lien system threatening debt and the loss of land, small landholders and tenants organized the Farmers' Alliance. Eventually numbering over two million people in forty-two states and territories, the Alliance sought to free the rural poor from dependence on local merchants and commercial banking elites through a cooperative crusade and a subtreasury plan that would make federal credit socially available. Formed in 1892, the People's Party expressed these economic goals as well as the larger collective ambition of recentering politics around the basic interest of laborers.[14]

Among those that gravitated to this Populist movement, the courts emerged as the target whenever concerns were raised about the federal Constitution. As I noted in chapter 2, by the turn of the twentieth century the salience of the federal judiciary, in particular, rose dramatically for everyday Americans. In the context of greater industrialization and emerging national markets, the issue of how to regulate this growing economy—and especially labor-business relations—became a central dilemma. Moreover, in a nation without an expansive central administrative apparatus, the courts, dominated as they were by pro-business appointees, increasingly employed powers of judicial review to claim for themselves such regulatory authority. Essentially, then, it was the courts that served as the *de facto* regulator and adjudicator of relevant debates.[15]

For many reformers and activists, this exercise of judicial review highlighted a profound illegitimacy in the courts' expanding role. Nowhere in the actual text of the 1787 document was there an explicit provision granting the federal judiciary the right to strike down government action, including congressional laws, as unconstitutional. Instead, the Supreme Court, through Chief Justice John Marshall's 1803 opinion in *Marbury v. Madison*, had claimed this power *for itself*. This fact, along with the judiciary's early institutional weakness vis-à-vis the other branches, explains why the Supreme Court in the years before the Civil War tended to tread carefully when invoking such authority. Indeed, after *Marbury*, it would not be until 1857—over half a century later— that the Supreme Court again declared an act of Congress unconstitutional. That infamous case, *Dred Scott*, denied federal citizenship under the Constitution to all African Americans, whether enslaved or formally free. It further held that Congress did not have the power to ban slavery in new territories, like those formed from the 1803 Louisiana Purchase. The ruling only inflamed anti-slavery hostility to the federal courts and further spotlighted the shaky grounds for a strong bench, let alone for broad readings of judicial review.

The fact that such review powers—in virtually any form—were a global outlier further raised suspicions about the bench's role. By comparison with Europe, American-style review was a clear anomaly. It gave a small number of unelected judges, appointed for life, the ability to strike down overwhelmingly popular decisions. And all this proceeded with virtually no chance of democratic rebuttal by representative institutions or popular vote. Congress could not use supermajorities to override a ruling, and federal constitutional amendments were notoriously hard to ratify.

Yet by the 1880s and 1890s, such federal judges appeared to be aggressively invoking these self-declared powers, setting themselves up as what amounted to a third legislative body. More or less all from elite class backgrounds, and with corporate sympathies, they overturned everything from labor laws to social welfare provisions and taxation schemes. Judges further influenced employer-employee matters by systematically privileging one side in negotiations—for instance, by criminalizing union organizing and protest.[16]

But crucially, as the Populist movement picked up steam, activists at first avoided viewing the extremism of American-style judicial review as emblematic of the larger failures of structural design. Instead, while reformers may have seen the federal bench as corrupt and to be deplored, they essentially treated the larger institutional and symbolic order as just and to be defended. It was problematic and elitist judges, along with the corporate bosses they served, who together stood in the way of addressing destitution and dependent working relations on the farm or in the factory. Focusing on the lack of a textual basis, these arguments tended to present the development of judicial review as a violation of the Constitution's true meaning and as an institutional perversion taken advantage of by pro-business judges.

Running in 1892 as the People's Party candidate for president, James Weaver referred to Marshall's decision in *Marbury* as a "gross usurpation" of power, which over time had allowed judges to operate as an "*imperium in imperio*"—a state within a state.[17] Not to be outdone, the Populist governor of Oregon, Sylvester Pennoyer, declared in another article condemning *Marbury* that "this unconstitutional usurpation of the law-making power by the Federal courts is productive alone of confusion, anarchy and judicial despotism."[18]

As the new century dawned, such claims about the courts spread far and wide, becoming a staple of political sentiment throughout the labor movement. Samuel Gompers, the founder of the American Federation of Labor (AFL), viewed the Supreme Court as little more than a class instrument and judicial review as legally illegitimate. He argued that "in exercising this prerogative the Supreme Court usurped power that did not constitutionally belong to it."[19]

Indeed, changes to the courts eventually became a critical piece of those reformist efforts that later coalesced under the broad umbrella of

Progressivism. By 1912, Oregon, California, Arizona, Nevada, and Colorado had all passed statutes at the state level authorizing the recall of judges. Moreover, none other than former president Teddy Roosevelt called for popular referenda on federal judicial decisions.[20] In broad strokes, the latter proposal became part of the Progressive Party platform. Formed in 1912 by Roosevelt in his effort to reclaim the White House, the new party "demand[ed] such restriction of the power of the courts as shall leave to the people the ultimate authority to determine fundamental questions of social welfare and public policy."[21]

Indeed, throughout the 1910s and 1920s, Progressives routinely proposed ideas that would have dramatically restructured the federal courts. At various points, this included pressing for term limits, retirement ages, expansion of the number of justices on the Supreme Court (to deemphasize the power of any one judge), direct election, and either the elimination of judicial review or significant changes to how review operated. Along with national referenda on judicial decisions, these reforms ranged from requiring supermajorities for Supreme Court decisions to be binding, to granting Congress the power to override court rulings through legislative action.

Many of these judicial alterations would have effectively ended the global anomaly of the American federal bench, bringing these courts closer to what would eventually emerge across much of the world, especially during the post–World War II years of decolonization and European reconstruction. More radically, some of these changes embodied a Progressive desire to make the courts as democratically responsive as popular legislatures across the range of their activities—from constitutional questions to typical matters of criminal and civil law.

QUESTIONS SPREAD BEYOND THE COURTS

If anger at the courts produced a broad-ranging reconsideration of the judiciary, things did not stop there. From the very beginning, concerns about the undemocratic nature of judicial power generated questions about the extent to which the constitutional system as a whole was truly democratic.

For instance, Weaver, the Populist presidential candidate mentioned above, may have believed that federal judicial review contradicted what the framers themselves intended. But he nonetheless admitted that the 1787 structure did include a variety of institutional features that, in practice, undermined popular power. Noting that in the 1890s only the

House of Representatives was actually elected by direct vote, let alone organized around popular rather than geographic representation, he acknowledged that "the fact remains beyond dispute that under our present system, three out of the four subdivisions of Government are practically placed beyond the control of the multitude."[22] Weaver addressed this seeming contradiction by holding—not unlike Frederick Douglass during Reconstruction—that although the constitutional order combined democratic and undemocratic components, the essence of the Constitution was expressed in the former, while the latter could be thought of as antiquated holdovers from a bygone time.

Still, Weaver's focus on the judiciary as the crux of problems faced an unavoidable fact: even on his own account, the undemocratic components of the Constitution far outnumbered the democratic ones. Alongside the courts, everything from the bicameral nature of Congress to the intricate federalist division between state and national authority seemed structured to place obstacles in the path of enacting widely backed responses to problems of immiseration and inequality. And as failed reform efforts mounted, popular criticism extended from the courts to these broader constitutional arrangements. Such voices argued that the issue was not a single faulty mechanism—say, federal judges claiming authority that did not belong to them—but the entire political system. Indeed, as early as 1893, the Populist journalist, activist, and politician Henry Demarest Lloyd, who would later become a supporter of the Socialist Party of America (SPA), declared at the AFL convention the collective need for a "grand international constitutional convention in which a new magna charta [sic], a new declaration of independence, a new bill of rights shall be proclaimed."[23]

The case of Walter Clark, the Populist chief justice of the North Carolina Supreme Court and one of the state's most popular politicians during the era, is also instructive. Like Weaver, he rejected judicial review and believed that the Constitution's framers did not intend it. But, writing in 1898, in the context of corporate success in pushing back Populist electoral efforts to control the federal government, Clark could not help but see his party's larger defeat as bound to those constitutional features previously noted by Weaver. It appeared to Clark that a key reason for both the success of judicial review and the Populist revolt's defeat at the national level—despite the intensity of mass support— was the fact that the entire governing order was "never democratic."[24]

For Clark, the country needed nothing less than a basic revision of its Constitution, through packaged amendments or even a new convention. So long as features persisted like the Electoral College, the indirect election of senators (at the time), and the lifetime appointment of federal judges, their interlocking effect would be the repeated frustration of mass reform politics. In his mind, these characteristics all highlighted the degree to which the founders' Constitution was fundamentally damaged by eighteenth-century monarchical thinking; the document was constitutively shaped by anti-democratic checks, like the presidential veto, that were "a survival from times when the people's representatives could not legislate without the assent of the monarch expressly given to each act."[25]

It should not be a surprise that Clark was both a white Southerner and a defender of Jim Crow.[26] His arguments combined in potent ways the white supremacy, economic populism, and sectional bitterness that circulated throughout the region. During the days of Reconstruction, as we have seen, national symbols generally—from the Constitution to the Declaration—became fraught for those whose allegiance to the Confederacy died hard or who saw the North and its army as an occupying power. But in a sense, antebellum Jacksonian politics, discussed in chapter 2, also highlighted how anti-elitist suspicions of the federal government—particularly as a threat to local white rule—had a long pedigree in the South.

In the early nineteenth century, settlers addressed this threat by vigorously policing the exercise of federal authority in communal life. They also invoked strict constitutional construction as a way of limiting what they saw as the illegitimate exercise of a monarchical prerogative. But by the end of the century, the dramatic and expanded everyday salience of the Constitution placed significant strain on this long-standing approach. The reality of an ever more integrated national economy alongside the experiences of the Civil War and Reconstruction made avoiding the tentacles of the Constitution's federal structures appear nearly impossible. Where past anti-elitist suspicions had comfortably fit within a politics of constitutional fidelity—so long as the Constitution was read narrowly and decision-making left to the local level—the seeming pervasiveness of national constitutional politics in shaping collective options on the ground made those old accommodations far less viable. Especially as economic depression and the collapse of independent landholding for white farmers came to dominate the political debate in the 1890s, the narrative began to shift. And a more overt class-based criticism of the Constitution—less concerned with surface fidelity and respect, and with roots reaching all the way back to eighteenth-century Anti-Federalism—became increasingly joined to white Southern discontent.

THE TRANSATLANTIC MOMENT, IMMIGRATION, AND AUGUST SPIES

One significant implication of the idea that the federal constitutional order was riddled with monarchical elements, as North Carolina Supreme Court Justice Clark contended, was that it challenged faith in American class exceptionalism. US judicial review, for instance, suggested that, to the extent that American practices were "exceptional," such exceptionalism was not something to celebrate; rather, it highlighted deeper social and institutional flaws. Such hard truths raised the possibility that not only were current US realities far more akin to the rigid hierarchies of Europe, but perhaps governing practices going back to the founding had never really broken from Old World forms of class rule. And critically, Clark's puncturing of settler mythology occurred just as academic and mass contacts between Americans and Europeans expanded. This increased connection directed attention toward seemingly common developments on both sides of the Atlantic.

During these years, a tremendous amount of political and scholarly exchange occurred between the two continents. Everyone from social scientists to municipal officials and national politicians engaged in continuous conversation with counterparts in Europe. So, if European reformers contemplated changes far and wide to the organization of state and economy, why not explore their relevance to a US context that appeared institutionally broken?

At the same time, European migrants surged into civic associations and social movements—especially the labor movement—infusing political debates with new vitality. Such arrivals were steeped in the ongoing social battles of their home countries and carried their own revolutionary and republican heritages. They were thus often less predisposed to take for granted venerative presumptions about American institutions and customs.

Writing as early as 1885, Woodrow Wilson himself concluded that the present generation of Americans had become "the first to entertain ... serious doubts about the superiority of our own institutions compared with the systems of Europe."[27] In a sense, patrician defenders of the established order were not wholly wrong to feel threatened by how exchanges and new arrivals appeared to unleash social and cultural change. In many ways, the transatlantic dimensions of the era offered the final ingredient shifting the terrain of acceptable political argument—spurring institutional experimentalism as well as competing, less exceptionalist accounts of national experience.

Spies's own autobiography, written from his jail cell and published by his wife, Niña van Zandt, just prior to his execution, emphatically decried pretensions of American superiority. Spies began the book by exclaiming, "'Barbarians, savages, illiterate Anarchists from Central Europe, men who cannot comprehend the spirit of our free American institutions,'—of these I am one."[28] Embracing his immigrant status, his words pointedly inverted the kind of bromides to the genius of American institutions given during the Constitution's centennial celebration that same 1887 September.

If business and governing elites blamed social unrest on the cultural failures of new immigrants, Spies argued that it was really native-born Americans—in particular, those in power—who seemed to blindly champion a monarchical and aristocratic world view, in the process rejecting both republican values and truly emancipatory economic arrangements. The fact that he was raised in central Germany, close to "the remnants of the old" feudal "castle[s]," argued Spies, meant that he knew what class rule looked like, even if the "intelligent American" called him a "Barbarian." He reminded his readers that his German birthplace was where the Reformation began, a "reformation . . . which started . . . in a country where four centuries later the 'Barbarian Anarchists' come from, 'who cannot comprehend the spirit of the American institutions' . . . [yet who] broke down the feudal barriers, which impeded human progress."[29] He too came from a society with its own education in meaningful self-rule. Thus, it was unclear to him why the American state and economy—especially in the context of its evident failures—should enjoy any special status.

Equally important, Spies's cultural background meant that he could tell when class oppressors used the symbols of government—the presumption of shared patriotism or the pomp and circumstance of long-standing state ritual—to convince workers to fight to uphold their own domination. In the United States, much of this ritual was now built around supporting an unreflective acceptance of supposedly free institutions. In reality, though, these practices protected the interests of property, and criminalized virtually any agitation on behalf of social change.

The result, according to Spies, was that for all the supposed differ-

ences between "Barbarian" immigrants and "intelligent American[s],"
"tell the Americans to fight for the maintenance of our commercial
robbing posts and fleecing institutions—tell them to fight for the protection of the *lawful* enterprises of our Board of Trade men, Merchant
princes, Railroad kings, and Factory lords—would they do it? Deplor-
able as the fact must seem—they would! Even more readily, I fear, than
those 'barbarians from Central Europe.'"[30]

According to national mythologies, Americans—with a sense of
shared identity forged through the rugged practices of settlement—
had an unbreakable commitment to their own independence and self-
rule. Yet the deference many showed to those in power suggested far
greater commonality with Old World hierarchy. It pointedly repudiated the idea, going back to J. Hector St. John de Crèvecoeur, that the
American was somehow a "new man, who acts upon new principles."[31]

Indeed, Spies challenged American laborers to display greater "rebellious spirit" than the generations of European serfs, many of whom
acquiesced to a self-defeating faith in feudal institutions. To the American readers who believed themselves better than those serfs of old or
who doubted that any society would survive with extreme injustice,
Spies taunted, "you don't believe the people would have born all these
outrages—? My friend, your rebellious spirit carries you away. The 'orderly and good people' suffered these atrocities just as silently as our
'law and order abiding workingmen' bear them to-day."[32] For Spies, in
keeping with his anarchism, the question for the future was not just
whether the prevailing modes of despotic and "imposed authority"[33]
could be cast aside. The more important question was whether American workers could be jolted out of their complacency and struggle on
behalf of genuine self-rule.

New Origin Stories Emerge

Although many critics of the system focused their attention on very
real immediate struggles, key thinkers also cast an eye toward the past.
And this eventually led to a striking and explicit reassessment of the US
founding. If the constitutional system protected such anti-democratic
interests, what might that say about those who designed it in the
first place?

Across the reformist spectrum, it became increasingly common
for activists to contend that a significant part of the problem lay with
the framers themselves: whatever the past toasts on July 4, the found-

ers never actually had been committed to democracy, and instead had sought to suppress the popular ambitions unleashed by the Revolution. Thus, change in the present would require coming to grips with the extent to which the federal Constitution was in fact a counterrevolutionary document.

THE POLITICS OF OPPOSITION AND A
RECASTING OF THE FOUNDING

August Spies may have been an executed anarchist and radical, framed as an outsider by those in power. But his basic analysis hinted at a counternarrative of American life that became increasingly commonplace after his death, particularly in the wake of Populist defeat. Across reformist camps, activists coalesced around the idea that Americans were not the "individual sovereign[s]"[34] they imagined themselves to be (to use Spies's language). Instead, most working people faced various modes of class rule.

Moreover, if in Europe reforms were historically thwarted by old constitutional orders—and the feudal elements that backed them— then perhaps in the United States too the constitutional order itself stood in the way. This indicated that the 1787 text, rather than being an embodiment of popular self-government, was what the Progressive economist, political scientist, and lawyer J. Allen Smith strikingly proclaimed: a "reactionary document"[35] that preserved the interests of the wealthy few.[36] Thus, Americans had to be disabused of the faith they had in the existing system. They had to see this legal-political order as an expression of aristocracy rather than its concrete repudiation. Only then would Americans be open to the potential changes essential to containing industrial hierarchies in both the US and Europe.

This critique was tied to a sustained argument about the Constitution's symbolic and structural role in society. Increasing numbers of activists, from remaining Populists to Progressives and members of the Socialist Party, contended that the constitutional system—by judicially entrenching property relations, as well as by dividing government power—quietly allowed socioeconomic elites to dominate the instruments of statecraft. This system made it very difficult for most citizens— whose only meaningful power derived from sheer numbers, as opposed to money or political connections—to use elections and mass pressure to overcome the variety of constraints built into decision-making. In this way, existing arrangements facilitated rule by the "Invisible Government"[37] of class elites, in the words of the journalist Charles Edward Russell, a co-founder of the National Association for the Advancement of Colored People (NAACP) and a politician on the SPA ticket. Reformers repeatedly described the period and its governing structures as "plutocratic," dominated by wealthy citizens to serve their own socioeconomic goals rather than those of the entire community.[38]

Reformers argued that, even worse, mainstream conversation around the document hid from workers and farmers basic truths about the nature of their own political community. As J. Allen Smith wrote, American popular culture treated the Constitution as "imbued with the spirit of political equality," thus keeping hidden from view "the fundamental nature of their system of government."[39] Americans still almost instinctively believed that their institutions, even if in need of some improvement, more or less expressed their actual desires and interests. In a sense, far too many remained the "law and order abiding workingmen" of Spies, accepting institutional arrangements that undermined their own basic self-rule. And business elites took advantage of precisely this faith in the legitimacy of the legal-political order to maintain power. In Europe, discourses around the crown or the church may have sustained deference to aristocratic elites. But in the United States, this role was increasingly played by the language and symbols of the republican tradition itself.

In trying to make sense of the psychology of American class deference, the editors of the *International Socialist Review* republished translations of large portions of the German sociologist Werner Sombart's writings on American political identity, which would be famously collected under the title, *Why Is There No Socialism in the United States?*[40] Sombart explained that the idea "drilled into the American worker from childhood" was that "the sovereign people alone decide what shall be legal in the realm of the American union." And this, he noted, had a profound popular effect. Even when government policies derived from the wealthy few, ordinary Americans tended to identify with those policies and to see them as expressions of their own political will. "However ... imaginary it may really be," concluded Sombart, the assumption that the sovereign people ruled in the United States instilled "in each individual a boundless feeling of power."[41] It also created a continuous psychic temptation among farmers and workers: to fall prey to the belief that the interests of powerful co-nationals were the interests of all, and so to accept elite authority.

The *International Socialist Review*, published out of Chicago by

Charles H. Kerr, may have been a leading organ of the SPA's left wing, but its focus on the destructive mythmaking around the Constitution placed it squarely within the broader reformist conversation. Across activist spaces, the question of the time was just how to break the culture of deference highlighted by Sombart. For more and more reformers, one method was clear. For over a century, notables had attempted to transform the framers of the Constitution, individuals like James Madison and Alexander Hamilton, into godlike figures. For some, their aim was partly to place existing institutions and hierarchies beyond popular critique. It was why the wealthy poured so much money and energy into festivities like the centennial celebration, which declared the genius of the founding fathers. All of this suggested that deepening the political mood of mass protest and opposition required contesting the exalted status of the framers themselves.

For this reason, reformers increasingly engaged in a profound retelling of the history of the federal Constitution's origins. They highlighted how the text's authors were flawed and self-interested in ways that led to class rule even after the American Revolution. These activists sought to replace one story of national founding with another, the latter of which would free ordinary laborers from myths that hindered social change. Indeed, these years witnessed a substantial cottage industry of constitutionally skeptical scholarly and journalistic writing questioning the framers' intentions.[42] The result of this literature, as distilled by the Progressive historian Vernon Parrington, was to depict the federal Constitution as nothing less than "a deliberate and well-considered protective measure designed by able men who represented the aristocracy and wealth of America; a class instrument directed against the democracy."[43] According to this reading, the Declaration of Independence and the US Constitution did not share a common animating purpose, as Lincoln or Douglass contended. Instead, the latter text was a direct assault on the principles of the former.

THE CRITIQUE SPREADS IN ESTABLISHMENT CIRCLES

Such views even took hold in key establishment circles. Take the perspective of Herbert Croly, who played a critical role in developing the ideological framework for Teddy Roosevelt's 1912 Progressive Party presidential campaign. Even after Roosevelt's defeat, Croly continued to enjoy a significant political footprint, as "Croly's *New Republic* became virtually the house organ for the Wilson administration."[44]

Croly bluntly stated that the implementation of the Constitution was a "kind of conspiracy" in which the "educated and wealthy classes bulldozed and cajoled the people into submitting to an alien and essentially obnoxious political system."[45] He concluded that "the Constitution was . . . 'put over' by a small minority of able, vigorous, and unscrupulous personal property owners."[46] Despite only amounting to "one-sixth of possible voters," pro-Constitution forces were able to win the day because of the wealthy's own intense internal cohesiveness as well as their pervasive social power and institutional control.[47] By contrast, those opposed to the Constitution failed to block ratification because they were "poor, scattered, disorganized, and unaccustomed to leadership and to united action"; they lacked the "class-conscious[ness]" of propertied elites.[48] Here too Croly reiterated activist worries about how popular deference to the wealthy subverted democratic practice and undermined republican liberties. That someone like Croly—trained at Harvard and a friend and confidant to presidents and judges—repeated such stinging critique of both the document and the framers themselves was indicative of the times.

The journalist William Allen White offers another germane example of how such skepticism had spread into the political establishment. Also an outspoken supporter of Teddy Roosevelt's 1912 Progressive presidential bid, White was hardly some wild-eyed agitator. As a young man, he had gained fame through a scathing 1896 attack on Kansas Populism, which he depicted as the destructive rise of an uncouth mob mentality.[49] But a little over a decade later, in the context of swirling industrial conflict and muckraking exposés of the Constitution, he himself began to rail against both industrial inequality and the governing political order, in language that was often more radical than that used by any of his old Populist foes. Speaking of the country in the 1910s, White wrote,

It seems necessary to inquire if this capture of the Constitution by our only aristocracy—that of wealth—was not in truth merely a recapture of what was intended in the beginning by the Fathers to belong to the minority. The checks and balances put in that Constitution to guard against the rule of the majority protected slavery for fifty years, and perhaps they bound the nation to the rule of the privileged classes in the Nineties. Perhaps these same checks and balances were put into the Constitution deliberately—the judiciary which annuls statutes and remakes laws, the rigidity of the fundamental law to amendment, the remoteness of the Senators from popular election and control.[50]

Even a relatively moderate political commentator like White questioned the very motives of the nation's founding "Fathers."

The historical analysis circulated broadly enough that it had regional inflections, with Woodrow Wilson hinting at a Southern white variation on the theme. Wilson, as we will see, ultimately pushed back decisively against constitutional opposition and developed his own venerative stance. But in his earlier years as a scholar, he too underlined the Constitution's anti-democratic features, which strengthened the position of the founding era's "ruling classes." He argued that this was not accidental, but rather due to its original purposes—the manner in which the Constitution was "organized upon the initiative and primarily in the interests of the mercantile and wealthy classes."[51] Wilson's post–Civil War context was one in which Northern commerce dominated, with Southern white constituencies often decrying how they were being reduced to economic appendages meant simply to provide raw material and hard labor. One could construe this association of the Constitution with commercial elites to imply that the rules did not operate impartially in these class *and* regional rivalries.

CHARLES BEARD AND MADISON'S ARISTOCRATIC THEORY OF POLITICS

During a period of deep social unraveling, these views of the Constitution genuinely vied with more venerative approaches for popular dominance. While this class-based counternarrative took many forms, it eventually became most closely associated with the historian Charles Beard.[52] It is unclear how many farmers and workers would have been directly exposed to Beard's seminal 1913 book, *An Economic Interpretation of the Constitution of the United States*. But its arguments influenced innumerable journalists, commentators, and activists, and it pulled together elements of the pervasive constitutional critique. Croly, for instance, explicitly referenced "Professor Beard's investigations" as the basis for his own interpretation of the constitutional founding.[53] For this reason, focusing on Beard tells us much about the specifics of the counternarrative. It also speaks to the depth of the era's critique of the framers themselves—how the substantive ideas of men like James

Madison were often depicted as aristocratic embodiments of an English colonial worldview.

In later years, Beard would contend that his book was not "written with reference to [the] immediate controversies" of the 1910s or its "profoundly disturbed" "'climate of opinion'" around the Constitution; it was simply dispassionate history.[54] But for many activists at the time, one could not read the book without connecting his story of the framing to ongoing Gilded Age developments. Implicitly, a reformist reader would see in these pages an explanation of the Constitution's twentieth-century failures. And these failures were not merely because eighteenth-century individuals understandably were unable to foretell the future. Rather, they derived from the fundamental defects in the political philosophy of the text's authors—a philosophy Beard elucidated.

Indeed, to unlock the real nature of the 1787 Constitution, Beard believed that the hidden key was the *Federalist Papers*, especially James Madison's *Federalist No. 10*.[55] He argued that *No. 10*, when read in combination with other *Federalist Papers* like *No. 51*, offered "the underlying political science of the Constitution."[56] These documents together indicated the framers' very particular—and to a reformist audience, troublingly aristocratic—understanding of the problem of arbitrary authority. For the framers, the major causes of potential despotism came from two principal sources: first, government officials; and second, "an interested and overbearing majority"[57]—those ordinary individuals with little or no property.[58] But Madison and others very consciously ignored a *third* source of political despotism: the destructive role that socioeconomic elites could play in political life.

According to *No. 51*, then, a key purpose of constitutional construction was to limit the ability of officeholders to claim absolutist rule, as in monarchical Europe, by dividing and limiting government power itself. For Madison, the most dangerous potential branch was the legislative. Thus, ensuring that officeholders did not wield power unjustly above all meant avoiding legislative supremacy: "The remedy . . . is to divide the legislature into different branches; and to render them, by different modes of election and different principles of action, as little connected with each other as the nature of their common functions and their common dependence on the society will admit."[59]

But why did Madison believe that legislatures were the most dangerous branch? Beard argued that the explanation could be found only by reading *No. 51*'s structural suggestions against the arguments in *No. 10* about factionalism. He contended that, when the framers focused on the sources within society that promoted the rise of despotism, they overwhelmingly emphasized worries about self-interested majorities, and especially how poorer citizens could use strong legislatures to undermine property rights. As a consequence, the Constitution was most directly designed to address the dangers to republican order that might be posed by public officials exercising power on behalf of the less affluent. And the framers pursued these ends by insulating political decision-making, to the greatest extent possible, from common citizens.[60]

Beard, along with many of his Progressive and Socialist readers, certainly appreciated that most of the framers would have likely opposed the extreme forms of inequality that marked the Gilded Age. Revolutionary-era political elites generally presumed that basic settler egalitarianism constituted a necessary sociological condition for free government: internal egalitarianism ensured that settler society was composed of economically independent citizens, with the everyday ethical training in self-rule to participate thoughtfully in politics. By contrast, great disparities in wealth went hand in hand with a propertyless and dependent mob, like those found in Europe—supposedly untutored in republican habits and enjoying no personal stake in the collective good. Such a mob could be easily swayed by demagogues and tyrants who promised revenge against the wealthy, and in the process would end the dream of republican liberty.[61]

But this admittedly indirect defense of egalitarianism, derived from the framers' presumptions about the preconditions for free government, was noteworthy in how it placed the primary blame for any collapse of free institutions on the poor themselves, who—if unconstrained—might take advantage of their numbers to act out fantasies of class revenge. As Beard quoted Madison's view (from a letter Madison wrote to Thomas Jefferson in October 1788): "In our Governments the real power lies in the majority of the Community, and the invasion of private rights is *chiefly* to be apprehended not from acts contrary to the sense of its constituents, but from acts in which the Government is the mere instrument of the major numbers of the Constituents."[62]

The deeper implication was that the 1787 structure—precisely because it viewed poor majorities as the real threat to stability and freedom—did very little institutionally to restrain the capacity of wealthy citizens to use their economic power to overrun the political process. According to Beard, "the economic corollary of this system is as follows: Property interests may . . . secure advantageous legislation whenever necessary, and they may at the same time obtain immunity from control

by parliamentary majorities."[63] In the words of the famed English reformers and future Labour Party stalwarts Sidney and Beatrice Webb,
whom the American socialist William Noyes quoted at length in his
assessment of American plutocracy: "The framers of the United States
Constitution . . . saw no resemblance or analogy between the personal
power which they drove from the castle, the altar and the throne, and
that which they left unchecked in the farm, the factory and the mine."[64]

For Beard, the framers' failure to provide vigorous controls for dominant socioeconomic groups—while carefully limiting the political power
of government officials and poor majorities—was not simply an oversight. The framers themselves came from the same class backgrounds.
They took for granted that although poor settlers were dependent and
selfishly wedded to their material interests, fellow class elites enjoyed
the economic independence and the education in self-rule needed to
exercise power wisely. Even while denigrating the material needs of the
poor as "partial" or "factional," framers like Madison simply treated
their own economic self-interest—that of the wealthy few—as if it were
the common good. Therefore, the entire constitutional project, according to Beard, was a product of class solidarity among revolutionary-era
elites: "The wealth, the influence, and a major portion of the educated
men of the country were drawn together in a compact group, 'informed
by a conscious solidarity of interests,' as President Wilson has so tersely
put it."[65] Thus, the governing structures that emerged aimed to serve
that group's specific material interests—even if they did so disguised as
general republican values.

This shared socioeconomic sensibility spoke to why the framers were
so deeply committed to entrenching, within the new federal structure,
classically aristocratic institutions such as the Senate. As Madison and
others well knew, from ancient Rome to Renaissance Florence, senatorial frameworks and upper houses helped to break up the majoritarian strength of the many; they offered wealthy citizens a concrete
institutional mechanism for maintaining political control. In keeping
with these ends, the American Senate—indirectly elected until 1913 and
thereafter still over-representative of particular regional interests—held
striking control over key policy matters. Precisely because the Senate
was not a majoritarian institution, the framers tasked it with confirm-
ing life-tenured federal judges as well as other senior officials of the federal government. Similarly, the Senate under the 1787 Constitution
was meant to have a decisive role in shaping foreign policy through
its authority to ratify treaties. Taken together, this decision-making

role underscored the extent to which the framers viewed counter-majoritarian bodies like the Senate as more than symbolic entities. They hoped to insulate decisive political spaces from mass intervention, allowing these arenas to serve as a practical vehicle for sustaining the political influence of the few.

Under a Beardian reading, all of this meant that the Constitution was best understood as a reversal—rather than an expression—of whatever democratizing forces had been unleashed by the Revolution. The framers may have opposed, on republican grounds, a society marked by extremes of wealth and poverty. Nonetheless, they also saw the preservation of elite class authority as a critical safeguard against property rights infringements, and ultimately against tyranny. They therefore constructed a Constitution that sustained elitist supervision, even after the end of British control, but under new, more ostensibly popular modes of political rule.

Men like Madison may have imagined that the Constitution would go hand in hand with ongoing settler egalitarianism. But a key narrative by the early twentieth century held that the document—by leaving unchecked the "personal power" operating "in the farm, the factory and the mine"—resulted, in practice, in a political order that exacerbated the society's hierarchical tendencies. The fact that this analysis had become increasingly commonplace suggests a notably demystified constitutional discourse—as invoking the framers or their desires would hardly have operated as a trump card in legal-political debate.

Progressivism, Suffrage, and the Presidential Solution

The spread of this Beardian framework, just as with Wilson's constitutional critiques and North Carolina Chief Justice Clark's call for basic "Revision of the Constitution"[66] spoke to a real development: the degree to which both class-based accounts and wholesale constitutional rethinking had become widespread. And such conversations emerged among judges, politicians, and academics, including those—like Wilson—who were hardly thought of as rabble-rousers.

This created a climate ripe for candid assessments of the institutional order, as underscored by two lasting constitutional legacies of the early twentieth century: women's suffrage and the rise of presidentialism. Today both of these developments are overwhelmingly read in venerative constitutional terms—as proof of the successful adaptability of the system and of its inherently egalitarian and regenerative features. But at the time, feminist camps divided over whether the struggle for the vote broke from, as opposed to completed, the constitutional order. Similarly, Progressive proponents of expanding presidential power may have embraced ideas of institutional adaptability, so as to address issues of national fracture and constitutional paralysis. But they nonetheless often took as given the class-based and skeptical narrative of the founding.

WOMEN'S SUFFRAGE: CONSTITUTIONAL FIDELITY OR CONSTITUTIONAL BREAK?

The women's suffrage movement sheds light on the uneasy status of straightforward Constitution worship, let alone inclusive creedal ideas of national identity, in what we now conceive to be "wins" of the American system. In recent decades, the overwhelming tendency in political life has been to depict the Nineteenth Amendment—which granted women the right to vote—as concrete proof of the perfectibility and goodness of the constitutional project, as well as of the idea that the United States has germinated a commitment to universal and equal liberty from the founding. And early suffragists, grounded in abolitionism and shaped by the Civil War, often presented their call in precisely these terms. As the writer and feminist activist Elizabeth Cady Stanton declared, voting rights for women simply fulfilled the "fundamental principle of our government—the equality of all the citizens of the republic."[67] In the words of the historian Mari Jo Buhle, such suffragists often "hailed the Constitution as a grand document lacking only in details of universal citizenship, and whose exceptions in regard to race and sex could now be struck out."[68]

But if the struggle for suffrage offers continuities with a venerative and creedal politics familiar to Americans today, it likewise suggests just as many breaks. To begin with, the failure of Reconstruction-era male politicians to extend the vote to women infused the feminist movement, in white circles, with explicit white supremacy. This fundamentally upended creedal links between feminist politics and racial equality. Stanton, Susan B. Anthony, and others increasingly invoked racial judgments of superiority and inferiority as a basis for asserting the unacceptability of providing the ballot to Black men but denying it to white women. In one letter to the *New York Standard*, Stanton wrote of the Reconstruction order, in deeply racist terms, that "the black man is . . . far above the educated white women of the country" and "it becomes a serious question whether we had better stand aside and see 'Sambo' walk into the kingdom first."[69]

The ultimate defeat of Reconstruction only intensified these trends in the mainstream suffrage movement. By the beginning of the twentieth century, activists like Carrie Chapman Catt, president of the National American Women's Suffrage Association (NAWSA), the country's largest suffrage organization, presented white women's suffrage as a critical method of safeguarding an appropriate racial hierarchy. Catt viewed opposition to women's suffrage as resulting in part from the "ill-advised haste" with which states during Reconstruction had enfranchised "the foreigner, the Negro, and the Indian."[70] And so she was at pains to underscore that the movement was pointedly not for *all* women, but for native-born white women.

Given these presumptions of white supremacy, the historian Michael David Cohen notes that "suffrage organizations in the twentieth century usually segregated along racial lines."[71] And groups like the American Women's Republic (AWR), founded by the Missouri-based publishers of the *Woman's Magazine*, with tens of thousands of members and chapters in over two dozen states, went further, explicitly restricting membership only to those "of the Caucasian race."[72] Thus Catt and other leaders certainly emphasized the compatibility of women's suffrage with the existing constitutional order. But they did so precisely to underscore how expanding the vote would not disrupt settler assumptions about white rule.

If such mainstream activists embraced the Constitution but rejected creedal values, more radical feminists often rejected any posture of constitutional fidelity. The anarchist Emma Goldman bemoaned the tendency of the official suffrage movement to use the case for the vote to defend the legitimacy of the constitutional order. In her mind, leaders such as Catt focused on formal political rights in ways that ignored the structural economic conditions facing most women. They thus exposed the "narrowness" of more establishment "conception[s] of women's independence and emancipation."[73] And Goldman was not alone in challenging the mainstream movement in these terms. Given the growing centrality of labor and industrial struggles, more and more feminists became invested in the connection between class and gender relations. As a result, a significant strand of activism saw the ballot not as an end in itself, but as a wedge for pursuing even more extensive changes.

Indeed, Stanton's own daughter, Harriot Stanton Blatch, underscored both the generational shift and the growing sentiment. For her, women's suffrage was hardly proof of the specialness of American democracy, given the extent to which the issue had swept Europe as well. If anything, American reformers were drawing from the militant tactics and political arguments of their European allies, many of whom had extensive ties to labor politics.[74]

In this context, a number of feminist reformers began adapting and reframing socialist critiques of capitalism. They presented patriarchal control of women's labor by men as the dominant and overarching relation of exploitation in society—instead of the employer-employee relation exclusively. And they saw such control as expressing a fundamental conflict between the sexes. Charlotte Perkins Gilman, a close friend of Blatch, argued that the struggle for suffrage would only generate real emancipation if it also challenged this material dependency of women on men, preserved through the prevailing gendered division of labor both within and outside of marriage. Such a gendered division left women either bound to the home in a sphere of domesticity—which denied them the possibility of controlling their own labor—or at the mercy of market forces and predatory wage relations. Gilman concluded, "a society whose economic unit is a sex-union can no more develop beyond a certain point industrially than a society like the patriarchal, whose political unit was a sex-union, could develop beyond a certain point politically."[75]

The rise of these voices spoke to a dramatic development within the women's movement. Some of its most influential figures had come to see the denial of women's suffrage not as a historical anachronism, out of step with the basic meaning of the constitutional project, as Stanton or Catt had contended. They rejected the idea that the ultimate constitutional victory of suffrage was therefore proof of the essential goodness of American institutions. Instead, disenfranchisement highlighted to them the patriarchal foundations of collective life, and also the fundamental need, as Mary Livermore—considered by many "the highest leader of the Gilded Age woman's movement"[76]—famously contended, to create a fundamentally new social order. This order would explode the gendered division of labor, be premised on "the omnipotence and happiness of cooperative work," and above all be "'superior to any existing society.'"[77]

This meant that constitutional changes like the eventual Nineteenth Amendment should be thought of as the first volley in a comprehensive effort to truly democratize the state and the society, rather than simply the final step in an already just framework. The hope was that reforms like women's suffrage, by elevating the practical power of an oppressed group, could provide an irruptive tool within the infrastructure of existing arrangements. A strengthened feminist movement, armed with the vote, would make it harder for the social order to persist and would help pave the way for a different constitutional system — one reconceived ethically and economically on emancipatory terms.

In a sense, the emergence of these distinct orientations within the women's movement once more emphasized a basic fact about the country in the years leading up to World War I. The social upheaval generated by industrialization and by basic economic transformations had thoroughly unraveled many of the truisms of settler society. It had created an environment best described as one of open possibility, in which new movements felt emboldened to imagine radically altered social conditions and to contest the legitimacy of prevailing institutions, including the 1787 Constitution.

It also speaks to another equally noteworthy development. The recent events of the Civil War and the pervasive climate of social conflict facilitated very specific accounts of solidarity. And these often placed one's status as a worker, white Southern sectionalist, Black person, or woman above ties based purely on shared nationality.

Even relatively mainstream suffrage organizations like the American Woman's Republic underlined this latter point. The AWR echoed Catt's more conservative belief that suffrage was consistent with the existing constitutional project, simply deepening its essential truths. Leaders even organized their association as a parallel "republic," with members termed "citizens" and with its own ratified constitution. The idea was that, by mimicking the practices of the 1787 framers and by engaging in self-government within the organization, members would gain the practical education needed once they gained the vote. But for all the ways these practices participated in traditional constitutional veneration, they nonetheless carried an incendiary undercurrent. Group leaders took as given that the country needed women's suffrage because male rule had failed catastrophically, as attested to by poverty and war. Their alternative Republic was thus also a separate government — outside the official one — run by white women and embodying their shared and specific interests. It had the whiff of a "secessionist group," as the historian Michael David Cohen notes, and implicitly presumed a divide between the basic values and orientation of empowered men and those of dependent white women.[78]

HERBERT CROLY AND THE PROGRESSIVE
SEARCH FOR A MIDDLE WAY

For many of the male leaders of the Progressive Party—a center of reformist electoral politics during these years—the rise of such subnational group identification was a matter of grave concern. According to Croly, to overcome social dissolution the country needed what he famously called a "new nationalism," a phrase that became the basic slogan for Roosevelt's 1912 campaign. Croly saw around him a class-ridden, localist, and disintegrating United States, and contended that the country would "become ... more of a democracy" only as it became "more of a nation."[79] And he argued, as did both Roosevelt and Wilson, that presidentialism offered the best institutional pathway to cohesive nationhood.

Their analysis pointed toward a twentieth-century adaptation of the 1787 framework. But it also spoke to the way in which many mainstream reformers now viewed the overall legal-political system as profoundly broken. As discussed earlier, Croly took for granted that the United States found itself subject to an "undemocratic Constitution," which, from the founding, amounted to "an imposition on the people rather than an actual popular possession."[80] He also repudiated the Constitution worship of business and legal elites, who in his mind transformed a legitimate "reverence for order" into a destructive "reverence for an established order."[81] He thus backed, at least in theory, calls for a second convention to rewrite the text and for a simplified amendment process—akin to what operated at the state level—to enhance the popular responsiveness and efficacy of the federal government. Indeed, in Croly's opinion, the existing "amending clause [was] the most formidable legal obstacle to the democratizing of the American political system."[82]

Consistent with these sentiments, the 1912 Progressive Party supported a series of institutional reforms consciously aimed at overcoming the counter-majoritarian tendencies of the 1787 Constitution. Along with popular review of judicial decisions, mentioned above, these included mechanisms such as "primaries, referenda, recall, initiative."[83] The 1912 platform also called for a constitutional amendment to establish the direct election of US senators. And most tellingly, "pledg[ed] itself to secure such alterations in the fundamental law of ... the United States as shall insure the representative character of the government," including by "a more easy and expeditious method of amending the federal constitution."[84] All of this highlights what the legal scholar Andrea Katz has called the era's "Progressive formalism,"[85] in which mainstream reformers and politicians embraced the idea of substantial written correctives to a document viewed as profoundly flawed.

Yet, over time, the dominant orientation of Progressive constitutional thinking at the national level deemphasized arguments for systematic formal rewriting through mechanisms like a second convention or a simplified amendment process. A significant reason had to do with the double-sided relationship between the nation and the Constitution. On the one hand, avowed nationalists like Croly saw the 1787 system as actually undermining patriotic commitment, especially by fracturing representative authority and so focusing attachment either at local levels or in one's particular social class. But they also worried that the conditions necessary for an actual second convention would have to approach open revolutionary conflict. For this reason, they increasingly turned to other pathways to graft change onto what they understood to be a misshapen governing framework.

Progressives such as Croly believed that there existed a cross-class common good—namely, recovery of the economic independence and participatory self-government they nostalgically associated with the "American pioneer." And, to achieve this common good, they contended that citizens needed to break from their deference to wealthy elites, in order to appreciate fully the need for change. Pro-business elites offered no viable path for cohering society because, in opposing labor rights, socioeconomic protections, and other much-needed reforms, they essentially opposed the public interest.

At the same time, Croly (along with many other Progressives) was also wary of how labor radicals placed working-class solidarity above all other attachments. Even though citizens had to break their deference to the wealthy few, these class-first mass movements presented their own risk of further social discord and communal breakdown. Croly certainly defended unionism and greater workplace participation as offering essential educations in republican self-rule.[86] And, within bounds, he accepted class consciousness as a productive counterweight to the economic solidarity of the wealthy. But, above all, he believed that the only way for individuals to create a new harmonious whole was for them to abandon their partial group identities—especially localist and class orientations—and come to think of themselves as members of a unified nation.

This call to place national attachment above all else is significant for the type of political sensibility it promoted. It meant that such Progressives—despite their vocal criticism of Madison and the other framers—in the final analysis tended to share elements of a traditional and anti-populist fear of mob rule by the poor. Not unlike the founding "Fathers" William Allen White or even Croly castigated, they too presented working-class allegiances, when left unchecked, as real threats to republican community. In particular, Croly worried that labor's focus on class struggle had the potential to see all forms of political order as the enemy—to become, effectively, a call for permanent revolution. And since he believed that "social justice depends upon order," Croly feared illegality and violence in this brand of insurgent radicalism. He concluded, "progressive democracy would cease to be progressive in case it departed for long from the use of essentially orderly methods."[87]

For many Progressives, the political challenge of the moment centered on how to steer the country between the perceived extremes of reactionary business elites and revolutionary labor activists. And, again, the amendment process offered little hope—"the existing method," Croly lamented, "calls for amendment practically by unanimous consent."[88] Such built-in ossification meant that only conditions similar to those that produced the Reconstruction Amendments could generate a second convention or a package of extensive structural reforms—again near revolutionary political circumstances, perhaps akin to Northern military rule of the South in the 1860s. But by then constitutional change would only be an aftereffect of dramatic and disruptive social upheaval.

THE TURN TO PRESIDENTIALISM AND CONSTITUTIONAL INTERPRETATION

Over time, this specter of revolutionary disorder pressed more establishment reformers to downplay any constitutive or wholesale constitutional break and to seek alternative methods for combining reform with social preservation. As the iconoclastic and Democratic Senator William Jennings Bryan maintained, political and legal reforms should, more than anything else, embody a commitment to constitutional "evolution rather than a revolution."[89]

Thus, while Croly and others still argued for amending the text, when possible, they increasingly sought to find informal means of shifting the direction of the overarching framework. And the best informal means, they concluded, was a strong brand of presidentialism. Croly and other aligned Progressives no doubt saw themselves as defenders of direct democracy and bottom-up participatory practices. But they also faced a hard truth: no cohesive national "people" in fact existed. In this context, they worried about the role played by existing political organizations, including the Socialist Party of America and various burgeoning socialist and anarchist labor institutions. In a sense, they feared that all the intermediary structures between the national "people" and a properly centralized government tended to entrench class difference or intensify regional conflicts—a special danger in a country so recently undone by violent civil war.

By contrast, they hoped that stronger presidential leadership—already embedded in the constitutional system—could offer an instrument for moving beyond destructive and partial associations. It could assist in generating national harmony and in balancing between the perceived dangers of reactionaries and revolutionaries. Croly thus called for a wise and energetic presidential power that facilitated a "discriminating exercise of the national will and intelligence" by "organizing and vitalizing the rule of the majority."[90]

For this reason, Croly and other Progressives gravitated to Roosevelt and then to Wilson out of a belief that, in the words of the historian Sidney Pearson, "a union between progressive intellectuals . . . and active politicians"[91] could steer the public toward the common good. Not surprisingly, these arguments also fit very comfortably with the emerging beliefs of both Roosevelt and Wilson, who imagined presidentialism as a solution to the problems of outmoded constitutional constraints. As Roosevelt famously proclaimed, "the President . . . is the steward of the people, and . . . he is bound to assume that he has the legal right to do whatever the needs of the people demand, unless the Constitution or the laws explicitly forbid him to do it."[92]

Wilson too now rallied to American presidentialism, although he once favored replacing the 1787 framework with something far more akin to parliamentarism: Wilson had spent no less than the July 4 centennial in 1876 writing apocalyptically in his college diary, "how much happier [the United States] would be if she had England's form of government instead of this miserable delusion of a republic. . . . I venture to say that this country will never celebrate another centennial as a republic."[93] But thirty years of class conflict and growing fears of revolutionary tumult left him increasingly uncomfortable with explicit calls for constitutional re-founding. Instead, he saw in the president all the energetic potential he had associated with a prime minister.

Critically for Wilson, this eventual embrace of presidential government was likely further buttressed by his own commitment to white supremacy and deep antipathy to Reconstruction. The legal scholars Nikolas Bowie and Daphna Renan suggest that Congress's efforts to uproot racial domination in the South also influenced his decision to abandon legislative supremacy. They note how Wilson described "the Reconstruction Congress as having 'no scruples about keeping to constitutional lines of policy. . . . The negroes were exalted; the states were misgoverned and looted in their name,' and 'the relative positions of the President and Congress in the general constitutional scheme of the government' were almost forever transformed."[94] In fact, the broader suspicion among white national elites, including many Progressives, of the Reconstruction project cooled commitments to parliamentarism. It fostered greater interest in other sites of energetic government such as the presidency.[95] Even if the framers may not have intended it, the executive offered the existing system an instrument suited to imposing national cohesion on a divided twentieth-century society. As Wilson now proclaimed in 1908, the president was nothing less than "the unifying force in our complex system, the leader both of his party and of the nation."[96]

For figures like Wilson, Roosevelt, and Croly, presidentialism had two great strengths. For starters, it focused popular attention on a single charismatic site of national attachment. Indeed, it was noteworthy that constitutional centennial celebrations only truly succeeded nationally when they pivoted toward a focus on Washington—a political leader who could galvanize patriotic commitment. And, perhaps most important, presidentialism offered a solution to the problem of unaccountable judges. Even if judges served for life and enjoyed powers of constitutional review, at the end of the day they were nominated by presidents. Thus, if effective leaders held the office of the presidency, over time they could also alter how the courts operated.

This relationship between presidentialism and a transformed judiciary suggested that the Constitution had more interpretative flexibility than a fixation on formal changes alone might suggest. As Croly himself noted, this interplay within the federal government underscored how, with the right people on the bench or in positions of institutional power, the document could be productively redeployed to "emancipate . . . democracy from continued allegiance to any specific formulation of the Law."[97] It was not the case that the text—short, open-ended, and vague—required the readings that a business-dominated court imposed on it. Rather, these readings were a product of who sat on the highest courts. This spoke to the need for presidents—as leaders of the nation—to reshape the ideological and interpretative orientation of the federal judiciary.

Ultimately, as the Progressive magazine the *Outlook* contended, there was no need to put a primary emphasis on formal constitutional change. The Constitution was not "a series of cast-iron rules" derived from mythic founders, but a document fundamentally open to the requirements of the public interest. As Wilson himself noted, "the Constitution contains no theories. It is as practical a document as Magna Carta."[98] In a sense, such Progressives argued that both hard-line defenders of the status quo and revolutionary critics tended to read the existing text as having only one true meaning for most issues of public import—and so as essentially outside the bounds of legal reinterpretation. The two sides may have coded the Constitution in opposite ways, but they both accepted an unduly formalist account of textual meaning. According to the *Outlook*'s editors, "the reactionary and the Socialist agree in their interpretation of the Constitution. Extremes meet."[99]

Such a combination of presidentialism and "transformative appointments"[100] to the judiciary became the core of how mainstream political actors sought to overcome the constitutional impasse of the late nineteenth and early twentieth centuries. This solution, though, underscored a basic tension in Progressive constitutional thought—one that would have profound implications for American life going forward. According to those like Croly, the 1787 framework was fatally compromised by how it undermined energetic government at the national level *and* by its undemocratic essence. But the rise of presidential government, while expanding centralized state power, had a far more ambiguous relation to popular self-rule.

Strengthening the presidency—and reducing the barriers between a national people and a centralized executive—presented a real danger of an empowered political entity eventually substituting its will for that of the public. Frederick Douglass expressed this concern about presidentialism, which he called "one man power,"[101] given how an emboldened and intransigent executive in Andrew Johnson had sought, systematically, to thwart Reconstruction. Furthermore, what assurances existed that an unleashed president would in fact confront plutocratic interests? More ominously, would a powerful presidency refrain from using the machinery of the state to attack political dissenters?

Finally, if constitutional change occurred primarily through judge-managed processes, what did that mean for participatory democracy? The relevant power brokers would inevitably be national politicians, lawyers, and judges. Even if the courts accepted Progressive interpretations of the Constitution, greater social welfare gains would not be won through a genuinely bottom-up constitutional politics—something Croly himself sought. They would instead result from a legal-political order in which most people had limited direct authority to devise and entrench essential rights schemes or to change the structural organization of government. Movements would operate within highly insulated institutional settings, which would force activists to translate their demands into registers acceptable to dominant political and legal actors. Even if this Progressive project succeeded, many questions would remain.

Conclusion: Adaptation without Veneration

If mainstream early-twentieth-century reformers ultimately rallied to ideas of constitutional adaptability—especially through the instrument of the presidency—these arguments had a very different register than today's more familiar creedal and worshipful tone. The potential for internal evolution was part of a broader debate about constitutional failings, and about whether meaningful reform could only occur through revolutionary rupture. Unlike in later years, advocates of the "evolution" approach did not necessarily present the institutional capacity to accommodate social change as proof of the genius of the framers, the inherent goodness of the text, or its perfectibility over time through an unfolding and inevitable progress.

And there were obvious reasons these reformers did not presume a link between a politics of veneration and defenses of the Constitution's potential for change. As highlighted by the 1887–1889 centennial celebrations and the business embrace of the Constitution, the language of constitutional reverence was primarily a conservative one, which held firm to the idea of the 1787 text as already perfect. By contrast, many of the Progressive reformers, who developed anti-formalist theories of constitutional interpretation and adaptability, took for granted a class-based counternarrative of the original framers.

These reformers and politicians did at times fall back on superficial veneration. Yet even those who, like Woodrow Wilson, increasingly emphasized the wisdom of the document had far more complicated relationships to the Constitution than more recent figures. As the author of *Congressional Government*, among other texts, Wilson's early scholarship had been widely associated both with class-inflected accounts of the framers' intentions and with the idea that their science of government may be an outmoded eighteenth-century holdover. But in the context of intensifying industrial conflicts and fears about revolutionary threats, Wilson muted his criticisms of the framers and pushed back against any implicit calls for sweeping formal changes. Given his emerging faith in presidential government, he began highlighting the internal capacity of the constitutional order to respond effectively to prevailing conditions. He praised the framers' overall thinking and argued that, while they were no doubt fallible—as are all people—the framers' act of construction "masterfully" "combined stability with liberty in the process of absolute self-government."[102] When running for president, he even hesitated to criticize the bench too extensively.

Still, Wilson, once in office—and even after expressing far less skepticism than Teddy Roosevelt, let alone Eugene Debs—seriously considered nominating to the Supreme Court perhaps the Constitution's most outspoken judicial critic, the fellow Southerner Walter Clark, whom he admired but worried was too old.[103] He also maintained close relations with Croly and the *New Republic*, as the magazine became a vocal defender of the administration. And these ties persisted despite Croly's continued emphasis on the counterrevolutionary meaning of the Constitution.

All of this speaks to the very different constitutional politics during the era, as compared to what would eventually take hold. A plethora of plausible views circulated, and the same actor—whether a Populist, a Progressive, or a feminist—could swing between praise and stinging critique. Indeed, of the four central candidates in the 1912 presidential campaign, only William Howard Taft—who finished third—was truly identified with constitutional veneration. And this fact went hand in hand with his status as the candidate of big business, a status which helped doom his run. It was thus conceivable both for a president to challenge the legitimacy of the Constitution and even for a potential Supreme Court justice, like Clark, to argue for its outright rejection.

Indeed, although many Progressives may have shifted toward adaptation through presidentialism, they were hardly the only reformist orientation with a broad audience and a significant constitutional platform. Throughout these years, the Socialist Party of America argued systematically for a fundamental constitutional break and re-founding, as opposed to a presidentialist turn. Even more significantly, they tied such re-founding to calls for genuine and continuous mass popular control over constitutional politics. And they also challenged the focus on the nation either as the primary site of political attachment or as essential to constructing meaningful solidarity and social order, just as Progressive reformers feared. Instead, as the next chapter details, socialists and more radical activists often embraced an internationalist and class-oriented politics as the basis for community, organizing, and democratic self-government.

CHAPTER 4

The Socialist
Constitutional Alternative

In the years leading up to World War I, the Socialist Party of America (SPA)[1] was a serious and growing political force. At the head of its ticket was one of the most charismatic and popular figures of the era: Eugene Debs, a founder of the American Railway Union (ARU), one of the first large-scale industrial unions in the country, and a candidate for president five times between 1900 and 1920. The last of these races he ran from a jail cell, imprisoned by Woodrow Wilson's administration during World War I for speeches opposing American involvement. As popular as Debs was, the party was more than a platform for an individual leader. It became a truly national movement. It had members serving in Congress, like Victor Berger out of Milwaukee and Meyer London from New York City; deep ties to both trade and industrial unions; and, by 1912, approximately a thousand elected officials throughout local and state governments.[2]

More than any other group in the country, the SPA became closely identified with the effort not just to adapt the Constitution, but to replace the existing system root and branch. The party worked assiduously to popularize the class-based counternarrative of the Constitution that had spread across reformist camps. As Debs would pointedly declare, the Constitution was "autocratic and reactionary," "not in any sense a democratic instrument, but in every sense a denial of democracy."[3] The *Appeal to Reason*, out of Girard, Kansas, once a key Populist weekly and by 1910 the most significant SPA newspaper in the country (with a circulation of over 500,000), routinely published revisionist accounts of the founding, with titles like "Tricked in the Constitution."[4] Other party organs like the *International Socialist Review* included countless essays on the failings of the Constitution. They also contained advertisements for anti-Constitution books and popular education courses that would instruct students about the text's flawed founding and the need for constitutional transformation.[5] In fact, such popular education efforts, aimed at building worker solidarity and class consciousness, were a central component of the party's overall activities. In New York City, SPA supporters founded the Rand School of Social Science in 1906, one of the first worker education schools, where for years none other than Charles Beard himself offered courses in constitutional history.[6] And on the Great Plains, socialist farmers—in keeping with populist traditions from the 1890s—staged massive encampments where, alongside speeches and music, lecturers taught the basics of American government, using anti-Constitution books such as J. Allen Smith's *The Spirit of American Government* as their guide.[7]

SPA constitutional ideas were very much of a piece with the reformist times. But in their calls for a basic constitutional break, party activists offered a radicalized version of more mainstream approaches, and so pushed the country in novel directions. As this chapter details, SPA activists contested the Progressive drift toward both presidentialism and judicial reinterpretation as meaningful solutions. Beyond that, they often articulated a vision of constitutions and constitutionalism distinct from conventional accounts both then and today. In particular, perhaps more so than any other reformist group, they tended to reject the focus on constitutions as fundamental law[8]—standing above ordinary legislative mechanisms and constraining popular will. Instead, they embraced new institutional arrangements in which mass publics could intervene continuously to ensure that both the economy and politics were infused with popular needs. As part of this overarching vision, they also embraced class-based institutions as essential intermediaries between the state and the individual. In effect, SPA activists often treated such institutions as key to maintaining what I would call a mobilized "government behind the government." Such permanent mobilization aimed to create the type of sustained democratic energy that could ensure that insulated elites did not subvert new constitutional processes for their own interests.

Moreover, the party—in conversation with the variety of competing socialist and anarchist voices that circulated around it—struggled with questions of transformative strategy and inclusive membership in ways that continue to resonate deeply today. These radical activists developed sophisticated accounts of how to engage with the existing constitutional order and fought among themselves over whether to prioritize direct action at the workplace or legal-political reforms. Unlike the vast array of white organizations in American life during the post-Reconstruction years, the SPA as well as connected groups like the Industrial Workers of the World (IWW) also became institutional spaces for articulating goals of racial equality. Leaders like Eugene Debs explicitly sought to build a truly cross-racial and class-conscious transformative majority. But these efforts were ultimately undone—both by deep-rooted racism among key party figures and constituents, and by the SPA's general difficulties in meaningfully intertwining race and class in its politics.

Thus, to the extent that the current moment, with its parallels to the first Gilded Age, raises questions once more about constitutional orthodoxies, the strengths and weaknesses of SPA constitutional politics, as compared to Progressive and other reform approaches, may well offer meaningful political lessons. In addition, given that today's legal scholars, including those concentrating on the Progressive period, have focused primarily on court-based litigation or congressional disputes over amendments and reform, commentators have tended to miss these alternative strands of constitutional thinking. Although such alternatives were once treated as real possibilities, even by ideological opponents, they have essentially been excised from both the scholarly record and cultural memory.

This excision has resulted in far less awareness of the wide-ranging quality of that past conversation, let alone of the profoundly *constitutionalist* nature of much socialist critique during the era. Indeed, the conventional focus has obscured a key element of the American story: the way in which, through multiple historical points, constitutionalism *as such* was not considered synonymous with one strain alone—namely, faith in the idea of a sacrosanct fundamental law and in its creedal constitutional embodiment.

Socialism and the Rejection of Fundamental Law

For many of those that gravitated to the Socialist Party, "the ultimate aim," as the 1912 platform declared, was the "realization" of what members often called "the co-operative commonwealth."[9] Such a society would extend democratic principles to the economy, in part by making "the instruments of wealth production the common property of all," in the words of the party activist, union leader, and journalist William Mahoney.[10] The result amounted to the overcoming of capitalism, with its exploitative and interrelated systems of wage labor, production, land ownership, and distribution. Socialists thus sought an order in which the mass of dependent laborers enjoyed the equal and effective freedom to shape the terms of their work lives.

Those in the SPA argued that a central means for moving toward this socialist alternative would be the working class winning control over government, and then implementing the "collective ownership and democratic management"[11] of the central industrial and financial elements of the economy. On its face, this goal may not necessarily suggest a particular orientation to, or even concern with, the federal Constitution. But SPA activists fundamentally linked the two. They contended that the US legal-political system was not a "popular government"[12] — of and by the people — but instead the instrument of an oppressive and ruling capitalist class. Socialists thus saw replacing the Constitution and replacing capitalism as deeply interconnected projects.

TOWARD A NEW WAY OF IMAGINING
A CONSTITUTION

If Progressive reformers increasingly tended to emphasize the flexibility embedded in the constitutional framework, the driving SPA approach opposed this turn.[13] According to growing Progressive critiques of formalism, the actual text was largely neutral with respect to the socioeconomic questions of the day. This argument held that the interpretive ambiguity built into the document meant that its provisions ultimately did not enhance any specific social base or assume a socioeconomic policy outcome. Invoking just this sentiment, Supreme Court Justice Oliver Wendell Holmes Jr. had famously rejected the pro-business idea of a constitutionally protected "freedom of contract." Writing in his 1905 dissent to the Court's infamous decision in *Lochner v. U.S.*, which struck down New York State maximum hour laws in the baking industry, Holmes contended — as Woodrow Wilson would also argue — that the Constitution embodied no "particular economic theory."[14]

Many Progressives, even anti-formalists, certainly accepted that the veto points embedded in federalism and in the broader system of checks and balances constrained government power. But for those like Wilson and Holmes, the degree to which these structural constraints fatally compromised policy-making was overstated. Indeed, cases like *Lochner* highlighted how pro-labor legislation was actually making its way through representative institutions, if only to be struck down by the courts. Thus, presidential leadership and key judicial appointments might well be enough to overcome the worst institutional dysfunctions. Without rewriting the text, politicians and publics could rebuild a framework in which the process of constitutional decision-making was separated from the substance of socioeconomic outcomes.

Socialists, however, tended to be deeply skeptical of this possibility. Wilson or Holmes may have been correct that, in theory, particular reforms could be pursued under the terms of the existing arrangements. The relative vagueness of the text largely avoided what the *Outlook* had called a "series of cast-iron rules." But the interlocking nature of the established institutions absolutely made certain outcomes far more likely than others. These formal structures organizing constitutional life—structures explicitly chosen by the 1787 framers, after all—strengthened the practical power of entrenched elites and undermined the aspiration toward a cooperative commonwealth. As 1916 SPA presidential candidate Allan Benson wrote in his muckraking exposé of the framers, *Our Dishonest Constitution* (1914), "the Constitution by no means makes majority rule impossible, but it makes rule by a compact, energetic minority exceedingly easy."[15]

Socialists also rejected the Progressive criticism that the SPA and its allies ignored the role—and the promise—of social forces in shaping the interpretations and outcomes of constitutional dispute, beyond the text alone. Instead, SPA activists argued that the entire problem was how institutional mechanisms (federalism, the Senate, the Supreme Court) *combined* with the greater material and cultural resources of socioeconomic elites to drive constitutional meaning down particular paths. As Debs pointedly declared, given the combination of undemocratic structures and the socioeconomic power of the few, "politicians and legislators are today the representatives, not of the people, but of the trustified capitalist class."[16]

For many Socialist voices, this sense of the relationship between process and substance led to two connected conclusions: First, activists had to care deeply about the constitutional system because it profoundly constrained any collective move away from capitalism. And second, they should remain suspicious of anti-formalist reform orientations that embraced interpretive flexibility as a lodestar and deemphasized the structuring impediments to meaningful change. The implication was that, in embracing textual openness, Progressives at magazines like the *Outlook* failed to reckon adequately with the fractured and countermajoritarian nature of legal-political design. Such fracture worked hand in glove with interpretive openness to allow the powerful to win con-

stitutional battles time and again—even when they had limited popular support.

All of this highlighted to many Socialists that changing the hardwired features of the existing constitutional order was ultimately unavoidable. More importantly, it also meant that Americans would have
to change their underlying ideas about the *very nature* of what a constitution should be. The framers had thought of a written constitution
as a relatively short document, one that laid out universal principles—
largely preserving property rights—and remained institutionally insulated from ordinary political contestation. Such an approach treated
the document as a higher and inviolate law that had to be safeguarded
from mass political activity. Indeed, under this classic vision, insulation stood at the heart of all constitutionalism—the promotion of a
law supreme over democracy, and worthy of reverence for precisely that
reason.

In response, such Socialists challenged underlying assumptions
about the appropriate length, focus, institutional structure, level of detail, and permanence of a constitutional document. Generally during
these years, Populists and Progressives had promoted competing theories of design—emphasizing flexibility, elaboration, and extensive
rights provisions—and had been implementing those approaches at the
state level. The SPA too embraced this reformist sensibility, also favor-
ing documents that bore a closer resemblance to legislative statutes. For
Benson, the framers' preference for a "short and obscure" constitution
was a response to their specific post-Revolution class predicament. Put-
ting the matter bluntly, he declared that such wealthy elites found themselves confronting "a majority . . . so restless that it seem[ed] expedient
to pacify them, yet so ignorant that they [could] readily be deceived."
Throughout history, he proclaimed, under such circumstances "it has
ever been the custom" of elitists like the framers or "gentlemen like Napoleon Bonaparte to favor 'short and obscure' constitutions."[17]

In addition to derisively rejecting the federal model's brevity and
lack of detail, the party went even further than other reformist groups
in championing both majoritarianism and experiments with the basic
units of American politics. In keeping with the party conventional wisdom, Benson asserted that a unicameral and near-supreme legislative
branch should be the heart of democratic politics: "A congress, composed of a single house," should act as "the chief instrument of government," because it "respond[ed] most promptly to the desires of the
people." He also saw the federalist system of states as ending with the

transition to a cooperative commonwealth. Since state-based organization in the US involved a malapportioned and deformed brand of representation, democratic improvements meant that "state lines would also largely disappear."[18]

Above all, these views fed into a sustained critique of *any* politics of constitutional sanctification—including about any new, more adaptable arrangements that might emerge. Socialists thus provided perhaps the era's most thoroughgoing rejection of the very idea of constitutions as fundamental laws. Instead, written constitutions may be a baseline or default, which would provide a backdrop, at least under capitalism, for ongoing legislation and reformed judicial practice. But precisely because of the persistent need for democratic experimentation with all the forms of legal and political decision-making, it would always be subject to meaningful change.

This rejection of the traditional framework was bound to the Socialists' analysis of capitalism and to their ideas about how class hierarchies inevitably interacted with legal-political processes. They argued that so long as Americans treated any written document—the 1787 text or a new one written for the twentieth century—as truly supreme, little ultimately would have changed. For the activist Crystal Eastman, this was because "the state under capitalism, whether it be democratic or an autocratic state, is bound to be, not a reconciler of, or arbitrator between classes, but an agent of the exploiting class."[19] She contended that political contests for power between business and labor inevitably took place on an unequal terrain. As corporate elites could bring to bear far more resources in potential conflicts, state processes inevitably reflected the fundamentally unequal nature of social arrangements.

This meant that even new constitutional orders tended to preserve—if not freeze—the society's existing power imbalances. As Debs also maintained, as long as capitalist economic relations persisted, any "government," "its constitutions and its statutes, its courts, its legislatures, and its armies . . . are institutions under class rule, expressly designed to establish the supremacy of one class and enforce the subjugation of another class."[20] Prior to establishment of the cooperative commonwealth, no ideal process could be assumed to serve as a neutral referee of class dispute. All arrangements had to remain open to ongoing popular mobilization.

Thus, the goal was not to imagine in advance some idealized law or set of governing processes, and then seek to ratify that law and place it above politics. Instead, working people should craft a set of institutional mechanisms that allowed popular majorities to negotiate and renegotiate the terms of the existing order in response to laboring interests. No "greater power" could "reside elsewhere than in the people themselves," Benson contended.[21] Otherwise, even with his preferred popular assemblies, any legislative decisions and governing structures placed beyond popular intervention could be usurped to entrench existing class arrangements. In direct opposition to the Madisonian vision, such a Socialist account aimed to collapse significantly the chasm between higher and ordinary lawmaking and to transform both modes into expressions of genuinely popular law.

For this reason, under this SPA constitutional theory, a central constitutional tool was a much easier amendment process—something that became a persistent national platform demand for the entire life of the party as a significant electoral power.[22] That change would make constitutional and legislative practice much more equivalent, and would render both far more responsive to mass democratic voice. This would result in an evolving text, one that resisted elite usurpation and that continually incorporated the types of working-class experiments with state and economy vital to constructing the cooperative commonwealth.

CONTESTING FAITH IN JUDGES AND PRESIDENTS

The Socialist approach to constitutionalism also had profound implications for the relationship between the existing text, courts, and presidency. Above all, Socialists contended that problems with "judicial oligarchy,"[23] to use a Progressive phrase, could not be solved so long as courts remained the central sites of constitutional politics. Again, under the emerging Progressive view, if presidents developed a strong direct bond with the people, then they would enjoy the popular legitimacy needed to drive legislation and to select judges that fit their ideological agendas. Furthermore, if those chosen judges were also term-limited and hedged in by various constraints, they would be more responsive to both presidential and popular demands. Court-based constitutional disputes would then generate very different results from those under the existing federal judiciary.

Socialists, however, often questioned whether this particular Progressive mix would, over the long run, produce genuine popular control, even if it offered real improvement over the established system. For starters, many Socialists believed that, as Progressives turned to anti-formalism, they often falsely treated court-based interpretation and formal amendments as normatively equivalent. Both were simply *means* to the end of implementing various technocratic fixes. Thus, if changes could be achieved through court-based interpretation, they should be pursued without worrying about the amendment process.

In response, Socialists suggested that judicial fixes, while important, addressed only one side of the problem. A large part of what generated judicial dominance over constitutional meaning was the fact that avenues for constitutional change outside of litigation were limited. Precisely because the amendment process was so profoundly constrained, the courts inevitably claimed greater and greater everyday constitutional authority. Thus, when push came to shove, the Constitution changed in practice only through judges' chosen interpretations of the existing text—and only through arguments they viewed as reasonable. In a sense, focusing on how to shift court-based interpretation did not reshape *who* counted as the basic participants in constitutional conversation. Even if new judicial interpretations took hold, American constitutionalism would remain by and large a body of laws primarily overseen by judges, alongside powerful politicians and lawyers.

This did not mean that the SPA opposed judicial reforms. Socialist voices strongly advocated for judicial restructuring and backed the most expansive Progressive ideas: from direct election of judges to a basic transformation in the organization of federal courts and the effective abolition of the Supreme Court as it currently existed. At the state level, where judicial elections existed the party even vigorously ran candidates to replace pro-business judges.[24] One can see this latter move as embracing that more radical Progressive aspiration to challenge the presumptive divide between courts and legislatures and to infuse, to the extent possible, the everyday operation of the judiciary with popular sentiment. It also indicated a drive to contest corporate state power in the here and now, even if one embraced a more sweeping critique of the legal system under capitalism.

Yet, alongside court reforms, party activists consistently presented popular referenda and a simplified amendment process as more than merely means to an end. A genuinely accessible amendment process, for instance, would alter fundamentally the terrain on which legal-political struggle took place. It shifted the terms of who owned the Constitution, moving away from constitutional *law* overseen by legal elites to constitutional *politics* pursued by organized mass movements. As Debs noted, when discussing the replacement of the old 1787 Constitution with new arrangements, it was essential that constitutional change "not be framed by ruling class lawyers and politicians."[25]

Unfortunately, so long as other constitutional pathways remained largely foreclosed, most constitutional life would devolve into a political fight over control of the judiciary. Popular debates may have occurred outside the courts—concerning everything from what rights the document should enshrine in the first place to what governmental structures were compatible with democracy. But to the extent that courts wielded dramatic authority over how constitutional change proceeded, they could effectively sweep critical reform objectives off the table. As such, everything ended up depending on who sat on the bench.

In a deep sense, these Socialist arguments also evinced a real wariness of presidentialism. For starters, SPA activists had concerns about whether presidents would be properly accountable to mass movements. If most political attention centered on charismatic leaders in the national government—with class-based and other intermediary associations diminished—how could a powerful and centralized state not dominate political discourse? Under such circumstances, presidents could use their charismatic and institutional authority to consolidate power almost regardless of popular will—all the while claiming to speak for the people's demands.

Moreover, Socialists doubted whether presidents could be truly counted on to push in transformative directions, including with respect to the judiciary. Under the existing social order, presidents continued to be beholden to background distributions of wealth and power, in addition to the distorting effects of the Electoral College.[26] As Benson noted of how constitutional arrangements intersected with money and party dynamics, "the people have never yet determined who their [presidential] candidates should be. Politicians, usually backed by great business interests, have always usurped this popular function."[27] Rather than contesting hierarchies, presidents have thus seemed far more likely to make common cause with elements of the legal establishment or to cut deals with corporate elites. Socialists learned lessons from both Teddy Roosevelt's and Woodrow Wilson's actual presidencies—namely, the willingness of ostensible reformers to accommodate private wealth and to use the state's force against working-class dissent.

But even if an ideal president employed the office to push aside the legal establishment, that would not adequately uproot the existing *mode* of constitutional decision-making. It would simply establish a new set of empowered judges and politicians to replace the old. Instead, the Socialist goal involved meaningful control by working people over the constitutional system as a whole. And for that to occur, judges and presidents could not serve as the decisive gatekeepers—court-centered constitutional law had to be displaced. Only a truly popular constitutional politics would ensure that workers' struggles were not moved back into insulated venues like the bench, with new forms of judicial dominance reemerging over time.

DEFENDING RIGHTS OUTSIDE THE COURTS

In response to these Socialist arguments, mainstream defenders of the Constitution often contended that without a powerful judiciary directing constitutional debate, individual liberties and basic rights would be swept aside by unchecked majorities. SPA voices, however, claimed that taking constitutional politics out of the courts would, over the long run, better entrench essential protections. Indeed, many were aggressive proponents of rights and saw both individual safeguards and mass democracy as facilitating the move toward a cooperative commonwealth.

Party activists repeatedly invoked the First Amendment and asserted the free speech protections they believed it defended. The 1912 platform—at the peak of the party's popularity—called for nothing less than "the absolute freedom of press, speech, and assemblage."[28] According to Socialists, the rights to dissent and to organize politically provided the foundation for any legitimate legal-political order. To this they added positive rights textually ignored by the federal Constitution— including union rights and a broad range of socioeconomic guarantees. Crucially, none of these liberties arose out of a special American experience, but instead from universal democratic principles.

Crystal Eastman, who became closely identified with the cause of free speech, perhaps best articulated the Socialist sensibility regarding the relationship between rights and democracy.[29] During World War I, Eastman co-founded the Civil Liberties Bureau of the American Union of Anti-Militarism, which eventually became today's ACLU. As for her connection to the SPA, she never actually formally joined the party. Her biographer, Amy Aronson, emphasizes her "principled nonconformity" and wariness of dogmatic party lines.[30] Nonetheless, Eastman identified strongly with the SPA and enthusiastically threw her support and activism behind many of its electoral, free speech, and labor campaigns. In the teeth of wartime crackdowns on the organization, she wrote in 1918 of its essential emancipatory role for the working class: "The Socialist party is only incidentally a political institution; it is something politicians cannot understand, a deep-rooted faith and a thoroughly understood intellectual conception which must grow because it satisfies the vital desires of real human beings."[31]

Eastman's commitment to socialism actually had begun "while [she was] still a college student."[32] She then graduated second in her class from New York University Law School in 1907, but faced profound difficulty in finding employment as a lawyer due to the legal profession's pervasive sexism.[33] Over the next two decades, her writing and activism intertwined socialism with feminist, labor, and anti-war commitments, focusing on legal-political strategies that would open up the constitutional system to fundamental reconstruction. Aronson writes that throughout these years Eastman had a "legitimate place in the leadership of many leftist movements."[34]

For Eastman, the drive toward the cooperative commonwealth rested on the organized power of the working class. And precisely because the state was always susceptible to control by entrenched elites, laboring publics needed the capacity to voice sustained opposition to governing policies and frameworks. As she declared, "without freedom of speech, of assembly, of the press, the principle of majority representation is a mockery. The denial of these rights is a virtual disenfranchisement of the workers."[35] Socialism could be neither achieved nor preserved without a system that protected the activities central to mass mobilization and protest. Only then could a laboring majority stand as what amounted to a government behind the government.

Indeed, the wish of some Progressives to build an immediate relationship between the president and the people served just the opposite aim. In hopes of expanding participatory engagement and direct representation, this focus undermined the actually existing institutional bases for collective organizing and sustained democratic voice. For this reason, Eastman and others defended—as free speech rights—everything from union drives to disseminating literature, picketing, boycotting, and engaging in sympathy or even general strikes.

Moreover, she argued that none of these essential protections could be left to the courts. This was because it was overwhelmingly the empowered few—rather than the tyranny of the majority, as Madison feared—who undermined the rights necessary for a legitimate constitutional order. Those wielding socioeconomic authority almost exclusively conceived of threats in terms of their own economic interest. And they elevated this interest to a fundamental right, through constitutional discourses around "freedom of contract" or guarantees for property. They then made every other element of the legal-political order bow to those considerations.

Such elites thus willingly trampled virtually all protections key to a functioning democracy, from the ability of ordinary people to organize at work or in politics, to basic speech protections, to the very right of the vote itself. And, to give legal cover to their violence, they took advantage of their dominance over the state's coercive apparatus, whether through the police, the army, or the courts. As Eastman concluded, "the ruling class . . . has proved that any inconvenient provision of the constitution can be set aside, and has taken a long bold step toward openly disenfranchising all who advocate fundamental changes in the form of government."[36]

All of this informed the SPA's propensity to reject an aspirational project that focused heavily on the conversion of judges as the pathway to meaningful change. Some Progressives may have seen reform-minded and well-placed judges as susceptible to new, creative textual interpretations. But for many Socialists, not to mention anarchists and other radicals, the long experience with "the policeman's club and the magistrate's edict symbolized the state's alliance with entrenched privilege," as the historian Melvyn Dobofsky writes.[37] They believed that, just as the courts had systematically preserved slavery in the antebellum period, they upheld industrial oppression in the early twentieth century. Thus, a system of meaningful safeguards could be achieved only through democratic transformations to state and society. For these reasons, Socialists time and again connected rights not with the judiciary or with the existing legal process, which tended to restrict them, but with mass action—through legislative means, through popularly enacted constitutional amendments, and through hard-won labor union victories.

If pro-Constitution figures saw limiting judicial review as a threat to liberty, Socialists took just the opposite position. Taking the Constitution away from the courts, more or less, would not only deepen majoritarianism; it would actually better protect individual and collective liberty. According to Benson, "the rights of citizens would be safeguarded" only if constitutional power was "vested in the people themselves," since "no flimsy words in a constitution ever safeguarded human rights." Indeed, "these rights" were "too precious to entrust" to any state officials, "even though they wear black robes and be justices of the United States

Supreme Court."[38] Unless rights were *popular* rights, they would inevitably be uprooted by socioeconomic elites, taking advantage of the existing instruments of minority rule. Sustained mass mobilization, activists concluded, offered the best long-run method for truly preserving the rights of the most marginalized. Rather than thinking of constitutional rights, democracy, and socialism as competing forces, Socialists thus emphasized the way in which the path to each rested on the strengthening of the other two.

Divergent Strategies to Get from Here to There

If party activists developed a powerful theory of constitutional design and politics, they faced a massive question. How should they interact with what they characterized as a fatally flawed constitutional system? And what strategic approach would facilitate the eventual construction of a cooperative commonwealth? This debate spilled beyond the party itself to involve labor radicals more generally, especially within the Industrial Workers of the World. Both SPA and IWW voices tended to agree that the constitutional order preserved capitalist domination and so had to be overcome. But these organizers often reached very different conclusions about the ultimate efficacy of grounding social change in strategies that emphasized electoral politics and constitutional reform.

Although the IWW had been formed by activists of various socialist and anarchist stripes, over time it became most closely associated ideologically with a brand of syndicalism, or what William "Big Bill" Haywood, one of the founders of the IWW, called "industrial unionism."[39] Under the banner of "one big union for all the workers,"[40] IWW organizers imagined replacing capitalism with a system in which unions would "control the industry in which they work,"[41] displacing both existing wage relations and the larger political state. This focus on direct union management contrasted with the classic SPA belief in the value of the state, at least for the foreseeable future,[42] given its critical role in transforming broader economic relations.

Most SPA figures contended that, although the state embodied the existing distribution of class power, elected Socialists could nonetheless employ state instruments to democratize society and to set the stage for more fundamental changes. IWW activists, on the other hand, were by and large far more skeptical, understanding the state as an inherently reactionary force. For them, the primary effort had to center on claiming worker control at the point of production, because state machinery—

even if controlled by ostensibly well-meaning Socialist politicians—would push toward the preservation of hierarchy.

Haywood himself often downplayed these sites of disagreement, and in the years before the First World War, IWW members (also known as Wobblies) flowed into the SPA, aligned especially with the party's left wing. Haywood was elected to the SPA's national executive committee and famously referred to industrial unionism—for all its anarchist implications—as simply "socialism with its working clothes on."[43] Nonetheless, SPA and IWW leaders eventually fell out over questions around economic versus legal-political approaches, vision, and tactics.

THE COURT AS A SITE OF STRUGGLE

To make sense of these tensions, it helps to start with where SPA and IWW activists found common ground. Radicals—whether socialist or industrial unionist, and whatever their ultimate view of the state's transformative potential—realized that they could not simply ignore the legal-political order, and especially the courts. The judiciary remained an extraordinarily powerful site for the application of state power, and so contestation had to take place within it, as expressed for instance by the SPA running candidates for judicial office. Thus, when faced with intense government crackdowns, party and union activists both repeatedly defended the constitutional legality of their practices, whether speaking and writing in opposition to World War I or organizing labor strikes, pickets, and boycotts. For instance, those in the IWW persistently argued—in the public square and before hostile judges—that their organizing tactics were protected by those "elemental rights guaranteed under the Constitution."[44]

Such radicals were clearheaded about the likelihood of judicial defeat and, pointedly, did not see defending the First Amendment as a means of venerating the wisdom and foresight of the framers. They saw their battles in the courts as serving a series of related aims. As the legal historian Laura Weinrib writes, IWW leaders "hoped that their rare courtroom successes would" facilitate the release of jailed organizers or "open up opportunities for soliciting members on street corners, outside the watchful gaze of employers."[45] Small-scale victories could also provide to those dispossessed a reprieve from the everyday violence they experienced—offering real and immediate improvements for the weakest in society. In this way, they would demonstrate to working-class and poor constituents the willingness of activists to face genuine personal costs for the well-being of the community, and also the potential effectiveness of various organizing strategies.

But besides these explicitly pragmatic aims, such court-based contests could also serve other ends. Radicals sought to reject the pervasive presentation by pro-business elites of socialist and labor activism as extreme and dangerous, and thus appropriately subject to the state's repressive might. The IWW and its leader, "Big Bill" Haywood, were especially tarred by opponents with what the historian Joseph Conlin called a "reputation for violence." It is true that Haywood during his earlier years in the Western Federation of Miners (WFM) had embraced the use of arms against business opponents, in a mining context in which "industrial disputes," says Conlin, "more closely resembled small wars."[46]

Yet, by all accounts, Haywood's WFM experiences led him to disavow armed confrontation. As he told one 1913 crowd, "I for one, have turned my back on violence. It wins nothing. When we strike now, we strike with our hands in our pockets."[47] Although revolutionary in ambition, IWW texts persistently rejected the use of force: "We do not advocate violence; it is to be discouraged."[48] They emphasized tactics of nonviolent mass protest and civil disobedience, or what they called "passive resistance."[49] And as Conlin concludes, their practice backed up these words; their union drives were "characterized by nearly complete nonviolence on the part of the Wobblies and sometimes vicious brutalities on the part of authorities."[50]

Given such systematic repression, IWW organizers, as well as socialists of various stripes, consciously employed the language of the Constitution—the very embodiment of the existing order—to highlight the degree to which their peaceful actions were lawful even under the terms established by the powers that be. For instance, the historian John Wertheimer notes how when police sought to shut down socialist open-air meetings, activists would commonly "flash constitutions and free-speech clauses . . . ritually inverting the assertion of legal authority, if only for a moment."[51] In this way, they aimed to underscore how those with authority were actually the ones that openly disregarded their own rules, as SPA member Eastman suggested. Indeed, in the 1887 Haymarket trial, August Spies himself had made just this point when addressing the court. Spies maintained that he simply had lawfully exercised his constitutional right to political speech, a right that the state then lawlessly attacked. This meant that he had been the one "who . . . upheld the constitution against those who tried to trample it under their feet."[52]

These court fights—including the ultimate Haymarket execution of Spies and others—exposed to the wider public the fundamental inconsistency between judicial lip service to rights and the practical reality of state and corporate abuse. Furthermore, for many socialist and radical voices this inconsistency indicated not only the hollowness of basic guarantees under the existing constitutional system, but also the related need to establish a fundamentally new social order. It emphasized how the real enjoyment of essential protections would be achieved only through a structural re-founding on genuinely class-egalitarian terms.

CONSTITUTIONAL LEVERS AS REVOLUTIONARY REFORMS

Still, SPA and IWW leaders tended to disagree about how much emphasis to place on concrete constitutional reforms as opposed to other strategies, in particular tools of direct labor action like the general strike. For those committed to taking over the state through electoral means, the centrality of implementing changes to legal-political institutions in the here and now was absolutely essential. Precisely because of the deep distortions in the existing design, alterations to capitalist relations would be near impossible absent the fundamental transformation of the constitutional process. For such Socialists, this meant that constitutional reforms should be understood *as* socioeconomic reforms, in keeping with their overriding opposition to dividing between legal-political process and socioeconomic substance. Calls for changes to society *and* calls for changes to the legal-political order: together, these provided a constitutively intertwined set of demands for a more democratic polity. Thus, all Socialist Party proposals, as the 1912 platform declared, aimed "to strengthen the working class" in the present, so that it could "increase its power against capitalist oppression" and better fight for that "ultimate aim," the creation of a "co-operative commonwealth."[53]

Electorally focused Socialists thus saw their relationship to the ballot box as both instrumental and normative. First, the vote afforded a useful tool for gauging mass support and for determining how much actual strength they could bring to bear in conflicts with corporate and state opponents. Beyond that, numerous party voices also believed that, under a genuine system of universal suffrage—in which all working people had access to the vote and their vote counted equally—Socialists had the real potential to win power and to implement the range of structural changes necessary to abolish capitalism. These activists viewed themselves as on the side of the many, even if at present that majority remained untapped.

Yet, alongside the strategic potential of elections, SPA politicians further backed electoral democracy out of a normative defense of majority rule. Only under conditions in which they had the concrete support of the many could activists fulfill a cooperative vision. If pursued through minority rule, the inevitable result would be sustained violence as the condition of social change. And imposing ends violently—without majority support—fundamentally broke with cooperative ideals of community and solidarity, in ways that would deform whatever social order emerged. Socialism and democracy were thus necessarily intertwined, because only through democracy could one build the type of political consciousness and identity required for cooperative arrangements.

This made constitutional levers a critical means of unleashing the democratic potential within electoral systems and so building a transformative political majority. In a sense, such levers could be imagined as pragmatic reforms, but with revolutionary implications. If implemented, they would, step by step, facilitate popular control of the state. This control would in turn dramatically expand the bargaining power and social position of working people in their contests with corporate employers—again driving home how pursuing democracy and pursuing socialism were practically one and the same.

The party's 1912 platform perhaps best captures this linkage of socialism and democracy at the core of SPA constitutional demands. For the intermediate term, the party sought a systematic reconstruction of the constitutional system in line with mass democratic and parliamentary modes pressed by fellow socialists in Europe. The program included calls for "proportional representation, nationally as well as locally"; "the abolition of the Senate and of the veto power of the President"; "the election of the President and Vice-President by direct vote"; "the abolition of the power usurped by the Supreme Court of the United States to pass upon the constitutionality of . . . legislation enacted by Congress"; "national laws to be repealed only by act of Congress or by a referendum vote of the whole people"; "abolition of the present restrictions upon the amendment of the constitution, so that instrument may be amenable by a majority of the votes in a majority of the States"; "the granting of the right to suffrage in the District of Columbia with representation in Congress and a democratic form of municipal government"; "unrestricted and equal suffrage for men and women"; "the election of all judges for short terms"; and, finally, "the calling of a convention for the revision of the constitution of the United States."[54]

In sum, the SPA in 1912 essentially pursued four types of reforms, as initial steps before more radical political experiments such as, for instance, breaking up the states: (1) extending voting rights; (2) checking presidential and judicial power; (3) improving the popular representativeness of Congress, as well as expanding its authority; and, of course, (4) enhancing the accessibility of the amendment process and creating other methods, like popular referenda, for mass legal-political intervention. Again, all of this took for granted that a strong, undivided majoritarian legislature, backed by mass mobilization, was far more compatible with continued social transformation than was the emerging American presidential focus. As Benson maintained, here echoing Frederick Douglass during Reconstruction, "it [was] more nearly safe to entrust congress with the task of declaring what is the popular will than to permit any one man, however exalted his station, to do so."[55]

Critically, these demands were not empty calls; they were central to how SPA politicians believed they could chart a path from the present to the desired future. For example, when Victor Berger was first elected to Congress from Wisconsin in 1910, he immediately pursued constitutional reforms. Despite threats of censure from conservative representatives, he introduced a resolution proposing a constitutional amendment to abolish the Senate, which he saw as standing for rule by the few. Berger described the upper house as an "obstructive and useless body, a menace to the liberties of the people," and declared that "the Senate has run its course" and like "the British House of Lords" must "yield" to principles of democratic self-government.[56]

For these electorally focused Socialists, the long-term goal remained the cooperative commonwealth, which would bear little resemblance to the existing society in governmental form or economy. Still, for the time being, these leaders also aimed to identify specific alterations to the existing institutional landscape that would disrupt status quo hierarchies. Activists were not necessarily opposed to one-off amendments, and often supported individual reform initiatives, including those that eventually became ratified as new amendments: women's suffrage, the direct election of senators, congressional authority to enact a graduated income tax. If achieved, these shifts—like a simplified amendment process or actual abolition of the Senate—would enhance the capacity of working people to pursue their shared interests.

Standing alongside these procedural reforms were the plethora of other economically grounded Socialist demands—sometimes explicitly framed as constitutional rights. In facilitating the "collective ownership and democratic management" of the economy, Socialists backed protections for the right to strike (including practices like secondary boycotts), an eight-hour day and maximum hour laws, unionization, a ban on child labor, extensive social insurance, a basic public provision of food, and "public works" jobs for the unemployed, among many others.[57] Socialists therefore put their primary emphasis on experimenting creatively with a variety of institutional changes—across state and economy—and on assessing whether those changes practically altered existing distributions of power.

This multiplicity of overlapping demands also indicated SPA skepticism that any single reformist or constitutional silver bullet existed to fix society. Again, party activists did not approach formal changes to the constitutional text technocratically, as a way of remedying an otherwise functional system. They primarily treated amendments as an alternative method, alongside an actual convention, for peaceably packaging demands in ways that could eventually lead to a thoroughgoing break from the founders' text and their very idea of constitutionalism. They focused on how to generate a wholly new governing economic and political framework, but through the infrastructural reality of a dense existing system. Such an understanding implicitly approached each economic or legal-political reform as a small-scale mechanism for making the daily reproduction of a hierarchical and capitalist order increasingly difficult.

THE IWW, DIRECT ACTION, AND BUILDING AN INSURGENT AND TRANSNATIONAL WORKING CLASS

By contrast, those that gravitated to the IWW tended to question the utility of the SPA legal-political program. These labor radicals focused instead on direct workplace action, seeing a problem in the constitutional reform agenda's obvious legal continuity with the prevailing order. Whether new formal amendments to the 1787 text or even a second convention, such reform proposals still used the very methods of constitutional change promoted by the framers. The strategy created the impression that the state's governing sensibility—and perhaps even its established institutions—could nonetheless provide a means for overcoming capitalism. Wobblies argued (along with some in the SPA's left wing) that for all the Socialists' vocal criticism of Progressives, in practice the SPA's legal-institutional platform could look very similar to more mainstream reformist ideas of evolution or adaptation.

A key issue for "Big Bill" Haywood was that electorally focused SPA politicians overestimated the party's potential at the ballot box. Haywood was certainly not opposed to voting strategies, given his position on the SPA's national executive committee. And he saw elections as a real tool for organizing workers and building union support. But this utility depended on the circumstances of the specific workers. Since Wobblies sought to organize all workers through "one big union," they appealed to immigrant, Black, women, and even child laborers. They reached out to the most dispossessed workers, including transient individuals who moved from place to place in search of a job and so were rarely residents in locations long enough to assert the right to vote. Thus IWW activists were fully conscious of the extent to which many of their members—given systematic disenfranchisement on race, sex, and other grounds—simply did not enjoy the franchise.[58]

For Haywood, this reality meant that pride of place should always be given to direct action or the "industrial ballot." In some settings, where workers enjoyed political representation and the vote could thus be an instrument for fighting capitalist opponents, electoral approaches could make sense. As he remarked, "I advocate the industrial ballot alone when I address the workers in the textile industries of the East where a great majority are foreigners without political representation. But when I speak to American workingmen in the West I advocate both the industrial and the political ballot."[59]

Still, the unavoidable fact of disenfranchisement meant that Haywood and other Wobblies were much less sanguine about the vote's overall value in effectively winning and holding power. IWW activists questioned whether Socialists could actually gain the electoral numbers to control the federal government and then to implement genuinely broad-ranging changes, including constitutional reforms. It was true that, in the lead-up to the 1912 elections, the party's support expanded exponentially. And that year Eugene Debs garnered nearly a million votes for president (6 percent)—despite facing reformist candidates in both Teddy Roosevelt and Woodrow Wilson. So, whatever the Wobbly doubts, this appeared to make the political strategy viable.

But IWW organizers also had further critiques of prioritizing the vote. They believed that it tended to warp the agenda of Socialist politicians, creating incentives to hold on to electoral power—including by responding to non-working-class anxieties and demands—rather than

to remain committed to class struggle. The lyrics to the famed IWW activist Joe Hill's song, "Mr Block," narrated the trusting worker's betrayal
by a Socialist politician:

Election Day he shouted, "A Socialist for Mayor!"
The "comrade" got elected, he happy was for fair,
But after the election he got an awful shock,
A great big Socialist Bull did rap him on the block.
A Comrade Block did sob,
"I helped him get his job."[60]

Hill and others were deeply concerned about the potential opportunism of elected politicians—not just Roosevelt or Wilson, but even Socialists like Berger. They contended that redirecting one's focus away
from workplace actions toward elections diverted energy from necessary industrial confrontations, and therefore would prove counterproductive in the long run.

Perhaps most fundamentally, Wobbly organizers worried that emphasizing electoral strategies, including constitutional reform projects,
suppressed rather than promoted the type of working-class consciousness conducive to more radical assaults on capitalism itself. Like many
Populists and Progressives, SPA and IWW activists argued that the
poor and the working class needed to break free from deference to socioeconomic elites. But they also rejected the idea, implicit in the notion of "the people," that there existed something like a shared public
good across the class divide.

Instead, they depicted society as marked by fundamental and irreconcilable conflicts of interest between workers and the owners of capital. And to the extent that capitalist relations persisted, especially those
of wage labor, there could be no such thing as a harmonious "we the
people." In the blunt words of Charles Edward Russell, the NAACP
co-founder and SPA politician, "so long as it [the working class] deludes
itself into the belief that it can trust anybody outside of its own class
it will thus be tricked fooled and defeated."[61] Thus, a properly oppositional relationship to capitalism—rather than simply to its most egregious and brutalizing manifestations—required breaking the idea that
workers shared a patriotic common ground with economic elites who
may be fellow nationals. Indeed, the editors of the *International Socialist Review* declared, "the working class has no country. The employing
class has stolen them all."[62]

SPA and IWW organizers thus tended to agree that the type of nationalism that Croly, Roosevelt, and others called for should be resisted. It offered a distorted account of social bonding, one that could ultimately only be enforced by preserving the existing structures of class hierarchy, even if in subtler forms. Both groups also rejected the idea that no viable alternatives for solidarity existed between nationalist cohesion and sectarian dissolution. But rather than building community on the accidental basis of where one was born, they sought instead to tie laborers together through their everyday experience of work. This concrete experience, when linked to the emancipatory project of creating a cooperative commonwealth, could provide the same kind of imagined community that grounded nationalist ideas of social cohesion. The effective implication for a working-class audience was that their class-based approach was no more fictive than the dominant politics of patriotism, or the traditional nineteenth-century idea of westward expansion as a shared enterprise in white republican self-rule.

Moreover, one's identity as a worker linked Americans in internationalist terms to fellow laborers abroad. No doubt, laborers would have to be organized where they were located. But under this alternative vision of solidarity, a worker's central ties of attachment would be to all other laborers—similarly situated and equally fighting for another world, both in one's local community and around the globe. In fact, for this very reason, issues of the *International Socialist Review* included sections like "The World of Labor," so as to highlight the shared efforts of workers everywhere—from Canada, Argentina, and the Dominican Republic to states across Europe—to bring socialism into being.[63]

Given this anti-nationalist vision of solidarity, Wobblies in particular worried that projects of evolutionary institutional change would be demobilizing. They saw constitutional reforms—dealing with the amendment process, federalism, bicameralism, the structure of the judiciary—as having a quality of abstraction disconnected from everyday work experiences, the heart of class solidarity. It seemed to require complicated conceptual gymnastics to link legal-political design to the underlying realities of immiseration and dependence facing those most dispossessed. According to the IWW activist Justus Ebert, "workingmen on the job don't care . . . they want practical organization first, all else after."[64] Ebert feared that the more abstract the demands became, the less workers would be willing to commit to the personal costs associated with political and industrial fights. Furthermore, such constitutional demands also blended in with other non-socialist reform efforts. They created not only the impression that perhaps change was possible under the existing terms of the state, but also the sense that maybe voting for the Socialist Party differed little from supporting the Progressive or any other nominally reformist enterprise.

THE PROCEDURALIST LIMITATIONS
OF SOCIALIST PRAGMATISM

For electorally minded Socialists committed to the constitutional platform, Wobbly suspicion of legal-political reform raised basic questions about the radical union's imagined path forward. In particular, many SPA thinkers believed that the IWW had no clear agenda for getting from the present-day status quo to a genuinely emancipated society: their focus on specific grievances in the workplace could also be co-opted by other reformist entities. Moreover, their overarching instrument for revolutionary change, the general strike, had a millennial and near-religious quality. Wobblies sought a steady escalation of mass protest leading to a series of general strikes, which would displace capitalist bosses and allow worker unions to claim ownership of the means of production. Under such circumstances, the existing state — including the constitutional order — would collapse, or, as Ebert wrote, "systems fall; the old society is destroyed; the face of modern life is transformed."[65]

By contrast with the Wobbly wish for a single, great revolutionary break, many SPA leaders saw elections and constitutional alterations as a step-by-step process toward building a genuine majority and improvising a new social order out of the old. Wobblies tended to move quickly between concrete immediate demands, like wage increases at work, and the emancipatory horizon of post-capitalist worker control. But SPA critics wanted an agenda that could attract large numbers of working people, from small-scale job improvements to fundamental transformations in society. In a sense, if Wobblies argued that abstract constitutional demands were demobilizing, Socialist politicians suggested that too big a gulf between immediate economic improvements and the cooperative ideal could create its own dispiriting effect. The steady achievement of intermediate reforms would heighten workers' bargaining power and thus create a cascading effect, especially as the possibility of a socialist alternative became clearer. Thus a utopian imaginative horizon would combine with practical goals in the here and now, eventually dismantling the extensive structural constraints that blocked the path to a genuinely different society.

This relative incrementalism led key SPA leaders to a more pragmatic relationship with not only the country's legal-political institutions but also its national symbols. The SPA's concern with constitutional arrangements in part emerged from a desire to ensure that a working-class popular majority could not only manage a transitional process away from capitalism, but also avoid elite usurpations of all sorts. Majoritarianism protected against the presidential takeovers that the Progressive embrace of executive power portended. And it safeguarded against a comparable authoritarianism implicit in simply destroying the existing state. Transitional phases required legal-political institutions organized to promote mass working-class participation and voice. Without them, it could become exceedingly easy for a small coterie of actors to subvert revolutionary developments. That coterie could claim control of administrative apparatuses and simply substitute its ends for the will of the working class.

Thus, for electorally focused Socialists, the fact that constitutional reforms maintained contact with the existing order was not entirely a negative. It provided a governing infrastructure within which working-class constituents were attuned to operating, and where they could more comfortably (if not always successfully) press for their goals. Furthermore, while SPA politicians too saw the need for an internationalist and class-conscious collective identity, they also believed that Socialists had to organize people from where they were—including by potentially using the symbolic and institutional tools available, even nationalist ones.

By contrast, IWW activists implicitly viewed this SPA electoralism and interest in constitutional reform as systematically downplaying the fact that a genuine move toward socialism might require breaking from the legal-political system and its processes. Even if the SPA somehow gained control over representative institutions through the ballot box, actual change could necessitate truly confrontational means— given counter-majoritarianism and the power of socioeconomic elites. These means might well include those nonviolent but highly disruptive direct-action tools, like the general strike, which some SPA figures castigated as quasi-millennial. Allan Benson himself ventriloquized this potential criticism of change through a smooth electoral and constitutional pathway, describing a skeptic as saying, "ah, but the capitalists will bedevil you still. . . . They will get into office by hook or crook and put your plans awry."[66]

By and large, SPA figures deemphasized such worries and proclaimed faith that socialism could nonetheless emerge without systematic norm-breaking. As Benson charted out the initial steps, Socialists would "gain control of this government" through the vote, "as we confidently expect to do before many years," and then implement their overarching agenda, including by "call[ing] a constitutional convention." When pressed on the question of institutional roadblocks and corporate backlash, Benson admitted that existing constitutional niceties might, if push came to shove, have to be abandoned: "If Socialism shall be too slow in coming, the tyranny of the trusts will undoubtedly compel the people to confiscate them, precisely as Lincoln confiscated the slaves."[67]

Yet, Benson appeared to treat this as a more remote possibility, given his faith in the SPA's electoral potential to overrun anti-democratic constraints. Even more significantly, in invoking the 1863 Emancipation Proclamation, he also left unstated the fact that abolition and Reconstruction took place against the backdrop of war and of a Republican Party willing to use federal troops and to break from procedural norms to impose constitutional change. Given the degree to which Socialists were presented by business elites and government officials as lawless and threatening revolutionaries, one can understand why Benson refrained from connecting those Civil War and post–Civil War dots. For instance, Benson in *Our Dishonest Constitution* does not elucidate how a new constitutional convention would emerge. Would it have to follow the process laid down by Article V, even if that process placed extreme hurdles in the way of popular organizing? Or could it be authorized through large-scale mass mobilizations outside the terms of the 1787 text? As hinted at in the previous chapter when discussing Croly's fears, would near or actual revolution be the precondition for a new convention? Benson and others tended to avoid explicitly detailing how they planned to engage with elite intransigence if opponents refused to quietly exit the economic and political stage.

But this avoidance embodied a significant hole in mainstream SPA constitutional politics. The early twentieth century was permeated by reactionary pushback: business opponents took advantage of the anti-democratic tools embedded in the legal-political system and routinely deployed intense state and private violence. These were real roadblocks to change and, if the SPA enjoyed increasing electoral success, such re-action would only intensify. Simply repeating faith in a steady road to socialism through elections, followed by the process-based implementation of reform, would not be enough.

In this way, Benson's close association with Socialist constitutional thinking, as author of *Our Dishonest Constitution*, reinforced a worry that interest in constitutional reform could at times devolve into its own preservationist brand of proceduralism. During World War I, Benson, already a more conservative figure within the SPA, proclaimed his support for the conflict, broke with the party, and denounced both the IWW and the SPA's left wing as insufficiently patriotic. He presented radical activists' anti-war views and continued class-based internationalism as un-American dangers to a nation under arms. Attacking the party for which he had so recently served as the presidential candidate, Benson wrote in 1918, "in order to be respected, the party must be respectable. In my humble opinion, it is not now respectable."[68]

This concern with "respectability" did not just lead Benson to drift toward more mainstream Progressive-era politics. The desire "to be respected" also indicated a broader sensibility, beyond simply the question of World War I. Benson, as well as some in the party's right wing, seemed especially focused on proving to a general public the conventional quality of their socialist ideas—including the possibility of socialist achievement without any unruliness or norm-breaking.[69] Indeed, at times and among more conservative SPA politicians, this extended even to proclaiming, as Milwaukee City Attorney Daniel Hoan did in 1913, that "carrying out the complete Social Democratic program of political and economic reform" could be done under the existing Constitution and without the structural rewriting the SPA's own platform called for. As he told the audience, "the constitution's all right, it's all a matter of interpreting it."[70]

The fact that it was Hoan making this point was noteworthy. He would go on to serve as mayor of Milwaukee from 1916 to 1940, aided in his early electoral fights by also breaking from the SPA's anti-war position and backing US involvement in World War I. As IWW activists had worried, these shifts—which had the benefit of assuaging middle-class voters—seemed to eliminate much of the ideological difference between Socialists and Progressives. Like many Progressives, Hoan too accepted an anti-formalist view of the Constitution in which the right judges could generate the right interpretations, and he also seemed to treat anti-war politics as a threat to national solidarity.

These tendencies among more conservative SPA politicians spoke to a larger tension in Socialist politics. For some on the party's right wing, the hope was that genuinely transformative changes could somehow occur without the legal-political or institutional disruptions and confrontations that might tar an activist as disreputable. That desire thus promoted a type of wish fulfillment, perhaps parallel to the one they saw in the IWW's embrace of the general strike. In truth, electorally minded SPA figures, not unlike Benson or even Hoan, never adequately addressed the question of how they intended to reckon with institutional impasses and reactionary violence. It would take later generations of activists to more fully conceptualize these dilemmas.

SYMBOLS OF THE STATE AND THE DECLARATION OF INDEPENDENCE

This desire to be seen as respectable may help explain why SPA criticism focused on the 1787 Constitution rather than that other, even more constitutive symbol of American nationalism—the Declaration of Independence. In a sense, both documents spoke to the idea that settlers—immigrant and native-born, and regardless of class background—enjoyed a common political destiny. And in many ways, the Declaration too was routinely employed by business groups and legal elites to inhibit class consciousness and to promote nationalist attachments. This was apparent in the mass celebrations around the hundredth anniversary of the 1776 adoption of the Declaration, which became a moment of collective patriotism and fellow feeling, despite class differences.

But there were two elements that separated the Declaration from the Constitution that perhaps accounted for the Socialist political energy focused on uprooting the latter. First, the Declaration had a far more ambiguous meaning in the present. On the one hand, it certainly fed into notions about class exceptionalism, as well as about an ostensible disjuncture between feudal Europe and democratic America. But on the other hand, it did not so easily assimilate into a defense of the status quo. Euro-Americans, across class and ideological divides, recognized the revolutionary meaning of the Declaration.[71] For generations of radicals, this indicated that the Declaration was one part of a collective tradition of institutional rupture. It embodied a useful tool for highlighting a distinctive American working-class history of rejecting oppressive authority.

In addition, and perhaps most critically, the Declaration did not carry with it any concrete set of governing arrangements. What made the Constitution so insidious as a symbol was how invocations of a democratic "we the people" were linked in political practice to institutions that facilitated class rule. Thus, many SPA activists saw a particular need to disabuse working people of whatever emotional bonds they might still have had toward the 1787 framers and their institutions.

Yet, whenever invoking culturally familiar symbols and narratives, there was always a fine line politically between using them for irruptive ends and becoming subsumed by them, as Benson's political evolution dramatizes. For many in the IWW, SPA stalwarts could too easily fall back into exceptionalist tropes about American institutions or even about capacities for capitalist reform and renewal. And, as noted in chapter 2's discussion of Black politics after Reconstruction, this fine line became a continuous challenge to any mass mobilizing on behalf of transformative change.

The Place of Race in the Fight for the Cooperative Commonwealth

Ultimately, the SPA's desire to remain connected to "where (white) workers were" entailed a profound moral and political flaw—namely, around that very question of race. The party and those that circulated around it, especially in the IWW, provided one of the white spaces most hospitable to Black inclusion at the time. This was underscored by the involvement of members like Charles Russell in the founding of the NAACP and by Eugene Debs's own persistent and outspoken commitment to absolute racial equality. Furthermore, as exemplified by the likes of Teddy Roosevelt and Woodrow Wilson, mainstream Progressivism tended to go hand in hand with a deeply held white supremacist worldview. But even if many white Socialists challenged the pervasive Jim Crow climate of their times, the failure of the party as a whole to seriously confront the distinctive role of race in American capitalism critically impeded its emancipatory vision and prospects.

SOCIALIST CLAIMS TO THE ABOLITIONIST MANTLE

During the period, radical activists that gravitated to the SPA or to the IWW often embraced the idea that they inherited the mantle of the great abolitionists. As the Wobbly organizer James Thompson proclaimed, in terms that were routinely invoked by socialists and anarchists of the time, "we are the modern abolitionists fighting against wage slavery."[72] And during World War I, when the federal government suppressed the *Masses*, a journal edited by Max Eastman, he and Crystal

Eastman, his sister, named their new monthly the *Liberator* after William Lloyd Garrison's famed newspaper.[73] They intended this as further expression of the continuity between abolitionism and American socialism.[74]

SPA activists also drew directly from the anti-Constitution analysis of past Garrisonians.[75] Such abolitionists had depicted the constitutional order as preserving American slaveocracy and, with it, feudal hegemony on the plantation. Foreshadowing Charles Beard or J. Allen Smith, these abolitionist arguments often focused too on the framers' intent, and on how their class identity produced a fundamentally counterrevolutionary document. In his 1867 article in the *National Anti-Slavery Standard*, the abolitionist, journalist, and Reconstruction-era South Carolina official James Redpath contended that the framers were ultimately responsible for the country's infrastructure of "oligarchy." As such, he hoped that the Civil War would produce "the destruction of all confidence in the 'wisdom of the Fathers.'" In Redpath's mind, the framers "took care to incorporate as little as was possible of the Democratic spirit into their nascent institutions." Instead, they implanted in American life "five fortresses of aristocracy": slavery, class rule, gentry military leadership, the Senate, and the Supreme Court. Through these mechanisms, the text's drafters, whom he derisively placed in quotation marks as "our Fathers," "forged iron, with equal impartiality, into tongues for liberty bells and manacles for negro slaves. The best thing we can do for them is to imitate the dutiful son of old Noah — to look away and cast a mantle of charity over their too open nakedness."[76] Thus, Redpath and other abolitionists had embraced the need for radical constitutional change and even re-founding, writing of the "five fortresses": "They must fall or they must stand together."[77]

Half a century later, Socialists explicitly claimed these arguments as their own, grafting the problem of entrenched industrial hierarchy onto that classic critique of the Constitution. For instance, the influential Chicago journalist Algie Martin Simons quoted extensively from Wendell Phillips's *The Constitution, A Pro-Slavery Compact*. Simons grounded his written histories of slavery in that text, along with his analysis of the Constitution's role in preserving economic oppression — despite the legal repudiation of formal bondage.[78]

One reason why early-twentieth-century activists like Simons and Crystal Eastman felt a kinship with these previous voices was because a key strain of radical abolitionism was itself explicitly socialist, as the historian Andrew Zimmerman has explored. During the Civil War, approximately 10 percent of the Northern military had been born in Germany, including many veterans of the 1848–49 Revolution.[79] Politically exiled in the United States, a significant portion of these emigrants had been radicalized by their past experience. And, in fighting the Confederacy, German radicals rose to surprising prominence in the Union army, with exiles from the 1848–49 Revolution serving in senior officer positions (including, in certain cases, as Brigadier Generals).[80] Wherever they enjoyed leadership positions, such radicals pressed for immediate and uncompensated abolition, regardless of constitutional niceties, and for the arming of those formerly enslaved and the transfer of slave plantations over to Black rural workers. Furthermore, many pointedly rejected the careful separation Lincoln and other Republicans made between slavery and presumptively legitimate modes of private property. Instead, some of these German radicals read enslaved production as only an extreme form of the oppressive structures dominating economic life more generally.

Not unlike rural freedpeople themselves, such soldiers at times imagined the war effort as not simply a battle against secession, but also a revolutionary opportunity to reconstitute the fundamental terms of Northern and Southern society. A figure that persistently articulated these socialist positions before and during the war was none other than Karl Marx. Marx maintained a strong relationship with the German exile community in the United States and even gained a significant American reading audience in the 1850s and early 1860s as a regular columnist for the *New York Tribune*.[81] As Marx famously wrote to Lincoln in 1864, "the slaveholders' rebellion" was nothing less than "a general holy crusade of property against labor." This meant that for the conflict— what Marx called "the American Antislavery War"—to be victorious, the "crusade" on behalf of property had to be defeated not only through formal emancipation, but also through revolutionary rupture. Such a break would be embodied, on the ground, in the end of the plantation system, and in its replacement with Black collective ownership and control. And all of this would usher in a "new era of ascendancy" for the "working classes" as a whole—regardless of race.[82]

AMBIVALENCE AND WHITE SUPREMACY AMONG LEFT RADICALS

Still, for all these clear inheritances from and continuities with past abolitionism, the Socialist party as a whole—along with the era's white radicalism more generally—equivocated on how to think about the relationship between racial domination and class oppression. White socialists and anarchists depicted the class prism as the universal framework within which to understand all social conditions. And depending on how activists employed it, this prism carried with it contradictory impulses—which could both challenge and preserve the politics of white supremacy.

On the one hand, labor radicals emphasized shared material interests among workers, which hinted at a truly inclusive vision of collective membership. In a context in which business and governing elites employed racial animus to pit native-born white workers against immigrant or Black wage earners, placing class first offered a direct repudiation to settler xenophobia. Take for instance Justus Ebert's framing of cross-racial class solidarity under the banner of the IWW, perhaps the white-run organization most committed during these years to comprehensive multiracial liberation. As Ebert declared, "the I. W. W. aims to organize every man, woman, and child that is in the leaking, rotten boat of capitalism, so that we can all pull together for the shore of social safety and freedom just over yonder."[83]

All laborers, regardless of race or gender (or even age), were equally subject to dependent wage relations and new forms of agricultural bondage. And this meant, for Ebert or the Socialist Debs (who was also a participant in the IWW's founding convention), that Black people, women, and European and Asian immigrants were all entitled to freedom and thus to equal membership in the liberated society to come. Recognizing this common condition scrambled the traditional settler assumptions about insiders and outsiders, and it tore down the instinctive racial solidarities and embrace of Euro-American "whiteness," which had long been the foundation of collective life. The universal dimension of this class analysis was a key reason why some of the most popular Black political figures of the time—like the labor organizer and politician A. Philip Randolph or the Harlem-based journalist and critic Hubert Harrison—were attracted to socialism and to the SPA.

On the other hand, if material alliances broke down or could not be clearly articulated, the embrace of racial outsiders also tended to collapse. Economic interest may have been the central building block of cross-racial and cross-ethnic solidarity: it provided the concrete justification and everyday shared experience to connect groups long pitted against each other. Yet if immediate interest did not, over time, evolve into a principled and common bond of working-class community, there was extreme danger—in a context of Jim Crow entrenchment and nativist xenophobia—of slipping back toward exclusion. This tendency meant that class analysis could press in the direction of radical racial egalitarianism. But it could also be combined with pervasive judgments about white superiority or be employed to minimize racial injustice.

Thus, for some SPA leaders, the emphasis on class allowed them to present racial domination as a less significant side issue. The result— according to Jeffrey Perry, Hubert Harrison's biographer—was a "general neglect [of race] in the party press; failure of the party to change racist membership practices in the South; the party position of non-interference in the internal matters of the AFL trade unions that left segregative and exclusionary policies unchallenged; the lack of strong opposition to lynching."[84]

For IWW critics of the SPA, this party willingness was tied, again, to the all-consuming focus of some Socialist politicians on short-term electoral viability and success. Given the realities of Black disenfranchisement, the party needed to win its support, overwhelmingly, among white voters, most of whom remained deeply prejudiced. In this context, refraining from too aggressively challenging racist practices offered a way to avoid disagreements among white constituents. But as Black socialists like Hubert Harrison or those in the IWW would conclude, it exposed the SPA as, in the final analysis, unwilling truly to embrace class solidarity—instead allowing a politics of whiteness to remain paramount. To make matters worse, for every Eugene Debs— genuinely committed to a multiracial cooperative commonwealth— there was a Victor Berger, William Noyes, or Ernest Untermann who openly espoused white supremacy. And numerous party stalwarts took as given a Wilsonian belief in an ethno-racial hierarchy of peoples.[85] Not unlike the Southerner Walter Clark, they saw little contradiction between internal white class equality and external racial control.

THE CONCEPTUAL SPACE FOR RACE IN A CLASS-BASED FRAMEWORK

Beyond troubling tactical choices and the explicit racism of some, white radicals at a deeper level often failed to grasp the racial dimension of American economic and state practices. Until his death in 1926, Debs fought consistently against efforts to divide the SPA or working people generally on racial lines—to place white solidarity above class alliances. He remained ever hopeful that, with the coming of the cooperative

commonwealth, racism would disappear "like mist before the sunrise."[86]
Still, he also infamously concluded that Socialists had "nothing special
to offer the negro"[87] because there was "no negro problem apart from
the general labor problem."[88] Indeed, even when Socialists attacked the
Constitution as a pro-slavery document, they often treated the institution of slavery through a class lens without engaging with its particular
and brutalizing mode of racial domination. They thus presented all the
flaws of the society and of the 1787 text as grounded in the inherent
defect of anti-democratic subversion by a wealthy few. Madison, as an
enslaver, may have participated in and entrenched a specific system of
racial economic exploitation, but he was to be repudiated above all as a
propertied elite.

In a sense, white radicals of various stripes deemphasized the settler
dynamics of American society. For all the discussion of slavery generally, they spent little time on the constitutive role of Native expropriation and coerced Black labor in the specific structure of American
settlement and economic development. They thus ignored the role of
racialized exploitation—before and after slavery—as a critical mechanism for promoting internal white class equality and economic independence. Racial hierarchy had been woven into the fabric of American
capitalism, in the context of both small-scale production and now large-
scale industrialization. Therefore, racial and class politics could not be
separated in any truly transformative response to settler conditions.

Such an assessment had long circulated in African American life. Indeed, it echoed a sensibility that ran through rural Black ideas of communal plantation control all the way back in 1865. And Black socialists
like Hubert Harrison, who were often frustrated by the party's failure
to take seriously these interconnections, would come to develop them
in trenchant detail.

This failure had even broader significance: when white SPA leaders
in particular pursued a class analysis divorced from race, their views
could easily feed into familiar variants of Jacksonian anti-elitism. Under those accounts, the evil of corporate industrialization centered on
its degradation of free white laborers, reducing them to the dependent
status of racial outsiders—whether Black or immigrant. Simply calling once again for class equality—without working through how such
equality had historically been sustained through racial domination—
left the door open for the old combination of economic populism and
white supremacy. This was certainly not what Debs wanted, but for
many potential constituents—whether the segregationist Socialist in

the South or in an AFL trade union—it seemed a far more culturally resonant way to entrench internal white equality.

Socialist constitutional critique faced the same limitation. Someone like the racist Berger may have focused on the aristocratic implications of federalism, the Senate, and the Supreme Court. But the most obvious way in which the constitutional order undermined democracy and imposed class domination was the violent return of white supremacy across the former Confederacy. Black workers found themselves consigned again to extreme dependent labor in the factory and on the farm. For Harrison this made Black Americans, "as the most ruthlessly exploited working class group in America," "more essentially proletarian than any other American group."[89] Further underscoring this exploitation, the old white ruling class continued to hold the reins of power, once more directing the government apparatus and denying Black workers the right to vote. This racist defeat of Reconstruction employed lawless means—from overthrowing elections to the lynching of Black people. But these lawless means were also facilitated by a legal-political system that allowed white supremacists at the state level to take advantage of the fractured nature of constitutional design to reassert white control.

In this way, the white authoritarianism prevalent across the South offered the most sustained expression of how the existing constitutional system combined class domination and autocracy. Harrison thus called on SPA supporters to appreciate the extent to which promoting Black rights, including the right to vote, was itself essential to the political organization of the working class. As he challenged white Socialist leaders disinterested in Black enfranchisement: "If the Negroes, or any other section of the working class in America, is to be deprived of the ballot, how can they participate . . . in the class struggle? How can we pretend to be a political party if we fail to see this fact?"[90]

Yet, white Socialists rarely highlighted these matters when attacking the constitutional order's anti-democratic features, and instead tended to deemphasize the way in which confronting race was itself central to reconstructing class relations. Those like Debs certainly sought a multiracial and class-conscious majority. But even he shied away from an aggressive and directed focus on uprooting racial control specifically—a focus that could have expanded the practical economic and political power of Black working people, especially across the South. In a sense, Socialists—in part due to transatlantic connections and European immigrant bases—still looked too closely to Europe for their understanding of capitalism's rise and perpetuation in the United States. They did not suitably confront the specifically American dynamics of a racially constructed system of capitalist production and extractive labor relations. In practice, this meant that SPA activists approached racial domination as an archaic holdover, perhaps a leftover from a pre-capitalist and feudal system of slavery, and generally separate from the core focus on capitalist domination.

A real consequence was a profound limitation in understanding how and why class solidarities broke down in the United States. For example, one feature of industrial life that undermined a sense of shared cross-racial material interest was a commonplace white worker view of Black labor as a potential source of strikebreaking. As the historian Eric Arensen writes, "in reality blacks constituted only a small if ultimately undeterminable percentage of strikebreakers in the history of American industrial relations." Nonetheless, "white trade unionists and, indeed, much of American society," against the backdrop of prevalent white supremacist attitudes, often conceived of Black labor through this lens.[91]

In doing so, such white labor unionists evaded a key reason why some minority workers may have crossed picket lines. As the Black newspaper the *Chicago Defender* declared succinctly, the problem derived from the white unions' "prejudiced clannishness."[92] According to Hubert Harrison, it was partly "thanks to exclusion from the craft unions" that Black workers both faced such extreme exploitation and questioned the "sincerity" of white labor's commitment to real class solidarity.[93] In fact, going back to Frederick Douglass, white union racism had a profound effect on how various African American figures approached the problem of the Black laboring community. Along with projects of individual homesteading and full civic inclusion, Douglass also backed Black worker-owned cooperatives, including an 1870s shipyard venture in Baltimore—a city where, as a young enslaved worker, he himself had "caulked ships."[94] But the historian David Blight notes that Douglass was deeply suspicious of African American engagement with white-led unions, given their "discriminatory practices against Black and Chinese workers."[95]

Yet, many white Socialist politicians and activists had difficulty making sense of the structural reasons why white and Black workers were pitted against each other. This was because their underlying theory did not appreciate the centrality of racial domination to the development and maintenance of the American capitalist order, and thus to segmenting the working class in ways that imposed white authoritarianism in the workplace and in government. Given the lack of an adequate link between racial domination and class rule, race was deemphasized as a site for waging sustained political struggle.

Instead, time and again, white racial prejudice became a place of compromise even for more racially inclusive SPA leaders such as Debs, if they felt that they needed to accommodate their white membership. Even when they publicly declared opposition to racism, Socialist politicians often avoided spending actual political capital to push back against party affiliates, potential labor allies such as in the AFL, or prospective voters on questions of segregation, lynching, or internal union discrimination. Taken as a whole, the party fundamentally failed to reckon with how the systematic disenfranchisement and dispossession of African Americans—a significant portion of the actual working class—proved a massive roadblock in the way of mobilizing labor power.

Conclusion: Group versus Nation in the Politics of Allegiance

In the end, many factors meant that Socialists, along with radical fellow travelers, were unable to bring into being the world they sought. For starters, they faced intense forms of state and private violence, which disrupted organizing activities, killed members, and imprisoned leaders such as Debs himself. And, as we have seen, hesitancy and capitulation in the face of virulent white supremacy embodied a fundamental constraint on the basic emancipatory potential of the SPA. Electoral Socialists also made a real strategic error when they removed the IWW leader, "Big Bill" Haywood, from the party's executive committee in 1913. Victor Berger and his allies believed that the Wobblies' millennial and revolutionary rhetoric scared off potential voters and that a purge of the union would open the path to greater victories at the ballot box. Instead, the opposite occurred, validating the IWW sentiment that its brand of class militancy and direct action actually built working-class support on the ground. Where the union was strong, the party had been strong.[96]

At a deeper level, the various sides had correctly highlighted the weaknesses of the other perspectives. This perhaps indicated that mass movement efforts required both direct action and political-legal agendas; the SPA and the IWW were strongest when they worked together. Under those conditions, electoral and non-electoral strategies built on each other. This expanded both the insurgent potential of spontaneous and mass protest and the organizational capacity of party institutions and leaders to gain state power and pursue economic and political reforms.

Despite its defeat, the Socialist project during these years provided a profound experiment in the content and possibility of a fundamentally different constitutional and socioeconomic pathway. It embodied a culturally resonant and radical alternative with which American legal and political elites across the ideological spectrum had to contend. Whether or not more moderate reformers explicitly acknowledged this role, SPA activism served as a backdrop enhancing the era's climate of experimentation. Indeed, one can read the passage of the Sixteenth and Seventeenth Amendments—relating to a federal income tax and direct senatorial election, respectively—as partly due to a recognition by establishment politicians that the only way to halt the momentum of radical forces was to capitulate to relatively piecemeal reforms that enjoyed widespread popular support.

Finally, SPA and IWW organizers offered their own competing vision of solidarity and collective attachment, in contrast with nationalist calls. No doubt the proliferation of various group identities during these years had deeply destructive effects. The intensity of such identities unleashed white violence on African Americans and, in the context of the North's own profound racism, produced the return of white authoritarian rule in the South. And it led new industrial robber barons to consciously think of themselves as an American aristocracy, building ostentatious mansions in the manner of European nobility and holding themselves apart from the rest of society.[97] But from Black colonization efforts in the South to suffragist activism and growing class radicalism, the language of group solidarity—and indeed the increasing suspicion of a harmonious "we the people"—also became a central tool in movement organizing and in the creation of an oppositional political culture. It provided the means for highlighting structural and irreducible conflicts within society, which had been papered over by political elites uninterested in confronting social grievances.

At their most expansive, radicals like Debs, Eastman, Haywood, and Ebert sought to mobilize class identity specifically as a mechanism for building a cross-racial and internationalist social fabric. They conceived of the United States as a potential experiment in forging a new sense of community and political possibility. For this to succeed, they took as given that the Constitution—a symbol and a concrete institutional embodiment of the old regime—had to be overturned root and branch. Furthermore, SPA voices combined this call with an argument about the need to change the very way Americans imagined constitutionalism. Thus, during these years of rising movement intensity, those at opposite ends of the ideological spectrum saw the potential for genuine transformation, whether they viewed this development with elation or dread. In a sense, regardless of what conservatives like William Howard Taft or Henry Cabot Lodge may have hoped, change in some deep way seemed unavoidable.

Questions remained, though, as to what such change would ultimately look like. One hint came from political encounters in places like Cuba, Puerto Rico, and the Philippines. As chapter 5 explores, the early-twentieth-century experiments in constitutional meaning and national identity occurring within the continental United States coincided with new experiments overseas. In particular, officials and politicians began to build the political infrastructure for growing American power, and to develop the narratives that justified such international authority. Eventually, these experiments abroad would combine with developments at home to create a brand of national allegiance that rose above all other attachments, including class. Perhaps more surprisingly, they would do so through a newly revived and modernized politics of constitutional veneration.

CHAPTER 5

Developing Universalist
Empire in the Philippines

On December 10, 1898, the United States signed the Treaty of Paris, ending hostilities with Spain. While the Spanish-Cuban-American War initially started over the future status of Cuba, American officials embraced victory as an opportunity to extract from Spain a wide-ranging overseas empire, extending from the Caribbean to Southeast Asia. The treaty's Article I held that Spain relinquished sovereignty over Cuba and gave the United States occupation authority under international law. Article II handed over sovereignty of Puerto Rico and Guam, while Article III ceded the Philippine Islands to the US for the price of $20 million. Along with Hawaii's annexation in the same year, these expansions fundamentally transformed the country's geography—particularly given that, excluding the Alaska Purchase in 1867 and the uninhabited Guano Islands, all American territories had been contiguous before the 1890s. Two years later, in 1900, the United States acquired eastern Samoa through treaty with Great Britain and Germany; and in 1903 the US gained the Panama Canal after an American intervention in Colombia.[1]

Such developments announced the US's emergence on the international stage as a significant global military and economic force. They also spoke to the desire of officials to join the European worldwide scramble for overseas colonial possessions.

But these global ambitions immediately faced profound difficulty. Most importantly, a defiant anti-colonial movement in the Philippines rejected the treaty, reasserted the sovereign authority of the First Philippine Republic, and continued its war of independence—now waged against the United States. And while American public debate paid little attention to the Philippines when the US geared up for conflict with

Spain, it became a focal point of intense political controversy as a new and unexpected war raged on the islands.

By the time President Theodore Roosevelt unilaterally and prematurely declared the Filipino independence fight defeated—on July 4, 1902, no less—a staggering price had been paid for what should have been a relatively simple pacification project: four thousand US soldiers and approximately 50,000 Filipino troops were dead, not to mention upward of a quarter million Filipino civilians. The fighting had featured atrocities on both sides, with the American army resorting to the large-scale use of torture as well as "reconcentration camps," where rural populations were forcibly garrisoned in a policy that the historian Paul Kramer describes as "the deliberate annihilation of the rural economy" through "the destruction of villages," "the burning of rice stores," and "the killing of livestock"—all of which led to mass starvation, disease, and death. Stories about the US army's atrocities circulated throughout the American press and even led to a Senate investigation initiated by Massachusetts Republican George Frisbee Hoar in the first half of 1902.[2]

Against this background, critics like Mark Twain, who had always been wary of annexation, wondered aloud, "why, we have got into a mess, a quagmire from which each fresh step renders the difficulty of extrication immensely greater."[3] Indeed, Roosevelt's declaration of victory was itself, in Kramer's words, "a beleaguered fiction that broke down in unflattering reversals: by 1905, parts of the provinces of Batangas, Cebu, Bohol, Samar, Cavite, and Albay would be returned to military authority due to continued Filipino resistance."[4] For all intents and purposes, the American twentieth century had commenced with near open class war at home and an actual brutal military fight abroad.

In the crucible of the Philippine-American War, US politicians and officials began to forge an account of the American global project—one that ultimately would have far-reaching ramifications, including in the domestic arena. Pro-war politicians and commentators had hoped initially to model the US role on that of other European empires, and especially on the British example. But the intensity of non-white political opposition in places like the Philippines, which they failed to anticipate, set them on a different path.

In particular, this context of growing anti-colonialism—which would come to define twentieth-century international relations—eventually altered how officials conceived of and organized US overseas authority. Colonial administrators and supportive politicians started to distinguish American actions from European states, depicting the latter as motivated primarily by wealth extraction and racial domination. In an unexpected historical twist, they reclaimed anti-slavery creedal narratives—pushed to the margins at the time within Euro-American society—to depict US power as grounded in an inherent and exceptional culture of universal egalitarianism and self-government. In the process, defenders of American interventionism focused on constitutional promotion as a critical component of foreign policy, venerating the 1787 text as an embodiment of the unique political lessons that the US alone could offer the world.

In an age marked by American political experimentation—often motivated by worries about collapsing settler bonds—this intertwining of creedal ideas, the federal Constitution, and an aggressive US global posture was perhaps the boldest and longest-lasting experiment. Colonial administrators in the Philippines and elsewhere were effectively developing the ideas and practices that would ground American intervention and international police power for the coming century. And this particular blending of creed and Constitution—far from simply an instrumental way for Americans to justify their overseas ambitions— eventually solidified into the dominant ideological lens through which the country understood its domestic history and its place in the world.

Through the following pages, I lay out in greater detail this surprising set of developments. And I contend that the US reaction to the Philippine-American War and related turn-of-the-century global episodes helps to explain a real puzzle of twentieth-century politics: In the depths of Jim Crow, why did politicians and officials, who were themselves deeply committed to white rule, nonetheless start reviving universalist ideas of American identity? How could this be, given the historic association of creedal politics with the likes of Frederick Douglass and with the deep fears of racial upheaval shared by many whites during and after Reconstruction? Exclusively internal accounts of American constitutional culture and development are far less equipped to address these questions, to the extent they ask them at all.

The chapter begins with how pro-business and upper-class fears of social disintegration led politicians, initially within the Republican Party, to see imperial assertiveness as a path out of the morass of domestic social strife. It also engages with how, at first, the language of constitutional fidelity was overwhelmingly the domain not of defenders but

rather of *opponents* of overseas empire—who feared both the risks embedded in imperial governmental overreach and the weakening of the
US settler republican identity in a far-flung global project.

I then detail how, when confronted by the Filipino independence
movement, white officials began reimagining the project of colonial administration in ways that diverged from straightforward racial domination and instead revived dormant narratives of creed and Constitution.
In particular, colonial officials in the Philippines sought to explain why
the US—although unlike European empires—should nonetheless enjoy a permanent right of intervention. To do so, they invoked claims
about the culturally exceptional history of Anglo-European settlement
in North America—given concrete proof by the writing and enactment
of the Constitution—to justify why, although all peoples may be on a
path to eventual sovereign statehood, in the here and now white US officials could reconstruct non-white societies as they saw fit.

In other words, places like the Philippines provided the experimen-
tal laboratory in which white policymakers not only combined creed
and Constitution in novel ways, but also reconciled anti-slavery narratives of equal liberty—a potentially threatening and even revolutionary
discourse—with the continuation of white rule. These policymakers essentially built an account of American power on the global stage that
avoided the perceived pitfalls of two negative models: Reconstruction's
multiracial democracy and Europe's imperial system. For white officials, themselves deeply racist, actual multiracial democracy only generated disorder; and, if projected onto the global stage, it would place
too much authority in the hands of culturally "immature" populations.
Yet, at the same time, they increasingly contended that the legacy of
European imperialism was wrapped up with destructive rivalries and
exploitative violence. More and more white policymakers thus maintained that neither alternative offered an appropriate model for how
the US should operate abroad.

By contrast, their own arguments rejected permanent racial domination but still justified the authority of empowered settler elites to
supervise the political maturation of supposedly less developed peoples
both at home and abroad. They thus presented overseas nation-building
as bound to constitutional replication in ways that both continued and
broke from past settler expansion on the frontier.

Of course, initially the idea of the US as exporting its creedal constitutional gifts to a world under tutelage held little appeal, and was often
mostly of interest to elites in the Republican Party. Frequently, it was

drowned out by suspicion over greater international involvement and by the dominant focus on domestic industrial and class conflict. And, as the chapter also explores, contemporaneous Black and Indigenous arguments about self-determination pushed back against these narratives, pointing out the limits of this emerging American vision of an inclusive empire.

Still, against this backdrop, creedal and constitutional claims about US power eventually moved outside the Republican Party, and in particular to Southern segregationists like Wilson, who found in them a means to distinguish American imperium from traditional European empires while still vindicating racial hierarchy and even reaffirming domestic Jim Crow. Furthermore, when the US entered the First World War, pro-war activists marshaled this same combination of creed and Constitution to gain public support, explicitly championing the 1787 text as a core component of national loyalty and a key facet of what Americans should fight for abroad. Thus, by World War I, a broad swathe of the establishment actively promoted creedal language to defend both the Constitution and the justice of American military involvement.

In the chapter's final section, I examine how Woodrow Wilson's vision for US leadership on the World War I–era global stage drew heavily from creedal constitutional politics, despite his complicated relationship with the 1787 text as well as his opposition to Reconstruction and his continued commitment to white supremacy. Foreign policymakers had by then effectively married discourses of creedal constitutionalism and white supremacy in ways that cut against the former's racially transformative potential. The section therefore considers the exclusionary dimensions of this emerging constitutionally inflected foreign policy vision. It also emphasizes how Wilson's relationship to the Constitution evolved, such that he eventually became—alongside Lincoln—the other central white American articulator of creedal nationalism.

Thus a marginalized account of American identity at the end of the nineteenth century—whose earlier iteration was sustained mostly by a Black counter-public in the context of a post-Reconstruction white backlash—found new life through colonial administrators and white supremacist politicians, eventually emerging as the core national narrative of a dominant global power. Of course, it would take nearly half a century (and a second world war) for mainstream US politicians and commentators to widely accept US international dominance as an unquestioned good. But when they did, defending global primacy and defending creedal constitutionalism had already become deeply linked in the minds of policymakers across both parties—so much so that they appeared as almost one and the same commitment.

The Initial Plan for a European Imperial Model

In 1898, when pro-war politicians and commentators reveled in the victory over Spain and the extraction of expansive new territories, they imagined a future strikingly molded in the image of other empires. England's approach served as the preferred template for many pro-annexationists, who often embraced what the political theorist Duncan Bell has described as the idea of "Anglo-American" global leadership and of a shared British and American imperial destiny.[5]

In keeping with the rampant white supremacy of the times, such actors were deeply suspicious of the self-governing capacities of non-white peoples, and they assumed that forcibly annexed polities should be governed as Europeans then tended to rule the colonized world. Officials and policymakers displayed little interest either in observing constitutional limitations overseas or in promoting the US Constitution as a nation-building model for those in the Caribbean or the Pacific. Indeed, this disinterest became a common focus of critique by anti-annexationists. Opponents of territorial expansion worried about the implications of European-style empire for American republican identity, even as they also often repudiated the idea that non-white societies were capable of genuine self-government.

ROOSEVELT AND THE RESPONSE TO A
FRONTIERLESS WHITE AMERICA

In order to make sense of this initial approach, it is useful first to take a step back and explore the motivations of the era's key defenders of overseas conquest. Few people were as closely identified with the Spanish-Cuban-American War in the public's imagination as Teddy Roosevelt. Indeed, the conflict had helped to make Roosevelt famous. At the outbreak of hostilities, he resigned from his position at the Department of the Navy and led a small regiment of soldiers in Cuba known as the Rough Riders, ultimately earning the Medal of Honor for his actions. And in the months following the victory, he became one of the most vocal supporters of territorial annexation. Although no single figure can capture the totality of views supporting the war and annexation, Roosevelt's justifications for an American global turn provide compelling insight into the mindset of many Republican Party officials and advocates of colonization.

For Roosevelt, defending the war—not to mention empire-building more generally—was not simply a matter of adventurism. For starters, he viewed an increasingly globalized world as inevitably placing into conflict European "civilization" and non-European "barbarism."[6] Unless the US projected economic and military power abroad, its own domestic security and peace would over time become imperiled. Moreover, the Pacific—where, according to the Navy admiral and historian Alfred Thayer Mahan, "the westward course of the Empire again meets the East"—embodied a central flashpoint of this confrontation, requiring an aggressive American posture.[7] Thus, even as the Philippine-American War broke out, Roosevelt initially remained absolutely committed to American annexation and colonial rule. He viewed the islands as a critical access point to China and a strategic possession in the battle between East and West.[8]

But beyond geostrategic considerations, Roosevelt's defense of empire emerged precisely out of an account of what had long forged social cohesion in the United States: territorial expansion across the continent. Not only had westward expansion provided the engine for "Americanizing" distinct European immigrants; it also provided a shared project—one that galvanized collective life, fostered great acts of heroism, and inspired individuals to subordinate their own private interest. Not surprisingly to Roosevelt, a frontierless America, without new land for settlers, had become consumed by internal class conflict. Both business tycoons and their labor antagonists stoked destructive social forces, since each was more committed to fighting over profits than to promoting the greater good.

For Roosevelt, global assertiveness therefore provided a means to reboot settler solidarity and with it a sense of national purpose. Speaking on April 10, 1899, before the Hamilton Club in Chicago, Roosevelt highlighted how the new call to empire continued the country's frontier expansionism, which had done so much to shape the essence of Americanism. Although it might be impossible for Americans to settle other continents as they once did North America, he argued that Euro-Americans through colonial rule could still do "our fair share of the world's work" and "strive in good faith to play a great part in the world."[9] Such rule would spur material progress, relieve domestic class pressure by turning conflict outward, and ultimately provide Americans with the sense of national mission absent from collective life.

In this way, empire-building offered a return to origins, and a mechanism to ensure that white settlers of competing class backgrounds focused not on what drove them apart but instead on what brought them together as a people. It meant embracing once more the ethic of self-sacrifice and hard work that had pacified the continent and transformed hostile country into a free white republic. Describing the values entailed by the imperial imagination, Roosevelt declared: "I wish to preach, not the doctrine of ignoble ease, but the doctrine of the strenuous life, the life of toil and effort, of labor and strife; to preach that highest form of success which comes, not to the man who desires mere easy peace, but to the man who does not shrink from danger, from hardship, or from bitter toil, and who out of these wins the splendid ultimate triumph."[10] In essence, he mirrored his friend Frederick Jackson Turner's arguments, which similarly focused on the centrality of conquest to the collective experience and the inevitability of an American projection beyond the continent. Turner too had concluded that "unless this training has no effect upon a people, the American energy will continually demand a wider field for its exercise."[11]

For all these reasons, just as westward settlement had been a Euro-American project, overseas empire was also explicitly understood in racial terms. It amounted to conquest of non-white peoples, or, as Roosevelt also declared in 1899, "gradually bringing peace into the red wastes where the barbarian peoples of the world hold sway."[12] Such racial views—which were ubiquitous among colonial officials—highlighted how, in dealing with Spain's former colonies (Cuba, Puerto Rico, Guam, and the Philippines), the initial US administrative position mimicked the overarching approach of other European empires. Actual local self-determination was considered profoundly politically dangerous. And, in keeping with pervasive Jim Crow ideas of the era, Northern Republican administrators—not unlike Southern Democrats such as Woodrow Wilson—believed that the world was hierarchically arranged into distinct peoples at different levels of development, with Anglo-Europeans at the apex. They viewed Cubans and Puerto Ricans (especially those in the upper class of fully Spanish descent) as higher on the hierarchy than either Filipinos—who themselves were divided into numerous racial categories—or the Chamarro people of Guam.

But even with respect to Cuba and Puerto Rico, officials expressed deep worries about not only the multiracial nature of the societies, but also the degree to which they were marked by racial intermingling. This meant that, for Elihu Root—the Republican Secretary of War under

McKinley and the key framer of American policy—Cubans, Puerto Ricans, and Filipinos were "all as incapable of self-government as children." For Cuba's Governor-General Leonard Wood, full representative government on the island would mean the "establishment of another Haitian republic." Similarly, for Puerto Rico's Military Governor George Davis, the local population was but "a few steps removed from a primitive state of nature."[13]

COLONIAL SUPERVISION AND THE REJECTION OF CONSTITUTIONAL PROMOTION

Given these judgments, administrators in the immediate post-1898 period largely took for granted that Cubans, Puerto Ricans, and Filipinos all should be subject to long-term colonial supervision, albeit adapted to the particularities of each society and its place in the racial hierarchy. As for Guam, the historian Lanny Thompson notes that cultural-political interest in the particularities of the Indigenous community was virtually nonexistent. Military rule through the navy was simply imposed, "in spite of attempts by the local population to organize a legislature (1899) and regardless of their petition for civil government (1901)."[14]

Especially relevant for our purposes, American officials across all these territories initially systematically avoided a proselytizing approach to the federal Constitution. As we have seen, the Constitution may have been a national symbol. But for individuals like Roosevelt, Americanism was tightly joined to settler expansionism, whereas concern for or focus on the federal Constitution (or even constitutionalism generally) was a decidedly secondary matter. American administrators therefore did not consider it self-evident that the project of empire required either being legally bound by domestic constitutional principles or advancing those principles abroad.

Above all, white official judgments about race decisively constrained the utility and value of constitutional promotion. At home, debates may have swirled over the anti-democratic limitations of the 1787 text. But for US colonial administrators, spreading the federal Constitution would have involved spreading a democratic system of self-government. Such a framework was appropriate to the United States—and not its new colonies—precisely because of the home country's Euro-American identity. Administrators thus rejected any full-throated creedal rhetoric and also believed that any meaningful replication of the US constitutional order would be a recipe for disaster, due to underlying incompatibilities between responsible self-rule and the ethno-racial makeup of overseas communities.

Indeed, as chapter 2 discussed, it had increasingly become conventional wisdom, even within the mainstream Republican Party, that Reconstruction had failed *because* of widespread Black male suffrage—whatever the Fifteenth Amendment appeared to require. Not unsurprisingly, then, Root and other colonial officials believed that significant restrictions had to be imposed wherever voting had to be allowed, and that independence was out of the question for both the Philippines and Puerto Rico. In terms of institutional structure, as the historian Sam Erman notes, "Root initially looked to British colonial models for inspiration, but soon concluded that non-democratic versions of US state governments were a better fit."[15]

For Root, the smaller and less complicated example of Puerto Rico offered a test case for whatever governance structure might eventually be adapted for the even less culturally developed Philippines. In 1900, this took the form of Puerto Rico's Organic Act (also known as the Foraker Act), which imposed a presidentially appointed governor and an eleven-member executive council that served as the upper legislative house. The only space for Puerto Rican representative voice was in electing a nonvoting Resident Commissioner to Congress and through a thirty-five-member lower house, which held strictly limited legislative power. The lower house depended on the eleven-member executive council to pass bills, and the US Congress could annul any law that did make it through both chambers.[16]

The Cuban experience offers even more insight about the initial US disinterest in grounding its international power in the promotion of either meaningful democratic self-government or a distinctly American constitutional model. And this disinterest is especially noteworthy for two reasons. First, providing Cuba with independence from Spain had been a central domestic justification for the war effort. And second, educated and wealthy Cubans of Spanish descent tended to venerate the US Constitution as a foundational example of a local and settler self-government in the New World.

On the centennial of the 1787 framing, José Martí, the Cuban author, journalist, and independence hero, famously extolled the document as near perfect, barring only the vexed issue of slavery. Where earlier constitutions were simply "artificial imitations from the Greek leagues," the 1787 document was the first to show "that government takes roots in a nation only if they are born in the nation itself."[17] If the centennial at home had hinted at a text that would become increasingly fraught politically, given the long shadow of the Civil War and emerging industrial conflict, such possibilities were not apparent among educated voices in Havana. And in fact, when delegates to the Cuban Constitutional Assembly met in late 1900 to write their new text, they consciously modeled their document on the 1787 document—complete with three branches of government and names drawn from the American example: a President, a bicameral legislature with a Senate and a House of Representatives, and a relatively independent judiciary. Although this project clearly operated under the shadow of American occupation, it progressed without explicit imposition from Washington and at least partly exhibited genuine reverence for the US federal document.

American colonial officials, however, did not consider the emulation cause for celebration. Those like Root and Governor-General Wood had pressed for suffrage restrictions in elections for local municipal office and for the Constitutional Convention. Even with these restrictions, US officials expressed frustration that middle-class and educated Cubans had voted into power individuals Wood described as "political agitators" rather than conservative planter elite.[18] In truth, such delegates were hardly radicals (as highlighted by their constitutional politics), but their general commitment to universal manhood suffrage made them threatening to Washington—despite their class status and European Spanish background. This commitment prevailed at the Cuban Constitutional Convention, nearly unanimously, with conservative opponents largely absenting themselves from the final vote tally given its certain victory.[19]

For Root and Wood, constitutionalizing the franchise undermined American dominance over the island and potentially handed over political control to ethno-racial groups considered "unfit" for self-rule. Thus, for US officials, the problem with the drafters of the Cuban Constitution—for all the ways in which they imitated US constitutional structure—lay in their split from the post-Reconstruction white American conventional wisdom on perhaps *the* critical point: they had backed the enfranchisement of Afro-Cubans. In doing so, they repudiated the racial assessments about hierarchy and readiness for self-rule that shaped prevailing opinion even among Northern Republican policymakers.[20]

This divergence overrode all the continuities between the Cuban and US constitutional vision. It is why Wood likened Afro-Cuban voting to the creation of a new Haiti. As a successful slave revolt, Haiti may have symbolized Black liberation to African Americans. But to white Republican officials, Haiti provided a dangerous racial precedent for a world turned upside down.[21] However much the Cuban delegates embraced Madison and the framers, on a central issue for colonial administrators—the political wisdom of multiracial democracy—those delegates broke ranks with pervasive Euro-American norms.

Indeed, in part due to anxieties over the potential implications of Afro-Cuban enfranchisement, colonial officials required Cuban delegates to accept the Platt Amendment as a condition of the US relinquishing formal sovereignty and withdrawing its troops. Among other features, the amendment—which the Assembly had little choice but to incorporate into the constitution—placed checks on Cuban foreign policy and commercial rights, required the country to lease land to the US military (eventually the Guantanamo Bay Naval Station), and gave the United States a permanent right to intervene in Cuban internal affairs whenever it deemed necessary.[22] In other words, American officials hardly viewed the comprehensive replication by Cuban delegates of US constitutional and representative practices as a stabilizing force. Rather, they understood it—especially when combined with universal manhood suffrage—as a threat to growing American imperium and presumptions about white supremacy.

Ultimately, Root's vision for Cuba did not include the spread of domestic American institutions, especially if combined with the uprooting of the established racial order. Instead, the secretary of war sought local practices compatible with permanent American supervision and notions of hierarchy. In particular, he hoped for a form of colonial management in the same spirit—if not necessarily the exact same form—as the British in Egypt, which he characterized as allowing "England to retire and still maintain her moral control."[23]

All this highlights how colonial administrators—in Cuba and Puerto Rico, not to mention the Philippines and Guam—presented US power as a fairly conventional extension of the European imperial project. For Root, Wood, Roosevelt, and others, the project of empire may have had elements of racial instruction and betterment. But they considered the "barbaric" or "immature" nature of non-European and racially diverse communities as a main source of international disorder, thus requiring indefinite and long-term white American rule as a precondition of global stability and peace. Empire, therefore, became a project of explicit Euro-American domination, often in keeping with the idea of England and the United States as specifically linked in a common global colonial enterprise. Such racial domination would protect civilization from potential threat, and also ensure that those lessons in "uplift" would actually take hold in the non-white world.

EXCLUSION AND THE "CONSTITUTIONAL FIDELITY" ARGUMENT AGAINST EMPIRE

The specter haunting all these conversations about American imperium was the Philippines. Overwhelmingly, both supporters and opponents of Philippine annexation assumed the essential whiteness of American ethno-racial identity. Thus, all sides had to grapple with the question of whether the Philippines' vastness and racial composition would destabilize the US demographic and cultural makeup.

For opponents, the Philippines' sheer size raised the prospect of fundamentally transforming the nature of the American settler project. They worried that only military government and near monarchical power could possibly maintain control over such extensive territory. And they wondered what it would mean demographically for a Euro-American polity to rule over such a populous society in which actual white settlement and racial displacement were a non-starter.

These anti-annexationist arguments tease out two key features of the legal-political debate at the time—features that make only more surprising how creedal constitutionalism emerged as a central discourse of American global power. First, the initial principal voices for constitutional fidelity were *opponents* of overseas territorial expansion. And while they rallied to the Constitution out of concerns that expansion would undermine legal constraints, they did so on decidedly *anti*-creedal grounds. Especially within the Democratic Party, their worry had less to do with the treatment of Filipinos and much more to do with how expansive powers abroad might be applied against free settler citizens domestically. As such, opponents invoked the Constitution *both* to defend the essential whiteness of the United States and to venerate the text's perceived checks on federal authority. And second, this further reiterates how the original arguments for international expansion appeared interested *neither* in the creed nor in the Constitution.

Yet Republican Party officials slowly began to shift, reclaiming creed and Constitution in response both to anti-annexationist opponents at home and to Filipino independence fighters abroad. And their eventual reclamation attended, in important ways, to arguments that circulated in Euro-American society against colonizing the Philippines.

Again, white opponents of all political stripes overwhelmingly focused on the implications of overseas expansion for internal politics. In particular, they invoked a classic republican suspicion: that entanglement in European imperial rivalries, by promoting large standing armies and executive centralization, abetted the rise at home of military despotism. This worry went all the way back to the founding, when men like Virginia Congressman John Randolph described professional militaries as "mercenaries" and "ragamuffins."[24] Even Alexander Hamilton himself argued that a key way to escape domestic tyranny was by creating social conditions that avoided the need for "extensive military establishments."[25]

For the Kansas Populist Jerry Simpson—according to one scholar, "the unofficial voice of the party in the House"[26]—the requirements of pursuing and maintaining an overseas empire created military conditions ripe for the domestic reduction of basic liberties. In the context of the Spanish-Cuban-American War, Simpson opposed new appropriations bills that would increase the army from 25,000 to over 100,000, asserting that "along with a scheme for colonial empire," pro-war politicians in Washington sought nothing less than "to place on the throne in this country William McKinley, President of the United States, Emperor of the West Indian Islands and of the Philippines, and then get a standing army to enforce the power of this new empire."[27] For this reason, opponents saw the willingness of annexationists to deny constitutional protections to new colonial dependencies as above all a sign of a creeping monarchism at home. As Justice John Marshall Harlan famously wrote in his dissent to 1901's *Downes v. Bidwell* ruling, in which the Supreme Court upheld the annexationist view and declared that Congress could establish differential legal regimes in overseas possessions, "monarchical and despotic governments, unrestrained by written constitutions, may do with newly acquired territories what this Government may not do consistent with our fundamental law."[28]

In this way, critics of overseas expansion framed McKinley and others as trampling on constitutional principles. This is evident not only in Harlan's dissenting language in *Downes*; it also permeated Democratic Party opposition arguments more generally. In William Jennings Bryan's speech accepting the Democratic nomination for president in 1900, he drove home the charge that McKinley and his colonial administrators pursued policies that would imperil constitutional government and basic liberties. Bryan declared, "there is no place in our system of government for the deposit of arbitrary and irresponsible power. . . .

That the leaders of a great party should claim for any President or Congress the right to treat millions of people as mere 'possessions' and deal with them unrestrained by the Constitution or the Bill of Rights . . . shows how far we have already departed from the ancient landmarks."[29]

In fact, the legal historian Gerard Magliocca details how anti-annexationist rhetoric was central in popularizing the very use of the phrase "Bill of Rights" to describe the first ten amendments.[30] Before Reconstruction, the amendments together were rarely referred to as a bill of rights.[31] The dominant view conceived of them as itemized constraints on federal power vis-à-vis the states, responsive to Anti-Federalist worries at the founding that the new governing structure took too much authority away from local decision-makers. It was only during Reconstruction that the idea of the amendments as constituting an individual rights charter began making political headway, with those like Ohio Republican Congressman John Bingham leading the charge—on one occasion invoking the phrase more than a dozen times during a day of congressional debate.[32]

But with the collapse of Reconstruction, this energy abated. By the end of the century, the amendments' status in the popular imagination remained marginal, as underscored by the fact that the centennial of the Bill of Rights in 1891—like the fiftieth anniversary in 1841—was almost entirely ignored. In part, this lack of interest indicated the real disagreement among political and legal elites after the defeat of Reconstruction about whether the Constitution included something like a national bill of rights.[33] Should there be interlinked guarantees providing extensive protections to all Americans, even including Black people, as national citizens and regardless of where they were on US soil? Simply put, reviving such questions did not aid the broader white elite desire to turn the page on sectional conflicts.

But now, in the context of the Philippines, anti-annexationists like Bryan began strenuously invoking a "Bill of Rights" as under siege by those defending overseas expansion. This refashioning, by Democrats no less, of Reconstruction-era arguments had the rhetorical power of dramatizing McKinley's perceived lawlessness and monarchical instincts. But it also highlighted the extent to which, at the outset of these debates, no one—pro- or anti-annexation—thought of new colonies abroad as relevant to promoting the Constitution. As discussed above, colonial administrators like Root and Wood appeared to have little interest in doing so. And the popular description of the administration's view— that maintaining dependencies was legal—was that McKinley and his

Republican allies simply did not believe that the Constitution "followed the flag," extended comprehensively wherever the US claimed territory. As for *Downes* itself, Court observers famously saw the ruling—specifically allowing Congress to impose special import duties on goods from Puerto Rico despite the Constitution's requirement of uniform duties throughout the country[34]—as less about constitutional integrity or respect, and far more about the Court falling in line behind the White House and Congress. The journalist Finley Peter Dunne's "Mr. Dooley" column, written from the perspective of an Irish immigrant and barkeep, declared of *Downes* (issued after McKinley's reelection victory over Bryan), "no matter whether the constitution follows th' flag or not, th' Supreme Court follows th' illiction [*sic*] returns."[35]

While most opponents of annexation did not voice their concerns on creedal or remotely inclusive grounds, there were some outliers, especially among those who gravitated to Populist and Socialist circles. In February 1900, the Nebraskan William Neville, who eventually would be the last Populist in the House, famously took to the floor of Congress to denounce the war in the Philippines as an illegitimate extension abroad of the type of unjust racial subjugation that marked American domestic treatment of Black Americans: "Nations should have the same right among nations that men have among men. The right to life, liberty, and the pursuit of happiness is as dear to the black and brown man as to the white . . . as sacred to the weak as to the strong, and as applicable to nations as to individuals, and the nation which subverts such rights by force is not better governed than the man who takes the law into his own hands."[36]

According to Neville, what made American global imperialism immoral was not simply its implications for domestic republican institutions. Imperialism treated non-European communities—entitled to equal respect and independence—as merely instruments for the achievement of white economic and political ends. Underscoring this point, the *International Socialist Review* noted the irony of Teddy Roosevelt using July 4 in 1902 to declare presumptive victory in the Philippine-American War. On a day marking US independence from an imperial master, Roosevelt busily extolled "crushing . . . the resistance of Filipino fighters for independence," "in close imitation" of the old English crown.[37]

But rather than following Neville's or the *International Socialist Review*'s lead, mainstream white anti-annexationists tended to use anti-creedal and explicitly exclusionary language. These voices, particularly Democrats, attacked overseas expansion by arguing that the call to empire was if anything *too* inclusive. Territories like the Philippines should not be annexed, because Filipinos supposedly lacked the fundamental capacity to acculturate in any meaningful sense into American values. J. Neal Steere, a professor at the University of Michigan and a persistent and influential opponent of global expansion, wrote of the Philippines, "I think if we annex the islands, with our form of government and our institutions, we will have an endless amount of difficulties. The Indians themselves are in a state of pupilage, with no experience in self-government, and are in no state to become citizens, less so than were the Africans in the South after the civil war." For Steere, both Native Americans and formerly enslaved persons were outsider groups, presenting a permanent threat to the racial coherence and internal democracy of the American community. Similarly, the inherent inferiority of non-European foreign populations raised grave concerns about the new imperial politics. In his view, expansion simply meant the inevitable and destructive "mongrelization" of a fundamentally white republic.[38] Indeed, a circulating explanation of American atrocities during the occupation emphasized how the war had facilitated white "degener[acy]" and "emulation" of native "savagery"[39]—especially through racial intermingling—instead of Rooseveltian uplift.

In a sense, these anti-annexationists argued that the problem with global expansion was that overseas empire constituted a break from, rather than a continuation of, settler practices of colonization. Roosevelt and Turner may have emphasized the link between their call to empire and invocations of "Manifest Destiny,"[40] which during the 1840s justified the takeover of Texas, the Mexican-American War, and continental conquest more generally. But those like Roosevelt ignored the centrality of actual Euro-American settlement to the classic method of territorial growth. The earlier wave of continental empire remade North America as a white society, dispossessing Indian nations and steadily incorporating new land into the republic on grounds of equal statehood.[41] New possessions like Hawaii, given its smaller Indigenous population and significant white settler presence—already nearly 20 percent of the overall population in 1900[42]—could one day be incorporated on these classic expansionist terms.[43] But most overseas territories, especially vast ones far from the continental United States with large, diverse populations, simply would never be colonized in this way due to the impossibility of extensive Euro-American migration. To make matters worse, these colonies could serve as a permanent supply of inexpensive labor and goods, undercutting white American business and laborers.[44]

As Carman Randolph, a law professor at Columbia University, contended, these facts combined with the racial incompatibility of Filipinos and whites presented grave problems for annexation. Maintaining the Philippines as a colony entailed ruling over a racially distinct people under conditions in which the territory could not be transformed demographically—and therefore politically—into a truly white polity. As Randolph concluded, "the United States . . . ought not to annex a country evidently and to all appearances irredeemably unfit for statehood because of the character of its people and where climactic conditions forbid the hope that Americans will migrate to it in sufficient numbers to elevate its social conditions and ultimately justify its admission as a state."[45]

Above all, such arguments underscored the extent to which, for many anti-annexationists, opposition stemmed not from a rejection of empire per se. Rather, those like Steere and Randolph worried about how global expansion threatened American racial identity and thus cut against the long-standing settler approach. As Sam Erman has compellingly demonstrated, part of what intensified these worries was that the meaning of the Reconstruction Amendments had not yet been fully settled, even after domestic decisions like 1896's *Plessy v. Ferguson* made clear the Court's abandonment of real civic inclusion. Although white national elites had shaped amendment interpretation to fit with racial segregation and the rise of Jim Crow, did these provisions still necessitate "statehood" within the union for overseas territories, as well as "citizenship . . . and rights for nonwhite residents" in these possessions? According to none other than Alfred Thayer Mahan, those and related questions were the "constitutional lion in the path" of expansionist aims.[46]

Further highlighting the racist backdrop of the debate over annexation, the central Supreme Court decision anti-annexationists relied on to question the constitutionality of colonial dependencies was none other than Roger Taney's notorious 1857 majority opinion in *Dred Scott v. Sanford*, in which he wrote that African Americans, again whether enslaved or formally free, had no meaningful legal rights under the US Constitution.[47] Taney also declared in the opinion that Congress was bound by constitutional constraints and thus did not enjoy discretionary power in the territories. As discussed in chapter 2, this meant that Congress could not outlaw slavery, and instead had to preserve the property rights white settlers held in enslaved persons.

Using Taney's framework, anti-annexationists therefore suggested that the "Constitution always follows the flag" idea supported two important and interrelated elements: a critique of colonial dependencies, with their risk of expanding despotic power at home, and an aggressive defense of racial domination. The worry with giving Congress such unchecked authority was far less about the imperial violence visited upon non-white societies abroad. The concerns often were practically the inverse: Would it mean extending rights to those societies in ways that mimicked the perceived problems of Reconstruction and undermined the established constitutional methods of expansion? Taney's pre–Civil War fear had revolved around how greater congressional authority— such as by banning slavery—would uproot settler frameworks of territorial governance. Such settler frameworks emphasized equal statehood but only through local white demographic and political supremacy.[48]

Chief Justice Melville Fuller, a longtime Democratic Party figure and the 1860 presidential campaign manager for Stephen Douglas, made *Dred Scott* a centerpiece of his own dissent in *Downes*, quoting extensively and positively from Taney's opinion.[49] For modern readers, the idea that, decades after the Civil War, justices would still cite *Dred Scott* as good precedent may come as a shock. But the use of *Dred Scott* by Fuller, who also had been part of the "separate but equal" majority in the post-Reconstruction *Plessy v. Ferguson* decision (1896), underlines the extent to which anti-annexationism could reinforce rather than subvert entrenched racial hierarchies. It also speaks again to the very different politics of constitutional fidelity at the outset of the conflict in the Philippines. Those who most aggressively invoked constitutional limitations hardly projected creedal and inclusive values; instead, their invocation served a central aim of preserving the explicit whiteness of the republic.

Recovering Both the Creed and the Constitution for the Philippines

Even confronted by anti-annexationist arguments premised on race and xenophobia, defenders of global expansion over time came to stress the inclusive attributes of empire. And they did so in large part because of unavoidable colonial developments on the ground. Above all, administrators did not bargain for the sheer intensity of the Filipino fight for independence. The local push for self-determination—backed by the

force of arms—set off a chain reaction in Washington, in which officials haltingly acceded to realities beyond their control, in the process
reframing the American project overseas.

THE REPUBLICAN PARTY, JAMES LEROY, AND
MEDIATED SELF-RULE IN THE COLONIES

With the Philippine-American War's "formal" end in 1902, Congress
approved the Philippine Organic Act, which provided a statutory basis for the creation of a Philippine Assembly and offered some degree
of Filipino self-government. As in Puerto Rico, this Assembly would
form a lower legislative house, with the president-appointed Philippine
Commission serving as the upper house. The new Assembly would take
effect once a series of conditions were met: (1) Filipinos ended their independence fight; (2) the Commission completed and published a national census; and (3) local recognition of American sovereignty had
produced at least two continuous years of peace following the census
publication.[50]
    Crucially, this move to a highly mediated form of Filipino electoral
representation—not to mention more general practices of power-
sharing between American colonial administrators and local elites—
was effectively imposed on reticent American administrators against the
backdrop of raging war. Many such officials expressed skepticism that
the islands were suited even for the partial self-rule provided to both
Cuba and Puerto Rico. But it became necessary for the US to offer this
plan simply to get minimal buy-in from entrenched local families—and
therefore to maintain rudimentary colonial control. As James LeRoy, the
secretary to the Philippine Commission, noted, "we have not given to
the Filipinos political concessions wholly out of hand.... In part we gave
them because they made us give them, with their knife at our throat."[51]
    Once these policies were implemented, Republican Party leaders
needed to explain why concessions to Filipino constituencies did not
signal imperial failure and instead could be defended as more than just
political expediency. Republican officials thus found themselves in a
difficult political predicament. Challenges in the Philippines necessitated the accommodation of local calls for self-rule, however partial.
But at the same time, criticism of annexation and of bills like the 1902
Organic Act (passed entirely on party lines, with Democrats voting no)
became increasingly framed in highly exclusionary terms, focused on
the fundamental limitations of non-European peoples. Both develop-

ments made Philippine colonization seem out of step with classic settler notions of racial hierarchy, not to mention constitutional fidelity.

Moreover, Republican expansionists also found themselves forced to square two seemingly contradictory positions. They had to defend new policies of mediated self-rule and thus argue on behalf of Filipino political capacities. But they also needed to articulate why such capacities did not make American colonization an immoral act of political subjugation, as the Filipinos engaged in armed resistance maintained. In fact, on the ground, the Congress of the First Philippine Republic had drafted and ratified its own governing text in 1899, informally known as the Malolos Constitution after the city where it was written. Given that the Philippine Congress was largely composed of Spanish-educated elites, the country's "illustrado" class, the document largely followed previous Spanish models. It also emphasized popular sovereignty as the legitimate ground of government and focused institutionally on an empowered unicameral legislative branch.[52] If US officials accepted that Filipino people were politically capable, how could the violent subversion of such local exercises in constitution-making be defended?

Slowly, Republican proponents began to reclaim universal elements of the Civil War creedal narrative to justify their unfolding policy choices. The original explicit pitch of racial domination—the US finally joining their European cousins on the world stage—now morphed into a very different set of arguments. This transformation entailed a rediscovery of the Constitution and a growing focus on constitutional promotion as a central component of American interventionism. Eventually, this shift transformed the basic rationales that administrators would apply to make sense of American power writ large.

Perhaps the imperial figure that best captured the process by which Republicans began to solve these dilemmas was the aforementioned James LeRoy. As secretary to the Philippine Commission, LeRoy not only saw the inner workings of the new colonial state; he also became a close ally of and advisor to future president William Howard Taft, who at the time served as the Commission's chairman and then as the Philippines's first civilian Governor-General. Surveying conditions in the country, it was clear to LeRoy that empire conceived in traditional European terms—and war understood as a project of explicit racial domination—had indeed failed, as powerfully captured in Paul Kramer's seminal book on American colonization of the Philippines, *The Blood of Government* (2006).[53] For instance, Kramer explores how LeRoy viewed the military quagmire as due in large part to the deep-rooted belief, among white soldiers and their officers, that the US was engaged in a race war and that their presence in the Philippines would help spread white supremacy around the world.

Writing in 1907 about what had stoked the Philippine-American War, LeRoy contended rather polemically that what local inhabitants found even more upsetting than the "water cure"—the infamous form of torture Americans used against Filipinos—was the everyday practice of white racism by the military establishment: "We do not make enemies for ourselves half so much by the occasional administration of the water cure or other forms of torture and barbarity as by a studied attitude of contempt, an assumption of racial and individual superiority, and the constant disregard of their petty personal rights and of the little amenities that count so much with them." For LeRoy, white racism was little more than a domestic "provincialism" that, when extended to the Philippines, generated massive problems for the successful administration of the colony. As he concluded, invoking dismissively Rudyard Kipling's famous phrase "white man's burden," "we have carried into the Philippines a petty race prejudice, the offspring of past provincialism and the inheritance of slavery with its residue of unsettled problems; and we are betraying a tendency to swagger under the 'white man's burden,' sometimes in the garb of commercialism, sometimes in the raiment of science."[54]

In fact, whatever success might be claimed in the Philippine experiment, LeRoy asserted, resulted not from the initial American design of those like Root. Instead, the dictates of simply keeping imperial order had required administrators to relax racial exclusions and collaborate with powerful local constituencies. In his widely read 1905 book on the islands, *Philippine Life in Town and Country*, LeRoy wrote that "the very force of political necessity has compelled the recognition of the native families of prominence, including many that, by talent or audacity, have forced themselves into recognition alongside the old half-caste aristocracy." Yet, this experience ultimately highlighted to him the skill and capacity many Filipinos possessed in self-government and state-building. "Political expediency"—the need to quell unrest—may have initially moved colonial administrators toward a "freer social *regime*," given that Americans were "in general, stronger in prejudices based on race and color than were the Spaniards." But nonetheless the move had made pacification and American colonial authority possible.[55]

For US officials, the struggle in the Philippines thus underscored a series of unavoidable facts. It spoke to the sense that the United States had appeared on the global stage at a decidedly late moment—not only because it came after the European scrabble for colonies, but also because such empires were already fraying under the weight of non-European contestation. And the American experience, not to mention global events more generally, underlined that European societies could not pacify colonial subjects simply by imposing their own permanent political will.

Perhaps nothing brought home this latter point more directly than Japan's stunning military victory over Russia, explicitly dramatizing the stakes of the struggle between East and West that Mahan had foretold. For politicians in the United States and in Europe's imperial capitals, it augured the reversal of centuries of world history. And for those colonized, the outcome had a galvanizing effect. None other than Mohandas Gandhi (later known by the honorific Mahatma) saw Japanese success as proving that "the peoples of the East will never, never again submit to insult from insolent whites."[56] For the Black American scholar, critic, and activist W. E. B. Du Bois, the war similarly destroyed that "foolish modern magic of the world 'white'" and gave heart to colonized peoples everywhere that "colored revolt against white exploitation" was possible.[57]

It was for all these reasons that Roosevelt felt the need to send naval ships on a tour of Australia and New Zealand, as proof to both Europeans and non-Europeans that white polities would not simply recede in the face of growing non-white power.[58] Thus, although they drew quite different conclusions, white colonial administrators too increasingly saw the world in terms that echoed Du Bois's famous declaration about the new age: "The problem of the twentieth century is the problem of the color-line,—the relation of the darker to the lighter races of men in Asia and Africa, in America and the islands of the sea."[59]

All of this suggested to Republican officials another way of conceiving of American imperium. They may have retained the Rooseveltian geostrategic goal of imposing peace and, with it, assuring American security under conditions of increasing global interconnection. But if non-European peoples could not be permanently subordinated, perhaps their political rise need not be considered only a danger.

LeRoy's conclusions with respect to the Philippines specifically shed light on this approach. In his mind, Filipinos certainly were not ready for political independence and complete autonomy. Even in attacking American prejudice on the islands, he nonetheless asserted that he did not "seek to gloss over Filipino defects" and that "we should . . . be honest with the Filipino in the matter of laziness."[60] And, just as earlier administrators contended, LeRoy too believed that Filipinos remained in a stage of political and cultural "immaturity," so immediate independence would only cause anarchy and require the return of American soldiers. At the same time, the skill of some local elites also indicated that even Filipino groups with no European ancestry were not culturally foreclosed from full self-rule, and indeed could eventually take their place as true equals on the world stage.

As a consequence, the emerging idea suggested that Americans should not think of their mission in the overseas colonies as indefinite presence—let alone territorial conquest akin to past continental dispossession. Rather, the United States played the role of educator, tutoring less developed peoples in the institutions and customs of democratic self-government. And through the very success of this mission, such possessions would inevitably disappear—in the Philippines, but also in Puerto Rico and elsewhere. These colonial territories would be replaced by independent and self-determining polities equipped to maintain internal stability without American supervision at all. Foreign communities, including in the non-European world, chafed against the established imperial order and argued for their own self-rule. So LeRoy and others started to contend that the United States could serve as an instrument not for extending European rule, but rather for facilitating that path from "immature" polity to "mature" self-governing republic. And all of this would be in the name of promoting international peace.

THE LEGACY OF THE MONROE DOCTRINE

What would this governmental education in the name of global peace look like as a model of international relations? Instead of claiming territory, the United States would assert a persistent economic and military power abroad. It would open new markets for American domestic goods and intervene wherever chaos threatened the possibility of peace. Such global authority would not require extensive colonial dependencies and would be justified in the name of stability and global self-government. From the discourse of tutelage, it would also draw the notion that American supervision was central to the proper exercise of local self-rule, as the United States provided a benevolent hand steering weaker nations in peaceful and prosperous directions.

In many ways, this account of American global power further developed the long-standing Monroe Doctrine, introduced in 1823 by then president James Monroe during his seventh annual State of the Union Address to Congress.[61] Under the doctrine, any attempts by European states to colonize land or to develop spheres of influence in the Americas would be seen by the United States as acts of aggression justifying intervention.

This foreign policy approach sought to undermine two early checks on American authority. The first was the continuing commitment of European empires to sustain an economic and political monopoly over Latin America. The second consisted of efforts by local governments to close their doors to US business or to limit external supervision of their economies.

As the political theorist James Tully notes, this US defense of free trade presupposed a set of international rights and duties, which were hardly universally accepted. American leaders like Monroe presumed that all European states—including their settler siblings such as the US—enjoyed a cosmopolitan right of commerce with non-European societies. At the same time, non-European societies had a correlated duty of hospitality to open their doors to foreign companies and trade.[62] The point of this right and duty was not simply to expand markets for American products, but also to "civilize" non-European peoples by entrenching broadly common institutions of state and market in neighboring countries. As a result, the right to free trade went hand in hand with a right both to military intervention and to economic compensation if local governments violated the duty of hospitality and closed their doors to American companies.

In the Pacific region, the great nineteenth-century extension of this approach involved Commodore Matthew Perry's 1853 expedition to Japan, in which, by threat of arms, the naval officer compelled the Japanese government to open its ports and trade to US merchants.[63] And in the 1870s and 1880s, John Bingham's ambassadorship to Japan reinforced both sides of the old Monroe Doctrine. Bingham, drafter of the Fourteenth Amendment and early popularizer of the "Bill of Rights," pressed during his twelve years as ambassador for two key policies: First, American access to Japanese markets at low tariffs. And second, a dismantling of the prevailing system of unequal treaty arrangements, which allowed European governments to dictate internal economic policy to Japan. In this way, Bingham's approach presented the American vision—even if grounded in forced economic entry—as an alternative to even more patently domineering European practices.[64]

During much of the nineteenth century, such American accounts of economic expansionism stood side by side with the far more central picture of US empire as settler colonization. Yet, with the end of the frontier, the Monroe Doctrine gained greater purchase in the American imperial imagination. Efforts in Latin America or Japan thus became forerunners of the "open door" foreign policy, associated with Secretary of State John Hay's 1899 and 1900 notes on US relations with China. Then, especially in the context of the Philippine-American War, the profound difficulties involved with creating formal dependencies pushed decisively against alternatives built around additional European-style overseas possessions.

The result was a transition in imperial understanding that made past debates about Philippine and Puerto Rican annexation moot. In one sense, the original American project in such countries (not to mention Guam and other territories) became a historical artifact—at least if framed as a quest to colonize new polities. As an example of actual overseas expansion, the Spanish-Cuban-American War's aftermath became an outlier, a move toward direct European imitation that was ultimately abandoned. But in another sense, the experience in the Philippines and elsewhere served as a model for the future. To the extent that these projects entailed conceiving of American power as creating a stable world of market-oriented and self-governing republics, they set a template for developments to come.

Perhaps the greatest indication of this transition can be seen in how Roosevelt struggled to recast his own views about the US's role in the world. As early as 1901, in his speech to the Minnesota State Fair, he said of the American goal in the Philippines: "We are not trying to subjugate a people; we are trying to develop them and make them a law-abiding, industrious, and educated people, and we hope ultimately a self-governing people." In this context, he also called on the United States to "speak softly and carry a big stick" in global affairs.[65] Whereas earlier he had emphasized the centrality of conquest and domination, he now underlined the country's attempt to foster free and eventually independent republics with a firm guiding hand.

Similarly, in his State of the Union message three years later, Roosevelt defended interventionism, especially in the Western Hemisphere—of the type the Platt Amendment had written into the Cuban Constitution—while at the same time disavowing any desire for permanent expansion. He remarked, "it is not true that the United States feels any land hunger or entertains any projects as regards the other nations of the Western Hemisphere save such as are for their welfare. All this country desires is to see the neighboring countries stable, orderly and prosperous." American intervention was therefore solely a product of the need to ensure such order and to protect the United States from chaos abroad: "If ever country washed by the Caribbean Sea would show the progress in stable and just civilization . . . all question of interference by this Nation with their affairs would be at an end."[66]

Even Roosevelt eventually came to believe that the annexation of the Philippines was itself a folly. He privately remarked that the colony had become the American "heel of Achilles," one moreover that unnecessarily antagonized Japan in its own natural sphere of influence.[67] Thus, by the beginning of World War I, the same man who had engaged in racist saber-rattling following the Japanese victory over Russia had come to see the politics of formal empire-building in distant lands as counterproductive in light of global realities.

AN INCLUSIVE POLITICS OF AMERICAN EXPANSION

Still, as these views gained prominence, a significant question persisted: Where did the American right to intervene come from, in Cuba, the Philippines, or elsewhere? Why did the country have the privilege to shape the terms under which foreign peoples enjoyed their own self-determination? Indeed, LeRoy's own analysis begged this very question. And, ultimately, other Republican policymakers broke from elements of LeRoy's initial account to develop their answer.

Recall that LeRoy saw the turn to facilitating self-government as forced by facts on the ground, and also as inconsistent with deep-rooted and racialized notions of American identity and power. LeRoy's experience in the Philippines emphasized to him the disconnect between his own more inclusive vision of empire and the assumptions that most white Americans carried to the islands. He found that they not only "preach[ed] inequality" but also "more or less openly pit[ied] . . . the promulgators of the Declaration of Independence" for their soaring egalitarian language.[68]

This meant that, for LeRoy, American colonial administrators had to depart from racist national assumptions in spreading principles of equal liberty among non-white peoples. To underscore the point, LeRoy hoped that tutelage would not be a one-way street, and that contact with the rest of the world would "draw us into a field in which ultimately our prejudices may broaden out, and in which our provincialisms must disappear." Empire could thus be a tool through which Americans "learn to shed" their reflexive racism as "we mingle more with the men of the world and think less of our cherished isolation." Effectively, LeRoy suggested that the global project challenged a quintessentially white republic to conceive of itself in more inclusive terms. And, particularly given that US administrators had been pushed against their will toward freer political arrangements, in a real sense stability and self-rule emerged *in spite of*—and not because of—American values.[69]

But in explaining the right to intervene, Republican policymakers rejected LeRoy's assessment of long-standing American racism; instead, they began to focus on how to differentiate between American power and European imperialism. And they did so especially by adapting and updating settler arguments about what made the United States an exceptional nation. Previous generations had argued that the United States, unique within the family of European states, was marked by internal class equality. But rising inequality and labor strife made such arguments increasingly hard to sustain. So, against the backdrop of industrial conditions and non-European political assertiveness, proponents of global power started to deemphasize claims about both class exceptionalism and white solidarity.

Instead, Republican elites presented the country's history as unique among European siblings precisely because it aimed to fulfill universally applicable Enlightenment principles. In effect, they began to revive and repackage creedal anti-slavery narratives about national founding and purpose, perhaps not entirely surprising given their identity as the party of Lincoln. In a more noteworthy move, party figures also increasingly returned to the federal Constitution as concrete proof of the distinctiveness of the American project. All this happened despite the fact that constitution-promotion had been fairly marginal to initial colonial thinking about American rule—and indeed explicitly rejected as a model for non-European populations—with opponents of overseas expansion criticizing McKinley and the Republicans, albeit in a different register, for their lack of constitutional commitment.

One could well argue that the domestic context was critical to the willingness of white policymakers to reaffirm both creed and Constitution in the Philippines. Creedal universalism had long been deeply associated in the white American imagination with a racially transformative anti-slavery politics. But under conditions in which the basic challenge to racial hierarchy embodied by Reconstruction and the Reconstruction Amendments had been largely contained, it became far easier for establishment Republicans to revive anti-slavery creedalism without having to fear its most threatening implications. They could even depict anti-annexationist worries about the dangers of expansion to American racial identity as overblown. And above all, such policymakers could still view the most radical elements of the Reconstruction project as ill-judged and a negative model, while nonetheless defending both creed and Constitution as embodiments of a basic American spirit.[70]

At the same time, the rhetorical and legal attacks on Republican expansionists as lawless and anti-constitutionalist clearly played a major role in pressing defenders of empire to embrace the document in these renewed arguments. As early as the 1902 Philippine Organic Act, alongside mediated self-rule, Republicans included language in the law extending some of the first ten amendments to the colony, establishing an equal protection clause modeled on the Fourteenth Amendment and prohibiting slavery in line with the Thirteenth. Indeed, Republican papers like the *New York Times* referred to these provisions as "The 'Bill of Rights' for the Filipinos," consciously seeking to defang Democratic uses of the phrase and to refashion imperial expansion as itself an exercise in spreading, even to non-white peoples, the benefits of constitutionalism.[71] While this emerging discourse of empire among Republican officials did not consolidate overnight, within a decade—and against the backdrop of war and reversal in the Philippines—the basic elements became increasingly entrenched.

In many ways, David Jayne Hill, a Republican Party stalwart, ambassador to Germany, president of Rochester University, and the highly influential author of *Americanism: What It Is* (1916), offered the most systematic account of this relationship between American imperium and a revived creedal politics—with the Constitution at the center. For Hill, what most distinguished the American character from Old Europe was the document and the political tradition it embodied. Whereas European communities resulted from feudalism as well as political and religious absolutism—and thus were predisposed to treat foreign populations instrumentally—the Constitution underscored how the American experiment had, from its genesis, attempted to make real the universal Enlightenment right of self-determination. Contrasting European monarchical despotism with the American commitment to self-government, Hill declared that the "original and distinctive contribution of the American mind to political theory" was the focus on eliminating "forever the recurrence of absolutism in *every* form, whether official or popular, whether of dominant individuals or of popular majorities."[72]

Furthermore, the reason the country's founders had so committed themselves to this constitutional principle—to *"the restrictions of the fundamental law"*[73]—was that they had been raised in a political community culturally attuned to practices of self-rule and principles of liberty. Thus, the distinctive cultural attributes of the North American colonies had allowed both creedal and constitutional values to flourish in the first place. According to Hill, the earliest settlers left monarchical England because of a "protest against mere power," and indeed the first truly American charter of liberty was not the Constitution but the Mayflower Compact of November 11, 1620. Long before England's 1647 "Agreement of the People" or the later writings of John Locke and Jean-Jacques Rousseau, initial settlers—"a company of plain men, sailing over wintry seas to an unknown land with the purpose of escaping the too heavy hand of an absolute government"—forged "the beginning of real self-government." Therefore, the Constitution, a century and a half later, was just the culmination of a specifically American cultural commitment to the "voluntary renunciation of arbitrary power."[74]

Just as important for Hill, if constitutional order and republican self-rule were the product of a settler political-cultural heritage, their enjoyment both at home and abroad could not be reduced purely to racial criteria. In fact, Hill argued that since the federal Constitution gave concrete substance to the universal aspiration that "absolutism in every form should be abolished,"[75] ultimately "Americanism" was a matter of one's political values rather than of ethnicity: "It cannot be maintained that Americanism . . . is a matter of race. Our country from the beginning has been populated by people of widely different ethnic origins. Some of their qualities are perpetuated with practically little effacement, others are obscured by the syncretism of races; but there is no definable ethnic type that is exclusively entitled to be called American."[76] Instead of merely an Anglo-European settler polity, no different than Australia or South Africa, the Constitution offered living proof that Americans had produced a phenomenon unique in global history: they had erected, out of divergent racial communities, a single, unified, and powerful nation. In effect, Hill mapped out nothing less than an early-twentieth-century variant of what scholars like Nikhil Pal Singh have called "American universalism"—the idea, with anti-slavery roots, that the United States is exceptional as the first nation truly grounded in equal liberty for all.[77]

This appealing idea was then taken up as the reason why an expanded American role abroad served the basic interests of foreign populations. According to Hill, European powers sought to divide the world based on the principle of "imperialism" and thus treated other communities as little more than material spoils. But precisely because American "constitutional" ideals, embodied in the 1787 text, were "antithetical to Imperialism, whose watchword is unlimited power,"[78] only the United States could offer the world, including non-white societies, a counterbalance to European hegemony. The constitutional principle meant that American authority was, in opposition to empire, centrally about creating the conditions for peaceful self-government in foreign societies.[79]

THE GLOBAL EXPORT OF CONSTITUTION-WRITING

Another reason those like David Jayne Hill turned so fully to constitutionalism as the language of US power clearly lay in its resonances with the frontier experience—an experience that remained ever present for white decision-makers across the political spectrum. It may have been evident to all that Euro-Americans could not simply settle foreign continents as they had the West. But that did not mean that the settler process—by which new territory had been transformed into presumptively "free republics" in the United States—had no relevance abroad.

Recall that writing state constitutions on the frontier had long been the final stage of reconstituting—demographically and politically—Native territory into a white American polity, admissible as a "sister state" in the union. Even if the Philippines could not be made demographically white, Republican officials contended that the polity could nonetheless be "Americanized" so that its legal, political, and economic order mimicked the basic American principles forged during frontier expansion and colonial settlement. And so it was only natural that constitution-writing became the critical last stage of reconstructing a less "mature" and non-white society, such as the Philippines, on US institutional and cultural terms. If nation-building effectively became a central function of American overseas power, such efforts also became inherently bound up with the writing of new constitutions.

While US officials drew inspiration and ideological sustenance from the American past, they diverged from vital aspects of settler-state constitutionalism in their plans for overseas territories. Such internal state constitutional writing efforts were largely decentralized, emphasizing the political autonomy of local white populations, and thus generated constitutional systems that often repudiated the 1787 federal text's model of governance and theory of institutional design. But for Hill and other Republican thinkers, the perceived lack of maturity within foreign societies meant that they could not be counted on to exercise the same basic autonomy. Moreover, colonial officials and supportive commentators overwhelmingly came from socioeconomic and political circles that were deeply suspicious of the era's domestic class-based critique of the Constitution, and of the ongoing US internal climate of "Constitution tinkering."

The result was threefold. First, it meant an overseas focus on top-down colonial supervision, rather than actual local control, in projects of foreign nation-building and constitution-writing. Hence, it was a non-starter to think of locally determined efforts, like the Malolos Constitution, as worthy of systematic implementation. Second, all of this suggested a dramatic narrowing in the relevant constitutional imagination promoted (or allowed) by American officials abroad. Thus the substance of constitutional politics was limited largely to the perceived terms of an idealized 1787 document—with Progressive experimentation in the United States or Filipino ideas of unicameral legislative arrangements both excluded.

Third, Republican officials, who were overwhelmingly pro-business actors, projected abroad the same conservative intertwining of aggressive market capitalism and federal constitutional deification that simultaneously faced profound opposition at home. Following tendencies going back to the Monroe Doctrine, colonial policymakers read Filipino—and more generally non-European—refusal of market access on American terms as "disorder" and as a threat to commercial peace. They also saw nation-building as significantly involved with establishing the type of legal-political arrangements protective of property rights and thus supportive of pro-business capitalist arrangements. At home, multiple groups were decisively contesting just this intertwining of hierarchical corporate power with constitutional checks and balances. But on the international stage, officials nonetheless joined together an aggressive promotion of both market capitalism and its perceived constitutional correlates—all bound to veneration for the 1787 text.

One clear consequence was that policymakers, through the language of constitutionalism, essentially laundered the imperial continuities between European and American economic dispossession and state violence. LeRoy had hoped that American engagement in the Philippines would, over time, distance the US from both its racially exclusionary inheritance and its extractive and brutal rivals. But Hill could now look back and describe American conduct on the islands as *proof* of American magnanimity and commitment to global democracy. Glossing over the actual history of race war and continued colonial suppression, Hill declared, "we have taken in tutelage a population in its political child-hood and conscientiously striven to lay the foundations for its future self-government." Although it may have required military imposition, Hill could nonetheless maintain that at stake in the Philippines was not imperial rule but the entrenchment of Filipino self-determination.[80]

Black and Indigenous Debates about American Power and Self-Determination

Still, this universalistic defense of American power marked an unde-niable move away from the most extreme racial judgments of the Jim Crow period. It inverted precisely why many white opponents of impe-rial annexation were wary of overseas possessions. Anti-annexationist had worried that American institutions would be compromised in a set-ting in which the country ruled over a broad array of non-white societ-ies assumed to be "unfit" for constitutional government. Now, expan-sionists declared the spread of such government to be the very purpose of American authority.

In fact, to the extent that similar universalistic arguments previously circulated in public debate they were often voiced by Black political figures—an indicator of their more marginal earlier status in white for-eign policy-making circles. Yet a closer interrogation of internal Black and Indigenous discussions about self-determination and rising Amer-ican power further highlights problems with this more inclusive narra-tive. These discussions speak directly to the unavoidable continuities between new US and Old European paradigms.

THE BLACK EXPANSIONIST IDEA OF EQUAL STATEHOOD FOR ALL PEOPLES

Hill's American universalism—linking global authority to the pro-motion of equal liberty—mirrored none other than Frederick Doug-lass's earlier vision of a "composite" nation and of the American role in the world. In 1871, President Ulysses Grant had appointed Frederick Douglass to the Commission of Inquiry for the annexation of Santo Domingo (the Dominican Republic). The project for annexation ulti-mately collapsed under the weight of classic settler concerns about de-mographics and racial incompatibility—arguments that came to the fore yet again during debates about the Philippines.[81]

In response to such claims about the Dominican Republic, Douglass had vociferously defended annexation, viewing American territorial growth as a mechanism for proving that all groups—regardless of color—were capable of republican citizenship. In presenting this argument, Douglass articulated how the domestic creedal story connected to a global one, offering his own sketch of American universalism: with slavery vanquished, the meaning of expansionism had fundamentally changed. In the post–Civil War period, territorial growth thus embodied above all the spread of freedom to peoples everywhere. "Since liberty and equality have become the law of our land," he wrote in his 1882 autobiography, "I am for extending our dominion whenever and wherever such extension can" be pursued "honorably."[82]

For Douglass in this context, the promise of constitutional redemption and universal equality was not just the true purpose of American history, but in a profound way the American mission to the world. In fulfilling the country's destiny, Americans would act in a way consistent with the interests of foreign peoples and, in the process, remake the international community in their own country's liberated image. In words not unlike those of President John F. Kennedy in his 1961 inaugural address, Douglass proclaimed: "It may, indeed, be important to know what Santo Domingo can do for us, but it is vastly more important to know what we can do for Santo Domingo."[83]

Douglass died a few years before the wars with Spain and the Philippines. But during the post-1898 debates over Philippine annexation, some Black commentators, especially within middle-class and educated circles, articulated a vision of expansion in ways that drew directly from his past arguments. Their willingness to accommodate the expansionist times partly resulted from partisan affiliations, given that Republicans—for many African Americans still the party of Reconstruction—were the face of overseas colonization and Democrats—the home of the Southern white oligarchy—its key domestic skeptics. Further buttressing this Black openness to empire was how Democratic opponents stoked fears about what a massive increase in new non-white subjects would mean for the country's presumptive whiteness. By contrast, these African American commentators viewed the same demographic implications as a potential lever for forcing whites finally to accept Douglass's dream of a universally inclusive United States.

None other than W. E. B. Du Bois's own initial and conflicted response to the American project in the Philippines captured these accommodationist impulses. In December 1899, Du Bois used his presidential address before the American Negro Academy to engage with the thorniness of US overseas colonization.[84] He no doubt made clear his distaste for conquest. He placed white American behavior toward Filipinos in a long line of European violence going "[b]ack to 1500," "when the hatred and dislike of foreigners made war a holy pastime, and patriotism meant the murder of those who did not speak your language."[85] Over the ensuing decade, one marked by ongoing brutality and American military reversals, Du Bois's condemnation would only intensify.[86]

But at least at the outset of annexation, that sentiment operated alongside claims that American expansion could nonetheless foster greater civic inclusion. If white national elites were committed to expansionism no matter what, overseas efforts could still serve positive ends. In the same 1899 speech, Du Bois remarked on how the Spanish defeat meant "that the colored population of our land is . . . about to be doubled," something that amounted to "the greatest event" for both the Black community and the nation "since the Civil War." Even with the Filipino independence fight against the US raging, Du Bois was willing to see in the country's "new imperial policy" a potential for the United States truly to become the first universal nation.

To make this possible, he called on African Americans to engage with Filipinos, Puerto Ricans, and other new colonial subjects in two basic ways. First, Blacks needed to approach these groups with an "attitude of deepest sympathy and strongest alliance"—to defend their interests in domestic politics against the prejudices of white racism. But at the same time, African Americans also had to engage in the hard work of infusing overseas projects with inclusive commitments. This meant not only contesting white racism, but also tutoring foreign peoples in the culture and practices of American institutions. Du Bois argued, "we must stand ready to guard and guide them with our vote and our earnings. Negro and Filipino, Indian and Porto Rican, Cuban and Hawaiian, all must stand united under the stars and stripes for an America that knows no color line in the freedom of its opportunities."[87]

At least in this moment, Du Bois, like Douglass before him, connected American imperium to broad civic and material uplift. He too seemed to imagine new territories, no matter how far-flung, as being incorporated not as colonial dependencies but on terms of absolute formal equality—what Douglass referred to as "our sisterhood of States."[88] If white anti-annexationists often depicted with horror the prospect of a Philippine state within the US, such Black voices suggested that eventual statehood for all territories—just as in the past—remained an essential way of ensuring that expansion actually fulfilled redemptive and egalitarian aspirations. In a sense, this more accommodationist perspective within Black politics simply extended the classic terms of settler territorial incorporation to their logical conclusion—complete with locally directed constitution-writing projects. If empire was a "fait accompli,"[89] they aimed to free this project of explicit white supremacy. They attempted to combine settler-imperial legal-political processes with a belief that the foundation of American global power would be universal self-government for all, regardless of race.

NATIVE POLITICS AND THE SETTLER
CONSTITUTIONAL MODEL

In important ways, both Douglass and Du Bois indicated a line of argument that some Native Americans themselves began pursuing with respect to federal territory on the North American continent. These same years saw a statehood push by the so-called Five "Civilized Tribes"—the Cherokee, Muscogee (Creek), Chickasaw, Choctaw, and Seminole Nations—who had been forcibly removed from their land during Andrew Jackson's Trail of Tears. Thousands had died along the way, with Native peoples relocated west of the Mississippi River to what the federal government called "Indian Territory," today part of Oklahoma.

In 1905, the Five Tribes held a constitutional convention to establish the US State of Sequoyah, named after the person central to the development of the Cherokee writing system, and petitioned Congress for admission. Just as had long been the practice among white settlers on the frontier, the Five Tribes—after drafting a proposed constitution—held a referendum in Indian Territory with over 75 percent of eligible voters participating and support for the constitution overwhelming, by a margin of 59,279 votes to 9,073.[90]

Moreover, the proposed constitution underscored the degree to which the Indigenous drafters were willing to embrace an account of political incorporation premised on replicating, within Native American society, the US Constitution's legal-political order. The framers of the Sequoyah Constitution not only accepted the legitimacy of American expansion, if organized through statehood for all—including for Native peoples—but also modeled their constitution directly on the 1787 text. The Sequoyah document mimicked the federal government, complete with a House of Representatives, a Senate, a Supreme Court, and Governor akin to the US president. Its preamble repeated exact language from the 1787 preamble and declared its "faith in the Constitution of . . . the United States." Indeed, the very first article was a "Bill of Rights" built around the first ten amendments to the federal Constitution.[91]

Republican politicians and white national administrators rejected the idea of Sequoyah statehood, like Philippine statehood, in large part due to their own persistent uncertainties about the possibility of full non-European cultural assimilation into the United States.[92] This despite the fact that, in the Sequoyah case, Indigenous actors acceded to white racial sentiments as a way of highlighting their own cultural similarities. The Sequoyah Constitution, for instance, included a provision for segregated schooling, so as to show respect for Jim Crow hierarchies and bind together whiteness and Indigeneity.[93] And in the late eighteenth and early nineteenth centuries, the same Five Tribes had pursued Black enslavement as part of similar efforts to signal to white settlers elevated Indigenous political standing.[94] In this way, the Sequoyah Constitution embodied one moment in a fraught settler-Indigenous dynamic in which some Indigenous elites sought to gain political respect through adaptation to oppressive racial norms.

But even if white Republican officials rejected these statehood claims and held firm to their own distinct judgments about racial hierarchy, the geopolitical tide had nonetheless shifted. After a decade in the Philippines, many of these same officials had effectively come to embrace a very similar creedal and constitutional vision of American imperium as that offered earlier by Douglass. Hill's basic outline of how American universalism and constitutional commitment fit together clearly resonated with a strain of Black and, to a lesser extent, even Native American politics. Presumed ethno-racial differences between groups may have made statehood impracticable for white officials. Yet the US's guiding purpose increasingly revolved around the promotion of constitutional democracy, framed as a universal goal that could be enjoyed by all peoples everywhere. Through this understanding, American expansion—on the continent and overseas—entailed nothing less than the proliferation globally of the institutions and principles of republican self-government.

ERASURE IN AN INCLUSIVE EMPIRE

For all its potential inclusiveness, from the very beginning this linkage of both creed and Constitution to American expansionism—even as

articulated by Black elites—reaffirmed the racial politics of settler supremacy that defined the era. This reality was implicit in competing
Black anti-imperial arguments against territorial absorption, even on
terms of equal statehood for all. And it was certainly present in contemporaneous Indigenous efforts at full independence.

For many Native peoples, the Sequoyah Constitution was at best a
defensive maneuver, in response to the systematic expropriation of Native land and the destruction of their status as separate and independent polities. Indeed, Native Americans in Indian Territory only converged around statehood and constitution-writing after two significant
developments: Congress's passage of the 1898 Curtis Act and the defeat
of the Snake movement. The Curtis Act sought to forcibly assimilate
members of the Five Tribes into a single framework of individual American citizenship, by eliminating tribal courts and governments in Indian Territory and by imposing federal jurisdiction on all Native American subjects. In response, the Muscogee leader Chitto Harjo, called by
white politicians "Crazy Snake," led a mass movement of 5,000 strong
to reassert Muscogee independence under treaties the US government
had persistently violated. Federal troops responded with violent suppression, including the arrest of Harjo and scores of supporters.[95]

It was only then, after independence had effectively been removed
from the table, that Indigenous groups turned toward the statehood
option. Even at that point, many Native peoples understood themselves
to be voting for a plan for self-determination and survival as a separate
political community, albeit under the terms left available by US absorption. Indeed, this was how the Sequoyah drafters defended the constitution to their communities, even though the actual document hardly
incorporated such Indigenous aspirations. As the legal scholar Robert
Tsai notes, the text "preserved no distinctly native organizations, institutions, or customs,"[96] and instead simply acceded to an individualized
framework for Native peoples that treated the territory and its inhabitants as politically identical to any other continental geographic space.

Thus, the Sequoyah Constitution diverged substantially from a long
history of Native American constitutionalism, going all the way back to
the Haudenosaunee (Iroquois) Confederacy, formed hundreds of years
earlier. These models often combined representative institutions with
plurinational arrangements that preserved the political autonomy and
Native organizations of the different Indigenous communities. Indeed,
a comparable vision had marked both the 1827 Cherokee Constitution,

with its creative synthesis of American and Indigenous structures, and the proposed 1870 Okmulgee Constitution, the most sustained previous effort at Indigenous constitutionalism and potential statehood in the Indian Territory. The latter ultimately failed to garner sufficient Native support at the polls due to concerns over tribal representation in its legislature. Unlike the Sequoyah text, however, the Okmulgee document conceived of a "confederacy" of Indigenous peoples, aimed at safeguarding "each of the nations" as a separate polity.[97]

By contrast, Sequoyah had no specific group rights or meaningful account of plurinationalism, even if the Native public on the ground conceived of the state in these terms. The reason for this erasure was that Sequoyah's drafters had to navigate the fact that white settlers in massive numbers had encroached even on Indian Territory, and so their bid required support from the local white population. Even more critically, leaders worried that any genuine effort to incorporate systematic protections for Native self-determination and autonomy would make Sequoyah a non-starter in Washington. Of course, it was a non-starter anyway, even with its replication of anti-Black settler judgments and professed devotion to and imitation of the 1787 Constitution.

Ultimately, the Sequoyah effort highlights how even the most radically egalitarian defenses of territorial annexation and of the US as a "composite" nation, offered by those like Douglass, fundamentally obscured the status of Native peoples as independent polities. To the extent that some within the Republican party, so-called Indian reformers, included space for a continuing Native presence inside the American state, it was on the same grounds of civic inclusion as that offered to previously enslaved persons or to European migrants. Such reformers argued that Native Americans should be given formal US citizenship, but on the condition that they abandon their own separate collective identity as autonomous political communities and thus incorporate themselves, as individuals, into American society. But, as with the Curtis Act, not to mention the earlier 1887 Dawes Act—which broke Indigenous land up into individualized parcels, ultimately leading to the expropriation of 60 million acres of Native territory—this was precisely the vision that troubled the vast majority of Native peoples.[98]

Neither Douglass nor Du Bois (at the time), let alone white reformers, had sufficient appreciation for the different structural position of Blacks and Native Americans in collective life. African Americans found themselves a coerced labor supply, while Indigenous nations constituted competing and distinct polities on the same territorial land mass.[99] This meant that any benefits that civic membership offered to previously enslaved persons ultimately embodied a form of brutal political erasure for expropriated nations.[100] And even when some Native peoples were willing to accept civic membership—as with the statehood bid—as the condition for warding off further expropriation and cultural destruction, they understood this as an accommodation to political realities.

In a sense, most anti-slavery Republicans, white and Black, were well aware of the sleight of hand involved in linking new European migrants and previously enslaved persons as similarly situated in the body politic. For rhetorical and socially cohesive purposes, they at times papered over the structural difference in arrival between settler migration and Black enslavement. But Republicans of virtually all stripes rejected the viability of providing for meaningful Indigenous self-determination, treating Native American polities as sovereign and political coequals of the American settler state, both in the present and going forward. Rather, Republicans overwhelmingly took for granted that Native peoples in the United States were a "dying race," one that, in its confrontation with the "irrepressible" force of "civilization," would inevitably "fade from the earth." As Lincoln had stated all the way back in 1863, the only future for Native peoples on a continent governed by "the white race" was "by living as they do," abandoning the goal of self-determination and assimilating politically and culturally.[101]

Even Frederick Douglass tended to repeat these settler truisms, in particular when he sought rhetorically to distinguish supposedly forward-looking Black citizens from backward-looking and autarchic Native Americans. "The Indian wraps himself in gloom, and proudly glories in isolation," Douglass declared in one 1862 speech. "He retreats before the onward march of civilization. . . . He sees the plowshare of civilization tossing up the bones of his venerated fathers, and he dies of a broken heart."[102]

Not unlike many white Republicans, Douglass assumed that the American state was the national inheritor of the territory—if anything, the civilizing and modern political successor to Native peoples, whose very survival depended on their willingness to abandon their "gloom" and accept historical inevitability. In this way, he engaged in his own mirroring of Indigenous elites when they drafted the Sequoyah Constitution. Those elites had sought to link Indigeneity and whiteness by reaffirming Jim Crow hierarchy. Similarly, Douglass aimed to bond whites and Blacks together by emphasizing a shared settler embrace of civilization vis-à-vis Native drives to preserve a distinctive cultural and political way of life.

Moreover, Douglass's creedal presentation of the country as a "composite" nation was, in many ways, a forerunner to the mid-twentieth-century idea of the United States as an "immigrant nation" in which Black people could be seen as just one of various migrant settler populations. They thus shared the same cultural story of movement and freedom as other new European communities on the continent. Douglass continued in the same speech that whites and Blacks enjoyed an "interior resemblance . . . greater than the exterior difference" of color, because—unlike Native peoples—the African American "clings to American civilization," that redemptive narrative of universal and equal liberty. This juxtaposition between Black people and Native Americans once more recast the latter not as sovereign and self-determining polities facing violent conquest, but instead as obsolete holdovers.[103]

In this way, the multiracial democracy of Douglass—whatever real freedom it offered Black Americans—still tended to participate in an extreme erasure of Indigenous presence. It reimagined the country's colonizing project as the opening of freedom to communities from around the world, and therefore American history as a progressive and universalizing march. But all of this meant that even more radical creedal accounts, with a universally inclusive national identity, reaffirmed a basic denial of Native self-determination.

BLACK DISAGREEMENT OVER EMPIRE

Although some Black elites used creedal constitutional language to defend a version of American expansionism, the policy framework proved a difficult fit in the African American community. For many Black opponents of overseas empire, the Native American example highlighted how a racialized settler politics appeared encoded into the emerging rhetoric of American universalism, from Indian Territory to the Philippines. While the intense xenophobia of many anti-annexationists had created space for Black openness to new territorial acquisition, the hopeful aspirations of the 1899 Du Bois—or of Douglass earlier—hardly monopolized Black thought on the matter.

Just as with the politics around the collapse of Reconstruction, African Americans split over the basic question of whether to keep faith in the national project, and therefore how to orient themselves toward American international power. Some Black journalists began from a position, not unlike Nebraskan Populist William Neville's, that— given white control over policy—expansion was inevitably a projection abroad of domestic white supremacy. But they went even further and argued that this meant that African Americans should identify not with the American state but instead with its Filipino opponents, and thus cast their lot with the Indigenous fight for self-determination at home and abroad.

Henry McNeal Turner famously described American suppression of Philippine independence as "an unholy war of conquest," not unlike settler subjugation of Native Americans, and called the leaders of the uprising "a feeble band of sable patriots" worthy of Black support.[104] The *A. M. E. Church Review* published an editorial contending that Filipino resistance spoke to how "a startling movement had begun . . . which shall in the cycles change the present relation of oppressor and oppressed." Similarly, the *Washington Bee* declared that it was no surprise that "a bond of sympathy" had sprung up between African Americans and Filipinos, since there was a clear "analogy between the struggle which is now going on among colored people for constitutional liberty and that of a similar race in the orient."[105]

These arguments tapped into entrenched African American judgments that whites and Blacks constituted opposed groups within society. As long as basic domestic relations of power remained undisturbed, Black support of US global imperium carried a deeply perverse consequence. It meant participating in the domination of non-whites abroad while reproducing conditions of domestic racial subordination. As the journalist and activist Ida B. Wells declared, "Negros should oppose expansion until the government was able to protect the Negro at home."[106]

Du Bois initially had sought to distinguish American power from European imperialism. At this stage in his political evolution, he still hoped—despite his real doubts—that the country could follow a creedal and constitutionally redemptive path. This meant both that the country would engage in racial amelioration at home and that its interventionism abroad could be redirected to promote inclusive freedoms for non-white peoples. Under such conditions, American efforts on behalf of self-government internationally would not mirror the exploitative racial domination practiced by other European states. But from the beginning, other Black opponents of empire contested the legitimacy of such a distinction. They questioned whether even an ideal of statehood for all peoples within the American polity, like that associated with Douglass, ultimately went far enough to uproot white supremacy.

For Douglass, again in the same creedal terms that had justified Native American displacement, the takeover of smaller Indigenous communities by powerful states was inevitable: "Nations must be able to exist either by love or fear and Santo Domingo can win neither love or fear . . . small and weak nations are plainly out of joint with our times and are going out of fashion."[107] Since Douglass's vision of empire saw expansion as almost preordained, republican self-government for foreign populations devolved into a project of incorporation as equals into presumptively free and large societies like the US. In a sense, Du Bois in 1899 fell into a similar trap of inevitability. By treating the "new imperial policy" as a foregone conclusion that Black Americans should seek to shape in better directions, Du Bois too implicitly affirmed that incorporation might be the only viable and rights-protecting path for Filipinos or Puerto Ricans.

However, Black critics highlighted how this creedal vision of extending liberty through assimilation into American citizenship fundamentally denied authentic and local self-determination over the institutions of collective life. Such assimilation might take place on terms of legal equality, and so be consistent with creedal and constitutional narratives. Nonetheless, it entailed the destruction of Indigenous societies as they were constituted and the rejection of their underlying autonomy. Thus a common Philippine poster during the war called on Black soldiers (and not without some success) to abandon the American side and refuse, as the historian Willard Gatewood writes, "to be the instrument of his white master's ambition to oppress another 'people of color.'"[108] Indeed, this underlying sentiment is part of what made David Fagen, the Black soldier who left his infantry troop to accept a Philippine commission — engaging in notorious guerrilla raids against the US army that garnered front-page coverage in the *New York Times* — both a folk hero to some Blacks and a figure of extreme racial anxiety for many white Americans.[109]

Ultimately, for Black critics of emerging creedal accounts of empire, self-government remained meaningless unless the American state fully respected the basic sovereignty of non-white peoples and allowed them to control their own political destiny as separate nations. This position repudiated all forms of imperial supervision and external control, from practices of colonial tutelage all the way to those of territorial absorption through equal statehood.

Thus, African American opponents like Turner looked upon expansion, even when justified in far more inclusive terms, as a new adaptation of white rule rather than its renunciation. Universalistic defenses of American intervention may have been premised on equal liberty. But they nonetheless ignored the nature of American continental conquest over Native peoples, and also allowed white national politicians on the global stage to set the terms for what constituted self-determination and how it would be fulfilled. Indeed, Du Bois himself would renounce whatever hope he initially placed in expansion. As the Philippine-American War dragged on, he too would make explicit the link between Indigenous dispossession and overseas imperialism. The biographer David Levering Lewis tells us that in stinging editorials Du Bois described "the 'Rape of Cuba and the Conquest of the Philippines'" as "the blackest deeds in American history since the Seminole Wars."[110]

Woodrow Wilson and Creedal Constitutionalism as a Language of White Supremacy

In essence, the growing justifications for American power—especially through arguments about exceptionalism and the constitutional tradition—combined seemingly conflicting political ideas of universalism and cultural superiority. Figures like David Jayne Hill may have believed in the theoretical fitness of all racial groups for full self-government. But transforming this theoretical fitness into reality entailed a sustained project of American stewardship, in which non-European communities in particular would be led from their "political childhood" into a "civilized" adulthood.

In this way, and perhaps counterintuitively, more and more white expansionists retrofitted ideas of equal liberty to defend both past conquest—whether in North America or the Philippines—and prevailing racial hierarchies. The return of creedal rhetoric may have been a response to global pressures and a move toward greater American inclusiveness. But its flexibility as a discursive tool for defending the racial order of the day made it increasingly popular even outside the Republican Party and among political figures long associated with die-hard and unreconstructed white supremacy.

WILSON ADOPTS THE CREEDAL CONSTITUTION

One can appreciate the resonance of Hill's formulation in the fact that presidents of both traditional parties, when pressed to justify American global power, began to do so in virtually identical terms. William Howard Taft, LeRoy's great benefactor, presented the "great principle" guiding American actions in the Philippines in the following way: "We are to govern the Philippine Islands in accordance with the maxim 'Philippines for the Filipinos.'" As with Hill, Taft believed that this "principle" made the United States unique among European states, separating it even from England, whose imperial approach of "enlightened selfishness" was "exactly the opposite of that which we have pursued in the Philippines."[111]

As for Woodrow Wilson, Taft's Democratic presidential opponent in 1912, he too—and perhaps more than anyone else—came to be closely identified with this vision. On first glance, this may be a surprise given his outspoken Southern rejection of Black political rights and his willingness, at the beginning of his academic career, to engage in damning critiques of the federal Constitution. He would hardly seem a natural figure for an American universalism that recovered Republican anti-slavery narratives and that emphasized the specialness of the country's constitutional tradition. But for starters, to the extent that Reconstruction and the Reconstruction Amendments' actual threat to white supremacy had indeed been pushed back, a Southerner like Wilson could be more open to extracting from the creed his own account of the national project. In fact, the new interventionist imagination was also attractive to Wilson—even if bathed in anti-slavery rhetoric—because of how it still fit into his own Southern-inflected account of self-government and racial hierarchy.

Recall that Wilson was deeply traumatized by the experience of Reconstruction, which he saw as the denial by a tyrannical North of political liberties to Southern whites, in a way that inverted the appropriate racial hierarchy among distinct "peoples" at different levels of cultural development. As Wilson turned to international debates, in many ways he projected these views onto the meaning of American power. Especially given the Southern white experience, if the US stood for anything it had to stand for the value of self-government—a value that was basic and universal.

But this did not mean that all foreign, especially non-European, peoples could live according to the principle in the here and now, since doing so first required a process of political maturation. As he declared in a 1907 lecture at Columbia University, "self-government is not a mere form of institutions, to be had when desired. . . . It is a form of character. It follows upon the long discipline which gives a people self-possession, self-mastery, the habit of order and peace and common counsel, and a reverence for law which will not fail when they themselves become the makers of law: the steadiness and self-control of political maturity."[112] In fact, "only a long apprenticeship of obedience can secure" less developed peoples "the precious possession" of real self-government—"a thing," as Wilson stated, "no more to be bought than given."[113] This suggested that, just as with Republican interventionists, the US had a particular role to play on the global stage: its primary purpose was to create a world of self-governing republics by shepherding less developed peoples on the path to freedom.[114]

Increasingly, Wilson too turned to the 1787 Constitution as proof of American exceptionalism and as the substantive educational content the country would offer other societies. As a younger scholar, Wilson may have drawn attention to how the framers were self-interested and shaped by their class position, and interrogated the real defects in their institutional design. He continued to believe—especially given twentieth-century domestic economic needs—that the 1787 structure required updating, which ideally could be achieved through a steady move toward presidential government. But Wilson's growing faith in the internally adaptive capacity of the constitutional order—not to mention his central fears that explicit constitutional rupture could further deepen class conflict and social disorder—pushed him to downplay constitutive constitutional flaws. By the time he ran for president in 1912, his embrace of anti-formalist interpretative flexibility meant that, by contrast with both Teddy Roosevelt and Eugene Debs, he deemphasized concrete formal changes to the Constitution.

In the context of Wilson's shifting sentiments, the turn to the global stage further reinforced his growing commitment to the federal constitutional project. Just as with Hill, he increasingly described the Constitution's writing and ratification as a truly world historical event; it established "enlightened processes of politics that were without precedent" in human experience. And equally important, the framers who devised these processes were only in a position to do so because of their ethno-racial background—the fact that they had "sprung from a race habituated to submit to law and authority" and from a "stock" that had "served the long apprenticeship of political childhood." In this way, the

Constitution offered nothing less than the culmination of a specifically Anglo-Saxon education in political liberty.[115] In 1876, Wilson may have believed that the Constitution produced a "miserable delusion of a republic,"[116] but those thoughts were now wholly rejected as juvenile reflections.

All this meant that when Wilson imagined the United States as promoting universal commitments to self-government, above all this increasingly entailed the promotion of Madisonian constitutionalism: the replication in foreign polities of the institutions and discourses that marked domestic statecraft at the federal level. In describing the American project in the Philippines, he asserted that the country must engage with Filipinos "in the true spirit of our own institutions," which more than anything else meant "giv[ing] the Filipinos constitutional government, a government which they may count upon to be just, a government based upon some clear and equitable understanding, intended for their good and not for our aggrandizement."[117]

In other words, for Wilson, the precondition for foreign self-determination was the replacement of local structures of authority with those that consciously mimicked the American federal constitutional framework—a project that was critically distinct from how Roosevelt, Root, and Wood initially imagined American ambitions in Cuba, Puerto Rico, and the Philippines. As president, Wilson's policies embodied this basic approach, highlighted by the 1916 Jones Act for the Philippines, which supplanted the Organic Act as the new governing document on the islands. The Jones Act disappointed Filipinos, who had hoped Wilson might fulfill his 1912 campaign goal of providing the islands with independence during his presidency. The Act did offer greater local autonomy and even, as the historian Anna Su writes, "officially put on record the promise of the US government to grant independence, the first act of such nature by any colonial power in history."[118] But this delayed promise came wrapped in practical policies that perpetuated the colonial state, as well as the administration's judgments about race and appropriate constitutional order.

The Jones Act's specific institutional structures copied the 1787 document in important ways, including establishing a Philippine Bill of Rights. As part of this, of course, the actual history of Filipino independence figures drafting their own bill of rights in the Malolos Constitution—the section had been titled "The Filipinos and Their National and Individual Rights,"[119] and focused especially on negative liberties and criminal procedural protections—was quietly forgotten.

The Jones Act also transformed the Philippine legislature into a fully elected body and endowed it with increased political control, subject though to the oversight of the American Governor-General. Most interestingly, the legislature was directly modeled on the US Constitution, with a bicameral structure complete with a new elected upper house called the Senate and the existing Assembly renamed the House of Representatives. Indeed, the similarly named Jones Act for Puerto Rico, instituted the following year, followed an equivalent framework and also paralleled American federal constitutional structures — implementing a Senate, a House of Representatives, and now a Puerto Rican Bill of Rights.[120]

As a result, each act suggested how Wilson conceived of American power in a world of supposedly distinct peoples, both racially and developmentally. On the one hand, the new framing document expressed American universal values — concretely embodied in the 1787 Constitution. But on the other, it accommodated judgments that Filipinos and Puerto Ricans remained unprepared for full independence.

Again, given Wilson's earlier academic suspicions of American checks and balances, on its face it would seem surprising that his policies so dutifully reproduced 1787 design features that he once viewed as compromising effective government. But in its own way this enthusiasm for federal mimicry in constitution-building mirrored practices of other European empires, especially Britain. As the historian Linda Colley notes, in the nineteenth and early twentieth centuries Britain too was involved in extensive enterprises of global constitution-writing, both directly in its colonies and indirectly across parts of Europe and Latin American.[121] This also seems unexpected given that British political officials largely forswore the need for any formal written constitution at home. But as with Wilson's view, British colonial administrators believed that what sustained domestic liberty in England was an ethno-racially and culturally grounded training in self-limitation and responsible government. Although such a culture might take centuries to develop, British imperialists could promote, through constitution-writing, an institutional distillation of Anglo civilization. Similarly, Wilson may have believed that the old 1787 Madisonian structure required considerable updating to adequately serve the needs of a modern and culturally mature polity like the United States. But, as underscored by the two Jones Acts, the old federal Constitution nonetheless provided the most effective building blocks and practical education for foreign peoples still in their "political childhood."

In the end, like the Organic Act before it, support for the Philippine Jones Act also fell along party lines, with Democrats in favor and Republicans opposed. But despite the partisan debates over how much self-rule was too much and how soon to disentangle the United States from the Philippines, Wilson's policies highlighted the growing convergence within certain policy-making factions of both parties. To the extent that Democrats like Wilson supported an aggressive American global presence, they legitimated this presence in well-established terms. For Wilson, the Constitution had its weaknesses, but now he also presented it as a sacred document, the product of centuries of cultural development and proof of the country's universal mission on the global stage. So when policymakers imposed familiar constitutional structures in foreign nations, those structures were tangible embodiments of American principles—proof of the self-abnegating commitment to equal liberty for all. As Wilson declared during the First World War, in words that could easily have been uttered by Frederick Douglass, his administration operated entirely by "the principle of justice to all peoples and nationalities, and their right to live on equal terms of liberty and safety with one another, whether they be weak or strong."[122]

LAYING THE FOUNDATIONS FOR EXTENDED TUTELAGE

Of course, in practice this ostensibly universalist commitment reaffirmed rather than undermined American supervision and interventionism. Indeed, the very continuity between US and British constitution-building enterprises (both as understood by Root and as implemented later by Wilson) dramatized how, regardless of emerging American self-presentations, the new American imperium still echoed the old European variety. Even the growing language of exceptionalism vis-à-vis other empires placed US foreign policymakers in a long line of European officials, who had also justified their nation's global power based on special cultural attributes and historic destiny. Perhaps most important, for those on the receiving end of American power during the period, the new politics of US global authority could seem awfully similar to its European rivals.

A quick glance at what this authority meant domestically and abroad drives this last point home. Within the US, for Wilson the vision of the country as grounded in principles of universal self-determination was not only consistent with, but in fact helped to explain why the rise of Jim Crow was a legitimate response to Reconstruction. After all, segregation reestablished the proper racial hierarchy and ensured that responsible white Southerners—not unlike administrators in the Philippines or elsewhere—could facilitate the political maturation of Black Americans. Overseas, this approach often linked political maturity to the willingness of non-white polities to accede to US market imperatives and capitalist legal arrangements—not unlike with Republican officials. The failure to do so signaled either "disorder" or an inability of ethno-nationally less developed peoples to live up to constitutional ideals. Under such circumstances, the United States was within its rights to assert tutelary authority and to impose political or even military order, as it did in settings from Latin America and the Caribbean to the Pacific.[123] And later, in the context of the League of Nations, these American experiences emphasized to Wilson the need for a mandate system. This system was again premised on white trusteeship, with American and European states serving as "tutors and advisers" to non-white peoples, always prepared to intervene if needed.[124]

For Wilsonian politics, the likelihood of necessary intervention remained high. Although the US could do its best to provide local inhabitants an education in constitutional government, at the end of the day real freedom was still, in Wilson's words, a "form of character and not a form of constitution."[125] This suggested that creating an international community of self-governing republics would take time, and would require not just American patience but also American fortitude in imposing its will on backsliding nation-states and peoples. However hard, this task ultimately fell to the United States. Europeans could provide assistance, but given their own internecine violence and history of absolutism, American state power and global guidance offered the last and best instrument for defending universal principles.

Thus, the actual substantive experience for non-white communities, whether at home or under US global authority, did not shift all that materially from 1898 to 1917. In practice, Wilson—just as with Root and Wood before him—used judgments about racial hierarchy to question the advisability of meaningful self-determination in the present and to defend highly mediated structures of colonial administration. But what had emerged was a new account of these broad policies, which was self-consciously universalist in presentation. And unlike the immediate post-1898 iteration, the updated account placed the promotion of the federal Constitution at the forefront of a narrative about the difference between American and European imperium.

THE LONG-TERM RAMIFICATIONS AND
CENTRALITY OF THE GLOBAL TURN

The fact that white supremacists like Wilson could see themselves in assertions of both the Constitution and the creed is significant. It speaks to a central reason why, over the course of the twentieth century, creedal constitutionalism spread across mainstream white politics. It was not simply, or only, that white American politicians and constituencies began supporting greater racial inclusivity due to the moral rectitude of the position—although some of them certainly did. Equally important, many politicians and commentators found a way to tell a story, centered on American global primacy, that combined creed and Constitution without necessarily repudiating the society's established hierarchies, including around race.

Without engaging with the country's early-twentieth-century overseas experience—and with how it was interpreted by key officials—it is difficult to explain the concrete circumstances under which past antislavery arguments took new forms and steadily regained political and cultural vibrancy. The internal containment of Reconstruction's promise certainly facilitated national elite willingness to reclaim anti-slavery rhetoric. Still, in the domestic arena that containment embodied a tense settlement in which, although the Reconstruction Amendments persisted on the books, pervasive white supremacist views treated Reconstruction as a wrong turn. However, through the overseas experience, this settlement—a potentially uncomfortable mix of universalism and white supremacy—became transformed. The effort to shape and justify American power infused this mix with ethical value and a sense of national mission that legitimated practices abroad as well as at home.

In addition, over time the American global turn provided real grounds for embracing the larger constitutional system in ways that buttressed existing, if imperiled, brands of support. When the US found itself trapped in a brutal war in the Philippines, there were essentially two domestic defenses of the Constitution widely circulating in white society. The first was the classic worship of the 1787 text as an embodiment of the founders' genius, both a skillful cross-sectional compromise and an essential mechanism for fulfilling the promise of American settler freedom. As we have seen, that worshipful pose came up against the breakdown of collective life—including civil war and intense industrial conflict—and the role of the legal-political order in that unraveling. Thus, this first defense oftentimes devolved into simply a business conservative championing of the Constitution as a bulwark safeguarding property and even capitalism itself. It had the benefit of deep cultural roots, but it offered a story of the text and the country facing real skepticism.

The second defense related to the developing Progressive argument about the malleability of the Constitution—its capacity to adapt to serve reformist ends. During these years, invoking this adaptability provided a rationale for why radical rupture or revolutionary change was not necessary to address large-scale social problems. But a Progressive contention that Americans could work around constitutional flaws was hardly a compelling reason to deify an antiquated text and system.

By contrast, the idea of the Constitution as embodying universal values of self-government that the US spread to the world was a profoundly romantic vision of national purpose. As pushed by pro-annexation expansionists in 1902, it no doubt faced just as much pushback as the more conventional defenses. Yet the more the US became a driving force in world affairs—and the more Americans fought and died in massive global conflagrations—the deeper these arguments struck as a persuasive story of mission and sacrifice.

In a sense, when scholars focus exclusively on the domestic sources of support for constitutional veneration, they ignore the real hollowness of these sources in the early twentieth century. They also profoundly undervalue the eventual affective and cultural appeal of connecting pro-Constitution sentiment to a new universalist *and* exceptionalist narrative of shared project.

Indeed, for actors across the political spectrum, this linking of the Constitution to both creedal ideas and an international purpose also infused other defenses of the text with higher meaning. It provided an explanation in public life for why pro-business invocations of constitutional property rights or of checks and balances were not just veils for the economic self-interest of a wealthy few. Rather, pro-war business conservatives could depict the American federal constitutional model—presented as bound tightly to an aggressive system of market capitalism—as essential to promoting a global community of stable, self-governing republics committed to peace, commerce, and prosperity.

Even if such a view faced intense and mass opposition at home, the connection between constitutional veneration and the global turn began a reframing of contentious domestic institutional arrangements. In the internal setting especially of class conflict, both the legal-political system and pro-business capitalist property relations were often depicted as elite power grabs over state and economy. But when conceived through American global engagements, the pro-business link between the 1787 text and capitalist entrenchment could be turned into an embodiment of a shared national history worth rallying around and protecting.

Conclusion: The Colonies as a Rehearsal for the Great War

By the time Americans began debating whether or not to enter World War I, pro-war defenders of an assertive global posture—Democrat or Republican—had a clear set of arguments to employ. These arguments creatively reconstituted creedal ideas, linking universal equality and constitutional commitment to American cultural exceptionalism and a special mission abroad. They embodied a meaningful ideological break both from preexisting notions of empire as a project of white settlement and from some of the most virulent forms of white supremacy that circulated during the time.

Still, they also preserved that past in key ways. One can see this in how figures like Hill reaffirmed the central markers of the settler experience—from Puritan colonization to revolutionary independence and from federal constitutional founding to continental expansion and the writing of new settler-state documents. This reaffirmation legitimated white dominance, albeit on revised terms, and presented the American international role as refashioning the world in its own image—both politically and economically. And while such remaking would not occur demographically, as settler colonists had imagined for North America, it certainly aimed to proceed both institutionally and normatively.

Thus, the emerging universalism projected onto the global stage and into a new historical epoch long-standing settler-inflected judgments about race, power, and privilege. The old settler vision of Indigenous erasure and absorption became transformed into a project of assimilationist replication, one that justified continuous overseas interference to reshape non-white societies into mirror images of the United States. As part of this project, US officials enjoyed both a right and a responsibility to replace local non-white modes of authority with institutional structures marked by federal constitutional statecraft and those private property relations consistent with US economic expansionism.

It is critical to reiterate that these arguments—on behalf of extensive American interventionism and federal constitutional veneration—did not enjoy a mass political base before World War I. They were the views of a narrow policy-making community, tied to disagreements in Washington around what do with overseas possessions and how to conceive of American international authority more generally.

However, in the context of the 1917 war effort, this emergent linking of creed, Constitution, and global assertiveness began to strike a nerve within public sentiment. And that change resulted, in no small part, from an aggressive campaign by political, military, and business elites that had no precedent in American history. As I explore in part II of this book, the pro-war campaign on behalf of the Constitution had reverberating consequences for the constitutional climate going forward. For the Wilson administration, in a time of global conflagration, past debates over questions like judicial review, whether to have a parliamentary or presidential system, or the pluses and minuses of bicameralism took on a new, more troubling hue. Wilson himself may have once imagined basic alternatives to the constitutional state. But to do so now meant throwing one's lot in with disorder in the global struggle between violence and democratic stability.

Defending the constitutional order both at home and abroad—and regardless of its weaknesses—became of utmost political importance. In this context, bills like the 1916 and 1917 Jones Acts, which imposed elements of the federal constitutional system on overseas possessions, gained an added significance. These policies did not simply educate less developed peoples in the mechanisms of constitutional self-government. They implicitly reaffirmed constitutional respect at home and dramatized to Americans that the national project was worth defending from external and even internal threat.

PART II

The Spread of a New Constitutional Citizenship, 1917–1945

But the war, which brought socialists and liberals together in the fight to maintain civil liberty, was as bad for the socialists as it was good for the liberals. The fight for free speech demanded constant reference to the Constitution and the Declaration of Independence. To demand that these documents be lived up to, was the most revolutionary thing a socialist leader could do, except go to jail. And from demanding that they should be lived up to, some of these leaders have apparently gotten into the habit of believing they will be lived up to, and that when they are, that will be the Social Revolution.

CRYSTAL EASTMAN, "THE SOCIALIST
PARTY CONVENTION" (1920)

Some say that President Roosevelt can be trusted but that future Presidents might pack the Supreme Court with corporation tools. Yes, if the voters elect a reactionary President and a reactionary Senate to confirm the nomination, it is possible that this will happen. But it is not likely. Public opinion will prevent the Court from ever again sinking to the depths the present majority has brought it down to.

LABOR'S NON-PARTISAN LEAGUE, "THE
SUPREME COURT VS. THE PEOPLE" (1937)

CHAPTER 6

World War I, the Security State, and Constitutional Loyalty

In April 1917, the same month that the United States entered into World War I, the recently formed National Association for Constitutional Government (NACG) published the first issue of the *Constitutional Review*. The group, whose president was David Jayne Hill,[1] the former American ambassador to Germany and president of the University of Rochester, included a manifesto explaining the reasons for its creation. According to the NACG, the country found itself surrounded by external and internal threats—ranging from German forces abroad to revolutionary socialists and anarchists at home. Indeed, radical domestic critics of the federal Constitution now numbered in the "several millions of Americans." Such critics had their "organizations," like the Socialist Party of America (SPA) and the Industrial Workers of the World (IWW), and "perfectly definite ideas as to the structural changes which they desire to effect in American institutions." Even worse, opponents of the Constitution were "energetic and persistent in presenting their platforms to the public mind." All of this meant that "the Constitution [was] in danger of assassination in the house of its friends."

For NACG, radical calls for transformation were more than just wrongheaded. With the country moving toward war, they destabilized the single entity—the federal Constitution—that, more than anything else, safeguarded the nation as a free republic. In effect, reformers, especially socialists, aimed to replace American "liberty" with "the chaotic rule of an irresponsible and absolutistic democracy." Facing such ideological menace, not to mention military threat, the NACG declared that "all right-minded men" needed to launch a concerted effort to revive "the real patriotism of the great mass of the American people" and to defend both the Constitution and the government it had established from assault.[2]

In many ways, both the editorial's claims and its alarmist tone were familiar. Such language had long been the bread and butter of those business and legal elites who championed the Constitution in the context of intense class conflict—groups the Progressive journalist Norman Hapgood derisively called "professional patriot[s]" committed to "defending the existing property and political system without change."[3] As the NACG's editorial suggested, these voices tended to feel beleaguered, given the outspoken constitutional criticism that circulated among urban reformers, industrial workers, poor African Americans, and even some pro-segregation white Southerners. But for all the familiarity of the sentiment, the *Constitutional Review* arrived at a decisive wartime moment in American politics—a moment that gave heightened resonance to its mission.

In particular, Europe's implosion exacerbated the sense of cultural and political crisis felt by many white citizens, especially native-born and Protestant Euro-Americans. In the half century leading up to US entry into the First World War, the basic elements that had long defined American identity faced extreme pressure—as a result of the closure of the frontier, the (purported) undoing of racial hierarchy, and upheavals in family structure and settler economic social mobility. This pressure had created the opening for wide-ranging reformist projects affecting everything from class and race to gender relations. But it also fostered xenophobia, the further entrenchment of white supremacy, and a pervasive and fearful worry that settler society was on the verge of collapse. With the country facing perceived threats abroad, more and more Americans reassessed their relationship to the discordant old order, and many began to rally around the existing symbols of the republic—with the Constitution chief among them. Whatever its weaknesses, the text nonetheless connected them, in the twentieth century and at a time of global conflict, to what many viewed as the country's golden age.

In this wartime climate, the NACG was just one of a plethora of associations, working in concert with politicians and military officials, that fed the shifting public sentiment. These actors collectively spearheaded a constitutional organizing and educational campaign at a national scale, unlike anything seen previously in US history. They presented constitutional commitment as fundamentally a national security imperative and sought to elevate the document above popular dissent. In classrooms and at mass celebrations, pro-Constitution advocates promoted loyalty to the 1787 text as *the* paramount prerequisite of patriotic citizenship, persistently fusing Americanism with constitutional reverence.

Still, even though world war and fears of revolutionary extremism invigorated pro-Constitution groups, opposition had not disappeared. Shifts in public discourse simply meant that real skepticism now continued to exist alongside a broader and far more activated base of public support. The same questions remained about the structural and anti-democratic weaknesses of the legal-political system, not to mention the ongoing connections between the constitutional system and elite class rule. Defenders thus confronted the daunting question of how to foster a general culture of unquestioned constitutional devotion—and with it, wartime devotion to the existing institutions of state and economy—in a context of persistent contestation.

In this chapter, I detail how pro-Constitution and pro-war organizations, along with public officials and corporate allies, responded through two overlapping approaches that have fundamentally shaped American political life. The first centered around making the Constitution a *positive* principle that would justify American militarism abroad as well as a robust new security framework at home. As part of this, supporters embraced that creedal constitutional narrative, honed in the wake of the 1898 Spanish-Cuban-American War, which had been adopted and retooled by colonial administrators in the context of early debates about global expansionism. Pro-Constitution activists going into World War I then presented this narrative as essential to national identity, and as distilling the values that Americans would fight for abroad and thereby extend to the world.

To help embed constitutional loyalty—as well as the emerging security state—in the American model, supporters energetically promoted patriotic education and pro-Constitution ideas of deferential citizenship. They eventually engaged in projects such as constructing a new, separate building exclusively for the Supreme Court—perhaps the ultimate monument to the constitutional order. In this way, the First World War launched the broad domestic spread of evolving accounts of creed and Constitution. In time, these accounts would become the dominant way Americans spoke to each other about the meaning of citizenship and its fundamental ties to the Constitution.

For the second approach, pro-war and pro-Constitution advocates took advantage of the war's patriotic energy to present constitutional critics as either consciously or unwittingly aiding overseas wartime foes. Rather than debate the specific details of constitutional design, they overwhelmingly presented the Constitution as a shared national symbol. They argued that its basic framework—understood to include the existing organization of state and economy—therefore must be placed beyond political dispute going forward. And given that anti-Constitution sentiment produced disunity and threatened the war effort, such opposition had to be vigorously, and even violently, suppressed.

Pro-Constitution activism during World War I did not simply proceed through open dialogue in the public square. Instead, supporters ensured adherence to the text and its associated institutions through methods common to many histories of modern state-building. These included practices most identified not with the rights-respecting civic culture often tied to constitutional support today, but rather with an extreme and belligerent nationalism: insistence on ideological uniformity, appeals to exceptionalism and cultural particularity, militarism, and political repression. Perhaps surprisingly, the basic policies that elected officials and military elites pursued during the era—centered on patriotic education, cultural assimilation, and the violent suppression of anti-Constitution sentiment—echoed similar nationalist enterprises at virtually the same historical moment in places like Germany, France, the new Turkish Republic, and elsewhere.

In this way, the official version of creedal constitutionalism, with its potential for egalitarian and inclusive politics, became tied to these repressive security origins—setting a pattern that would recur multiple times over the twentieth century. As a result of this dual approach to establishing constitutional fidelity, the war fundamentally altered how many Americans thought the document should be understood and debated. The pre-war popular discussion often depicted the Constitution as simply a governing framework: a decision-making process and legal infrastructure directing the contours of legislative, judicial, and executive authority. To the extent that basic features of both state and economy might require substantial revision, the text was one of many institutional features of collective life potentially open to modification.

But the wartime constitutional campaign deemphasized this focus on the Constitution's actual functioning and practical effects—including the ways in which it might not meet social needs. Instead, pro-Constitution voices sought to remove basic structural and economic questions from active contestation. In exchange, they reoriented conversation around an emerging story of the creedal Constitution, with the document playing a central role in helping Americans advance a universal project of constitutional self-government and market capitalism. Whereas pre-war veneration had been closely (and unflatteringly) associated with business elites, now a freshly burnished patriotic Constitution offered protection to economic orthodoxy. By contrast, calls to change the country's legal and economic structure, including through the constitutional system, were increasingly characterized as anti-patriotic.

This reconfiguration may not have won comprehensively at the time. Against the backdrop of both the Great War and the Russian Revolution, 1917 to 1919 were years of intense labor uprising, in which groups like the IWW imagined themselves as potentially on the precipice of a new world. Even after their defeat, both constitutional skepticism and anti-capitalist politics remained vibrant and then gained prominence in the context of the 1930s Depression.

Nonetheless, pro-war and pro-Constitution advocates succeeded in permanently linking constitutional support with American patriotism in the general collective imagination, and in further identifying both with faith in market capitalism. Over time, this change placed critics of both the Constitution and the society's underlying economic system on the political defensive. It pressed many, even self-avowed communists (as we will see in chapter 7), to make arguments in constitutionally venerative terms.

A Popular Base for Constitutional Devotion

The 1910s and 1920s witnessed deeply interconnected calls, largely from establishment elites, for a robust security infrastructure and a public culture of constitutional respect. Most of the key figures pressing for greater constitutional reverence were central to war mobilization efforts and also had strong corporate ties. This overlapping membership underscored the symbiotic relationship between wartime constitutional discourses, security practices, and pro-business sentiment: just as creedal constitutional claims helped infuse security practices with a higher normative purpose, concerns about external threat and internal social disorder buttressed the sense that the Constitution, bound closely to the existing economic system, should be treated as an unassailable foundation for shared national identity. Taken separately, those various commitments—to heightened militarism, to the Constitution, and to market capitalism—all faced profound opposition during the era. But the wartime fusing enhanced the popular legitimacy of all three positions.

THE BUSINESS FOUNDATIONS OF PRO-CONSTITUTION AND PRO-WAR ACTIVISM

Tracing membership across these groups offers a glimpse into how these projects became intertwined. And a good place to begin is with the author, diplomat, and university president David Jayne Hill himself, whose 1916 book *Americanism: What It Is* outlined a revived creedal constitutional politics as a means to ground American imperium. Hill helped to found the National Association for Constitutional Government, served as honorary vice president of the American Defense Society,[4] and spoke routinely on behalf of the National Security League (NSL).[5] The Defense Society and the NSL, two of the most prominent military preparedness organizations, were early champions of a permanent civilian defense infrastructure. Operationally, these groups advocated for the expansion of military funding, the creation of executive branch institutions overseen by military experts to coordinate defense policy, and compulsory peacetime military service and training for all able-bodied male citizens.[6]

Hill's movement between the NACG, the Defense Society, and the NSL was hardly novel, and indeed common membership and leadership were widespread across the various groups and among pro-Constitution and pro-security activists more generally. For example, Nicholas Murray Butler, president of Columbia University for the first four decades of the twentieth century, was both a frequent author for the NACG's *Constitutional Review* and an executive committee member of the National Security League.[7] James Beck, Solicitor General between 1921 and 1925 and author of countless books and articles praising the wisdom of the Constitution, was also heavily involved with the NSL. He participated in its "patriotic education" campaigns during the war, writing the preface to one of the group's speaker handbooks.[8] After the war, the NSL independently distributed his reflections on the Constitution, for example by sending out 10,000 free copies of his 1922 collected volume, *The Constitution of the United States*.[9] The NSL had a similar relationship with Charles Warren, Wilson's former assistant attorney general, an editorial board member of the *Constitutional Review*, and a Pulitzer Prize–winning constitutional scholar.[10]

Given this overlap of membership and ideological goals, it is hardly surprising that pro-Constitution and pro-security organizations often worked together on joint initiatives. Many even formed umbrella groups to coordinate their efforts, like the 1922 establishment of the Sentinels of the Republic, which united the American Defense Society, the NACG, the Constitutional Liberty League, and the American Legion, a powerful veterans group formed in 1919.[11]

At an organizational level, this overlap resulted in large part from the sources of funding and energy behind the drives for military preparedness and for greater constitutional loyalty. For most of these civic associations, the central financing came from the business community in New York City. For instance, NSL's main donors included corporate tycoons such as George H. Putnam, Cornelius Vanderbilt, Henry C. Frick, and Simon Guggenheim.[12]

This concentration of influence was hardly uncommon during the age. As the historian Sven Beckert writes, at the turn of the twentieth century the city's mercantile elite faced the particular ire of reformers attacking the plutocratic tendencies of American industrial capitalism. These critics argued that the same individuals, often city neighbors, "dominated the nation's trade, production, and finance" and enjoyed an outsized political power that "reverberated . . . from City Hall to the White House."[13] Underscoring the point, when Robert Lee Bullard, US Army general during World War I and president of the NSL in the 1920s, retired from the military following the war, he relied not on the federal government but on private capital for his financial security. New York City businessmen, including Vanderbilt, raised $20,000 as a lump sum retirement fund and then facilitated his rise to presidency of the League.[14]

Perhaps the primary concern of the New York City mercantile elite—as had long been the case for business defenders of the Constitution—revolved around maintaining property relations. They saw supporting the war and popularizing the Constitution as of a piece with safeguarding the existing economic system from internal and external threat. As Michael Kammen writes of the umbrella group Sentinels of the Republic, "its organizers hoped to persuade one million people 'to pledge themselves to guard the Constitution and wage war on socialism.' Their battle-cry became the following: 'Every citizen a sentinel, every home a sentry box.'"[15] Mobilizing patriotic fervor on behalf of both the Constitution and a strengthened security state thus aided an aggressive brand of Americanism and cast critics of capitalism as enemies of the nation.

THE CONSTITUTION AS A POSITIVE
PRINCIPLE FOR A NEW SECURITY STATE

Buttressed by such pro-capitalist business sponsorship, a profound symbiotic relationship emerged between security politics and Constitution worship. But advocates of military preparedness and American entry into World War I faced a familiar and widespread criticism—one with strong roots in American life—that fueled anti-war sentiment and created a deeply divided public during the conflict. This was the long-standing idea, powerfully voiced during the post-1898 debates over the fate of Puerto Rico and the Philippines, that military despotism undermined free government. Relatedly, the best way to avoid such despotism—as George Washington had cautioned in his 1796 Farewell Address (coauthored by Alexander Hamilton, who had articulated similar sentiments in the *Federalist Papers*)—was through isolation from Europe and its internecine conflicts.[16] Such anti-interventionism and anti-militarism now counseled against the push by pro-war activists toward both far greater global authority and its related domestic requirements. And these entrenched views raised significant doubts about the "Americanness" of preparedness efforts, let alone of the broader militarization of civilian life.

In response, members of the Defense Society and the NSL began to reiterate precisely the creedal arguments that colonial officials had increasingly used to justify empire in the Caribbean and Asia. Hill's 1916 *Americanism: What It Is* not only helped to make sense of the American role in places like the Philippines. It was written during the push for American entrance into World War I and in the context of ongoing debates over compulsory peacetime military training. For Hill, defending these wartime projects—along with American global power more generally—required a clear account of why the United States was exceptional and why American authority served both foreign and domestic needs.

The answer, for him and other pro-war activists, lay first in an assessment of the extreme threats the United States faced: as those like Teddy Roosevelt, Elihu Root, and Alfred Thayer Mahan had long argued, the US had no choice but to claim a greater interventionist presence, given the extent to which global disorder now imperiled Americans as well. The war in Europe highlighted that, if the US did not enter the conflict and shape it on favorable terms, the country would be subject to instability and violence unleashed from abroad.

Indeed, the global repercussions of the Russian Revolution—generated by the fallout of the war—meant that, for these activists, the threats were no longer theoretical and had in fact reached American shores. According to the National Security League's Executive Committee, revolutionaries of all stripes, emboldened by events in Russia, were massing in the United States to "overthrow" both the Constitution and the system of capitalism, which together embodied "American institutions and ideals."[17] In fact, given the degree to which the "civilized world . . . has been shaken to its foundations," Hill concluded that unless Americans were "disposed to sacrifice every interest, to forego every privilege, and to renounce every right," they would have to ignore anti-war cries about the evils of "militarism" and instead embrace preparedness and the global fight.[18]

But why should Americans believe that joining the European struggle for global domination—especially by mimicking the aggressive and militarized policies of imperial adversaries—would make the country or the world any safer? Would it not simply reproduce in the United States the politics of rivalry and confrontation destroying Europe? For pro-war voices, the brand of creedal constitutionalism reclaimed during turn-of-the-century imperial adventures helped to answer these questions: US power had a salutary effect domestically and internationally because of the country's historical and cultural exceptionalism. If the European imperial "watchword" was "dominion," according to Hill, the American watchword—forged through settlement and frontier expansion—was constitutional democracy. Combining the language and principles of the Declaration of Independence and the Constitution, Hill declared that the United States rested on a "simple creed," one "needing no enlargement" and "no argumentative justification": "that government should exist for the sake of the governed" and "that a just government is based upon the equal rights of all the people to life, liberty, and the pursuit of happiness."[19]

For pro-war voices, moreover, one need not worry that this "creed" would be damaged by militarization, given that these values were so deeply embedded in the life of the country. As Hill and others noted, the "creed" had taken institutional and written form through documents like the Constitution because it embodied cultural values that had emerged over centuries—and therefore could not be easily extinguished. For Ralph Barton Perry, the Harvard-based philosopher and staunch advocate of preparedness (who took part in the voluntary military training camp organized by pro-war activists in Plattsburgh, New

York), worries about rights infringements and security excess were
overstated: unlike the country's adversaries, American culture was constitutively bound to individualism and toleration. Through these arguments, Perry and others incorporated an element into the creedal
constitutional discourse that would become even more critical to later
anti-Nazi and Cold War–era thinking. As the political theorist Alexander Livingston writes, they contrasted the "universalism, limited government, toleration, and humility of American liberalism"[20] with the
collectivist authoritarianism of its rivals.

According to this view, Germany—alongside the new Soviet Union,
which pro-Constitution voices viewed as embodying the "absolutistic
democracy" socialists would destructively impose on the US—not only
exemplified a generalized European commitment to imperialism. Such
societies were also defined by authoritarian cultural values antithetical
to Americanism. As Perry wrote of Germany specifically, its domestic
community "sacrificed individualism" and accepted "authority too easily." It had no space for the pluralistic commitments that made American culture so exemplary. If the United States, as expressed in the Declaration and the Constitution, was the quintessential "tolerant nation,"
Germany instead embraced a "Nietzschean" will to power as its "national self-consciousness," combining a closed domestic order with violent conquest abroad.[21]

Indeed, Hill and others maintained that this American cultural embrace of inclusive and individualistic ideals, written into the country's
governing texts, "attracted the oppressed of all nations to these shores."
And it meant that the furtherance of American global authority (unlike that of German power) served the interests of all peoples everywhere. But according to Hill, the United States for too long had been
a "voice crying in the wilderness." Given that "the rights of people have
nowhere been respected . . . except where they were defended by force
of arms," Americans would have to impose their will—through force if
necessary—on the world.[22]

This vision of national identity had a series of related effects. First, it
placed the Constitution at the heart of American exceptionalism, also
providing an implicit justification for the war. It therefore buttressed
the larger worldview promoted by pro-war champions: belief in the
need for greater militarism generally and, with it, far greater US global
authority. At the same time, just as American constitutionalism justified
military preparedness and international police power, the reverse was

also the case. Security claims helped to activate and broaden a popular base of support for what had often been a beleaguered pro-business position in the US with respect to the Constitution. If the circulating prewar argument had emphasized that the constitutional state's connection to the existing economic order produced class domination rather than democracy, wartime exigencies highlighted the destabilizing dangers of such attacks on established institutions and practices.

Against the immediate backdrop of the European conflict—as well as the long-term context of settler ideological and legal-political unraveling—the idea that so-called "100 percent Americanism"[23] required total fealty to the Constitution emerged as a defining mass political commitment. Such sentiment was particularly strong among native-born and Protestant Euro-Americans. Indeed, despite its top-down New York corporate sponsorship, "by mid-1916," according to the legal scholar Mark Shulman, "the NSL had some 50,000 members nationally, organized into 155 branches in 42 states. By the end of the year, membership had doubled, with 250 chapters and 100,000 members."[24] In large numbers, returning soldiers joined veterans' groups like the American Legion, which adopted not just national loyalty but constitutional loyalty as a guiding principle. As part of this, the Legion and similar groups embraced the need to protect the Constitution absolutely from all perceived threats—whether overseas foes or domestic socialists and anarchists.[25]

Indeed, to an important degree, the rise of the second Ku Klux Klan, born in 1915 and a creature not just of the South but of the North and West as well (with strongholds in Indiana and Oregon and over 4 million members by the mid-1920s), spoke to the power of such pro-Constitution organizing.[26] The Klan rallied aggressively to the 1787 text and repudiated any of the old sectionalist suspicions of the document. Although the group pointedly rejected Hill's and Perry's creedal universalism—viewing the Constitution as an Anglo-Saxon and exclusive inheritance—it nonetheless placed extreme commitment to the Constitution alongside white Protestant supremacy as cornerstones of its ideology. And it further understood backing the Constitution as bound explicitly to protecting American capitalism from unfolding socialist and labor radical opposition. Dramatizing the Klan belief in the tie between text and country, during its initiation or "naturalization" ceremonies new members were questioned about the seven sacred symbols of Klankraft and what they represented; one of these symbols was the flag, and it denoted the Constitution.[27]

Fusing Americanism and Constitutional Faith

Such mobilizations around the Constitution as a positive symbol, along with the shifts they embodied in popular mood, energized business elites and public officials during and after the war. They also went hand in hand with a series of civic and governmental strategies aimed at producing uniform affective attachment to the federal Constitution across the country writ large. Through this, pro-Constitution advocates sought to inculcate a new type of American citizen, one that psychologically identified with the constitutional state and was willing to defend it against external and internal foes, through violence if necessary.

PATRIOTIC EDUCATION IN A SECULAR CREED

Although constitutional veneration increasingly tapped into a mass base during World War I, officials and pro-Constitution activists fully understood the challenges ahead. They faced real constitutional distrust and a profoundly divided public across key elements, from the war effort to the legal-political system to the basic arrangements of industrial life. In response, politicians and civic leaders employed a common method to eliminate existing bases of opposition, whether to the constitutional state or to the economic system: a vigorous education campaign to "Populariz[e] the Federal Constitution."[28]

Since 1875, the document itself had been kept in cellar storage in the State Department. But in 1921, in the context of these pro-Constitution efforts, President Warren Harding ordered the text to be moved to a place of honor at the Library of Congress, where Americans could view it and reflect upon its special meaning.[29] As the editors of the *Constitutional Review* asserted, although socialists and anarchists were "impervious alike to logic and to facts," most Americans would come to identify with the Constitution if properly taught about its essential features. Calling for "a campaign of counter-education," the *Review* stated that "the great mass of intelligent American citizens, who are in danger of being misled and corrupted by . . . insidious propaganda, should be thoroughly instructed in the fundamental principles of the American system of government and the contents and meaning of the great charter of their liberties."[30]

For all the ways that those like Perry, the Harvard-based philosopher, claimed that American culture, as emblazoned in the Constitution, did not "sacrifice individualism," these efforts moved in other directions.

Their core ambition was to generate social cohesion by fostering within citizens a reflexive sense of respect for governing institutions. Collective education around the document especially aimed to stamp out individual dissent and enforce political agreement—to shape Americans into the type of citizen-subjects who would be obedient to the existing social order and committed to the state's security objectives. As the motto for one widely read pamphlet, *The United States Constitution Simplified*, declared: "Don't Quarrel with Your Government; Read Your Constitution."[31]

Constitutional education programs were distinctive in the extent to which they did not cover interpretive doctrinal debates or questions of institutional design. Instead, the programs emphasized, in broad terms, the essential justness of the Constitution, and behind it the broader system of market capitalism. Pro-Constitution activists saw attacks on the Constitution as a stand-in for wider challenges to fragile collective institutions during a time of war and unfolding threat. They therefore aimed to silence first-order disagreements in society about whether to retain existing institutions at all. Educational campaigns, at root, aimed to fundamentally tame dissent, promoting universal loyalty to a background set of legal, political, and economic processes that would be placed beyond dispute.

Take for example nationwide contests, like that devised during the war by New York State Commissioner of Education Henry Sterling Chapin to write "The American's Creed." The effort was systematically backed by corporate figures, publishing heads, and government officials. And its organizers very consciously understood the contest as a way to link the war effort to national loyalty. William Tyler Page, who would later become Clerk of the US House of Representatives, wrote the winning "creed" (out of over three thousand entries). Upon winning his $1,000 prize at an event held in the US House of Representatives, Page spent the money on war bonds for the military effort abroad.[32]

In terms that were becoming increasingly familiar given pro-war rhetoric, Page's winning "creed" combined the language of the Declaration, the Constitution, and the Gettysburg Address to articulate a basic statement of universal shared values. It read in part, "I believe in the United States of America as a government of the people, by the people, for the people . . . a perfect union, one and inseparable; established upon those principles of freedom, equality, justice, and humanity for which American patriots sacrificed their lives and fortunes." And it concluded by tying Americanism to loyal obedience to the institutions of state: "I therefore believe it is my duty to my country to love it; to support its Constitution; to obey its laws; to respect its flag, and to defend it against all enemies."[33]

Indeed, the contest used the religious language of "creed"—in keeping with how Hill and other pro-war voices similarly appropriated the term—precisely to establish a deeper foundational agreement regarding collective institutions. For Page—himself a descendant of both President John Tyler and one of the Declaration's signers—the whole point of writing out the statement was to make clear to a divided public the extent to which documents like the Constitution embodied a secularized version of "the Apostles' Creed." Page maintained that he explicitly incorporated language from the Declaration and the Constitution, because they were to him "my American bible," sacred and holy texts that should not be critically interrogated but instead accepted unconditionally and on faith.[34] These claims embodied a twentieth-century expression of those early nineteenth-century Protestant arguments in which, to use Lincoln's 1838 words, the Constitution amounted to the "political religion of the nation."[35]

Above all, the pro-Constitution educational campaign during the era hoped to instill a deferential identification with the constitutional state. The NSL pressed for September 17—unevenly remembered in 1887— now to be designated as a national holiday, called "Constitution Day." They aimed to use commemorative events to teach "the people in true Americanism and sound and intelligent patriotism," and thus to dispel the seductiveness of socialist "cults" like "bolshevism" which were "attacking the foundations of our institutions."[36] Although it would take eight decades for Congress to eventually establish the holiday, the NSL, working in concert with other like-minded groups such as the Constitution Anniversary Association, did succeed in generating widespread observance of the day during and especially after World War I.[37]

A large part of this success resulted from focusing on the Constitution as, above all, a "creed," and thus deemphasizing any substantive disputes about constitutional rights, interpretation, and structure—those profound disagreements over how to read the text or assess the democratic content of the institutions themselves. This de-emphasis of the sites of ongoing controversy allowed advocates to connect with a far wider audience than business elites had previously been able to reach.

Nonetheless, pro-Constitution advocacy in the 1910s and 1920s featured centrally in the era's conservative politics. Along with backing all the counter-majoritarian elements of the legal-political system, conservative politicians and lawyers often subscribed to a formalistic theory of constitutional interpretation—one bound to respect for property rights, the defense of limited federal government, and skepticism of both "class legislation" and perceived democratic excess. As the NSL's Executive Committee proclaimed, American identity itself sprang "only from the protection of personal liberty and the right of property—the right of individual possession as guaranteed by the Constitution. He who does not believe in this cannot be an American."[38]

Still, the actual programs pursued by groups like the NSL focused surprisingly little on conservative theories of constitutional interpretation—for example, on how one should defend strong property rights as a matter of legal doctrine and textual argument. Rather, pro-war and pro-Constitution voices sensed the document's untapped potential, at a time of security threat, for mobilizing a broader range of citizens behind a defense of the system writ large. Their approach thus suggested less interest in publicly relitigating interpretive or institutional design debates, though their views generally benefited from increased constitutional support. Instead, they sought, through organized events and celebrations, to galvanize a public on behalf of the overarching order generally.

And given the context of war—including the heightened receptivity to calls for national unity that it produced—the focus on the Constitution as a shared collective symbol struck a meaningful chord. Activities such as mass celebrations of the Constitution or school-mandated textual lessons gained support and participants well beyond the political Right alone. The year 1919 saw governors of twenty states issue official proclamations declaring September 17 to be Constitution Day. Governor Alfred Smith of New York announced, "I know that the citizens of this state will welcome the opportunity of demonstrating their love of country by participating in the nation-wide celebration of the signing of the Federal Constitution."[39]

That year, some twenty thousand meetings were held across the country in celebration of the text. As the *Constitutional Review* breathlessly told its readers, "if the average attendance was no more than five hundred persons, that would mean that, on that day, ten million of our people renewed their allegiance to the Constitution, were instructed as to its transcendent merits, and recorded their purpose to uphold its [*sic*] against all assaults."[40] By 1923, observance had grown to such an extent that the American Bar Association (ABA) and the National Education Association labeled the whole week "Constitution Week" and strongly encouraged schools to use part of each day for constitutional instruction. The War Department even ordered all military bases to engage in commemorative exercises.[41]

The educational campaign also included broad distribution of constitutional material, comprising countless pamphlets praising the document (such as those already mentioned, by James Beck and Charles Warren) as well as copies of the text itself. For example, the NACG published what it called a *Pocket Edition of the Constitution of the United States* and distributed 50,000 copies in 1920.[42] According to the historian Kathleen Blee, the Women's Klan similarly produced "a detailed guide to the proper display of the American flag and a pocket-sized version of the US Constitution," each booklet emblazoned with the Women's Ku Klux Klan logo.[43] The NSL even provided summer correspondence courses on the Constitution for adults.[44]

Also beginning in 1919, chambers of commerce, Rotary clubs, the ABA, and over a thousand newspapers worked together on the National Oratorical Contest, in which private and public high school students gave speeches on the virtues of the Constitution. According to the ABA's Committee on American Citizenship, by the mid-1920s "more than a million and a half young people" took part annually, in the process becoming "thoroughly educated in the Constitution."[45] Of the 1924 contest, Michael Kammen writes that the "seven finalists spoke for twelve minutes . . . at the DAR [Daughters of the American Revolution] auditorium in Washington before an audience that included Calvin Coolidge and the president of the American Bar Association. Secretary of State Charles Evans Hughes and four associate justices of the Supreme Court served as judges."[46]

Perhaps the most central constitutional educational initiative focused on compelling all schools, from grade school to university, to impose constitutional instruction as a requirement for graduation. Combining forces with the ABA's Citizenship Committee, the American Political Science Association in the early 1920s put together a model statute for state adoption. Samuel Weaver of the Washington State Bar Association described the basic elements of the proposal:

1) Below the eighth grade the teaching of patriotism and citizenship; 2) beginning with the eighth grade, regular but elementary instruction in the principles of government; 3) no student to be admitted to a high school or a normal school without having met these requirements; 4) in all high schools, colleges, and universities regular

courses of study of not less than three full periods per week throughout the school year; 5) no person to be granted a certificate to teach until he shall have passed a satisfactory examination upon the provisions and principles of our constitutional system. This law would require not only that the Constitution be taught in the school, but that the students should be required to study it and to pass a satisfactory examination upon its principles.[47]

And these calls to action paid immediate dividends. According to the historian Jill Lepore, over the course of the 1920s the number of states mandating constitutional instruction rose from twenty-three in 1923 to forty-three by 1931.[48]

DEFERENTIAL ATTACHMENT IN THE
POLITICS OF CONSTITUTIONAL RESPECT

Taken together, these educational initiatives, motivated by the need to establish the boundaries of acceptable disagreement and thus tame dissent, highlighted three aspects of an ever more prominent and deferential model of citizenship: ideological uniformity, a sense of constitutional duty or obligation, and reverence for founders. Through school instruction and also through immigrant naturalization processes, government and civic actors prioritized absolute constitutional support above all else. This was far more important than substantive engagement with, or open inquiry into, the nature of the system itself.

For backers of school bills, ranging from professional bodies and veterans' groups like the American Legion and the Grand Army of the Republic to explicitly pro-Constitution organizations and even the KKK,[49] the goal was not just *any* mode of constitutional education. Instead, they sought what Weaver called a "uniformity of instruction." For these associations, no effort would be successful unless schools across the country employed the same nationalized teaching material. Only then could "universal loyalty" to the Constitution be "secured" "regardless of state lines."[50]

These actors would likely have chafed at the suggestion that they sought to impose an unthinking conformity, which they associated with authoritarian Germany or the Soviet Union's "absolutist democracy." They would have contended that their goal was a cohesive but horizontal community, in which the divisive group identities of the recent past — especially those grounded in class or immigrant ethnic background —

receded before a primary individualized attachment to the nation as democratic citizens. Moreover, such attachment to the nation and its institutions would lead Americans, consciously and spontaneously, to defend the republic from perceived threats if necessary.

The problem, of course, was that the mechanisms for forging such attachment emphasized precisely a culture of political obedience, especially given elites' deep anxieties about the dangers posed by undirected discussion and untamed criticism. The plethora of classroom manuals and booklets generated by the National Security League and other associations put this clearly on display, framing the right type of instruction as an exercise in ritual and memorization.[51] One commonly used text, *Our Constitution in My Town and My Life* (1924), written for twelve-to eighteen-year-olds by Etta Leighton (the Civic Secretary of the National Security League), consisted of over a hundred mechanical questions and answers:

> 84. What has our Supreme Court . . . been called? "The balance wheel of the Constitution. The high guardian of the Constitution itself.". . .

> 91. What distinguishes our Government and makes it a safer guardian of the people's rights than the governments of Great Britain or France? "The Supreme Court, because it protects the people even from tyranny of the Government itself."[52]

The same tendencies shaped the period's approach to naturalization processes. Since the first federal naturalization law in 1790, prospective citizens had been required to take an oath of allegiance to the country, which included an oath to uphold the Constitution as the new law of the land.[53] But throughout the nineteenth century, the actual administration of these naturalization processes had been left to local and state courts. These judges, as the historian Dorothee Schneider tells us, were often "themselves appointees of the [local] political machine." By the end of the century, they worked with local ward bosses who sought to naturalize as many potential voters as possible, so long as they might be sympathetic to the party, even "transform[ing] hundreds of petitioners into newly minted Americans in a single day." In this context, taking the constitutional oath, let alone actually demonstrating textual commitment, was a mere formality. The main limitation on naturalization in most cities typically revolved around partisan affiliation, since "immigrants who were unlikely to vote for the political party in charge were naturalized in much smaller numbers."[54]

Given the Democratic Party makeup of many of these city machines, anti-immigrant fears about "fraudulent" naturalizations become a Republican legislative matter. This led a Republican Congress in 1906 to pass a new naturalization framework aimed at "restrict[ing] the courts empowered to naturalize, establish[ing] standardized procedures, and impos[ing] new penalties... for fraud and corruption."[55] In part due to the Republican Party's pro-business bent and its deepening association with immigration restrictionism, the bill also added that prospective citizens had to show both knowledge of English and "attachment to the principles of the Constitution."[56]

But it was not until the wartime context that actual constitutional education proliferated as part of naturalization processes. And, just as with teaching material for children, the emphasis for new citizens was on accepting the text and its institutional order as essentially sacred and above question.[57] The North American Civic League for Immigrants, out of Providence, Rhode Island, spelled out exactly the degree to which constitutional commitment rested not on respect for individualized dissent but rather on unconditional support for existing institutions. The League prepared 65 questions and answers for prospective citizens, a list even more ritualistic than those written by Leighton for teenagers:

6. Q. Do you believe in our form of government?
A. Yes.

7. Q. Will you support the constitution?
A. Yes.

8. Q. What do you mean or understand by supporting the constitution?
A. By living according to its laws, and seeing that all others do the same, and if necessary fight for its defence [*sic*].[58]

As for New York State's *Citizenship Syllabus*, Michael Kammen tells us that it too ended "with a similar catechism" and also declared that "every man living in America, working in America, and having a family in America should have instilled in him the ideals of America...."[59]

Federal District Judge Martin Wade underscored the connection between constitutional instruction and the creation of ideological consensus, whether for schoolchildren or prospective citizens. In an address published in the *Constitutional Review*, he proclaimed that anyone who questioned the viability of the Constitution should not be allowed to instruct students: "I would not have in an American college a teacher or professor who . . . even harbors a dream that some day this government will fail. . . . I would not tolerate a teacher . . . who cannot find in discussing problems of American government more to glorify than to condemn."[60] Similarly, according to one 1923 ABA report, "the schools of America should no more consider graduating a student who lacks faith in our government than a school of theology should consider graduating a minister who lacks faith in God."[61]

Alongside uniformity, constitutional education also upheld a particular theory of political membership. For all the talk of individualism, pro-Constitution activists at the time commonly emphasized the importance of developing within Americans a greater awareness of the duties and obligations of citizenship. They also aimed to enhance their devotional capacity and willingness to sacrifice personal ends for the nation. According to the same ABA report quoted above, "the gravest danger is the gross indifference of our people to the duties of citizenship."[62] Expanding on the point, Robert Lee Bullard, NSL president, often gave a stump speech called "The Meaning of Citizenship." In it, he argued that the Constitution established a system of government that could not last without the willingness to fight on its behalf—politically and militarily: "We hear all together [*sic*] too much about 'rights' . . . and too little about duty, obligation and responsibility. . . . The outstanding obligation is by force of arms to defend our government and maintain the Constitution of the United States."[63]

This notion that citizens should feel a sense of duty to sacrifice on behalf of the Constitution highlights why constitutional champions like Bullard also defended universal and mandatory military training, even during peacetime. In fact, support for such training became a central point of contact between pro-Constitution and pro-security advocacy. As Henry Litchfield West, the executive secretary of the NSL and former commissioner of the District of Columbia,[64] warned, "citizenship means everything or nothing."[65] That is, if Americans had neither the capacity nor the willingness to bear arms for the republic, citizenship itself remained an empty concept. And for David Jayne Hill, constitutional instruction and armed instruction went hand in hand, as military training offered another critical avenue for teaching the importance of respect for the constitutional state. Arguing for the basic interconnection between the two forms of education, he told one audience, "every able-bodied young man in our country should first be well instructed in the meaning and value of our free institutions, and taught a wholesome respect for civil authority, and then be impressed with the privilege and obligation of a full preparation of mind and body to defend them."[66] In a sense, even if Americans should ideally have horizontal and non-hierarchical relationships with each other as democratic citizens, getting to that point required a degree of compulsion. Imprinting respect for instituted authority, including through mandatory training and instruction, ensured a citizen's central attachment to the nation-state rather than to divisive class or ethnic identities.

Finally, in addition to ideological uniformity and a sense of duty, pro-Constitution voices sought to elevate the status of the text's framers in their educational campaigns. If Americans embraced the genius of the framers, and saw them as uniquely skilled in political creation, they would be more willing to identify emotionally with the document itself. Thus, the pamphlets, speeches, and teaching material generated during the period focused overwhelmingly on the virtue and wisdom of the founders, often using near prophetic language. For Leslie Shaw, former governor of Iowa and Treasury secretary under Teddy Roosevelt, "the Constitutional Fathers" were a "picked body of men . . . recognized as surpassing any equal number ever gathered for any purpose."[67]

George Washington, in particular, enjoyed an exalted status in this discourse; he was described time and again as the framer most central to the decision to hold a convention and later to the text's ratification. According to Charles Warren, "without [his] ardent advocacy . . . and the confidence inspired in the people by his support . . . the Constitution would never have been adopted."[68] Similarly, for James Beck, it was Washington who convinced Americans that a new constitution was needed: "Turning his back upon the sweet retirement of Mount Vernon," "once again the father of his people came to their rescue."[69] In emphasizing Washington, advocates mirrored the centennial move from 1889 to connect the constitutional state to the appeal of the first president.

By focusing on Washington, Warren, Beck, and others also sought to respond to a persistent criticism from constitutional skeptics: namely, that the revolutionary experience—complete with the Declaration of Independence—fundamentally differed from the counterrevolutionary constitutional founding a decade later. Washington's position as both wartime commander in chief of the Continental Army and presiding "father" of the Convention allowed pro-Constitution activists to present the text as the ultimate fulfillment of the revolutionary project, instead of its negation. As such, the focus on the first president was part of a sustained effort to respond to widespread class-based critiques around the document's meaning. Glorifying Washington as a transcendent figure recast the significance of the Constitution and aimed to quell doubt about its revolutionary and democratic credentials.

Such glorification—of all the framers—also served an additional and equally central purpose. The early decades of the twentieth century saw a revival across the political spectrum in organized political interest in the framers, as well as extensive scholarly work on the activities of the Philadelphia Convention, aided by the historian Max Farrand's publication in 1911 of his three-volume *Records of the Federal Convention of 1787*. But, as discussed in chapter 3, the heightened interest in and interrogation of the founding generation hardly meant their deification. Given the context of post–Civil War tension and massive industrial strife, closer inspection of the framers' words, internal debates, and socioeconomic backgrounds often fed into class-based critiques of men like Madison and Hamilton. Those analyses depicted the framers as driven by material interests and thus committed to constructing a constitutional order that, for selfish purposes, preserved economic privilege and constrained popular power.

If anything, due to the prominence of intellectuals like Charles Beard, J. Allen Smith, and Herbert Croly in the years before World War I, one may contend that the greater political presence of the eighteenth-century framers tended to go hand in hand with *decreased* faith—at least as expressed in the public debate. Activists, organized movements, and even elected officials openly asked whether the arrangements of the founding generation were still worth defending institutionally. As noted in chapter 2, the journalist and newspaper editor E. L. Godkin quipped: to the extent that elements of the existing constitutional order should be preserved, this was because the country had in truth initiated a second republic—during the Civil War—with Abraham Lincoln and wartime Republicans as the *real* founders, aiming to address the failures of the first.

For many pro-Constitution figures, this pervasive critical conversation demeaned the heroism of the nation's 1787 "fathers" and created a dangerous climate open to revolutionary projects of reform. Giving one of the many university lectures established to honor the text (the Cutler

Lecture at Rochester University), Charles Warren—seeking to defend the existing constitutional state—declared, "to describe the Constitution as simply the product of class interests or of propertied selfishness, is to assert that such motives as patriotism, pride in country, unselfish devotion to the public welfare and belief in fundamental principles of right and government, did not exist or control."[70] Such views besmirched true statesmen, and even worse, made Americans in the twentieth century believe that they could do better and thus embark upon widespread institutional experimentation. Reminding the public of the gulf between the incorruptible framers on the one hand and contemporary politicians and radical agitators on the other, Warren remarked, "they were great men, employed upon a great task, and moved by high impulses. . . . When you are asked hereafter to consider amendments to that instrument, it would be well to consider carefully whether the men who urged such changes are equally great and whether their motives and ideals are equally high."[71]

Thus, in emphasizing the genius of a Washington or a Madison, Warren and others aimed to underscore that, although acts of new political construction may have been appropriate for the late eighteenth century, they were no longer appropriate in the present. Americans should not seek to emulate that earlier generation; rather, they should show deference to their institutional handiwork. This paramount concern with protecting the institutions by elevating their creators reinforced how the educational campaigns of the time promoted hierarchical ties between the citizen and constitutional government. More than anything else, proponents of the text sought to transform the ordinary American's encounter with the document and its institutions. The Constitution should be understood not as one historical path out of many. Instead, citizens should approach the Constitution as an almost biblical inheritance from mythic (or perhaps prophetic) founders, and as fundamentally outside the bounds of legitimate opposition.

THE SUPREME COURT BUILDING AS A
MONUMENT TO CIVIC OBEDIENCE

Perhaps nothing better underscored these interrelated educational goals than the project to erect a new and separate building to house the Supreme Court. Finally completed in 1935, it represented pro-Constitution activism's greatest and most lasting aesthetic creation during the period, powerfully dramatizing the emerging vision of the ties binding Americans to their governing text.

Tasked with designing the building was Cass Gilbert, a well-known architect with close ties to the American Legion, the American Defense Society, and the National Security League. During the war, Gilbert had played a notable role in government propaganda as the associate chairman of the Committee on Public Information's Division of Pictorial Publicity.[72] Gilbert wanted above all to make the building an imposing historic monument to the Constitution, one that would inspire awe in Americans and also melt away suspicion of the Court. For this reason, his plans were controversial at the time, with some architectural critics worrying, in the words of the historian Paul Byard, that "the authority it meant to convey was easily confused with authoritarianism."[73]

The concerns focused on how Gilbert imagined the individual's aesthetic experience on viewing and entering the building. More specifically, he aimed to overwhelm the individual with the majesty of the Court. And he hoped that this experience would instill an emotional willingness within citizens to subsume their particular identities in favor of a deep attachment toward both the Court and the constitutional state it represented.

During these years, Gilbert was influenced by the revival of classical Roman iconography and design in 1920s Italy. An admirer of Benito Mussolini, with whom he had a personal audience while selecting marble for the Supreme Court building, Gilbert expressed approval of the patriotic education in Mussolini's Italy: "Patriotism is taught to the children and to grown people alike, and when a whole people is convinced of the greatness of their country and the wisdom and greatness of their leader that country is to be respected."[74] Perhaps unsurprisingly, Gilbert chose an idealized and grand variation on ancient Roman architecture as the basis for the new building. He sent Mussolini photographs of his Supreme Court drawings,[75] and handpicked the marble in Siena himself.[76]

Clearly, not all defenders of the Constitution during the period were sympathetic to Mussolini.[77] Still, Gilbert's design vision and intentions for the building aligned with the broader civic culture promoted by such groups. Pro-Constitution figures may have commonly invoked the idea of Americanism as tied to a tolerant and open individualism, which they even counterposed to a collectivist and authoritarian politics. But at the same time, many of these same writers maintained that, under circumstances of external and internal threat, individualistic values would only survive if citizens showed deference to institutions and to heroic leaders.

Indeed, given the extent to which first-order disagreements about state and economy remained a powerful force in public life, such deference was considered foundational for social cohesion and for cutting against divisive alternative political and cultural attachments. Compliance might thus be necessary to preserve the US as *the* quintessentially "tolerant nation." In this way, whatever the rhetorical claims about American openness, constitutional education in practice—through speeches, mass celebrations, textbooks, naturalization exams, and even architectural monuments—constructed affective bonds through explicitly top-down forms of allegiance.

The Constitution's Enemies as the Country's Enemies

The forceful educational approach blended pro-Constitution activism with a muscular commitment to government repression—one that often specifically targeted socialists and labor radicals as national security dangers. All this proceeded despite assertions by people like Ralph Barton Perry that fears of political authoritarianism in the US were unfounded thanks to the country's unique culture of individual liberty. Crackdowns took place through a framework of laws and executive actions that intertwined Constitution defense with a coercive security apparatus, and that sought to tie together criticism of market capitalism, anti-Constitution arguments, and sedition.

FRIENDS, ENEMIES, AND SEDITIOUS SPEECH

In general, wartime defenders of the Constitution repeated that the vast majority of citizens and new immigrants were "well-meaning people"[78] who could be made patriotic through popular education about the text. However, at the same time, they insisted that there existed a small group of enemies to the Constitution who would never be persuaded through education. According to one wartime National Security League pamphlet, these enemies were often "Secret Americans": individuals who might not openly admit their support for the German cause or for Russian revolutionaries, but who quietly stood behind arguments about pacifism or the evils of militarism to undermine the constitutional system.[79] The pamphlet continued, "the only safe rule is to regard all of these as unconditional traitors."[80] As the pages of the *Constitutional*

Review maintained, these anti-war activists exemplified how "the enemy [was] within our gates,"[81] "covertly at work to undermine the Constitution."[82] Indeed, this internal threat, spearheaded by foreign agitators and revolutionary extremists, had "made great headway"[83] and had "become a focus of infection for others."[84]

As a result, educational efforts alone were not enough; American values could only be preserved if groups promoting views outside the bounds of acceptable opinion were confronted and their threatening ideas eliminated. Pro-Constitution forces therefore appealed directly to all like-minded citizens to take matters into their own hands and to defend the political community by actively suppressing dissent. This meant that a significant element of pro-Constitution argument during the war and its aftermath not only called for dramatically expanding the domestic security apparatus. It also called on citizens to participate in acts of surveillance and, when necessary, violent reprisal.

In addition, the American Defense Society demanded "increased vigor of the interning of aggressive pro-German sympathizers, whether German citizens or not."[85] Arguing for the country to follow the lead of England's mass German internment, the Society noted that, after the arrests, "malicious plots and propaganda ceased."[86] Such groups further called for the complete exclusion of the Socialist Party from politics. In the context of the war, this position met with some success, as Wisconsin Socialist Victor Berger was twice elected to Congress in 1918 and 1919 but denied his seat by a special committee in the House of Representatives, due to his anti-war statements and his speech-based conviction on sedition charges.[87] Similarly, in 1920, the New York State Assembly suspended and then expelled on ideological grounds five SPA politicians who had been elected to the body.[88]

In fact, pro-Constitution activists frequently claimed that the Wilson administration, notorious during the period for its harsh crackdowns on dissent,[89] actually did too little to eradicate internal threats. George Sutherland, the former Utah senator and future Supreme Court justice, and himself a contributor to the *Constitutional Review*, declared in 1918 that administration actions "did not go far enough." In his view, during wartime there was no place for "scurrilous and abusive criticisms of our form of government, our Constitution and our institutions" because "an unbridled tongue may be as dangerous as a wicked hand."[90]

One famous voice of criticism came from within the administration itself. Charles Warren, in many ways the most respected intellectual face

of pro-Constitution activism in the 1920s—as well as a powerful presence in the Democratic Party and a friend to presidents and Supreme
Court justices[91]—played an especially aggressive role in debates within
the Justice Department. While assistant attorney general, Warren was
the principal drafter of Wilson's two 1917 Proclamations regulating the
conduct of "alien enemies," not to mention the Espionage Act (1917),[92]
the Trading with the Enemy Act (1917),[93] and the Sedition Act (1918).[94]

These laws provided the legal infrastructure for a massive and historically unparalleled federal assault on speech, dissent, and the rights
of European immigrants. Among other things, they led to the first government censorship boards;[95] the outlawing, according to the historian
Robert Goldstein, of "virtually all criticism of the war or the government";[96] and the summary arrest of "alien enemies."[97] Other measures
to control enemy nationals included their mass registration, as well as
a complete ban on their entering Washington, DC.[98] To give a sense
of the coerciveness of security practices during the war, some 2,000
people were prosecuted under the Espionage and Sedition Acts, mostly
for speech crimes (including some of the most well-known and popular Socialists of the time, such as Eugene Debs and Victor Berger).[99]
Over 6,000 "alien enemies" were detained under presidential warrants
issued by the attorney general, the vast majority interned in army detention camps.[100]

Warren considered the writing of these bills his greatest achievement
while in office.[101] But he was nonetheless angered by what he viewed as
the weakness of the Justice Department in combating seditious speech.
In particular, he believed that existing treason laws should be more "vigorously enforced."[102] This, he contended, would ensure that all US civilians who gave "aid or comfort"[103] to the enemy—through, for example,
nonviolent political advocacy of anti-war positions—were fully prosecuted. As for noncitizen civilians, they should face court-martial for
analogous crimes.[104]

When these views met with some internal resistance—and it became clear that the Justice Department was skeptical of his proposed
mass treason trials—Warren reached out to extreme pro-war senators
like Lee Slater Overman from North Carolina and George Earle Chamberlain from Oregon. Working with the senators, Warren drafted a new
bill providing for the military trial of civilian citizens and noncitizens
alike for all speech crimes,[105] with punishment by death at the discre-
tion of the military judges.[106] As Warren told Overman, in his view the

lack of vigilance in the Justice Department made clear that military involvement was the only solution: "For nearly a year I have been convinced that the only effective way of dealing with enemy activities in this country was by the military.... I do not believe that war can be effectively carried on by the criminal courts."[107]

After Chamberlain introduced the bill in the Senate, Thomas Gregory, the attorney general, was furious at Warren's insubordination and forced him to resign. Warren's actions, however, made him a *cause célèbre* in Washington among security hawks. And for those following the news of the day, his actions helped to further entwine the linkage of pro-Constitution and pro-war commitment.[108]

Such activists did not stop with calls for new, more coercive security measures. They also pursued separate nongovernmental actions against perceived constitutional enemies. For instance, the National Security League widely circulated a wartime manifesto by none other than Teddy Roosevelt, despite his pre-war critiques of the constitutional system. The manifesto declared: "We ask that good Americans ... uphold the hand of the Government at every point.... Furthermore we ask that where government action cannot be taken, they arouse an effective and indignant public opinion against the enemies of our country, whether those enemies masquerade as pacifists, or proclaim themselves the enemies of our Allies, or act through organizations such as the I. W. W. and the Socialist party machine, or appear nakedly as the champions of Germany."[109]

Indeed, a combination of belligerent nationalism and constitutional devotion—in which defenses of the text required popular campaigns of social censure, civic participation in government crackdowns, and even independent political violence—became part of the public culture of the times. Bar associations routinely imposed "punitive professional sanctions,"[110] like disbarment, for those lawyers who defended or associated with dissidents. Constitutional loyalty, as the historian Jerold Auerbach notes, meant "cleansing the bar."[111] At universities, professors who took anti-war stances or who were viewed as otherwise ideologically suspect found themselves without employment. At Columbia, university president Nicholas Murray Butler, an outspoken pro-Constitution voice, stated that there would be "no place" on campus for people who countenanced "treason." Butler oversaw the firing of numerous academics, eventually leading the historian Charles Beard himself to resign in protest.[112]

Patriotic speaking tours, such as those of Robert McNutt McElroy, Princeton professor and NSL educational director, also embodied this militant spirit. As McElroy told the *New York Tribune* after a preparedness trip to Wisconsin, the whole state was effectively committing treason, given its large German population and "100,000 disloyal votes"[113] for Socialist candidates (long one of the most popular parties in the state). Calling for government investigations and, failing that, action from loyal Americans, he declared, "I was out there when the news of the German advance was coming through, and from the reception it got you would scarcely have gained the impression that it was a blow to America. You would have been far more likely to suppose that it was somehow a cause for congratulation in this country."[114] These cries of treason and calls for action stirred various groups to respond. The most notorious was the American Protective League, which during the war enjoyed a quasi-official status, engaging in raids and surveillance of suspected German sympathizers with the backing of state and federal authorities. Following the war, the American Legion—again with government complicity[115]—similarly initiated violent attacks on those it deemed constitutional enemies and thus security threats, focusing on radical unions and organizations like the IWW and the SPA. As the journalist Norman Hapgood reported at the time, by the end of 1920 the American Civil Liberties Union had verified over fifty coordinated acts of violence nationwide by Legionnaires.[116]

In effect, pro-Constitution advocacy closely bound itself to a remarkably authoritarian statecraft, one that tarred anti-war, anti-Constitution, and anti-capitalist speech as interrelated threats to Americanism. Under this framework, dissenting activists, such as in the IWW or the Socialist Party, were constitutional enemies beyond reasoned debate. One need not engage with the actual ideas of someone like Eugene Debs, Crystal Eastman, or "Big Bill" Haywood, because they were not "well-meaning people." Instead, they were "impervious alike to logic and to facts," and so "a focus of infection for others." Precisely since these actors could not be reasoned with, government officials and civic associations defended everything from bans on political parties to speech restrictions, arrests, and deportations.

Crucially, such coercion was justified precisely in terms of the Constitution. Only security vigilance would ensure the survival of the constitutional state and, with it, the very Americanism championed by the likes of Perry and David Jayne Hill. Thus, pro-war and pro-Constitution advocates could describe an inclusive and open-minded America, while at the same time exercising repressive power to protect such values from external German actions or internal socialist threat.

The institution principally tasked with guarding the constitutional state was none other than the "commander in chief," the president. The wartime experience thus also highlighted how the politics of constitutional defense and of presidential expansion—not to mention violent excess—fed each other. In a sense, the war cemented Wilson's full identification with the Constitution and even with the politics of Constitution worship—a complete reversal from his earlier sentiments. For all intents and purposes, he now oversaw a security apparatus that authorized the arrest and imprisonment of dissenters for attacking the Constitution. There was an obvious irony in Socialists facing potential prison sentences for statements hardly more extreme than Wilson's 1876 diary description of the Constitution as creating a "miserable delusion of a republic." But Wilson had left those assessments behind, embracing the presidency as a robust and flexible tool of both policy-making and security control. Furthermore, he clearly appreciated how, during a time of war, the hyper-nationalism associated with constitutional devotion could be a useful means for strengthening the power of the office.

In this way, Wilson's wartime security practices vividly embodied just those pre-war SPA fears that saw the Progressive turn toward presidentialism as the solution to an anti-democratic Constitution. Socialists had worried that, as an end run around the broken features of the 1787 framework, executive power would simply unleash discretionary violence, while failing to adequately address deep-rooted and structural flaws. Presidentialism might promote energetic power, but at the cost of reinforcing the anti-democratic nature of the existing order. And those anxieties hardly seemed far-fetched, given that politicians and labor activists had been imprisoned, the SPA and IWW had both seemingly been declared seditious, and loyalty campaigns were proliferating.

Today we tend to think of the Constitution as a central tool for pushing back against just these types of security excesses. But Wilson's combination of venerative politics and robust presidential authority suggests that this is only part of the story. The wartime experience directly intertwined a culture of Constitution worship with growing and unchecked executive power. And, as will be discussed in later chapters, this combination was hardly unique to World War I. It reemerged time and again as a significant feature of twentieth-century American security politics, eventually reaching its zenith during the Cold War.

THE CULTURAL EFFECTS OF VENERATING
A CAPITALIST CONSTITUTION

This pro-Constitution turn to repression, especially of anti-war and anti-capitalist groups, resonated deeply with the authoritarian nationalist politics gaining strength elsewhere in the world at the time. And the intertwining of constitutional loyalty with an aggressive security politics highlights a profound tension in the type of constitutional culture that the events around World War I helped to foster in the US. As the next chapters explore, once the war's jingoism receded, the increasing identification of constitutional loyalty with egalitarian creedal terms provided a rhetorical basis for defending religious toleration, dissenting speech, women's rights, immigrant inclusion, and protections for Native Americans and Black citizens—even in the depths of the Jim Crow 1920s. Thus, one piece of the war's legacy aligns with how current scholars and commentators often depict the Constitution's salutary function in collective life—facilitating a common public culture dedicated to sober reflection and civil liberties, and skeptical of belligerent nationalist appeals.[117]

At the same time, pro-war political and legal elites did not generate an historically unprecedented mass politics of constitutional loyalty by fostering self-reflective citizen-subjects. Instead, they employed the entire apparatus and repressive potential of the state to entrench deferential citizenship, using the perceived need for greater social cohesion to systematically feed practices of top-down conformity and assimilation. Therefore, for all the talk of the Constitution's centrality to protecting liberty, very little of the period's organizing focused on valorizing the types of civil libertarian commitments, especially freedom of speech, that one might expect. Rather, pro-Constitution figures often viewed crackdowns on dissent as critical to protecting the constitutional state, or as the NACG manifesto proclaimed, to "inculcat[ing] ... respect for the organic law of the land."[118]

For pro-war and pro-Constitution advocates, supporting the Constitution and aggressively policing political speech went together. In fact, Socialist Party and IWW invocations of their First Amendment speech rights were often dismissed out of hand as a way for dangerous revolutionaries to avoid appropriate suppression. This all underscores how today's standard linkage of a civil libertarian Bill of Rights with constitutional commitment remained relatively tangential to that era's pro-Constitution organizing. As the historian Gerard Magliocca notes,

"Wilson never referred to the Bill of Rights in any public statement over his two terms of office."[119] Indeed, it would take the specific dynamics of a second world war against Nazi Germany for now familiar discourses around the Bill of Rights to take center stage in how governing elites celebrated the Constitution.

The World War I era's far different constitutional rhetoric speaks to how a new constitutional citizenship spread in the United States in tandem with the development of a security apparatus, reinforcing and legitimizing emerging modes of coercive power instead of simply limiting such coercion. The way pro-Constitution advocates linked devotion to the document with both heightened militarization and a defense of American international police power therefore had long-term implications for the country's constitutional culture. In particular, these security origins embedded lasting ideological continuities between the inclusive and the repressive dimensions of the American constitutional experience—continuities built into official versions of creedal constitutionalism.

Finally, such repression brought with it a noteworthy reframing of pre-war debates about the Constitution's relationship to capitalism and socialism. Before the war, the close business identification with the Constitution was a genuine liability in popular politics. To the extent that the Constitution seemed to operate in conjunction with an aggressive brand of market capitalism, this raised the prospect that meaningfully addressing economic grievances might require significantly rewriting the Constitution. Indeed, as noted in chapter 3, some Progressive reformers sought to push back against this growing presumption by defending the Constitution's interpretive and structural flexibility. They claimed, in opposition to SPA and IWW activists, that one should not associate the Constitution with pro-business orthodoxy because the Constitution had no preconceived economic theory, and changes to production and distribution *could* occur under the existing legal-political system.

But for many Americans who rallied to the military cause during a time of patriotic fervor, the Constitution's association with capitalism was more to be defended than critiqued. Government and civic actors specifically targeted socialist and labor radicals, especially in the SPA and the IWW, as threats due to their combined anti-war and anti-Constitution beliefs. Pro-Constitution efforts thus helped to promote a far broader identification of socialism with un-Americanism, well beyond the old bastions of the business Right.

At a time when more and more Americans were taking part in mass celebrations of the Constitution, that existing connection in the public mind between socialist politics and opposition to the text had a further consequence. The simultaneous attack on socialism and constitutional dissent intensified a cultural embrace of market capitalism as a critical part of both national identity and an American order in need of preservation. The war—and the patriotic mood it generated—thus became a key moment in advancing a capitalist ethos in the popular imagination, as a worthy component of what Americans should fight for when they defended Constitution and country.

Conclusion: The Long Shadow of Wartime Constitutional Devotion

The intensity and pervasiveness of pro-Constitution activism had a striking effect in the years following the war, both on opponents of state security crackdowns and on public life more generally. Mass inculcation of constitutional devotion certainly revolved, to a large degree, around top-down projects of repression and propaganda. Yet there also existed a genuine and substantial popular appetite for just these projects. The war's added sense of threat helped to transform fears about social breakdown—in the face of class conflict, massive numbers of new immigrants, and challenges to the racial order—into far more than simply the anxieties of a wealthy few. Leaders of groups like the NSL or the American Legion, not to mention the Ku Klux Klan, found more and more Americans "search[ing] for order"[120] in the face of near continuous upheaval. Many such citizens found new meaning and security through the collective effervescence and affective power produced by mass political rituals—not unlike publics in Europe during the same years.

Therefore, wartime recitations of constitutional faith, complete with celebrations of the document and its framers, cannot simply be reduced to a false consciousness perpetuated by business and governmental elites. These practices spread so widely because they also responded to a real wariness many Americans felt about the trajectory of pre-war public life—including the rise of socialist and anarchist politics— while embodying a desire to take pride in a shared history of achievement, irrespective of that history's flaws.

Pre-war social movements had sought to better their members' lives by challenging the value of existing structures and settler norms, from the nature of the economy and the state to the organization of family and race relations. In the post-war period, these movements' leaders faced the question of how to sustain that energy for change in a time of intensifying popular concern with social disorder: How does one argue for transformation when the collective focus on national pride and unity increasingly collapses into a defense of the existing system—including through state and private violence? How should reformers relate to those working-class white citizens—especially men returning from war—who now deeply identified in patriotic terms with the nation-state they fought to defend? And, relatedly, what to do with the increasingly pervasive political discourse that treated anything with a whiff of socialism, including anti-Constitution arguments, as tantamount to disloyalty?

Past activists may have unapologetically called for constitutional rupture and comprehensive social reconstruction. But after the war, reformers became more reticent to directly oppose the intertwining of Americanism and constitutional support. It would take another intense social crisis—the Great Depression—for radical anti-Constitution opposition to reclaim the political offensive. But even then, World War I's legacy of pro-Constitution and security-driven nationalism would cast a long shadow.

CHAPTER 7

Inclusion and Exclusion in Interwar Americanism

In the depths of World War I, it hardly seemed self-evident that the 1920s would witness a growing sense, even among previously skeptical reformers, of the need to speak in a register that combined American-ism with constitutional veneration. The war certainly tapped into a substantial base for Constitution worship, gaining emboldened defenders especially among native-born Euro-Protestants and even working-class white Americans. Still, assertions about the Constitution's genius often continued to carry the mark of empty, business-sponsored cliché, despite such claims enjoying deeper political and cultural resonance. And the war itself remained highly contentious, with mass draft evasion and profound opposition across labor, immigrant, and Black constituencies in particular. Furthermore, 1917 was a dramatic year in world history—punctuated not only by American entrance into the war but also by the Russian Revolution, whose ultimate outcome and meaning remained open. For those in the Socialist Party of America (SPA), the Industrial Workers of the World (IWW), and other radical organizations, profound changes seemed inevitable within the United States as well. In this moment of radicalization, and even in the face of well-funded and energetic pro-war and pro-Constitution efforts, systemic critiques of the existing governing framework appeared ascendant rather than on the verge of retreat.

Yet, as this chapter explores, over the course of the 1920s the charge of un-Americanism increasingly stuck to such opposition, which found itself facing genuine marginalization. Two developments in particular fed into this shift. First, as discussed in chapter 6, at a time of patriotic ferment, growing mass weariness of domestic social conflict, along with the continued state crackdowns on dissidents, placed almost all reform-ist politics on the defensive. Second, pro-Constitution advocates combined universalistic appeals with a rhetoric of cultural chosen-ness in ways that played into the deep-seated white supremacist impulses continuing to permeate collective life.

In particular, as this chapter first lays out, pro-Constitution advocates engaged in a sustained effort to racialize constitutional opposition. At a time when alternative constitutional models appeared everywhere—and neighboring Mexico embarked upon writing its own new revolutionary document—various defenders of the 1787 text cast all these projects as foreign and dangerous. And they suggested that, if competing constitutional ideas percolated in domestic life, such ideas must result from the ethno-racial cultural immaturity of new immigrants and nonwhite constituencies. Underscoring the discursive plasticity of pro-war brands of creedal constitutionalism, these advocates even routinely made common cause with groups like the Klan. In doing so, they presented anti-Constitution sentiment not as a long-standing staple of American political discourse, or even as dangerous just for any association with socialism. Instead, they increasingly constructed all anti-Constitution sentiments as racially foreign and for that reason a distinctive threat.

These claims hint at why an aggressive nationalist politics was so powerful during this specific period, certainly by comparison with the pre-war years. The combination of external war and internal ethno-racial and religious pluralism tapped into deep-seated Euro-Protestant anxieties about the implications of growing diversity. Pro-Constitution advocates and increasing numbers of native-born white citizens saw the country's heterogeneity as a profound source of disunion and social conflict, precisely at a time when the nation itself seemed to be in peril. All of this fed a rallying effect around an intensified vision of the American nation, bound to judgments about both race and Constitution in ways that contrasted with long-standing traditions of institutional experimentation and reform.

The chapter also considers how this marshaling of race to stamp out opposition, along with the war context and the period's mass education campaigns, generated profound internal debates within immigrant, Indigenous, Black, labor, and feminist movements. While exclusionary nationalism met with genuine success during and after the war, the pro-war focus on the creedal Constitution also embodied a significant rhetorical opening for these opponents. Such movements thus struggled to define their appropriate relationship to the Constitution and to American nationalism. Many pre-war Socialist and labor radicals had outspokenly rejected both "Americanism" and the Constitution, since they described patriotism as a kind of class treason and viewed the existing legal-political system as inherently undemocratic. But new movement leaders and reform institutions were shaped by the war, the state's crackdowns, and the ethno-racial climate.

As such, they became unwilling to directly challenge the terms of debate, even if they may have believed in principle that the Constitution was fundamentally broken and should be rewritten wholesale. Instead, reformers across a variety of movements—especially immigrant, labor, civil libertarian, and feminist—began to emphasize how their claims were grounded in the Constitution. They especially focused on First Amendment protections connected to free speech and religious toleration, and in the process repurposed creedal ideals for more inclusionary ends. These activists effectively decided that, if the spreading constitutional citizenship could not be straightforwardly rejected, perhaps it could still be made compatible with meaningful change. And this political repurposing won tangible policy victories, even against the larger context of political reaction.

This strategy also fed into that steady and ongoing transformation of radical constitutional skepticism—once a common opinion held by reformers, politically engaged Americans, and even establishment officials—into a position ever more associated with a lack of adequate patriotism. The chapter thus concludes by considering the lasting effects of the inter-war era's racial politics of disloyalty. Especially for white reformers, the framing of constitutional support and constitutional opposition as wrapped up with who could claim status as a "true" American significantly redirected political discourse and reformist strategies.

Yet, the final shift would have to wait for a later period. Even during these inter-war years of political suppression, robust critiques of American nationalism and of constitutional fidelity still circulated. But in contrast to the years before and during World War I, they circulated most aggressively within Black and Indigenous counter-publics: dissident groups already cast as ethno-racial outsiders and thus often less concerned with being targeted as un-American. In fact, it was Black radical critiques—which intensified due to the period's Jim Crow violence and extremism—that provided a thread of continuity between pre–World War I radical constitutional opposition and its partial revival during the New Deal social struggles to come.

For the main histories of American identity, all of this might seem a bundle of contradictions. Scholars like Gary Gerstle, Rogers Smith, or

Michael Ignatieff certainly accept that the US has competing traditions of what we might call civic and ethnic nationalisms—notions of collective identity grounded in liberal pluralism as well as those grounded in "illiberal" and inherited racial, cultural, and religious ties.[1] But it is hard to explain, through those existing accounts, why American ethnic nationalism generally speaks in the "civic" and presumptively inclusive language of the creedal Constitution. How did creedal constitutionalism become the discursive framework not only for civil rights promotion but also for racially restrictive accounts of national identity and membership? Is it merely a cynical smokescreen?

The inter-war era's affirmations of creed and Constitution point to at least a partial answer, suggesting, for instance, that recent anti–"critical race theory" politics is a contemporary manifestation of argumentative strains dating back a century. As discussed in chapter 5, American expansion in the Philippines and elsewhere elaborated a set of claims about how creedal constitutionalism—a potentially revolutionary and threatening ideology for white settler society—could nonetheless align with the segregationist commitments of people like Woodrow Wilson. During and after World War I, the new mass politics of Constitution worship went even further, with many proponents investing deeply in the idea that the creedal Constitution emerged in the US *precisely because of* Anglo-European chosen-ness. At the same time, white politics during these years also asserted, time and again, that Black critiques of white racism were an unpatriotic attack on the creedal nation.

All of this made commonplace a stunning reversal within mainstream politics. African Americans, who had long been the cultivators and champions of creedal constitutionalist language, found many of their own egalitarian efforts at basic civic inclusion—not even radical transformation—recast by conservative forces as a "fifth column" threatening the creed itself. In fact, especially in the North and West, white voices increasingly defended the existing racial order not through classic arguments about biological superiority and essentialism. Rather, such voices presented an Enlightenment American creed as imperiled by radical and foreign reformists of various stripes.

This politics of the inter-war period thus also helps to explain a significant puzzle in more recent American life. A key rhetorical feature of the "white nationalist" political revival intensified by the Trump years has been an aggressive embrace, by many proponents, of a version of creedal constitutionalism. Certainly, some voices have explicitly asserted white supremacist views. But more commonly, aligned politicians and commentators will attack "multiculturalism"[2] and anti-racist teaching in schools, or defend harsh crackdowns on immigrant rights, by claiming to stand for both the universalistic principles of "1776"[3] and the Constitution.

Indeed, the 1920s and 1930s proliferation of education bills—from state-mandated constitutional instruction to English-only classrooms—serve as the historical lineage for today's more recent public-school interventions. For example, a 2021 Texas bill bans teachers from presenting "slavery and racism [as] anything other than deviations from, betrayals of, or failures to live up to, the authentic founding principles of the United States, which include liberty and equality."[4] The bill is part of a sustained conservative reaction against contemporary Black political efforts at racial reform; such reactions present public engagement with the history and ongoing practice of racism—rather than resurgent white supremacy—as the *actual* threat to a creedal constitutional order. This pushback mobilizes ideas of American inclusion and universalism precisely as a way of forestalling a sustained examination of what genuine equality may entail. And it emphasizes, once again, the flexibility of creedal constitutionalism as well as the long-standing paradoxical quality of its entanglement with American ethno-nationalism.

Racializing Constitutional Opposition

It may seem counterintuitive that any version of the creedal Constitution can fit so comfortably with a politics of white nationalism or function to strengthen nativist political objectives. But in the years after World War I, many pro-Constitution activists pursued precisely this set of ends and alliances through the language of the creed. In doing so, they successfully pushed back against a political view circulating at the time: the thought, present for decades, that native-born Americans might look abroad and to new immigrant communities for possible alternatives to their own legal-political order. In the process, these activists also mobilized white racial solidarity as an engine for entrenching constitutional loyalty.

THE MEXICAN CONSTITUTION AND THE QUESTION OF FOREIGN MODELS

To make sense of the racial dynamics of pro-Constitution advocacy, it helps to appreciate how the dislocations of World War I—for all the ways in which it promoted jingoistic politics—also spread cosmopolitan ideas of transnational change and institutional borrowing. The rise of the Soviet Union made real the idea that workers and their allies could actually establish an alternative to capitalism in the here and now. And, although less commonly remembered today, 1917 witnessed another remarkable event outside the national border: the Mexican adoption of a new constitution during its own revolution. This adoption, like the Russian Revolution, spoke to the existence of non-US models for how to govern political and economic life.

The Mexican constitutional founding had great appeal to labor and radical activists at home. And it could not simply be cast aside by pro-Constitution figures as Bolshevism—despite the efforts of business elites to do so.[5] For some domestic observers, what made this adoption so significant was how it implicitly challenged the efforts of pro-Constitution advocates to depict a constitutional tradition, writ large, as a uniquely US inheritance and cultural project—or to present the global spread of constitutionalism as the spread *specifically* of 1787 principles and institutions.

The Mexican example thus spoke to the fact that the US was not the only society, in the Americas or elsewhere, that claimed an Enlightenment heritage or whose members embraced ideals of free self-rule. It became part of a broader debate not only about constitutional possibility, but also about whether the pro-war focus on a distinctive and exceptional American way of life—tied to the existing federal Constitution—was itself a deeply limited parochialism. Why should one view the prevailing US constitutional order, riddled with corporate influence and anti-democratic constraints, as the best expression of a broader and potentially universal Enlightenment tradition?

As for the text of the Mexican document, the constitution was a mixture of different models and theories of design. Like the 1901 Cuban Constitution, the document drafted by future president Venustiano Carranza and groups allied to him preserved a Madisonian separation of powers, with a president, bicameral legislature, and federal judicial power complete with a Supreme Court. And it also formalized various individual and negative rights evocative of the US 1787 text, with respect to matters like criminal process or the quartering of troops in private homes. But alongside these provisions, the new constitution encapsulated key aspirational commitments of an international and broadly social-democratic Left.

In particular, the 1917 Mexican Constitution broke from the American federal constitutional model in including a long list of detailed policy goals aimed at fulfilling popular needs, and above all at incorporating extensive socioeconomic rights. Articles 27 and 123 especially highlight such rights, focusing on land reform and worker status respectively. The former constitutionalized the state's right to regulate "natural resources" to ensure a "more equitable distribution of public wealth," including by taking "necessary measures . . . to divide up large landed estates." The latter article—a landmark globally for the labor movement—constitutionalized, among a list of social protections, the right to unionize, to the eight-hour day, to the strike, to minimum wage, to social security, and to equal pay for equal work regardless of sex or race.[6]

In 1901, the US Constitution had been the ideological horizon for many educated and wealthy Cuban nationalists. But by 1917, the Mexican constitution—at least, the elements that addressed the "social question"—implicitly repudiated the 1787 text's focus on property rights and limited formal protections for poor and working people. Instead this Mexican model, which soon spread across Latin America and Europe, helped set the terms of constitutional debate for the Weimar Republic in Germany and for Russian revolutionaries of various stripes.[7]

In reality, the ideological divisions evident in the writing of the document meant that most of its transformative socioeconomic potential remained unfulfilled—though other countries eventually brought these concepts to greater fruition. But the idea of the Mexican Constitution nonetheless provided a powerful counterexample to the US federal model. SPA and labor activists thus embraced the Mexican development as a dramatic victory for the working class, and as a new opening for conceiving of a constitution's relationship to rights. Moreover, it upended judgments about racial hierarchy and institutional diffusion—since here learning moved from a former colony read as non-white to Europe and its settler polities, rather than vice versa.

In taking seriously constitutional alternatives such as the Mexican example, activists within the United States also implicitly suggested a reevaluation of the status of immigrant communities at home: looking abroad for potential insight highlighted the value of learning from a broad range of domestic newcomers as well. As August Spies had proclaimed all the way back in 1887, he too came from a community (in

Germany) that had struggled to overcome feudal oppression, and that might have lessons to teach native-born Americans confronting evolving iterations of the old hierarchies.

In fact, immigrant voices, who had long been central to building both the labor movement and radical politics more broadly, came to play a powerful role in speaking out against American military involvement as well as the new constitutional loyalty. In the process, they questioned how war support had become an instrument for defending both political repression and the prevailing class-based status quo.

PRO-CONSTITUTION ADVOCACY AND THE FOUNDATIONS FOR FORCED ASSIMILATION

Despite the mass celebrations and flag-waving, pro-war and pro-Constitution advocates could not avoid confronting the question of whether the overseas events of 1917 compelled Americans to consider fundamentally revising their own institutions. Answering in the negative, these voices returned again to the now familiar focus on American cultural particularity: the historical uniqueness of the American experience suggested that the Constitution was a sacred document, arising from a culturally exceptional Euro-American settler community, and it could not simply be replaced. In this way, such advocates aggressively framed opposition to the Constitution as not only unpatriotic, but also as a destructive product of unassimilable and threatening ethno-racial outsiders.

In the pre-war years, constitutional skepticism had been voiced widely, well outside new immigrant and labor radical circles and by such exemplars of respectable white Protestant opinion as Woodrow Wilson and the journalist William Allen White. In fact, at the beginning of the twentieth century, the precise contours of the "American model" remained contested. Recall that proliferating state constitutions often diverged sharply from the US federal system, with long and detailed texts, flexible amendment processes, more majoritarian structures, and some socioeconomic rights protections. And these experiments in constitution-writing were perhaps even more quintessentially "American" than the 1787 text, given that settlers replicated them time and again as they expanded across the country. As such, in important ways, the Mexican constitutional experiment actually paralleled developments percolating throughout the United States.

But political discourse around the Mexican example took a different turn. Instead, efforts to associate constitutional experimentation with immigrant activists at home or Mexican politics abroad prompted an explicitly racialized counterreaction. Pro-Constitution advocates rejected the idea that native-born and Euro-Protestant Americans had anything to learn from perceived outsiders. They presented rallying around the federal Constitution—as a symbol of the nation and as the definitively "American" model—as an essential way to separate the Euro-Protestant American republic from racially and culturally unfit alternatives. In the process, such arguments further entrenched the idea that the federal model, rather than other ongoing experiments within the country, counted as the American exemplar.

As chapter 6 suggested, the war's climate of constitutional celebration, as well as of looming threat, gave added vitality to preexisting business claims that socialist and labor activism, including "Constitution tinkering," was un-American and a project of external meddling. Those claims increasingly melded with nativist rhetoric that racially suspect foreigners were pressing these ideas on "true" Americans. Whether non-European neighbors like Mexico or southern European immigrants, none of these communities supposedly had the same long-standing education in self-rule as native-born white Americans.

As Burton Alva Konkle, a Swarthmore College history professor and frequent contributor to the *Constitutional Review* in the 1920s, wrote of recent arrivals, "instead of coming in a profound thoughtfulness for the blessings of free institution, some place their raw Utopian theories on their banners and ask us to adopt them."[8] Or, as David Jayne Hill similarly concluded, in order to sustain the Constitution—a national inheritance with roots extending back to the Pilgrims themselves—immigrants would have to shed their Old World and "un-American" "ideas and sentiments."[9] In this way, "Americanization" and imposing constitutional commitment became one and the same, the essential method of "'assimilating' the new elements that enter into our population."[10]

All of this spoke to how the version of creedal constitutionalism developed by Hill, Wilson, and others, which spread broadly during the war years, hardly constrained a racialized discourse of repression and forced assimilation. On first glance this might be surprising, given how creedal rhetoric about American exceptionalism—even from the likes of Woodrow Wilson—rested on universalistic Enlightenment claims. But emphasizing the need for various groups to identify as democratic citizens of the nation, rather than as members of immigrant or class-based communities, did not mean a displacement of *every* ethno-racial affiliation. Instead, it implicitly reconceived the abstract and individualized citizen of the nation-state as someone who, in reality, had properly acculturated into *one* of the various competing affiliations—a Euro-Protestant and native-born identity. This segment of society, whose values and self-understanding enjoyed elevation as the collective standard, became the presumptive cultural norm establishing proper citizenship and nation-state attachment.

This construction of domestic citizenship also related to culturally particularist arguments about the US's appropriate place in the global order. Specifically, as discussed with reference to the Philippines in chapter 5, such a definition of citizenship explained why native-born Euro-Americans enjoyed the moral right to assert international police power and to reconstruct in their own image both outsider communities at home and foreign societies abroad. This exceptionality justified the United States' special and redemptive global project, embodied by the war effort, and emphasized the domestic importance of preserving the country's distinctive constitutional heritage.

The circulating discourse of creedal constitutionalism certainly had tendencies toward both more and less inclusion. But in the context of war and domestic pressure, pro-Constitution advocates ultimately embraced the exclusionary potential of American exceptionalism. These advocates saw growing ethno-racial heterogeneity, alongside mass political dissent in a time of national peril, as essentially pluralism gone awry: destructive and discordant rather than inculcating a unifying civic culture. In line with their focus on ideological conformity, such concerns pushed pro-Constitution figures to reinforce the cultural dominance of Euro-Protestant settler identity as a necessary prerequisite for social cohesion and consensus.

This increasingly dominant approach thus married universalism *and* racial hierarchy. And the combination allowed Wilson to speak of the universal right of all peoples to self-determination, while simultaneously defending Jim Crow and worrying, on the eve of World War I, that European internal fighting imperiled the future of "white supremacy on this planet."[11]

CONSTITUTIONALIST NATIVISM AND THE KLAN

Shared assumptions about the ethno-racial foundation of American identity help explain why establishment pro-Constitution groups could nonetheless make common political cause with explicitly white supremacist organizations like the Klan. The Klan's aggressive targeting of Jewish and Catholic immigrants alongside African Americans may seem out of step with an ostensible embrace of universalist values. But the ways in which powerful figures implemented creedal constitutionalism meant that, in practice, it could be difficult to distinguish these groups' preferred policies in key areas of American life.

Figures like Hill certainly disagreed with those in the Klan over the extent to which American values could be fully internalized by non-white peoples. Recall that for him Americanism was not reducible to "a matter of race." Such disagreement played out, for instance, on issues related to the US's global role and the value of spreading constitutional self-government abroad. Like more extreme nativists, Hill opposed Wilson's efforts to incorporate the country into the League of Nations. But as a Republican internationalist, Hill's opposition was based on his belief that the League would actually hinder the exercise of American international police power. He worried it would subject an exceptional and universal nation—not to mention its project of global primacy—to supervision by less free societies through an incipient world government.[12] Thus, over the long run, it would undermine rather than strengthen a redemptive American project.

By contrast, extreme nativists mirrored past anti-annexationist arguments in the debates over Puerto Rico and the Philippines, tying isolationism to xenophobia and a closed border. They opposed the League based on a suspicion that foreign communities would threaten a Euro-Protestant settler identity at home. Individuals like Senator William Borah of Idaho, who combined isolation with aggressive anti-immigrant rhetoric and policy arguments, or Tom Watson, a white supremacist out of Georgia, called for international retreat in tandem with defenses of racial purity and exclusion. Indeed, these views were powerful enough to forestall Wilson's hope of the United States taking a clear leadership role in the post-war era, not to mention the push by global interventionists in both parties to claim control over the state's foreign policy. It would take Pearl Harbor and World War II for the imperial internationalism associated with both Wilson and Hill to gain permanent political victory and to proceed unconstrained by a decisive isolationist check.[13]

These disagreements nonetheless took place against a shared set of judgments about the settler past. Hill may have rejected the idea that greater global engagement would undermine domestic American cohesion. But he also accepted the centrality of Euro-Protestant experience for national identity and purpose—an experience shaped by a unique cultural heritage extending from the Mayflower Compact to the federal Constitution. For Hill, just as for explicit white supremacists, it spoke to the political maturity of English and later Euro-Protestant settlers by comparison with other peoples. As the editors of the *American Standard*, the Klan's widely circulated journal, wrote of the Constitution, in terms consistent with more establishment pro-Constitution advocacy, the document "put into written form the immortal principles of liberty, popular government, and equal justice, which were the fruitage of Anglo-Saxon character."[14]

In effect, Klan leaders and establishment pro-Constitution figures shared an account of the exceptionalism of Euro-Protestant settlement and a diagnosis of 1920s America: ethnic, religious, and racial heterogeneity fed socialist disorder and constitutional disloyalty, undermining the cultural foundations of the republic.

This shared viewpoint meant that both establishment pro-Constitution groups and Klan activists rallied around aggressive Americanization efforts that combined education and immigration initiatives. As discussed in chapter 6, these included state-mandated constitutional instruction. They also entailed stamping out foreign languages in schools and in political life. Promoters believed that an exclusive focus on English would standardize national identity and ensure that new communities embraced a properly American ideal of liberty, order, and self-government. In addition, they contended that such efforts would help to overcome the destructive effects of socialism, ethnoracial heterogeneity, and lingering anti-war sentiment.

Calls for English-only measures had gained prominence during World War I and focused especially on the German language, which was associated with everything from Old World monarchism to Nietzschean and collectivist authoritarianism to anarchist and revolutionary socialism. Hill's American Defense Society demanded that state and local governments eliminate the use of German in schools and fight to make "the German language . . . a dead language."[15] At the same time, the NSL began a national campaign "with the object of destroying the German-language press"[16] through mass popular rallies and pressure on advertisers and news dealers.[17]

Critically, when the war ended, English-only proposals did not recede. They actually grew beyond the wartime focus on German identity. By 1923, the number of states that required English-only instruction stood at thirty-five, up from just nine at the end of the nineteenth century.[18] Capturing the Americanization sentiment in 1919, the famed Harvard academic Albert Bushnell Hart—a president of both the American Historical Association and the American Political Science Association, and the NSL's Education Director of the Committee on Patriotism through Education—remarked that "any adult immigrant who comes to this country and is found three years thereafter unable to use English for the ordinary communications of life should be repatriated." In his view, "no public or private schools ought to be allowed to educate in any racial language except English," and suffrage should be limited solely to "those who can read and write English, not merely a few stock phrases and sign their name, but can actually communicate with people in the ordinary daily life."[19]

Hart's words highlight just how easily pro-Constitution voices moved between creedal universalism and exclusionary politics during the era. Hart very explicitly contended that values of inclusion were central to American constitutional identity; indeed, he had been one of W. E. B. Du Bois's professors at Harvard and served as a trustee of Howard University.[20] But all groups were only *theoretically* fit to enjoy a universal American freedom. Transforming this theoretical fitness into reality required employing government power to impose a standard "American" identity on those viewed as politically and culturally unprepared. It essentially suggested maintaining over all outsider communities—from new immigrants to African Americans, Chinese, Mexicans, and Indigenous peoples—the same brand of "tutelage" that the US engaged in abroad.[21]

This sentiment led more establishment pro-Constitution advocates—whether Hill, Hart, or the author and former Assistant Attorney General Charles Warren—to become closely associated with the era's restrictionist immigration policies, alongside groups like the Klan. In the 1920s, nativist politicians finally succeeded in closing the open door for European arrivals, with the passage in 1917 of a literacy test for immigrants and the implementation in 1921 and 1924 of the first numerical quotas, limiting annual immigration from abroad entirely—well beyond those of Chinese descent.

The second of the quota laws, 1924's National Origins Act, targeted southern and eastern Europeans specifically, dramatically reducing the numbers admitted from those regions. It also explicitly excluded from the quota system Asian immigrants ("aliens ineligible to citizenship and their descendants") and Black people from the Caribbean ("the descendants of slave immigrants"). The result was that in the ensuing years the share of entrants from northern and western Europe rose to 84 percent, and official immigration from many non-white communities essentially disappeared.[22]

These practices no doubt perpetuated classic settler exclusivities, re-inforcing the idea of whiteness as crucial to American belonging. But they did so on terms that highlighted the extent to which the centuries-long project of territorial expansion and settlement had become a thing of the past. If the open door for European migrants had been a product of settler demographic needs, by the 1920s that project was complete. And even many European newcomers—once viewed as potential co-ethnic settler participants—faced nativist barriers to entry.[23]

Threatened communities contested all of these policies. But strik-ingly, pro-Constitution advocates often responded by simply embrac-ing ethno-racial arguments to explain away internal resistance or to articulate why security requirements justified the exclusion of some groups. Hill's discussion of the Pilgrims may have left the point implicit, but Iowa Governor Leslie Shaw reminded Americans that the Consti-tution had arisen from an English and Euro-Protestant social environ-ment. He reiterated the view that Americanization projects, and indeed the Constitution itself, faced opposition because, by the early twentieth century, that identity was disintegrating under the pressures of racial and religious heterogeneity. From African Americans to Roman Cath-olics, the United States found itself attempting to integrate increasingly diverse populations—and "many of them," Shaw argued, were "biolog-ically unable to think in terms of Anglican liberty."[24]

In this way, the boundary between more establishment pro-Constitution advocacy and Klan argument often became difficult to delineate. Many promoters of the Constitution during and after the war may have broadly disseminated the new creedal politics. But this vision of creed and Constitution did not displace white supremacy. In-stead, the variation aligned with efforts to update and project it into the future.

In particular, such ideas allowed civic and government actors to as-sert universalistic and inclusive commitments in theory, while in prac-tice arguing that the basic order required defending classic settler hi-erarchies and imposing coercive policies premised on the need to eliminate difference. And this helped to reframe constitutional opposi-tion not simply as a competing legal-political viewpoint, but as itself an embodiment of a foreign and racially suspect infiltration. If anything, the connections between supposedly liberal universalistic principles and culturally grounded historical arguments only encouraged the state's coercive apparatus. It also reinforced that apparatus's focus on those groups deemed outsiders as the preeminent dangers to a Euro-American way of life.

In some ways, the uneasy but allied inter-war relationship between establishment and Klan pro-Constitution figures presages elements of today's political linkages—in particular between more conventional conservative opposition to contemporary anti-racist activism (often in creedal constitutional registers) and explicitly white nationalist opposition to the same. The two current strains of right-wing opposition are ideologically distinct, and contemporary conservatives who strongly identify with the creedal Constitution would condemn any suggestion that their education or immigration policies have any connection to racism. But these present-day perspectives similarly can share common political objectives in part due to often overlapping narratives about a unique, glorified, and racially inflected American cultural heritage—one seen as worthy of veneration and as under threat in the classroom or at the border.

Pluralistic Creedal Reform and Its Limits

The intertwining of Americanism, cultural homogeneity, and constitutional devotion during the inter-war period placed reformers and activists in an uncomfortable position. In the years following the war, the climate of mass celebrations and state crackdowns essentially transformed an accusation of constitutional opposition into a charge of national disloyalty—one with clear ethnic and racial undertones. Real social bases certainly remained open to constitutional skepticism and to fundamental changes to state and economy. But the aftereffects of World War I altered the terrain on which general debate occurred. In a meaningful shift from the pre-war era, the concerted civic, business, and government campaign had succeeded in forcing anti-Constitution sentiment into a long-term retreat, even with its later revival during the Great Depression.

At the same time, the pro-Constitution campaign's creedal rhetoric also created avenues, even in the 1920s, for constitutionally grounded counterclaims about the centrality of inclusion and social change. One way for reformers to avoid being tarred as unpatriotic or as a foreign cultural and racial threat was to invert, and thereby attempt to expand, judgments about Americanism. They argued that pro-war nativists failed to embody creedal values, and that instead defenders of pluralism had properly embraced the ideals embedded in the Declaration and the Constitution. Perhaps most effectively during the inter-war years, immigrant activists and allied religious clergy creatively deployed creedal constitutional rhetoric for reformist ends. Despite the era's anti-immigrant national currents, their ideas thus developed and disseminated a competing and constitutionalist embrace of ethnic, religious, and racial difference. Still, these arguments had their own limitations, which became especially pronounced when reformers applied them to the position of Indigenous peoples in American life.

IMMIGRATION AND CREEDALISM'S INCLUSIVE POTENTIAL

Pro-immigrant activists pushed back against the period's xenophobia by casting nativists as deeply un-American. As the Presbyterian minister Everett Clinchy argued in the 1934 book *All in the Name of God*, which in many ways summarized the emerging response, nativists reproduced precisely the cultural attributes that many pro-Constitution advocates decried as defining autocratic Germany and Bolshevik Russia. Whatever their claims to be "100 percent American," groups like the Klan rejected the essential element of Americanism: individualism. This was because they ignored the constitutive link between individualism and diversity or difference, instead embracing a "cultural monism"—"a stream whose source is the idea of the totalitarian state." Moreover, anti-immigrant voices ignored the long-standing tradition of toleration, especially religious toleration, embedded by the framers in the American Constitution. Clinchy argued that Washington, Jefferson, and Madison were all defenders of religious inclusion. This highlighted how "the American ideal summons its citizens to regard all forms of religious belief and cultural tradition as personal characteristics which enrich" the country.[25]

Clinchy and others also embraced the religious implications of how pro-war and pro-Constitution figures had invoked an "American creed," but for different ends. If notions of toleration, inclusion, and self-government were an American secularized faith, this faith was not solely a product of Anglo-Protestant theology. Given the degree to which the American population had been reshaped through broad European immigration, the American creed in truth resulted from shared

Catholic, Jewish, and Protestant values. As the historian Kevin Schultz writes of pro-immigrant argument at the time, these values meant that "if America was to continue to be a beacon of liberty, it would have to accept its fate as a tri-faith nation."[26] Fundamentally, this meant treating more recent immigrants—especially non-Protestants, including from southern and eastern Europe—with the same approach of cultural respect and political and economic inclusion that marked earlier generations of northern and western European and Protestant newcomers.

Over time, the frequent *New York Times* contributor P. W. Wilson's 1931 phrase, "Judeo-Christian" values, became most associated with the idea of the country as tri-faith. The historian K. Healan Gaston writes that from the mid-1930s, "Jewish and liberal Protestant commentators increasingly invoked that term as they called for open-ended tolerance of all belief systems." According to this framing, "authoritarianism and Judeo-Christianity [were] mutually exclusive principles."[27]

Even in the face of a pervasive nativist climate, this approach to creedal constitutionalism won real victories in the 1920s. In 1923 and in 1925, the Supreme Court struck down state bans on foreign language educational instruction and Catholic private parochial education as unconstitutional.[28] The former case concerned a 1919 Nebraska law that was the product of wartime anti-German frenzy; the latter case emerged out of the Klan's anti-Catholic campaign in Oregon. In both settings, the Supreme Court, hardly a bastion of immigrant protection, appeared to reaffirm the idea of toleration and religious acceptance (the right, according to Justice James McReynolds, "to worship God according to the dictates of his own conscience"[29]) as central to American notions of constitutional liberty.

In fact, these arguments gained a significant foothold in government policies well outside defenses of Catholicism and Judaism alone. At virtually the same time as the Supreme Court engaged with issues of immigrant religious rights, the federal Office of Indian Affairs, later renamed the Bureau of Indian Affairs (BIA), struggled with its own forced assimilationist efforts to eliminate Native American practices such as ceremonial dances. For white reformers troubled by coercive treatment of Indigenous communities, the language of religious toleration became a powerful tool for redeploying the charge of un-Americanness and for underscoring how prevailing policies undercut national values.

No one better embodied this than John Collier, who founded the American Indian Defense Association in 1923 and would later become

the head of the BIA under Franklin Delano Roosevelt, where he oversaw the "Indian New Deal." Collier was profoundly steeped in the politics of immigrant rights, including religiously inflected creedal constitutional arguments. He had spent twelve years as secretary of the
People's Institute, a Progressive and reformist association focused on
supporting immigrant communities and defending their cultural traditions. For Collier, the ceremonial practices of Indigenous nations like
the Pueblo peoples were religious ones, no different than more familiar Christian customs. And if Americans took seriously the idea that
a creed of religious acceptance united them, then Native Americans
should be included as equals on terms no different than those of Jewish
or Catholic communities. Collier argued that the Pueblo mode of worship and "sacred secret knowledge [was] just as holy as are the secrets
given to Catholic priests in confession." Likewise, principles of "Americanism" condemned attacking Pueblo practices just as they condemned
"legislat[ing] that the Catholic priests shall reveal the secrets of the confession, if we believe in religious liberty."[30]

Such an approach won partial victories from the Office of Indian
Affairs during the period. The office stepped back from its aggressive
opposition to Pueblo practices, for example allowing a small number of
boys to be kept out of school while they completed their ceremonial initiation, on First Amendment free exercise grounds. And when Collier
took over the agency during the New Deal, these claims—in keeping
with that period's pro-immigrant politics—became part of a larger defense of internal Indigenous autonomy, albeit ultimately under federal
supervision.

In fact, as the historian Tisa Wenger notes, the relative success of
creedal constitutional claims in defending Native practices led some
Pueblo leaders to begin embracing the rhetoric of religious freedom
during the inter-war years, as a way of highlighting to whites the Americanness of respecting Native American customs. Such voices consciously re-described broad aspects of Indigenous life as "religious,"
precisely to gain greater autonomy over internal decision-making. One
example from Wenger's work: "In 1925 one All-Pueblo Council petition
'to the President of the US, the Congress, and Our Friends the American People,' once again protested against the BIA's efforts to restrict ceremonial dances," connecting these efforts "to new disputes over tribal
governance" and "as further proof of the government's 'interference in
religious liberty.'"[31]

THE LIMITS OF TRI-FAITH POLITICS AND
THE EXPANSION OF WHITENESS

These Native American efforts clearly mirrored how Native peoples in "Indian Territory" had attempted creatively to invoke constitutional commitment, through the proposed 1905 US State of Sequoyah, as a way of maintaining a degree of political independence and control. But just as with that earlier experiment, the redeployment of wartime creedal arguments on behalf of cultural toleration came with its own drawbacks—and not just for Native peoples.

To begin with, the religious grounding of civic inclusion in American life did little to confront wartime and 1920s anti-socialist and anti-communist extremism. If shared interdenominational faith was the cultural foundation of American tolerance, where did that leave labor radicals who argued against organized religion on the basis that it often fed a deferential respect for class elites and for oppressive institutions? In a sense, the emergence of tri-faith or "Judeo-Christian" America may have allowed for immigrant and even some Indigenous incorporation on cultural terms. But it entailed its own ideological exclusions and construction of foreign outsiders—especially when it came to those who could be tarred as atheistic.

Thus, as the historian K. Healan Gaston explores, alongside its more pluralistic variations, a clear strain of Judeo-Christian politics was deeply "anti-secular," and by the 1940s and 1950s Cold War it often framed nonbelievers as inherently disloyal and on the side of "godless communism."[32] During periods when radicals of all stripes faced suppression, imprisonment, and deportation, this focus on a Judeo-Christian basis for creedal ideas had two sides. It could serve both as a politics of immigrant acceptance and as justifying a crackdown on presumptively "un-American" groups.

Even within the broader 1920s immigrant politics, the jingoistic wartime and post-war climate promoted just these repressive tendencies. Italian, Irish, and other ethnic societies may have embraced a pluralistic reading of American identity, connected in key ways to emerging tri-faith ideas of belonging. But the historian Jonathan Zimmerman notes that such pluralism did not stop a number of these societies from actively participating in conservative and pro-business campaigns to stamp out any critical characterizations of the eighteenth-century "Founding Fathers."[33]

Indeed, for some new Euro-Americans, hero worship of the revolutionary generation became a cultural mechanism for demonstrating one's absolute patriotic and hyper-nationalistic devotion. It amounted to additional proof that immigrants and European "ethnics," rather than Protestant nativists, were the real Americans. The Knights of Columbus, the "country's largest Catholic organization," offers a telling example of how these groups championed pluralist inclusion even as they engaged in jingoistic suppression. Edward McSweeney, who chaired the Knights' historical commission, viewed the Knights as embodying true 100 percent Americanism in ways distinct from both anti-immigrant conservatives and Progressive and Socialist reformers, including prominent historians like Charles Beard. He held that genuine patriotism entailed teaching children that "each racial group [had] made a substantial contribution" to pushing the national project forward. Yet he also contended that "treasonous" texts, which questioned the genius of the founders, had to be eliminated from the classroom.[34] This repressive politics ultimately generated troubling and strange bedfellows. Zimmerman writes that Irish American groups in Wisconsin went so far as to "eagerly lock arms" with anti-Irish and anti-immigrant patriotic organizations to pass a 1923 state law that banned any text from being taught in the public schools that "defames our nation's founders."[35]

At the same time, the emphasis on the US as a tri-faith Judeo-Christian nation did not in all cases actually repudiate a hierarchical theory of ethno-racial development. Instead, it could go hand in hand with simply re-envisioning that hierarchy as including a broader segment of Europeans at the cultural apex than the era's nativists might have allowed. At a deep level, Christianity and Judaism were understood as European cultural creations and inheritances. Such an interfaith creedal language could thus promote both immigrant inclusion and an expansion of the category of "whiteness." Furthermore, not unlike the settler and "composite" Americanism of Teddy Roosevelt and Frederick Jackson Turner in an earlier era, this creed could do so while still holding firm to prior judgments, particularly about perceived non-white cultural failings. And this is partly why, in the post–civil rights period and with the end of racially restrictive immigration policies in 1965, the notion of Judeo-Christian America was often invoked to resist the country's growing religious and ethnic multiculturalism.[36]

Just as important during the inter-war years, even when such creedalism embraced the idea of universal racial inclusion and repudiated Jim Crow politics, the idea of the "Europeanness" of religious ideas had additional implications. It ignored the power and originality of African American theological traditions. Above all, it tended to reinscribe a version of whiteness, even if more expansively conceived, as the presumptive American mainstream. The focus on new immigrant acceptance implicitly placed Blackness as outside this mainstream, and it deemphasized the centrality of Black enslavement and ongoing oppression to the historical and current project of real inclusion. Often, to the extent that Black oppression was engaged with at all, any act of racial ameliorism, no matter how minor, would be used to highlight the generosity and aspirational consistency of a white and immigrant majority. The implication of this was that such acts deserved gratitude from non-white communities, whether or not they led to material improvements.

IMPLICATIONS FOR INDIGENOUS RIGHTS

As hinted at above, these problems were similarly present in the extension of arguments about religious toleration to Native Americans. This was apparent in Pueblo internal debates over how and whether to invoke the Constitution as a guarantor of ceremonial practices. If some leaders embraced the rhetorical potential of religious liberty, others expressed wariness about conceiving of dances and initiation rituals as embodying a Pueblo "religion."

For many Indigenous leaders, such ceremonies were above all understood as inseparable from the exercise of sovereign control over their own land and the maintenance by Pueblo nations of a distinct identity as separate and autonomous peoples. As the Pueblo delegates to Congress declared in 1923 before the Senate Committee on Public Lands and Surveys, ceremonial rights were part of a larger struggle for independence, which required the ability to maintain an autonomous way of life alongside its necessary correlate—control over land on Indigenous terms: "May God forbid that anyone refuse us the right to live. Land and water means the life of the Pueblo Indians; without these we cannot survive."[37]

Crucially, Indigenous inclusion on the same conditions of religious toleration as immigrants erased the fundamental fact that European migrants and expropriated Native peoples found themselves in structurally distinct positions. It treated Native peoples as if they were simply another migrant settler population. But for Indigenous groups, the re-description of cultural practices as religious worship, akin to

Catholicism, ignored the centrality of these practices to political self-determination. It implicitly reduced Native Americans to the same status as any other religious minority. In this way, the tri-faith politics of religious inclusion perpetuated a settler imagination, precisely because it offered Indigenous inclusion only on terms that erased Native American status as independent and prior political communities.

For related reasons, efforts during the 1920s to expand US citizenship to Indigenous peoples, culminating in the Indian Citizenship Act of 1924, faced extensive opposition within Native American communities. White reformers viewed such measures in creedal terms—as highlighting the inclusive nature of the national polity—just as, a generation earlier, such reformers had depicted Sequoyah and Native incorporation through statehood in a similar way. Now they celebrated the bill—which extended citizenship to 125,000 Native Americans at the very same time that the National Origins Quota closed the door to Asians, Africans, and southern and eastern Europeans—as a significant moment of creedal victory in a sea of nativist reaction.

But for some Indigenous leaders, like the famed Tuscarora Chief Clinton Rickard, extending US citizenship was no cause for celebration. As he later recalled, "our citizenship was in our own nations" and the result of these reforms would be that "we would lose most of our independence." Rickard appreciated that white activists may have had a "sincere" desire "to do what they felt was right by us." But such efforts essentially sought to transform Native peoples into, in his succinct phrase, "imitation whites"—a "plan" that "was a lot more flattering to whites than it was to us." Even if theoretically inclusive, this reformist ambition presupposed the negation of Indigenous self-determination: "United States citizenship was just another way of absorbing us and destroying our customs and our government."[38]

These concerns about settler erasure were also at the heart of Laura Cornelius Kellogg's efforts to develop alternatives to more mainstream reform projects. Kellogg, an Oneida activist and founding figure in the Society of American Indians (SAI), strenuously advocated during the 1920s on behalf of what she called the "Lolomi Plan," perhaps the most innovative attempt during the era to conceive of the meaning of Indigenous self-determination in the face of an entrenched US settler state.[39] Like Rickard, Kellogg rejected the presumption that English settlers brought democracy to North America and that the federal Constitution thus offered the mature expression of an exceptional Euro-American political culture.

Her 1920 book, *Our Democracy and the American Indian*, instead offered what the political theorist David Temin calls a profound "counternarrative" of creedal assumptions. Invoking the Haudenosaunee (Iroquois) Confederacy, Kellogg began by declaring that "the idea of the League of Nations and Democracy originated on the American Continent about 600 years ago. It came from an American Indian." For this reason, not only did Indigenous absorption into the American project violate the political independence and autonomy of Native peoples; it also was premised on the false assumption that Indigenous polities needed to learn about constitutional government from Euro-American settlers. If anything, the great Indigenous innovation was plurinational federative arrangements—"freedom and equal opportunity to each nation"—something that US legal-political structures seemed to have forgotten.[41]

Yet, unlike Rickard, Kellogg doubted that, in the face of a dominant settler state, Indigenous nations could return to their absolute "former independence." Instead, she imagined a framework of "self-government" that attempted to build Native self-determination into a transformed US-Indigenous governing framework. Her Lolomi Plan would have eliminated the Office of Indian Affairs, along with "the status of wardship," and returned to Indigenous polities their land and resources. Each such polity would be a "self-governing body" under an expanded system of federation. In this way, Kellogg imagined a plurinational structure in which Native peoples—although not formally independent—nonetheless would enjoy political and economic control over their material land base.[42]

At the heart of the Lolomi Plan was what Kellogg viewed as an adapted version of "Indian Communism," which rejected the privatization and breakup of Indigenous land, instead conceiving of Native peoples collectively directing "our natural resources by ourselves."[43] Temin highlights "five key planks" of the Plan:

(1) Reservation lands would be recognized as the collective title of the tribe. (2) The people would pool assets to form worker-run cooperative enterprise, with the aim of mitigating economic dependency and creating work meaningfully related to community needs and self-understandings. (3) Citizen-workers would hold shares, with decisions made on the principle of one person, one vote. (4) Property would be held in fee simple—with underlying title in the tribe—but could not be sold to anyone outside of the tribe.

(5) Profits from any enterprise would fund health care, education, housing, and cooperative stores.[44]

Temin characterizes these ideas as amounting to an early version of "decolonial-democracy," one that Indigenous activists would continue to develop over time. Such efforts "challenged settler-imperial domination by bringing together a project of Indigenous self-determination with reimagined democratic narratives, values, and institutions."[45] It also implicitly suggested a fundamentally reconceived US constitutional project, which would ground settler-Indigenous interaction in transformed arrangements of plurinational and concurrent sovereignty.

In their own distinct ways, both Rickard and Kellogg attempted to reassert Indigenous self-determination in a context of fundamental settler disavowal of such autonomy, even among white reformers promoting notions of inclusive citizenship. They both highlighted the basic tension between creedal constitutional politics and Indigenous freedom, which remained a persistent problem even within the far more consciously anti-racist social movements of the later civil rights era. For those post–World War II movements, as discussed in later chapters, it would take real conceptual ingenuity to build solidarity between Indigenous and other non-white communities, given the distinct relationship of Native peoples to the US nation-state.

Black Radicalization and Constitutional Skepticism during the Inter-War Years

Non-Indigenous radical activists during the inter-war years tended to ignore these tensions between civic inclusion and genuine Native American self-determination. But when it came to issues of class, race, and gender, radical voices were more attuned to concerns with wartime creedalism and its post-war reformist uses. Particularly within the Black public, the war and its domestic effects actually facilitated the growth of a robust anti-imperial, internationalist, and constitutionally skeptical posture. An official and more venerative Black politics tended to circulate especially among educated and wealthier African Americans, and such a venerative posture often found itself on the defensive. It was strenuously criticized by Black nationalist, socialist, and communist entities, which spoke to and for mass bases radicalized by the failure of Black wartime participation to alter the basic domestic experience of racial domination.

WHITE VIOLENCE AND BLACK POLITICAL
DISCONTENT IN WARTIME

One can appreciate the era's emerging Black political discontent by turning to the pages of the *Messenger*, the most significant Black periodical connected during the era to the Socialist Party, with a peak monthly circulation in 1919 of 26,000 (the NAACP's *Crisis* reached 95,000 at the same time). The *Messenger* maintained a consistently critical view of both the war and constitutional support during and after hostilities.[46] Edited by Chandler Owen and A. Philip Randolph, the magazine was perhaps best known for its intense and mocking attacks on establishment Black voices, notably W. E. B. Du Bois and Booker T. Washington. Owen and Randolph focused their animus especially on the Black embrace of wartime creedal rhetoric, such as Du Bois's much-publicized call in the *Crisis* for African Americans "while this war lasts" to "forget our special grievances and close our ranks" on behalf of the war effort.[47] Their critiques of the conflict were similar to those made by Black anti-imperialists during the Spanish-Cuban-American War. According to the *Messenger*, Americans promoted abroad the same instincts of racial domination and hierarchy that defined domestic political life. In the Philippines, it meant "driv[ing] Spain out" and "keep[ing] what we took." And during the First World War, despite Wilson's universalistic rhetoric, for the non-white world it simply entailed replacing "one set of usurpers" with "another set of usurpers."[48]

Owen and Randolph similarly decried the willingness of more moderate Black periodicals to accede to the constitutional celebrations of the times. Those periodicals, wary of being labeled unpatriotic, would repeat bromides about the wisdom of the founders and even support Constitution Day events organized by the likes of the National Security League.[49] By contrast, the *Messenger* found this participation deeply troubling. According to Owen and Randolph, in keeping with past Black radical and SPA arguments about the Constitution, the very best one could say for the document was that it was "good in parts, but badly executed." They compared its more egalitarian and rights-protective language to the "concessions" offered to Black workers by conservative and exclusionary trade unions in "the American Federation of Labor,"[50] not to mention by business antagonists. The *Messenger*, aligned at this moment with the IWW and highly critical of the AFL,[51] declared bluntly of both those economic concessions and of the Constitution, "we are by no means too sanguine over the possibilities of the sop which was granted."[52] The problem specifically with the document was that provisions like the First Amendment and the egalitarian Reconstruction Amendments were little more than "dead letter articles."[53] These provisions simply dramatized the extent to which, in practice, the constitutional order actually suppressed dissent and preserved white supremacy.

Therefore, Owen and Randolph were hardly surprised that the funders and promoters of Constitution Day events were "a group of reactionaries"[54]—the very same entities that whipped up war fervor and called for the imprisonment of both labor activists and wartime dissidents of all stripes. Indeed, they had been arrested and charged during the summer of 1918 with sedition for distributing the *Messenger* and for speaking out publicly against the conflict.[55] All this underscored how Constitution worship served a particular and undemocratic constitutional state, oppressive on both racial and class grounds.

For this reason, the editors were similarly not surprised that the peak of constitutional veneration matched the peak of mass violence against both African Americans and labor union members. Rather than spurring the "enforcement" of the text's Reconstruction language (which "has not been" and "is not now being enforced"),[56] constitutional celebrations helped to unleash a violent antipathy toward anyone viewed as outside the body politic—especially due to their critiques of white supremacy or capitalism. The *Messenger* noted the degree to which, for all the invocations of constitutional commitment, "lawlessness in America proceed[ed] apace," with countless Black people during the war "lynched—many of them burned at the stake" and "real labor leaders, I. W. W.s" "also victims."[57]

Randolph and Owen voiced a percolating Black disdain of what amounted to a common educated and middle-class African American hope during and after the war: the belief that if Black people proved their loyalty to whites—by pledging faith in creed and Constitution and by fighting and dying for the security ends of the state—then meaningful citizenship would follow.

Indeed, in many ways the war effort highlighted the plausibility of this claim, at least when it came to the issue of voting rights for white women. As late as 1917, Woodrow Wilson continued to maintain that women's suffrage was a state rather than a federal issue. But the increasing wartime language of American universalism and creedal inclusion—not to mention the fact that many leaders in the mainstream suffrage movement rallied around the war effort—shifted the administration.

Wilson famously appealed in 1918 to the more recalcitrant Senate to approve the amendment proposal, declaring that constitutionalizing the right of women to vote was critical to "the realization of the objects for which the war was being fought."[58] George Creel, the head of the wartime propaganda effort at the Committee on Public Information, similarly concluded that "Equal Suffrage is part and parcel" of the war's "great big struggle for equal justice and real democracy."[59] In so arguing, Wilson also highlighted white women's uniformed participation—although not as frontline soldiers—along with their factory role on the home front, engaged in the industrial work men on the battlefield traditionally occupied, as proof of their worthiness to be voting citizens: "This war could not have been fought, either by the other nations engaged or by America, if it had not been for the services of the women,—services rendered in every sphere,—not merely in the fields of effort in which we have been accustomed to see them work."[60]

But if a wartime embrace of creedal constitutionalism spurred women's suffrage, this was in large measure due to the profound differences between the position of white women and Black people (regardless of gender) in collective life. White women had long found themselves subject to patriarchal control and viewed in society as natural inferiors to men. But settler women had always been treated—not unlike settler children—as integral elements of the community rather than an outsider population or external threat. Their status derived from hierarchies within the family structure, rather than from imperial colonization and its related practices of enslavement. In reality, this of course still entailed profound and gendered experiences of exclusion and powerlessness. Nonetheless, it established very different organizing relations between settler men and settler women.

Moreover, establishment suffrage supporters of both sexes often presented women's voting as a mechanism for constraining the political power of new immigrants, Black Americans, and Indigenous peoples. As such, there increasingly existed a built-in basis of white male acceptance. For instance, some of the first states and territories to extend the vote to women were on the frontier in the post–Civil War period, and explicitly imagined suffrage as a way to attract white women to help settle and demographically control the territories. Thus, even before the passage of the Nineteenth Amendment, "15 states had granted women full suffrage, 2 southern states had given women the right to vote in primary elections, and 13 states had awarded women the right to vote for president."[61] The war and its discursive justifications may have provided suffragists with a fortuitous set of circumstances, but the seeds for white male support of the Amendment had long been set.[62]

However, for Black people, conditions—and especially the extreme resurgence of explicit white supremacy during the decades following Reconstruction—were quite different from those facing white women suffragists. And the early-twentieth-century context of African American communities also proved critically distinct from that of Black soldiers and enslaved persons during and after the Civil War. After all, over time, that war had been fought precisely on grounds of slavery's illegitimacy.

By contrast, against World War I's particular political backdrop— not to mention the nativist xenophobia it spurred—Black efforts to link citizenship to security and loyalty implicitly reinforced a long-standing settler suspicion. This was the idea that African Americans were a dangerous "fifth column" who—if they *did not* demonstratively prove their loyalty—were rightly subject to rights infringement. In fact, some conservative Black voices willingly said as much. For instance, Emmett Scott—a close associate of Booker T. Washington at the Tuskegee Institute and the highest ranking African American in the Wilson administration—declared that "the moment the American Negro failed to perform all of the duties of citizenship, he immediately abdicated the right of claiming the full privileges of citizenship."[63]

Black radicals understood the obvious cost of demonstrably embracing all the "duties of citizenship." It implicated African Americans in the violence and militarism of the same state that oppressed them at home. And it also failed to appreciate that, no matter how much "loyalty" Blacks displayed, white American society appeared unwilling to treat African Americans as equals.

The *Messenger* may never have had the same circulation as the *Crisis*. But for many in the Black audience, the publication's critique of Black war participation and civic loyalty struck a real chord. Randolph would later recall that "the Negro community basically was friendly to our antiwar position, but the leadership was not."[64] And Roi Ottley, the seminal African American journalist and correspondent for the *Amsterdam News*, concluded in the 1950s that "the truth is, Negroes exhibited little enthusiasm for" World War I. "They held British imperialism, ruling millions of their African brothers, was no less savage than German conquest of the Cameroons. Nor did they feel the United States was altogether virtuous."[65] Following the war, the rise of the Ku Klux Klan, white race riots, and anti-Black lynchings together highlighted the extent to which Black participation in the war had not changed white "hearts and minds" at home. If anything, the war and its associated narratives had generated yet more internal violence.

BLACK INTERNATIONALISM AND THE POLITICS OF SELF-DETERMINATION

Increasing numbers of white Americans, including working-class citizens, may have begun espousing an aggressive Americanism after World War I, bound up with constitutional devotion and national pride. But Black public life in this era moved in the opposite direction. Starting in the immediate post-war years, even previously moderate Black political figures started to adopt a more critical posture. In some cases, this meant embracing explicitly internationalist suspicions of *any* attachment to the American nation-state, creedal constitutional or otherwise.

It is important not to overstate these developments, especially in characterizing the actual power radical forces could effectively wield in society. The wartime and post-war "Red Scare" crackdowns weakened reformist institutions in general, including Black institutions. And the sheer intensity and violence of Jim Crow conditions in the 1920s created profound disillusionment within the Black community, undercutting faith in the viability of any meaningful racial reform—whether through the political process, union organizing, or other mass protest campaigns. It also placed a continuous shadow of state-sanctioned threat over all organizing that could be labeled "red" or radical.

One sees this especially with the steady deterioration of the Socialist Party as an effective electoral alternative to the Democrats and Republicans. As the historian Theodore Kornweibel Jr. writes, "militancy in general was on the defensive, whether in third-party politics, in labor, or in racial protest. Even the established groups like the NAACP and the Urban League were on the decline." By the end of the 1920s, the NAACP's *Crisis* had a monthly circulation of 30,000—less than a third of its 1919 peak. Meanwhile, a lack of available financing for the *Messenger*, a central radical Black outlet during a period of conservative reaction, doomed the smaller magazine.[66]

This crackdown—while certainly weakening key institutions—generated new cycles of radicalization among Black activists, as well as among poor and working-class African Americans. In a sense, the extremism of the disjunction between establishment Black wartime hopes—overseas loyalty leading to domestic freedom—and violent white supremacist realities had its own reverberating implications. It created the conditions for expanding urban support for explicitly race-conscious entities, like Marcus Garvey's Universal Negro Improvement Association (UNIA), as well as for the growth of the Communist Party of the United States of America (CPUSA)[67] among the rural Black poor.

Although these Black political blocs had significant internal differences and often competed with each other, one thing that stitched them together was a newly cohesive internationalism—the product of an inter-war emergence of an assertive and global anti-colonialism. In a sense, post-war Black radicalization, fed by deep discontent with white American society, occurred at a decisive historical moment. Blacks could concretely imagine their own community as linked not to an American "we the people," as pro-Constitution forces demanded, but instead to an inchoate and growing non-white and anti-colonial international.

Following World War I, Hubert Harrison was perhaps the Black intellectual and movement leader who most comprehensively sought to attach African American political identity to the growing sense of global anti-colonial solidarity and community. The Harlem-based Harrison moved through a variety of radical and Black organizations, from the Socialist Party to Garvey's UNIA. Although less well known today, Harrison was an electric speaker and among the time's most popular African American public figures.[68]

Harrison's popularity was due in part to his uncompromising stances. For Harrison, the destructive racial consequences of the First World War—which facilitated the extension of colonialism abroad and Jim Crow at home—underscored that the "color line" was an international issue. It also spoke to the fact that African Americans shared far more in common with other colonized peoples than with white co-nationals. This meant that Black participation in the US state's global interventionism created the perverse consequence of African American acceptance of the state's security agenda, which fought against fellow colonized peoples on behalf of the very white business and government elites that sustained their domestic oppression.[69]

According to Harrison, to the extent that African Americans were part of any community, it was an international community of "darker races," who shared the same interest in economic and political self-determination free from all colonial rulers. Emphasizing the tie between American settlerism and European practices of empire, Harrison contended that any brand of American nationalism—including one tied to the Constitution—was profoundly flawed as a ground for pursuing Black freedom. Harrison wrote in 1921, "we have appealed to the common patriotism which should bind us together in a common loyalty to the practice rather than the preachments of democracy, and in every case we have been rebuffed and spurned." The only solution was to link the Black struggle in America with that of "subject peoples of all colors" who, across the globe, sought "their own enfranchisement from the chains of slavery, social, political and economic."[70]

As a significant indicator of the times, Du Bois—long a figure of establishment Black politics—came to embrace, far less equivocally during these years, that American global authority replicated rather than challenged European colonial hegemony. Du Bois had been deeply disappointed by Wilson's refusal to take decolonization seriously during negotiations at Versailles and in the genesis of the League of Nations— not to mention outraged by the intense post-war racial violence in the United States. As such, he eventually found it impossible to continue repeating creedal constitutional claims. Indeed, Du Bois began a systematic march away from the brand of American universalism he had previously articulated during the initial days of the Philippine-American War and then during World War I.

In these inter-war years, Du Bois remained unwilling to abandon entirely the idea that empire could be in the service of liberating non-European peoples. He imagined the rise of a non-European power that could provide a counterpoint to white domination, and especially championed imperial Japan. This was not only because of Japan's global ascent, though its defeat of Russia in the 1905 war and its inclusion as one of the five victorious powers at the 1919 Paris Peace Conference marked a remarkable shift in the racial tides of international affairs. Du Bois also supported Japan because it had championed the inclusion of a racial equality clause in the Covenant of the League of Nations—a clause defeated by strenuous opposition from the United States and Australia, the two English settler siblings in the non-European world.[71]

This episode left a lasting impression on many African Americans, and Du Bois enthusiastically conceived of Japanese might as holding out that old aspiration—going all the way back to Frederick Douglass—of imperial expansion in the service of universal equality. As late as 1937, he described Japan as having "the responsibility of proving to the world that colonial enterprise by a colored nation need not imply the caste, exploitation and subjugation which it has always implied in the case of white Europe."[72]

Of course, Black opponents of empire argued—just as they had during the Spanish-Cuban-American War—that subjugation was inherent to the colonial enterprise itself. Regardless of the nation-state's racial identity, colonialism necessarily ignored the right of local communities to shape their own political destiny. As the *Messenger* put it succinctly, "we have no more right in the Philippines than Japan has in Shantung."[73]

Still, at a deeper level, Du Bois embraced the emancipatory potential of these statist projects—whether the US immediately after the Spanish-Cuban-American War, Japan in the 1920s and 1930s, or later China under Mao Zedong in the 1950s[74]—in part due to an essential problem facing anti-colonial efforts to remake the international order: if the colonized world would eventually fundamentally redistribute global economic and political power, it needed clear transformative agents with the institutional capacity to implement these shifts. Time and again, Du Bois returned to strong nation-states as entities with this institutional capacity. Other Black internationalist voices were correct to highlight the imperial pretensions or internal authoritarianism of such statist projects, even if pursued by non-white leaders in Japan or China. But they nonetheless would have to answer the question: How could movements build the type of power necessary not only to ensure formal independence for ex-colonies but also to alter, systematically, the terms of the international system? As discussed later in the book, African and Asian anti-colonial leaders would imagine a world order in which newly independent countries created federative arrangements among themselves, to guard against dependencies in the global economy and build meaningful political authority vis-à-vis past rulers.[75] But Du Bois, certainly in the inter-war period, considered strong non-white states as central to any successful outcome.

Yet, even if serious questions persisted about how to relate to non-European powers like Japan or later China, all Black internationalists in the US could agree on the need, in the here and now, for concrete transnational connections. Black American and Asian and African publics had to be structurally linked together into new communities of struggle and liberation. These years thus saw a variety of such organizations spring up to house an emerging Black politics committed to confronting racism and colonialism, both at home and abroad. Before his own untimely death in 1927 at the age of forty-four, Harrison founded the International Colored Unity League (ICUL) as a mechanism for stitching together domestic and international anti-colonial activism. By the end of the 1930s, the entity in Black American life most strongly identified with such transnational politics was the International Committee on African Affairs (later renamed the Council on African Affairs), which rallied strenuously on behalf of independence and labor campaigns across Asia and Africa. The renowned Black singer, thespian, and radical activist Paul Robeson served as its chair during most of its existence, with Du Bois himself as vice chair.[76]

This spread of Black internationalism provided the conditions for perhaps the most striking feature of Black politics during the period: the emergence in the Deep South of a sizable base of support among the Black rural poor for the Communist Party by the 1930s. As detailed in the historian Robin Kelley's seminal book, *Hammer and Hoe* (1990), for a period the party created real institutional roots in states like Alabama, shaping the direction of organized struggle and challenging established Black organizations such as the NAACP for overall political leadership. The party became so popular among African American farmers and workers because of its distinctiveness relative to existing groups, both white and Black. Unlike other white reformist institutions, the party, at least for a time, showed a real commitment to Black leadership as well as an investment in the promotion of Black culture, art, and literature. And unlike Black middle-class institutions like the NAACP, the party took far greater pains, as Kelley notes, to combine a "militant opposition to racism"—expressed, for instance, through courtroom struggles like the Scottsboro case (where "nine young black men [were] falsely accused of raping two white women in Alabama")—with a "fight for the concrete economic needs of the unemployed and working poor."[77] It thus spoke to a grassroots desire both for radical insurgency and for Black preeminence and centrality in any revolutionary project. In this way, the party's concrete aims as well as its embrace of Black self-assertiveness resonated profoundly both with Black poor and working-class aspirations and with their profound distrust, during the depths of Jim Crow, of white society.

At the same, the CPUSA pursued an emerging theory of liberation premised on the idea, as Kelley highlights, of "the 'black belt' counties of the American South as an oppressed nation."[78] The historian Beverley Tomek contends that the Black belt thesis was largely "imposed" on the CPUSA "from the outside," pushed by figures in the Soviet-led Communist International (Comintern or Third International) based on a hastily drawn comparison between the Black experience and that of various national communities across the new Soviet Union. Indeed, most American party leaders, both white and Black, were suspicious of the thesis, especially as its seeming invocation of racial separatism ran counter to the long-standing aim of building cross-racial class solidarity. They also saw little African American working-class appetite for the idea of a distinct political state.[79] Still, the Comintern adopted the thesis in 1928 as its organizing framework. Kelley writes that under the resolution, Black people "[a]s a nation, like the Lithuanians or Georgians of the old Russian empire . . . had a right to self-determination."[80] As an organizing tool, American Communist skepticism of the position was certainly borne out by the facts. Kelley concludes that the call for Black self-determination "did not persuade black Communists to attempt to seize Mississippi and secede from the United States, nor did it bring black folk to the Party in droves."[81]

Nonetheless, a group of Black activists in the CPUSA, chief among them Harry Haywood, did embrace this principle of self-determination. In their hands, they transformed what had been an underdeveloped slogan into a specific critique of how the structure of American statecraft preserved white planter rule across the Jim Crow South. According to Haywood, Reconstruction's defeat was intrinsically bound up with the ultimate failure to abolish "the plantation system" and therefore the persistence of deeply oppressive structures of racial capitalism. He believed that genuine freedom for Black people across the South could not be achieved without confronting the question of land and property. This was because African Americans in the counties associated with the Black belt—stretching from eastern Virginia to eastern Texas—were a distinct and cohesive economic and political community. They had been enslaved on this land and they continued to provide the oppressed labor for the plantation economy. Haywood maintained that "there is no escape from the conclusion that freedom and prosperity for the people of the South, Negro and white, can be won only through drastic overhauling of the present system of land ownership and agrarian relations of the region. The fight for such radical change must be placed in the very heart of any effective program."[82]

Critically, such a project was near impossible to achieve under the existing legal-political institutions. Black people were not only systematically disenfranchised through explicit Jim Crow policies that denied African Americans the vote; they were also disenfranchised by the very structure of Southern state boundaries and administrative units. Haywood writes that these "boundaries . . . arbitrarily crisscross the area of contiguous Negro majority breaking up this area into a maze of governmental administrative, judicial, and electoral subdivisions, which in no way correspond to the life needs of its people."[83]

Moreover, white authoritarian results were the conscious political project of planter elites. "These divisions are purposely maintained — in many cases are even gerrymandered — by the South's rulers with the aim of continuing the political suppression of the region's predominant colored population." All of this meant that as a programmatic agenda, "the abolition of these bureaucratic and arbitrarily established boundaries and their replacement by truly democratic ones, conforming not with the needs of the bourbon oppressors but with those of the oppressed, is a key task of American democracy."[84]

For Haywood, this call for African American "political self-rule" in the Black belt did not necessitate actual secession.[85] But it did entail recognizing that African Americans were a revolutionary entity in their own right, separate from the larger white working class. In a departure from the position of some in the CPUSA — not to mention past white SPA politicians — Haywood held that American capitalism was constitutively shaped by racial domination, and so race could not simply be subsumed into class. For this reason, Black people had to be organized in pursuit of their own economically grounded but very specific emancipatory interests.

This sense of a distinct Black freedom project alongside the broader American working-class struggle was a key reason why Haywood embraced the idea of Black people as "an oppressed nation."[86] Such a framework spoke to the underlying structural differences between white and Black working-class and poor experiences. It also connected Black Americans to non-white anti-colonial projects around the globe — beyond comparable projects in the old Russian Empire. Indeed, it even had clear parallels with Kellogg's approach to Indigenous freedom in her Lolomi Plan.

Perhaps most significantly for our purposes, Haywood's elaboration of the Black belt thesis was grounded in a specific vision of constitutional transformation. He called for "full equality throughout the country" alongside "self-determination in the South."[87] Haywood thus defended the importance of ongoing struggles across the United States for Black labor and political rights. But in the South, to the extent that the Black belt remained part of the country, a new "governmental and administrative structure" had to replace the old states. These institutions would facilitate Black democratic majoritarianism and would serve as popular instruments for redistributing land from the white "oligarchs" to the working poor, both Black and white.[88] As Haywood concluded, such Black "self-government" meant "a regrouping of county and administrative districts to guarantee full proportional representation for the Negro people in all areas of government." It amounted to "a simple democratic demand, in full conformity with the principles of majority rule."[89]

This version of the Black belt thesis faced obvious issues of practical viability.[90] Nonetheless, Haywood's ideas clearly connected to a long Black radical imagination. Its vision of both struggle and freedom was especially reminiscent of nineteenth-century projects among the Black rural poor: It echoed the 1865 hope of a Christmastime jubilee and the emigrationist and later anti-imperial crusades of Henry McNeil Turner. It rejected any false faith in a shared American "we the people" and saw the existing constitutional system as an impediment to Black freedom. And it focused on structurally transforming the Southern economy. More broadly, many of the Black leaders ultimately drawn to the CPUSA came from families with roots in the old radical Black institutions, like Turner's African Methodist Episcopal (AME) church. Al Murphy, for instance, one of the most dynamic Black Communist organizers and secretary of the Share Croppers' Union (SCU) in the early 1930s, grew up in a politicized household in which his grandfather had been an AME elder under Bishop Turner.[91]

White Reformism and the Charge of Disloyalty

All of this highlighted how the pro-war and pro-Constitution campaigns' effects on the Black public were hardly straightforward. And the campaigns certainly did not quash dissent, especially among those truly at the margins of settler society. Yet for much of reformist white politics—for instance, anti-war activism, labor organizing, and the women's movement—the post-war story took a different route: namely, those same loyalty campaigns had far more success in suppressing radicalism.

In a sense, the accusation of disloyalty was less personally stinging for many poor and working-class Black people than for white reformers and constituents. The Black relationship to the larger community inherently encompassed greater ambivalence, given how settler society had always framed African Americans as outside the political community. By contrast, appeals to patriotism resonated more deeply in white working-class settler life, however much August Spies may have found such views counterproductive. As Spies and others contended, building class-based solidarities among white Americans therefore required extensive political work, in order to undermine the nationalist claims of pro-business conservatives. And now, under the intense onslaught of the state's pro-Constitution campaign, violent crackdowns on dissent, and the larger xenophobic climate of nativism and Jim Crow, white activists found themselves pressed to prove their genuine Americanness.

CIVIL LIBERTARIANS, UNIONS, AND COMMUNISTS DECLARE THEIR ALLEGIANCE

Groups like the IWW had always viewed such exercises in national fealty as necessarily losing propositions. Proving one's Americanness often devolved into embracing false nationalist attachments and suppressed the real and internationalist solidarities that existed among working classes both at home and abroad. But given how the war's new nationalism had generated real shifts in white working-class identity and politics, many reformers worried that they had no choice but to respond to these changes or face losing cultural contact with elements of their social base. The result was that, even among radical white voices, there existed tremendous pressure to reframe demands through state-sanctioned narratives of Americanism, constitutional respect, and patriotic identification.

One can see this most explicitly with the Civil Liberties Bureau (CLB) of the American Union Against Militarism, the forerunner of the ACLU. The CLB co-founder and anti-war critic Crystal Eastman had long espoused the common socialist position that there was nothing distinctively "American" about respect for civil liberties or democratic self-rule. Indeed, the domestic constitutional order—exemplified by slavery, segregation, and the criminalization of labor protest and organizing—spoke to the extent to which the American legal-political system in fact negated effective popular freedom.[92] As Eastman continued to maintain after the war—even as other reformers increasingly claimed the language of creed and Constitution—American institutions from their genesis had not been "of much practical value in protecting the poorest workers."[93] In this way, she offered a clear class-based internationalist alternative to the internationalisms of Wilson, Hill, and Ralph Barton Perry. Rather than combining creedal nationalism with a push to global empire, Eastman saw her wartime opposition—as well as her broader vision of anti-imperialism and anti-militarism—as essential to preserving solidarities between working and colonized peoples *everywhere*, regardless of nationality.

Nonetheless, she creatively invoked existing constitutional language to oppose state violence and to defend the democratic value of dissent. In response to pro-war and pro-business Constitution Day initiatives in 1917, the CLB circulated a letter, co-signed by Eastman, calling for members and supporters to organize their own counter-events on Constitution Day, aimed at emphasizing the centrality of "free speech, free press and liberty of conscience" to any defensible interpretation of the text.[94] Eastman appreciated that, in the depths of wartime extremism, sometimes "the most revolutionary thing" a "socialist could do, except go to jail," was to demand that the "Constitution and the Declaration of Independence" "be lived up to."[95] In her view, the purpose of such efforts, including counter–Constitution Day events, was again to illustrate the profound illegality and political bankruptcy of the very forces that claimed the constitutional mantle. Indeed, the 1917 events that took place starkly dramatized the point: federal and local police broke up the meetings, arrested participants, and denied speakers the opportunity to discuss the merits of the First Amendment.[96]

For this reason, "while we shall continue to exercise our political rights, whenever and wherever a capitalist government allows us," Eastman maintained, it was critical not to fall prey to nationalist pressure or to engage in actual Constitution worship. She saw all around her, even in the Socialist Party, the pull toward restorationist language, to declare one's "everlasting allegiance to [the Constitution]" or to make arguments premised on "bring[ing] this erring national back to the faith of its father." She viewed with profound disappointment the way Socialist politicians like Charley Solomon, one of the five expelled on ideological grounds from the New York State Assembly, responded to the crackdown. Rather than emphasize the inadequacy of the constitutional system and the hollowness of rights under capitalism, he proclaimed, "I am one hundred percent American" and "I support the Constitution."[97]

These moves struck her as willfully ignoring the extent to which the country—shaped by wartime reaction—was in the midst of a "complete breakdown of the most essential democratic institutions." In failing to directly address this reality, even these SPA leaders acceded to authoritarian trends, both reinforcing the preservationist climate and undermining the oppositional ethic needed in working-class communities. Such actions validated those long-standing IWW charges that some SPA politicians cared more about getting elected than about over-coming capitalism.[98]

Although throughout the 1920s there were white reformers such as Eastman who refused to accept the new constitutional citizenship, they became increasingly isolated. More and more activists, including Social-ist politicians, retreated from wholesale constitutional opposition un-der the prevailing attacks. In fact, one can see this retreat beginning in the letter to affiliates that Eastman herself had signed off on, which in-cluded the claim that defending free speech was also about "stand[ing] by the great principles of liberty for which the Constitution stands."[99]

As the historian John Witt details, over time other bureau leaders, particularly fellow co-founder Roger Baldwin, increasingly tended to insist that they were "'loyal' to the 'American ideal' of freedom."[100] Just as significantly, this insistence eventually went hand in hand with a narrowing of what constituted the core of ACLU activism. According to Crystal Eastman's biographer, Amy Aronson, this included "disso-ciat[ing]" presumptively patriotic free speech defenses "from interna-tionalist campaigns for global democracy and world peace."[101]

As late as 1929, Baldwin was still attempting to combine a language of constitutional fidelity with the type of anti-imperial sensibility that Eastman embraced. That year Baldwin and others on the executive committee—who throughout the 1920s persisted in engaging with Left organizations in Europe—"advocated" extending the ACLU's work to include activism against "control of weaker nations by the United States." However, in a telling indication of the group's emerging ap-proach, the historian Laura Weinrib notes that "reactions" to this anti-imperial call from other leaders within the ACLU, including Harvard law professor and future New Deal Supreme Court justice Felix Frank-furter, "were unexpectedly hostile."[102]

It was not only anti-war and free speech activists who found them-selves accommodating a more constricted political climate. Many white labor leaders also responded to the security crackdowns and the overarching nationalist environment by seeking to prove their pro-Constitution and Americanist bona fides. The violent government sup-pression of the IWW—a group that had explicitly denounced patriot-ism as a tool of class oppression and rejected the Constitution in similar terms—led a new generation of labor activists to rally instead around both nation and text. John Lewis, president of the United Mine Work-ers and eventually a central figure in establishing the Congress of Industrial Organizations (CIO), responded to the anti-union retrenchment of the 1920s by reframing the labor movement as an extended enterprise in constitutional veneration. Writing in 1925, Lewis contended that "the government structure of the Republic" was "broad, sound, and foresighted." In restorationist terms that ignored Eastman's admonitions and instead echoed his business foes, he referred to the UMW's goals as simply "a return to the first principles—a reassertion in practice of the rules laid down by the Fathers of the Republic."[103]

This discursive move had lasting ramifications. Even during the greater political openness of the later New Deal period, some radicals believed they had no choice but to speak in the language of creed and Constitution to successfully parry charges of un-Americanness. The eventual fate of the US Communist Party offers perhaps the greatest illustration. In the mid-1930s, Soviet policies shifted toward support for the "Popular Front," in which the party in the United State pursued coalitional alliances with New Deal reformers and more traditional elements of the labor movement. A significant goal of the shift was to build support among white constituencies, including in the South. This did not mean abandoning the commitment to racial equality; throughout the mid-century, the CPUSA would remain associated, within both the Black and the white imagination, with a fearless commitment to Black freedom. But it did entail substantial policy changes and transformations in affiliated institutions, so that both might be made more palatable to white audiences.

In particular, the party—which had been remarkable in viewing African American workers as the revolutionary lead and in promoting Black people in leadership roles—abandoned the idea of the Black belt and of African American self-determination. It also replaced Black leaders like Murphy at the Share Croppers' Union with white activists who would be more acceptable to Southern white racial sensibilities.[104] Ultimately, the goal of organizing whites in the South largely failed, and the policy's long-term effect was a collapse of the party's Southern Black base. This failure reopened the space for the revival and eventual dominance of traditional organizations like the NAACP.

Whatever these later consequences, it is noteworthy that the Communist Party—a revolutionary organization—believed that a strategic desire to expand white working-class support required it to burnish its patriotic bona fides. This meant adjusting its racial politics and, not unrelatedly, fully embracing Constitution worship. Not long before, Communists had called for a systematic overhaul through the breakup of the states and Black control over newly devised Southern political and economic units. But now in the mid-1930s, the party wrapped itself in flag and text.

During the 1936 election, Earl Browder, executive secretary of the party, went out of his way to convince constituencies of the ideological continuities between communism and the Constitution. In the presumptive spirit of the 1936 platform, which famously stated "Communism Is Twentieth-century Americanism,"[105] he stumped across the country carrying a copy of the Constitution in his pocket, a document meant to symbolize his "rights as a citizen."[106] And in 1938, the party added to the preamble of its own constitution language that creatively mirrored—if adapted—the very militancy of the pro-war and pro-business Constitution campaigns, committing Communists to "defend the United States Constitution against its reactionary enemies who would destroy democracy."[107]

This new embrace followed some two decades of "Red Scare" tactics and loyalty campaigns. But for a group linked in the white public imagination to the Soviet Union—and, just as critically, to Black radical politics—there was no better way to prove one's local and national authenticity than by emphasizing devotion to the Constitution.

DEFENDING WOMEN'S RIGHTS
DURING A TIME OF REACTION

The same accommodationist tendencies shaped the trajectory of the women's movement as well. Especially in the depths of 1920s political reaction, feminist leaders—like white labor and civil liberties activists—often saw the post–Nineteenth Amendment viability of the women's movement as requiring a demonstration to male government and business elites that sex equality was compatible with the new nationalism and constitutional citizenship.

As discussed in chapter 3, suffrage efforts—not unlike Black politics—had always contained two competing orientations. One orientation, embodied by Carrie Chapman Catt, the president of the National American Women's Suffrage Association (NAWSA), presented women's right to vote as a natural fulfillment of the American constitutional tradition. This orientation also tended to disconnect the project of extending voting rights for white women from issues of both class and race. Indeed, leaders like Catt were willing to use racist rhetoric, and even make common cause with pro-business and pro-segregation groups, in order to facilitate the success of white women's suffrage. And during the war, Catt and NAWSA embraced both the war effort and pro-Constitution activism as a tool for highlighting the Americanness of women's suffrage and the patriotism of the larger women's movement.

But there had always been a second orientation, expressed institutionally in the fight over the Nineteenth Amendment by the National Woman's Party (NWP), headed by Alice Paul, and in which Crystal Eastman also played a central role. The NWP distinguished itself during the war years by the militancy of its suffrage tactics, famously maintaining a picket of the White House despite pressure from groups like NAWSA to close ranks behind the president.

These tactics spoke to the fact that many activists within the NWP held a broader vision of what women's emancipation entailed. They believed that liberation might well require transforming the gendered division of labor between men and women, which otherwise maintained structures of patriarchy both at home and at work. Outspoken activists also viewed political rights for women as one piece of overcoming the intertwined and oppressive forces of sexism, economic dependency, racism, and militarism that dominated American life. The NWP's openness to these beliefs—as well as the NAWSA's complicity with wartime jingoism and repression—led socialist and anti-war feminists like Eastman, as well as Black feminists like Ida B. Wells and Mary Church Terrell, to associate with the group.[108]

But the combination of the passage of the Nineteenth Amendment and the government's crackdowns on radicalism sucked the popular energy from the NWP. Paid membership fell from 50,000 in 1919 (in the heady days of suffrage amendment victory in Congress) to only 151 by the early 1920s. Alice Paul believed that a significant reason for this decline was the group's identification with socialism and other brands of radical politics, all framed as dangerously un-American in the postwar years. This view led Paul to press remaining activists to focus exclusively on a single-issue agenda, aimed primarily at the ratification of a new constitutional amendment: the Equal Rights Amendment (ERA). In its 1923 version, the ERA read, "men and women shall have equal rights throughout the United States and every place subject to its jurisdiction. Congress shall have power to enforce this article by appropriate legislation."[109]

For Paul, the goal of achieving the ERA meant taking a page from the playbook of the rival NAWSA, now renamed the League of Women Voters (LWV). This entailed framing the ERA as a project of constitutional fidelity that fulfilled rather than challenged the larger principles of creedal constitutionalism. It also deemphasized efforts to revive grassroots energy within the NWP, and focused instead on lobbying in Washington, building links with national white male politicians who might be persuaded to push for the amendment. Finally, it necessitated delinking the project of feminism from any association with anti-nationalism, anti-militarism, socialism, and Black activism. With respect specifically to the issue of race, although Ida B. Wells and Mary Church Terrell had strongly backed the NWP's picketing during the war, after the war the NWP largely avoided incorporating Black voices or concerns into its agenda.

Indeed, under Paul's leadership, the NWP tended to view even Southern race-based violations of the Nineteenth Amendment as not truly about women's rights. Instead, the NWP treated these as a matter of racial politics, and so outside the organization's single-issue focus. At the same time, Paul pushed hard to ensure that the NWP's national conventions also voted down resolutions supportive of the disarmament work of anti-war activists, including Eastman and those more broadly connected to the peace movement.[110]

All of this meant that whenever the 1920s NWP saw a move toward greater formal provision of equal rights for women, it championed that move as a victory. And it did so regardless of what the practical effects may have been for cross-movement solidarities or for women on the ground, especially poor and working-class women.

Take for instance the NWP's response to the Supreme Court decision in *Adkins v. Children's Hospital*, which struck down a sex-specific minimum wage law for women.[111] The Court maintained that the passage of the Nineteenth Amendment extended full membership to women and ended their dependent status. As such, if minimum wage laws during the era violated a man's right to "freedom of contract," women as free citizens equally enjoyed those same constitutional liberties. In this way, the case mirrored the NWP's ERA discourse, which emphasized the constitutional importance of equal treatment of both sexes under the law.

But at the same time, the decision also pitted the goal of formal equality against both material improvements for poor and working-class women and the labor movement's hope to expand workplace protections. Rather than confronting this tension—between formal rights and substantive material equality—the NWP's newspaper simply hailed the decision. Indeed, the paper rejected the idea that questions of economic structure were relevant to feminism at all: "It is not within the province of the Woman's Party, as a purely feminist organization, to discuss the constitutional question involved [i.e., the idea of freedom of contract] or the merits of minimum wage legislation as a method of bettering labor conditions. On these points we express no opinion."[112]

Crystal Eastman was dismayed at the narrowing of the movement during these years, and its focus on formal law to the detriment of class and racial conditions. Along with Alice Paul, Eastman had been one of the coauthors of the Equal Rights Amendment. And she had imagined a very different path for feminist politics in the wake of the suffrage victory. In line with her overarching approach to constitutionalism, Eastman had seen the Nineteenth Amendment not as an act of constitutional fidelity or redemption; instead, she saw it as offering a tool for both providing practical rights to women and steadily dislodging the broader constitutional order. She hoped that, with white suffrage achieved, the goal would shift to a further radicalization of feminist ambitions, in keeping with the desire to transform the fundamental economic, familial, and racial structures of society.

Of course, Eastman also rejected the exclusive focus on class that shaped the politics of many of her male Socialist Party colleagues. In her speech "Now We Can Begin," published in the *Liberator* in December 1920, she reiterated that women's emancipation could not be reduced to socialism or to economic change alone. Just as Charlotte Perkins Gilman had maintained, the basic problem of sexism was the gendered division of labor, which shaped the constitutive terms of the family itself. Unless society confronted this basic division, even "the downfall of capitalism" would not ensure "her complete emancipation."[113] And Eastman pressed for the ERA in part due to this belief: in her mind, the amendment highlighted the extent to which the division of labor transformed vast domains of collective life into gendered sites of differential rights and power.

Still, in keeping with Eastman's larger constitutional vision, this new amendment would not aim to complete the American constitutional project. Rather, it provided yet another lever for opening up how collective life could be organized: truly making good on the commitment to "equal rights" would substantively reconstruct the basic terms of women's experience. It entailed nothing less than "arrang[ing] the world so that women can be human beings . . . instead of being destined by the accident of their sex to one field of activity—housework and childraising."[114] For Eastman, equality meant doing away with sex-specific laws. But a genuinely feminist remedy could not entail ratcheting down labor protections so that no one had them. Instead, it required expanding them to all and, more broadly, generating the actual economic and cultural conditions for women's material and psychic independence. Eastman thus also saw the ERA as a path to a broad transformation in the marriage laws, and in what the historian Nancy Cott describes as the laws of "inheritance, divorce, child custody, and sexual morality."[115]

Above all, the constitutional shifts would go hand in hand with recognizing women's household labor as work of equal value—and, through state-sponsored assistance, distributing the provision of child care and housekeeping fairly across both sexes. As Amy Aronson writes, "her plan was to facilitate a relational model of shared childcare by bringing both mothers and fathers into the home."[116] First, this entailed a "revolution in the early training and education of . . . boys and girls," underscoring joint responsibility and practical knowledge by all of reproductive work. And second, since society at present essentially compelled women to provide this uncompensated labor, they should be properly paid for it by the state through a "motherhood endowment." Speaking of the long-standing subordination within the family of women as dependent caregivers, she declared, "the only way we can keep mothers free . . . is by the establishment of a principle that the occupation of raising children is peculiarly and directly a service to society" and those who "perform this service" are "entitled to an adequate economic reward from the political government."[117]

Notably, this approach, which in the 1970s (as we will see) would become associated with "Wages for Housework" campaigns, deviated from other feminist calls during the early twentieth century, associated with Charlotte Perkins Gilman, to "outsource motherhood to trained professionals."[118] Both Eastman and Gilman sought to overcome the gendered division of labor in part by socializing reproductive work. But Eastman worried that outsourcing, without a transformation in the culture and education of society, would simply replicate the patriarchal terms of who inevitably ended up being consigned to this labor. She also was committed to a framework in which both men and women within the family could freely choose whether to pursue child care and reproductive work or modes of labor outside the home. By contrast, those that backed government provision of child care saw proposals like the "endowment" as far more entrenching of gendered work expectations than professionalized care. Its very framing in terms of "motherhood" reinforced cultural assumptions about how the family unit was organized.[119] Eastman would have countered that when other reforms and cultural changes shifted gender norms, such a funding program would lose its association with "motherhood" alone and thus liberate both men and women to decide on the terms of their work life. These debates would persist among feminists across the century.

Beyond the question of an "endowment," Eastman argued that for women to be meaningfully free they also had to control the initial choice of whether to have families and also how large those families should be. Without such control, it would remain impossible to break both the gendered division of labor and broader system of patriarchal domination. Real emancipation thus necessitated ending the criminalization of birth control and affirmatively providing ready access to it. Eastman maintained that without reproductive freedom, women could not control the terms of both intimate and public life: "The immediate feminist program must include voluntary motherhood."[120]

Eastman thus rejected the idea that feminism could be collapsed into socialist politics. Still, she saw a feminist agenda as part and parcel of a wider ambition to eliminate all the structural and material dependencies that shaped the experiences of those subordinated—whether their subordination was on class, racial, or gender grounds. And while she believed that key ameliorative improvements could be made within the existing legal-political framework, ultimately the entire social order would have to be thoroughly reconstructed for genuine transformation to occur. She viewed the unwillingness of the NWP to take seriously this overall agenda as ignoring the extent to which women's emancipation was not a single-issue project that could be safely disconnected from other spheres of injustice.

Ultimately, Eastman considered the direction of the NWP—not unlike the era's broader reformist turn—as accelerating rather than addressing the falling popular energy behind the women's movement. If Alice Paul and others believed that feminism's association with radicalism led to declining numbers, Eastman's approach suggested that retreating into a status quo politics was not the solution: it gave young women and those attracted to reform movements no imaginative horizon worth fighting for and therefore no reason to join. By acceding to a limited vision of freedom and by accepting the post-war strictures of Americanism and constitutional faith, the tendencies within official feminism—now including the NWP—effectively gave up on the movement's transformative ambitions. Even worse, organization leaders who embraced a politics of formal equality could become complicit in sustaining the hierarchies that structured collective life.

Conclusion: The Unaddressed Crises of Gilded Age Politics

If reformist anxieties about being labeled unpatriotic spoke to the power of the pro-Constitution campaign, the persistence—and even growing cohesion—of a constitutionally skeptical Black internationalism highlighted the campaign's limitations. The World War I–era effort to bind militarism, constitutional devotion, and unquestioned allegiance to the constitutional state clearly had met with real success. And this success resulted in no small part from the emergence of a receptive mass popular base, concerned with the seeming breakdown of settler social order and committed to aggressively protecting existing racial, family, and economic hierarchies. In such a climate, and with constitutional opposition cast as a foreign danger, professing constitutional commitment became proof of one's American-ness, coded in highly racial terms. Taken as a whole, the effort forced many constitutional opponents into long-term ideological retreat, and also pressed more moderate reformers to rearticulate their claims within a constitutionally respectful register, thus proving their national and ethno-cultural loyalty.

Still, the pro-Constitution campaign offered little sustained rebuttal to the extensive structural and rights-based critiques that had shaped Gilded Age debates about the constitutional order. Indeed, throughout the 1920s, the very same crises that had fed earlier constitutional disillusionment persisted. Industrial society continued to generate heightened inequality and to subject factory workers to poverty, hazardous conditions, and the ever-present threat of joblessness. Political institutions marked by extensive veto points, which business elites employed to defeat social programs and other popular reforms, proved fundamentally powerless to respond. Even worse, these institutions seemed complicit in sustaining these hierarchies. As for race relations, the further entrenchment of Jim Crow highlighted how state-based representation and federalism—and the power it gave to Southern white elites at all levels of government—only strengthened the political grip of a white oligarchy, regardless of Black aspirations for the Reconstruction Amendments. The Nineteenth Amendment gave millions of women the right to vote—a massive achievement—but access to this right was racially circumscribed. Furthermore, it did not go hand in hand with meaningful shifts in the roles to which women found themselves assigned within society or in the broader structures of family and economy.

State-sanctioned violence, organized constitutional celebrations, and ritualistic school exercises may have altered the cultural terrain in favor of pro-Constitution voices. But the failure to address these underlying conditions left real and persistent cracks in the legitimacy of the governing order. As I detail in chapter 8, nothing brought this fact home more than the Great Depression, which again unleashed all the internal social conflicts that had been contained, if only superficially, by World War I and its aftermath.

CHAPTER 8

Transformation and Preservation in the New Deal

In 1936, during the depths of the Great Depression, Franklin Delano Roosevelt and his New Deal allies retained power in a stunning reelection victory, the greatest in American history. Roosevelt won 46 of 48 states in the Electoral College and over 60 percent of the popular vote—the largest share since James Monroe ran essentially unopposed in 1820. Democrats increased their representation in both houses of Congress to three-fourths, with effective margins brought even higher by additional support from Progressive-aligned Republicans and some third-party independents.[1] Congress had not been this lopsided since the early days of Reconstruction in 1866, when Radical Republicans pursued military control over the defeated Confederacy and refused to seat Southern Congressional candidates who had won in whites-only races.

FDR's win offered a resounding endorsement of the New Deal policies implemented in the preceding years to combat the Great Depression. The 1930s had witnessed an economic collapse of staggering proportions, which dramatically remobilized poor and working-class Americans. The Depression had generated nearly wholesale joblessness, as unemployment figures rose from 429,000 in October 1929 to over 15 million—one-third of the labor force—in 1933. Without work, men and women were left absolutely destitute, facing eviction and foreclosure and unable to feed their families.

In the past, poor relief had been a largely haphazard enterprise, usually provided locally and through private charities. But these methods were woefully inadequate to deal with the massive economic crisis. As a result, the unemployed took to the streets in marches, rent riots, and even mob looting. Cities, already nearing bankruptcy from new municipal relief efforts, teetered on the edge of actual collapse. And even those who still had jobs faced serious financial pressure, due to a precipitous fall in wages. In response, industrial workers sought to protect their interests by developing a large-scale new union movement, which in 1934 involved 1.5 million people in strikes. This movement eventually centered in the emergent Congress of Industrial Organizations (CIO), which, paralleling the efforts of the unemployed, called above all for social and economic protection.[2]

Roosevelt and his New Deal coalition aggressively responded to these overlapping crises. But their efforts faced a massive roadblock in the Supreme Court. A stronghold of the conservative economic and social order, the Court struck down central pieces of Depression-era legislation. This judicial intransigence appeared to confirm all the earlier doubts about the constitutional system as a whole: existing arrangements pitted an overwhelming supermajority of Americans against a small number of judges—unelected and serving for life—and gave primacy to the views of the latter. And that fact alone seemed to make the post–World War I rhetoric of constitutional genuflection newly absurd.

The Great Depression thus raised fundamental questions about the future viability of both capitalism and the Constitution, especially in a global setting of financial ruin and rising new and revolutionary political ideologies. It also called into question the reformist potential of earlier Progressive aspirations, going back to Woodrow Wilson and Herbert Croly, for informally adapting the constitutional system through court interpretation and presidential leadership. If World War I's language of creedal constitutionalism was to become broadly convincing, there would need to be significant transformation in the everyday experiences of ordinary people, including across class and racial lines. And perhaps, at the end of the day, the legal-political order was too brittle and inflexible to survive twentieth-century realities without a formal break and a thoroughly rewritten text.

Yet the spring of 1937 witnessed a remarkable turn of events: the Supreme Court capitulated, shifting its jurisprudence and even upholding the National Labor Relations (or Wagner) Act—the labor movement's prize victory, which strengthened the capacity of unions to press for higher pay and better conditions. Writing in the *New Republic*, the political scientist (and perhaps the era's defining constitutional scholar) Edward Corwin concluded that all this entailed a constitutional "revolution" unlike any in American history. Court interpretation had changed before, but no changes had been "so radical, so swift, so altogether dramatic."[3] Moreover, as the next few years unfolded without Supreme

Court pushback, FDR and his backers succeeded in profoundly reorganizing the nature of the bureaucratic state.

New Dealers thus embraced and seemingly fulfilled the Progressive ambition of grafting a new system of presidential government upon the 1787 framers' original design. They expanded the powers of the federal state, built an administrative framework for economic regulation, and centralized much of this decision-making within the presidency—in effect constructing the executive branch as the main focal point for lawmaking.

For FDR and those around him, these transformations infused the existing system with far greater political energy and popular legitimacy, especially through a more direct relationship between the president and the people. The Constitution's words may have remained the same, but its meaning and its actual institutions had undergone a significant overhaul. All of this seemed to vindicate that earlier Wilsonian faith in constitutional adaptation. And it is also why scholars today often follow Corwin's analysis at the time, depicting New Deal constitutional politics as a project that aspired to—and significantly achieved—basic legal and political reconstruction.[4]

Yet, as I argue in this chapter, for all the genuinely transformative implications of the era's constitutional innovations, New Deal changes nonetheless had their own profoundly preservationist dimension. For starters, FDR very consciously defended New Deal adaptation as constitutional restoration—as a way of redeeming the constitutional project and thus protecting American institutions from both pro-business reactionaries and revolutionary extremists. And at a structural level, the entrenchment of presidentialism took for granted the permanence of central features of the established constitutional order, including an extraordinarily difficult amendment process, an ultimately unreformed federal judiciary (complete with lifetime judges who still enjoyed strong powers of review), and an overarching system of state-based representation (with rippling implications including through the Electoral College and the malapportioned Senate).

The New Deal framework thus quietly rejected the alternative theory of design that had defined Socialist constitutional argument as well as much of Populist and Progressive state constitutional practice during the preceding half century. As discussed in chapter 4, perhaps the most sustained Socialist argument against the 1787 order, not to mention against the presidentialist solution, was that it failed to institutionalize popular participation adequately. New Dealers did experiment with sites of participatory involvement, particularly within the administrative state. But the failure to confront existing constitutional structures warped these efforts. In the end, the new managerialism tended to focus constitutional politics around the interplay of legal elites in the executive branch and in the judiciary. By contrast, Socialists and other radical activists had long sought to create a mass participatory infrastructure in which organized working-class constituencies could intervene continuously everywhere—reshaping, as necessary, existing arrangements in ways that fused democracy, evolving rights commitments, and ongoing changes to the economy.

As I detail in the first section of the chapter, intense constitutional criticism returned in the mid-1930s, along with debates about how to transform the existing system—whether by rewriting the text or by informally reconstructing it under presidential guidance. I also discuss W. E. B. Du Bois's Depression-era assessment that, even more important than the selection among transformational means, reformers had to confront the rippling racial and economic hierarchies generated by state-based representation. Failing to do so would, according to Du Bois, permanently damage any project of true democratization. Judged against these broader alternative visions, FDR's presidentialism ultimately accepted a key dimension of the existing system: its highly insulated nature, reinforced by the degree to which direct popular power remained deeply fractured by multiple and overlapping veto points in a state-based system.

The chapter then develops these arguments by focusing specifically on the court-packing episode, which is usually depicted in terms of its norm-breaking qualities as well as the constitutional changes generated by eventual Supreme Court acceptance. Instead, I explore how the court-packing debate and outcome—despite the goals of many of its backers—had the perhaps unintended effect of contracting constitutional conversation. I argue that the heavy emphasis on Supreme Court membership tended to drain energy away from other political discussions about how to genuinely democratize the constitutional system as a whole. Moreover, this narrowing—which ran counter to the goals of some New Dealers—aligned with FDR's own instincts: that is, in support of presidential management and an overall safeguarding of state and economy. I also assess the reasons why labor leadership ultimately rallied around the New Deal language of constitutional restoration, and the consequences of this choice.

This chapter therefore offers a reading of the late 1930s that brings home the striking duality of the period, which is often deemphasized in scholarly discussion: FDR's management of judicial reform both facilitated and contained constitutional change. It is true that New Deal consolidation was a legal-political reconstruction that reoriented constitutional politics. But at the same time, it also *circumscribed* the possibilities for the future.

This latter aspect is often overlooked by legal scholars, perhaps due to a common focus on the legislative and judicial wrangling in Washington at the time. The Washington-based analytical lens focuses attention on the difference in constitutional vision between FDR and his anti–New Deal opponents, especially business conservatives. But if one broadens the scope to incorporate the aspirations of the era's reformers and movement activists, the options under debate and the range of constitutional possibility spill well beyond FDR's updating of Progressive presidentialism. Thus, by connecting FDR's choices to many of his own more radical supporters—emboldened Progressives, Socialist politicians, Communist Party newspapers, Black intellectuals, labor leaders, and even New Deal lawyers—one can more fully appreciate both the transformative and the preservationist dynamics of the period.

Ultimately, dramatic reform did indeed arrive, in ways that must not be underemphasized. But it did so through processes that remained wedded to central constitutional structures of representation, not to mention the courts, all wrapped in a language of textual fidelity. The New Deal workaround thus led to major achievements of the mid-twentieth century. But it also left for future generations—including our own—the persistent problems of anti-democratic and system-wide defects.

The Return of Constitutional Skepticism

Upon first taking office in 1933, FDR oversaw a variety of legislative measures aimed at assisting those inside and outside the labor force. New federal insurance schemes provided for the aged and jobless, while massive public works programs gave millions employment. As for those already employed, minimum wage laws ensured against the most extreme pay cuts. Above all, the Wagner Act, passed in 1935, strengthened the bargaining capacity of unions and created a new labor relations board with enforcement capacities: the Board would preside over employee elections, prohibit employer interference, and compel companies to negotiate labor contracts with elected union representatives.

Such collective bargaining was in many ways the central goal of the union movement, which saw this legislative triumph as finally eliminating the near absolute power management enjoyed over the terms of work. Since the rise of industrial wage labor a century earlier, employers had benefited from a radically unequal bargaining position: they could dictate the conditions of employment in ways that sometimes mimicked feudal master-servant relationships. Now, through collective bargaining, workers—in the form of their union representatives—finally had the opportunity to participate alongside business and state actors in shaping their own employment.[5]

But despite overwhelming popular support for these measures, the Supreme Court—long a bastion of business elites—continued to fight a rearguard battle against New Deal legislation. In 1935 and 1936, the Court struck "down a half-dozen regulatory schemes on the ground they were beyond congressional authority." These included some of the most high-profile New Deal recovery measures, like key parts of the National Industrial Recovery Act (NIRA), with the Court strongly "reasserting its own authority to review the merits of state economic legislation."[6] Even more ominously, despite the 1936 election returns, new court challenges meant that the justices appeared poised to invalidate the heart of the great New Deal achievements for poor and working-class Americans, including the Social Security Act and the Wagner Act.[7]

These developments buttressed the classic Progressive view of the courts as a judicial oligarchy. They also spread such sentiments across large swathes of the New Deal coalition. Increasingly, many New Dealers and their supporters agreed that significant changes to the constitutional system would have to be implemented. The debate then moved to how to pursue fundamental shifts, revisiting and revising the key prewar questions in Progressive and Socialist circles: Should politicians, lawyers, and movements primarily focus on formal alterations to the federal Constitution? Or would informal and interpretative adaptations prove sufficient?

PROGRESSIVE-ERA CONSTITUTIONAL
CRITIQUE RECLAIMS CENTER STAGE

After the First World War, schoolchildren may have found themselves declaiming the genius of the Supreme Court in constitutional education classes. But those lesson plans ran headlong into the troubling realities of the federal judiciary's operations during the Great Depression. The courts' actions reenergized the Progressive-era suspicion that, as Sidney Hillman—one of the most popular leaders of the CIO—declared in a CBS radio network broadcast, the Supreme Court was nothing less than a "judicial dictatorship."[8] Speaking at the Labor's Non-Partisan League (LNPL) convention, Wisconsin Senator Robert La Follette Jr., the fiery Progressive Party ally of both labor and the New Deal, similarly referred to the ability of a bare majority on the Supreme Court to strike down legislation and to "stubbornly cling to an outmoded philosophy which the people of the country have emphatically renounced" as "a threat to a functioning democracy."[9]

La Follette Jr.'s words in many ways articulated a central conviction of his own father, La Follette Sr., the Wisconsin congressman, senator, and governor, not to mention the 1924 Progressive Party candidate for president (winning 17 percent of the vote). During the post–World War I years of constitutional celebration and school-taught genuflection toward the Supreme Court, La Follette Sr. perhaps did the most to keep alive in the electoral imagination the profoundly anti-democratic potential of judicial power. He asserted, for instance, that "it is typical of the Supreme Court . . . that whenever Congress has sought to enact progressive and human legislation which was offensive to great financial interests to strike it down." And he had famously called for the elimination—if need be, by constitutional amendment—of the ability of lower federal courts to declare acts of Congress unconstitutional, with Congress able to overrule a Supreme Court decision by simply reenacting the bill.[10]

La Follette's son now took up the mantle of judicial reform, along with labor, and with intense conviction. The LNPL had been founded in 1936 as what the political scientist Eric Schickler calls the "brainchild" of both Sidney Hillman and John Lewis at the CIO. The organization expressly aimed to mobilize labor voters—regardless of race or gender—to back FDR in that fall's momentous reelection campaign. The CIO and LNPL raised the bulk of the nearly $800,000 spent by labor during the election and played a central role in shifting Black American support toward FDR and away from its traditional home in the Republican Party. Their effort was widely considered crucial to the campaign, with the *New Republic* writing in September 1936 that "more significant than anything Mr. Roosevelt may say is the support he is receiving from the Labor's Non-Partisan League." Indeed, in the aftermath of the election, commentators described it as just as much a victory for labor as it was for FDR, with the *Nation* claiming that "[labor] now emerges from this election with greater political prestige than it had ever had before in American history."[11]

But for labor activists, electoral victories would be meaningless if business allies in the courts—long a concentrated site of elite socioeconomic power—continued to have final say over what Americans could legislate. As one popular LNPL pamphlet declared, "the reactionaries are trying to use the Supreme Court to nullify the election."[12] With key new cases looming, labor voices saw an insulated judiciary as undermining mass democracy at multiple levels, reversing the overwhelming popular will expressed through the vote. At an even deeper level, federal courts undermined the conditions necessary for working-class Americans to enjoy full inclusion as democratic citizens: those in the CIO and the LNPL believed that without union protections and a robust safety net—which they understood as positive socioeconomic liberties—working-class and poor constituents were denied the practical ability to be free and equal members of society.[13] Moving the country toward a real democracy thus entailed establishing a system in which the state had affirmative duties to provide everyone with these basic needs and protections.

As during the pre-war years, this conversation about the courts and democracy also spilled over into wide-ranging debate about the degree to which judicial dictatorship was indicative of the constitutional order more generally. Speaking of the times, the Yale law professor Thurman Arnold, later the head of the Antitrust Division at the Justice Department and a federal circuit judge on the United States Court of Appeals for the District of Columbia, mocked the continuing effort of business elites—in the face of utter institutional failure—to invoke faith in the Constitution as a way of calming political nerves. He noted sardonically how papers like the *New York Herald-Tribune* "printed as the head of its editorial columns the President's oath to support the Constitution" as if "somehow they are making the country safer by this gesture." For Arnold, the times were such that only "timid people wave the Constitution," believing that by invoking the words of the document like a "prayer" they could ward off radical change. Even these pro-business elites understood the weakness of such gestures, for the simple reason that the constitutional order had proven itself unequal to the challenges of the day. As Arnold declared, "it [was] the failure of the practical institutions to function which has raised doubts in the hearts of conservatives." Surveying the economic crisis and both the political agitation and the malaise that it had generated, Arnold concluded bluntly, "there is no settled faith in our form of government as the only workable type."[14]

In this context, a variety of reform figures reasserted the need to address once and for all the democratic limitations of the constitutional system. Not surprisingly, these individuals often had deep links to previous Progressive-era efforts, and saw the New Deal as an opportunity to overhaul structural flaws papered over by wartime jingoism and postwar political retrenchment. Take as one example the National Popular Government League (NPGL): a long-standing reform organization that had been an outspoken critic of post–World War I "Red Scare" crackdowns[15] and whose membership drew from activists and backers of the old Progressive and Socialist movements as well as from labor. The NPGL was headed by Judson King and Bertha Hale King (in the 1920s the latter had been the first woman to serve as executive secretary of the Socialist Party). The League declared in a bulletin to its members and supporters that "the evils of a quarter-century [ago] return to face us in aggravated form" and that this fact required recommitting to "the promising beginnings of reform made in the 1910 period" before they "were swept aside by the World War and its aftermath of reaction under the Harding-Coolidge-Hoover regime."[16]

Above all, for activists like those in the League, Americans should not focus exclusively on the problem of the Supreme Court. Instead, they must recognize the extent to which the whole 1787 constitutional framework operated exactly as the founders intended. Norman Thomas, six-time presidential candidate for the Socialist Party (from 1928 to 1948) and a founding member of the ACLU (along with Crystal Eastman and Roger Baldwin), drove home the point. He argued that economic change proved so difficult in the United States because the entire political structure was organized to constrain mass democracy. In words that mirrored Progressive-era arguments, he wrote: "A system in which there is so much final legislative authority in the Supreme Court; a system under which the President might be easily elected by a minority; a system under which the state of Nevada, which has less than a hundred thousand people, has the same rate of representation in the powerful Senate as the State of New York with more than twelve millions—such a system may perhaps be defended on various grounds, but certainly not on the ground that it is democratic."[17]

In Judson King's view, the most striking example of this problem of minority rule was not even judicial review. Instead, it was the degree to which the Constitution itself proved virtually impossible to amend. It was true that "five men on the Supreme bench can now block any law passed by a majority of the 531 members of Congress." But, alongside this, "thirty-three senators can now block the submission of an amendment to the Constitution" and "representatives of 2,895,237 people, in the 13 smallest states, or less than 2.4 percent of the population . . . can block the adoption of an amendment if submitted."[18]

Drawing from the likes of J. Allen Smith, Charles Beard, and Allan Benson, King contended that this difficulty of amendment aimed precisely to preserve class rule. Reminding Americans of the counterrevolutionary nature of the 1787 Constitution, the NPGL declared, "it has always been the habit of the masses of all nations to cheer the Declarations of Independence . . . and then permit the conservatives to write the constitutions and fix the laws of property. Years later, the people awake to find that they still have the declarations . . . but the Tories have the goods."[19] For both King and Thomas, the crisis of the Court thus should be treated as an opportunity to reconceive, finally, the organizing principles of the established system.

ARGUMENTS FOR A NEW FORMAL CONSTITUTION

Given the context of economic depression and institutional intransigence, the question for an ever-assertive collection of constitutional critics—inside and outside government—was not merely *whether* to redesign the political framework. Taking this for granted, reformers focused on *how* to change the existing order in ways that would make it far more amenable to mass popular goals.

Not surprisingly, the internal disagreements tended to map onto the old debates within Progressive and Socialist circles over how much effort to put toward actual textual alterations. Crucially, this discussion embodied more than just a disagreement over pragmatic political calculations regarding, for instance, how to head off conservative stonewalling in the courts. It also entailed a deeper debate about how formally to read legal texts, and also which kinds of actors—especially experts or citizens—should lead the actual constitutional politics of interpretation and reform.

Arguing for formal changes were those like Norman Thomas, Judson and Bertha Hale King, and the firebrand New York City lawyer and congressman Vito Marcantonio (who was closely identified with the Communist Party, although not a member). Elected to office in the 1934 midterm, Marcantonio immediately pushed for efforts to systematically rewrite the Constitution. He defended changes that would nullify the Supreme Court's powers of judicial review. And along with three other representatives (all Progressive midwestern allies of La Follette Jr.), he even introduced a bill before the House calling for a new convention, with La Follette Jr. placing their joint statement into the official Senate Record.[20]

In the statement, the congressmen declared that, given recent judicial rulings, it had become obvious that "twentieth-century problems cannot be seriously dealt with under the eighteenth-century interpretations of the Supreme Court." This reality, along with the structural weaknesses of the existing political order, spoke to the immediate need to "take steps to call a convention to revise the Constitution in the light of present-day requirements."[21] In many ways, Marcantonio's role in pressing for a politics of constitutional overhaul also highlighted the malleability of the Communist approach to the Constitution during the Popular Front era. Even after moving away from the Black belt thesis, activists and politicians connected to the party were still more than willing to engage in radical constitutional critique, irrespective of the general posture of Constitution worship being promoted simultaneously by Earl Browder, the CPUSA executive secretary.

Norman Thomas, the Socialist Party presidential candidate, also agreed that the "country needed a new fundamental law." But in his view, an actual second constitutional convention was both highly unlikely and, at that moment, probably counterproductive. The New Deal electoral coalition remained a patchwork of often competing interests, rather than a unified and revolutionary base. As a result, it had not set forth a comprehensive vision of institutional reforms akin to the Socialist agenda in 1912. Any convention in this context, spearheaded under FDR's leadership, would implement an "extraordinary hodgepodge" of policies rather than a coherent alternative design.[22] Marcantonio too eventually deemphasized the convention call,[23] perhaps persuaded by these arguments about the cumbersome nature of a second convention and the still limited revolutionary potential of the existing New Deal coalition—especially given its alliances in the South with a white oligarchy.

Both Thomas and Marcantonio thus focused on a constitutional amendment, which would clarify Congress's authority and entrench basic labor rights and positive socioeconomic guarantees. In 1935, Marcantonio introduced into Congress an amendment that received extensive support within the unions[24] and from Thomas: the Farmers' and Workers' Rights Amendment aimed to establish congressional authority for the implementation of wide-ranging legislation—including child labor regulations, minimum wage laws, maximum hour provisions, unemployment insurance, pension schemes, and collective bargaining—as well as laws regarding public ownership of utilities, natural resources, and other economic sectors.[25] Interestingly, the amendment did not explicitly constitutionalize the Wagner Act, in part because of some radical and Communist Party concerns with the bill.[26] Despite their support for collective bargaining, party activists expressed concern about the tripartite and corporatist structure of the Act, which managed labor disputes through government, business, and labor partnerships. They worried that this could, over the long run, shift too much power away from the independent capacity of the union to impose its will at the point of production, especially by regulating and containing shutdown methods such as strikes and sympathy boycotts.[27]

Still, regardless of the details of the amendment, both Marcantonio and Thomas hoped that, once this expansive legislative power was formally constitutionalized, labor's continuing capacity to provide the New Deal with supermajorities would in time radicalize the New Deal agenda itself. These supermajorities would sweep away the remaining conservative electoral constraints and create the terms for a rolling reconstruction of both state and economy. Ideally, they would do so through additional packages of constitutional reforms and eventually, when the time was right, through an actual convention.

Judson King partially diverged from Thomas and Marcantonio. He viewed the amendment revision initiative—"a change in the amending clause of the Constitution which will make that instrument flexible"— as even more important than the Farmers' and Workers' Rights Amendment.[28] As many pre-war Socialists—and even Progressives—had maintained, King believed that such a shift was essential to creating the type of governing order responsive to mass democratic pressure. A simplified amendment process was the precondition for cumulatively implementing just the systemic changes Thomas and Marcantonio sought. He worried that without it, reformers would remain captive to pro-business judges appointed for life, the divided structure of legislative decision-making, the inhibiting effects of federalism, and the representational dysfunctionality of the states.

In a sense, those like King may have worried that activists could not expect labor to sustain its overwhelming supermajorities indefinitely. These, after all, were the product of economic crisis and extraordinary mass mobilization. Consequently, only by changing the amendment process could reformers ensure that popular policies, under less extreme circumstances, would actually overcome the Constitution's numerous veto points.

Other constitutional critics, however, feared that Thomas's and Marcantonio's ultimate concerns about an actual convention applied just as much to the equally cumbersome amendment process. Specifically, amendments would prove too slow in the context of immediate crisis and with court cases looming on the horizon. These critics also believed that after years of constitutional celebration, explicitly arguing for fundamental textual revision would swim too quickly upstream for many Americans (and not only business conservatives)—even during times of extreme economic dislocation. Thus, for pragmatic reasons, they felt it might be best to avoid linking reform to actual re-founding or wholesale structural revision.

ANTI-FORMALIST INTERPRETATIONS AND THE RISE OF THE LIVING CONSTITUTION

Further buttressing these pragmatic considerations was a belief that focusing on formal changes to the Constitution misunderstood the nature of the document, in a deeper sense. According to various New Dealers, one could achieve nearly all the policy reforms while superficially holding on to the 1787 text. This was because, for the most anti-formalist of these constitutional critics, the document had minimal intrinsic textual meaning outside of what empowered officials could impose at particular historical moments. Therefore, so long as Americans embraced its open-endedness, they could transform the existing Constitution into a pliable instrument of social improvement.

The legal figure within the Roosevelt administration who did the most to articulate this radically anti-formalist reading of the Constitution was none other than Thurman Arnold. For Arnold, the politics of the era highlighted a notable disjuncture. Large numbers of Americans had concluded that the basic institutions of state and economy needed a fundamental overhaul. And yet, many of these same Americans would likely balk at explicitly discarding the Constitution—even though, in practice, it was the very document that established and protected those troublesome institutions. For Arnold, this was because the Constitution in American life had come to function less as a concrete framework for governmental decision-making and far more as a "creed" or "unifying symbol." In a sense, the World War I–era pro-Constitution project had effectively succeeded in reshaping the popular relationship to the document. But for Arnold, "the beauty of this" was that, in the United States, the actual "language of the Constitution" was "immaterial," since "it represent[ed] current myths and folklore rather than rules." And critically, these "myths and folklore" were "very elastic"—in fact, they were more or less infinitely flexible because they could "be used on both sides of any moral question without the user being bothered by what the Constitution actually says."[29]

All of this made it both fundamentally unnecessary and also politically counterproductive to focus on rewriting the Constitution, since this would court significant opposition. Virtually any political objective could be achieved—whether it concerned new positive socioeconomic rights or the rise of a centralized administrative state—even while proclaiming surface fidelity to the document. In a sense, Arnold took the past Progressive idea that the Constitution had no embedded economic theory to its ultimate conclusion: the Constitution had no genuinely fixed meaning. If Earl Browder could convince enough Americans that the right interpretation of the Constitution required communism, who was to say he was wrong? In Arnold's view, this indicated that the political battle should be over changing institutional and popular interpretations of the text—and altering the symbolic meaning individuals ascribed to an open-ended document—rather than formally shifting its "immaterial" language.[30]

Arnold's ideas enjoyed particular prominence among New Deal lawyers. And they extended what Charles Beard himself had developed as a theory of the "Living Constitution," a phrase which, as the legal scholars Joseph Fishkin and William Forbath note, "he put into general circulation."[31] By the late twentieth century, the phrase would become a staple of liberal constitutional politics. Beard had been foundational in historically underpinning the class-based critique of the Constitution, and his words were often cited by those Socialists and Progressives who backed a formal overhaul. But by the New Deal, Beard had concluded that a focus on the seemingly hardwired elements of the text overstated the degree to which legal-political consequences were determined in advance by either the Constitution's written language or its main design features. Beard accepted that the text laid down "some core reality and practice" on which there existed a "general consensus":[32] for instance, the reality of a bicameral Congress, state-based representation, or the fact that a person had to be thirty-five years of age to run for president.

But Beard contended that this "core reality" was actually far narrower than Socialists had supposed.

In particular, Beard argued that most of the Constitution's textual language was unavoidably indeterminate, a collection of "vague words" and "ambiguous expressions." He wrote that this ambiguity cloaked constitutional meaning in "huge shadow[s] in which the good and wise can wander indefinitely without ever coming to any agreement respecting the command made by the 'law.'" The language was largely "immaterial," to use Arnold's word—not because lawyers and publics simply ignored the text, but because the document's brevity and openness meant that the language alone could not resolve constitutive ambiguities.[33]

According to Beard, these ambiguities underscored that there existed nothing talismanic about the text: "The words and phrases cannot rise out of the Constitution and interpret themselves. Some human being, with all the parts and passions of such a creature, must undertake the task of giving them meaning in subsidiary laws and practices." At the end of the day, the Constitution-in-practice emerged from the document's implementation on the ground by actual people—"citizens, judges, administrators, lawmakers." These actors held the power to read the text to suit their purposes; they could "bring about changes in the relations of persons and property" or they could "preserv[e] existing relations." The Constitution was thus a "living thing," mostly the product of what electoral coalitions and their representative officials could achieve through political action: "The Constitution . . . is what living men and women think it is, recognize as such, carry into action, and obey. It is just that."[34]

This idea of the Constitution as "living" had two related political implications. First, it suggested that, if reformers and movement actors did not like the interpretations conservative judges imposed on the Constitution, they should develop alternative jurisprudential arguments. And then—through electoral victories—they could refashion constitutional meaning across the federal government, including in the courts themselves through new nominations and openings.

Second, and relatedly, Beard as the author of *An Economic Interpretation of the Constitution of the United States* certainly accepted that the structural design of the Constitution was riddled with countermajoritarian roadblocks. As Socialists had argued, constitutional processes made certain economic distributions and political outcomes more likely. But Beard did not view these structural realities as insurmountable for making basic changes to labor relations or property rights. Instead, he considered them a problem for political organizing. And, with FDR's popularity rising and a New Deal coalition taking shape, Beard believed that the sheer number of New Deal voters could overcome existing veto points and enforce new theories of constitutional meaning.

As Beard concluded of the Constitution's Article II, which laid out the executive office, "Article II of the parchment may repose peacefully in the archives, but the Article that counts most in real life is the personality occupying the White House."[35] The words written by the framers may have included counterrevolutionary features, but at the end of the day they were less important than who held the office and how that person wielded power. As long as working-class constituents controlled Congress and the presidency—and through those representatives shaped both the judiciary and a new administrative civil service—there was no need for a different document.

Therefore, Beard disagreed with anti-Constitution formalists who argued for a new text, not only out of pragmatism but also due to a different vision of constitutional change. He suggested that those like Norman Thomas inadvertently promoted a theory of the law that assumed the existence of objectively valid resolutions to these legal debates: they desired formal changes because they believed the text mostly to have a finite and fixed meaning. Beard worried that such an approach to the Constitution in particular demeaned rather than heightened the self-assertiveness of mobilized constituencies, especially by viewing workers as the passive subjects of the law. As such, this formalism ignored the extent to which the Constitution was a creation of active and ongoing agency, and therefore already open to whatever transformative changes majority coalitions could impose.

Under a Beardian reading, proponents of a new constitution fell into two conservative traps. First, since an objectively accurate interpretation of the text could be reached, debates about the Constitution were perhaps best left to experts. In this way, such critics unwittingly deemphasized the most popularly accessible method of change in the here and now: ongoing textual reinterpretation in Congress and in the courts by social movements, politicians, and their aligned and partisan lawyers.

Just as significant, anti-Constitution formalists seemed to accept that the only way of implementing genuine change involved following the paths prescribed by the framers themselves: holding a convention or writing new language. They thus engaged in their own kind of

Constitution worship, though centered on the means rather than the ends. By contrast, for Beard, the New Deal project highlighted how one could inscribe social-democratic values into the existing system through other unconventional means. Even if the Senate or state-based representation remained, bills like the Wagner Act, along with new administrative agencies, could create innovative business, labor, and government structures to appropriately govern the increasingly complex economy and society. This new institutional infrastructure aimed at full employment, economic redistribution, and broad socioeconomic liberty. And it amounted to a constitutional overhaul—whether or not the amendment procedures laid out by Article V of the Constitution had been used.

Significant disagreements existed between formalist and anti-formalist critics of the Constitution. But one should not lose sight of the real continuities across these camps. Just like Norman Thomas and Judson King, Beard and Arnold were deeply suspicious of investing the 1787 text with overweening ethical value. And they both also believed that the Constitution-in-practice required radical alteration.[36]

In fact, this version of a "living Constitution" did not rest on American exceptionalism and institutional greatness or invoke a narrative of creedal redemption. Unlike the Professional Patriots in the ABA, with their "cult of constitutional certitude," Beard understood the Constitution to be what Americans accepted at any moment in time—and this meant denying the text a hallowed status. Rather than "a 'sheet anchor,' a 'lighthouse,' an 'ark of the covenant,' a 'beacon,' and a 'fundamental law,'" the Constitution was simply a collection of good and bad legal and political practices. "These symbols," Beard wrote, "are supposed to represent some reality, something tangible, a substance which all good and wise men can see and agree upon. Yet in truth they are mere poetic images that correspond to no reality at all, and the employment of them is sheer animism."[37]

Indeed, by refusing to view the Constitution as infused with telos, people like Beard believed they could sever whatever destructive function the text played as a source of conservative reaction: "If the Constitution is a sheet anchor, then it may be 'lost.' If it is a lighthouse, then a storm may bring destruction. If it is an ark of the covenant, the wicked may steal it away. A beacon can be 'extinguished.'"[38] But if, on the other hand, the Constitution was seen as none of these things—as rather a practice rendered fungible for countless innocent and wicked purposes—then the document could move wherever the public took it. During these years of the Great Depression, Beard suggested that a productive ambivalence toward the Constitution—rather than reverence or even an overly formalist attentiveness—was the best affective relationship. Such ambivalence enhanced the collective willingness to engage in political experimentation, and it fought against the temptation to collapse back into latently preservationist postures.

DU BOIS, DEMOCRATIC INSURGENCY, AND THE QUESTION OF MEANS AND ENDS

Given that formalist and anti-formalist critics both embraced legal-political experimentation and tended to back the most radical redistributive efforts of the New Deal, such positions were two sides of a common political effort at constitutional overhaul. And W. E. B. Du Bois perhaps articulated most profoundly the need to combine these two orientations in any effort to transcend the constitutional system. Du Bois today is rarely read by legal scholars as a significant constitutional interlocutor. But his arguments—especially in the 1930s and 1940s—offer among the most sustained accounts both of the limits of the federal constitutional model and of how to conceive of legal-political change.

Above all, Du Bois refused to treat the debate between formalists and anti-formalists as a hard binary. Instead, he approached the matter through an overriding question about how means related to ends. Postwar racial violence, 1920s Jim Crow extremism, and the Great Depression had all combined to radicalize Du Bois. He viewed the constitutional order as implementing deeply undemocratic arrangements that sustained both economic and racial hierarchy. Indeed, by this point in his life, he regarded American capitalism as a system interwoven with white supremacy. And he further believed that overcoming the latter required replacing the former, along with all the legal-political structures that preserved both.

In assessing reform tools, then, the primary questions for Du Bois centered on which means—available in the here and now—did the most to disrupt the country's racial capitalism. And Du Bois's answer developed, but also engaged with the potential weaknesses within, 1910s Socialist Party constitutional politics. Not unlike Eugene Debs or Crystal Eastman, he believed each reform approach should be assessed based on how it altered the basic distribution of power and thus made it more difficult for the established social order to persist. Du Bois's framework then proceeded by drawing from both formalist and anti-formalist insights. Like anti-formalists, he rejected any fixation on existing constitutional process—amendments, conventions—as the necessary or even privileged instrument for change, viewing this as its own form of Constitution worship. But like formalists, he nonetheless believed that hardwired features of the system—which profoundly compromised representation and limited mass popular involvement—could not be wished away. In the final analysis, he believed, there would have to be an actual institutional rupture from the 1787 framework.

These views were most thoroughly developed in two texts that bookended FDR's presidency: 1935's magisterial *Black Reconstruction in America, 1860–1880* and 1945's *Color and Democracy.* The first book highlighted the multiplicity of ways Americans—especially in the years during and after the Civil War—implemented revolutionary change: formally amending the document, but also devising new textual interpretations and, most importantly, pursuing extralegal acts of mass rebellion. This history meant that in the present it was essential to experiment broadly with a variety of revolutionary means, which together could chip away at the prevailing legal, political, and economic systems.

Black Reconstruction is remembered today as a landmark response to the dominant American historiography of the post–Civil War years, shaped by the Columbia professor William Dunning and others sympathetic to white supremacist interpretations.[39] Du Bois argued that the end of slavery was the product not of white political largesse, but rather of a massive "general strike" of Black enslaved workers, as hundreds of thousands of African Americans shut down the Southern economy, took up arms against their enslavers, and, through their own actions, fundamentally linked emancipation to the war effort. Du Bois also systematically repudiated the pervasive and racist conventional wisdom that Reconstruction ended because of Black political limitations. Emphasizing a class-based structural analysis, Du Bois instead underscored how the ultimate détente between Northern industrialists and the Southern planter class led to the rise of the Jim Crow order, with Republican Party complicity. In the process, he challenged white assumptions that Black-run and interracial governments were corrupt and mismanaged, demonstrating in profound detail the remarkable achievements of the era—from extending the vote to both poor whites and Black men formerly enslaved, to building new public school systems, to confronting questions of landlessness and material access.

But the book was also, in ways we now tend to forget, a sustained examination of the symbolic and structural role of the Constitution in shaping the terms of economic life, race relations, and democratic possibility. *Black Reconstruction* implicitly and explicitly reflected on the problems of the 1930s and the type of radical political thinking and energy that would be necessary for addressing them. Du Bois published the book at a moment when his relationship with the NAACP, an institution with which he had been deeply identified in the public imagination, had frayed badly. This led to his resignation from the editorship position at the NAACP's *Crisis* and then from the NAACP entirely. For Du Bois, the combination of extreme Black immiseration and persistent white racial hostility made highly suspect the idea that effective Black freedom could be achieved through formal legal equality and civic inclusion. As he wrote in June 1935, "the colored people of America are coming to face the fact quite calmly that most white Americans do not like them, and are planning neither for their survival, nor for their definite future if it involves free, self-assertive modern manhood."[40] Such skepticism led Du Bois to question the benefit of focusing on desegregation as the central political strategy. It even led him to call for building Black economic cooperatives and separate institutions, much to the consternation of his former allies in the NAACP.

But Du Bois's comments about separation were not a matter of retreating from politics or of accepting the Black conservatism of those identified with Booker T. Washington. Instead, given this skepticism of relying too heavily on interracial alliances within the United States, Du Bois hoped that, through Black-run producer and consumer cooperatives, African Americans could develop their own independent power and employ such power to confront white supremacy. Rather than aligning primarily with white reformers at home, Du Bois believed that an organized Black political and economic base should then also build strategic links with anti-colonial movements abroad.

In keeping with his own growing internationalism, discussed in chapter 7, Du Bois increasingly contended that, to the extent that the Black poor were part of any community, they were part a global community of colonized labor. The lesson of the international economic crisis—and not simply of the American Great Depression—was that members of this transnational community all suffered under modes of coercion and violence that mirrored, in new forms, the enslavement African Americans experienced in the years before the Civil War: "In Africa, a black back runs red with the blood of the lash; in India, a brown girl is raped; in China, a coolie starves; in Alabama, seven darkies are more than lynched."[41] Emancipation had required a revolutionary assault on the slaveocracy through a collective and organized resistance on the part of Black enslaved workers. So too in the 1930s, Du Bois argued, genuine transformation would require a similar and sustained effort—only now at the global level, and by institutions of resistance that stitched together colonized labor.

Du Bois thus rejected ideas of American creedal redemption, as well as the faith that one could count on meaningful transformation occurring through a politics of constitutional rule-following, as even earlier Socialists like Allan Benson seemed to hope. In his view, the Civil War and Reconstruction had taught that—given the depth of white supremacy and the prevailing institutional order—actual change required significant norm-breaking on behalf of genuine democracy. Such norm-breaking had taken a multiplicity of forms: an insurgent and mass Black rebellion, or "general strike" against slavery; military rule in the South to ensure Black voting rights; and even the refusal to seat white Southerners in Congress as a means to facilitate the passage of the Fourteenth Amendment.

Civil War and Reconstruction-era achievements had necessitated using all the revolutionary tools available to Black people, as well as their allies in the Republican Party, in order to democratize a fundamentally undemocratic constitutional system. None of these means were in the spirit of the Constitution; indeed, they were pointedly *un*faithful to the 1787 institutions. Even the use of constitutional amendments rejected any sacrosanct attachment to the Article V process and bent the established procedural rules. Such changes were predicated instead on the belief that "rule-following, legal precedence, and political consistency are not more important than right, justice and plain commonsense."[42]

In fact, Du Bois contended that African Americans and Radical Republicans had, in truth, re-founded their country, even if they had not formally held a convention or written a new document. They nonetheless had "formed a new United States on a basis broader than the old Constitution and different from its original conception." In this assertion, Du Bois paralleled earlier arguments by the journalist E. L. Godkin, who during the 1887 constitutional centennial celebrations had declared that those like Lincoln—rather than Madison or Hamilton—were the current constitutional order's real framers. Now, Du Bois explicitly added to the pantheon of true founders the great heroes of Radical Reconstruction, who like Thaddeus Stevens "crashed" "through the cobwebs" of "rule-following" on behalf of a democratic and multiracial "political power built on slavery smashed."[43]

For Du Bois in the 1930s, all of this indicated a similar need to reject any "fetich-worship [sic] of the Constitution." Genuine transformations to the social order likely would have to proceed through a variety of creative and even disruptive means. These might include mass civil protest alongside institutional innovations, which—whether through amendment, legislation, administrative regulation, or textual interpretation—did not pay undue respect to the formal requirements of the Constitution. In fact, the country would only be transformed if Americans rejected "legalist" beliefs either in the wisdom of existing structures or in the idea "that consistency with precedent is more important than firm and far-sighted rebuilding."[44]

Still, if Du Bois embraced a multiplicity of potential means, he nonetheless believed that, at the end of the day, one could not avoid confronting the structural problems of political representation in the United States, as he highlighted in the later *Color and Democracy*. Above all, he saw overcoming both capitalism and white supremacy as requiring sustained power-building among the most oppressed segments of the working class, the Black poor chief among them.

But this power-building was fundamentally compromised by the voting system embedded in the actual written terms of the Constitution. That state-based framework, along with the rest of American federalism, placed a massive thumb on the scale in favor of the forces of white supremacy—with rippling effects for who served as president, who sat on the Supreme Court, and what policies were contemplated. It helped ex-Confederates to reclaim power in the context of Reconstruction. And once Black people were again disenfranchised, it so dramatically overrepresented Southern white constituents that Jim Crow politicians effectively determined the extent of any practical changes to the social order.

For Du Bois, even Norman Thomas and Judson King, let alone Thurman Arnold and Charles Beard, failed to adequately appreciate how the constitutional system entrenched American authoritarianism. Such voices—not unlike white Progressives and Socialists in the 1910s—focused in general terms on the undemocratic nature of representative institutions. But they failed to contend with how those institutions specifically elevated the authority of Southern reactionaries in ways that encoded even into the New Deal economy a politics of racial hierarchy.

Simply put, nearly a century after the Civil War, the country still found itself subject to the dictates of a white planter elite, because white Southern votes counted for drastically more in the legal-political system. "This lack of democratic methods not only gives the South four times the political power of the Middle West," Du Bois contended, "but also gives it control of some of the most powerful committees in the Senate." All of this meant that "the race problem has been deliberately intermixed with state particularism to thwart democracy."[45]

For this reason, while Du Bois supported the New Deal, he always remained skeptical that the Democrats would, when push came to shove, actually press for the interests of all workers regardless of race — precisely due to the stranglehold white supremacist elites had over the party's Southern wing. He was not surprised that, in passing the Wagner Act, New Dealers bowed to racist politicians and rejected efforts that would have prohibited racial discrimination by unions. They also declined an amendment proposed by Vito Marcantonio to extend the bill to farm workers, who constituted a substantial portion of the Black working class in the South. FDR had even failed to back anti-lynching legislation. The overall result was a national system of government that "turn[ed] 13,000,000 Americans into second-class citizens"; so long as it remained in place, the country could never truly be "rational and progressive."[46]

In a way, Du Bois echoed the Black CPUSA activist Harry Haywood's analysis of how the existing state system divided Black and poor political power, embedding a politics of minority rule at virtually every level of government. Emphasizing how capitalist and racial domination fit together, Du Bois noted of state politics, especially in the South, "monopoly and industry can by this rotten-borough system turn the state into a medieval fief and usurp" any representative government. "This extraordinary situation" — embodied in everything from the Supreme Court and Senate to the power local white and business elites enjoyed through federalism — had "neither rhyme nor reason." It was rather "a survival of an eighteenth-century American Tory hatred and fear of democracy, surviving as a fetish" in the form of Constitution worship. Du Bois believed it had more in common with the authoritarianism of "German particularism" than with real democracy — whatever the pro-Constitution advocates said.[47]

Ultimately, Du Bois's analysis did more than merely combine existing anti-formalist and formalist critiques. It called on the likes of Arnold, Beard, Thomas, and Judson King to all be bolder both in terms of ends and means. The ultimate goal had to be more than simply a social safety net that protected the poor from the worst excesses of the economic order. It needed to encompass an uprooting of racial capitalism itself, as well as of the institutions of government that sustained it. Otherwise, the system would inevitably return power to the same white oligarchy that had defeated Reconstruction.

As for political strategy, confronting the connected evils of economic and racial exploitation certainly required both formal structural changes and new textual reinterpretations. But none of this would be possible unless a powerful and insurgent movement of working people drove social change and placed continuous pressure on existing institutions. Such a movement, not unlike the abolitionist general strike during the Civil War, should remain open to exercising whatever irruptive power it enjoyed—from large-scale work stoppages at the point of production to mass civil disobedience of the laws generated by the "rotten-borough system."

Given the degree to which those marginalized, particularly the Black poor, were systematically excluded from actual economic and political decision-making, a reliance on solely legalistic methods for constitutional change would be deeply self-defeating. Those methods all emerged out of processes that critically misallocated power and voice, due to the brokenness of American representation. And they overwhelmingly proceeded in settings from which the most marginalized had been largely removed.

Du Bois's arguments certainly invoked aspects of the old Industrial Workers of the World (IWW) syndicalist position, as discussed in chapter 4, and implicitly critiqued the process fixation and avoidance of norm-breaking that shaped some of the more conservative SPA leaders. Still, he was far from utopian about social revolution. Nor did he embrace direct action whatever the consequences. As the historian Timothy Shenk notes, Du Bois reminded Black radicals farther to his left that partial New Deal achievements were nonetheless worth defending. Therefore, it was important to calibrate means through a realistic assessment of the array of forces at play, and to expand on the real and ongoing achievements of FDR policies. Rather than "sneer[ing]" at New Dealers, all of this countenanced engaging in mass actions—whether inside or outside the established legal-political system—in ways that could facilitate rather than undermine emerging changes.[48]

But critically, whatever the means chosen, the overall relationship to the existing Constitution had to be instrumental. If the opportunity emerged, one had to be willing to think in truly transgressive terms about, for instance, breaking up the states or eliminating the Senate— irrespective of the constitutional text or the dictates of norm-following. For this reason, Du Bois saw Constitution worship as a political threat— even the surface-level fidelity that Thurman Arnold was willing to engage with. The post–World War I climate of constitutional celebration perpetuated a culture of deference to the state, and of general fidelity to the existing processes, regardless of how they systematically enhanced the power of the few. If change proceeded in ways that still mouthed respect for the Constitution—despite how "it all add[ed] up to one result: the frustration of popular rule"[49]—this inevitably would result in the containment of transformative energy. Du Bois placed democracy, and with it the basic principle of an equal and effective vote for all, at the center of his normative lens. From this point, he argued for a willingness to bend the other elements of the constitutional order, those "Tory" holdovers, in service of genuine democratic expansion.

Court-Packing and the Politics of Constitutional Change

In this overarching political climate—one of spreading radicalism vis- à-vis the Constitution, and of widespread popular distrust of the judiciary specifically—FDR introduced his court-packing initiative. In February 1937, he proposed the Judicial Procedures Reform Bill, which included a provision allowing the president to nominate a new Supreme Court justice whenever a sitting one, having served for at least ten years, reached the age of seventy. At the time this would have resulted in some six additional appointments.[50] Such an increase to the Court's size would swamp resistance, effectively allowing New Deal legislation to proceed without the specter of five unelected justices striking down widely supported measures.

In many ways, court-packing was precisely the type of creative means—unconstrained by narrow "legalism"—that Du Bois called for. And indeed he backed the effort, writing that he "believed very strongly that the power of the Supreme Court should be curtailed" and considered "Roosevelt's plan," given "pressing necessities," to be "the best practical effort."[51] But ultimately, for reasons both expected and unexpected, the politics unleashed by court-packing forestalled as much as it facilitated comprehensive change—certainly of the type Du Bois defended. The effort tended to center criticism around the composition of the Supreme Court, rather than the structural organization of the institutions. And when the justices on the bench began upholding New Deal policies, such conversation buttressed sentiment that perhaps the constitutional system as a whole—especially the existing modes of representative government—was not as broken as the critics contended. Moreover, FDR clothed the entire debate about the courts in a language of constitutional restoration, validating radical fears of veneration and its possible long-term effects.

THE NEW DEAL CONFRONTS JUDICIAL DICTATORSHIP

At least initially, it was hardly clear that FDR's approach to judicial reform would end up having preservationist implications. Many of the staunchest critics of the Constitution, both formalist and anti-formalist, backed the court-packing initiative and saw it as a pathway toward reducing the structural authority of the judiciary. If successful, Supreme Court expansion would limit the power of any specific justice and would also open space for yet further shifts in the organization of the federal bench—whether through term limits, supermajority requirements when the Court struck down congressional legislation, or the establishment of legislative overrides of judicial review.

For Thurman Arnold, FDR's action was precisely the informal adaptation the moment required: it refused to be imprisoned by the words on the page or by counterproductive formal mechanisms. Such an approach recognized that the Constitution was ultimately what individuals interpreted it to be. Indeed, relying primarily on formal amendment would ignore the fact that, if the same conservative justices remained, the Constitution-in-practice would continue to depend on the will of entrenched New Deal opponents, no matter what the new words in the text said.[52] This was another lesson of the Reconstruction Amendments: despite being a tool of racial equality, these amendments had been twisted by judges into an interpretative device for the protection of business. This point was certainly not lost on Du Bois, and it informed the reasoning behind his strong approval.

Even those most identified with the goal of formally rewriting the document ultimately endorsed court-packing. Judson King at the NPGL saw liberalizing the amendment process as the most important innovation on a path to constitutional transformation. Nonetheless, he argued for the immediate "enact[ment] of 'the President's plan.'" In his view, "then later let the progressive forces of the Nation press steadily forward for" more far-reaching structural changes.[53] Norman Thomas too contended that despite the fears over presidential power—as well as the failure of the plan to directly address the nature of congressional authority—the bill was an acceptable stopgap measure. Responding to more conservative anxieties about whether FDR was setting himself up as all-powerful, he wrote that "a democracy impotent to act because it is paralyzed by a . . . judicial oligarchy would be more likely to invite a strong man to step in as Dictator."[54]

As for Vito Marcantonio, he actually was an early and vocal defender of court-packing. As the 1930s proceeded, in many ways his constitutional approach came to mirror that of Du Bois. While Marcantonio was associated among labor activists with the project of formal change, he nonetheless increasingly combined a flexible account of means with a long-term agenda of structural institutional overhaul. For him, what mattered most was responding immediately and comprehensively to social crises and doing so through a variety of pathways, informal and formal—all linked by a commitment to building both economic and political power among working people themselves. In fact, before FDR publicly took up the position, Marcantonio began calling in early 1936 for adding new justices to the Supreme Court, regardless of legal niceties.

Marcantonio too saw this as the kind of necessary political experimentation that could go hand in hand with explicit constitutional revision down the road.[55] Jurisprudential shifts, once achieved through court-packing, could then be entrenched through actual textual changes in the Constitution. This all meant that when additional amendments were implemented, the new written language would not be compromised by a holdover bench.

For Marcantonio, again akin to Du Bois, the best historical comparison to the Great Depression was the crisis faced by the country during and after the Civil War. In a speech to Congress on the occasion of Lincoln's birthday, Marcantonio noted that when Lincoln found himself faced with a Court that might strike down war measures, including the Emancipation Proclamation, "he simply turned around and he changed the Court. From 5 members he increased it to 10 members on March 3, 1863, by act of Congress."[56]

For both formal and informal critics of the Constitution, the central problem was that the overall institutional order blocked popular sentiment—something that Supreme Court intransigence vividly embodied. Therefore, moving beyond this particular Court's dominance over constitutional decision-making did not undermine judicial independence per se; it merely would begin to institutionalize a meaningful mass democracy. The judicial reform bill may have amounted to a small step, but it nonetheless took a step in the right direction, and with an immediate effect—especially essential given the precarious legal status of important socioeconomic measures.

This sense of exigency, along with the broader belief that the Supreme Court as currently composed stood in the way of democracy, helps to explain why both labor and Black activists backed the plan so strongly. According to a pamphlet widely circulated by Labor's Non-Partisan League, "Packing the Supreme Court or Petting the Sweat Shop," court-packing would "free the legislature from the dictatorship of the Court."[57] For George Berry, the LNPL's president, supporting the effort was "of first importance to the workers of this country,"[58] and it became the central objective of labor in early 1937. The group immediately went about organizing mass meetings across the country in defense of the initiative, with CIO unions urging their members "to make known TODAY, through letters or telegrams to every Congressman and Senator of your district and State, that the President's proposal for judicial reform has your complete support."[59]

Similarly, the Black press featured numerous editorials defending the bill. As one *Chicago Defender* article declared, court-packing held out "enormous possibilities for Negroes." Not only would a new Supreme Court back laws "giv[ing] working people greater share in national wealth"—something African Americans would benefit from since Blacks were "preponderantly working-class people." It would also generate a potential transformation in the jurisprudence of the Reconstruction Amendments: "Roosevelt court would never have declared Reconstruction Federal Civil Rights bill unconstitutional, nor would permit Grandfather clause, interstate jim crow trains as conservative court did."[60] Making the same point, the *New York Amsterdam News* described how the Harlem Lawyers' Association had endorsed FDR's plan in significant part because of the implications of a changed bench—namely, the inclusion of those with a "more moderate and liberal attitude"—for racial equality.[61] Many Black commentators rallied to the plan in part due to the long experience with judicial curtailment of the Fourteenth Amendment. They subscribed to the view that, especially given the pressing political moment, what mattered at the end of the day was whether racial conservatives or racial liberals were interpreting the document.

Nonetheless, the bill faced extensive pushback from the remaining conservatives in Congress, who saw it as a power grab by the president, and even from some New Dealers, who were wary about the long-run implications for executive power.[62] Such opponents often employed the language of constitutional preservation, and they emphasized the threat court-packing posed to the rule of law. New York Governor Herbert Lehman, a strong FDR ally, published a letter to this effect in the *New York Times*, addressed to Senator Robert Wagner. He emphasized that while he believed the New Deal legislative program "represented the greatest step forward in social reform that any nation has undertaken for many years," he could not support the court-packing plan. He worried that it would create "a greatly dangerous precedent which could be availed of by future less well-intentioned administrations for the purpose of oppression or for the curtailment of the constitutional rights of our citizens."[63] Similar concerns within the ACLU led the organization—while very supportive of the New Deal agenda and deeply critical of existing Supreme Court doctrine—to withhold official endorsement of the bill.[64]

And in Congress, Burton Wheeler, the New Deal Democratic senator from Montana, argued that even if it were slower and more cumbersome, principles of constitutional fidelity required using the amendment system rather than short-circuiting that established process by adding members to the Court. According to Wheeler, the most constitutionally respectful approach would ratify a new amendment that clarified Congress's legislative power, leaving no room for the Supreme Court to see otherwise.

In response, FDR reminded the public during his March 1937 fireside chat of the very problems with the amendment process itself. He noted that the process's veto points did not just generate "delay"— they meant that reactionary forces could well misdirect and "sabotage" any effort. And even if a new amendment were enacted, "its meaning would depend upon the kind of Justices who would be sitting on the Supreme Court bench."[65] Court expansion ensured against the possibility of continued intransigence by conservative justices, even in the face of a changed constitutional text. In a sense, Wheeler's position highlighted Charles Beard's—as well as Du Bois's or for that matter the 1910s IWW's—point about the politics of formal amendment: in the hands of more moderate figures, it could also easily devolve into a brand of Constitution worship that deified the framers' established pathway for change and employed veneration to limit more creative efforts to re-mold the existing system.

But what doomed the bill—FDR's first legislative defeat—was the fact that, in the midst of public debate and congressional wrangling over court-packing, the Supreme Court pulled back from the precipice. On March 29, 1937, the Supreme Court reversed its position on the constitutionality of minimum wage regulation, upholding a Washington state law in *West Coast Hotel Co. v. Parrish*. Even more momentously, on April 12, the Court handed down its landmark decision in *NLRB v. Jones & Laughlin Steel Corp.*, which upheld the legality of the Wagner Act. When the latter decision was announced, workers across the country broke out in spontaneous celebrations, with those in Aliquippa, Pennsylvania, the site of a massive plant owned by Jones & Laughlin Steel, "pil[ing] into cars and parading through town, horns blaring."[66] And then on May 18, Willis Van Devanter, one of the four justices that made up the conservative faction on the Court, announced his retirement. Later that same day the Senate Judiciary Committee failed to vote out of committee a court expansion bill. Significantly weakened, the fight over some compromise form of expansion would still proceed through the summer before finally dying in the Senate.[67]

With respect to *West Coast Hotel Co.* and *NLRB v. Jones & Laughlin Steel Corp.*, Justice Owen Roberts, after previously striking down New Deal legislation as unconstitutional, cast the deciding vote sustaining the laws. Roberts likely shifted sides in late 1936—that is, *before* FDR announced his court-packing initiative, and (at least in part) in response to the landslide election returns that underscored how out of step the Supreme Court was with public sentiment.[68] But the popular narrative quickly took hold that his decision was a direct response to FDR's proposal. This was called "the switch in time that saved nine," treated in political commentary as a judicial capitulation to FDR that ultimately kept the Supreme Court at its current, still unaltered size. Whatever the internal motivations that drove Roberts (or for that matter Van Devanter[69]), it was no doubt the case that after doctrinal changes and a key judicial retirement, more voters, including many FDR supporters, saw the immediate threat posed by the judiciary as diminished. That threat was increasingly outweighed by worries about the plan's precedent for future presidential power. By June of that year, according to one pollster, 59 percent of responding Americans had come to oppose congressional passage of FDR's plan.[70]

FDR'S POLITICS OF CONSTITUTIONAL RESTORATION

Court-packing became a notorious defeat for FDR, the moment scholars often point to as when the president overran his popular support.
Yet, in many ways, it served both the transformative *and* preservationist ends that FDR himself intended. The initiative, and the "switch in
time" that followed, facilitated a tremendous constitutional overhaul.
Even if the reform bill did not make it through Congress, many of its
goals succeeded: from shifting judicial interpretation to fortifying a
new administrative state armed with the power to pursue social welfare
ends. And despite the pushback, the court-packing episode established
a key precedent for what the legal scholar Bruce Ackerman calls "transformative judicial appointments": the self-conscious use of court nominations by presidents to impose constitutional change on a recalcitrant
judiciary.[71] Over time, these transformative appointments, as employed
by Roosevelt and his successors, became a central tool in entrenching
an assertive brand of presidential government—one aspect of which
became the executive's construction, through judicial nominees, of federal courts compatible with its own ideological agenda.

At the same time, FDR's changes stopped at genuinely altering the
nature of American representative and judicial institutions, whether the
state-based electoral system or the organization of the federal bench.
Roosevelt very consciously promoted the initiative as an act not of radical transformation but instead of small-scale reform in keeping with a
general reverence for the Constitution. As the political scientist Keith
Whittington has concluded, "the administration hoped to harness
the power of the Court, not destroy it."[72] In effect, he got his wish: enhanced presidential government alongside preservation of the basic
constitutional infrastructure.

More radical reformers and New Dealers had imagined court-
packing as a wedge that would eventually generate even more expansive
and fundamental shifts to state and economy. But FDR, from the very
beginning, was notably wary of these agendas. He promoted reform as
effectively about, in the words of legal scholars Fishkin and Forbath,
"sav[ing] capitalism and the Constitution."[73] FDR argued that there
was "nothing novel or radical about this idea" and that it simply aimed
to do two things: first, address inefficiencies in court adjudication by
"mak[ing] the administration of all Federal justice speedier and . . . less
costly"; and second, inject new blood into the legal system ("younger

men who have had personal experience and contact with modern facts and circumstances under which average men have to live and work"), thereby ensuring against the "hardening of the judicial arteries."[74]

Above all, FDR, in his March fireside chat and even more pointedly in his Constitution Day speech—the latter honoring the document's one hundred fiftieth anniversary on September 17 (by then the fixed date of constitutional founding)—located himself within the post–World War I tradition of Constitution worship. His approach, he told American listeners, was governed by an abiding belief that the Constitution was a document of "enduring wisdom"[75] and should be treated like a "bible," "read again and again."[76] Rather than imagining dramatic structural alterations, FDR sought to protect the constitutional order from out-of-date judges who would reduce a "layman's document" to a "lawyer's contract."[77] For this reason, it was essential to have new blood on the Court who would interpret the text in keeping with the living tradition both Beard and Arnold defended.

But this language of fidelity underscored a real difference from Beard's and Arnold's version of that living tradition. Recall that they may have emphasized interpretive flexibility, but in the name of pursuing radical institutional and ideological departures and of rejecting the treatment of the 1787 text as a "lighthouse" or "beacon." Their "living Constitution" might eventually bear little relationship to the existing legal-political order or to the frameworks one associated with the text. Roosevelt, by contrast, used the idea of a living Constitution to embrace that document's status as a "beacon." And the constitutional system's capacity for change offered proof of the country's ability to achieve a historic promise—one present from the very founding.

FDR's language of devotion and restoration no doubt derived from genuine pragmatic considerations. Arnold himself had noted how shifts in constitutional culture made it challenging, even during the Depression, to directly reject the document. By embracing constitutional reverence, FDR could deflect conservative accusations that he was behaving both unpatriotically and unconstitutionally in confronting the Supreme Court or in avoiding the amendment path.

Yet beyond pragmatism, investing in the symbolism of the Constitution had additional political stakes, and FDR may have preferred this approach to fully opening up the Constitution to formal changes. In Roosevelt's hands, the court-packing debate focused above all on the views of individual justices. It channeled conversation into a matter of who was on the Supreme Court, rather than into questions about the basic nature of the institutions themselves—and especially whether those institutions actually supported a mass democracy.

An amendment avenue could certainly be a project of constitutional fidelity, aimed at shoring up the state and reaffirming the processes laid down by the framers, as imagined by Senator Burton Wheeler. But the choice might also unleash mass mobilization over the fate of a range of legal-political institutions. After all, such popular engagement would have happened at a time of intense social unrest. And it may have proceeded down pathways, implicating various structural features of government, over which FDR had less control. Indeed, as FDR himself had implicitly done in his fireside chat, all of this could have called into question the Article V process itself: Perhaps formal change, authorized through mass mobilization, should break from the terms laid out by the existing document?

Roosevelt's approach thus did not just question change by referendum; it more broadly evinced skepticism of constitutional change by mechanisms initiated and directed from outside government through mass popular action. It should be underscored that in questioning the amendment avenue Roosevelt saw himself as primarily "in a crusade," as Fishkin and Forbath write, "against the 'economic royalists' and their new 'industrial dictatorship.'"[78] As he declared of the threat from the business Right in his Constitution Day speech, "we have those who really fear the majority rule of democracy, who want old forms of economic and social control to remain in a few hands."[79] It was these "royalists" who disingenuously called for using the amendment route, as a way of actually forestalling reform and holding on to minority rule.[80]

Yet at the same time, Roosevelt was fearful too of the spread of revolutionary socialism and the potential for radical energy to sweep away institutional respect and with it established legal-political process. As he also noted in that 1937 Constitution Day address, "we have those who are in too much of a hurry, who are impatient at the processes of constitutional democracies, who want Utopia overnight and are not sure that some vague form of *proletarian* dictatorship is not the quickest road to it."[81]

In navigating between these perceived extremes, FDR unsurprisingly trusted his own judgment about the pace and mode of constitutional change. Institutionally, his approach reinforced the power of the presidency, since FDR would ultimately dictate which justices would interpret the law. In this way, court-packing fit nicely within Roosevelt's own vision of expansive executive authority—in keeping with the constitutional politics of both Teddy Roosevelt and Woodrow Wilson. At root, privileging the presidential appointments of judges entailed cementing presidential guidance as a dominant framework of constitutional reform.

ELITE EXPERTISE AND THE CORROSIVE
EFFECTS OF THE OLD ORDER

FDR may have been wary of mass political action driving constitutional change. But he and those around him nonetheless did imagine a role for popular participation. Many New Dealers intended such presidentialism, especially when it came to the administrative state, to go hand in hand with real shifts in political and economic decision-making. Still, over time, the failure to pursue significant structural constitutional reforms had corrosive effects on the nature of such decision-making. It compromised efforts to incorporate popular voice and it pushed the overarching New Deal framework down pathways of insulated and elite management.

For starters, a goal of court-packing certainly was to move power away from the judiciary—even if only to "harness" that power, as Whittington writes. Yet, without any structural changes to the federal courts or to the constitutional amendment process, it proved incredibly difficult to alter how American legal-political practice operated. The judges themselves ultimately remained appointed for life, and they continued to wield extensive authority to rule on what counted as law. For now, following the "switch in time," they just exercised this authority in ways that met with FDR's approval. Neither adding six justices to the Supreme Court nor leaving the size unchanged actually permanently reshaped the underlying power of the institution.

Perhaps, above all, this was because FDR seemingly had little appetite for arguments from those like Judson King—in keeping with a long line of Socialists and even some Progressives—regarding the need for a simplified amendment process. Without other viable pathways for constitutional change, the mechanism by which change occurred overwhelmingly involved fights over interpreting the existing text. This had real consequences, in particular for which institutions and actors would be the main sites and players. Inevitably, the individuals empowered to participate in debates about interpretations would be legal elites and presidential appointees—regulatory administrators, executive branch lawyers, and ultimately judges as well.

FDR's hesitance regarding opening up the constitutional system to broad popular intervention kept a fundamental bottleneck in place. Essentially, the courts remained the central site for determining what counted as a constitutional question and how those questions should be resolved. Again, earlier Socialists had treated judicial reform and changes to the amendment process as two sides of the same coin. One could not systematically rein in judicial power *without* establishing spaces for ongoing and genuinely popular constitutional agency. And so, unsurprisingly, the courts—given that they were the institutionally entrenched venue for constitutional politics—regained the upper hand. This funneled constitutional debates into venues largely insulated from direct involvement by mass publics.

Still, some around FDR sought to mitigate this insulation through a more participatory vision of the administrative state. Such participation coincided with FDR's account of governance, in part because it operated under presidential oversight. In particular, throughout the 1930s, New Dealers developed a host of new institutions—housed in the executive—for the implementation of economic management and social provision. And, at times, they experimented with arrangements that would give working-class majorities—through their union institutions—far greater authority in the organization of the economy.

Yet, in grafting presidentialism and administrative government onto the constitutional system, FDR essentially left untouched the existing terms of political representation. That fact had rippling consequences for the ability of New Deal statecraft to incorporate sustained and direct involvement by mass publics.

One can see this in the story of bills like 1938's Fair Labor Standards Act (FLSA). Fishkin and Forbath write how the FLSA used "tripartite 'industry committees' composed of union, employer, and public representatives to hammer out rules and standards for their respective industries."[82] Recall that, within elements of the labor movement, whether Communists or old AFL leaders, there were real concerns that a tripartite and corporatist framework would undermine labor's independence.[83] Yet, if that was a danger embedded in corporatist forms, these new institutions nonetheless meaningfully unleashed "workers' collective power"[84] within both the administrative apparatus and the economy. The legal scholar Kate Andrias describes how "FLSA's administrative scheme made clear that employers would have to negotiate as equals with unions both in the marketplace and in government. In this way, FLSA and the NLRA [National Labor Relations Act] together 'provided the most hospitable climate ever fashioned in American history for trade unions and for decent enforceable conditions of employment.'"[85]

Unfortunately, though, even when New Deal administration expanded the bargaining power and decision-making authority of working-class institutions, it remained hamstrung by the electoral and constitutional processes that encased the overarching state. With respect to the FLSA, Southern white Democrats had succeeded in ensuring an extensive "agricultural exemption" so as to preserve racial hierarchy in the labor market.[86] Furthermore, in the context of an unreconstructed electoral system, "Southern employers routinely failed to comply with the law, while pressing Congress for amendments to curtail both FLSA and the NLRA," as Andrias notes.[87] Over the ensuing decade, these forces increasingly succeeded in "dismantl[ing] state-sponsored bargaining and . . . curtail[ing] workers' rights more generally."[88]

For our purposes, conservative reaction bore fruit in no small part because the constitutional system provided institutional advantages to business and Southern white opponents of the New Deal. FDR no doubt realized the centrality of Jim Crow structures across the South to undermining the scope of socioeconomic reforms, including in bills like the Wagner Act and the FLSA. In the context of systematic Black disenfranchisement, Southern white Democrats increasingly turned on New Deal efforts out of the desire, as Fishkin and Forbath write, "to insulate the region's separate, racially segmented, caste-ridden labor market."[89]

In response, FDR "attempted an unsuccessful purge in 1938 of southern members of Congress who had begun to resist his legislative agenda," as the political scientist Ira Katznelson has elaborated. Yet, as Katznelson also notes, FDR was wary of explicitly challenging the South's "racial order," given the potential implications for the Democratic Party coalition: "He 'seemed ready enough to leave well enough alone in questions that involved white supremacy.'"[90] In practice, this meant that Roosevelt may have fought to unseat Southern Democratic opponents at the ballot box. But he also sought to avoid a broader confrontation with the pervasive role of racial domination in Southern society.

Katznelson highlights how, at the very same time that Roosevelt pressed an election campaign against the region's conservative Democrats, the New Deal's National Emergency Council was generating a report on "economic conditions of the South." At FDR's behest, the council "stressed the region's poverty, and its underutilized human and physical resources," while making "no mention whatsoever of segregation." In this way, FDR both seemed to recognize that race could not be cordoned off from matters of social welfare and constitutional innovation and persisted in the "forlorn hope" that such a cordoning might still succeed.[91]

In a sense, FDR's broader constitutional politics—combining veneration with a focus on individual Supreme Court justices as the problem—spoke too to this desire to "leave well enough alone." This fact was not lost on Du Bois. Writing at the end of FDR's presidency, Du Bois stingingly concluded in *Color and Democracy* that such New Deal constitutional fidelity approached the state-based system, including the "composition of the Senate," as a "national tabu [*sic*]," a "situation" that "must not be discussed."

FDR and other governing elites may have pushed back against individual judges or sought to remove the worst Jim Crow politicians from office, but they left uncontested the language of "States' Rights," along with the assumption that deifying the states somehow promoted actual "local government"—democratic rule on the ground by a Black and white working class. In fact, "states rights and local government [were] two contradictory terms." Even after the replacement of conservative judges, these representational consequences, Du Bois declared, fundamentally "crippled" "the democratic process in the whole nation." Whether in Congress, the courts, or the new administrative state, they impeded the country's ability to deal forthrightly with all manner of concerns, including "poverty, illiteracy, and disease."[92] Simply put, there was no end run around confronting the destructive effects of the old 1787 infrastructure.

In this way, the issue with the administrative state paralleled that of the courts. In the courts, one needed changes both to the bench and to the amendment process to avoid power steadily reverting to the judiciary as the dominant constitutional arena. Similarly, without significant transformations to the constitutional mechanisms of political representation, participatory achievements in the administrative system would almost inevitably be undermined. One needed an administrative framework *and* a system of popular voting and representation to ensure the ability of working-class majorities—regardless of race—to intervene meaningfully in decision-making. By 1949, Congress had "effectively abolished" the FLSA's tripartite industry committees, as

Andrias tells us, and comparable experiments in using administration to expand worker authority more or less "disappeared from the core federal statutes."[93]

With respect to the administrative state, the resulting political containment of worker representation and power also further elevated more insulated modes of decision-making. By eroding alternatives, it tilted the broader framework in the direction of expert-led managerialism. From the beginning, such an orientation had circulated among central New Deal architects who—when push came to shove—placed more faith in expertise than in mass publics. Thurman Arnold, for example, preferred greater presidential and administrative leadership precisely because of how it could liberate economic management from too much popular meddling. Arnold believed in the necessity of a functioning electoral system to put into office representatives broadly committed to social-democratic ends, or what he called "humanitarian ideals"[94]—hence some of his suspicions of the 1787 framework. But, in his view, more shielded institutions were far better equipped to actually fulfill these ideals.

The Columbia economist Rexford Tugwell, who was part of FDR's first-term "Brain Trust" and served as undersecretary in the Department of Agriculture (and later as the Washington-appointed governor of Puerto Rico), embraced a comparable vision of experts and citizens. A proponent of more top-down managerial control, Tugwell in the 1970s even wrote a new constitution for the United States as a thought experiment. It formalized robust presidential power and created additional planning and regulatory branches of government.[95] In the mid-1930s, the editorial page of the *New Republic* circulated ideas like Tugwell's, and in essays like "Social Control vs. the Constitution" argued for constitutional overhauls premised on establishing a new "Supreme Planning Council" composed of "experts in social and economic management" "entrusted with hammering out long-time policy."[96] Under all of these accounts, the public primarily existed to provide an occasional electoral mandate, and then mostly as the beneficiary of enlightened and socially responsible government.

In effect, as experiments with extensive worker representation broke down, what persisted was a New Deal tendency toward faith in professional expertise, social science, and insulated statecraft. And the power of the unreconstructed bench further buttressed that tendency. Indeed, the bench itself remained compromised by the unreformed electoral system. Nomination processes continued to run through the states—

the presidency with its electoral college, and the Senate with its segregationists who controlled committees and oversaw confirmations. This meant that, even if in retreat, the same reactionary forces, enabled by the constitutional order, still retained disproportionate influence, including over who served in the federal judiciary and in the administrative state.

To a significant degree, then, court-packing and its fallout—shifts in jurisprudence and the entrenchment of presidential administration—papered over what Du Bois called a "lack of democratic methods" in the underlying constitutional system. Due to a combination of pragmatism and preservationist sensibility, FDR declined to take up broader questions that reemerged in the context of the Depression: Should federal court appointees serve for life, let alone have powers of judicial review (both open matters for many movement activists during the New Deal)? Should the amendment process itself be altered to decrease its extreme counter-majoritarianism? And, above all, should state-based representation for all of these institutions—the Senate, the electoral college, the amendment system, and even indirectly the Supreme Court—be significantly revised?

Instead, the perceived success of New Deal reforms established a clear framework for how change would occur—and in a way that left decisive aspects of the existing legal-political infrastructure in place. Constitutional change in this model proceeded primarily through the interaction of presidents, administrative officials, and business and labor leaders with lifetime judges. These interactions were mediated by a state-based system of political representation that shaped which laws could be passed and which officials could be appointed. The resulting conversation heavily emphasized the views of legal elites, whether in the executive apparatus or in the judiciary, and centered on their creative textual and jurisprudential interpretations. Labor groups no doubt became crucial actors, even at times enjoying some forms of representation in the administrative state. They pressed for their own statutory and constitutional interpretations, and they defended hard-won victories. But the fight was now far less about first-order questions, including regarding the basic terms of legal-political process. As Socialists had long worried, the new constitutional compact made it very difficult for mass movements to introduce those foundational matters—or to challenge whether legal elites should play the primary role in determining the actual language and terms of constitutional dispute.

LABOR DECLARES ITS FAITH IN THE
AMERICAN REPRESENTATIVE SYSTEM

Ultimately, it should not be a surprise that the "switch in time" and the capitulation of the Supreme Court produced a decline in searching public debate about the problems of constitutional design. FDR's decision to avoid matters of constitutional representation and the amendment process may have left unaddressed profound electoral disparities in influence as well as a bottleneck when it came to constitutional decision-making. Yet, FDR had succeeded in ending court intransigence and in installing effective presidential and administrative management. Fulfilling these goals seemed to redeem the constitutional system as a whole. With supportive officials more or less filling the Senate and the Supreme Court, the old Progressive-era critiques of counter-majoritarianism appeared less relevant. Even for many poor and working-class Americans — natural constituents for those arguments — New Deal victories dramatically reduced the perceived exigencies of the topic.

Still, it is worth noting the extent to which labor's most significant leaders in the CIO and the AFL refrained from continuing to press these critiques of the Constitution. They had been vociferous defenders of court-packing and powerful opponents of judicial dictatorship. The CIO especially was also a natural successor to pre–World War I's labor radicalism, long associated with deep constitutional skepticism. Furthermore, even after the achievement of the Wagner Act, the country continued to be roiled by social upheaval and class conflict. Thus, a noteworthy piece of the story is the degree to which labor leadership joined FDR in backing constitutional innovation through the same language of restoration.

There were certainly pragmatic reasons for this choice. FDR's approach had gone hand in hand with labor victories, the likes of which the country had not previously enjoyed. Labor leaders too increasingly found themselves with a seat at the political table, whether on Democratic Party matters or regulatory agency deliberations. Whatever the flaws of the 1787 system, presidential leadership and the emerging administrative state were finally making good on long-standing movement aspirations.

This pragmatism was further buttressed by those same background shifts in constitutional culture. Figures such as John Lewis, AFL President William Green, and Sidney Hillman all operated in a world *already* constrained by the World War I–era politics of constitutional veneration. The state destruction of the IWW and the general tarring of labor as unpatriotic during that period had clear political effects. Above all, for the next generation of leaders it underscored the need to couch any economic changes in a language that nonetheless highlighted one's constitutional commitment and, through that, one's national attachment. If FDR himself appreciated the patriotic power associated with constitutional veneration, this was hardly lost on labor.

In a sense—precisely because of the World War I wedding of capitalism, constitutional attachment, and patriotism, along with that era's Red Scare crackdowns—many labor activists were deeply conscious of how a challenge to the existing distribution of property and wealth left them open to charges of disloyalty. And so, not unlike the CPUSA at the time, they sought to parry these attacks by locating worker rights and control in their own constitutionally faithful language of Americanism.

When Labor's Non-Partisan League organized mass meetings across the country on behalf of court-packing, it planned to hold those meetings on April 19, 1937—Patriot's Day, commemorating the first revolutionary battles against the British in Concord and Lexington.[97] And in describing court-packing, leaders went out of their way to emphasize their own reverence for the Constitution and the preservative nature of the initiative. Green presented court-packing as of a piece with conceiving of the Constitution as a living thing, "broad, comprehensive and flexible enough to meet the expanding economic and social conditions of a constantly changing world." But this interpretative flexibility did not drain the text of normative substance; instead, it spoke to the genius of the founders and to the inherent promise embedded in the constitutional project. According to Green, "the wisdom of its designers is reflected in its adaptability," and it was "inconceivable that our forefathers intended to set up a rigid law that would prevent us from progressing in our expansion as a nation, and . . . from securing a realization of our economic and social institutions."[98]

As for Hillman, court-packing had the benefit of being not only "direct" and "courageous" but also "the lawful and constitutional way to meet the needs of the times"—rather than a step toward even more far-reaching institutional overhaul.[99] Indeed, the LNPL's 1937 Supreme Court handbook emphasized how the initiative actually protected society from further constitutional upheaval. It would leave "our system of 'checks and balances' . . . unchanged" and "undisturbed"—and, in fact, by creating greater alignment between judicial decision-making and popular sentiment, it "would increase respect for the Courts."[100]

Du Bois certainly would have recognized a deep irony to this labor defense of constitutional "checks and balances." By the 1940s, the CIO fully understood that the only way to sustain labor gains across the country was to organize industry in the South, bringing together Black and white workers through campaigns like "Operation Dixie." These campaigns ultimately failed, as the historian Barbara Griffith details, in large part due to the white authoritarianism that defined Southern states. Political power, she writes, was organized through "naked mechanisms of social control that enforced inherited class and caste relations" in ways that proved difficult for union organizers to disrupt.[101] Critically, "checks and balances"—or, more specifically, connections between federalism, the Electoral College, and the Senate—played a key role in preserving the ability of a white economic and political elite on the ground to dictate these policies. Yet by acceding to what Du Bois called that "national taboo," labor unwittingly accepted a political playing field profoundly stacked against it for the long run.

The reason for the choice, though, connected to the sense that proving labor's patriotism was more politically crucial than pressing forward with radical constitutional critiques. In the 1910s, groups like the IWW may have emphasized an unapologetic working-class internationalism and treated patriotism as essentially a poisoned chalice. Whatever its discursive benefits, for "Big Bill" Haywood and other IWW leaders patriotism ultimately was a tool of breaking class bonds, undermining an oppositional political culture, and promoting a false presumption of national harmony. Given society's irreconcilable conflicts, one's primary attachment had to be with fellow workers, wherever they were and regardless of race or nation.

A quarter century later, labor's main American leaders still passionately embraced the view of irreconcilable conflicts between business and the working class, and they still viewed class as one's central site of allegiance. In fact, for many CIO activists, true class consciousness also required building multiracial organization and democracy.[102] But, shaped by the lessons of the 1910s and 1920s, those like Lewis and Hillman explicitly attempted to marry working-class opposition with the politics of patriotism. This entailed presenting labor's struggle as a continuation of the American Revolutionary tradition embodied in the first battles against the British. Given the growing popular symbolic identification of the Constitution with nationhood, it also entailed presenting the Constitution—and therefore even its counter-majoritarian features—

as an instantiation of the Revolutionary project. Such framings turned away from the Progressive-era judgment that the constitutional founding in fact repudiated the ideals of the 1776 Declaration. Crucially, all this meant that, during debates over court-packing and other reforms, labor leaders followed FDR in highlighting how working-class struggle—for all its transformative implications—was more an exercise in political *restoration* than in revolution.

This spoke to a built-in tension in the emerging posture of labor leadership. To the extent that national politics was dominated by the demands of labor, then working-class identity—now combined with a commitment to the national project and its existing institutions—acted as a powerful engine for social change. But what if labor lost its political grip, and the institutions again became stumbling blocks—precisely the developments that hamstrung the FLSA as well as the 1940s Southern organizing drive? What would this mean for the internal coherence of a brand of working-class nationalism built around reverence for the founders and their "checks and balances"?

At the high-water mark of the New Deal era, such questions were put to the side as overly abstract. According to the LNPL, there was no need to worry about future presidents packing the Supreme Court with "corporation tools," because that would require working-class voters, labor's base, to elect "a reactionary President and a reactionary Senate"— something that was "not likely." In a sense, such labor groups believed that they had successfully fulfilled Beard's call to political organizing: labor now had at its disposal a permanent and broad popular coalition able to overcome whatever dysfunctions and misallocations of power were embedded in constitutional design. As the LNPL concluded, "public opinion will prevent the Court from ever again sinking to the depths the present majority has brought it down to."[103]

For someone like Norman Thomas, this specific fusing of class and national attachment—grounded as it was in constitutional commitment—may have warded against conservative charges of labor disloyalty or lawlessness. But Thomas expressed concern that, over the long run, the cabining of structural constitutional reform—including over the judiciary—would be profoundly self-defeating. As he told Roger Baldwin, the ACLU co-founder, "it is amazing . . . to find organized Labor, with its traditional distrust of government by courts, waxing so enthusiastic for fifteen judges instead of nine."[104] He seemed to realize that labor's organizational power, not to mention the intensity and cohesiveness of working-class identity, might well abate in the future. Such abatement could generate the potential for a new era of political reaction, with all its inevitable effects.

At a deeper level, labor fixation on the immediate judicial amelioration also fundamentally obscured the nature of the constitutional problem facing the country. The underlying issue was not simply bad decisions by a specific set of judges. It was, as it had been for over a century, the underlying constitutional infrastructure—constructed as an impediment to mass democracy and as an instrument for the entrenchment of minority rule by economic and, indeed, racial elites. Thomas worried that labor leadership had essentially allowed a bloc of conservative justices on the Supreme Court to serve as an alibi for the Constitution, a mechanism for absolving the sins of the larger governing arrangements. Going forward, all of this would reaffirm rather than undermine the continuing power of the courts to operate as central determiners of constitutional politics and of possible constitutional change.[105]

Such an absolution may have aligned with FDR's preservative instincts. But they did not serve labor's own long-standing agenda of greater democratization and transformation. Forces within the labor movement, especially those associated with various socialist groups, certainly perceived this danger. And they explicitly sought to maintain a constitutionally critical stance. Both the *Socialist Call*, a weekly based in New York and later Chicago, and the Communist-affiliated *New York City Daily Worker* continued to intensely defend basic changes to the judiciary and the broader constitutional structure, well after the Supreme Court's "switch in time."

Although court-packing's legislative defeat now seemed inevitable, given the "switch," labor and socialist organizations generally refused to give up the fight. However, in contrast to AFL and CIO leadership, these radical papers presented FDR's initiative as just a partial move toward more fundamental constitutional alterations. According to the *Call*, the Supreme Court's "recent decisions" did not mean that they might not "slide back into the old routine of handing down reactionary" rulings. This suggested not just the need to pack the court now, but also a refusal to allow the jurisprudential shift to "placate and pacify . . . American workers," or to "put them into a more genial mood by a few crumbs of comforting labor decisions."[106] These papers argued for the need to think of FDR's plan as simply a "step," in the words of the *Daily Worker*, hopefully leading to expansive reforms that "permanently strip the judicial oligarchy of its usurped power."[107] Court-packing alone "would change nothing,"[108] according to the *Call*, because it would not transform the overall structure of the governing system.

At least at first, there remained a potential audience open to conversations about these structural alterations, despite the public gravitating away from court-packing specifically. In the spring of 1937, even after the Supreme Court's initial shift, large majorities continued to support basic constitutional reforms to the judicial system. In fact, 64 percent, according to the American Institute of Public Opinion, backed an amendment that would end lifetime Supreme Court tenure and require "justices to retire at some point between 70 and 75."[109]

Yet even these more moderate reform ideas had little place in the emerging constitutional settlement. And for many labor leaders and union members alike, the Supreme Court's quick consolidation behind the New Deal agenda in the late 1930s affirmed the constitutional order's adaptability and the benefits of the developing presidentialism. Just as crucially, it also seemed to demonstrate labor leadership's political wisdom in deciding to criticize judges in the language of constitutional restoration rather than revolution—as a way, according to the LNPL, of actually raising the esteem of the courts and protecting the rest of the system.

Ultimately, labor's discursive and strategic choices embodied an assessment of the political times. Implicit in Du Bois's vision of mass insurgency and constitutional experimentation was a recognition that genuine democratic change might require significant acts of norm-breaking in ways that opened the country to greater instability. For many Americans—and not only white citizens—the Civil War and Reconstruction examples suggested a degree of political struggle that seemed unsettling, even against the backdrop of a depression. And as Thomas himself admitted when assessing whether a new constitutional convention would lead to a better document, it was unclear just how revolutionary the times were, or how much opportunity existed for truly radical change. Was there enough of a consolidated and transformative working-class majority to push for more than that "hodge-podge" of policies Thomas feared would result? Given these questions, New Deal achievements felt like a very substantial victory indeed to many union leaders and workers.

But in important ways, FDR's and labor's constitutional pathway also seems a missed opportunity. At the end of the day, there was real validity to the view, espoused by Thomas, Judson King, Marcantonio, and Du Bois, that entrenching permanently democratizing reforms probably required formal textual changes—whether through a diminution of the judiciary's outsized power over constitutional politics, the establishment of public goods (housing, health, jobs, education) as basic rights, or fixes to electoral distortions. As Du Bois suggested, a key way to ensure that informal creative adaptations actually stuck was to have them institutionalized and memorialized, especially by changing the terms and language of the existing constitutional system. Such a concretization would hardly be foolproof, but it would be far more likely over the long run to resist the embedded tendencies of the legal-political infrastructure to aid conservative retrenchment.

Even if the times were not genuinely revolutionary, there was certainly potential political will for significant, if medium-scale, reforms across the 1787 structure. This will, ultimately left untapped, could have been mobilized to push the federal system in a direction more explicitly comparable to the era's state constitutions and to global social-democratic constitutional developments. In keeping with the ideas floating in the 1930s, actionable alterations could have involved judicial restructuring, the amendment process, formal rights guarantees, and even reforms—however incomplete—to state-based representation, such as eliminating the Electoral College or weakening the Senate.

But all of these ideas—from the small-scale to the truly radical—disappeared from the agenda after the "switch in time" and court-packing's demise. New Deal constitutional reform choices meant that the moment effectively passed for more durably remaking judicial and representative institutions. And it would take years—perhaps not until the more open discussions of the twenty-first century—for Americans broadly to begin to appreciate what might have been possible and what had been missed.

Conclusion: Making Peace with Madison

For all the labor talk of constitutional restoration in the 1930s, movement voices—not to mention many New Dealers—hardly worshipped framers like James Madison. A common view persisted that the 1787 drafters, whatever praise they deserved, nonetheless had created an unwieldy governing framework—one requiring a presidential and administrative grafting in order to survive. Mainstream union leaders by the 1930s were certainly far more hesitant to assert the old critique of the framers as consciously promoting class rule. But New Dealers of various stripes still widely emphasized the disconnect between twentieth-century realities and the institutional compromises that produced the 1787 text. With Supreme Court intransigence overcome, New Deal elites may have made their peace with Madison. However, in the 1930s, they had not entirely discarded old Progressive-era skepticism of Madisonian constitutionalism.

Over the next two decades, the climate changed dramatically, as figures central to the New Deal coalition began explicitly identifying with the framers and their constitutional politics. This move from accommodation to unequivocal reverence can only be explained by foregrounding global developments. As chapter 9 explores, the specter of European dictatorship and the rise of Nazi Germany recast the stakes of constitutional skepticism. These events promoted a far more thoroughgoing identification with figures like Madison, who became increasingly deified for establishing within the United States an approach to politics that seemingly avoided the fate of either fascism or Stalinism. Indeed, even by the early 1940s, with the US at war with both Germany and Japan, virtually nothing of the mid-1930s debates about the Supreme Court remained—let alone the discussions about whether and how to scrap the Constitution.

This shift would dramatically alter the terrain of constitutional possibility. At the edges, radical constitutional critique persisted, once more especially within elements of Black politics, where it returned with intensity during the late 1960s and early 1970s. But the era of aggressive white labor opposition to the Constitution had ended for good. And this closure ultimately undermined any real likelihood, in the following decades, for large-scale structural alteration—beyond, that is, the further consolidation of presidential and administrative power.

CHAPTER 9

The Good War and Constitution Worship

As early as December 1939, when the Roper research company and the magazine *Fortune* polled Americans for their views of the Constitution, the results were striking. With attention turned to the Nazi invasion of Poland and war in Europe, more and more Americans began assessing the US constitutional project against the backdrop of dangerous alternatives. Sixty-four percent of respondents now agreed that "our form of government based on the Constitution is as near as perfect as it can be and no important changes should be made in it." Only 19 percent argued for the document to be "thoroughly revised to make it fit present-day needs."[1] In short, by the early 1940s, issues of fundamental reform no longer shaped the constitutional discussion. Instead, conversations reflected a consolidating faith that the document was central to an anti-totalitarian American way of life, which culturally and politically safeguarded citizens from dictatorship.

How did the popular conversation around the Constitution change so quickly and so dramatically? It was true that FDR had succeeded in pushing New Deal policies and administrative innovations past court intransigence. Moreover, his success clearly helped to shift public sentiment in favor of the overall governing order. But ultimately that paints only part of the picture. The change in mood cannot be explained without considering the political currents affecting Europe and in particular the rising tide of fascism and the brutal Stalinist crackdowns in the Soviet Union. Indeed, the pervasive language of "dictatorship" in the 1930s—both in labor's criticism of the Supreme Court and in conservatives' attacks on FDR's presidential initiatives—highlighted the extent to which, across the ideological spectrum, American constitutional debates became colored by new and unsettling forms of European authoritarianism.

As the country headed toward war with Germany and Japan, Americans completed a remarkable and rolling two-year celebration of the Bill of Rights' sesquicentennial and, by extension, of the constitutional system as a whole. These celebrations spoke to the degree to which veneration increasingly extended beyond the traditional social bases of Constitution worship: namely, business elites and their conservative allies. Arguments about the anti-totalitarian values of the Constitution were repeated time and again by a broad swathe of left-of-center national political elites: New Dealers, labor leaders, a growing number of Black activists, and even classic Progressive-era critics like Charles Beard.

In this chapter I show how more and more Americans—including labor and civil rights reformers—viewed the specter of European-style dictatorship as a real threat domestically. With this shift, the potential stakes of reworking the constitutional system seemed to increase as well: constitutive changes to the governing order *might* generate a more democratic society; but pressing for such changes also created the possibility that the country could find itself marching toward Stalinist purges or fascist tyranny.

In this setting, many New Dealers rediscovered and rallied around the inclusive and rights-protecting values in the constitutional text—especially in the first ten amendments—as a safer way to press for social improvements while avoiding destructive excess. Yet, just as during World War I, this expanding support for an elaborated creedal constitutionalism did not shed its ties to aggressive security politics. And this fact would persist during the Cold War and beyond.

I therefore focus especially on two dramatic constitutional episodes from the period. I first detail the Bill of Rights celebrations and the political culture they promoted. And in the chapter's final pages, I turn to the mass Japanese internment initiated at essentially the same historical moment. To the extent that accounts of the era explore these episodes, they are almost always kept politically separate. Under conventional readings, the story of the Bill of Rights highlights the development of an American civil libertarian culture, in which constitutional commitment increasingly facilitated liberal practices. As for Japanese internment, it speaks to the historic failure to live up to those ideals and the continuing well of racist sentiment shaping American life.

Despite the clear tensions between these episodes, it was not simply a coincidence that constitutional celebrations and mass internment overlapped in time. Both were grounded in notions of American exceptionalism as well as in the perceived wartime necessity of promoting American values against potential threats. In a sense, they presented two sides of the same constitutionally venerative posture: protecting the constitutional state justified both an inclusive and pluralistic politics of rights-enhancement *and* harsh crackdowns on perceived enemies.

Implanting the Bill of Rights in the Creedal Constitution

Although World War II veneration ultimately sustained the coerciveness of earlier national security Constitution worship, there were profound cultural differences between the politics of the two wars. World War I's conservative pro-Constitution voices had consciously focused on the text as a symbol of national unity, deemphasizing its actual functioning as a structure of representative decision-making. But in the early to mid-1930s, against the backdrop of economic collapse and the risk of Supreme Court nullification of legislative victories, New Deal supporters of virtually all stripes pushed back decisively against this pro-Constitution move. Even when labor leaders and New Deal officials expressed their constitutional fidelity, they emphasized the perceived failures of the existing mechanisms and their limitations-in-practice vis-à-vis other possible modes of representative democracy.

However, in the lead-up to World War II, New Deal backers increasingly began to consider how best to highlight to Americans the historically unprecedented dangers embodied by Nazi Germany, Fascist Italy and Spain, and Stalinist Russia. These dangers were patently evident abroad in the German push toward global conquest. And they seemed potentially present at home in the extent to which the country's own convulsive social crises might—by opening the door to radical political alterations—create the potential for authoritarian takeover. In confronting these developments, a growing number of left-of-center commentators and reformers did more than just pull back from debates about fundamental structural change. They also rediscovered and embraced key aspects of the Constitution's eighteenth-century inheritance—in particular, the Bill of Rights—as safeguards against emerging dangers. And New Dealers began promoting this inheritance as shaping a distinctly American culture and way of life—one that pressed against a European totalitarianism in which the state exerted absolute control over an individual's activity and thought.

THE NEGLECTED BILL OF RIGHTS

In many ways, the turn to the Bill of Rights was surprising, as the actual history of the Bill of Rights largely involved haphazard application and limited focus on the first ten amendments as collectively embodying a distinctive and individual rights charter. At the very least, the presentation of these amendments as highlighting a deep and abiding cultural contrast between American liberalism and European totalitarianism seemed historically suspect.

As chapters 5 and 6 noted, for most of American history the amendments enjoyed no special or exalted status. The 1841 and 1891 anniversaries of their ratification had passed with little fanfare, and well into the late 1930s three states (Massachusetts, Connecticut, and Georgia) had still never formally ratified them.[2] Even after its revival through the debates over the Puerto Rican and Philippine annexations, invocations of the Bill of Rights and its rhetorical use in politics remained less common than one might expect. The historian Gerard Magliocca found only two perfunctory references by US presidents to the phrase "Bill of Rights" between 1921 and 1934. And "the Supreme Court noted the existence of the Bill of Rights only once between 1919 and 1937 in a case that was not from the Philippines or Puerto Rico."[3] When the actual document of the Constitution was moved out of storage in 1921, the first Congress's proposal of what would become the ten ratified amendments remained in the State Department basement. They would only be transferred to the National Archives and to a location accessible to the public in 1938, as efforts to commemorate the Bill of Rights' anniversary started to get off the ground.[4]

Furthermore, the idea that the Bill of Rights' political purpose and effect had been to articulate a sphere of liberal autonomy, free from government coercion (be it state or federal), hardly withstood scrutiny. As a charter of individual liberties protecting free exercise and political speech—not to mention establishing a broader realm of personal autonomy as a privileged domain of freedom—the amendments had rarely operated to meaningfully constrain overweening government power. For example, Madison and Jefferson argued that 1798's Sedition Act—criminalizing criticism of the federal government—violated the First Amendment. But the Act was never appealed to the Supreme Court and, until it expired in 1801, remained both good law and the legal basis for prosecuting numerous high-profile Jeffersonians.[5]

Moreover, there was no popular sense of the first ten amendments—
with their speech and religious liberties guarantees, property protections, judicial process safeguards, and account of federal authority as cabined by powers reserved to the states and to the people—as
a unified rights charter. Even Madison and Jefferson never made the
rhetorical move to say that the Sedition Act threatened the "Bill of
Rights," explains Magliocca, "though that would be an obvious point
to make now."[6]

As for any Supreme Court history of invoking these amendments
or their underlying principles of civil libertarian autonomy, the record
was checkered to say the least. Roger Taney's *Dred Scott v. Sanford* ruling, discussed in earlier chapters, did rely heavily on the Fifth Amendment. But it invoked that amendment to defend the property rights of
enslavers in the territories, regardless of congressional prohibitions on
the practice.

This troubled history for the amendments' liberal credentials continued into the twentieth century. The Court had little difficulty upholding World War I crackdowns on dissent under the Espionage Act, finding such suppression consistent with the First Amendment.[7] In 1927's
Buck v. Bell, in an opinion written by Oliver Wendell Holmes Jr. and
signed by all but one justice, the Court upheld the state of Virginia's
compulsory sterilization of the intellectually disabled. Repeating eu-
genicist language that would become common throughout fascist Europe, Holmes declared that "it is better for all the world, if instead of
waiting to execute degenerate offspring for crime, or to let them starve
for their imbecility, society can prevent those who are manifestly unfit
from continuing their kind."[8]

And, finally, in the midst of the Bill of Rights celebrations themselves, the Court in 1940's *Minersville School District v. Gobitis*, again
in an 8-1 decision, ruled that the First Amendment did not prohibit
schools from compelling children to salute the flag or recite pledges
of allegiance, despite their religious objections.[9] Notwithstanding the
1920s Supreme Court victories on the right to foreign language education and to the provision of Catholic private parochial schooling, the
overall record was fairly dismal. Pro-eugenicist decisions like *Buck v.
Bell* did not just underline the Court's failure to protect liberal autonomy. They also spoke to the extent to which any presentation of the
"Bill of Rights" as at the long-standing core of national identity would
be a political fiction.

REDISCOVERING AMERICA'S CHARTER OF LIBERTY

Nonetheless, in the late 1930s and early 1940s a broad range of actors embraced this reimagining. They began to depict the first ten amendments as a charter that embodied a 150-year commitment to anti-totalitarian values, deeply embedded in the cultural life of the republic from the founding.

In some ways, this framing echoed that of the philosopher Ralph Barton Perry during World War I. He presented American culture—given concrete expression in the Constitution—as above all grounded in a sustained respect for toleration and pluralism. Yet pro-Constitution advocates in the 1930s and 1940s diverged from World War I–era champions, particularly in which features of the constitutional order they held up as especially praiseworthy. During the First World War, pro-war voices—to the extent they highlighted specifics to venerate the Constitution—engaged in generalized invocations of the value of checks and balances or of the Supreme Court as a safeguard of liberty. And these voices generally avoided wading too deeply into thorny questions about interpretation or about the Constitution's institutional design and capacity to address large-scale governance problems.

But New Dealers in the late 1930s found it hard to similarly praise long-standing decision-making structures, like the Supreme Court, as a key protector. After all, many had argued only recently that these constitutional arrangements imperiled basic social provisions. Instead they turned to the first ten amendments. Even when inadequately enforced through the governing institutions, these amendments established the textual anchor for promoting a culture respectful of basic civil liberties. In this way, the Bill of Rights—as national symbol and ethical core—could constrain the domestic spread of global authoritarian currents. And as the country seemed headed for war, it also could articulate the values the country should fight for abroad.

Indeed, such arguments about American civic culture were a significant part of why FDR very self-consciously refused to call himself a "Progressive." He believed the label had been burdened by the conflicts of the past, and instead reclaimed the term "liberal." Liberalism had long been associated with nineteenth-century ideas of limited government and a self-regulating commercial society. But FDR now reconceived it as a shared commitment to personal autonomy.

His vision of autonomy had two interrelated sides. First, individuals had to enjoy basic financial and workplace security from the vicissitudes of economic life. And such security then facilitated the capacity to live as one chose in private: free from the coercive interference of the state, and based on the rights of association, movement, religion, and speech.[10] These rights—so essential to what FDR called "personal living, each man according to his own lights"[11]—were what the Constitution's first ten amendments espoused.

As the 1941 anniversary approached, government and civic actors embarked on a sustained multi-year celebration of the amendments and of their centrality to national identity and exceptionalism. The three not-yet-ratifying laggard states quickly addressed their omission. FDR and Congress officially proclaimed December 15—the specific 1791 date on which the ten amendments were ratified—as "Bill of Rights Day" in a joint resolution, and 19 state governors and 86 city mayors followed suit.[12]

By the time it passed, Americans were swept up in one of the most extensive mass celebrations in national history, far greater than any previous constitutional anniversary.[13] And while strongly backed by government entities, these celebrations were a remarkably inclusive affair, by contrast with the Constitution's 1887 centennial. Labor organizations, chambers of commerce, the NAACP, the ACLU, and countless civic and religious associations all promoted the events. "Fully one quarter of the nation's population," details the historian John Wertheimer, "belonged to organizations that 'actively supported' the celebrations."[14]

Meanwhile, major cities hosted an endless stream of events. For example, at a designated hour, Chicago essentially stopped for a simultaneous reading of the Bill of Rights in all 83 local neighborhoods.[15] Across the country, countless editorials and newspaper articles extolled the wisdom of the first ten amendments, with the *New York Times* publishing them in full as a tribute to Bill of Rights Day.[16] On the radio, Bill of Rights Day festivities included patriotic music, speeches from entertainers and former Supreme Court justices, and even a radio play on the amendments' history starring Jimmy Stewart, Edward G. Robinson, Lionel Barrymore, and Orson Welles. All of this was then capped off by FDR's evening address, carried live nationwide by all of the networks.[17] Thus, even for those that could not attend, the celebrations were ubiquitous and unavoidable.

Among the most noteworthy features of these rolling celebrations was how they helped to shift the cultural meaning of the Constitution, its framers, and its founding. One can see this at play in one of the first commemorative events, the Civil Liberties Commission (CLC) of

Massachusetts's sesquicentennial dinner in February 1939, held at the
Boston Chamber of Commerce. The CLC was a local anti-censorship
group formed in the late 1920s and headed by Orville Poland. Poland's
speech, given before Massachusetts's Republican governor and the
state's various business elites, is remarkable for the degree to which it
is dismissive of the actual 1787 text drafted in Philadelphia. He begins
his speech by declaring, "Yesterday I re-read the Constitution of the
United States and I was once more impressed with the fact that the original Constitution . . . contains nothing, if we except the separation of
powers, which marks it as the charter of our democracy." For him, that
text appeared as a somewhat misshapen set of compromises among the
drafters. Perhaps the best that could be said for it was that "the founding fathers were so harassed in determining means that [they] could not
achieve ends." By contrast, the Bill of Rights, without which the document would never have been ratified, gave the whole enterprise ethical
meaning: "With the incorporation of the Bill of Rights the skeleton
Constitution took on new significance—it became a charter of liberty;
the keystone of the structure of democracy."[18]

If the previous half century had witnessed intense dispute over the
basic legitimacy of the constitutional order, the competing sides nonetheless shared a common account of what they were debating when they
argued over the Constitution. For the most part, the Constitution referred to a structure of governance and decision-making, as well as a
set of rights protections, chief among them property rights. And, for
many Progressive-era critics, it was precisely the anti-democratic weaknesses of the prevailing judicial and representative structure, as well as
the fixation on property rights, that exacerbated social conflict and undermined necessary reform. Moreover, all of these flaws could be traced
back to choices made by the framers themselves—shaped as they were
by class status, concern for their own economic position, and their
related suspicions of poor and working people, not to mention their
views of women and non-whites. Even after the triumphs of the New
Deal over judicial and other roadblocks, it remained hard to conceive
of these hard-won triumphs as simply a product of the Constitution's
genius or of a wisdom passed down from the framers. Rather, recent
successes, as Orville Poland himself hinted at, seemed to occur *in spite
of*, rather than because of, the constitutional system.

But the political rediscovery of the Bill of the Rights provided a crucial step in what would, over the following decade, become a thoroughgoing reevaluation of the framers. If the Constitution was bound less to

a structure of governance and to property rights alone, then the framers' inheritance was not just one of outmoded institutions and cycles of contention. Rather, as expressed in the first ten amendments, the framers' document above all carried forth an overriding faith in the centrality of liberal autonomy to a free and open society. As FDR declared in his Bill of Rights Day speech, men like Madison deserved worshipful adoration because they had created a "declaration of human rights" unlike any in the history of the world. Indeed, according to FDR, "no date in the long history of freedom means more to liberty loving men in all liberty loving countries" than December 15, 1791.[19]

This reevaluation of the framers, facilitated by the renewed attention to the Bill of Rights, thus altered the classic Progressive-era debate about whether the Constitution was best read as a defeat of the American Revolution's democratic potential. Now FDR and other New Dealers suggested a distinct basis for burnishing the revolutionary credentials of the document. As Roosevelt declared, the Bill of Rights entrenched the values of the Declaration of Independence; it concretely embodied how "the Founders of the Republic" saw the "rights to life, liberty, and the pursuit of happiness" as "inalienable."[20] In other words, to the extent that the Revolution was a struggle on behalf of personal autonomy broadly understood—against overweening state power seeking to stamp out independent belief—the Bill of Rights enshrined liberal ethical ends for all time.

Furthermore, the coming war with Germany seemed ultimately to be a test of whether the US would slide into fascism or stay true to the values of its framers. And these values were now presented as principles that had, to date, protected American citizens from totalitarian takeover. If the country—and indeed the whole world—faced the menace of Nazism, and of what New York Governor Lehman called "foreign 'isms'"[21] of all kinds, then the Bill of Rights constituted a cultural gift from the founders, which preserved a liberty-regarding ethic in the face of demagogues and tyrants.

FDR's Bill of Rights address was delivered just eight days after the bombing of Pearl Harbor, seven days after the declaration of war against Japan, and four days after declarations against Germany and Italy. Infused with the moment, the speech juxtaposed Jefferson and Madison on the one hand against Hitler on the other. Expanding on World War I–era critiques of German politics as "Nietzschean," Roosevelt described Hitler as the visceral and complete repudiation of liberal autonomy in favor of total domination by the state over all aspects of personal

life: "What we face is nothing more nor less than an attempt to overthrow and to cancel out the great upsurge of human liberty of which
the American Bill of Rights is the fundamental document: to force the
peoples of the earth, and among them the peoples of this continent and
this Nation, to accept again the absolute authority and despotic rule
from which the courage and the resolution and the sacrifices of their
ancestors liberated them many, many years ago." Thus, for FDR, honoring the Bill of Rights meant nothing less than a call to arms. It required
defending—if need be, by force—the principles of the founders against
"Hitler and his fellows," who viewed the ten amendments as "empty
words" and "proposed to cancel them forever."[22] In this way, FDR's language proclaimed the essential and foundational worth of the Constitution and its eighteenth-century drafters. Presented most starkly, one
could either side with Madison, the author of the Bill of Rights, or with
the violence and brutality of Hitler.

NEW DEALERS ENGAGE IN MASS CELEBRATION

As a result of this rediscovery, a remarkably broad variety of political
voices rallied around the Bill of Rights—and by extension, around the
Constitution. These included those who, during World War I, had expressed deep suspicion of that period's jingoistic language of Constitution worship. The new focus on the Bill of Rights, even if based on
a fiction, led many reformers and organized groups to now embrace
their own politics of Constitution worship, especially in the context of
a global and unparalleled Nazi threat.

Indeed, the rolling Bill of Rights celebrations very clearly built on
that version of creedal constitutionalism promoted by immigrant and
religious activists during the inter-war years. It especially fit with the idea
of a tri-faith and pluralistic Judeo-Christian America—championed
by the minister Everett Clinchy and others—that, from its birth as a
nation, repudiated "monism" and championed religious and cultural
difference.

In many ways, this connection of Bill of Rights celebrations to tri-
faith and Judeo-Christian pluralism was a natural extension of the New
Deal coalition. A significant part of the coalition drew on recent immigrant communities from eastern and southern Europe with large
Catholic and Jewish populations. The New Deal's dependency on these
voting blocs meant that the version of Americanism and Constitution
worship that Roosevelt and other politicians promoted had to be far

more inclusive than that exhibited during World War I. At the same time, such immigrant and working-class constituents experienced the New Deal itself—complete with jobs, a social safety net, and the Popular Front cultural embrace of difference—as genuinely embodying their incorporation into the American project. Thus, for many in FDR's working-class base, celebrating the Bill of Rights and celebrating the achievements of the New Deal became almost one and the same.

During the mid-1930s period of heightened social conflict, with the goals of mass democracy and the realities of the legal-political order pitted against each other, linking a tri-faith creedalism to Constitution worship would have been far more difficult: the constitutional system seemed a profound roadblock to New Deal aims. But now the Supreme Court no longer appeared to be an obstacle, and popular attention had turned to Europe. In this context, the Bill of Rights anniversary spoke to how supporting the New Deal, affirming one's belonging as an American, and backing the Constitution all fit together. For many Americans, the most significant threats to New Deal achievements increasingly came from abroad, in the form of wartime enemies. Thus, rallying to the creed and the Constitution embodied one clear way to show one's pride in the successes of the preceding decade.

The Bill of Rights also served as an apt site for national rallying because those ten amendments, collectively, gave virtually all the bases of the New Deal coalition something tangible to defend as their own. For the hundreds of new religious and culturally inclusive civic associations, many formed in the late 1930s and early 1940s against the backdrop of coming war, the Bill of Rights celebrations spoke to both immigrant inclusion and a defense of pluralism against fascist threat. The Council Against Intolerance in America offered one telling example. Their Sesqui-Centennial Commission, composed of religious leaders of various Christian and Jewish denominations, spearheaded countless commemorative events, provided educational material to schools on the genius of the ten amendments, and even convinced FDR to serve as honorary chairman.[23]

For labor groups, commemorating the Bill of Rights became a way of celebrating the freedom of association and freedom of speech guarantees in the First Amendment. Union activists had invoked these rights for decades—largely unsuccessfully—when defending the legality of organizing, picketing, secondary boycotts, and other labor tools. But if earlier union activists, like those in the Industrial Workers of the World (IWW), had seen the substantive violation of these rights as proof of the inherent violence of the whole constitutional system, New Deal victories altered the climate. Labor leaders joined in the celebrations, without the internal ambivalence that marked Progressive-era debates over rights. Underscoring the value of the Constitution specifically for labor—a point activists would likely have treated with real cynicism not long before—FDR's November 1941 speech, proclaiming December 15 to be Bill of Rights Day, referred to unions as one of the critical "institutions of a democratic people," and one "which ow[ed]" its "very existence to the guarantees of the Bill of the Rights."[24]

At the same time, the close association of Nazism with racism created a push by Bill of Rights advocates to highlight differences with European fascism. In particular, they claimed with renewed vigor the importance of racial equality for an exceptional and distinctively American creedal constitutionalism. This was evident in various commemorative events, like the 1939 ACLU-sponsored conference, overseen in part by Eleanor Roosevelt, intended to kick off a "civil rights year." This included a focus on the "civil rights of Negroes" alongside sessions on censorship, academic freedom, and religious liberty—all presented as under threat from *external* forces.[25]

The emphasis on racial equality also emerged in associated speeches, such as the one given by Harvard English professor Howard Mumford Jones at the same Civil Liberties Committee banquet attended by Orville Poland. Jones emphasized how the word "race" did not appear in either the 1787 Constitution or the first fourteen amendments. And he asserted that this omission was consciously made, speaking to the fact that "the American way, the way of the Bill of Rights [was] not the way of Germany or Italy."

During these years, Bill of Rights advocates routinely championed the framers by linking them to the values of liberal autonomy, and by deemphasizing the compromises of the constitutional structure. But people like Jones went even further. They began reading back into the 1787 framers both a liberal *and* a racially egalitarian ethos. Essentially fusing the framers with later post–Civil War and Radical Republican figures, Jones declared that the "founding fathers"—that is, men like Madison, Hamilton, and Jefferson—"knew racial conflict, and they did not want any more of it." According to this view, honoring these founders in the twentieth century thus entailed rejecting archaic European racism: "If racial antagonisms are abroad in the world, let us keep them outside our gates."[26]

These arguments became a common way of tying Jim Crow to fascism and of underlining the un-Americanness of racism. They depicted racism as a foreign influence or an anachronistic holdover that did not speak to the essence of American identity, either at the founding or in the 1930s and 1940s.

Of course, such arguments engaged in a profound act of political erasure. First, they treated enslavers like Madison as the intellectual predecessors of abolitionist politicians like Charles Sumner. Just as egregiously, this approach cloaked the extent to which sustained racial subordination embodied a constitutive and ongoing feature of the American experience. Instead, such subordination was presented as out of step with the essential truth of the framers' own project, regardless of the settler underpinnings of the country's economic and political development.

Even if African Americans largely understood this rewriting as a falsehood, given the specter of Nazism, Black people—across class and ideological divides—rallied to the war effort and increasingly to this presentation of the national project. If the First World War had been marked by mass Black opposition, the historian Gary Gerstle notes that African Americans "responded to the Selective Service Act of 1940 and the initial calls for soldiers with much greater enthusiasm than the army had anticipated."[27] African American newspapers called for a "Double V": victory over fascism on the global stage, and victory over racism at home.[28]

Indeed, such support even informed the more radical wings of Black internationalism. The historian Penny Von Eschen tells us that none other than George Padmore, the influential Trinidadian socialist and Pan-Africanist, "enthusiastically promoted the use of black American and African troops and argued for their importance to the Allied war efforts." These Black voices, within and outside the United States, had not given up on their critiques of American imperialism. Nor had they closed their eyes to the colonial domination of Asia and Africa by US allies like England and France. But, as Von Eschen writes, they nonetheless joined with mainstream Black figures and effectively treated the "Double V" as a "Triple V"—seeing the "fight against Jim Crow . . . as inseparably linked to the fight against both imperialism and fascism." From Padmore to the editors of the *Pittsburgh Courier* and the *Chicago Defender*, a broad collective of activists and writers hoped that wartime victory, with Black participation playing a critical role, would steadily sweep away all three evils.[29]

Buttressed by this Black wartime support, mainstream Black leaders aggressively promoted inclusive narratives of the national project grounded in the Bill of Rights. Groups like the NAACP also championed the amendments as textual proof of true Americanism, linking patriotic loyalty to anti-racism, anti-fascism, and even opposition to European colonialism, whether pursued by allies or by foes. The organization became a central sponsor of the Council Against Intolerance in America's sesquicentennial events.[30]

And Black activists and performers, such as the famed concert singer Marian Anderson, played a very public role in the day's festivities. Two years earlier, in 1939, the Daughters of the American Revolution had denied Anderson use of its Constitution Hall, due to a bar on non-white performers on the stage, creating a national incident in the process. In response, Eleanor Roosevelt publicly resigned her membership in the organization[31] and worked quietly to help stage Anderson's landmark outdoor concert at the Lincoln Memorial—attended by 75,000 people and broadcast around the country by radio.[32] Now, Anderson opened the Bill of Rights luncheon at the Commodore Hotel in New York City by singing the national anthem, with Eleanor Roosevelt in attendance.[33]

Indeed, one of the most significant artistic creations of the era—the song "Ballad for Americans"—emphasized just how far Black inclusion, and especially Frederick Douglass's old idea of a "composite nation," had spread culturally. The music was written by Earl Robinson, a Communist Party member, and performed on CBS radio in November 1939 by the Black singer and activist Paul Robeson. The song was among the most popular of the era, a moving articulation of the US as a home for peoples from across the world, in which African Americans were as welcome as any other community. As Robeson intoned, "I'm just an Irish, Negro, Jewish, Italian, French and English, Spanish, Russian, Chinese, Polish, Scotch, Hungarian, Litvak, Swedish, Finnish, Canadian, Greek and Turk, and Czech and Double Czech American."[34]

BEARD, RANDOLPH, AND OTHERS RECONSIDER THE CONSTITUTION

This focus on the Bill of Rights, in the context of the fight especially against fascism, did not just push Constitution worship to the center of New Deal political and cultural life. It also altered how some past critics related to the text. And this shift, as we will see, would become more and more pronounced over the following years.

Take for example the ACLU, whose essential involvement in the sesquicentennial events completed a remarkable transformation over the course of two decades. When ACLU co-founder Crystal Eastman defended the principles of the First Amendment during World War I, she—like those in the IWW—did so from a position of both deep anti-nationalism and constitutional suspicion. She emphasized those First Amendment principles in order to underscore the legality of labor and anti-war activism, the actual lawlessness of constitutional fetishists, and the large extent to which the overall constitutional structure effectively nullified basic civil libertarian values. Moreover, for these earlier thinkers, the fact that free speech ideals were written in the document did not make them the *product* of American exceptionalism. Rather, they were universal and internationalist ideals, which had been given some grounding, albeit weak, within domestic law.

Beginning in the inter-war years and solidifying in the context of Supreme Court acquiescence to the New Deal and the fight with Nazi Germany, the ACLU took a different stance. The organization—and its executive director, Roger Baldwin—became virtually synonymous in the public's mind with the promotion of the Bill of the Rights and with an intertwining of patriotism, American exceptionalism, and constitutional devotion. And it did not just stop there. As mentioned earlier, in 1939, the ACLU sponsored a conference meant to kick off a "civil rights year" in honor of the first ten amendments. This was overseen by none other than William Allen White,[35] who in 1910 had decried the Constitution as binding "the nation to the rule of the privileged classes"[36] during a time of industrial strife. But, as the terms of constitutional conversation shifted and with the ever-present threat of totalitarian alternatives, White changed perspective and came to chair the ACLU's sesquicentennial committee. He had come to think of the Constitution as an inclusive and rights-protecting inheritance and those eighteenth-century framers as liberal champions, whatever their class-driven limitations.

Within Black public life, a key figure who revised his position was A. Philip Randolph. Randolph was especially concerned with the growing presence of the Communist Party in African American politics. As discussed in chapter 7, the party very consciously embraced constitutional veneration in the mid-1930s as part of its Popular Front strategy; "Ballad for Americans" can in many ways be thought of as tied to the CPUSA, given Earl Robinson's membership and Robeson's sympathetic views on the Soviet Union. In fact, due to the role of the CPUSA in pressing for racial equality, many Black activists at the time—like Robeson or party members such as Claudia Jones and Harry Haywood—

conceived of communism as an allied philosophy; they thus had absolutely no problem distinguishing it from fascism. Indeed, they viewed racism and colonialism as embodiments of a fascistic thinking deeply embedded in both European and white American culture, and saw various communist groups as in solidarity against such oppression.

Randolph, by contrast, became profoundly suspicious of the Soviet Union. This was due to both the intensity of the Stalinist purges and his perception of the CPUSA's opportunism within Black politics. The party's willingness to dramatically switch position due to policy changes in the Soviet Union left him deeply concerned that it was driven not by local needs but by external objectives. Closed to free thinking and to meaningful democratic debate and self-rule, party decisions struck him as secretive, guided not by "logic, reason, and fact" but by "a caucus under the control of an outside organization." In this way, "totalitarian communism," for Randolph, ultimately aligned with fascism. It was "committed to an anti-democratic program" and "had to be ruled out as a solution to the Negro problem."[37]

Yet, despite this opposition, during the 1930s Randolph was still willing to pursue collaborative projects with communist activists. He served as the first president of the National Negro Congress (NNC). Founded in 1936, with the critical involvement of Howard University professor Ralph Bunche, the organization brought together Black and white activists across the era's broad Popular Front, including liberals, socialists, and communists. As the historian Thomas Sugrue writes, the NNC—and the expansive coalition it embodied—underscored how a wide swathe of the period's Black political voices came to agree "that the problem of racial equality was fundamentally economic and that the solution required addressing the impoverishment and exploitation of black and white workers alike."[38]

Yet, four years later Randolph left the Congress amid the Soviet nonaggression pact with Nazi Germany (a pact that would prove short-lived when Germany invaded Russia). In the context of that pact, the CPUSA followed the Soviet line and opposed any coming conflict. The historian Glenda Gilmore writes that Communist activists pushed the NNC Resolutions Committee to "pass a motion against U.S. involvement in the 'imperialist war.'" For Randolph, that sense of top-down directive from the Soviet Union to the CPUSA further cemented his belief that, while the United States was deeply flawed, the world's most profound threats came from "Nazi Germany and Communist

Russia and Fascist Italy." Of the Soviet Union, he declared the country to be a "death prison where democracy and liberty have walked their 'last mile.'"[39]

Randolph's intensifying anti-communism led him to adjust his own past critiques of the Constitution. On its face, this may be surprising since Communists like Browder had rallied around the Constitution. But for starters, Randolph did not trust CPUSA assertions of constitutional devotion, given its internally secretive practices and increasing identification with Stalin. More importantly, Randolph's strong support of the war, in a context of mounting authoritarian extremism, led him too to view the Bill of Rights and the language of the Constitution in general as bulwarks against dictatorship and global tyranny.

Randolph certainly rejected the illusion, promoted by some white backers of Black civil rights, that the United States had been committed to equality from the founding, declaring pointedly that "American democracy is no lily of purity." But he contended that avoiding the paths of both fascism and communism meant discarding a utopian faith in any radically new political order. Given the very real and dangerous alternatives to the US's incomplete democracy, the best practical agenda for Black Americans was to embrace the constitutional order as more or less legitimate, and to enforce through legal and legislative processes those rights embedded in the document. Indeed, whatever its "sins," the existing "American democratic system" seemed the only viable path for Black freedom. Despite the depth of American racism, at least in the United States Black people, Randolph concluded, "have the right" under the constitutional system "to fight for their rights." This fact was "more important than all the other rights for which Negroes . . . are fighting." Thus, an open-eyed brand of constitutional fidelity provided the best practical mechanism for "cleansing" the country "of its sins against minorities."[40]

For those like Randolph, the very different response of white national politicians to racial reform during World War II, by contrast with that during the First World War, offered proof of the wisdom of this approach. When Randolph threatened to stage a massive march on Washington in 1941 to protest discriminatory employment conditions, FDR sought to head off the march by issuing an executive order prohibiting racial discrimination in the defense industries and in federal agencies, and by establishing the Fair Employment Practices Commission. All of this fed Black political aspirations that, unlike twenty years earlier, an

African American embrace of both creedal constitutionalism and the war effort—itself against a racist menace—could actually bring tangible benefits. The desire of white politicians to differentiate themselves from Nazi Germany, along with FDR's far preferable views of race relations compared to those of Woodrow Wilson, meant that, this time, that double victory at home and abroad appeared more plausible.

But perhaps the historian Charles Beard's evolving views offer the greatest illustration of the general shift in constitutional climate from just a decade earlier—let alone the years before World War I. In 1943, Beard published *The Republic: Conversations on Fundamentals*, a striking wartime reappraisal of both the 1787 document and the framers themselves. Although it is less remembered today, in his final years he looked upon the book as his personal favorite, and it became the defining popular work on the Constitution during World War II. *The Republic* was a massive commercial and critical success, to a degree unparalleled in his long career. It went through five printings in its first six months, selling over 180,000 copies. Henry Luce's *Life* magazine took the step of serializing the book, and it eventually sold more than four million copies.[41] Along with glowing reviews in pro–New Deal outlets like the *Nation*, it was also "hailed" as "classic" in Luce's other publication, the conservative and business-friendly *Fortune* magazine. Indeed, the fact that none other than Henry Luce himself now championed the work of Beard, an historian and critic notorious in business circles, was a striking development. The Harvard political scientist and constitutional scholar Carl Friedrich commented in his own 1944 review that "there must be something exceptional about a book when" both the left-leaning *Nation* and the more right-wing *Fortune* magazine "offer unstinting acclaim."[42]

The Republic was structured as a dialogue about the Constitution, its history and meaning. Modeled after Plato's own text, it consisted of a series of imagined conversations at Beard's New Milford, Connecticut home with neighbors and interested acquaintances of varying ideological perspectives. Over the course of these conversations, Beard effectively offered a sustained defense of the wisdom of the 1787 framers' basic vision and the built-in capacity of the American constitutional order to adapt in the face of emerging problems while remaining true to foundational principles. For decades, Beard's name had been synonymous for academics and activists with a class-based critique of the Constitution. But against the backdrop of New Deal successes and, especially, concerns with European fascism, his defense of the framers suggested just how much the tide seemed to have turned away from Progressive-era skepticism[43]—a fact further underscored by the obvious popular appetite for the book as well as its cross-partisan elite appeal.

If Beard had once famously emphasized class interests in discussing the founding, he now declared, "I sometimes think that politics is more of a determining force in history than economics," and contended that the Constitution was not simply the product of a conflict between "radical or agrarian forces" and those of "conservative or capitalistic reaction." Rather, a second, even more significant battle had been waged at the founding: "an influential group on the extreme right" saw events like Shays's Rebellion as an opportunity to establish a "thoroughgoing military dictatorship." This meant that, as it turns out, one should not view framers such as Alexander Hamilton and James Madison as counterrevolutionary class elites engaged in anti-democratic reaction. They were instead best understood as truly heroic actors, seeking to thwart the rise of a potential proto-fascist dictatorship; their overarching project constituted an effort to protect a free political order from absolutist tyranny.[44]

With Nazism on his mind, Beard now asserted that the 1787 Constitution embodied nothing less than "an eternal contradiction to despotic and irresponsible government, such as Caesar's or Napoleon's or Hitler's." "Leaders among the framers of the Constitution," Beard maintained, "regarded the resort to constitutional government instead of a military dictatorship as their greatest triumph. In my opinion they were entitled to view their achievement in that way."[45]

In keeping with his anti-formalist 1936 account of the "Living Constitution," Beard continued to view the constitutional text as a flexible and open-ended outline, capable of being interpreted and reinterpreted to address modern challenges and incorporate evolving values. Moreover, the constitutional entrenchment of the New Deal highlighted just this capacity for adaptation, as well as the lack of any need for significant formal revisions, let alone wholesale rewriting. The document proved more than capable of adjusting "to the storms of the ages" and was "as flexible as American intelligence and character may make it."[46] But Beard's analysis in *The Republic* more explicitly emphasized a redemptive vision of the founding. The Constitution may have been malleable for countless good and bad purposes, but he now underscored the importance of how it carried with it a political and moral core against "dictatorship." It was indeed a sheet anchor, lighthouse, or beacon, and its ratification launched the nation on an improbable project in constitutional democracy.

Beard concluded of the "founding fathers" that their "will to exalt civilian power above military force" and their "attempt to institute government by plan, proposal, discussion, and popular decision" provided twentieth-century Americans a political inheritance of "extraordinary historical significance." And in part due to this inheritance, Beard maintained that he did "not believe that even in a great national crisis we shall . . . subject ourselves to totalitarian government." Americans just needed to protect "the blessings of liberty" and to infuse whatever changes they implemented with "the letter and spirit of the Constitution." As he succinctly described ongoing projects of reform, "we could work wonders without altering a line of the document." In a way not totally dissimilar to David Jayne Hill, Beard too suggested that the Constitution had, over time, helped to inculcate a set of cultural values that sustained rights-respecting and democratic practices in the United States. These values steered Americans away from dangerous European extremes. Beard declared the genius of the American founding and the framers themselves, in terms that might have shocked some of his Progressive and Socialist readers in the 1910s: "If modern Europeans had devoted to the study of *The Federalist* the attention they gave to Plato's *Republic*, they would have been far better off in every way."[47]

Given Beard's near deification of Madison and Hamilton—whom he presented as "fathers" of American freedom and greater philosophical thinkers than Plato—it was not a complete surprise that *Fortune* would praise the book. But Beard's anti-formalist and living constitutional framework remained central even in this embrace of veneration. His approach still very much vindicated the New Deal state and repudiated the old pro-business line.

The elite cross-partisan appeal of *The Republic* thus also spoke to an emerging ideological convergence among Center-Left and Center-Right. Unlike during World War I, when celebrating Constitution Day often had the quality of fairly empty jingoism, the political sides appeared to find some common ground on thorny questions of political economy and governance. Refracted through the dangers of European dictatorship, both New Dealers and their erstwhile opponents began to look upon the preceding decade as perhaps a narrow escape.

Rather than falling prey to extremes, the constitutional system had managed to survive a series of crises. For some on the business Right, that survival suggested the benefits to social order of entrenching some economic regulation and social welfare structures. And for New Dealers, it suggested that checks and balances were not the immovable and anti-democratic objects they may once have appeared. Indeed, as Beard would write in 1944, recent events proved that such checks and balances offered a valuable middle ground—flexible enough to implement popular policies, while rigid enough to ensure that "at no time could the 'snap judgment' of popular majority prevail in all departments of the federal government" and thus subvert basic civil liberties.[48]

BARNETTE AND *SCHNEIDERMAN*: THE NEW CONSTITUTIONAL CULTURE REACHES THE COURT

Above all, Beard's own evolution vividly highlighted how the fight over the Supreme Court and the wartime context entrenched a new American constitutional culture. The half century between the end of Reconstruction and the New Deal legislative and judicial victories had been a period punctuated by widespread constitutional critique, focused especially on the document's failures as a system of governance. As the country's attention shifted to the war, some still treated the structure as an imperfect compromise. But for many, the Constitution had increasingly become a site of conscious and affective attachment, even among figures like Beard or William Allen White who were fully aware of these imperfections. If anything, this embrace by past Progressive-era intellectuals mirrored broader trends within constituencies that had been home to constitutional skepticism, whether working-class white Americans now deeply committed to the New Deal order or growing numbers of patriotic Black citizens who volunteered to fight against Nazism.

World War I may have created a mass base open to constitutional veneration. But these later developments truly expanded that base well beyond the political Right. As World War II progressed, creedal constitutionalism became nothing less than a deepening staple of New Deal liberalism—the way in which many leaders and supporters conceived of and began describing the country and its meaning. While not the only account of national identity, it nonetheless emerged as the leading collective narrative; it was no longer just one among a variety of competing orientations to politics.

According to this developing conventional wisdom, the Constitution was best understood as an anti-totalitarian and rights-protecting text. It carried within it universal values of immigrant and racial inclusion as well as associational rights for labor, religious protections, and speech guarantees for all. Thus, the Constitution was not an anti-majoritarian roadblock to economic and social reform. Instead, it offered a charter of personal autonomy—one that clarified the moral differences between an American way of life and that of fascist adversaries abroad.

For those like Randolph or the ACLU's Roger Baldwin, this new iteration of creedal constitutionalism was compelling precisely because it diverged from the aggressive, xenophobic, and anti-labor constitutionalism that defined World War I's pro-war politics, not to mention nativist reaction after the war. It had been grounded explicitly in the Bill of Rights, and it categorically invoked anti-racism as part of the fight against fascism.

As discussed in chapter 7, some reformers had strategically responded to the mass constitutional celebrations in the 1910s and 1920s by redeploying veneration to defend reformist and inclusive goals. Now that strategy finally appeared to bear real fruit, both within the culture and even in the courts. In 1938, the NAACP won a striking legal victory, when the Supreme Court declared in *Missouri ex rel Gaines v. Canada* that Missouri violated the equal protection clause of the Fourteenth Amendment by failing to provide in-state law school education for Black students.[49] And in 1943 the Court issued two rulings grounded in the idea that an anti-totalitarian Bill of Rights stood at the core of American constitutionalism.

First, it overruled its own decision from just three years earlier in *Gobitis*, now holding in *West Virginia Board of Education v. Barnette* that the First Amendment protected students from being compelled to salute the flag or to recite a pledge of allegiance. As Justice Robert Jackson, who served as FDR's attorney general until 1941, pronounced for the majority, "if there is any fixed star in our constitutional constellation, it is that no official, high or petty, can prescribe what shall be orthodox in politics, nationalism, religion, or other matters of opinion, or force citizens to confess by word or act their faith therein."[50]

And then, just as remarkably, in *Schneiderman v. US*, the Court addressed the question of what exactly the 1906 naturalization law, requiring "attach[ment] to the principles of the Constitution of the United States," commanded of prospective citizens. In 1939 the federal government had moved to denaturalize William Schneiderman, a CPUSA activist and candidate for governor of Minnesota, based purely on his beliefs rather than on any unlawful actions or criminal charges. The move occurred at a time of fractured US-Soviet relations, again in the context of the latter's nonaggression pact with Nazi Germany. It also aligned with 1940's Smith Act, which targeted both communists and fascists by making it a crime to advocate the government's violent overthrow or to be a member of any group engaged in such advocacy. These actions spoke to both how global dynamics were raising fears about Soviet sympathies and how retrenchment against the most radical edges of the New Deal were shifting domestic life. They also presaged the Red Scare politics that would follow World War II, once the US-Soviet military alliance against Nazi Germany was no longer necessary.

The lower courts backed Schneiderman's denaturalization on grounds that would have been familiar to World War I–era constitutional advocates: according to both the federal district and circuit courts, one could not oppose capitalism and be attached to the Constitution. As the Ninth Circuit Court of Appeals stated, "there was substantial evidence . . . that the Communist Party held and advocated that private ownership of the agents of production was wrong; that the agents of production should be confiscated by the government without compensation to the private owners thereof." "It is obvious," the Ninth Circuit concluded, "that these views are not those of our Constitution."[51]

But when the Supreme Court finally ruled—not coincidentally, at a moment of repaired US-Soviet wartime relations—it reversed these earlier decisions, placing central constitutional priority on civil libertarian concerns. Justice Frank Murphy's majority opinion emphasized the seriousness of the rights infringement entailed by denaturalization "twelve years after it was granted," an action requiring "the clearest sort of justification and proof." Moreover, to the extent that the Constitution had any defining value, it was "freedom of thought." As Murphy declared, "criticism of, and the sincerity of desires to improve, the Constitution should not be judged by conformity to prevailing thought, because, 'if there is any principle of the Constitution that more imperatively calls for attachment than any other, it is the principle of free thought—not free thought for those who agree with us, but freedom for the thought that we hate.'" Even if anti-capitalist and communist ideas were un-American, according to this line of reasoning, it was far more un-American to abandon the Bill of Rights and deny individuals their First Amendment protections. In both *Barnette* and *Schneiderman*, the Court's language thus came to mimic the anti-totalitarian creedalism that had so dominated Bill of Rights celebrations in previous years.[52]

Wartime Devotion, *Korematsu*, and the Security State's Violence

In some ways one could tell a triumphal story of liberal and rights-protecting values, rediscovered through the Bill of Rights and then increasingly embedded in constitutional culture. Yet the New Deal marriage of constitutional faith and national security also projected into the future many of the problems that had defined earlier pro-war constitutionalism. In particular, it implicitly granted an often racially defined group the power to determine whose rights deserved protection. And even those claiming to champion this updated version of the creedal constitutional framework acquiesced to practices that violated civil libertarian ideals.

THE DOUBLE-EDGED SWORD OF LIBERAL EXCEPTIONALISM

It is true that Bill of Rights creedalism, complete with its full embrace of American exceptionalism, fostered a popular culture more attuned to civil liberties and open to racial reform. But these were not the only political implications that derived from reading the United States as having a special destiny and as the world's last, best hope against the rise of global tyranny. That vision of the country could easily slip into assumptions that state security prerogatives—no matter how intensely rights-infringing—were inherently liberal and constitutionalist.

Under those readings, whatever protected the constitutional state from threat necessarily promoted liberal values, both in the US and around the world. In this way, constitutional veneration continued to operate on both sides of the ledger: It created the terms for inclusion and rights protection, and it could in key moments push back against specific abuses. But it also buttressed an overarching account of American power and purpose, which time and again justified coercive practices in the first place.

This aggressive interlocking of security and constitutional veneration circulated even as part of the broader festivities surrounding the Bill of Rights. Take the role in Los Angeles of John Lechner, who was executive director of both the local Bill of Rights celebration committee and the Americanism Education League.[53] In a February 1941 speech before the Los Angeles City council celebrating Americanism Day, he declared that, as war loomed, Americans "faced a withering barrage from . . . the combination of dictatorship nations . . . and from selfish hate-spreading anti-American groups within our own borders." These facts required an unequivocal embrace of the constitutional state, because "in order to preserve the Constitution and our Bill of Rights," "and in order to protect the integrity of minorities worthy of protection," "unlimited freedom of speech, press, and assembly should be removed from all subversive groups . . . whose ultimate aim is the destruction of the American way of life."[54]

It was no coincidence that such language came from California, which became the epicenter of calls for the mass internment as seditious enemies of all those of Japanese descent. During World War I, National Security League education director Robert McNutt McElroy had infamously referred to the entire state of Wisconsin as effectively treasonous, because of its German population. Now, such views of the Japanese spread among white citizens on the West Coast.

In response, in March 1942—only three months after the rapturous culmination of Bill of Rights celebrations—the military began implementing Roosevelt's Executive Order 9066. This order, as well as supportive congressional legislation, ultimately led to the internment in prison camps of approximately 120,000 people of Japanese descent.[55] And, in keeping with Lechner's fears about those "within our own borders," internment was understood in part as an effort to defend the constitutional project against tyrannical dangers at home and abroad.[56]

A racialized construction of just who counted as the Constitution's enemies fueled the internment. And this construction fed on longstanding ideas about the ethno-cultural basis of the national project, ideas that even rights-committed New Dealers—who would have opposed internment—still implicitly repeated.

Recall that for those like the Harvard English professor Howard Mumford Jones, the best way to defend anti-racism as American involved rewriting the history of the founders themselves. This amounted to a serious historical distortion. Yet the real dilemma with claiming the founders for contemporary egalitarian ends was that it could unwittingly reproduce—rather than counteract—the past pro-war intertwining of exceptionalism and cultural particularity. Claims about the founders tended to emphasize the sense that a specific group of European settlers in the New World had created an historically unique society, one that truly embodied Enlightenment principles. And such claims often presented "mainstream" Americans—implicitly defined as white—as cultural inheritors of this project. As such, mainstream Americans stood as gatekeepers, responsible for determining which communities were capable (or incapable) of inculcating basic values—particularly during a time of war—not to mention the appropriate process and speed for including racial outsiders.

These cultural understandings were at play in Lechner's own striking assumption—offered while simultaneously defending inclusion and constitutional toleration—of an effective white right to decide which minorities were "worthy of protection" and which crackdowns were necessary to safeguard the Constitution. In a sense, the era's broader constitutional and national narrative of egalitarianism failed to address the structural roots and persistence of American racial subordination. Instead, it highlighted the specialness of Euro-American framers, distinctively capable of creating a universally inclusive society.

In this way, the narrative had the cultural effect of bestowing on empowered white political elites a type of moral privilege. To the extent that white Americans were the cultural and intellectual descendants of those initial colonists, they had the right to shape the terms of membership and to determine what counted as security threats. And, in the especially destructive hands of individuals such as Lechner, who became a vocal proponent of mass interment, this meant that anyone of Japanese descent was cast as an unassimilable enemy of the constitutional project. For Lechner, defending both the Bill of Rights and the American war effort *required* truly extreme crackdowns.

AMBIVALENCE AND EXCLUSION IN WHITE SOCIETY

Speaking to this interplay between rights-protective language and acquiescence to large-scale oppression, even the ACLU equivocated in its opposition to Japanese internment. While the group participated in the cases challenging Executive Order 9066, the national organization's approach focused on the arbitrary implementation of the order rather than its inherently unconstitutional nature. Indeed, the historian Greg Robinson tells us that, much to the chagrin of founding member Norman Thomas, "in June 1942, the ACLU national board voted by a decisive margin not to oppose the [basic] constitutionality of Roosevelt's order." Thomas struggled throughout the war to build mass opposition to the internment, and he looked with disdain on the ease with which presumptive civil libertarians in the ACLU accommodated themselves to racist assessments of Japanese threat. Writing shortly after the board vote in the *Christian Century*, Thomas concluded: "In an experience of nearly three decades I have never found it harder to arouse the American public on any important issue than this. Men and women who know nothing of the facts (except possibly the rose-colored version which appears in the public press) hotly deny that here are concentration camps. Apparently that is a term only to be used if the guards speak German and carry a whip as well as a rifle." Thus, at the most decisive moment, all the era's praise of the Bill of Rights nonetheless went hand in hand with the same violent security politics as World War I's mass constitutional celebrations.[57]

Indeed, when the matter reached the Supreme Court, Justice Murphy, who wrote the majority opinion in *Schneiderman*, found himself in dissent in *Korematsu*—a case he declared to be "the legalization of racism."[58] The very same justices decided these cases, just eighteen months apart. And while in *Barnette* they struck down the government's ability to force children to salute the flag, and in *Schneiderman* limited denaturalization powers, they upheld a coercive right to collectively imprison—on national security grounds and without any individualized process—an entire ethno-national community. And the Court did so even though such actions had obvious resonances with fascism—or, as Thomas repeated time and again, amounted to "totalitarian justice."[59]

Yet two obvious differences between *Schneiderman* and *Korematsu* may help explain why Murphy could not convince his colleagues in the latter case. First, on a Supreme Court now fully composed of FDR appointees (only Owen Roberts remained from the pre–New Deal era), the domestic political and geopolitical implications of the opinions were distinct. Preserving Schneiderman's nationality in 1943 was consistent with US-Soviet comity and the president's war effort. Similarly, constitutionalizing Japanese internment shielded Roosevelt and his wartime policies from scrutiny. But just as critically, ethno-racial questions also implicitly circulated about who could and could not embrace national values. That background combination of American exceptionalism and cultural particularity may have made it far easier to imagine every person of Japanese descent as a potential security danger than to suspect the same of a Euro-American immigrant in the country since the age of two.

In fact, the evolving national narrative suggested that, in the conduct of the war, certain types of prejudice—against European immigrants, but also against Black citizens—began to appear as injustice, whereas others disappeared from view. If African Americans had been treated as a dangerous fifth column during World War I, more and more government officials embraced the idea that Black people, by fighting and dying for the republic, were now proving their citizenship—especially against the increasingly pervasive ethos of a "composite nation."

Indeed, officials began to recognize the ubiquitous discrimination Black serviceman faced as a threat both to the war effort and to national ideals. Such soldiers, Gerstle writes, fighting on behalf of presumptively egalitarian American principles, found themselves "routinely denied the basic liberties accorded their white counterparts"—either barred overseas from accessing military clubs and facilities or subject to daily harassment and indignities when training at home. In response, Secretary of War Henry Stimson created monitoring offices to react to outbreaks of white violence against African American soldiers. And as the war progressed, the army and the navy both began small-scale efforts to integrate facilities and crews, ultimately leading to President Truman's post-war 1948 executive order desegregating the armed forces as a whole.[60]

But for citizens and noncitizens of Japanese descent, their presence on the West Coast and the specter of Asian power in the Pacific led many whites to desire comprehensive exclusion. Some white Americans perceived those of Japanese descent as maintaining too close an attachment to foreign and illiberal cultural values. This made them, according to Lechner and others, potential threats to the inclusive commitments of the US constitutional project. This was so even if there were Japanese Americans, as there were African Americans, who fought in the war with great distinction. Such military service was not necessarily enough to establish the loyalty of the group as a whole or to diminish their imagined threat to the well-being of the constitutional state. Indeed, FDR's move to internment in mid-1942 was significantly an election-year effort; it maintained white support on the West Coast for New Deal policies and for World War II, especially given that the war initially focused more on Germany than on Japan.[61]

In this way, American wartime creedalism remained more than adaptable enough to fit with classic settler binaries and with an extreme brand of racial subordination. Internment amounted to the culmination of a long history of exclusion and population control, which had shaped the collective experience of Asian Americans for the better part of a century. While the door had remained open in the late nineteenth century for European migrants participating in frontier expansion, Asian migrants faced forced removal and systematic discrimination if they remained. Seen both as economic threats to white farmers and laborers and as culturally unassimilable, Chinese workers, for instance, were subject to harsh exclusion laws and the first sustained federal deportations in American history. All of this dramatically decreased their numbers domestically, even before the 1924 quota eliminated Asian entrance entirely.

At the same time, Japanese migrants out West in the late 1800s (along with all others judged to be of Asian descent) found themselves part of a new legal category—"aliens ineligible to naturalize"—explicitly barred from ever becoming formal citizens through naturalization. Western states then incorporated new alien land laws specifically to target Japanese farmers and to prevent "aliens ineligible to naturalize" from owning land. White settlers thus succeeded in disinheriting Asian immigrants from access to the nation's territory—much as they had succeeded with earlier generations of Blacks, Mexicans, and Indigenous peoples.[62]

Now, during World War II and in the face of racial tension and perceived economic competition, the Roosevelt administration again marked out the Asian population for collective punishment. Noncitizens from Germany and Italy faced individualized processes for detention—effectively protected as co-ethnics of Euro-American immigrant communities now incorporated into the New Deal coalition and its ideas of composite American identity (whatever Elroy may have wanted during World War I).[63] The Japanese ethnic community alone found themselves subject to mass internment.[64] In this way, the spread of constitutional devotion in the 1930s and 1940s maintained space for serious security abuses and racial definitions of threat—both of which one might have expected to fall away in the face of inclusive and civil libertarian creedal constitutional narratives of patriotism and American exceptionalism.

THE PERSISTENCE OF UNDERLYING CONSTITUTIONAL QUESTIONS

Alongside these troubling dynamics, the wartime championing of the Constitution obscured another key dilemma of American politics. The era's arguments papered over the same persistent structural concerns about the constitutional system that World War I pro-business activists had consciously sought to suppress. Even if the late 1930s and early 1940s marked the flowering of a New Deal embrace of the Bill of Rights, the structural flaws of the legal-political system persisted. Tellingly, the era also embodied the containment of the New Deal's broader domestic economic agenda, and especially those efforts to move beyond a limited social welfare state to a more comprehensively social-democratic one. Whereas labor activists had imagined that Court acquiescence to the New Deal would create the conditions for new and rolling legislative victories, this would not come to pass.

For Du Bois, as discussed in chapter 8, the main roadblock remained the same as always: a broken and fundamentally undemocratic system of state-allocated constitutional representation allowed Southern white conservatives to wield outsized power over congressional decision-making and to stall legislative initiatives. In his view, a recognition of these basic facts did not entail adopting a politics of dictatorship. Du Bois certainly respected the intense activism of many Black Communists. And at the very end of his life he became a member of the CPUSA, in part due (as we will see in chapter 11) to the persistent repression he experienced from the US government. But in 1944, he pointedly declared that he "did not believe that the Communism of the Russians was the program for America; least of all for a minority group like the Negroes."[65]

Indeed, socialist and radical voices often agreed with many of the critiques A. Philip Randolph made of the CPUSA, including around its willingness to completely abandon principle when Soviet policy changed. For Norman Thomas, the party's vociferous wartime backing of Japanese internment was a profound moral stain and made it fundamentally untrustworthy. While Thomas, with the support of Du Bois, organized petitions demanding that FDR rescind Executive Order 9066 and attempted to build a socialist, liberal, and civil libertarian bloc against internment, the CPUSA moved to sabotage these efforts. Thomas later described the party's leadership as "212 degree Fahrenheit patriotic because of our necessary alliance with Stalin," and therefore willing even to "break up . . . meeting[s]" Thomas "organized in [sic] behalf of the outrageously dispossessed Japanese and Japanese Americans."[66]

These CPUSA actions followed the changing winds in Moscow. As illustrated by struggles within the National Negro Congress, after the Nazi-Soviet pact, the party—much to the anger, it should said, of many of its grassroots activists and members—rejected Popular Front and New Deal alliances and opposed any coming war. But then, when Nazi Germany invaded the Soviet Union, it switched again and became among the most militant pro-war voices in the US—supportive of whatever measures FDR deemed necessary.

Yet, whatever one thought of the Soviet Union, or of the CPUSA, this did not absolve the American constitutional order of its significant flaws. For Thomas and Du Bois, it did not mean accepting that criticism of American legal-political institutions should be rendered more or less off limits. According to Du Bois, the condition for meaningful Black freedom—not just piecemeal amelioration—remained the same, and started with a dramatic reconstruction of basic democratic process, regardless of new wartime Constitution worship. Reflecting on the US as the country faced World War II—and against the backdrop of a now rediscovered and celebrated Bill of Rights—Du Bois nonetheless declared that there remained a continuing need for a mass insurgent politics on behalf of genuine democracy: "The democracy which the white world seeks to defend does not exist."[67]

Conclusion: Setting the Stage for Cold War Nationalism

These constitutional doubts still expressed by Du Bois and others were far less pronounced throughout the nation than during World War I. And as World War II gave way to a new Cold War with the Soviet Union, the previously widespread anxieties about the existing political and legal order were pushed decisively to the margins. The Supreme Court's New Deal shift and the vision of World War II as the "good war"[68] served as critical pillars for the expansion of creedal constitutionalism and the entrenchment of constitutional legitimacy across the political landscape.

Indeed, growing numbers of white Cold War commentators and politicians reimagined as virtues the very features of the US Constitution that had previously promoted deadlock. Take for instance the Supreme Court itself. Earlier Progressive-era reformers had highlighted the relative exceptionalism of American-style judicial review—in which lifetime judges could overturn national legislative decisions, while publics had limited opportunities to respond, given the difficulties of amendment and the lack of any congressional override. Progressive reformers argued that such exceptionalism demonstrated the extremism of American-style counter-majoritarianism, and suggested how far domestic institutions lagged behind democratic innovations elsewhere.

But a new conventional wisdom emerged following World War II. Now, judicial review itself—so beleaguered in the preceding half century—offered an example of why American society had avoided Europe's dictatorial turn. And the institution's status as a global outlier spoke to a broader and positive national exceptionalism. It exemplified the way in which a US system of checks and balances warded off totalitarian tyranny: limiting the authority of government actors, allowing power to counteract power.

Under this view, the constitutional structure hewed as closely to the ideal as any liberal-democratic arrangements actually could in the real world. Whatever the old Progressive, Socialist, and even New Deal suspicions, the Constitution-in-practice promoted a civic culture that valued moderation, compromise, and reasoned debate. Thus, the Constitution charted an ameliorative path between fascist and communist extremism. In part for this reason, the global spread of the institutions of American constitutionalism—judicial review chief among them—gained renewed policy-making importance in the post–World War II years.

The Cold War years also saw a remarkable transformation in constitutional politics at home. Well into the 1930s, the Constitution still faced deep skepticism from center-left academics, lawyers, activists, and New Deal politicians. But by the early 1960s, liberal elites approached the document with unambivalent patriotic attachment. And although it continued to face pushback within the Black counter-public, the Constitution nonetheless reached deeper into African American life than perhaps at any period since Reconstruction. Furthermore, in white working-class culture, constitutional attachment went hand in hand with a fundamental reshaping of the labor movement's self-understanding and political impulses. Union leaders and members increasingly embraced even class-harmonious accounts of nationalist American belonging. For many, the dramatic labor and global successes of the New Deal and World War II were all the proof one needed of American exceptionalism and of constitutional greatness.

Creedal constitutional ideas, and their connection to global American primacy, had been so beleaguered at the beginning of the century. And yet, as the following chapters show, they now became firmly embedded as the principal way white Americans spoke to each other about their nation.

Those willing to challenge this Cold War nationalism found themselves lonely voices under threat and, as in the case of Du Bois, forced into political exile. If reformist opponents of the Constitution in the 1910s believed, perhaps too optimistically, that their views had the potential to convince most Americans, by the early years of the Cold War that door had shut. New Deal successes and wartime creedalism disconnected radical constitutional skeptics from their putative white working-class base. And this raised profound questions for the future about what kinds of change, and on what terms, would be possible in the United States.

PART III

Consolidating the American Model, 1945–1965

According to the political power which each actual voter exercised in 1946, the Southern South rated as 6.6, the Border States as 2.3 and the rest of the country as about 1.

When the two main political parties in the United States become unacceptable to the mass of voters, it is practically impossible to replace either of them . . . because of the rotten borough system based on disenfranchised voters. . . .

This spells danger: danger to the American way of life, and danger not simply to the Negro, but to white folk all over the nation, and to the nations of the world.

The federal government has for these reasons continually cast its influence with imperial aggression throughout the world and withdrawn its sympathy from the colored peoples and from the small nations.

> W. E. B. DU BOIS, "INTRODUCTION," IN
> *AN APPEAL TO THE WORLD* (1947)

The intellectual liberals who twenty years ago wanted to pack the Supreme Court as frustrating the will of the masses . . . and who were quoting Charles Beard to show that the Constitution is a mere rationalization of economic loot—those same liberals today are hugging for dear life that same court and that same Constitution, including its Fifth Amendment. They are hugging those two most conservative of "outdated" institutions as their last life preservers against the McCarthyite version of what their Henry Wallaces used to call "the century of the common man."

> PETER VIERECK, "THE REVOLT
> AGAINST THE ELITE" (1955)

CHAPTER 10

Launching the American Century

In 1941, Franklin Delano Roosevelt delivered one of the most famous speeches of his presidency. His 1941 State of the Union Address, popularly known as his "Four Freedoms" speech, called on the country to abandon a position of isolationism, to assist allies ensnared by war, and ultimately to commit to transforming the world in keeping with American values. Precisely because domestic life was grounded in constitutional "respect for the rights and the dignity of all our fellow men," declared FDR, "so our national policy in foreign affairs has been based on . . . respect for the rights and dignity of all nations."[1]

Such creedal constitutional ideas definitively moved to the center of American public life during World War II, uniting a broad swathe of the population behind a shared vision worth fighting for in the face of fascist global threats. And the years following the war saw the country experience an equally dramatic intensification of constitutional veneration: for governing elites, the Constitution became much more than just a workable institutional mechanism for navigating domestic social problems, and one source of national pride. Instead, for both previously skeptical New Dealers and their conservative opponents—not to mention various influential scholars and commentators—veneration became constitutively bound up with Americanism *as such*. A broad swathe of the political, business, and intellectual classes came to embrace the Constitution as the American "night sky,"[2] in the legal scholar Laurence Tribe's evocative words—less a contingent political fact and more an almost natural and permanent feature of collective life. As the famed sociologist Seymour Martin Lipset concluded in 1963, it became simply "unthinkable" that the Constitution could "be abolished or fundamentally revised"[3]—whatever the domestic political traumas of the century's first four decades.

This complete embrace of the constitutional system extended key elements of New Deal–era constitutional culture, but also broke from it in important ways. 1930s New Dealers may have eventually pledged their loyalty to the document. But, like earlier twentieth-century Progressives before them, they tended to emphasize its openness to economic experimentation, as part of the "living" nature of the text. FDR no doubt presented his wide-ranging economic agenda as a form of constitutional restoration designed to save capitalism rather than to overthrow it. Still, from Bill of Rights celebrations to the Supreme Court's *Schneiderman* decision overturning a Communist Party member's denaturalization, 1930s and wartime constructions of constitutional meaning tended to prioritize civil liberties and socioeconomic guarantees over classically capitalist values.

By contrast, early Constitution Day advocates all the way back in 1917 had aimed to create a national consensus that treated both legal-political *and* market arrangements as practically pre-political and inevitable. And while the disruptive experiences of the Great Depression at least partially stalled those efforts, they returned and flourished across policy-making sites after World War II. Commentators and decision-makers began to treat the Bill of Rights' civil libertarian protections as the other side of a capitalist coin—fusing two elements that many had understood as separate only the decade before. In the process, these thinkers essentially pulled together all the pieces that would become the durable official ideology of American constitutional reverence going forward.

In this updated form of veneration, to be a believer—both in the text and in the nation—meant increasingly just affirming that the existing constitutional structure embodied a near perfect realization of the representative ideal. It also involved treating anti-totalitarian personal rights protections as connected to market capitalism, with the market conceived of as an essentially just mechanism for distributing material wealth and economic power—requiring only a minimal degree of managerial guidance. Furthermore, all of these intertwined values would be preserved by American global power, which safeguarded liberal democracy from both domestic and foreign threat.

This consolidating constitutional politics sought to remove from public dispute critical questions that had long been central in American public life—questions about the basic organization and principles of the legal-political system, the economy, and the emerging national security state. The new politics deemphasized the ideological flexibil-

ity historically embedded in past combinations of creed and Constitution. In the preceding century, these combinations spilled well beyond
FDR's welfarist and regulatory framework. At times, they could even
go hand in hand with revolutionary and norm-breaking means: during
Reconstruction after the Civil War, Radical Republican supporters of a
multiracial democracy viewed long-term military rule over the former
Confederacy as necessary for any redemptive effort. And the US Communist Party, during its "Popular Front" period in the 1930s, combined
creed and Constitution to proclaim that "Communism Is Twentieth-
century Americanism."

Despite this past openness, by the late 1950s creedal constitutionalism had been transformed into a correlate of capitalist democracy,
bound closely to reverence for a set of existing legal-political institutions. Such reverence lavished praise especially on those institutions associated with checks on majority rule, and it voiced deep opposition
to change through any potentially unruly or non-legalistic means. In
effectively a single generation, the political conversation in Washington converged exclusively on *one* account of the Constitution, and even
one account of *constitutionalism*. For policymakers and academics, being a constitutionalist in the United States—or even having a constitutional politics at all—became reduced almost exclusively to a particular
model and mode of politics, defined as the only truly American version.

This critical shift raises a basic question about post-war constitutionalism: Why did governing elites rally so dramatically around a specific,
ever more rigid account of the creedal Constitution? In this chapter,
I argue that engaging with the ideological terms of rising American
global primacy offers the best answer. I also contend that this context
both framed the terms of the emerging US-led global order and narrowed the possibilities of constitutional change within the country
itself.

Focusing on the elites that shaped post-war American foreign policy, I suggest that their intensifying veneration was influenced by two
decisive developments that marked the post-war period from the mid-
1940s to the late 1950s. First, the war itself and the confrontation with
Nazi Germany created near unanimous support within national policy-
making circles for building "the first great American century," in the
famous words of the media magnate Henry Luce.[4] At the national
level, commitment to American international police power definitively
won the day over long-standing pockets of isolationist sentiment. Sec-

ond, against this backdrop of essentially uniform faith in American imperium, the country increasingly engaged in ideological and material
struggle with the Soviet Union for global dominance.

Both developments had profound effects on the political and cultural
meaning of the federal Constitution within the United States. Going all
the way back to the occupation in the Philippines, defenders of greater
international power had embraced constitutional self-government as
perhaps their central language of justification: an exceptional tradition
in political liberty, emblazoned in the 1787 Constitution, supposedly
distinguished legitimate American authority from the European empires of old. In the post-war moment, the promotion of an American
Century became closely bound up with reconstructing the global community in the US's own constitutional image—both with respect to the
internal structure of foreign states and in the design of new multilateral
institutions.

In the first section of this chapter, I highlight the role of constitutional discourse in the establishment of the American international order. I focus especially on the construction of the United Nations and
the writing of new constitutions in defeated powers like Germany and
Japan. The section explores those projects by linking them to the era's
key texts—such as the Swedish sociologist Gunnar Myrdal's *An American Dilemma*—and also offers a glance back to earlier 1930s efforts
at large-scale US constitutional promotion among Native American
peoples, which provided a template for the massive post-war projects.

I then turn to the context of Cold War rivalry—particularly over
the allegiance of non-white societies in newly independent states. With
US elites embracing the effort to entrench an American global order
against a socialist adversary, creedal constitutionalism—especially in its
pro-war and pro-business association with capitalist entrenchment—
became further elevated in policy-making circles. It developed from a
common political language, albeit one facing various competitors, into
something closer to a secular theology. This overarching ideological
framework became the central way Cold War officials spoke about the
US role in the world, as well as the rightfulness of the country's special
global status.

These American officials increasingly presented the choice for publics at home and abroad in Manichaean terms: one could select either
American market capitalism and liberal constitutionalism or socialist
terror. Policymakers and commentators contended that the Soviet claim
to be a "people's democracy"—despite its evident authoritarianism—

exposed the dangers of a tyrannical majority and the ease with which democratic excess could descend into totalitarian pathology. They argued that the American constitutional system—with its counter-majoritarian veto points and its rights commitments, including to private property—ultimately offered the only sustainable model for joining together democracy and liberty.

In this way, earlier Progressive-era accounts of constitutional design—which emphasized the need for more rather than less popular participation and control—were reconceived as threats to both *true* constitutionalism and democracy. For an emerging generation of Cold Warriors, constitutionalism thus became narrowly associated with an experiment in capitalist democracy, grounded above all in Madisonian checks and balances.

Ultimately, this effort to build an American Century on updated creedal constitutional terms produced dual incentives among officials in Washington. On the one hand, it created the need to prove genuine commitment to universalist ideals—including racial equality—and to demonstrate actual material benefits from participation in the US orbit. Governing American elites grounded the new international order of independent nation-states in ideas of collective rule-following, and on principles of civil and political liberty. These practices clearly pressed against the old European-style imperialism, offering decolonizing elites both legal and institutional bases to challenge the actions of powerful states—including the US.

But the new mode of American global power—like its Wilsonian predecessor—had much in common with those earlier, now ideologically disavowed imperial projects. As I argue in the chapter's final section, this updated creedal constitutionalism fed suspicions in Washington that any anti-colonial project with socialist tendencies necessarily signified Soviet domination, and thus would inevitably lead to authoritarian outcomes and global instability. As a key consequence, for all the official invocations of legal self-restraint, constitutional language justified foreign interventions and lawlessness abroad just as often as it limited discretionary violence.

In academic writing today, *constitutionalism* and *empire* are often presented as conflicting practices. This basic scholarly approach echoes David Jayne Hill's World War I–era juxtaposition, and it depicts imperial excess as arising from an abandonment of constitutional commitment. In addition, scholars today often explain the 1950s elite political consensus through the lens of Cold War rivalry. Yet such work, especially in the law, rarely asks *why* that consensus entailed such an intense embrace of the federal Constitution in particular. The existence of an ideological adversary need not have entailed elevating the Constitution or the existing legal-political institutions specifically.

This chapter's exploration of the entrenchment of a specific mode of constitutional politics among post–World War II US officials—a type of imperial constitutionalism—engages with these features of American scholarship. I argue that the 1940s and 1950s highlight how the establishment of American global primacy, complete with the exercise of a continuous international police power, became ethically rooted in the constitutional commitment of US policymakers. This constitutional commitment, joined as it was to the ideological edifice of American primacy, in turn narrowed the domestic scope of acceptable argument about the Constitution—now an important symbol of the US's unique position in the new world order. In effect, the post-war political settlement within the United States was fundamentally an imperial settlement: It presumed a background agreement on the centrality of American international dominance to global stability and domestic largesse. And it normatively centered both that stability and that largesse on an official version of creedal constitutionalism, simultaneously inclusive and tied to capitalist economic and political relations.

The Constitution and American Primacy in the Wreckage of European Empire

It is perhaps surprising that a capitalist-inflected politics of constitutional veneration emerged as one important outcome of fighting Nazi Germany. Anti-fascist sentiment was a cornerstone of Popular Front culture in the 1930s—in art and writing as well as left and liberal coalition-building. As illustrated by the constitutional skepticism of those radical activists and even some New Dealers, one did not have to defend the wisdom of American constitutional design or the genius of the framers to contest rising authoritarianism. Indeed, anti-fascist politics in Europe during the war years displayed very little of the American fixation with constitutions. Nonetheless, as the war effort became bound up with the project of American global dominance, policymakers in Washington began systematically describing the meaning of the American project at home and abroad in constitutional terms.

World War II had generated a fundamental policy-making consensus in Washington, and increasingly in the academy as well, around the idea that American primacy would be essential for any stable postwar order. Within elite policy-making circles, the historic isolationist block—particularly with respect to intervention beyond the Western Hemisphere—fundamentally collapsed.[5] And to distinguish US might from European powers' colonial projects, officials and elected representatives returned to the same constitutional language that past supporters of American international assertiveness had used.

For half a century, this language had served as a central way of defending such assertiveness as the opposite of extractive empire. And it transferred naturally to new efforts to promote and institutionalize American authority throughout the world. For this reason, to the extent that national elites converged around commitments to US primacy, they almost inevitably also converged around these commitments' established creedal and constitutional justifications. If building a new American Century emerged as an immovable and practically pre-political article of elite policy-making faith, a creedal Constitution gained the same exalted status. They became practically inseparable commitments, and believing in one meant believing in the other.

WORLD WAR II CREEDALISM AND THE IMPERATIVE OF A NON-IMPERIAL AMERICAN POWER

Roosevelt's 1941 State of the Union offered one of the most notable early interlinkings of American global power and constitutionalism. In terms highly reminiscent of David Jayne Hill or Woodrow Wilson, FDR suggested that the centrality of the creed and of the Constitution to national identity meant that American interests were essentially equivalent to the world's interests. And only if the US imposed these constitutionally grounded values everywhere would global peace be established.

Indeed, the "four freedoms" Roosevelt described in the speech were at their root a New Deal–inflected and welfarist version of the creedal constitutional faith, steeped especially in that year's ongoing celebrations of the Bill of Rights. They included freedom "of speech and expression," freedom "of every person to worship god in his own way," freedom "from want," and freedom "from fear." Moreover, decisively repudiating isolationist sentiment, FDR ended his invocation of each freedom with a call, repeated in an almost liturgical manner, for Americans to entrench these values "everywhere in the world."[6]

FDR and other officials may have followed the framework laid out by earlier pro-war and pro-expansion figures like Woodrow Wilson. But, critically, many now leaned far more heavily on the inclusive dimensions of constitutionalism and global power, given their growing wariness of Wilsonian white supremacy.[7] While much remained continuous in the underlying racial logic of how US power operated abroad, especially in the non-European world, the rhetorical shift was nonetheless noteworthy. And over time this shift brought with it a real transformation in how most white national elites spoke about the country at home and abroad. US officials increasingly desired to avoid the appearance of racism in international affairs; eventually, this helped to transform how these elites came to internalize the meaning of the national past.

As I discuss more fully later in the chapter, this effort by post-war officials to strip both American primacy and constitutionalism of any explicitly white supremacist valence took place against the backdrop of profound structural changes in the international system. If the first half of the twentieth century had been marked by rising non-European political assertiveness, World War II dramatically escalated this process. The war's end entailed more than just the defeat of the Axis powers or even the eventual genesis of a new Cold War, the latter marked by American struggle with the Soviet Union for global dominance. In addition, the near total destruction of Europe—for the second time in three decades—set in motion the ultimate collapse of the old empires themselves, in a way that fundamentally differentiated the effects of World War I from those of World War II.

In 1945, the Allied powers may have won, but Germany had devastated its European enemies, leaving them either occupied or financially destroyed. These states—England, France, Belgium, and Holland—had been the central colonial powers, and they now scrambled to hold on to their imperial possessions. Meanwhile, the war had also dramatically improved the position of nationalist forces across Asia and Africa. And just as the conflict with Nazi Germany strengthened anti-racist and creedal discourse within the US, the ideological terms of the war also strengthened the hand of anti-colonial movements arguing for an end to empire and for equality at the international level. Ultimately, in the twenty years following World War II, almost every former colony gained independent nation-state status.[8]

These global changes had long-term consequences for American officials. The collapse of the old empires left the United States in a clearly preeminent global position, as the world's most powerful economic and military force. Yet these officials, deeply invested in entrenching global primacy in line with the country's strategic and financial interests, had to reckon with two emerging realities: a genuine ideological competitor in the Soviet Union, and also a world comprised overwhelmingly of decolonizing and non-white states—the latter highly suspicious of anything that looked like the old imperial hierarchies. Thus, as Cold War competition with the Soviet Union came to define the post-war years, this competition increasingly focused on which power could gain the allegiance of polities across the Global South.

But US efforts in the decolonizing world faced a real problem. The country was an old English settler colony, still governed in the mid-twentieth century by Jim Crow laws. As such, it seemed in many ways out of step with the decolonizing times—a reminder rather than a repudiation of the closing age of European empire. As one leading Indian newspaper pointedly declared in 1948, "the prevailing racist spirit in the U. S. A. is not consistent with America's claim to the moral leadership of the world."[9] Indeed, by contrast with the United States, the Soviet Union, particularly through the Communist International (Comintern), founded in 1919 following the Russian Revolution, had long been associated globally with anti-colonial independence projects.[10] And within the US, the Communist Party often stood at the forefront of civil rights battles.[11] As for the Soviet Union's 1936 constitution, it certainly imposed no real constraints on Stalin's dictatorship. But its Article 123 declared the equality of all Soviet citizens "irrespective of their nationality or race, in all spheres of economic, state, cultural, social and political life."[12] This led Paul Robeson to assert, based on a 1930s visit to the country, that Article 123 was "an expression of democracy, broader in scope and loftier in principle than ever before expressed."[13]

For many Asian and African political elites, not unlike Robeson, Soviet declarations seemed more than empty rhetoric because of the extent to which the Soviet Union—as well as aligned groups—had provided genuine material support for anti-colonial and Black struggles. The United States had remained mired in slavery and segregation at home since its founding, and it maintained imperial alliances abroad with the likes of France and England. Meanwhile, entities like League Against Imperialism and Colonial Oppression (LAI), founded with the backing of the Comintern, had organized to directly contest the League of Nations' mandate system.[14] The LAI's 1927 inaugural conference in Brussels was a remarkable gathering of global anti-colonial activists, including such figures as the future Indian Prime Minister

Jawaharlal Nehru, the Indonesian President Sukarno, the South African trade unionist James La Guma, the Senegalese nationalist and politician Lamine Senghor, and the great Mexican artist Diego Rivera.[15] These political efforts were even more significant given the relative material limitations of both the Soviet Union and various international communist organizations vis-à-vis the US.

All of this created a context in which post–World War II American officials were at pains to establish the non-racist and non-imperial nature of a US-led global order. As Eleanor Roosevelt stated in 1948, "our open discrimination against various groups [is] the one point which can be attacked and to which the representatives of the United States have no answer"[16]—emphasizing the problem of domestic American racism for US international authority. These worries, given Soviet anti-colonial associations, provided the background against which policymakers in Washington committed ideologically to the framework of creedal constitutionalism and also sought to demonstrate—through rhetoric and practice—the genuine global universalism of this framework.

GUNNAR MYRDAL AND THE HOPE OF
THE CREEDAL NARRATIVE

Unsurprisingly, many of the era's landmark political texts engaged with precisely this desire to affirm and cement the country's egalitarian essence. Perhaps none was more important than Gunnar Myrdal's *An American Dilemma: The Negro Problem and Modern Democracy*.[17] Released in 1944, the book was a major publishing event, and it circulated broadly across elite Washington circles. As the historian David Southern notes, *An American Dilemma* was the culmination of "a huge collaborative effort, sponsored and . . . financed by the Carnegie Corporation," to study the issue of race in the United States. It "became an instant classic"—read and debated by everyone from foreign policy officials to presidents and Supreme Court justices and immediately recognized as a pervasive and influential reference point at the highest levels of government.

As for its academic reception, the renowned sociologist Robert Lynd proclaimed in the *Saturday Review* soon after the text's publication that *An American Dilemma* was nothing less than "the most penetrating and important book on contemporary American civilization that has ever been written." Indeed, in 1964, when the same *Saturday Review* polled twenty-seven esteemed scholars and commentators for their opinion of a book "published during the past four decades" that "most significantly altered the direction of our society," *An American Dilemma* came in second only to John Maynard Keynes's *General Theory of Employment, Interest and Money*.[18]

For starters, *An American Dilemma* further drove the spread of the term "American Creed,"[19] invoked, as we have seen, since at least World War I. But, far more importantly, for policymakers in DC the book provided a framework for answering a basic and increasingly persistent question: Why were the universalist claims elites now asserted on the global stage not fundamentally compromised by the country's own sustained history of white supremacy? In other words, how could the United States claim to be a repudiation of European colonial rule—and thus different from England, France, or even Nazi Germany—given its deep-rooted structures of racial subordination?

Myrdal's arguments offered a resolution to this tension between stated ideals and ongoing practices—an analytical response that became definitive for national political elites in their justifications of American primacy and thus of the American Century. He contended that, going all the way back to the founding, the country's "high national . . . precepts"—its collective values when articulated on a more "general plane"—were not those of racial prejudice. Instead, they consisted of an inclusive and egalitarian "American Creed," as expressed in the Declaration of Independence.[20] Myrdal declared, "the nation early laid down as the moral basis for its existence the principles of liberty and equality."[21] There no doubt existed a deep conflict within white American society—the "moral dilemma" of the book's title—over whether to give priority to "local" and "individual" values of "group prejudice," embodied in Jim Crow policies, or to the "high national" ideals of the Declaration.[22] But, as I quoted in this book's introduction, Myrdal declared that, ultimately, "the main trend in [American] history [was] the gradual realization of the American Creed" and thus the completion of its foundational project.[23]

In this way, although white society clearly struggled with competing "value premise[s],"[24] the American story was one in which exclusionary commitments were losing out over time. Collective life had a hopeful direction—promising an eventual, if bumpy, overcoming of the racist past and a fulfilling of liberal-egalitarian principles.

Myrdal did recognize the persistence of racial discrimination within the United States. Still, he offered an optimistic vision of how, especially through domestic racial reform, the US could still claim interna-

tional leadership in an overwhelmingly non-white world. And it gave
scholarly support to officials' beliefs that the country, even if stained by
slavery and segregation, was fundamentally inclusive and non-imperial,
unlike its European rivals, and therefore worthy of global leadership.
Whatever the Jim Crow realities of the present, the American future
lay in redeeming its creedal potential—and thus in offering the world
a path beyond European colonial domination and toward a free and
equal order.

In his final reflections, Myrdal went so far as to contend that ongoing racial segregation was "not only America's greatest failure but also
incomparably America's greatest opportunity for the future." If the
country embraced its "own deepest convictions" by ending formal discrimination at home, this would aid both domestic "well-being" and
"American prestige and power abroad." In living up to the nation's core
values, the United States could complete its historical progression and
also ensure that American international authority was truly grounded
in the creed. As a result, nothing less than the long-standing dream of
"American patriots, that America should give the entire world its own
freedoms and its own faith, would come true." Myrdal proclaimed that
he believed in this eventuality, in part because he saw creedal faith as
shaping American behavior in ways small and large—underscored by
how "Americans stand warmheartedly against oppression in all the
world." Despite its internal failures, and unlike the disintegrating European empires, "what America is constantly reaching for is democracy at
home and abroad."[25]

For US officials, Myrdal's analysis reaffirmed faith in the goodness
of American primacy. It also further emphasized the need to fuse US
global authority with both domestic and international creedal commitments. But, interestingly, Myrdal himself did not view such creedalism
as necessarily requiring constitutional veneration. A Social Democratic
member of parliament in Sweden, Myrdal's view of the Constitution
hewed closely to the old Progressive-era critiques. In fact, according
to David Southern, Myrdal's account of the document "relied almost
exclusively"[26] on work by none other than Charles Beard. And he relied not on 1943's *The Republic*, which through a series of Socratic dia-
logues in important ways defended what Beard believed to be the framers' constitutional vision. Instead, he drew from Beard's 1913 classic, *An
Economic Interpretation of the Constitution of the United States*, with its
implication that the Constitution was an anti-democratic and counter-

revolutionary act by class elites. Following Beard, Myrdal wrote in *An American Dilemma* that the Revolution and the Constitution were motivated by a "difference in spirit," with the Constitution "conceived in considerable suspicion against democracy and 'fear of the people.'"[27]

But despite this critique, Myrdal nonetheless concluded that, whatever the problems of the 1787 text, "the common American is not informed on the technicalities and has never thought of any great difference in spirit between the Declaration of Independence and the Constitution. When he worships the Constitution, it is an act of American nationalism, and in this the American creed is inextricably blended."[28] Thus, for all practical purposes, Myrdal accepted that, by the mid-twentieth century, supporting the US creed entailed supporting the Constitution and vice versa. If radical nineteenth-century abolitionists like William Lloyd Garrison once argued that beliefs akin to the egalitarian creed actually required a repudiation of the 1787 text, for Myrdal the two could nonetheless be merged together. This meant that Myrdal's readers in Washington could quietly ignore his skepticism of the Constitution. And just as Myrdal accepted the cultural entanglement of creed and Constitution, when the US promoted an American model abroad, its brand of universalism and of constitutionalism ended up being one and the same.

A CONSTITUTION FOR ALL PEOPLES

All of this spoke to the fact that, as US officials began concretely shaping the terms of the post-war international system, they placed creed and Constitution front and center as the definitive account of national identity as well as of American leadership. With the old European imperial order collapsing, US policymakers saw the international replication of internal American values and legal-political practices as the key to a sustained peace.

First and foremost, this required the creation of rule-based and multilateral institutions, as well as the promotion of basic principles of equality and personal liberty. This two-pronged effort can be understood as an application of creedal constitutional means to solve the problem of global governance. The goal was to establish both a tight web of interlocking institutions—directing everything from international monetary policy and global trade to health, education, and scientific cooperation—as well as background constitutional norms that would shape intra- and interstate behavior. In this multilateral framework, the United States would serve as the global hegemon and ultimate military and economic backstop.[29]

The US would take on this responsibility due in no small part to the fact that, as the dominant political voice and market actor—with its currency the global reserve currency—the country would reap disproportionate economic and strategic gains.[30] But the legitimacy of the overall order—especially given the prospect of global decolonization—depended on American respect for constitutional self-constraint as well as for the formal sovereignty of all nation-states. And only through such respect could Americans ensure consensual participation by others.[31]

Along with the creation of the Bretton Woods economic institutions, this constitutional vision was best illustrated by the formation of the new United Nations, and especially its Charter and Universal Declaration of Human Rights. As FDR asserted in his March 1945 speech to Congress on the Yalta conference on the post-war European settlement, European rivalries had essentially led the world into a morass of global cataclysm and material ruin. The problem was that European powers had imagined that they could establish collective security through classically imperial means: "The system of unilateral action, the exclusive alliances, the spheres of influence, the balances of power and all the other expedients that have been tried for centuries—and have always failed." Instead, he called for the creation of a "universal organization," which would be unique due to its grounding in the values of equal respect and shared legal commitment that marked the domestic American constitutional order.[32] And indeed, when the UN Charter was adopted later that year, its preamble mimicked that of the federal Constitution—beginning with the phrase "We the peoples of the United Nations," echoing "We the people of the United States."[33] This choice had been suggested by the US delegate, Sol Bloom, a committed FDR ally, New York congressman, and central organizer in Congress of 1937's US Constitution Sesquicentennial Exposition.[34]

Just as important, American officials pressed aggressively for the post-war creation of an "international bill of rights" to parallel the domestic American one, in the form of what became 1948's Universal Declaration of Human Rights (UDHR). Indeed, the UN General Assembly resolution adopting the UDHR was titled the "International Bill of Human Rights," with the Declaration viewed as a centerpiece of that overarching project.[35] For US officials such as Louis Hyde, a delegate to the UN Economic and Social Council, the drafting and ratification of the UDHR in particular meant nothing less than the spread across the globe of "traditional American rights and freedoms."[36] Eleanor Roosevelt oversaw the writing of the Declaration itself, as the first chairperson of the UN Commission on Human Rights, and it was steeped in American constitutional language—and especially creedal discourse.[37] Along with New Deal social welfarist commitments, it lifted heavily from the US Bill of Rights and from the Fourteenth Amendment, invoking equal protection, due process, and the right to property, as well as free speech, assembly, and free exercise rights.[38] During the drafting process, official reports back to Washington happily confirmed that "the US position was accepted on all important points."[39]

A CONSTITUTION FOR EACH PEOPLE

But American officials did not stop at recasting the international system in a US constitutional image. They also maintained, in keeping with a half century of global interventionist beliefs, that the world would only be secure if foreign states were *themselves* reconstructed along American institutional and ethical lines.

These views were, perhaps, the natural culmination of claims that had emerged following the Spanish-Cuban-American War. And they concerned the centrality of constitution-writing to overseas nation-building. In the nineteenth century, the drafting of new US state constitutions on the American frontier had been the final stage of full territorial inclusion, as mentioned in chapter 2. Likewise, for decades in the twentieth century, it was commonplace among officials to think of US-led exercises in constitution-writing as part of the process by which culturally and politically threatening polities became incorporated into the broader American project. According to those in Washington, such reconstruction—aimed at inculcating constitutional norms within unstable or newly independent states—was key to ensuring an international order actually organized on terms of mutual restraint and therefore collective security.

In the years before World War II, perhaps the most sustained embodiment of this US project in constitution-writing came in the form of New Deal–era policies toward the Philippines and Native Americans. Given the Philippines' centrality to the development of the US brand of imperial constitutionalism, discussed in chapter 5, its ongoing role is hardly a surprise. By the 1930s, pressure from a divergent array of groups pushed FDR to accept an explicit transition to formal Philippine independence, albeit after a decade-long waiting period. These groups included Filipino nationalists, but also, most significantly, anti-immigrant voices, especially in the American West, who viewed Filipino presence in the United States as an economic and racial threat to white citizens[40]—echoing the racist anti-annexationist sentiments of the 1890s.

The resulting Tydings-McDuffie Act, passed in March 1934, was a major win for nativist politicians. At independence, Filipinos in the US would lose their US nationality and would be deported unless they gained appropriate immigrant status. But such status would be virtually impossible to achieve, given the intensity of racially restrictive quotas and the fact that, as Asians, they continued to be deemed "aliens" ineligible for naturalization—no matter how long they may have lived in the country. Furthermore, before independence, only fifty visas would be allocated yearly for Filipinos interested in emigrating to the United States.[41]

Still, Filipino independence leaders by and large accepted the bill—even with its extended transition and racist immigration provisions—as the best practical means for ending formal colonization. Critically, as part of the process for the transfer of sovereignty, the Act mandated the writing by Filipinos of their own constitution through a convention, followed by popular ratification of the document. But under the law, the United States would not approve just any document. The proposed constitution would have to preserve certain American trade and military privileges, not unlike the Platt Amendment with respect to turn-of-the-century Cuba. And it would have to incorporate key constitutional components, which, going back to the 1902 Philippine Organic Act, had been central to justifying the American project there—like a bill of rights, a republican form of government, and religious toleration.

In theory, there was within these terms potential space for experimentation. But the legal scholar Leia Castañeda Anastacio tells us that, given the backdrop of US power, Filipino elites involved in drafting the 1935 Philippine Constitution "opted for the familiar." They established a structure of "authority and rights" comparable to the "Insular Government," built around a presidential system (adapting the US colonial Governors-General), a Supreme Court, and, with additional amendments in 1940, a bicameral legislature once more named the

House and the Senate. The result was a legal-political order marked by what Anastacio calls "incompatible tendencies"—torn between the entrenchment of American interests and organizing assumptions on the one hand, and ongoing local demands for economic and political self-determination on the other.[42]

In 1934, months after adopting the Tydings-McDuffie Act, Congress also passed the Indian Reorganization Act (IRA). The bill was the centerpiece of the "Indian New Deal," and it initiated a parallel constitution-writing project, with many of the same strengths and enduring weaknesses as the Philippines effort. John Collier, the reformer and advocate for greater respect for Native American culture and practices, had by then been appointed commissioner for the Bureau of Indian Affairs (BIA). He became the public face of a broader 1930s effort to provide Native peoples with tangible improvements, aimed at reversing the late-nineteenth-century project of forced assimilation and land privatization.

In keeping with Collier's long-standing reformist goal of promoting greater respect for Indigenous cultures and institutions, the IRA set out, as the political scientist Kevin Bruyneel writes, "to recognize and foster the presence and role of tribes as political, socioeconomic, and cultural communities on reservations throughout the nation."[43] Native nations remained subject to the greater administrative authority of the federal government. But the bill nonetheless sought to strengthen internal self-governance and "to support tribal reservation economies through development programs, including financial and lending services."[44]

Crucially, although Native peoples were not formally required to do so, Indigenous constitution-writing became, yet again, a key step in the practical process by which the US government extended recognition to Indian nations and then provided them with necessary funds.[45] Spearheaded by the BIA, the immediate period after the enactment of the IRA saw some ninety-six new tribal constitutions implemented by Indian nations.[46] This was not only a remarkable project of constitution-promotion by the federal government, but also a natural extension of both the American approach to statehood on the frontier and nation-building overseas. In a sense, through the exercise of constitution drafting and ratification, Indigenous nations adopted a mode of governance that US federal authority could perceive as legitimate—in part because it replicated settler practices. For this reason, such efforts, as they did in the Philippines, embodied many of the same internal tensions that would come to define post-war constitutional promotion in overseas polities.

For Felix Cohen, who as assistant solicitor in the Department of the Interior became the central legislative drafter of the IRA, it was crucial for white American officials to appreciate the fact that Indigenous peoples had their own rich history of constitutionalism. Just as the Oneida activist and writer Laura Cornelius Kellogg had argued in 1920, Cohen too contended in one 1939 article that "tribal constitutions, after all, are not an innovation of the New Deal." He stated that "the history of Indian constitutions goes back at least to the Gayanashakgowah (Great Binding Law) of the Iroquois [Haudenosaunee] Confederacy, which probably dates from the 15th century."[47] Therefore, Cohen believed that if Native American nations wanted to write new constitutions as part of their assertion of self-government and autonomy, then these constitutions should be expressions of internal political values.

Nonetheless, the BIA produced its own "model" constitution for Native peoples, which officials on the ground circulated among Indigenous nations. As the scholars Vine Deloria Jr. and Clifford Lytle note, the result was that the mid-1930s IRA constitutions tended to "resemble" one another and to have a "distinct Anglo-American flavor,"[48] despite the diversity of Indigenous peoples and histories. In fact, in keeping with the US Constitution and the future UN Charter, the BIA's model constitution for Native nations too began with the phrase "We, the people of ___ tribe."[49] As the political scientist David Wilkins writes, BIA officials were torn between their respect for Indigenous practices and an overarching belief in US political wisdom: "On the one hand, they wanted to facilitate and encourage a degree of Indian self-rule; on the other hand, they were operating under certain cultural and political presuppositions that elevated their own values and governing systems over those of indigenous nations."[50]

In this way, the pre-war US experience with Philippine and Native American constitution-writing reinforced already established dynamics, which would soon define future American practices on the broader global stage. It highlighted the centrality of constitution-writing to US notions of nation-building, as well as the importance of such exercises in how officials sought to distinguish legitimate American leadership from old-fashioned and disreputable colonialism. But the experience across these cases also spoke to the background pervasiveness of US interventionist power, as well as to the tentative—at best—commitment to real sovereignty on the ground.

GERMANY, JAPAN, AND THE AMERICAN MODEL

In the immediate post-war moment, these dynamics came into play in the approaches taken toward the defeated Axis powers, Nazi Germany and Imperial Japan, which so recently had subjected the world to such destruction. In the German context, the US found itself navigating among a variety of competing actors and interests, in ways that inhibited the ability of officials to impose something like a straightforward American model. In particular, with the war's end, the four Allied states—the Soviet Union, Britain, France, and the United States—divided Germany into distinct zones under each power's authority.

One feature that clearly distinguished the American zone from the others was the commitment of US officials to constitution-writing. In the British zone, officials delayed the drafting of new constitutions by the local states for several years, maintaining, as the historian Harold Zink writes, that in the context of rolling economic crises there was "no great hurry"[51] to focus on the technicalities of institutional design. Yet American military authorities immediately pressed ahead with having states establish election procedures, elect members to the state legislatures, and draft new constitutions. General Lucius Clay, who in 1947 would become the military governor of the American zone in Germany, wrote that constitution-writing was nothing less than "the way to democracy." It had to be pursued "quickly at the local levels" and was foundational to uprooting totalitarianism and to imposing liberal-democratic order.[52]

As the Cold War rivalry with the Soviet Union divided Germany into east and west by 1949, US officials again strongly backed the formulation of a new constitution that would structure the terms of the West German Federal Republic. The specifics of 1949's Basic Law drew especially from the constitution of Germany's earlier Weimar Republic, and the process was not an American-dictated affair. But the suggestions made by US policymakers highlight what they viewed as the particular wisdom of the American constitutional example. Throughout the drafting process, Military Governor Clay especially pressed for strengthening the powers of the local states and for modeling institutional design on Madisonian federalism. In keeping with how the specters of fascism and communism had shifted New Deal–era debates about American checks and balances, Clay and other officials viewed federalism as essential to blocking the type of consolidated power that generated Nazi despotism.

If the American drive for constitutional self-replication faced various roadblocks in Germany, no such limitations existed in the Japanese context. Today the Japanese Constitution, which went into effect in 1947, is perhaps most famous for its Article 9, in which "the Japanese people forever renounce war as a sovereign right of the nation."[53] But it is also noteworthy for the extent to which it was a constitution imposed from above, drafted by a small coterie of American officials working for General Douglas MacArthur, the Supreme Commander for the Allied Powers (SCAP).

MacArthur very much conceived of this project as demonstrating the genius and global applicability of the American constitutional model. He declared the draft document written by his staff as nothing less than "the most liberal constitution in history,"[54] and thus a representation of the full flowering of long-standing American constitutional values. He implicitly presumed that as Japanese elites and publics internalized these commitments, the country would become a source of international stability, rather than a danger to its neighbors and to the global system.

For this reason, the text of the 1947 Constitution of Japan is infused with creedal constitutional language and mimics elements of the US Constitution. Like the UN Charter and the BIA model for Native American constitutions, it echoes the American preamble, beginning with the phrase "We, the Japanese people."[55] It is structured around three branches of government—executive, legislative, and judicial—with key institutions named after their American counterparts. The high court is called the Supreme Court and enjoys powers of judicial review. The lower house of parliament is known as the House of Representatives. Furthermore, not unlike the 1787 American Constitution, the Japanese document is relatively difficult to amend, requiring two-thirds support in both houses of parliament before being submitted for popular ratification.

It also follows the US text in its brevity, comprising only 5,000 words. As for the document's rights provisions, akin to the UDHR, the Japanese Constitution incorporates guarantees for speech, religion, assembly, due process, and property rights (complete with a takings clause) in ways that mirror the words found in the US Bill of Rights. Similarly, the document includes an equal protection clause modeled after the Fourteenth Amendment, which reads: "All people are equal under the law and there shall be no discrimination in political, economic, or social relations because of race, creed, sex, social status or family origin."[56] The inclusion of sex equality here is striking and, along with an additional article entrenching women's rights in the context of marriage and family, was inserted by Beate Sirota, an interpreter on MacArthur's staff.[57] These elements were a notable victory for the feminist construction of the creed, fulfilling abroad the type of constitutional goals that American women's rights activists of the time, associated especially with Alice Paul, had long hoped for at home in their fight for the Equal Rights Amendment.

The egalitarian provisions of the Japanese Constitution, especially the strengthened equal protection clause, also reiterated the now critical status, among white foreign policy officials, of universalist rhetoric for national self-image—and indeed, for what counted almost definitionally as the American model itself. American officials did not promote abroad a version of US constitutionalism that focused just on checks and balances, federalism, or civil libertarian guarantees. This model was permeated with expansive egalitarian language.

MacArthur's role and evolution here is telling. Five years earlier, in 1942, MacArthur had arrived in Australia, fleeing a Japanese assault on the Philippines that removed the US from its key decades-long strategic outpost in the Pacific. Speaking to a parliamentary dinner in Canberra, MacArthur underscored the deep personal importance to him of the warm Australian reception, especially given recent events. He declared, "although this is my first trip to Australia, I already feel at home. There is a link that binds our countries together which does not depend on written protocol, upon treaties of alliance or upon diplomatic doctrine. It goes deeper than that. It is that indescribable consanguinity of race which causes us to have the same aspirations, the same hopes and desires, the same ideals and the same dreams of future industry."[58] In the moment, MacArthur's words invoked a common settler experience linking the United States to Australia, not to mention South Africa. Just as Teddy Roosevelt and countless earlier American political elites had maintained for generations, MacArthur's focus on "that indescribable consanguinity of race" hinted at how these societies were at root experiments in the spread of Anglo-European settlement, in which English colonists successfully wrested political and cultural supremacy from non-European Indigenous groups.

In 1942, MacArthur thus implicitly imagined the war in terms of racialized antagonists, a struggle for global dominance between the descendants of Europe and a rising Asian power. That very same year, such a racial imaginary also justified mass Japanese internment across the

West Coast of the United States. In this ideological framework, Australia embodied nothing less than an outpost of Anglo-American rule and Anglo-American values in an otherwise treacherous region. Aligning with this cultural affinity and respect, MacArthur implemented the segregation of American soldiers in Australia—given the Australian government's initial desire to exclude Black American soldiers entirely from the country and its strident opposition, under its "white Australia" policies, to any racial intermingling.[59]

But five years later, MacArthur noted with pride the bestowal on Japan of the world's "most liberal constitution." And he approved an even more comprehensively egalitarian version of an equal protection clause than that found in the American Fourteenth Amendment. MacArthur presented the US role in Japan not as racial domination, but instead as fundamentally concerned with the spread of universal constitutional commitments, with racial equality and women's rights chief among them.

The difference of course between the early and late 1940s was not only the centrality for US officials of underscoring how American primacy entailed the repudiation of the type of explicit white supremacy embodied in Nazism. In addition—in a world of declining European empires and emergent independence movements across the Global South—it became increasingly relevant how non-white societies would view the American approach to non-white Japan. Therefore, in treating constitution-writing as an exercise in the promotion of liberal equality, political elites underscored the ideological tie between American primacy and an inclusive constitutionalism. As MacArthur wrote that same year in *Life* magazine, the purpose of transforming Japan in American constitutional terms was to demonstrate that these values were "no longer peculiarly American, but now belong[ed] to the entire human race."[60]

Of course, from the very start such post-war experiments did not truly cut the Wilsonian, and ultimately settler, knot between constitutional promotion and racial hierarchy—as hinted at in the narrative embrace of American exceptionalism and greatness. In Japan, to an important degree, the whole project was conceived of as a gift from white American benefactors. Moreover, this gift was only given after dropping two atomic bombs and the indiscriminate mass death that resulted.[61] The US may have asserted such control over the Japanese constitutional process, as opposed to the German one, because of the American need in Europe to negotiate with a variety of competing Western states and internal German constituencies. Yet judgments about relative cultural maturity and advancement, implicitly invoking Wilson's old theories of racial development, also certainly influenced the American willingness during the Pacific war to use especially brutal measures in imposing total defeat.[62] After the war, these views would similarly have shaped treatment of Japan as a blank slate, open for comprehensive constitutional experimentation. This tutelary role aligned with an overarching belief in the singular genius of American customs, and with the related commitment to full political and institutional management when aiding less mature, overwhelmingly non-white societies.

Such racialized tendencies persisted under the emerging form of American creedal constitutionalism, becoming hard-baked into Cold War dynamics. Still, one should not dismiss the real rhetorical power with which US officials presented the national project, even for those in the Global South. By grounding American primacy in constitutionalism—and especially by linking domestic values of equality with an international system premised on mutual consent—US policymakers and commentators offered a new generation of non-white leaders an alternative means for interpreting American objectives and actions. The US's rise—and thus its behavior overseas, however incoherent at times—could be framed as more than simply a project of white settler supremacy, no different than Australia or South Africa. Instead, it might be read as part of a general replacement of European empire with a new, universally inclusive global order.

Anti-Colonialism, Socialist Democracy, and the Capitalist Logic of American Primacy

For officials to succeed in imposing US authority on the world, they would have to establish more than a white American respect for non-white peoples—or an acceptance of their basic humanity despite the prevalence of domestic racism. Officials would need to show newly independent states that accepting an American framework for global order and internalizing American institutions were both affirmatively advantageous.

Two dynamics underscored the difficulty of successfully convincing decolonizing leaders and communities. First, emerging anti-colonial politics ran counter to the increasing conjoining of market structures to American constitutionalism and power. Furthermore, US officials

had to demonstrate why their preferred vision of liberal constitutionalism and market capitalism improved upon a viable Soviet alternative—
both as an institutional model and as a source of potential alliance.

THE CHALLENGE OF A NEOCOLONIAL
CRITIQUE OF CAPITALISM

For those in the decolonizing world, the Soviet Union's anti-colonial
and anti-racist rhetoric and practice were not the only elements giving
the country international appeal. Although the USSR was not nearly
as wealthy as the United States, it offered a clear example in the post-
war years of an impoverished state that had rapidly industrialized. This
example better approximated the circumstances across both war-torn
Europe and postcolonial Asia and Africa than did American economic
and political history.[63] Thus, for all of the United States' overall military and financial dominance, officials could not claim that the specific
American model provided the only path to material prosperity.

Critically, for many anti-colonial leaders, the Soviet alternative offered value independent of whether their countries actually sought
inclusion in a Soviet sphere of influence. For most leaders, replacing
formal European colonial domination with subjection to either American or Soviet directives hardly amounted to genuine independence. As
Ghana's first president, Kwame Nkrumah, famously proclaimed, the
great struggle for Asian and African countries after the end of the old
imperial order was to resist a new condition of "neo-colonialism." He
argued that decolonization may have altered the juridical status of African countries, but it had not produced substantive independence.

Indeed, in place of direct control, postcolonial societies now faced
a variety of economic, financial, and trade restrictions imposed by former imperial masters like England and France, as well as by new global
superpowers like the United States and the Soviet Union. These restrictions reduced nominally sovereign states to the level of dependent sat-
ellites, with limited capacity to dictate the terms of their own collective
future. As Nkrumah declared, the postcolonial state was "in theory, independent . . . [with] all the outward trappings of . . . sovereignty," but
"in reality its economic system and thus its political policy is directed
from outside."[64]

Independence leaders like Nkrumah were not interested in being Soviet puppets. Instead, a new generation of Asian and African decision-
makers saw in the Soviet example choices beyond whatever the old

empires now sought to impose. Many paths, especially to economic development, seemed available.

This sense of possibility was especially significant because of the extreme poverty and entrenched, colonially generated economic inequalities confronting various independence forces. For the Kenyan anticolonial activist and first vice president, Oginga Odinga, British rule had been marked by economic extraction and theft, leaving countless people landless and immiserated. As he titled his autobiography *Not Yet Uhuru* ("Not Yet Freedom"), in an agricultural society like Kenya, only a systematic transfer of land to those on the ground would grant them liberation from hierarchy and dependence.[65]

Moreover, Odinga was highly skeptical that the American model—now seemingly grounded in market capitalism above all—could meaningfully solve these local challenges. Countries like Kenya required a thoroughgoing project of material redistribution, which Odinga saw as essential to democracy and, relatedly, to actual self-determination in a world of formally equal but substantively unequal states. Without control over the material resources of the society, ordinary people would not possess the power within their own communities to truly govern themselves.[66]

In addition, simply allowing market prerogatives to dictate who possessed property after independence offered no genuine alternative. Even if one believed in the efficacy of markets in certain contexts, this approach failed to address the drastically and forcibly uneven distribution of property and power that resulted from colonialism. It simply meant that a combination of British settler elites and multinational corporations, alongside their wealthy African clients in the country, would end up claiming all the land and natural resources.

Odinga himself believed the best alternative to this eventuality was the domestic creation of "organized cooperative societies." These "societies" would be composed principally of the many "landless Africans" who had been expropriated and left destitute by the colonial state, or made to farm the great colonial landholdings. The hope was that with independence these communities would gain control over the land, working collectively to direct the production and enjoy the wealth of such property.[67] Indeed, alongside representative political institutions, Odinga presented entrenching the cooperative ideal as foundational to decolonization and to democracy—to actual rule by the people and therefore to any legitimate economic system. In the United States, as discussed in chapters 2 and 4, such an argument would have been familiar to previously enslaved Black plantation workers who sought a "jubilee" after the Civil War or even to some past white Socialist defenders of the "cooperative commonwealth."

Odinga viewed this economically driven vision of socialist democracy as essential for ensuring that independence did not slip into neocolonialism. According to him, a key problem with market capitalism was how it allowed a country's resources—which should be distributed on the principle of equal provision and power—to be sold to the highest bidder. In a world marked by profound global wealth inequalities, and particularly one shaped by a colonial past, such market relations tended to inure consistently to the benefit of foreign actors, who could bid the highest.

Indeed, Odinga read the desire of departing British colonial administrators to create a distinct class of propertied African elites in precisely these terms. British officials hoped that, through the "temptations" of "property," they could empower a constituency of local actors who would be "moderate and easily controlled" due to their economic ties.[68] Since the wealth of this new propertied elite would depend on capitalist market relations—as well as on financial ties to London—they would have a self-interest in dividing the national spoils between themselves and multinational corporations.

Thus, for Odinga and others, genuine independence—beyond merely the formal transfer of sovereignty—required ensuring that no such governing class emerged, beholden to foreign benefactors rather than to local communities. And this meant resisting the domestic consolidation of what many considered a predatory and global capitalist order.

A GLOBAL MONROE DOCTRINE AND THE MID-CENTURY VISION OF SOCIOECONOMIC RIGHTS

Such Third Worldist and anti-colonial accounts of socialist democracy presented American officials with a real ideological challenge. The American post-war international order took for granted the centrality of entrenching individual property rights and capitalist relations of production—regardless of how those rights and relations had first come about. And American interventionists going all the way back to President James Monroe and his Monroe Doctrine had long seen international stability as profoundly wedded to the promotion of American commerce with non-European societies. Such interventionists believed that expanding markets for American products and providing US business with access to raw materials fostered the commercial power of the United States. Supposedly, the benefits were not just a one-way street: greater commercial links enhanced cosmopolitan sensibilities within the receiving state, limiting their willingness to resort to violence by creating financial incentives for a durable peace.[69]

Defenders of global primacy after World War II similarly embraced these premises, along with the inherent and universal value of market capitalism and its related legal institutions—even as they backed certain social welfarist safeguards. Indeed, as the scholar Neil Smith contends, many of the American architects of post-war institutions, including the UN system and its governing documents, believed they were finally making good on the effort to create a "global Monroe Doctrine."[70] Woodrow Wilson, with his aspirations for the League of Nations, may have hoped to project such ends onto the world stage—combining American oversight and market access with principles of self-government. But now, the UN—as Smith writes of how officials understood the creation of the new multilateral order—"was to be the organization that successfully absorbed and displaced local territorial and political conflicts, [and] decoupled them from the free operation of a world market in which the United States inevitably dominated."[71]

Thus, when policymakers pressed for the constitutionalization of individual and corporate property rights—both at the international level and within foreign polities—they viewed such efforts as essential to implementing the US model. They were not an optional part of the system, which states could simply ignore while maintaining good standing under the terms of American leadership. Indeed, for officials who promoted a vision of American primacy, this meant that creedal constitutionalism was, to a significant degree, conceived of as an experiment in and expression of capitalist democracy.

American policymakers expressed this sentiment even when they sought to hold on to the more expansive social welfarist ambitions of the New Deal. FDR's most important wartime constitutional initiative, the Second Bill of Rights—proposed during his January 1944 State of the Union address—offers a telling example. The initiative consciously aimed to make good on the aspirations in his earlier "Four Freedoms" speech, and especially on the "freedom from want." Tying the provision of economic security to the fight against totalitarianism, FDR declared in 1944 that "'necessitous men are not free men.' People who are hungry and out of a job are the stuff of which dictatorships are made." He thus called on Congress to pass an extensive set of socioeconomic programs, which he viewed as basic positive rights—just as significant to preserving constitutional democracy as the negative civil liberties of the first ten amendments:

> The right to a useful and remunerative job in the industries, or shops or farms or mines of the Nation; The right to earn enough to provide adequate food and clothing and recreation; The right of every farmer to raise and sell his products at a return which will give him and his family a decent living; The right of every businessman, large and small, to trade in an atmosphere of freedom from unfair competition and domination by monopolies at home or abroad; The right of every family to a decent home; The right to adequate medical care and the opportunity to achieve and enjoy good health; The right to adequate protection from the economic fears of old age, sickness, accident, and unemployment; The right to a good education.[72]

The framing of this legislative agenda was absolutely steeped in creedal constitutional discourse, starting with the decision to refer to these policies as a "bill of rights." Moreover, just as the first Bill of Rights linked the Constitution to the Declaration of Independence—by entrenching "truths" from the Declaration that were "self-evident"—this second charter similarly safeguarded "economic truths" that, in the face of modern realities, had now "become accepted as self-evident." At the same time, the charter spoke to the universally egalitarian spirit of the American project, since the goal of the Second Bill of Rights was to ensure, in keeping with the nation's founding promise, that "security and prosperity can be established for all—regardless of station, race, or creed."[73]

Crucially, FDR's vision of socioeconomic rights was fundamentally distinct from how socialists, including those in the Socialist Party of America (SPA), often championed similar policies earlier in the twentieth century. As discussed in chapter 4, radical labor activists tended to frame these rights as gains that working people wrested from business elites through class struggle. Their call for socioeconomic rights highlighted the degree to which society remained riven by fundamental and irreconcilable class conflicts. They aimed not simply for state provision of the elements required for basic security. Instead—as with demands around a broad right to strike—socialist and labor voices often saw socioeconomic provision as a way to alter the underlying structure of domination that marked the condition of work, in which most people had no choice but to enter into a fundamentally oppressive labor market in order to survive.[74] They hoped that, by delinking work from the constant threat of precarity, workers would flip the power relations that existed between them and business employers. They would thus gain the material resources necessary to press for yet further transformative changes to state and economy.

Roosevelt's claim that "necessitous men are not free men" moved through a fundamentally different conceptual framework. For past SPA voices, such a phrase may have suggested that, if a person constantly worried about bare survival, they could not truly confront the economic elites that wielded power over them. By contrast, FDR's anti-totalitarian worry—echoing a long line of politicians going back to Madison—was that poverty made individuals susceptible to demagogues, who could prey on their insecurity to claim dictatorial power. In essence, social welfare provision—even something as extensive as a Second Bill of Rights—should actually aim to defuse class conflict in society, and thus to entrench the overall legitimacy of background property relations.[75] In important ways, this approach resonates with FDR's constitutionally restorationist tendencies, discussed with reference to the New Deal constitutional changes in chapter 8.

To emphasize the point, for Roosevelt these socioeconomic rights belonged to *citizens*, not to the working class as such. They were meant to establish a direct connection between the state and its members, and to underscore how one's primary political attachment was to "we the people" and the nation-state, rather than to working-class institutions. There would be no need for class struggle because the society would provide each person, as an individual citizen, with basic goods.

In fact, FDR saw such provision as not only perfectly consistent with capitalist democracy, but as speaking to a bedrock class harmony and shared Americanism that existed within society. It highlighted how capitalism—if hedged in with the proper safeguards—could enhance the interests of all, workers and businesspeople alike. Indeed, underscoring that the charter served everyone, regardless of class position, the Second Bill of Rights went so far as to include anti-monopolistic rights for "every businessman, large and small."[76] Thus, even during these later efforts to revive declining New Deal energy, American officials clearly diverged from more critical visions—as would increasingly be voiced by those skeptical of postcolonial capitalism. Such visions countered mid-century American accounts of both a harmonious "we the people" at home and a harmonious "we the peoples" on the international stage.

THE CREEDAL CONSTITUTION VERSUS
THE PEOPLE'S DEMOCRACY

In line with this conceptual framework, officials and academics associated with the American project systematically pursued two joined arguments. First, they aimed to discredit the idea of socialist democracy. And second, they sought to prove that capitalist democracy could provide for the social welfare of all, echoing initiatives at home like the Second Bill of Rights.

For starters, they aimed to convince uncertain publics everywhere that the socialist vision failed both as a matter of democratic theory and as a workable politics in the world. Such policymakers and commentators often contended that the very idea of socialist democracy was a contradiction in terms—fundamentally antithetical both to real democracy and to real constitutionalism. They pursued this line of analysis by, most importantly, reducing all socialist experiments to Soviet and Chinese examples. They thus raised questions about the compatibility between personal liberty and any radical project aimed at altering the basic economic relations within society.

In the post-war period, a variety of states associated with communism, or in the Soviet Union's orbit, had claimed the language of democracy to describe their own political projects. Specifically, they used the language of "people's democracies" or, as in the case of China under Mao Zedong, a "people's democratic dictatorship." The supposed democratic characteristic of these states was that they nationalized industry, land, and private wealth and then, at least partially, provided socioeconomic guarantees to their publics. But these modes of economic redistribution went hand in hand with an extreme centralization of political power within a single party apparatus, across countries in eastern and central Europe as well as in Asia. Although the party leadership running "people's democracies" was meant to represent the interests of society's various constituencies, the results were deeply oppressive. Those in power systematically substituted their own will for that of the public writ large, ruthlessly imposed policies, and denied citizens meaningful civil and political liberties.

US policymakers, therefore, rightly highlighted the deeply undemocratic nature of these regimes. For President Harry Truman, the US—as the essential backstop of the global order—had a responsibility to resist the spread of Soviet-style authoritarianism. This entailed asserting an international police power throughout the world to counter Soviet geopolitical influence and to "support free peoples who are resisting attempted subjugation by armed minorities or by outside pressures."[77]

Committed to the project of American primacy, these policymakers also contended that the world increasingly offered only two opposed choices: either a totalitarian path, falsely packaged in the language of the "people's democracy," or a genuinely free alternative in the form of the American model, which combined democratic self-government with liberal autonomy and constitutional respect. Such a framing provided the ideological core of the famous "Truman Doctrine," announced in March 1947 before a joint session of Congress. In the speech, Truman proclaimed:

> At the present moment in world history nearly every nation must choose between alternative ways of life. The choice is too often not a free one. One way of life is based upon the will of the majority, and is distinguished by free institutions, representative government, free elections, guarantees of individual liberty, freedom of speech and religion, and freedom from political oppression. The second way of life is based upon the will of a minority forcibly imposed upon the majority. It relies upon terror and oppression, a controlled press and radio; fixed elections, and the suppression of personal freedoms.[78]

The sharpness of Truman's oppositional categories had profound implications for how US political elites increasingly defined the entire socialist tradition, and not simply Stalinist state socialism.[79] In particular, they argued that state socialist invasions of personal liberty—when it came to speech, religion, or association—were intimately joined to the type of economic order such polities promoted. Efforts at radical economic redistribution evinced a basic disregard for the status of the individual—one's property and thus one's identity separate from the group as a whole—in a way that promoted a collectivizing authoritarian impulse. Crucially, such a claim intrinsically joined political and civil liberties to capitalist property rights, viewing the protection of the former as bound to that of the latter.

This view was a key reason why Truman, although a New Dealer, became wary of FDR's Second Bill of Rights framing—a phrase that, as president, he abandoned, never referencing it again after 1946.[80] FDR's proposal and vision may have been meant to entrench capitalist democracy. But Truman's avoidance of it indicated a growing Cold War worry that establishing such affirmative socioeconomic guarantees as imperatives of the state amounted to a possibly dangerous step—whatever the earlier New Deal energy behind such efforts. These affirmative constitutional duties potentially empowered the state, and constrained the individual's market relations, in a manner too closely aligned with the Soviet model.[81]

The British philosopher Isaiah Berlin, perhaps the defining political theorist of the early Cold War in both England and the United States, famously teased out the intellectual foundations of these fears. As the political theorist Joshua Cherniss discusses, Berlin explored how Soviet-style dictatorship was indicative of a push to "uniformity and authoritarianism" within certain socialist strains.[82] His famed 1958 Oxford lecture, "Two Concepts of Ordered Liberty," gave theoretical heft to arguments circulating since at least Truman's speech. Berlin contended that the history of political thought in the West had been shaped by two distinct ways of conceiving of freedom: negative and positive liberty. The former consists in the aim to be free *from* the coercion of others, and to enjoy a meaningful sphere of personal autonomy. The latter entails the affirmative desire for "self-mastery," the aspiration to control all of the primary decisions that affect one's life. For Berlin, a genuinely free order should be pluralistic, able to hold together the competing values implicit in both negative and positive liberty. In particular, this involved taking seriously both the desire for "self-mastery"—through representative electoral institutions—and the negative ends of non-interference, through various liberal constitutional constraints on state power.

The problem with the version of socialism spreading globally was that it unleashed the impulses driving positive liberty in ways that undermined the equally essential negative component. As Berlin declared, the revolutionary's "wish for the emancipation of my entire class" easily devolved into a willingness to disregard the individual rights of others, and indeed even of oneself. "So much" may a member of the working class "desire this" group emancipation that, in their "bitter longing for status," they will "prefer to be bullied and misgoverned by some member of my own . . . social class."[83]

When it came to the matter of anti-colonial liberation movements, Berlin distinguished between their internal logic and that animating Soviet dictatorship. According to the theorist Aaron Gavin, Berlin saw the fight against colonialism as "allow[ing] individuals who were previously . . . oppressed to regain their sense of humanity," and therefore "not reducible to the totalitarian logic." Yet as with the politics of class struggle, anti-colonial movements too could fall prey to the destructive dynamics embedded within the desire for positive liberty.[84]

Such movements often combined a push to free oneself from the shackles of European imperial masters with the goal of dramatically altering the underlying relations of economic power. The twin logics of national self-determination and economic redistribution, including through socialism, propelled various anti-colonial efforts in directions that disregarded negative liberty. Driven by the "great cry" to be "recognized as a man," Asian and African publics were often willing to accept dangerous infringements on individual autonomy. In seeking "self-mastery" for both one's class and one's nation, non-white societies could be led to accept that they will "not get 'negative' liberty at the hands of the members of my own society," but at least they will be "underst[ood]" and thus feel a "sense of being somebody in the world."[85]

Thus, Berlin implied that the possible socialist threat to pluralist freedom came not only from direct authoritarian takeovers by party elites, as with the Soviet Union and China. It also emerged in contexts when societies too hastily implemented pure majoritarianism, especially when the voting public was largely composed of either historically marginalized working-class constituencies or previously colonized non-white peoples. Just as FDR had worried that "necessitous men were not free men," long-oppressed groups under such conditions might willingly abandon negative liberty in the search for "self-mastery" and recognition. For this reason, Berlin suggested that even when national liberation movements in the Global South proclaimed faith in socialist economic transformation *and* in preserving representative government, the danger of potential illiberalism persisted.

THE ANTI-POLITICAL VIRTUES OF THE US MODEL AND THE REWRITING OF AMERICAN SOCIALISM

Among US officials and commentators, such arguments provided an analytical basis for claims that only the existing American model presented a genuinely free expression of democracy, because it alone could balance positive and negative liberty: the model combined respect for individual rights guarantees, including property rights, with the commitment to electoral majoritarianism. But such majoritarianism was constrained by checks and balances that counteracted the power of both government officials and tyrannical majorities.

One can see the centrality of these ideas in American propaganda in Europe during and after the war. As the American struggle with the Soviet Union began to take center stage, the US Office of War Information's magazine for Italy, *Nuovo Mondo*, included multiple articles on the genius of the American constitutional system. These articles focused especially on how the system preserved essential rights through its delicate institutional balance. July 1945's "Guardians of American Freedom" highlights the beauty of the state system and federalism, how it "serves to secure the freedom of individuals."[86] And in October 1945's "The Guardians of the Constitution," American officials offer a glossy pictorial introduction to the sitting Supreme Court justices, hailing them as critical protectors of "fundamental laws of liberty," especially "the first ten amendments, that guarantee to all citizens their fundamental freedoms." Depicting the overall model—complete with its checks and balances and Bill of Rights—as an ideal distillation of free government, the article concludes, "the constitution... remains the guiding light for those who guard the American democracy, the democracy that allowed a group of less than 4 million individuals to grow and to become a nation of 130 million citizens."[87]

This specific focus on the constitutional model as balancing institutional powers and defusing potential tyrannical majorities—such as through judicial wisdom and "guardianship"—indicates how US policymakers increasingly defined the distinctions between the American and Soviet alternatives: the creedal constitutional approach delimited the scope of politics, precisely by containing the impulse toward absolute "self-mastery." Wary of utopian beliefs that political action could overcome all injustices, officials emphasized the dangers of such action. And they viewed the American system's circumscription of the political domain as one of its great strengths.

As the seminal post-war sociologist Edward Shils concluded, the model Americans promoted on the world stage was in truth the culmination of a fundamentally "antipolitical tradition." Operative in domestic life for "more than a century," it was bound especially to the ideas of Madison—given concrete expression in the 1787 Constitution— and premised on an awareness of the need for political humility in the face of competing and often incommensurate individual and collective values within society.

For Shils, whose views became highly influential in foreign policy circles, this meant that the American example was so worthy of emulation because of its particular fusing of constrained majoritarianism with protections for personal liberty. Shils argued that, in a world of communist totalitarianism and collapsing European empire, the American historical example provided the only true "system of pluralism": a "system of many centers of powers, many areas of privacy and a strong internal impulse toward the mutual adaptation of the spheres rather than the . . . submission of any one to the others."

This meant that the American combination of market capitalism and liberal constitutionalism ensured that, unlike under state socialism, "the economy [was] not run by the government." At the same time, the commitment to pluralism meant that "government" too was "not run by the owners or managers of the economy." For Shils, the latter point drove home the falsity of the classic socialist critiques that American legal-political institutions were simply dominated by class elites and thus did not embody real democracy. In line with other long-standing defenses of the 1787 Constitution, he suggested that the checks built into the legal-political order ensured that no single social class or constituency held overweening authority, and that all political power *as such* remained constrained.[88]

Shils may have been right that the owners of capital did not directly control the state as an exercise in straightforward class domination. Rather, following the early-twentieth-century journalist Charles Edward Russell's notion of an "Invisible Government," Socialists and many Progressives had argued that the sheer diffusion of veto points fractured the practical voting power of the poor and historically oppressed— even after they were reluctantly granted suffrage by those in power. This allowed other resources, especially wealth and cultural influence, to circulate as decisive factors in political decision-making. In this way, American checks and balances did not equally check all forms of problematic self-dealing. Instead, the constitutional system constrained certain forms of political authority—especially that of one person, one vote—while unleashing other less democratic and even violent modes.

Indeed, Shils's apparent presentation of the socialist tradition— whether that of Eugene Debs, W. E. B. Du Bois, or Oginga Odinga—as contrary in its entirety to true constitutionalism, civil liberty, and democracy was, in many ways, a remarkable claim. It fundamentally refashioned how many socialists in the United States had understood their own project, and their relationship both to the constitutional language of rights and to the democratic principle of one person, one vote. Indeed, over the first four decades of the twentieth century, the SPA had been closely associated with the projects of extending civil libertarian protections and of democratizing institutions of representative government. Two of the initial founders of the ACLU, Crystal Eastman and Norman Thomas, were deeply invested in socialism and in the Socialist Party. Defenses of free speech emerged especially in the context of socialist and anarchist protest by labor radicals and by anti-war activists before and during World War I. The socialist Thomas himself, and figures like Du Bois, were strikingly lonely voices of strident opposition to Japanese internment during World War II.

For many of these activists, the United States had never been truly democratic. They believed that implementing a genuine mass democracy—along with those critical civil libertarian, political, and socioeconomic rights protections that strengthened the power of oppressed groups—was essential to equal and effective freedom. And, again contrary to Shils's presentation of the socialist tradition, neither Thomas nor Du Bois, for instance, rejected checks and balances as a general matter. But they and others concluded that the American legal-political order was permeated with excessive veto points—to an extent that fundamentally compromised the basic underlying principle of majority rule. In addition, Du Bois had long emphasized how the state-based system of American electoral representation profoundly undermined the foundational democratic idea of counting the votes of all citizens *equally*.

If the analysis of Shils and others refashioned the relationship of socialism to the American constitutional experience, it similarly obscured the anti-democratic (and anti-"constitutional") role played by past governing elites. This was especially true when it came to the presentation of earlier defenders of global interventionism—the actual intellectual predecessors of 1950s Cold Warriors. For example, men like Woodrow Wilson had rejected Black enfranchisement. Just as telling, during and after World War I government elites had systematically opposed civil liberties protections and instead cracked down brutally on labor and anti-war protest. And they did so while ignoring or even excusing racist violence against African Americans. In short, earlier promoters of both the Constitution and market capitalism had hardly been defenders of negative liberty and free elections. Instead, the actual "anti-political" constitutional tradition had seemingly stood on the other side, blocking real democratization and criminalizing political dissent.

But in the new Cold War context, the concrete historical record of the American struggle for a constitutional democracy receded from view. American officials and commentators focused on accentuating the contrast between the United States and the Soviet Union, in ways that reframed the meaning of past events. A long line of American socialists may have understood their politics as driven by an effort to truly combine constitutionalism and democracy. Yet, in a world defined by Manichaean options, socialism in all its forms became reduced to what Truman described as the Soviet path—one of "terror . . . and the suppression of personal freedoms."

To the extent that any attention was given to previous socialist defenses of basic rights or of representative institutions, these defenses were understood as merely instrumental efforts to destabilize capitalist societies. The presumption was that all socialists, akin to the Bolsheviks in Russia, backed guarantees like free speech or free elections only as long as they were useful, and that they would abandon them as soon as they became a hindrance.

MODERNIZATION THEORY, CONSTITUTIONALISM, AND THE PROMISE OF SHARED PROSPERITY

In seeking to win hearts and minds globally, American policymakers thus increasingly framed the American model as the only genuine path for spreading internationally connected principles of post-imperial equality, civil libertarian protection, and representative government. This framing certainly emphasized the clear authoritarian limitations of Soviet and Chinese alternatives. Still, genuinely moving leaders and publics—especially in the decolonizing world—would require addressing the social problems raised by Odinga, Nkrumah, and other independence leaders.

American officials worried that, if given a choice between an impoverished but politically free society and a prosperous state socialist example, foreign peoples might willingly choose the latter. Consequently, defenders of American primacy had to demonstrate two things: Within new nation-states, they had to show that a domestic model of market capitalism and liberal constitutionalism in fact fulfilled welfarist demands. And internationally, they had to prove that the American-generated infrastructure for the emerging global economic system did not simply enhance the international position of US elites or direct wealth back to American coffers. This infrastructure also had to share American largesse with poorer nations. Indeed, to truly be in the world's interests, such global wealth promotion needed to proceed even in contexts where the US's immediate goals might countenance the domestic hoarding of resources.

Simply put, officials' desire to gain political buy-in across the Global South required a concrete demonstration of the economic benefits of both inclusion within the American orbit and the domestic replication of US legal-political institutions. In the words of Max Milliken, head of the Center for International Studies at MIT, "the best counter to Communist appeals is a demonstration that these same [development] problems are capable of solution by other means than those the Communists propose."[89]

In explaining just how the American model solved endemic problems of economic inequality through non-communist means, US officials converged especially on modernization theory as their driving account of economic development. Indeed, this account became perhaps the dominant discourse of early Cold War foreign policy, and a central way of articulating the specific material benefits of both market capitalism and liberal constitutionalism.[90]

For modernization theorists, "modernity" entailed the institutionalization of a set of values and practices broadly associated with the Enlightenment and concretely exemplified by mid-twentieth-century American life. But in keeping with American universalism, Shils—a key intellectual force in shaping modernization theory—declared that while modernity was "western" in origin, it offered a developmental path for all societies and thus could be "detached . . . from its geographical origins and locus." Crucially, officials and academics hoped that this path would appeal to decolonizing societies, precisely because it did not involve the type of unconstrained capitalism that marked the pre–New Deal United States. In a 1959 conference keynote address on the future of "new states" across Asia and Africa, Shils contended that "'modern' states are welfare states," "democratic and equalitarian, scientific, economically advanced and sovereign." In this way, the project of modernization offered the happy and natural consolidation of capitalism with representative institutions, a social safety net, and faith in technology and scientific progress.[91]

American policymakers appreciated that many in the Global South remained apprehensive about what modernization entailed: including the entrenchment within decolonizing societies of property rights, market structures, and US statecraft more generally. Following Odinga's concerns, publics worried that, to the extent that anyone domestically would benefit, it would be historic elites now able to tighten their grip on economic and political power. In response, officials and academics underscored that the United States was committed to ensuring that this did not occur. For starters, Shils noted that such an outcome would be profoundly incompatible with the ends of modernization. The American development vision was anti-aristocratic and sought to "dethrone" "the traditionally privileged from their positions of pre-eminent influence." In disestablishing such old feudal classes within foreign states, modernization aimed to create an "economy based on modern technology," "industrialized," and with a universal and "high standard of living."[92]

In pursuit of this end, academics and policymakers argued that foreign states, especially in the Global South, could not simply be left to sink or swim in a world of unequal economic conditions. Dean Acheson, secretary of state under Truman, declared that the US had no choice but to treat its national wealth as a resource to entrench the American model abroad and thereby make good on the material promises of modernization. Especially given the Soviet counterexample, the US had to "use material means to a non-material end."[93] Acheson considered it vital to have institutions—like the eventual US Agency for International Development (USAID)—providing financial and technical assistance to decolonizing states in the Global South. US investment across the world—in everything from foreign infrastructure to public education—should make clear the existence of a meaningful alternative to socialist expropriation.

Such assistance embodied genuine concern, at least for many of the individuals implementing these programs. But not unlike 1930s New Deal policies at home, assistance was joined to preservative ends as well, for the overarching economic system. By increasing the social welfare capacities of poorer nations, the US staved off their more radical calls for internal and external change, and thus mitigated potential dangers to an American-led international order.

Going hand in hand with development assistance, officials also attempted to distinguish American economic practices from past European empires. As Republican and future Secretary of State John Foster Dulles had declared as early as World War II, the American post-war aim was "growth without imperialism."[94] US officials understood themselves as instituting multilateral arrangements that aimed to embody constitutional principles of self-constraint, rather than an exercise in imperial plunder. While American political elites were central in the genesis of these legal rules, they alone did not determine their content. And these rules placed certain limitations on how the United States could itself operate on the global stage, emphasizing that the American model grounded capitalism in principles of the rule of law and shared prosperity widely.[95]

The early Bretton Woods institutions and the European Recovery Plan, better known as the Marshall Plan after George Marshall, Truman's secretary of state before Acheson, perhaps best illustrated this official story of American largesse and legal self-constraint. But it also illustrated how this narrative could be self-serving. As with future American practices in the Global South, the Marshall Plan and the Bretton Woods arrangements were premised on the free flow of American capital. In a deep sense, this ultimately created a system that clearly benefited the US, particularly in allowing American corporations to penetrate new markets, often exploitatively. For example, the Marshall Plan ultimately assisted only US-aligned European states. Among its key geostrategic aims were to strengthen internal support for non-communist political forces and to undermine the attractiveness of any broadly socialist alternative, even if not aligned with the Soviet Union.[96] Later development assistance in Latin America, Asia, and Africa aimed to win over wavering elites and publics, in keeping with Acheson's motivations. At the same time, this assistance reconstructed local markets and legal frameworks in ways pliable to both US investment and anti-Soviet security objectives. Whatever the claim of American officials, the United States still leveraged its dominant status to obtain economic and strategic dividends from its aid recipients.

Nonetheless, these institutions and initiatives were largely rulebound and multilateral. And they were rooted in the premise that the United States, as the dominant economic power, had a responsibility to guarantee a global financial system aimed at promoting reconstruction and development. Although driven by superpower rivalry with the Soviet Union, Acheson, Marshall, Dulles, and others did seek to demonstrate that the American intertwining of constitutionalism with market-driven economic growth improved conditions abroad and checked the old mercantilist tendencies of past empires.

In this way, American power could arguably be conceived of as fundamentally *non-imperial*. It was imagined as providing for the basic social welfare of the global community, and officials understood themselves as constitutionalizing meaningful checks into the international order. These checks—which preserved the overarching system—were meant to be universally operative, even when they pushed against immediate American self-interest. The hope among officials was that such a vision would avoid any need, in the words of longtime American diplomat and Ambassador Charles Bohlen, "to force 'the American way.'"[97] It would instead convince those abroad not only that American-style capitalist democracy brought prosperity, but also that—both in theory and in practice—US objectives genuinely aligned with the world's interests.[98]

RESONANCE AND AMBIVALENCE AMONG POSTCOLONIAL LEADERS

This vision of the meaning of American primacy—constitutionally self-limiting, racially egalitarian, and capitalist—paid real dividends. For a range of elites across Europe and even in the decolonizing world, the American commitment to bilateral assistance, multilateral economic and security institutions, and a global rights regime all sustained faith that American imperium actually might lift all boats. And, as the next chapters will discuss, by the 1950s dramatic US economic growth and racial reforms, however halting, also burnished the general appeal at home of this American "model."

From the perspective of some in decolonizing societies, the American model may have been incompletely pursued by white national politicians—whether within the US or as part of the American-led international order. But in principle, the framework might well be a worthy and broadly accessible global example.[99] And specific Soviet actions as the Cold War intensified further aided these perceptions—in particular, rising authoritarianism within the Soviet sphere of influence and the country's crushing of uprisings like the Hungarian revolution in 1956.

One early and telling illustration of the American allure can be found in the ultimate transfer of sovereignty from the US to the Philippines in 1946. The day established for Philippine independence from the US was July 4—the same date that, in 1902, Teddy Roosevelt had (prematurely) declared victory in the Philippine-American War. American officials no doubt used July 4 to emphasize that the transfer should be read as one in which a mature constitutional democracy completed the process of preparing another for self-determination, rather than one in which an imperial conqueror now had to give up power. The festivities even included elderly Filipino veterans of the 1890s revolutionary fight, suggesting that the US had somehow always been on the side of Philippine independence.

At least some Filipino elites embraced this framing. The newly elected

president, Manuel Roxas, who represented conservative and landed interests and enjoyed US backing, offered an inaugural address wrapped in
appreciation for American stewardship. "As we are masters of our own
destiny, so too must we bear all the consequences of our actions," Roxas
proclaimed. "But we have yet a greater bulwark today . . . the friendship
and devotion of America. . . . Our safest course is in the glistening wake
of America whose sure advance with mighty prow breaks for smaller
craft the waves of fear."[100] Along with significant elements of the landed
elite, Roxas had worked with the Japanese during World War II, holding
a cabinet position in "the Japanese-backed government." But after the
war, he was deemed a reliable American ally and had been exonerated
by MacArthur of accusations of collaboration.[101] Roxas now effectively
wrapped himself in the joint Filipino and American post-independence
project, in a way that clearly served his personal interests. Yet it also
spoke to a genuine sentiment—especially among those whom Roxas
represented—that the American model and American leadership could
bring Filipinos prosperity and well-being.

    That real potential appeal of the American model was also powerfully
illustrated, in somewhat less poetic language, by the great Indian independence figure and first prime minister, Jawaharlal Nehru, who visited
the United States in 1949 on a three-week goodwill tour. As a symbolic
matter, his October 1949 visit with President Truman and speech to
Congress were important signs of the changing times: an Asian leader of
a newly independent non-white polity being hosted at the highest levels
of American government. In this way, the visit spoke to white American
recognition of the need, in a world overwhelmingly composed of non-
white peoples, to demonstrate racially egalitarian respect.

    For his part, Nehru went out of his way to distinguish between En-
gland's and other European states' destructive colonial imagination and
the new anti-colonial global vision he presented Americans as sharing.
Indeed, his remarks were noteworthy for the extent to which they were
infused with reverence for the 1787 Constitution and for the creedal
account of US national identity. Nehru described the United States as
fundamentally unlike European empires and as having a political project far more in line with India's own. Namely, both countries were born
through an independence struggle *against* imperial domination: "Like
you, we have achieved our freedom through a revolution." Nehru explained that in part due to this common origin, he viewed his visit to
the United States as motivated by the desire "to learn something of your
great achievements."[102]

Indeed, Nehru focused in particular on the value of the 1787 American Constitution. He read the document in classically creedal terms: as giving real teeth to the ideals of the Declaration of Independence. As such, he argued that, as part of a global project of mutual exchange, India and other countries across the Global South could learn much from the eighteenth-century framers. He described the likes of Madison and Hamilton as "torchbearers of freedom, not only for this country but for the world."[103]

Nehru spent little time on the differences in design between the recently drafted Indian constitution and the American example—the Indian text was notable for its length as well as its formal incorporation of extensive socioeconomic principles.[104] He instead continued by asserting that in "drafting the Constitution of the Republic of India, we have been greatly influenced by your own Constitution," mentioning the shared foundational commitments to equality, civil liberties, due process, and federalism. Nehru especially highlighted the similarities between the American and Indian constitutional preambles, with the Indian document also starting "We, the people of India"—a variation on the now familiar 1787 phrase. As Nehru declared, "you will recognize in these words . . . an echo of the great voices of the founders of your Republic. You will see that though India may speak to you in a voice that you may not immediately recognize . . . yet that voice . . . strongly resembles what you have often heard before."[105]

In important ways, Nehru's speech embraced much of the US national self-conception. Like American officials, he underlined the non-imperial nature of US power by highlighting how Americans operated from a principle of inclusive constitutionalism rather than colonial dependency. And he presented American legal-political institutions as an appropriate example for the world because they embodied globally universal values of civil and political liberty.

In fact, such references by independence leaders to a shared American and Asian or African anti-imperial heritage became more and more common over the ensuing decade. Perhaps the most striking invocation of shared anti-imperial history came in 1955, when Indonesia's revolutionary leader and first president, Sukarno, opened the famed Bandung Conference of Asian and African states. American diplomats had told Indonesian officials that the conference was set to begin on the 180th anniversary of Paul Revere's midnight ride, which informed settler militias of advancing British forces prior to the battles of Lexington and Concord.[106] Inspired by the fact, Sukarno declared in his speech, "the battle against colonialism has been a long one, and do you know that today is a famous anniversary in that battle? On the eighteenth day of April, one thousand seven hundred and seventy five, just one hundred and eighty years ago, Paul Revere rode at midnight through the New England countryside, warning of the approach of British troops and of the opening of the American War of Independence, the first success-ful anti-colonial war in history." In this way, Sukarno presented post–World War II independence struggles as the historic completion of a global anti-imperial project, with the United States as the effort's first victory: "But remember, that battle which began 180 years ago is not yet completely won, and it will not have been completely won until we can survey this our own world, and can say that colonialism is dead."[107]

Still, neither Sukarno nor Nehru, the central organizers of the Band-ung Conference, agreed with every facet of American institutional life, and both were deeply committed to Cold War neutrality. Indeed, during his 1949 trip, Nehru refused to simply parrot American judg-ments about the necessary connection between constitutionalism and market capitalism—one of the tensions the trip exposed between his and Truman's visions of the world. Even when speaking before Con-gress, Nehru made clear the potential need to break from market-based assumptions. He declared, not unlike the Kenyan leader Odinga later, that while India, in keeping with American constitutional ideals, had "achieved political freedom," the task before it was "to remove . . . pov-erty by greater production, more equitable distribution, better edu-cation and better health."[108] All of this would require a massive state-building effort,[109] joined to a willingness to upend capitalist property rights and relations of production, for instance by ensuring "that the fruits of cultivation should go to the tiller of the soil."[110]

Much to Truman's chagrin, Nehru refused during the visit to budge from India's position of Cold War neutrality. And Truman in turn re-fused to offer economic assistance. The refusal was a significant disap-pointment to Nehru, and it further reinforced global worries that—whatever US officials claimed—the American-led order might not prove a clear break from the old sphere-of-influence imperial past.

Sukarno also was wary of neocolonial politics, including in the form of US meddling. And both Sukarno and Nehru rejected American ideas of the country's exceptionalism and thus its unique capacity to spread values of self-government. In a sense, someone like Nehru sought a new global pathway that combined constitutional restraint with socialist eco-nomic possibility—a pathway that treated both the United States and the Soviet Union as ideological resources rather than rigid ideological constraints. As the legal scholar Madhav Khosla writes of Nehru's vision, "what India required was an adaptation of the Soviet experiment—a commitment to socioeconomic transformation without violence to civil rights," and thus "through the means of democratic constitutionalism."[111]

Indeed, India and other similarly situated countries effectively sought to transcend the categories of East and West, and to imagine a new and truly global universalism—embodied by both the United States and more recent decolonizing nations, all able to learn from each other as equals.[112] As the Cold War began, and even despite Truman's refusal of economic aid to countries that declined client status, postcolonial leaders maintained a degree of hope in the United States. For this reason, in the early to mid-1950s, someone like Sukarno still critically distinguished between the United States and the Dutch authorities that had previously ruled Indonesia.

In retrospect, Sukarno's speech at Bandung, referencing Paul Revere's midnight ride, was especially poignant. American officials would eventually support his overthrow, out of their desire to have a more pliable government in the strategic Southeast Asian state.[113] The resulting dictatorship of General Suharto, again with US complicity,[114] then engaged in what the historian Stuart Schrader has called "an anticommunist genocide of staggering proportions in 1965 and 1966, killing at least half a million people and imprisoning another million."[115]

Tellingly, in the 1940s and early 1950s both Nehru and Sukarno genuinely appeared to see the United States as part of a shared universalist and anti-imperial story, even as they refused client status. In a sense, their focus on a common US and Indian or Indonesian move from colony to independent nation-state spoke to the enduring ideological strength of the American language of constitutionalism, which framed the country's global power. The North American colonies had once used the writing of a new constitution, in part, to proclaim their independence from a European empire and to assert their equal sovereignty on the world stage. Now, postcolonial states across Asia and Africa associated constitutions with similar ends.

These parallels gave real cultural resonance to the US embrace of the written constitution specifically as the privileged mode of domestic and international governance. As discussed above, such resonance existed even within the territorial United States, partly explaining why many Native American nations implemented New Deal–era tribal constitutions—however top-down—to proclaim their own sovereign status. Internationally, whatever the substantive differences between the constitutional systems in the US and in the Global South—or between capitalist and socialist theories of economy and democracy—the American focus on constitutionalism thus fit with the decolonizing times.

Constitutionalism and the Persistence of Imperial Violence

Despite the resonance key postcolonial leaders felt with the US, the American fusing of primacy and creedal constitutionalism remained caught in the same tensions that had long defined accounts of the country's power, both on the American frontier and abroad. On the one hand, the US had committed to the promotion of formal equality, shared wealth, and legal self-constraint as the governing values of the global order. And this commitment was marked by America's willingness to submit itself to new multilateral institutions as well as to invest in development projects abroad.

On the other hand, this period was filled with gross US violations of those very values. These included wartime atrocities and mass killings; the embargoing and economic immiseration of socialist-leaning societies; anti-democratic overthrows; political assassinations; and support for friendly dictatorships, even when those dictatorships carried out extreme mass violence, as in Indonesia. The US found itself persistently departing from the very creedal constitutional principles that its officials asserted were the primary benefit of American authority—a point ultimately brought home to the domestic audience by the war in Vietnam.

PUERTO RICO, RESISTANCE, AND RACIALIZATION IN UNIVERSALIST RHETORIC

One can appreciate these embedded tensions—between spreading self-government and preserving hegemonic power—in the American post-war decision on the status of Puerto Rico. In a decolonizing era, American rule of the island amounted to a significant source of "anti-American propaganda," according to State Department officials.[116] Moreover, by 1950 Puerto Rico was in the middle of an armed uprising led by independence leaders like Pedro Albizu Campos. Yet, for all the focus on how American power was unlike European imperialism, granting Puerto Rico independence was effectively a non-starter in Washington, DC. FDR had called Puerto Rico the US's "island shield," protecting American control over the Panama Canal along with its hemispheric dominance.[117] With the British example very much in mind, US naval leadership referred to it as nothing less than "our Gibraltar in [the] Caribbean."[118]

In the end, US officials sought to square this circle by granting Puerto Rico "commonwealth" status under continued American sovereign control. As the political scientist Pedro Cabán notes, this shift provided greater internal autonomy and self-government for the island, but on grounds that were "always provisional," since Congress never "relinquish[ed] its constitutionally delegated powers over the territories."[119]

Critically, officials shaped the move to commonwealth status again around the politics of constitution-writing. The US once more created a process by which Puerto Ricans would draft their own constitution through a convention and then ratify that document by popular referendum. Only then would Congress approve the new government. In keeping with the American model, US officials required the document to embody "a republican form of government and . . . include a bill of rights."[120] And while the resulting text did entail more expansive socioeconomic protections than the American Constitution, it nonetheless largely mirrored the 1787 framework. It starts with "We, the people of Puerto Rico," incorporates key elements of the US Bill of Rights and the Fourteenth Amendment's equal protection clause, and then provides for an executive governorship, a bicameral legislature with the branches named the Senate and the House of Representatives, and a Supreme Court.[121]

On the one hand, Puerto Rican participation in this process, and the overwhelming ratification support for the document, indicated how the American constitutionalist language of power spoke to the times and reaffirmed principles of self-government. But on the other hand, the intensity of the simultaneous US military crackdown against the armed Puerto Rican independence movement underscored the linkage between the provision of American-style constitutionalism and the suppression of anti-colonial resistance.[122] As Cabán concludes, constitution-making was, in many ways, an effort to get Puerto Rican "consent to their continued colonial subjugation."[123]

In fact, this was how Vito Marcantonio, who represented a heavily Puerto Rican New York Congressional district, viewed the American approach. He had been one of Albizu Campos's lawyers when the independence leader was convicted in the 1930s of conspiracy to overthrow the US government.[124] And he pushed repeatedly not just for Puerto Rican independence, but for independence on genuinely *decolonial* terms that would liberate local communities from economic dependence and immiseration.

Under Marcantonio's reading, Puerto Ricans might be willing to accede to the half-loaf of greater autonomy under persistent American colonial rule in part because formal independence offered its own predations. He thus believed that independence had to go hand in hand with reparative economic and political commitments from the United States: "Puerto Rico, taken as the booty of war from Spain," Marcantonio declared, "has been successively ruined." The only solution was to tie formal independence to a series of truly transformative measures. In the independence bill he championed before Congress, these measures, as his biographer Gerald Meyer writes, "provided that Puerto Rico be indemnified and no tariff be levied on Puerto Rican products shipped to the United States, and . . . that no other restrictions be placed on the importation of Puerto Rican products or on Puerto Rican immigration to the United States."[125] Not unlike Nkrumah later, Marcantonio expressed critical concern with evolving modes of imperial domination — even as a territory's legal status shifted — and so focused on economic redistribution and open migration as centerpieces of meaningful decolonization.

None of this, of course, was remotely on the table for Truman and those around him. Indeed, Marcantonio's approach — including its rejection of restrictive border policies — was more or less the opposite of what US policymakers had imposed on the Philippines in the 1930s and 1940s as part of its independence process. In that context, while US extractive practices continued to shape the local economy, bills like 1934s' Tydings-McDuffie Act aggressively controlled Filipino movement. As for Puerto Rico, the American refusal of both formal independence and the tools to enable real economic autonomy underscored the limitations of the US brand of constitution-promotion as a framework for actual self-determination.

Ultimately, this type of uneasy fit between US words and actions made it difficult for defenders of American primacy during the Cold War to fully establish the legitimacy of global authority to non-US publics, whether in Puerto Rico or elsewhere. The US did gain significant consent from decolonizing societies. But it also experienced sustained opposition, on terms not unlike those presented by Nkrumah or implied by Nehru. Such opposition meant that the Cold War period was marked by periods of active resistance in the Global South, with one hot spot often replacing another in a continual cycle of pacification, disaffection, and crisis. In a deep sense, this cycle was hard-baked into the structure of how foreign policymakers sought to marry universalist claims—especially about capitalist democracy and liberal constitutionalism—with the projection of coercive US power.

Indeed, for all their growing racial enlightenment, American officials struggled with the same questions that had structured interventionism going back to the Spanish-Cuban-American War and its aftermath. Just as half a century earlier, post–World War II officials needed to explain why the US had the authority—given its ostensible commitment to non-white self-determination—to reconstruct unwilling societies abroad. In particular, why should American notions tightly yoking together market capitalism and liberal constitutionalism predominate? Officials may have sought to operate through soft power, to win hearts and minds and to gain consent for an American-led order. But what if foreign leaders and publics remained opposed? What if they held firm to institutional alternatives and regional orderings that they believed were compatible with local self-determination, but that Americans viewed as inconsistent with international stability?

As before, the basic response was interventionist. And during the Cold War period, this entailed military operations across the globe, oftentimes covert—including, as the political theorist Mark Neocleous notes, "in Greece, Italy, France, Turkey, Macedonia, Ukraine, Cambodia, Indonesia, China, Korea, Burma, Vietnam, Thailand, Ecuador, Chile, Argentina, Brazil, Guatemala, Costa Rica, Cuba, the Dominican Republic, Uruguay, Bolivia, Grenada, Paraguay, Nicaragua, El Salvador, the Philippines, Honduras, Haiti, Venezuela, Panama, Angola, Ghana, Congo, South Africa, Albania, Lebanon, Libya, Somalia, Ethiopia, Afghanistan, Iraq, and many more, and many of these more than once."[126]

As Neocleous references, the Philippines too became a site, yet again, of ongoing military confrontation. While the new president, Manuel Roxas, was extolling "the friendship and devotion of America," his government faced an intense peasant uprising known as the Hukbalahap Rebellion. The rebellion was spurred by continuing discontent with the extractive practices of the landed elite, seen also as Japanese collaborators during the war. It would take a decade of fighting and extensive "economic, military, and technical assistance from the United States government" before the rebellion was quelled.[127]

In a way that remained consistent with past European powers, US offi-

cials often fell back on accounts of American cultural exceptionalism—
and implicitly ethno-racial developmentalist narratives—to defend this
continuous assertion of international police power. Indeed, this tendency was present in Luce's own initial depiction of the American Century, which mirrored the earlier views of David Jayne Hill or Woodrow
Wilson: Americans enjoyed a right to supervise foreign states and to
intervene whenever US interests—read as the world's interests—were
endangered, precisely because Americans were nothing less than, in
Luce's words, "inheritors of all the great principles of Western civilization."[128] This language of exceptionalism placed US policymakers in
a long line of European imperial officials who had also defended their
nations' authority based on France's or England's presumed cultural distinctiveness and historic destiny. Critically, this meant that, even in the
post–World War II era of decolonization, the connection of a constitutionally grounded American universalism with racial hierarchy did not
truly disappear.[129] Although almost always implicit, it remained essential to justifying the expanding Cold War politics of a continuous and
permanent US police power.

This fact is most powerfully underscored by modernization theory. Despite Shils's claims to its universalist essence, the approach carried with it many of the historic Wilsonian ideas of racial tutelage.[130]
During these years, modernization theorists, both in the American
social sciences and in government, did not simply emphasize the origins of modernity as Western. Following Wilson, they also routinely
described the world as on a relatively linear path from traditional to
modern society.[131]

As discussed previously, modern societies combined liberal-democratic
constitutionalism with economic growth, urbanization, and high educational attainment. By contrast, the historian Nils Gilman writes that
traditional societies were understood by advocates of modernization
theory to be "inward looking, inert, passive toward nature, supersti-
tious, fearful of change, and economically simple." Moreover, the overarching American model was depicted as the ideal historical endpoint
of modernity. Meanwhile, the totality of the non-European world was
generally presented as "traditional."[132] For this reason, officials and academics often dismissed opposition to American market and security
prerogatives in the Global South as motivated by "traditionalist" fears
and by cultural immaturity.

Those like Nkrumah and Odinga viewed this dismissal as evincing a
profound and racialized disrespect for non-white societies. It suggested

that US officials, whatever the creedal claims, at the end of the day remained unable to take local demands seriously on their own terms. Politicians in Washington instead remained wedded to treating previously colonized peoples as instruments in the service of American power.

In a deep sense, this way of dichotomizing the world—between free Western and modern societies and unfree traditional ones—inevitably generated profound pushback. It helped to produce the basic paradox noted above: throughout the Cold War, promoting creedal constitutionalism abroad often seemed to *require*—as a matter of sustained practice—the undermining of real self-determination on the ground. Some leaders, like Nehru, may have invoked the universalist promise of American national identity. But others saw in US rhetoric—especially that fusing of modernization, capitalism, and liberal constitutionalism— an imperial continuity: a racially inscribed project of material extraction and political dependency. All of this meant that while US policymakers presented the spread of an American-led order as operating through global consent, the actual process of entrenchment often bore very little relationship to that rosy self-presentation. Indeed, the specific joining of constitutionalism and American primacy proceeded as much through coercion and lawlessness as it did through legal self-restraint and mutual collaboration.

INTERNATIONAL POLICE POWER
IN A MANICHAEAN WORLD

A series of related factors reinforced this reality of increasing extralegal coercion. First, US policymakers often contended that the American position as both the creator and the ultimate protector of the new international order brought with it profound responsibilities. In particular, for the system as a whole to generate security and prosperity, the US—given its status as the dominant superpower—would still at times have to step outside the terms of mutual self-constraint in order to exercise international police power. As the first nation among equals, it would face situations that required unilateral action to preserve the system as a whole. As Dulles declared as early as 1945 about the soon-to-be UN Security Council, "if [a permanent member] vetoed action to prevent aggression in the Western Hemisphere, we would be entirely free to use force."[133] Americans could not let unflagging rule-following undermine the nation's security and its responsibility to both neighbors and the world. And precisely because of the country's underlying values and constitutional commitments, those abroad could remain confident that the US would exercise this power judiciously. Such action would be taken only with the utmost seriousness and deliberation, pursued exclusively as a last resort.

Unfortunately, the Manichaean vision that politicians like Truman imposed on the world—capitalist democracy versus socialist tyranny, liberal modernity versus authoritarian traditionalism—fed the temptation to turn ever more to coercive and discretionary means. Policymakers often interpreted local opposition to US security goals or postcolonial arguments about "neocolonialism" through a combined prism of Cold War Soviet rivalry and non-white cultural immaturity.[134] And at times they would even treat such local pushback as a potentially existential threat to the overall order itself.[135] Thus, in the service of protecting creedal constitutionalism, the US increasingly saw the need to deviate from actual principles of constraint and to operate both unilaterally and in violation of basic legal precepts. With respect to the Soviet Union specifically, officials contended—with reason—that Stalin and his successors spread their sphere of influence through violence and terror. But these arguments also ignored the real and deep unpopularity of many American policies. The US imposition of market relations and related governing institutions and its sabotage of redistributive reforms, viewed as too socialistic, tended to strengthen the power of propertied elites—whatever the claims of modernization theorists.

Even worse, the American Manichaean approach validated fighting the Soviet threat, which American officials perceived everywhere, with the counterviolence of coups, assassinations, and covert operations.[136] Such validation at times went so far that acts of American violence themselves fed into defenses of US moral authority: violence highlighted an ethical bind facing the United States, with the country depicted as an exceptional nation forced against its own actual preferences to employ dirty political means in a world of disorder and threat. The discomfort Americans experienced with this harsh reality allegedly showcased how the country was fundamentally both moral and true to its own constitutional values.[137] The overall result was a US approach to the world in which creedal constitutional promotion became seemingly inseparable from unilateralism and discretionary violence.

Further reinforcing these dynamics, the American program—marrying constitutionalism and primacy—could easily collapse into clearly racialized and authoritarian justifications for the direct subversion of democracy itself. US scholars and officials did wrestle with why their policies—which were in keeping with the world's interests—often met with such profound skepticism on the ground. But the common turn to "traditionalism" as an answer led in deeply anti-democratic directions. And Washington's fears of totalitarian pathology under unconstrained majoritarianism devolved, at times, into outright disavowal of the very principles of electoral democracy and majority rule.

In explaining away resistance, some commentators and officials—especially those associated with modernization theory—held that, in the Global South, the transition from traditional to modern society might be threatened if local communities too hastily embraced free elections. Not unlike how Wilson had once defended Black disenfranchisement under Jim Crow, such societies supposedly did not have the cultural and economic prerequisites for mass publics to exercise majority rule wisely or to avoid demagoguery. As Nils Gilman details, this strain of analysis maintained that anti-Americanism derived from the dysfunction, in the Global South, of mass democratic pressure combined with economic underdevelopment. This especially combustible combination could lead societies to the "pathological" form of modernity epitomized by the Soviet Union.[138]

Critically, these arguments countenanced delaying electoral democracy and instead imposing pliable autocrats throughout Asia, Latin America, and Africa. Such autocrats would serve internally as stewards of modernization: promoting property rights, literacy, and technical and administrative expertise, even if they constrained political liberty. As such, US-supported autocrats would facilitate the preconditions for both market capitalism and liberal constitutionalism.

Oftentimes, the constitutional imagination was joined to these rationalizations for what amounted to American lawlessness. Even in the extreme case of Indonesia, the historian Geoffrey Robinson notes that US officials actually defended General Suharto's "move against Sukarno as 'constitutional' and 'bloodless,' as though it were quite unrelated to the violence that preceded it and was still going on in some parts of the country."[139] Around the world, the American interventionism repeatedly resulted in de-democratization and mass rights infringements. And yet, violations tended to be subsumed within an official story about the overarching establishment, under American auspices, of self-governing and constitutionally wedded states. In effect, US actions—even those that directly violated stated legal principles—were always imagined as still in line with constitutionalism. And when this official narrative proved implausible, constitutional violations were reduced either to mere aberrations or actually to the fault of the communities themselves, due to local cultural limitations.[140]

The result was a remarkable duality that shaped the American-led order. For key elites in the Global South, the American example did remain alluring despite its interventionist damage. Indeed, leaders from Turkey to post-Sukarno Indonesia often internalized judgments about traditionalism and modernity, and so accepted implicitly racialized development narratives about the path to prosperity.[141] Despite its internal tensions, that 1946 transfer of sovereignty from the US to the Philippines mentioned above offered another noteworthy illustration of the willingness of some in the Global South to embrace American leadership.

Even for those across the non-European world that rejected these narratives, the aspirational ideal of the American model—despite its flaws—had genuinely emancipatory potential, especially when juxtaposed against Soviet dictatorship. Thus, for all the profound violence and real democracy *demotion* during the post–World War II years, US officials succeeded in disseminating liberal constitutionalism as effectively the emerging "default design choice,"[142] especially for nation-states in the American orbit.

In fact, the American "constitutional consultant" became a common figure of Cold War politics. As the political scientist Barbara Perry writes, US-aligned states engaged in constitution-writing would often "contact the United States Embassy in that country" and then the request for "consultants" would be "channeled through the State Department or USIA [US Information Agency], which" would reach out to "one or several" academics and lawyers "in the network."[143] By the late twentieth century, such consultancies had become one coordinated mechanism for linking together the academy and the US security world, with "consultants" spreading the wisdom of the American model across Latin America, Asia, and Africa.[144]

For those abroad, this meant that an uneasy combination of resistance and buy-in marked the outside perspective of the American project. Many had a degree of faith in, or at least acceptance of, the overarching discourse of shared constitutionalism, with its domestic arrangements, multilateral institutions, and bilateral investment projects. But at the same time, there existed a wariness of the country's international police power and economic dominance. And none of this altered the essentially imperial nature of American primacy, whatever officials held to the contrary. For all the claims that the United States was not an empire, policymakers nonetheless effectively presumed that the country—alone in the world—enjoyed a permanent international police power, which brought with it the right to reconstruct foreign societies whenever it deemed necessary.

In this way, creedal constitutionalism served two functions. It articulated how and why American power could be constrained through commitments to equal formal sovereignty and to the international rule of law. But it also served as a constant prompt to see potential threats everywhere and to step outside legal constraints—to refashion the world in an American image, independent of the demands of local populations. David Jayne Hill had argued that the United States was not imperial because it was constitutional. But the country's imperium operated by grounding an exceptional right to intervene in the language of constitutional legitimacy—a type of imperial constitutionalism. In this way, the version of the creedal constitution that American officials promoted abroad wove both rights expansion and authoritarian violence—both legality and lawlessness—into the post-war international order.

Conclusion: The Cold Warrior as Constitutional Believer

Through the New Deal struggles of the 1930s, US political elites around FDR—not to mention social movement leaders and activists—held strikingly divergent views about the continuing utility of the existing federal constitutional system. But national policymakers across both political parties closed ranks dramatically and relatively quickly, whatever those past disagreements. As officials embraced the American Century, they similarly embraced a now established constitutional language for justifying global power. For a converging and bipartisan governing elite, this account of national meaning and purpose was no longer simply the leading way, among many possible ways, to make sense of the country. Instead, it became elevated to effectively the only true narrative.

Furthermore, in this Cold War context the focus on constitutionalism as the discourse of American power had real implications for cultural and political life. It embedded a basic duality between violence and constraint into the post-war order. It made creedal constitutionalism more politically rigid: fused to defenses of market capitalism and suspicions of unchecked democracy. And the project of the American Century spread Constitution worship into elite pockets previously impervious to its charms.

Again, for the sociologist Seymour Martin Lipset in 1963, it was "unthinkable" to replace the Constitution, because the document was nothing less than the "supreme symbol of authority," a galvanizing core of American nationalism and identity. Moreover, this status was justified, given the constitutional system's vital importance in promoting exactly the type of "democratic stability" that made the US a model to other postcolonial states. Just as Shils had venerated the American "antipolitical tradition," Lipset—also a significant modernization theorist—seemed to embrace how the Constitution defused politics, insulated market capitalism from counterproductive attacks, and constrained democratic excess through extensive veto points and rights guarantees. Indeed, the very fact that the constitutional order was "beyond the direct reach of the elected representatives and . . . not easily amended" helped to "institutionalize separation of the *source* from the *agencies* of authority" and so preserve the republic over the centuries.[145]

Like Shils, Lipset also worried that, as societies in the Global South made the transition from traditionalism to modernity, decolonizing publics might well proceed too rashly in attempting to address endemic problems of poverty and inequality. Especially if their constitutional systems allowed for relatively unconstrained majoritarianism (exacerbating the "demagogic license afforded by universal suffrage"), the results could descend into socialist tyranny—even if unintentionally. Avoiding these pitfalls would be hard, as democratic maturity was a long road, something that could not "be created by fiat." Still, one could look upon the US Constitution as offering a meaningful example of how to combine constitutionalism and democracy.[146]

Lipset's general sensibility was hardly unfamiliar in American history. After all, related claims had been the bread and butter of conservative and business elites during the Gilded Age. But Lipset was no pro-business conservative, championing constitutional loyalty to shut down labor activism or social welfare programs in the vein of those earlier proponents. As a student, he had been the National Chairman of the Young People's Socialist League, the official youth arm of the Socialist Party.[147] He presumably came of age in the 1930s and 1940s well aware of SPA critiques of just those anti-democratic elements of the Constitution he now praised. For multiple generations of aligned reformers, the existing constitutional structure had imposed overwhelming hurdles to the implementation of labor and racial reform. Rather than promoting "democratic stability," these hurdles exacerbated social crises and worked hand in glove with state-sanctioned violence against those marginalized and poor. And while Lipset remained a New Deal supporter, he now appeared to echo at least some elements of past pro-business constitutional argument, offered in the 1920s by the likes of the American Bar Association, the National Security League, and various "professional patriots."

Lipset's shift spoke to a crucial ideological turn within academic and policy-making circles—and a distinctly American response to the changing global conditions under which the US state operated. In the wake of Nazi defeat and European imperial collapse, Lipset and others believed in the profound importance of American leadership to ensuring international peace and prosperity. Given the realities of Soviet competition and non-white decolonization, he worried about the world's prospects if some version of the American legal-political order did not become the global standard. Like nearly all those in the postwar governing elite, Lipset embraced a Manichaean version of both the American Century and the Cold War—and thus implicitly a romance about the meaning of the country.

This romance became deeply bound up with a creedal constitutional story—which politicians, academics, and commentators told themselves and others—that presumed inherent, if not always evident, American goodness. And with this story came the prerogative and the moral worthiness of imperium abroad. New Dealers in the 1930s like Thurman Arnold may have reached a pragmatic détente with the Constitution. But Cold Warriors two decades later had now committed to the text wholeheartedly, and often with deep emotional connection. For all their differences with the old National Security Leaguers, they carried into the American Century many of the affective bonds and visions of national attachment that had been asserted—and resisted—so strenuously during and after World War I.

CHAPTER 11

Red Scare Constitutionalism

Though now long forgotten, the years 1945 and 1946, immediately following World War II, witnessed an explosion of open class conflict. As the historian George Lipsitz reminds us, "more strikes took place in the twelve months after V-J Day than in any comparable period in American history."[1] Abroad, political elites promoted an official American model—a combination of market capitalism and liberal constitutionalism—as the linchpin of the American Century and the ideal endpoint of political modernity. But at home, that same model found itself mired in industrial strife and white racial violence.

In many ways, the mid-1940s echoed the years between 1917 and 1919, when widespread social upheaval led radical organizations like the Industrial Workers of the World (IWW) to see dramatic change on the horizon.[2] As Truman's own attorney general, and future Supreme Court justice, Tom Clark concluded bluntly in 1946, "the aftermath of war has brought its characteristic cynicism, disillusionment and lawlessness"—effectively analogizing the times to that earlier period of institutional uncertainty and violent struggle.[3]

Yet by the late 1950s these elite fears had disappeared almost entirely from political discourse. Government officials and business conservatives proudly proclaimed that, in the United States, working-class consciousness did not exist. Instead, Americans of all backgrounds shared a common cultural unity.

How did governing elites during the 1950s so successfully entrench their version of creedal constitutionalism that they saw virtually no sustained ideological dissent within mass politics? Relatedly, what transformative effects did this process have for existing social movements—especially labor and Black activism—that had long been spaces associated with radical opposition, including around the Constitution?

The previous chapter argued that the American drive for global primacy facilitated an elite policy-making consensus around a specific vision of constitutional democracy. In the following pages, I contend that the same imperial backdrop, especially given Cold War rivalry, had profound domestic consequences as well. In particular, this backdrop pressed officials to seek conditions at home in which no meaningful ideological competitor to the official American model existed.

Just as they did overseas, policymakers pursued this project domestically through a combination of consent and coercion. They realized that in order to create a genuinely stable framework within the United States, they would need significant buy-in from society at large—especially from white working-class and African American constituencies. This buy-in called for a set of political and economic reforms that aligned with claims around the moral and material benefits of the consolidating order. But it also necessitated establishing, through a sustained climate of repression, that seeking radical alternatives carried extreme political and personal costs.

It should be noted that government actors embraced both reformist and repressive dimensions out of a real faith in the essential goodness of the Cold War project and profound concerns over threats to it. And this faith included, for many, a growing commitment to the underlying substantive reforms as a fulfillment of the country's true meaning and destiny. Yet, as with the circulation of American power on the global stage, the consequence was a similar—and similarly uneasy—combination of rights-respecting legality and coercive violence.

In this chapter, I focus in particular on governing elites' top-down imposition of ideological conformity. The discussion begins by detailing the extent to which the immediate post–World War II moment remained marked by real ideological conflict and fluidity. At the time, movement activists raised foundational questions about American primacy, the necessity of a Cold War, and even creedal constitutionalism itself.

I then turn to how, during the second "Red Scare," government officials fostered a climate of fear and suspicion as a way to suppress all opposition to the American state, and to related ideological commitments to capitalist democracy and global power. Just as during World War I, officials linked such an effort with the promotion of mass displays of political loyalty built around Constitution worship, perhaps most concretely embodied in the Freedom Train, a joint business-government enterprise that toured the country during the late 1940s.

It would take more than just this heightened climate of repression and ideological conformity to convince key social movement leaders, especially within labor and Black politics, to line up behind the Cold War project. Chapter 12 thus explores the reformist and inclusive dimensions of the post-war settlement, highlighting the consent-based conditions promoting bottom-up social support. For all the concerns with US state crackdowns, many activists were rightly suspicious of the Soviet brand of authoritarian politics. They also increasingly saw themselves as stakeholders within an emerging domestic socioeconomic and racial order — one that provided their constituencies with real improvements.

Still, in reading the repressive and reformist aspects of this story together, this chapter counters a conventional interpretation in legal scholarship of the Red Scare. Constitutional scholars tend to present the late 1940s and 1950s crackdowns—not unlike Japanese internment—as a failure to abide by constitutional principles. For such scholars, the country today is more committed to civil libertarian values precisely because it has come to look back on that period as a *violation* of the Constitution.[4]

But this standard approach ignores the centrality of constitutional consolidation and promotion to the terms of American post-war imperium — including its domestic developments. Thus, the conventional narrative insufficiently accounts for *why* these years marked a high tide both for the specific and genuine worship of liberal constitutionalism — including invocations of American faith in free speech and personal liberty—*and* for national security excess. This chapter therefore extends into the domestic context the basic analysis of how a context of American overseas primacy helped join together constitutionalism and discretionary violence.

In short, both the external and the internal realms of mid-century US constitutional politics were marked by parallel dynamics. The project of American power bound together reformist and coercive elements, with Cold Warriors working assiduously to impose, abroad and at home, an American legal-political model. Internally, this entailed militant Red Scare tactics, with key figures, like Truman, believing—in terms familiar from a half century of national security politics dating back to World War I—that repressive means served constitutionalist ends.

Dissensus at the Dawn of the Cold War

Why did American officials, commentators, and business leaders all feel
such a pressing imperative to impose a systematic Cold War constitutional consensus? To appreciate the urgency, it is essential to revisit the
climate of social conflict in 1945 and 1946. These were years marked by
real social and political uncertainty as well as by activist projects—for
instance within the peace movement and the Black counter-public—
that challenged the appropriateness of American primacy as well as central tenets of the presumptive US model.

POST-WAR LABOR STRUGGLE AND WHITE VIOLENCE

Unsurprisingly, much immediate post-war discontent stemmed from
the destabilization of the economy that followed the end of the war. Production demands during the war had provided jobs and wage increases—
due to the need for overtime work—to countless Americans. But the
return to peacetime conditions brought spiraling unemployment, with
one in four workers hired to fill wartime needs now left unemployed.
In October 1945, two million people were jobless and real incomes had
dipped by 15 percent. To make matters worse, millions of soldiers were
returning to the country. They too would be competing for a seemingly
shrinking supply of jobs, alongside women who had joined the workforce during the war.[5]

   In this context, commentators wondered if the United States might
be plunged into a new depression. In fact, a September 1946 *Fortune*
survey of public opinion found that 73 percent of respondents pre-
dicted that the country would have another "widespread depression"
within five years.[6] Not unrelatedly, spontaneous strikes—in many cases,
unauthorized by union leaders—spread nationwide and affected everything from the steel, oil, and auto industries to electronics and public
works. In 1946, general strikes hit numerous cities small and large, with
Houston, Rochester, Pittsburgh, Oakland, Stamford, and Lancaster
among the sites of mass labor protest.[7]

   At the same time, the post–World War II moment also mimicked
1919 in that the conclusion of both wars coincided with an eruption of
intense white racial violence and lawlessness. It may have been the case
that white national politicians—invested in spreading global power
during a decolonizing era—were voicing support for racial ameliorism
more broadly than their counterparts had in the years following World

War I. But regardless of the rhetoric in Washington, explicit and virulent white supremacist sentiment remained widespread among white constituents across the country, with returning Black veterans often bearing the brunt of this animus.

For example, "local public-housing authorities" in the North "often gave preferences to veterans," *including* African Americans, in housing placements. This meant that Black veterans found themselves moving into the region's previously all-white communities; they were thus effectively at the forefront of efforts to desegregate neighborhoods. The results could be brutal, as in Chicago in 1947 when a white mob stoned police officers and attacked African American passersby at the Fernwood Park Homes.[8]

The white response to returning Black veterans in the South was even more extreme, with incidents across the region of whites physically assaulting or gunning down African Americans seeking to register to vote or asserting their rights in other ways. As just one example, in 1946 in Athens, Alabama, "a mob of up to 2,000 whites rioted, injuring more than one hundred black residents," as noted by the historian Wendy Wall.[9] As had long been the case, it was not simply that white officials often failed to prosecute acts of violence. Such lawlessness essentially enjoyed local sanction as an extralegal means of enforcing racial control. This was particularly true at a time when white segregationists worried about the political restiveness of Black veterans. After all, they were returning from a war fought ideologically against Nazi racism.

For those in Washington, what made all the social unrest disconcerting—whether in the form of labor strikes or white racist violence—was how it undercut what officials believed to be the necessary domestic foundations for an American-led order. In the wake of World War II, policymakers were focusing abroad on the centrality to new global arrangements of American-style market capitalism and liberal constitutionalism. But in order to entrench American imperium, these actors also believed that the country could not be mired in internal instability; leaders had to tap into deep national reserves of agreement and shared political commitment. Underscoring the sentiment circulating among governing elites, Thomas D'Arcy Brophy, head of the Kenyon & Eckhardt advertising agency, declared the necessity of "re-sell[ing] Americanism to Americans." Successfully projecting international authority and police power required broad-ranging political unity at home.[10]

Such unity was particularly critical because the American position faced a significant economic and military competitor in the form of the Soviet Union. Again, the Soviet Union during these years—despite its Stalinist terror—offered a clear and ascendant ideological alternative. Politicians and commentators worried that this alternative could tempt communities overseas, especially in the Global South, but also disaffected constituencies in the United States.[11]

At the dawn of the Cold War, policymakers thus saw two sources of potential domestic danger. As noted in chapter 10, the Soviet Union had long defended principles of racial equality, which those in Washington feared could carry real appeal for Black Americans. At the same time, the immediate post–World War II context was one in which state socialism as a model of economic management appeared to be a success story: the Soviet Union seemed to have developed rapidly while explicitly eschewing capitalist principles. Thus, officials were also genuinely concerned that—especially during times of economic downturn and social conflict—citizens might question the inviolability of capitalist democracy, including the basic sufficiency of the New Deal social welfare framework.

Immediate post-war public opinion data suggested the plausibility of these fears and the generally unsettled nature of the overall climate. Such data is not always the best indicator of deeply held convictions, since the way questions are worded can structure the responses given. Still, surveys from the time speak to the period's discontent and the real space within mass sentiment for ideological fluidity. In the same September 1946 *Fortune* survey mentioned above, 73 percent of respondents were concerned enough about continuing economic crisis that they backed measures for "the government . . . to provide for all people who have no other means of obtaining a living."

This indicated an appetite for large-scale initiatives like FDR's Second Bill of Rights. But it further raised the specter of substantial support for even more radical alterations to the economy—alterations that would break definitively from the terms of capitalist democracy. Indeed, when asked "which of the following most nearly represents your opinion of the American form of government?" 43 percent did answer, "our form of government, based on the Constitution, is as near perfect as it can be." But 46 percent said either "it has not kept up with the times and should be thoroughly revised" or "the present system of private capitalism and democracy are breaking down and . . . we will have to have a new form of government."[12]

The Roper Center for Public Opinion Research has maintained survey data on general sentiment about the Constitution since 1936. Tellingly, this 1946 finding remains the one time more people opposed than supported constitutional preservation, instead backing a new form of government—and with it, potentially, basic transformations in the economic and political order.[13]

ONE-WORLDISM AND THE ABOLITION OF WAR

Further underscoring the ideological fluidity of the immediate post-war moment, it was not only that public life was marked by general institutional disillusionment and even a surprising degree of constitutional skepticism. Various social movement actors also challenged—both directly and indirectly—the governing project of an American-led world order, one linking creedal constitutionalism and global primacy.

In particular, the era's peace movement and Black politics offered two striking spaces of dissent from the official narrative. For starters, the absolute destruction wrought by World War II, as well as the specter of new, even more technologically dangerous weapons—like nuclear bombs—fueled grassroots peace activism. Activists worried that future wars, especially between the United States and the Soviet Union, could lead to human annihilation, as the US's own devastating atomic weapons use in Japan made disturbingly real. In response, activists began to organize around efforts both to ban nuclear weapons and to abolish war itself. And this effort ultimately joined calls for creating a single world government. In contrast to the United Nations, such a world entity would be a fully sovereign and supranational federation, enjoying the ability to proscribe war and to enforce such legal limitations.

The Federation of Atomic Scientists became associated broadly with these views, producing a monograph in 1946, *One World or None*, which sold over 100,000 copies. The book's popularity suggested a genuine appetite for both world government and the banning of atomic weaponry.[14] On the student activism front, Harris Wofford Jr., who would later become a US Senator from Pennsylvania, established the Student Federalists while at the University of Chicago. The group was committed to "mak[ing] world citizenship in a world community a political fact,"[15] and had chapters on 111 college campuses by the end of 1946, with an estimated membership of 4,000 to 5,000 members. Early the following year, it merged with other world government groups to form the United World Federalists (UWF), an entity with upward of 200 local chapters nationwide.[16]

Especially between 1944 and 1947, calls for world federalism highlighted public willingness to consider alternatives to a confrontational
posture toward the Soviet Union, and even to the global primacy of the
American nation-state. Significantly, those involved at the time with
federalist chapters viewed the US establishment of multilateral institutions, including the UN, as falling well short of the goal of a world order
truly committed to the overcoming of war. Activists worried that, precisely because these institutions were so closely bound to American security interests, they inevitably preserved nation-state competition and
would foster emerging Soviet rivalry. In fact, this was why the very first
Student Federalist electoral statement in 1944 had backed Vice President Henry Wallace, who would become deeply identified with opposition to the Cold War, instead of Roosevelt himself.[17] As Student Federalist President Thomas Hughes declared to members in a September
1946 lecture, the moment required nothing less than "break[ing] the
vise of nationalist rivalry while we still have time."[18]

With respect to US power, they also worried that any global order
built on the dominance of a particular state, however beneficent, would
eventually generate interstate rivalries that would precipitate yet more
warfare and violence. Quoting a fellow one-worlder, Hughes maintained that the best way to avoid confrontation with the Soviet Union
was for the United States and Britain to disavow their interests in carv-
ing up spheres of influence and "pledg[ing] themselves to the abolition
of war through world government." He concluded that "unilaterally
try[ing] to force the Kremlin to change its policy" without "identical
changes of policy for all governments concerned" would only produce
a ratcheting up of global conflict. If, instead, American citizens pressed
their political elites for a truly inclusive world government in which the
US abandoned its hegemonic status, these dangers could be avoided.[19]

Still, many of the students involved in one-worldism eventually
settled comfortably into careers in the Cold War state. Like Wofford, Thomas Hughes went on in the 1960s to serve as State Department director of intelligence in both the Kennedy and Lyndon Johnson administrations.[20] But this is not a total surprise, since one-world
advocates—while disavowing single-state dominance—often clung to
a deeply venerative approach to the American project, and to the US
Constitution. After all, the United World Federalists' founding in 1947
was meant to coincide with George Washington's birthday,[21] and the
group's use of the term "federalist" honored the 1787 framers. Paralleling FDR's vision of the UN, the group's idea for a world government

effectively involved the establishment of a creedal constitution for the globe. As an early student federalist policy statement maintained, this "international federal constitution" would "extend those basic freedoms" that the United States fought for during the war to everyone globally and would even include a "bill of rights."[22]

Given their own brand of creedal constitutionalism and Myrdallian faith in American goodness, most one-worlders eventually backed the new Cold War—especially as US officials pressed the country toward greater confrontation with the Soviet Union. They may have maintained their commitments to multilateralism and global rule-following.[23] But those that made their way into the foreign policy establishment came to interpret the Soviet desire to maintain a sphere of influence as proof that, whatever their earlier hopes, the US had no choice but to assert global authority.

Moreover, from the beginning, the federalists' version of world government conceived of anti-colonial independence demands principally through a lens of destructive European nationalism. Student federalists certainly embraced anti-colonialism, and participated in efforts on behalf of Moroccan independence from France, for instance.[24] But they tended to offer in world federation a cosmopolitan utopia, devoid of any sustained analysis of what independence leader Kwame Nkrumah would call "neocolonialism," as discussed in chapter 10, or the embedded structural inequalities between Europe and its historic colonies. One-worlders never adequately engaged with how, under pure global government, non-white communities could ensure their own meaningful self-determination as a matter of economic policy and institutional power.

In this way, past world federalists often fell into the same interventionist mode as some Radical Republicans who, in the nineteenth century, had argued for annexation in places like the Dominican Republican on grounds of absolute formal equality. Similarly, mid-twentieth-century postcolonial states may have been formally equal within this idealized world federation. But they would still face sustained power imbalances that shaped the actual terms of decision-making, and they would be subject to a framework conceived in American terms. For this reason, as US competition with the Soviet Union intensified in Asia and Africa, past one-worlders often retreated into a defense of American leadership. At its worst, this could devolve into familiar Cold War readings, in which non-white suspicions of US power were simply a matter of local communities lacking an adequately cosmopolitan vision, or remaining too wedded to their own destructive nationalisms.

Still, whatever the limitations of one-worldism, it is nonetheless worth underscoring its far greater ideological flexibility compared to the consolidating Cold War account of the American project, including with respect to the Constitution. World federalists effectively called for the United States to abandon any privileged status in the global system just as it approached the apex of its power; to replace its existing form of government with a new, truly supranational legal-political order; and to fundamentally subsume the nation's geostrategic security interests. Although widely derided by foreign policymakers in Washington, the number of political and cultural elites willing to lend their credibility to the cause was striking. Those associated to some degree with world government ran the gamut from Albert Einstein and the Manhattan Project's Robert Oppenheimer to Oscar Hammerstein, John Steinbeck, Supreme Court justices William O. Douglas and Owen Roberts (the latter of "switch in time" fame), A. Philip Randolph, and United Automobile Workers (UAW) President Walter Reuther.[25] The breadth of these associations speaks to the ideological openness immediately after the war. It shows how a Cold War Manichaeanism, not to mention the basic terms of American global primacy, were not nearly as entrenched across domestic political voices as they would eventually become.

THE CHALLENGE OF BLACK POLITICS
TO AMERICAN PRIMACY

Ultimately, though, the most searching critique of American primacy at the time—including of what would become Cold War orthodoxy—came from the Black counter-public. The post-war combination of economic crisis and extreme white violence made it especially difficult for African American communities to accept official narratives. And it pressed even moderate Black institutions to push beyond redemptive reform strategies that presumed an egalitarian American creed.

For instance, Black activists called for anti-racist action at new international institutions like the UN. Critically, they did not do so out of presumptive faith in American global leadership. Instead, they were motivated by the belief that the international community—especially decolonizing non-white peoples—could be organized as allies in contesting US practices. Even if international forums were largely built by the United States, many activists hoped to subversively redeploy them as spaces independent of American dominance, which could aid in exposing domestic racism.

One sees this especially with the petition *An Appeal to the World*, submitted by the NAACP to the United Nations on October 23, 1947. The petition described the systematic violation of African American rights, ranging from lynching to segregation to voter disenfranchisement to extreme inequalities in health, education, and housing. It called on the global community and the new United Nations specifically to redress these ongoing deprivations.[26] Overseen by W. E. B. Du Bois, after he decided during World War II to rejoin the NAACP, *An Appeal to the World* was infused with his own Black internationalist sensibility—quite distinct from the creedalism of white students in the United World Federation.

In fact, *An Appeal* further underscored how the wartime years had brought many Black radical and more liberal voices together around a shared agenda of global decolonization, which they connected to a double victory over fascism and racism. Such interconnections were perhaps best expressed by the Council on African Affairs (CAA). From its initial founding in 1937 as the International Committee on African Affairs (ICAA) through its wartime reorganization as the CAA, the Black-run organization was a critical instrument, as the historian Penny Von Eschen writes, for "keep[ing] the issue of colonial liberation on the US agenda and provid[ing] links to international anticolonial networks and African liberation groups."[27]

As mentioned in chapter 7, the organization was led by Black Left figures like Paul Robeson and Du Bois. More establishment African American elites often maintained their distance, especially given the key role of activists with ties to the Communist Party (CPUSA). For instance, by 1940, in the context of growing suspicions of the CPUSA as well as Soviet-Nazi accommodation, Ralph Bunche resigned from both the National Negro Congress (NNC) and the soon-to-be-renamed CAA. Bunch, the famed Black political scientist and diplomat—who joined the CIA precursor, the Office of Strategic Service (OSS), during the war before becoming a central advisor to Eleanor Roosevelt and a drafting figure in the 1948 development of the United Nations Declaration of Human Rights—found the CAA's Communist associations disqualifying. But especially while the war with Nazi Germany proceeded—and so with anti-communism somewhat abated—the CAA became an embodiment of Black Left-liberal cooperation on the global stage.[28] As for the immediate post-war moment, Du Bois's close ties to both the group and the NAACP indicated how *An Appeal* embodied shared anti-colonial sentiments and internationalist strategies among Black liberal and more radical voices.

All of this speaks to how Du Bois's understanding of the African American experience in the United States as a particular variant of Europe's larger colonial legacy circulated well beyond Black radical spaces. Through the petition, the NAACP connected confronting racial discrimination at home to decolonization everywhere. In his introduction, Du Bois underscored how racial discrimination within the US promoted a white supremacist mindset, which, if allowed to persist, would undermine emerging global anti-colonial efforts. As he declared, Jim Crow "cannot be persisted in, without infringing upon the rights of the peoples of the world." The petition also pointedly critiqued emerging anti-communist rhetoric, famously holding that "it is not Russia that threatens the United States so much as Mississippi; not Stalin and Molotov but [pro-segregation Mississippi congressmen] Bilbo and Rankin; internal injustice done to one's brothers is far more dangerous than the aggression of strangers from abroad."[29]

Thus, in the immediate post-war moment, the NAACP was willing to place the US in a long line of colonialist states, to contest anti-communist red-baiting of civil rights activism, and to do both in a highly publicized international setting. Such a move challenged various presumptions of the more rigid creedal constitutionalism then consolidating among white foreign policy officials. It suggested that, rather than universal egalitarianism being the inherent truth of the national project, the US might best be viewed as an extension—rather than a repudiation—of European imperialism and racial domination.

It also foregrounded for both international and national audiences internal Black skepticism about whether exclusively US-focused reform strategies—emphasizing court-based litigation and moral suasion of white politicians and publics—were destined to succeed. The problem was that a white majority, not unlike its cultural and racial allies in apartheid South Africa and elsewhere, might at the end of the day remain fundamentally opposed to Black freedom and to the broader interests of the racially oppressed. For this reason, internal change could well only come by forging solidarities with a non-white global majority and employing international pressure against recalcitrant white co-nationals.

The internationalist strategy further questioned, at least implicitly, the notion that the American model best fulfilled commitments to basic civil and political liberties. *An Appeal*'s focus on the systematic discrimination facing African Americans emphasized Du Bois's profound belief in the discourse of rights and in its emancipatory potential. But it also indicated his related belief in the hollowness of US rhetoric about democracy, let alone civil and political liberty for all, under the existing constitutional system.

In fact, Du Bois used the stage of the NAACP petition to repeat, at times verbatim, his critique in *Color and Democracy* of the constitutive flaws of the federal Constitution and its representative institutions. In *An Appeal*, he again argued that whatever the rhetoric, in reality both democracy and rights were dead letters in the United States for Black Americans, and hardly more secure even for "white folk all over the nation." Once more, he outlined the undemocratic implications of the Constitution's state-based electoral structure—which he again called a "rotten-borough system"—intensified by white authoritarian rule and Black disenfranchisement across the South. Updated with new post-war voting data, Du Bois wrote, "according to the political power which each actual voter exercised in 1946, the Southern South rated as 6.6, the Border States as 2.3 and the rest of the country as about 1."[30]

This meant that "the rulers of this nation [were] chosen and policies of the country determined" by a "disenfranchised vote"—one that fundamentally misallocated voice and practical political power. The resulting system of minority rule handed white supremacists in the South a governing veto, and embodied "a danger not simply to the Negro" but to everyone everywhere—"to the nations of the world." These legal-political structures explained how domestic racism threatened global anti-colonialism: it gave white authoritarians within the US outsized political power, which they then could project onto the world. This meant that an American-led order, whatever the aspirations, was nonetheless likely to be infused with troubling racial, political, and economic values. As Du Bois concluded bluntly, "the federal government has for these reasons continually cast its influence with imperial aggression throughout the world and withdrawn its sympathy from the colored peoples and from the small nations."[31]

Du Bois's introduction, promoted by the NAACP, thus rejected any exceptionalist view of an American model as a gift to the world. Instead, it raised the specter that, without significant internal reform, the US could be a de-democratizing global threat. Such contentions were striking throwbacks to earlier generations of Black socialist argument. But they also highlighted how Du Bois, in this post-war moment, saw decolonization as heralding a new rights vision—an opportunity to learn from global experiments abroad. Like independence leaders such as Nehru, Du Bois rejected a simple framing of Western modernity versus

Eastern traditionalism. He sought instead to promote a new and genuinely global universalism. This account would connect socialism with the fulfillment of mass democracy and "human rights"—the latter understood to entail both civil libertarian protections and broad-ranging guarantees of socioeconomic welfare and freedom.

Rather than the United States spreading an American model to the world, it was the world—particularly decolonizing societies—that could help steer the United States toward a more emancipatory horizon. This vision emerged partly because Du Bois remained skeptical of the official association US foreign and domestic policymakers made between democracy and rights rhetoric and the American constitutional system. If the actual American legal-political order had instead produced sustained racial violence and rights infringements, then why should the Global South take its lead from the United States—rather than the other way around?

In a deep sense, Du Bois's internationalist strategy rejected the legitimacy of American global hegemony. It presented US officials not as champions on the global stage of genuinely egalitarian values. Instead, it portrayed them as far more likely to project abroad the same Jim Crow logics and colonial structures that existed at home. For Du Bois, true global peace and prosperity certainly required a new international order. But these ends could not be achieved through American primacy. Problematic and dominant nation-states—and governing elites within them—should not enjoy a monopoly over the terms of the global commons. Instead, new and bottom-up frameworks had to be put into place to meaningfully disperse power to historically marginalized people and communities.

Although these were Du Bois's foundational and more radical suspicions about the American project, even the more moderate NAACP or someone like A. Philip Randolph were not unmoved by them. Randolph, long a labor and civil rights leader, may have become an ardent anti-communist. He now deemphasized his past opposition to the Constitution, and he had come to see constitutional fidelity and a redemptive nationalism as likely the best long-term mechanism for social change. But in the wake of the Second World War, Randolph's own skepticism led him to defend multiple racial reform approaches. Some aligned with the official presentation of national identity and purpose. But others appeared to repudiate all the emerging terms of American imperium, as racial violence and post-war social conflict made Randolph open, still, to more confrontational rhetoric and strategies.

Perhaps most famously, President Harry Truman called on Congress to impose peacetime conscription in 1948, as part of the acceleration of the new Cold War with the Soviet Union. Randolph responded by declaring that Black Americans should resist the draft so long as the military remained segregated. At a charged Senate committee hearing on peacetime conscription, white politicians like the longtime civil rights ally and Republican senator from Oregon, Wayne Morse, told Randolph that such a response was almost treasonous, given security objectives abroad: it would lead white Americans to view all Black people as a dangerous fifth column.

Randolph's response, for all intents and purposes, reiterated the position he and Chandler Owen staked out in the *Messenger* as young Black radical activists during World War I: regardless of what African Americans did, they were already treated as a community apart, and they could not rely on moral suasion to convince a white majority of their basic humanity. Change might only occur through more irruptive political strategies—including perhaps the creation of a world government (which he politely supported for a period).

At home, this meant the intensification of Black civil disobedience and nonviolent resistance to white institutions—even if it entailed facing extreme white violence in response. As Randolph declared to the committee: "I would anticipate nationwide terrorism against Negroes who refused to participate in the armed forces, but I believe that this is the price we have to pay for democracy that we want. In other words, if there are sacrifices and sufferings, terrorism, concentration camps, whatever they may be, if that is the only way by which Negroes can get their democratic rights, I unhesitatingly say that we have to face it."[32] Moved in part by his antipathy to the Soviet Union, Randolph had become more amenable to working collaboratively with white establishment politicians and in some cases adopting their narratives. But as with the NAACP's *Appeal to the World*, he also appreciated that more conciliatory reform approaches could fail—just as they had in the past.

The image of the "concentration camp" clearly evoked the Nazi genocide of Jewish people in Europe. In using it, Randolph went much further than the Swedish Myrdal in underlining the embedded racism of white society. Jim Crow was not simply a competing but irrational value premise in American life; it was, for Randolph, a homegrown American fascism, which might ultimately only be eradicated under conditions of heightened and revolutionary struggle—perhaps akin to the Civil War.

Randolph seemed to tell his white national audience that he may

have preferred a creedally framed and constitutionally respectful reform pathway—one built on shared faith in universalism, a common
American peoplehood, and perhaps even the legitimacy of US global
might. But if that strategy failed, there remained no reason for African
Americans to stay true to a nation that oppressed them, as Reverend
Henry McNeal Turner remarked all the way back in the 1880s. Indeed,
just as Randolph had argued during the First World War, to fight and
die for the international dominance of such a state would be a profound
disservice to one's own sense of self-worth, community, and freedom.
Just as in 1917, Randolph was attacked by more moderate Black leaders
in the African American press. And yet, echoing that earlier moment,
an NAACP poll found that 71 percent of Black college students supported him and intended to resist the draft.[33]

The Constitution and the National Security Project

Standing in the backdrop of this swirling post-war ideological dissensus was the challenge posed by the Soviet Union. For Truman and key
members of his administration, like Attorney General Tom Clark, the
American political environment was fracturing just as the country embarked on an existential competition with a totalitarian foe. In the mid-
1940s, voices of skepticism seemed to proliferate across collective life.
They could be found among labor activists engaged in wildcat strikes;
ordinary white citizens questioning whether the American form of government needed to be fundamentally revised; Black leaders and mass
publics contesting peacetime conscription or comparing the United
States to Nazi Germany or European colonialist projects in Africa;
and even white educated elites in the universities, including scientists
like Oppenheimer, who had been directly involved in the most sensi-
tive military and national security projects and now called for world
government.

In ways akin to World War I's earlier Red Scare, US officials offered
the most immediate and sustained response by aggressively intertwining security politics and pro-Constitution advocacy. In the context of
an escalating Cold War, those around Truman emphasized the need
for a robust security apparatus to project American power internationally and preserve American values at home. This new apparatus further
consolidated presidential government, drawing from institutional developments under both Woodrow Wilson and FDR to complete the

entrenchment of bureaucratic centralization and growth as constitutive features of the American state to this day.

THE RETURN OF THE RED SCARE

The National Security Act of 1947—echoing the name of the old World War I–era National Security League—took effect six months after the Truman Doctrine speech. It provided the core administrative infra-structure for the Cold War state, as detailed by the political scientist Douglas Stuart: "It created a National Military Establishment, which became the Department of Defense in 1949. It gave the Air Force an in-dependent status and provided the Joint Chiefs of Staff with statutory identity. It established the National Security Council (NSC), the Cen-tral Intelligence Agency (CIA), and a cluster of lesser-known institu-tions, including the National Security Resource Board, the Munitions Board, and the Research and Development Board."[34] These changes had long-term implications for the nature of American government. In par-ticular, they created a permanent and peacetime structure for gather-ing intelligence, elevated the policy-making responsibility of military officers, and dramatically expanded the executive agencies tasked with issues of defense.

This embrace by officials of a securitized politics of constitutionalism not only entailed fulfilling, finally, the classic aspirations of old mili-tary preparedness advocates, complete with an empowered presidency. It also went hand in hand with a systematic policy of ideological repres-sion. Those like Truman and Clark may have defined the United States externally in terms of its personal liberties and anti-totalitarian essence. But in the context of perceived existential struggle, they—not unlike National Security Leaguers before them—presented most dissent from the security state's objectives as assaults on the sanctity of the Ameri-can constitutional model. Thus, confronting public dissensus became, first and foremost, a matter of wide-ranging and top-down government suppression.

Today, Americans typically remember this Second Red Scare through the false accusations and wild excesses of Wisconsin Senator Joseph McCarthy. They also recall a handful of high-profile cases, such as the trial and execution on espionage grounds of Julius and Ethel Rosenberg or the House Un-American Activities Committee (HUAC) attacks on Alger Hiss. But the full government response was breathtaking in its scope, far exceeding in reach any similar state-initiated effort in American history.

Ten days after his Truman Doctrine speech, Truman, with Attorney General Clark's assistance, established by executive order the Federal Employee Loyalty Program. This aimed to remove all subversives and potential Soviet sympathizers from the government. At the same time, the Justice Department began deporting noncitizens on ideological grounds. Between 1947 and when Truman left office in 1953, approximately 350 federal employees were fired because of loyalty concerns, and another 2,200 employees chose to leave their jobs rather than face an investigation process.

But these firings were only the tip of the iceberg. In those same years, more than 4.7 million people were investigated by the federal loyalty program. The ubiquity of such investigations created an atmosphere in which any past statement or personal friendship could be used to suggest someone's "un-Americanness" or to end their career—even if they were, ultimately, expeditiously cleared of "disloyalty."[35]

In Congress, HUAC had a similar cultural effect. The committee had been established in 1938, operating during that pre-war period of crackdowns on perceived Nazi and Soviet sympathizers. Now, its anti-communist actions truly ramped up alongside Truman's parallel efforts in the executive branch. Only two federal employees were ever criminally convicted as a result of the committee's efforts (one being Alger Hiss), and both were convicted solely on perjury rather than on actual espionage charges. But as the legal scholar Geoffrey Stone details, "from 1945 to 1957, HUAC heard testimony from more than 3,000 witnesses and cited 135 individuals for contempt—more than the entire Congress had cited for contempt in the entire history of the United States to that point." Most significantly, Stone notes that the committee "amassed dossiers on hundreds of thousands of Americans who had done nothing illegal, or even wrong."[36]

HUAC's project was, at root, a massive propaganda undertaking. Many Americans at the time had understandable concerns about the nature of the Soviet Union and about Stalin's own tyrannical politics. But HUAC's reports and hearings—with their claims about subversive activity being rampant across government, labor, and Hollywood—helped to fortify a general climate of crisis in which Soviet-backed communism was depicted as on the march abroad and entrenching itself dangerously at home.

This atmosphere profoundly damaged the careers of high-profile celebrities and cultural elites—including Paul Robeson and Robert Oppenheimer. But, more generally and perhaps more importantly, both HUAC and Truman's loyalty program fed local and business crackdowns on anyone with broadly leftist sympathies, through blacklists, firings, and acts of vigilante violence. In addition, and just as significantly for political life going forward, it made individuals with radical or even critical views incredibly hesitant to voice them publicly. And neighbors or fellow citizens who may previously have been open to those positions became wary of the personal costs of any "subversive" associations.[37]

COLD WAR CONTAINMENT OF LABOR AND BLACK POLITICS

This climate had profound implications for leaders within both the labor unions and the Black freedom movement. Labor and African American politics had long been critical social bases not just for constitutional opposition, but also more generally for the articulation of radical alternatives to the existing political and economic order. Now, however, many movement elites felt compelled to rally around Cold War strictures and even to denounce past allies the state viewed as potentially subversive.

These developments were not entirely novel. The late 1930s government repression of the CPUSA and those viewed as fellow travelers had already had rippling effects within civil rights institutions and unions. Such earlier repression was part of the context in which, as described above, more mainstream activists began disassociating from CPUSA-linked groups or individuals. But the move to cut ties and to prove one's loyalty mushroomed in ways that had far-reaching impacts on how reformers presented the meaning and objectives of their own projects.

In particular, the Cold War climate created incredible pressure not only to depict reforms in creedal and constitutionally respectful terms. It also pressed activists to make demands in ways that nonetheless displayed one's Cold War commitment. As such, many increasingly found themselves expressing basic support for market capitalism, existing state institutions, and security prerogatives at home and abroad.

Union politics illustrated all of these tendencies. As loyalty tests proliferated in government, unions too initiated a massive purge of suspected Soviet sympathizers. In fact, CIO President Philip Murray enjoyed the ability to expel members without a vote. Mimicking Truman's terms, he declared that such actions were necessary because subversives were secretly attempting "to corrupt and destroy if possible the trade union movement in America."[38]

For those like Murray, part of the willingness to close ranks around Cold War orthodoxy had to do with post-war shifts in the public view of the labor movement. The 1946 strike wave may have been a dramatic show of strength, but the overall popular response was far more anti-labor than many union activists expected. In part this was due to the improved position of the movement itself, which was more dominant perhaps than at any moment in American history. In 1945, union membership reached 14.3 million people, with 27 percent of the entire workforce unionized.[39] Now a significant number of Americans outside the labor movement saw new work stoppages and demands as irresponsible, however warranted past actions may have been.

In this context, government claims about Soviet infiltration and sabotage provided a ready language for articulating anti-labor sentiments.[40] One Gallup poll in 1946 found 38 percent of respondents concluding that suspected communists wielded a "great deal" of influence in unions. Such findings were somewhat ironic; the actual CPUSA position, in keeping with wartime "Popular Front" commitments, pointedly favored labor peace. The party had in fact opposed radical efforts to pursue wildcat strikes and tended to shut down spontaneous grassroots uprisings, much to the chagrin of local activists.[41] Nonetheless, for Murray and others, regaining broader white American confidence in the labor movement became connected to demonstrating one's anticommunist bona fides.

This meant that union purges went hand in hand with a remarkable transformation in labor rhetoric. Key post-war leaders essentially abandoned the focus on class conflict, now too closely associated with Marxism and the Soviet Union, that had defined labor politics for nearly a century and throughout the 1930s. As Murray wrote in June 1948 of labor's patriotic Cold War credentials, "we have no classes in this country; that's why the Marxist theory of the class struggle has gained so few adherents. We're all workers here. And in the final analysis the interests of the farmers, factory hands, business and professional people, and white collar toilers prove to be the same."[42]

It was not simply that the CIO's leadership embraced a working-class nationalism. It also did so in a way that deemphasized any specifically class-based nature of political solidarity and community. Instead, establishing oneself as a loyal anti-communist required elevating one's attachment as a citizen of the American state above all else, and thus subsuming class affiliation vis-à-vis that larger state's security projects. If, in the 1930s, working-class and nationalist solidarities combined in an occasionally uneasy ideological framework for CIO labor leaders, the latter affiliation now gained the clear upper hand.

In this time of heightened crackdowns, the NAACP responded similarly to fears of being tarred with any subversive associations. For key leaders, the Cold War context required ensuring that the project of racial reform did not fall prey to accusations of Soviet infiltration. As with labor, this meant demonstrating Black loyalty to the security state. The 1950 NAACP national convention established an internal committee to ferret out subversives and, if need be, even to eliminate local branches suspected of Soviet sympathies. Although the leadership did not really believe the threat to be serious, their actions made clear a willingness to accept Cold War anti-communism and to refrain from connecting domestic Black conditions to direct challenges to US global authority or security objectives.[43]

In fact, the NAACP willingly participated in attacks on those few Black activists that remained opposed to the Cold War. The NAACP's Executive Secretary, Walter White, along with his close ally and future executive secretary, Roy Wilkins, made a special point in the early 1950s of trying to destroy the popular image of radicals such as Paul Robeson. Robeson, not only targeted by HUAC, was personally denounced in the NAACP's official paper, the *Crisis*, as everything from a "Lost Shepherd" to a "Kremlin Stooge."[44]

These attacks on an African American icon like Robeson spoke to a subtle but significant narrowing, even within Black politics, of the acceptable terms of creedal constitutionalism. Robeson, the singer of "Ballad for Americans," had been the face of Popular Front–era creedalism. Indeed, despite his praise for the egalitarian language of the Soviet text, Robeson persistently championed the potential embedded in the US Constitution. As a college student at Rutgers, Robeson wrote his undergraduate thesis on the egalitarian promise of the Fourteenth Amendment, declaring it to be, in creedal terms, "the Sleeping Giant of the American Constitution."[45] Robeson had once planned on a career in law—he graduated from Columbia Law School and worked for a period at a New York firm specializing in estates. But after facing racial slurs in the office and discrimination from potential white clients,

Robeson abandoned the vocation. He commented in the 1930s that he could not pursue "any profession where the highest prizes were from the start denied to me."[46]

Still, in keeping with a radical strain of Popular Front politics, Robeson's rhetoric and speech-making tended to combine revolutionary social change with a creedal Constitution—linking together Black freedom, overcoming capitalism, and anti-colonial efforts abroad. Not unlike some earlier abolitionists and Radical Republicans, Robeson often presented creedal and constitutional redemption as entailing potentially dramatic alterations to race, economy, and state. No doubt Robeson, like many Black activists before and after him, maintained an ambivalent relationship to American nationalist narratives, including with respect to its legal-political institutions.[47] But perhaps more than any other Black figure in the mid-twentieth century, he pressed as aggressively as possible to expand the discursive boundaries of creedal constitutionalism and to push against its preservationist uses.

But for those in the NAACP, and indeed within the Cold War Black leadership more generally, accepting anti-communism as the condition for racial amelioration came with clear expectations from the state. It meant limiting the terrain of contestation almost exclusively to domestic questions of race. And it involved accepting the basic terms of the emerging Cold War compact, tied to both capitalist democracy and American primacy.

Perhaps the most striking indication of these developments involves the chain of events that led to Du Bois's final break with the NAACP. This chain of events included the organization's repudiation of Du Bois's internationalist strategy, embodied in 1947's *An Appeal to the World*. Former First Lady Eleanor Roosevelt was a member of both the US delegation to the UN and the NAACP's board. And Roosevelt was vocally opposed to efforts like *An Appeal* to internationalize issues of Black subordination—seeing this as a propaganda coup for the Soviet Union. Indeed, she threatened to resign from the US delegation if the NAACP petition was introduced to the UN General Assembly. Walter White agreed not to press matters further, and *An Appeal* was introduced instead in a UN subcommittee, where US officials were able to suppress it for procedural reasons.[48]

White and the leadership at the NAACP had certainly seen the potential utility of employing internationalist strategies. However, they also recognized that white national politicians appeared more movable than ever before—now loudly proclaiming abroad their post-war investment in egalitarian values. They further concluded that, in an increasingly Manichaean political context, there would be real costs for falling on the wrong side of the Cold War framing of friends and enemies.

Individuals like White had spent years building up political credibility in Washington, and did not want to jeopardize either their leverage or their access. Therefore, when Henry Wallace ran for president against Truman in 1948 on a Progressive Party ticket emphasizing fundamental racial reforms, Du Bois and Paul Robeson were outspoken supporters. But White instead repeatedly reproached Du Bois for backing Wallace, and even became an official consultant that year to the US delegation for the UN's Paris meetings. In the end, Du Bois's anger over the burying of *An Appeal to the World*, along with his complaints about the group's suppression of his support for Wallace and White's willingness to take part in a state delegation, all led to his termination by the NAACP board.[49]

Du Bois's final break from the group spoke to a leadership judgment that any whiff of Black opposition to the Cold War would be strategically disastrous. To a large extent, it explains how the organization behaved when Du Bois again participated in an internationalist pressure campaign against the US government, this time through the Civil Rights Congress (CRC). In the 1940s and 1950s, the CRC was perhaps the most powerful Black radical entity in the country. In fact, in 1947 the CPUSA, now in firm control of the National Negro Congress, effectively chose to shut down the NNC. Those remaining in the NNC leadership eventually moved its "remaining assets" and memberships to the Civil Rights Congress.[50]

But while Black Communists, like William Patterson, held prominent roles within the CRC, the group attempted to draw together a relatively broad coalition. The historian Glenda Gilmore notes that the CRC's "initiating committee" included Black and white activists of various ideological stripes, with only "a few Communists present at the planning meeting . . . very few."[51] This Popular Front approach dovetailed with that of the 1930s NNC and the Council on African Affairs.

Politically, the new CRC sought—not unlike those organizations— to connect the fight against domestic racism to a critique of global capitalism and of colonial oppression. This move pushed the groups in more radical directions than the emerging drift of mainstream civil rights activism. In 1951 the CRC submitted a new petition to the UN—signed by Du Bois as well as by prominent Black Communists like Claudia

Jones, Harry Haywood, and William Patterson, and delivered in New York City by Paul Robeson—called *We Charge Genocide*. The very title spoke to the petition's confrontational posture. By framing American racism as genocide—once more invoking the Nazi Holocaust against Jewish people—the CRC rejected any redemptive presentation of the US as merely incompletely liberal, scarred only by a formal inequality that the country was on the path to overcoming.

It also reiterated Du Bois's skepticism regarding whether the American constitutional system encompassed anything like an expansive rights vision, rather than its basic denial. For the CRC, the Black experience combined an economic immiseration and sustained physical violence that met the 1948 Genocide Convention's test of "deliberately inflicting on the group conditions of life calculated to bring about its destruction in whole or in part."[52] This reality was not accidental; it was rooted in the foundational economic and political infrastructure of American society—its structural combination of white authoritarianism and exploitative capitalism. It therefore required a concerted international response, akin to global efforts against fascism, in order to be defeated. Simply put, the petition directly rejected—and on a global stage—every feature of American Cold War self-understanding.

Much like *An Appeal to the World*, the petition was denounced by Eleanor Roosevelt, with the State Department pressuring more mainstream Black elites to rebut the claims. Despite the fact that much of *We Charge Genocide*'s evidence of anti-Black violence came from NAACP sources, the group complied, wiring a rebuttal to Paris, where the CRC aimed to deliver the document to a UN meeting. At the same time, the State Department organized the presence, on the ground in Paris, of what the historian Carol Anderson calls a "Who's Who of Black America" to defend the country against the charges. This included Eleanor Roosevelt's close ally, Ralph Bunche, now a formidable US diplomat and Nobel Prize winner for his UN-related work in the context of Israel/Palestine.[53]

As a pragmatic matter, this Black liberal decision to side with the US government against the CRC made sense. It indicated a strategic judgment that, under Cold War conditions, it was better to pursue ameliorism alongside white officials than more radical changes against the backdrop of extreme state repression.

Indeed, that context of repression made *We Charge Genocide* the last major initiative of the era's Black radical voices, who faced an intense crackdown of prosecutions, deportations, and blacklistings. William

Patterson was detained abroad after delivering the petition in Paris, and had his passport taken by the government when he returned to the US. Robeson and Du Bois also had their passports revoked during this period.[54] Robeson, moreover, had already been attacked in Congress by HUAC and blacklisted from performing in the United States. Now the removal of Robeson's passport was meant as a type of state-enforced internal exile. Unable to travel overseas, he was both isolated politically from international allies and denied the ability to earn a living.[55] As for Claudia Jones, the Trinidadian-American activist was imprisoned on and off in the late 1940s and 1950s on ideological grounds for being a member of the Communist Party, before finally being deported in 1955 after having lived in the country since the age of eight.[56]

Along with the internal exile entailed by the travel ban, Du Bois also faced persistent government harassment, including being brought to trial in 1951 on charges that he was an unregistered foreign agent—a charge of which he was ultimately acquitted. Du Bois's alleged criminal liability resulted from his circulation, as the chairman of an anti-war organization, of a petition started abroad to ban nuclear weapons. Only five years earlier, such a letter was a fairly uncontroversial exercise of peace activism, of the type that prominent scientists and student federalists may have embraced. Indeed, in Europe the petition had been signed by many luminaries including "Marc Chagall, Thomas Mann, Pablo Picasso, and future French president, Jacques Chirac."[57]

But the times domestically had shifted, and the episode only further embittered Du Bois toward more establishment Black figures. Once he was under indictment, his lawyers had trouble finding prominent Black voices, in mainstream groups like the NAACP, to serve as character witnesses or to sign public statements of support. Similar problems plagued a testimonial dinner timed for his eighty-third birthday. Mordecai Wyatt Johnson, president of Howard University, and Charlotte Hawkins Brown, a famed North Carolina educator and author, "declined to speak," and Bunche "refused to cosponsor the dinner."[58]

The CRC's fate as an institution was no different. Under continual state threat and listed as a subversive organization through the McCarran or Subversive Activities Control Act (1950), the CRC eventually disbanded in 1956.[59] The Council of African Affairs—which shared many activist members in common with the CRC and which for nearly two decades had embraced a capacious Black internationalism linking together anti-racism, anti-fascism, and anti-colonialism—similarly faced charges as a subversive organization. Notably, the government claimed that its support for African anti-colonial and anti-apartheid groups, like South Africa's African National Congress (ANC), indicated pro-communist connections and service to a "foreign principal." Under the weight of government prosecution, the organization finally collapsed in 1955.[60]

The demise of both groups, not to mention the state's harassment of their central members, made clear the risk of holding any commitments seen as contrary to Cold War orthodoxy. This precarity would have been especially present for those in historically marginalized communities. But it was nonetheless a widespread social experience. If Truman, Clark, and others were concerned with the political dissensus and conflict marking the mid-1940s, they responded by comprehensively embracing the old basic playbook of aggressive security violence—but now in the name of protecting the constitutional state.

The Freedom Train and Cold War Creedal Celebration

The effort to hold down political discontent involved not only the application of repressive power. Akin to the old National Security League, the Truman administration (and later the Eisenhower administration) combined anti-communist crackdowns with new mass campaigns of constitutional education and celebration. These campaigns eventually gained the acceptance even of working-class and many left-leaning groups, especially as the American state muted other critical voices and the CPUSA discredited itself in part by an unwillingness to dissociate from Soviet authoritarianism.

THE EXPANDING TERRAIN OF REVERENTIAL CONSTITUTIONAL POLITICS

For a range of government officials, the central mechanism for promoting ideological unity involved a combination of the state's suppressive capacity with a sustained government-led effort to promote popular attachment to the terms of Cold War constitutional politics. In one slightly later example of such efforts, President Dwight Eisenhower in 1958 bestowed the new name of "Law Day" on May Day—the international workers' day, celebrated across the globe on May 1 in memory of the American nationwide general strike for an eight-hour day, as well as the related Haymarket affair of 1886. Charles Rhyne, Eisenhower's legal counsel and the president of the American Bar Association (ABA), had promoted the idea, whose purpose, as one planning guide declared, was to show "the contrast between the rule of law in the United States and the rule of force and fear under communism." During the late 1950s and 1960s, the ABA spearheaded efforts by local bar associations and legal educational groups to organize public events and school visits focused on the special genius of the federal Constitution—the great embodiment of American law—with planning themes like, "The Law . . . Wellspring of Liberty."[61] These events targeted May Day as inherently un-American, despite its historical genesis in the United States. They constituted one piece of an overall effort by governing elites to frame the entire socialist tradition as foreign and as antithetical to constitutional liberty.

During the earliest days of the Cold War, the extravaganza of the Freedom Train offered the greatest illustration of a sustained state effort to inculcate mass commitment to the official account of creedal constitutionalism and American primacy. The train toured the country between 1947 and 1949, visiting "322 cities in all forty-eight states" and offering displays and educational programming on the particular character of American freedom.[62] Underscoring the centrality of Constitution worship to the enterprise, the tour began in Philadelphia on September 17, 1947—Constitution Day—with patriotic songs, speeches, and "a mass recitation" before a "star-studded crowd" led by Supreme Court Justice Owen Roberts of the "Freedom Pledge." The pledge combined the anti-totalitarian rhetoric of American civil libertarian commitment with an invocation of the necessity of American global mission and leadership:

> I am an American. A free American.
> Free to speak—without fear
> Free to worship God in my own way
> Free to stand for what I think right
> Free to oppose what I believe wrong
> Free to choose those who govern my country.
> This heritage of Freedom I pledge to uphold
> For myself and all mankind.[63]

The campaign emerged out of the Justice Department, with Attorney General Clark viewing it as a way to respond to the labor unrest and social discontent in the war's immediate aftermath. He began advancing the idea that a train be equipped to travel the country carrying the defining documents of American freedom, accompanied by a large-scale advertising and teaching initiative to instruct citizens in true Americanism and in the country's essential values. The project was initially led by staffers at the National Archives, but it was soon taken over by business and advertising executives, who formed the American Heritage Foundation. In an effort at labor inclusion, William Green at the AFL and Philip Murray at the CIO were listed as vice presidents of the Foundation. But its board of trustees and main decision-makers were composed, above all, of the country's most significant CEOs.[64]

The items selected bore the stamp of the Foundation's business tilt, and more generally highlighted how Cold War officials increasingly defined the terms of the American model. The Foundation built its exhibits around originals of the Declaration of Independence, the 1787 Constitution (indeed, Washington's own copy), the first ten amendments or Bill of Rights, the Gettysburg Address (but notably paired with General Robert E. Lee's 1865 letter calling on citizens to bind up the wounds of the Civil War), the Emancipation Proclamation, the Thirteenth Amendment, and the flag raised on Iwo Jima. Alongside these items were additional display cases, including an entire case devoted to the constitutional genius of Alexander Hamilton.[65] Taken together, the items' message reinforced all the elements of the American model that policymakers were promoting abroad.

To begin with, the exhibits constitutively joined faith in market capitalism to any legitimate account of constitutionalism. The fate of FDR's Second Bill of Rights as part of the Freedom Train was telling: at first, National Archives staffers had proposed an entire exhibit on the train devoted to "Economic Rights,"[66] focusing on social welfare provisions and labor's right to collective bargaining, and including a booklet on the Second Bill of Rights. But, just as Truman had completely ceased mentioning the Second Bill of Rights, the Foundation dropped the whole exhibit.

In the course of three years, FDR's socioeconomically focused initiative had essentially gone from the centerpiece of an imagined post-war domestic order to a practically discarded relic. The Foundation's leadership seemed to view such an exhibit as muddying the sharp divide between US capitalist democracy and Soviet socialist tyranny. They wanted the campaign to juxtapose American individualistic freedoms from state interference—including both property rights and personal liberties—with the Soviet Union's collectivizing impulses.[67] Whatever someone like Robeson may have argued, being a creedal constitutionalist now entailed taking established property relations as an ethical and political given.

As for the subject of race, the Freedom Train's displays embraced inclusive rhetoric as important to American national identity. Even the Texan Tom Clark declared at the Philadelphia Constitution Day kickoff event that "all of us must be free or none of us are free. No man can have freedom for himself unless he is willing to share it with all, regardless of race, color, or religion."[68] Critically, this brand of universalism cut against how Du Bois's and the NAACP's *An Appeal to the World* presented the United States—indeed at virtually that same moment—to the global community. Rather than an embodiment of colonial power in the non-white world, the presumption behind the train's exhibits was that the United States—even if marred by the sin of slavery—had been built on liberal equality, and now was peacefully fulfilling its ineluctable egalitarian mission.

Relatedly, in seeking broad unity on creedal terms, the exhibits also systematically downplayed any hint of internal tension within society, whether on class or racial grounds. For this reason, the train was at pains to imply shared cultural commitments and thus near complete social harmony, even in the distant past. Hence the inclusion of Lee's letter alongside Lincoln's Gettysburg Address, together offering proof of an abiding American faith in reconciliation, compromise, and agreement.

Finally, this combination of creedal inclusion, liberal constitutionalism, and capitalist democracy were all wrapped up together in an overriding defense of American global primacy. The overwhelming focus of the twentieth-century items displayed as part of the Freedom Train revolved around the virtue of the US military effort during World War II.[69] The displays presumed American exceptionalism as well as the centrality of US international police power for world security. In this, Clark and the American Heritage Foundation board members essentially mirrored the efforts of US officials at the international level. They treated the promotion of creedal constitutionalism and of US imperium as two sides of the same coin: inculcating popular commitment to the former inevitably aided the cause of the latter.

To appreciate the extent to which the Freedom Train reflected a Cold War joining of constitutionalism with aggressive security politics, it is helpful to note differences between the American Heritage Foundation's project and the Bill of Rights anniversaries that had occurred on the eve of World War II. The earlier anniversary celebrations no doubt served a propaganda function for FDR, as he readied the country for war with Nazi Germany. But they did not go hand in hand with a comprehensive state crackdown on ideological dissent or on the Left broadly. Those celebrations were also notable for the extent to which labor and civil rights organizations, as well as their underlying memberships, were critically involved in the construction of the basic events. They were both top-down and bottom-up affairs.

By contrast, and far more closely mirroring pro-business and pro-war constitutional events during and after World War I, the Freedom Train was almost exclusively directed from above. It was carefully orchestrated by Cold War political and business elites, complete with pre-arranged "Rededication Week" events to precede the train's arrival in any given city. Leaving nothing to spontaneity and chance, the Foundation supplied local officials and volunteers with everything from editorials, stories, and cartoons for the city newspaper to advertising copy for businesses to speeches for dignitaries to instructions even on the minutiae of store window displays. As the historian Wendy Wall notes, rather than anything "grassroots," this choreographed affair "looked remarkably similar from Savannah to Spokane."[70]

In this way, despite all the celebration of American individualism and anti-statism, the Train carried with it a brand of authoritarian statecraft and a drive for ideological conformity that paralleled the very first Constitution Day events. Even the vision of free speech extolled in the Freedom Pledge that kicked off the tour spoke to how individualism and repression were stitched together. Mirroring the tenor of National Security League celebrations, government officials and business leaders in the American Heritage Foundation no doubt believed that political disagreement and expression were essential to American liberty. Yet certain types of dissent—forms of association and speech that officials felt threatened their vision of a free republic—had to be eliminated. Thus, Clark and others could both defend free speech and engage in subversive suppression due to a pro-security and pro-Constitution framework that presented state coercion as necessary—precisely so that true Americans could enjoy the benefits of an open society.

CROSS-CLASS ACCEPTANCE AND
COMMUNIST PARTY APOLOGETICS

The troubling nature of these conceptual aggregations was not lost on radicals at the time. The great Trinidadian journalist, critic, and socialist C. L. R. James noted in 1949 the striking contradiction of government officials claiming to protect civil liberties by cracking down on dissent and pursuing mass loyalty campaigns. For him, while Stalinist and fascist terror proceeded by "smash[ing] democratic rights as an open antagonist of democracy ... the American oligarchs abrogate the rights of the people in the name of the struggle against 'dictatorship' and 'totalitarianism.'"[71] Like virtually every other Black radical voice opposed to the Cold War, James would experience this contradiction firsthand. He penned these words under a pseudonym, given the repressive climate; four years later, despite being an outspoken socialist critic of Stalin and having lived in the United States for fourteen years, he found himself deported on ideological grounds. As for the Freedom Train, the CPUSA issued a memo condemning the project: "We cannot go along with the NAM [National Association of Manufacturers] and the Chamber of Commerce in helping to create this illusion of 'national unity.'"[72]

But such opposition faced an uphill battle. As the Red Scare picked up steam, large numbers of Americans took on board the Manichaean terms of Cold War politics. They were genuinely wary of Soviet-style dictatorship, and they accepted the proliferating claims about Soviet infiltration and subversive threats. Taking part in Freedom Train events became a way to demonstrate one's loyalty. In a context in which Americanism was rigidly juxtaposed against totalitarianism, participation highlighted the desire of many citizens to choose the "American" side—regardless of its ideological conditions and strictures.

Indeed, however top-down the project, boarding the Train or taking part in the Foundation's "Rededication" events generated a genuine outpouring of patriotic enthusiasm, especially from white citizens of all class backgrounds. Some 3.5 million Americans boarded the train, often waiting on seemingly endless lines to do so—a powerful visual expression of national devotion.[73] According to Wendy Wall, "as many as one in three participated in Freedom Rallies, Freedom Fashion Shows, and other events staged to celebrate the train's arrival in their towns."[74]

The willingness of white working-class constituencies in particular to embrace these events—even despite the lack of coverage of the labor movement and its ends—shaped how radicals approached the campaign. For instance, rather than calling on workers to boycott the train, the Communist Party was reduced to urging left-leaning organizations and activists to organize tours in which they could educate Americans about "the significance of the documents in relation to the current struggles of the people."[75] Earlier 1910s and 1920s Constitution Day celebrations had certainly helped to generate a mass base for veneration, but those events had nonetheless operated in a broader context of real political conflict and rolling discontent. Now, however, only a year or two removed from the largest strike wave in American history, essentially no direct and organized pushback emerged from within white working-class constituencies. The combination of repression and mass celebration had proven a dramatic ideological victory for Cold War elites.

To make sense of this victory, it should be noted that the CPUSA's internal contradictions made even many left-leaning citizens more likely to accept the era's Manichaeanism, and with it, projects like the Freedom Train. The party had put down real domestic roots in the 1930s as an American institution, with American leaders and a reform vision pegged to the particularities of the society. Many of the country's foremost writers, activists, artists, and scholars—white and Black—circulated in and out of the party during the heady days of the New Deal.

These party members and fellow travelers were not merely the "stooges" of the Kremlin, as Cold Warriors routinely claimed. Rather, they were often committed defenders of an anti-racist and anti-capitalist politics. Indeed, the party had gained a mass base during the 1930s precisely because local members—motivated by their deep moral commitments—were repeatedly willing to place themselves in the way of profound personal harm in order to defend society's most marginalized and violently oppressed communities. Moreover, such efforts were pursued independent of Soviet directive and in keeping with a genuine responsiveness to local needs.[76]

At the same time, A. Philip Randolph's long-standing worries about the party were clearly legitimate. Its national leadership had a secretive decision-making style and would switch overall policy orientations seemingly in response to missives from Moscow. As the legal scholar Geoffrey Stone notes, "newly available information" since the "collapse of the Soviet Union" "confirm[s] that the Soviets exercised considerable control over the CPUSA."[77] Indeed, for many local activists and fellow travelers, this sense of external direction was especially infuriating. And it had the effect, over the long run, of disconnecting the party from the mass base that activists had so painstakingly built. Indeed, for many Black Communist organizers in the South, the steady loss of that mass base was the evident consequence of mid-1930s strategic decisions imposed from above.

Now, given a Red Scare context of fear, more and more citizens refused to parse the political complexities. They worried about potential

Communist spies in government, and they rightly saw the willingness of CPUSA leadership to apologize for Stalinist terror as a profound moral failure. Such apologetics made it easier for citizens to accept state efforts that banned and totally suppressed the party, as well as those that infringed on the rights of members, fellow travelers, or even left-wing activists more generally. This was regardless of whether the specific organizations or individuals targeted actually engaged in any spying, sabotage, or criminal behavior at all. In a sense, the link between the Communist Party and the Soviet Union—along with the ways the former depended on the latter—led many to view the party as nothing more than a troubling Stalinist beachhead in the United States. Moreover, those very few Americans who seemed to back Soviet-style authoritarianism—a far smaller number than those circulating in and out of the party—served in this climate to delegitimize all socialist politics, even that of individuals like C. L. R. James who detailed explicitly the failures of post-revolutionary Russia to embody socialist values.

In essence, the government offered a stark choice between American capitalism and Soviet tyranny—and choosing the "American" side meant effectively repudiating socialism as such. This was despite the fact that, in the United States, the socialist tradition had actually been associated historically with efforts to deepen constitutional democracy: by marrying political and economic self-rule with civil rights and civil liberties. Yet, given the power of the Manichaean framing, the Communist Party's connection to the Soviet Union buttressed ideological objectives undergirding campaigns like the Freedom Train. At a basic level, it meant that any CPUSA challenge to the Train or to other loyalty campaigns could be rejected as merely Soviet propaganda—a key reason why these critiques gained so little steam.

At a deeper level, the connection between the party and Moscow further allowed governing elites to tar, more or less, any self-avowed instantiation of socialism—whether a state authoritarian or democratic variety—as inherently oppressive. It facilitated the Cold War presentation, as on the Freedom Train, of "freedom" itself as definitionally capitalist—even if myriad capitalist dictatorships existed abroad.

Conclusion: Critique and Legitimation in Cold War Constitutionalism

As the twentieth century proceeded, the definitional association of capitalism with liberty and socialism with oppression helped to hardwire into American politics a striking characteristic. Today, American governing elites might look back at a previous era's excesses as out of step with a national culture of civil rights and civil liberties, reinterpreting past practices like mass Japanese internment or the worst aspects of Red Scare crackdowns as aberrational national disgraces. But at the same time, ideas of American exceptionalism and necessary global authority generated near continuous growth in the domestic footprint of the security apparatus—punctuated time and again by failures in rights protections and violent reprisals against political dissenters.

As with oversees interventions, coups, and assassinations, officials and commentators differentiated between US domestic security violence and Soviet examples. As C. L. R. James suggested, government actors argued that American excesses were committed out of a desire to protect rights, precisely given the US global model's essential connection to free government. If anything, internal opposition within the United States to these regrettable practices—as well as later official condemnations—highlighted the real ethical distinctions between American capitalist democracy and its socialist enemies. The space within the US for self-reflection about past wrongs served as proof that the country embodied the open society it claimed to represent.

Over time, these arguments about the American project—and the Constitution's role within it—certainly curbed the most extreme violations of basic rights. But especially when framed in the Manichaean terms of American moral exceptionalism, frameworks of creedal and constitutional redemption nonetheless also operated to legitimate the basic contours of a now consolidated security apparatus. To a profound extent, both the expansion of that security state and the persistent breakdown in basic safeguards were shaped by a political culture that tied interventionism abroad and aggressive practices at home to the protection and promotion of American values, with the Constitution at their core.

As I will return to in part IV, for instance in the context of Vietnam, this overarching framework had real consequences going forward. Even when mainstream reformers and commentators decried national security violence or sought to restrain presidential abuse, they overwhelmingly tended to focus on symptoms rather than root causes. During and even after the Cold War, such voices routinely asserted the need to be true to the Constitution and to balance civil liberties and national security—through greater judicial oversight or even congressional legislation directly constraining executive authority. However, these constitutionally venerative reform projects overwhelmingly assumed the necessity for and permanence of American primacy, complete with the imperatives of global police power.

The result has been a habitual weakness of such efforts in practice to rein in the expanding security apparatus. To the extent that officials take as given a security vision entrenched during the Cold War, the consequence is often a dynamic of legal limitation in theory and political defection from rule-following in reality.

CHAPTER 12

Cold War Reform and the
Reframing of American Identity

In a special 1951 issue of *Fortune* magazine, the editors happily declared, "never have left-wing ideologies had so little influence on the American labor movement as they have today." They titled the issue "U. S. A.: The Permanent Revolution" as a playful appropriation of the revolutionary socialist phrase, and they noted with satisfaction that American workers did not identify with a "class-war union" as their primary site of political attachment. Instead, workers were Americans first, committed to national greatness abroad, and striving above all else for "middle class status and full citizenship" as individuals within the state. *Fortune* concluded confidently, and with much relief, "American labor is not 'working-class conscious'; it is not 'proletarian' and does not believe in class war."[1]

In a sense, the magazine merely repeated the earlier anti-communist rhetoric of major union leaders like the Congress of Industrial Organizations' (CIO) Philip Murray. But notably, the editors understood that rhetoric as more than labor's self-protection against Red Scare accusations. Rather, they saw across white working-class publics a deep investment in the Cold War terms of the American project. This marked a complete shift from the surveys that the same *Fortune* magazine had published only five years earlier, which reinforced business and government fears of intensifying post–World War II class conflict and mass disillusionment.

What had changed to make those worries seem so decisively a thing of the past? The Second Red Scare's national security constitutionalism, discussed in chapter 11, certainly provides a piece of the story. But the effective establishment of popular Cold War ideological agreement would not have been such a success if it relied only on violence and loyalty campaigns, even against the backdrop of fears regarding the

Soviet Union and the Communist Party's (CPUSA) ethical and political failings.

Ultimately, the type of political attachment *Fortune* highlighted and
celebrated also took root because of choices made by business and governing officials in the years following World War II. During the 1920s,
Constitution worship was still associated with business conservatism
and the political Right, including groups like the National Security
League and the American Protective League—and so was often connected to their extreme opposition toward any meaningful economic or
social reform. By contrast, Cold War governing elites took seriously that
widespread domestic buy-in could not be entrenched without actual
material improvements to the daily experiences of those traditionally on
the outside—especially white working-class and Black communities.

In important ways, the same officials operated through parallel methods in the international and domestic arenas. They defended American
primacy abroad through interventionist violence, but also through investment in multilateral institutions and in the extensive provision of development assistance. At home, political and business leaders similarly
contested the Soviet model by balancing state repression and mass celebrations with attempts to make good on creedal constitutional claims.[2]

This chapter explores the genuine achievements of such economic
and racial reforms and considers how they generated real buy-in to the
Cold War project from potentially restive social bases. I begin by detailing the terms of labor-business compromise as well as the emergence
of a substantial body of labor movement elites, not to mention union
members, who rallied to the Cold War cause. I also tease out comparable developments in the context of race, which resulted in Black leaders and their constituents backing—more fully than ever—reform
projects rooted in redemptive narratives of nation and Constitution.

I then examine the broader cultural developments that promoted
such buy-in, especially among African American elites, many of whom
now championed the American Cold War project in far less politically
ambiguous terms than in earlier eras. I contend that one key development involved the striking transformation of how white national politicians and commentators presented basic American identity. In the
context of Soviet rivalry and decolonization overseas, the consolidating version of creedal constitutionalism repudiated more stridently
than ever the presumptive Americanism of white supremacy, whether
expressed through domestic Jim Crow politics or shared white settler-
state solidarity abroad. In fact, white national elites increasingly pre-

sented Southern proponents of segregation, such as those in the Klan, as the very antithesis of Americanism—"hooded" threats akin to previous Nazi enemies—despite the Klan's association with constitution-promotion efforts in earlier eras.

These dynamics shifted the self-conceptions of both white and Black elites, as well as their views of the nation and their role within it. By the early 1960s, more and more white politicians had internalized a racially inclusive account of national identity. And they began to affirmatively identify their own historical past with that of non-white peoples, especially those engaged in independence projects abroad—precisely those communities long viewed as outsiders in the American story. Not unrelatedly, the same years witnessed an emerging group of Black Cold War elites who embraced the essential compatibility of pursuing both anti-racism and anti-colonialism along with the promotion, on the global stage, of the American model and post-war vision.

Through a consideration of how the Cold War compact gained meaningful domestic consent, this chapter also addresses a classic puzzle in American life: How did the members of a white, exclusivist, settler polity come to no longer recognize the central role of that history in structuring their own collective institutions and cultural past? The United States may share basic traits with various British settler colonies in the non-white world. But, as hinted at in chapter 1, Americans today—regardless of race—rarely think of themselves as part of an imperial family of racially constructed settler polities. Instead, most citizens seem to generally conceive of the country as quintessentially *anti*-imperial and inclusive. In fact, Americans have so thoroughly reframed their relationship to the national experience that what once might have been intuitive now appears to have little purchase on collective self-understanding.

While this overarching change did connect to the practical requirements of asserting global power over a decolonizing and overwhelmingly non-white world, this strategic dimension alone does not offer a full explanation. White political elites, and eventually the broader public, began to deeply internalize a universalistic and anti-imperial national narrative. In particular, white commentators began to link their own sense of personal political identity, and with it the creedal constitutional project, to two related accounts of belonging: first, the idea of the United States as a nation of immigrants; and second, as the "first new nation"—the initial decolonial domino that precipitated the fall of the old imperial order.

In other words, elites during these years began to conceive of themselves as situated similarly to non-white persons—whether migrants or
decolonizing peoples everywhere. And this self-understanding broke
critically with settler global affinities and a presumptive shared white
identity. Eventually, it also provided further narrative reinforcement for
civil rights transformations and thus for profound cultural and material
improvements across a broader swathe of society.

Still, for all these real benefits—which cannot be underestimated—
such narratives came with their own attendant costs. As I will explore in
part IV of the book, the country's shift in identity and self-understanding
effaced elements of the settler context from collective self-recognition.
And this in turn meant that Americans often avoided confronting—or
even failed to fully register—the country's ongoing colonial infrastructure or the living legacy of its settler history.

Building Cold War Domestic Consent

Although new narratives eventually reframed elite white American self-
awareness, broad domestic support for the Cold War project rested on
important material foundations. It connected centrally to an increasing
belief, among both movement leaders and mass publics, that constitutionally venerative and reformist strategies were succeeding—whatever
the claims of the country's remaining radical voices. Working-class citizens could look upon more conservative social groups, especially connected to business, and see those actors appear to make peace with
the New Deal economic order. And larger numbers of Black Americans perceived tangible improvements in their prospects through the
NAACP's litigation strategy and growing ties to the Democratic Party.

WHITE LABOR'S COLD WAR BOOM

The case of the United Auto Workers (UAW) offers striking insight into
both the depth of workers' demands and the management response. In
1945, during the height of the strike wave, the UAW not only called
for 30 percent pay increases for workers; to ensure that costs were not
passed on to consumers, the UAW also demanded that General Motors open up their books to the union. Unions effectively challenged
managerial prerogatives over the terms of production and distribution,
including how to price goods. In so doing, they asserted the need for a

new type of industrial democracy, in which workers shared in basic economic decision-making.[3]

For business executives, the domestic power of labor combined with the overseas example of Soviet economic success suggested real potential threats to corporate control. Furthermore, post-war labor protest—not far removed from the convulsive 1930s industrial struggles—had brought parts of the economy to a halt and had also indicated a potential social base for truly revolutionary changes. All of this convinced key business leaders—the very individuals spearheading the Freedom Train discussed in chapter 11—that unless some accommodations were made for labor, social unrest could well continue. And any such unrest could increase interest in Soviet-style state socialism, even at home. As UAW demands suggested, significant structural economic interventions that would systematically strip business of its discretionary authority were hardly off the table in the United States.

These labor pressures, with the Soviet specter in the background, set the stage for General Motors' famous 1950 agreement with UAW President Walter Reuther on a five-year collective bargaining plan. In return for the union's ensuring labor peace and abandoning earlier assertions of worker democracy, the company, according to the legal historian Reuel Schiller, provided "a substantial wage increase, the most generous pension plan in industrial America, medical insurance, annual cost-of-living increases, and a union shop."[4] As a commentator at the time detailed, that union shop in particular required "that all new employees"—although not existing non-union employees—"join the union and pay dues for at least one year."[5] *Fortune* declared the agreement the "Treaty of Detroit." And, as the country moved further away from the post-war strike wave, the agreement would establish the parameters for American labor-business cooperation and industrial life more generally.[6]

The fact that such arrangements coincided with improved economic conditions nationally further solidified the new settlement. The federal government's commitment to Keynesian stimulus spending increased domestic consumption and helped to facilitate a rising standard of living for white workers. And the material benefits of American global primacy provided the broader context for this boom, as the United States transformed from one among various global players to the dominant economic force in the world. Through the carrot of development assistance and the stick of military intervention and violent coups, the

United States was reconstructing foreign states in its image, and in the process opening markets for American goods. These developments, alongside the country's centrality to the global financial system (especially given the dollar's hegemony), provided the international underpinning for white middle-class prosperity.

All of this taken together made it seem that perhaps the global promotion of market capitalism—if hedged in with social safety nets, an enlightened corporate elite, and the right monetary policy—could well lift all boats, at home and abroad. As the editors of *Fortune* breathlessly declared of the Cold War economic project, in that same 1951 special issue,

> Fifty years ago American capitalism seemed to be what Marx predicted it would be and what all muckrakers said it was—the inhumane offspring of greed and irresponsibility. . . . But American capitalism today is actually nothing of the kind. There has occurred a great transformation, of which the world as a whole is as yet unaware. . . . There has been a vast dispersion of ownership and initiative, so that the capitalist system has become intimately bound in with the political system and takes nourishment from its democratic roots.[7]

American material largesse could thus offer important evidence for official claims that a capitalist system was the one true way to marry civil and political liberty with social welfare.

By the early 1950s, this sense of Cold War optimism spread to labor leadership and even to many white working-class citizens. To begin with, Reuther and other union officials were ultimately willing to leave managerial prerogatives to employers, so long as there were real material victories for their members. As even Reuther's more left-wing rival within the UAW, R. J. Thomas, commented during the earlier 1945 strike year, "I don't know much about the class struggle. I'm interested in wages, hours and working conditions."[8] And the trade-off with business appeared to provide just these ends, at least for those workers in industries where unions were strong. The scholar Jack Metzgar, the son of a steelworker, poignantly recalls the dramatic economic improvements his family enjoyed during the period: "If what we lived through in the 1950s was not liberation . . . then liberation never happened in real human lives."[9]

Labor leadership's acceptance of the trade-off was also bound to the very different political position of unions in the post-war period: New Deal victories meant that unions were increasingly an institutionalized player within state-business alliances, and indeed, within a more general governing elite. Given fears about being tarred with communism and labeled as disloyal, the era's union heads had no desire to jeopardize their newfound status or to be perceived as anything other than responsible Cold War actors. Indeed, Reuther himself emerged as a central figure within the highest echelons of the Democratic Party, enjoying in the 1960s close ties to President John F. Kennedy and becoming no less than President Lyndon Johnson's "confidant," according to Reuel Schiller.[10]

Such union leaders thus accepted a Cold War compact: labor focused exclusively on domestic wages and benefits, leaving business the right to shape the basic terms of production and workplace life. But this compact also effectively meant that labor granted the American state an unfettered right to pursue its anti-communist security objectives and global interventionist projects. Earlier generations of labor activists had often conceived of the movement as an insurgent and transnational mass democratic project, reaching everything from the basic terms of American capitalism to the state's overseas economic and military practices. But leadership now, in keeping with the Cold War linkages of market capitalism, liberal constitutionalism, and American primacy, abandoned whatever remained of an independent foreign policy.

This move extended naturally from labor's push for inclusion within the state's governing framework—as illustrated by its participation in anti-communist purges and acceptance of post-war business compromises. It also went hand in hand with Murray's declaration that the United State was a classless society. As opposed to past labor radicals, such figures essentially embraced the Cold War security state as representing the interests of all Americans—promoting shared and universal ideals abroad rather than primarily the material interests of a class elite.

This meant that labor, as it did during the Second World War, had a responsibility to sign on to the project of an American Century. Whatever the post-1945 dabbling of those like Walter Reuther in world federation, the Cold War nationalist goal became clear: to participate, through work at home and war abroad, in achieving the ends of the state. In fact, in 1961, the now merged AFL-CIO established its own American Institute for Free Labor Development (AIFLD), which aimed to shape the global labor movement on terms that dovetailed with American security objectives. This effort at times even meant undermining

unions elsewhere and making common cause with pro-business dictatorships, especially when foreign labor activists were viewed as insufficiently anti-communist.[11]

When union leaders had misgivings about Cold War practices, the
depth of their investment in the ties between labor, the state, and the
Democratic Party often undercut their willingness to push back. For
instance, despite Reuther's personal qualms about the Vietnam War,
his loyalty to Johnson led him to defend the administration in international settings. The historian and biographer Nelson Lichtenstein
writes that Reuther "put all his prestige on the line to forestall" efforts
in Europe, like that of the 1965 Amsterdam conference of the International Confederation of Free Trade Unions (ICFTU), to debate and
potentially condemn the American war effort.[12]

Union leadership's Cold War commitment was clearly motivated by
genuine ethical hostility to Soviet authoritarianism, in addition to strategic calculations.[13] But union officials were also responding to the role
of Cold War primacy in buttressing this post-war labor-business-state
settlement. One cannot underestimate the extent to which economic
growth and the enhanced position of many white workers in the 1950s
seemed, as it had during World War II, to go hand in hand with military expenditures, global interventionism, and a permanent wartime
footing.

Those in the IWW had once maintained that American imperialism fundamentally worked against the liberation of working people
at home and abroad. Now, however, at least for the white male unionized worker, domestic welfare gains and overseas war-making actually
fit neatly together. Indeed, whatever may have been lost in giving up
workplace control, labor leaders and many union members could look
with awe at US military and diplomatic might, and at the industrial
achievements of the country's domestic economy. As a new American
Century dawned, they could feel pride and a sense of collective purpose
in the working of American institutions. In a sense, Cold War politics
and the related post-war settlement fundamentally altered how union
institutions and many workers themselves related to the prevailing economic and political order. The experience of what Metzgar described as
"liberation" created a labor leadership—responsive to a growing base—
more invested in preserving the status quo than in cultural and political
opposition.

The intensity of this sentiment was such that even the Republican
passage of the Taft-Hartley bill in 1947—which significantly modified

the 1935 Wagner Act, labor's great New Deal achievement—did not puncture the mood of labor confidence. The success of the bill was a profound defeat for pro-labor forces, and it indicated how the labor unrest of 1945–1946 had affected public sentiment, aiding a powerful managerial offensive against unions. As the historian Jefferson Cowie writes, just a decade after the Wagner Act, the new bill "required union leaders to sign anti-communist affidavits, enumerated management's rights, allowed states to establish 'right-to-work' laws, limited the unions' political powers, and eliminated secondary boycotts, in addition to a host of other curtailments."[14]

The long-term effects would prove disastrous for the labor movement. The Taft-Hartley bill systematically purged unions of Left activists, who had been most committed to maintaining labor's organizing energy and momentum—including among Black Americans, women, and other communities historically deemphasized by union leaders. It also constricted labor's achievements in terms of both geography and economic sector—further ensuring that domains like agriculture and large swathes of the country, especially the South, would remain subject to the type of oppressive arrangements that operated before the New Deal.

Yet in the late 1940s and 1950s, although they railed against the bill, labor leaders could nonetheless place this setback in context. They could note that even business conservatives in Congress did not feel empowered to fully repudiate the Wagner Act and collective bargaining. And they could tell themselves that Taft-Hartley was a temporary reversal, which would be repealed in the short or medium term—even if, of course, that repeal never came. Unlike in the inter-war years, new examples of conservative reaction, such as Taft-Hartley, were not read as proof that the legal-political order itself had failed. Instead, they became subsumed within an overall account of the American economic and constitutional model as, by and large, a success story for the working class.[15]

LABOR'S GROWING DISCONNECT FROM BROADER SOCIAL MOVEMENTS

In important ways, the labor movement's increasingly conservative tendencies limited the scope of its demands and narrowed its viewpoint. It transformed the union itself into something more like a special interest group—focused above all on the economic status of dues-paying

members, rather than on broader social transformation. More generally, acceptance of the post-war settlement culturally and politically disconnected the movement, step by step, from related freedom struggles,
especially around Black and feminist liberation.

On matters of race, the labor movement remained an ally of traditional civil rights. But it steadily retreated as a leading strategic voice and
organizational arm of Black freedom efforts, as it had been for someone
like the union organizer and activist A. Philip Randolph. Randolph had
seen his work as president of the Brotherhood of Sleeping Car Porters
(BSCP) as intimately connecting questions of economic and racial justice. Yet the failure in particular of "Operation Dixie"—that 1940s effort of CIO organizers to create a cross-racial Southern union base—
meant that labor leadership, while calling for creedal inclusion, more or
less separated their bread-and-butter economic agenda from the project
of racial reform.[16]

Further reinforcing this tendency, many of the unions purged during
the anti-communist expulsions had high numbers of African Americans,[17] given the CPUSA's long-standing status within the Black community. The overall effect was a reification of the category of labor as
itself almost definitionally white: an amalgamated collection of the
various European immigrant and native-born communities stitched together through the ever more established tri-faith Judeo-Christian idea
of a pluralistic Protestant, Catholic, and Jewish American culture.

On matters of gender, the heart of the labor-business accord was
the creation of an American standard of living in which the primary
breadwinner—presumptively the male head of household—received a
"family wage" high enough to care for all of his dependents, his wife included.[18] Early-twentieth-century activists like Crystal Eastman, Emma
Goldman, or Harriot Stanton Blatch had previously linked feminism
and labor struggle together. Such voices often contended that transcending capitalism was bound to the overcoming of a destructive and
gendered division of labor, which reduced reproductive work to the
hidden and dependent labor of women alone.

But in many ways the post-war settlement was built on the same patriarchal assumptions that had shaped white labor's sociopolitical inclusion going all the way back to the Jacksonian period. The male union
member gained respectability and social standing through economic
arrangements that entrenched his dominance within the family unit.
And such dominance in fact constituted one of the principal psychic
and status benefits of the domestic Cold War compact itself. Indeed,

despite the achievements of the suffrage movement, the era became infused with a gendered politics of domesticity, shaping legal decision-making as well as the culture more broadly.[19] As late as 1961, the Supreme Court upheld a Florida law that included women on juries only if they requested to be added, on grounds that "a woman is still regarded as the center of home and family life."[20]

This dynamic severed most of what remained of the old Progressive and New Deal–era alliances between labor and feminist politics. Throughout the early Cold War period, feminism in general was in retreat, given the centrality of a gendered "cult of domesticity" to the entire post-war culture. This made it hard for feminist organizations to recruit new members—Alice Paul's National Woman's Party (NWP) had only about two hundred active members in the early 1950s[21]—and it structured who chose to join these groups.

In addition, most union leaders for decades had backed sex-specific protective legislation for women, along with the newer gendered "family wage" of the labor-business compact. Over the years, this tension between labor and feminist politics led the main women's rights organizations, especially supporters of proposed amendments like the ERA, to become strongly anti-labor. Thus, as Alice Paul told an interviewer about the political leanings of NWP activists, "so many, almost all our members seemed to be of the conservative school."[22] Given the demographics of who joined such groups, this was hardly surprising. During the 1950s, those involved in feminist activism were almost exclusively white and, as the historians Leila Rupp and Verta Taylor note, they were also an aging group that "by birth, marriage, or occupation [were] middle, upper middle, or upper class."[23]

Eastman had once hoped that labor and feminist constituencies could work together in ways that effectively radicalized each social movement, pushing society at large beyond the existing terms of both the state and the economy. But instead, as feminism became ever more isolated from other social movements, labor included, the opposite seemed to occur during the Cold War's first decade. The driving figures in what survived of the women's rights movement almost single-mindedly pursued formal equality and elite female access to positions of power. So long as male politicians were willing to support measures like the ERA, many of those remaining activists seemed fully willing to sign on to the projects of the state, including anti-communist crackdowns. And they also continued to be suspicious of any effort to expand the terrain of reform to include substantial racial or economic changes.

Similarly, the new union politics increasingly saw the primary achievement of the times as a middle-class American standard of living—one
union officials often treated as threatened by feminist critiques of male
authority.[24] Above all, the cultural drift of both movements—which
had once embodied truly significant challenges to the political order—
often shifted toward preservationist orientations. If anything, white labor politics and post-war feminism seemed at ease invoking a rigid new
brand of Cold War nationalism and constitutional commitment.

As discussed in chapter 8, during the 1930s key labor leaders had acceded to FDR's path of restorative and ameliorative reform, grounded
in narratives of constitutional commitment and national redemption.
In the wake of the Supreme Court's New Deal accommodations and
the rising threat of Nazism, those radical activists who had been committed to more revolutionary action—including fundamental institutional ruptures—effectively lost the internal struggle over the labor
movement's basic direction. And now those increasingly purged activists faced even more difficult circumstances: post-war union leaders appeared to believe as strongly in the genius of the American model as
their business opponents in Congress did. They seemed to line up as aggressively behind the security state, existing legal-political systems, and
even market capitalism—albeit hemmed in by social programs—as
their erstwhile class antagonists did. And union members gave little
hint of breaking with their leadership. In the context of an expanding
economic pie and Red Scare fears of foreign subversion, mass working-
class sentiment seemed to fall strikingly quiescent almost overnight.

The transformation of the labor movement's basic institutions went
even deeper than a rejection of the old class-based skepticism regarding
the constitutional system or an embrace of nation over class as the principal site of Cold War solidarity. In the Cold War public conversation,
union leaders acceded to a Red Scare climate in which not only "class
conflict" but even the notion of a coherent "working class" was treated
as a suspicious socialist concept. Politicians and commentators instead
used the increasingly ubiquitous phrase "middle class" to describe most
Americans—an essentially amorphous term that blurred the competing sides of the old social struggles.

The term spread, though, because it also spoke to shifting realities
among white union members themselves. The rising economic tide,
along with federal support for the mass production of new American
suburbs—critically, on racially segregated terms—gave white workers
broad access to homeownership. It created new, often racially exclusive

communities outside the cities, in which the social experiences of many union members began to replicate those of salaried employees and even workplace bosses.[25]

Over time, labor radicals found themselves confronting a social base fundamentally different in cultural identity from what had existed previously—a group far more invested in preserving gains than in opening the post-war settlement for revision. In a sense, the growing conservatism of union leadership and the cultural transformations within labor constituencies fed off each other, reinforcing an overall drift toward Cold War orthodoxy.

THE COLD WAR EMBRACE OF CIVIL RIGHTS

The other central means by which governing elites sought to gain public buy-in for the Cold War project was through racial reform. Truman and officials in Washington not only believed that sustained racial conflict was a continuous source of national disunity. As discussed in chapter 11, they also remained attuned to the profound transformations in the international system as the United States ascended to global dominance. As Truman famously quipped of how domestic racial reform and American primacy went hand in hand, "the top dog in a world which is over half-colored ought to clean his own house."[26]

In short, in a decolonizing world where American policymakers were locked in ideological struggle for the allegiance of non-white peoples, Jim Crow domestic practices made winning hearts and minds especially difficult. They directly undermined American claims to be any different than apartheid South Africa, let alone to be an inherently anti-imperial and universalist project in liberal equality. If policymakers hoped to cement national consensus and to project an image of racial inclusion to the globe, they would have to respond tangibly to civil rights demands.

As a result of this dynamic, Black activists faced a dual response from white national officials. Black radicals who identified with opposition to the Cold War—like W. E. B. Du Bois, Claudia Jones, Paul Robeson, and C. L. R. James—experienced intense state repression. But if activists accepted the state's security prerogatives at home and abroad—including the Cold War fusing of capitalist faith with creedal constitutionalism—then genuine improvements seemed possible. In fact, the NAACP's leadership soon concluded that white elite receptivity in Washington made for a fundamentally different moment than after World War I.[27] As long as African American leaders embraced Cold War nationalism, their accommodation would seemingly be repaid with legal and political victories.

This sense was evident even during the most intense days of post-war white violence against returning Black veterans. In December 1946, Truman put together the President's Committee on Civil Rights to address domestic race relations. One NAACP board member, Channing Tobias, was appointed to the committee, and both Walter White and Thurgood Marshall (then head of the NAACP's legal defense fund) appeared as witnesses. And just days after Du Bois's *An Appeal to the World* was introduced at the United Nations, a moment discussed in chapter 11, the presidential committee issued its own report, *To Secure These Rights*. The report called for various anti-discrimination measures, including a federal anti-lynching bill and a ban of the poll tax, and eventually became the basis for eliminating segregation in the armed forces. As the historian Manfred Berg notes, it "corresponded closely to the NAACP's own program" and was infused with creedal and Myrdallian language, declaring segregation to be "inconsistent with the fundamental equalitarianism of the American way of life."[28]

Politicians in Washington not only adopted NAACP initiatives; they also responded directly to African American pressure campaigns. Take for example the effort of activists to contest the decision of cities in the South to segregate viewing of the Freedom Train, with whites and Blacks entering it at different hours. As the famed Black author Langston Hughes wrote in his widely circulated 1947 poem, "Freedom Train," recorded for radio by none other than Paul Robeson:

If my children ask me, *Daddy, please explain*
Why There's Jim Crow stations for the Freedom Train,
What shall I tell my children? . . . *You* tell me—
'Cause freedom ain't freedom when a man ain't free.
But maybe they explains it on the
Freedom Train . . .[29]

Under fire from groups like the NAACP and facing impending stops across the South, the American Heritage Foundation's board and the train's government backers were pushed into a firmer and more public position than they had initially desired. Attorney General Tom Clark issued a letter to local mayors declaring that there would be no segregation aboard the train. And when Southern cities like Memphis and Birmingham publicly balked at integrating train viewing, the Foundation eventually canceled stops in those cities—a decision that led the NAACP to award the Foundation its highest honor. Indeed, even the Communist-affiliated *Daily Worker*, despite its qualms about the overall ideological project of the train, had to conclude that the train's trip to the South amounted to a "spectacular victory over the Jimcrow system."[30]

Even A. Philip Randolph's more confrontational 1948 call for mass Black resistance to the new peacetime conscription—unless the military was desegregated—also paid an immediate dividend. Randolph may have been attacked as un-American, and he surely would have faced real personal consequences if he had actually followed through with the call. Still, Truman and other officials sought to head off any mass action, and to ensure that someone like Randolph—who had been outspokenly anti-communist—could be convinced to abide by Cold War terms. The same month that he called on Congress to reintroduce the draft, Truman issued Executive Order 9981 ending segregation in the armed forces.[31] Like virtually all the post-war racial reforms, implementation happened only fitfully and would not be completed for years. Yet Truman's order highlighted the real vulnerability of Cold War politics to organized pressure from Black leaders and mass movements. Such activists appreciated how the shifting global dynamics of decolonization and Soviet rivalry created clear political openings. As the NAACP's Walter White told Truman at a White House meeting, racial "discrimination" was "being used abroad to discredit the United States and convince the people of the world that Americans were incurably addicted to bigotry."[32]

In keeping with those global dynamics, the growing embrace by white governing elites of racial inclusion, which became central both to their own sense of national identity and to the projection of American power abroad, had significant strategic implications for Black politics. It fundamentally tilted the historic debate among Black activists about whether to abide by redemptive and nationalist reform narratives. If African American politics had long been marked by an ambivalent attachment to the rhetoric and symbols of the nation-state, post-war leaders increasingly suppressed such ambivalence. The overwhelming Black elite position instead consisted of rallying around the Cold War version of creedal constitutionalism as the primary mode of Black political argument vis-à-vis the society at large.

This decision meant lining up decisively behind Truman. The 1948 presidential election provided an initial demonstration of Cold War fidelity for Black elites. For civil rights leaders like White, Roy Wilkins, and others, Truman was effectively the first sitting president running on genuine racial reform. Whatever Du Bois and Robeson may have felt about Progressive Party candidate Henry Wallace's deeper egalitarian commitments, a Black embrace of the anti–Cold War Wallace—especially at a moment of intense anti-communist fervor—could threaten the gains already achieved. White and others believed, not unreasonably, that if instead African Americans stood behind Truman, it would show white politicians the electoral utility of an anti-discrimination platform.[33]

Critically for future strategy, the Black public at large appeared to agree with the NAACP and the rest of the traditional leadership. The ensuing decade became a boom period for NAACP expansion, and the organization's dues-paying membership increased to 240,000 in 1953 and more than half a million in the early 1960s.[34] As for the election itself, despite Henry Wallace's civil rights credentials and the unflagging support he received from both Du Bois and Robeson—figures with great personal standing in Black life—Berg writes that "about 70 percent of blacks . . . voted for Truman and not more than 10 percent for Wallace." In fact, "solid backing from black voters allowed Truman to carry California, Illinois, and Ohio; without them he very likely would have lost the election."[35]

Moreover, the 1948 election as a whole indicated that Black and labor constituencies appeared to side with the emerging post-war domestic and international compact. Wallace had not only been FDR's vice president; he had also been perhaps the most popular 1940s New Deal figure in FDR's administration. In 1946 Truman fired him as secretary of commerce because of his public opposition to a confrontational approach to the Soviet Union, and in many ways Wallace's presidential campaign became a referendum on the Cold War itself. This meant that, for Black and labor elites who sought to derive meaning from the election returns, the conclusion seemed clear. Even within previously radical social bases, there appeared to be support for the Cold War framework—so long as this support led to actual economic, legal, and political protections. Highlighting both the intensity of the Red Scare climate and the unwillingness of Black and white working-class communities to take political risks at a moment of meaningful improvement, Wallace received no electoral votes and only 2.37 percent of the overall tally—the latter less than Strom Thurmond's Southern segregationist States' Rights candidacy.[36]

THE BLACK POLITICAL TURN TO
CONSTITUTIONAL LITIGATION

A second related and key strategic implication for Black politics was the African American post-war leadership's turn to constitutional litigation as the basis for overcoming Jim Crow segregation. Given white elite receptivity to racial reform, Black legal activists such as Thurgood Marshall very consciously applied the official language of creedal constitutionalism as part and parcel of a broader litigation approach.

Previous radicals—for instance, those involved with the IWW in the 1910s or with Communist Party legal challenges in the South during the early 1930s—had employed the courts as a defensive maneuver to protect union members or poor African Americans from jail. And cases like the Scottsboro trial also aimed in part to expose to public censure the lawlessness of the constitutional system as a whole. In other words, earlier litigation strategies did not necessarily entail the acceptance by radical lawyers of the legitimacy of either the courts or the legal-political order.

The overall NAACP move to the courts was not itself novel. It had actually begun in the inter-war period, though very much as a product of necessity. Those were years in which both major political parties, for distinct internal coalitional reasons, were uninterested in racial reform. Furthermore, Southern white Democrats maintained a stranglehold on key congressional committees through seniority. With the parties uninterested and the legislative process blocked, "the NAACP," as the political scientist Sidney Tarrow writes, "turned to the institutions that were furthest from representative politics—the courts."[37] Strikingly, that decision underscores how the initial shift to litigation resulted from the very brokenness Du Bois attributed to American representative institutions.

Yet, in the 1930s and especially in the 1940s, as the Supreme Court began altering its approach to civil rights, not only did the NAACP commit to a broad court-based campaign against segregation.[38] The context also shaped how Black lawyers articulated the meaning of engaging in the legal process. These efforts were not defensive maneuvers that displayed the lawlessness of the American system, nor were they purely borne of necessity due to the undemocratic essence of the constitutional structure.

Rather, Marshall and others presented the litigation strategy as demonstrating the very capacity of the constitutional system to fulfill its historic promise—to show the world the genuinely liberal and egalitarian truth of the American project. This rhetorical emphasis shone through, for instance, in the ubiquity of references to Gunnar Myrdal's *American Dilemma* by civil rights lawyers engaged in desegregation cases.[39]

The landmark 1954 Supreme Court decision *Brown v. Board of Education* confirmed the wisdom of both litigation and rhetorical investment in creed and Constitution. It offered perhaps the greatest example of what the historian Mary Dudziak has called the era's "cold war civil rights."[40] The decision struck down school segregation as a violation of the Fourteenth Amendment's equal protection clause and declared "separate but equal" to be inherently unequal.[41] The case once again highlighted how the global context created an environment particularly conducive to Black legal and political strategies grounded in constitutional redemption. The Justice Department took the step of filing an amicus brief in which it emphasized the international imperative to end Jim Crow. The brief included a lengthy quote from then Secretary of State Dean Acheson, in which he concluded bluntly that "the undeniable existence of racial discrimination gives unfriendly governments the most effective kind of ammunition for their propaganda warfare."[42]

Explaining the decision later, Supreme Court Chief Justice Earl Warren, a longtime Republican Party stalwart and former California attorney general and governor, would declare that the country faced a "contest for the hearts and minds of people" and that "our American system like all others is on trial both at home and abroad. The way it works; the manner in which it solves the problems of our day; the extent to which we maintain the spirit of our Constitution with its Bill of Rights, will in the long run do more to make it both secure and the object of adulation than the number of hydrogen bombs we stockpile."[43]

Indeed, Warren's own path offered further evidence of the shifts in white elite self-consciousness. Although as attorney general of California, he had argued for mass Japanese internment, by the 1950s he felt, in his posthumously published words, deep regret at "the removal order and my own testimony advocating it, because it was not in keeping with our American concept of freedom and the rights of citizens." He now fully embraced a Myrdallian vision of national life, and believed the Cold War would be won only if Americans lived up to their creedal ideals.[44]

For Black leaders, these victories—symbolized by *Brown*—provided tremendous demonstrations of the reform potential of Cold War constitutional politics, whatever their associated strictures. And not unlike the gains made by white working-class constituencies, they had a striking impact on Black rhetoric and increasingly on how African American leaders as well as constituents conceived of their own politics and relation to the United States. If ameliorative racial reform could proceed under the existing institutions—and moral suasion could convince white national elites to change policies—perhaps Black people should indeed understand themselves as part of a shared community with whites, maintaining allegiance to both Constitution and country.

Shifting White and Black Perceptions of Self and Nation

Eventually, the steady success of reforms profoundly altered how key Black leaders approached larger questions about the American project. These improvements did more than simply encourage acceptance of a pragmatic compromise with the Cold War security state. Instead, they seemed to validate the official US presentation of the country— affirming and legitimating the Cold War linkage of market capitalism and liberal constitutionalism to defenses of global dominance. This heightened legitimacy made key figures far more willing to unabashedly identify as Cold Warriors themselves.

The depth and breadth of this shift drew in part from the degree to which ameliorative reforms went hand in hand with cultural shifts in self-understanding among white national elites. Such elites increasingly understood segregationism as a threat to a free and multiracial America, and as fundamentally unpatriotic. They even began identifying themselves and the US culturally and politically not with a transatlantic white world—as earlier establishment white officials had done— but instead with non-white decolonizing societies.

WHITE SEGREGATIONISM AS ANTI-AMERICAN AND ANTI-CONSTITUTIONAL

Given greater Black support for Cold War objectives, more and more white politicians of both parties started to juxtapose Cold War nationalism not against Black disloyalty, but instead against the "un-American" nature of white supremacist organizations like the Ku Klux Klan. Indeed, as white and Black national elites converged on the same language of racial reform, white officials found it easier to depict both communism and segregationism as outside a common and liberal American identity—one shared across the racial divide.

A striking and early illustration of this phenomenon was offered by

Republican Pennsylvania Senator Edward Martin's Constitution Day speech in Philadelphia for the 1947 launching of the Freedom Train. Martin was a strident Cold Warrior, considered by labor opponents to be a reactionary or "'mossback' conservative." Following a long line of pro-business elites, Martin spoke of the Constitution in worshipful tones. In his 1967 *New York Times* obituary, the paper quoted him, describing his own views, as above all seeking to "defend America from enemies at home and abroad [and] to preserve the American system of government and the sacred heritage of freedom and independence handed down to us by the heroes and patriots of past generations."[45] In this way, he sounded remarkably similar to the pro-business and pro-war defenders of the Constitution in the 1910s and 1920s, including within the Klan itself.

But unlike those previous conservatives, Martin made clear in his Freedom Train speech that Americanism, understood in creedal constitutional terms, was under threat from "hooded men" as well as from socialists and communists. Indeed, it was vital to repudiate Jim Crow, because "persecuted Americans will turn in bitterness from Americanism to Communism. Inadvertently we shall be building a fifth column within our gates."[46] Here, Martin raised the old specter of Black Americans as a "fifth column," but, critically, he placed the blame squarely with white segregationists. Moreover, he directly attacked groups like the Klan, which had long declared themselves to be "100 percent American," as in truth inherently un-American.

This framing of the Klan as something atavistic and outside the American project had an additional implication. During the early decades of the Cold War, national policymakers in Washington cast Southern segregationism in particular as not only anti-creedal but also anti-constitutional. And this was despite the extent to which groups like the Klan had long wrapped themselves in the 1787 text and been deeply involved in 1920s Constitution worship.

During Reconstruction, of course, anti-Constitution sentiment had spread among bitter Southern sectionalists. And it remained at the edges of white Southern politics, articulated most notably by the historian and social critic Frank Lawrence Owsley, an outspoken member of the "Southern Agrarians": a collection of Vanderbilt academics committed to defending the South's way of life from perceived cultural and political attack. In a series of essays, especially his widely read 1935 piece "The Pillars of Agrarianism," Owsley presented the constitutional system as dominated by "particular sectional interests"—essentially a political imposition on the South of the aims of the wealthy North. With the Confederacy defeated and Southern independence in the twentieth century no longer possible, Owsley believed that abandoning the Constitution might offer the only solution to maintaining the South's distinctive racial hierarchy and cultural identity. He called for a new mode of government that ensured de facto autonomy to the various regions of the country, with only minimal federal intervention.[47]

Such views were distinctly out of step with the dominant defenses of both Southern segregation and white identity, which had by now fully embraced the Constitution. In no small part this was due to the successful re-consolidation of explicit white supremacy in the former slave states, and the extent to which the constitutional system itself aided such re-consolidation—particularly through state-based representation and related structures of federalism. And, of course, the late-nineteenth-century Supreme Court had moved aggressively to defang the Reconstruction Amendments and to give white rule its constitutional imprimatur, even beyond legalizing "separate but equal" through cases like *Plessy*. For instance, when white officials on the ground overthrew multiracial and democratically elected Reconstruction governments or imposed Jim Crow practices, they often worked hand in glove with private citizens exercising extralegal violence, for instance through the lynching of African Americans. But according to the Supreme Court in cases such as 1883's *U.S. v. Harris*,[48] Congress did not have the capacity under the Fourteenth Amendment to authorize the federal government to prosecute "private" rather than official state violence, if local authorities refused to do so. They held this to be the case even though, in truth, local authorities and elected politicians were often complicit or even directly involved in white attacks on Black individuals and communities.[49]

By the 1950s, few bothered to follow Owsley down the rabbit-hole of imagining new regional confederations. Instead, the most common way to defend segregation was to simply invoke constitutional fidelity and the importance of respect for Supreme Court precedent, as illustrated by the 1956 Declaration of Constitutional Principles. The Declaration, informally called the "Southern Manifesto," was written by Senators Strom Thurmond and Richard Russell as a response to *Brown v. Board of Education* and signed by 101 white Southern congressmen. The manifesto repeatedly proclaimed reverence for the Constitution "as the fundamental law of the land" and attacked the *Brown* decision for the extent to which it diverged from long-standing judicial case law and the framers' principles of states' rights and federalism: "We decry the Supreme Court's encroachments on rights reserved to the States and to the people, contrary to established law, and to the Constitution."[50]

Significantly, this constitutionalist position was hardly implausible at the time as an assessment of post-Reconstruction Supreme Court jurisprudence. Indeed, one of the most distinguished constitutional scholars of the early Cold War, Columbia law professor and Northerner Herbert Wechsler, contended in the *Harvard Law Review* that *Brown's* legal reasoning was faulty. Wechsler was not a segregationist and approved of the decision's outcome. But he argued that, by overturning school segregation on grounds that it "generate[d] a feeling of inferiority" among Black children "unlikely ever to be undone,"[51] the Court rested its ruling on the subjective and perhaps shifting experiences of those who were "affected" by the law—rather than on supposedly "neutral principles" that would "transcend any immediate result."[52] In the years since, Wechsler's argument has "become infamous" in the legal academy "for being obtuse."[53] Its implicit concerns about whether there are "neutral principles" to reject segregation, or if segregation necessarily entails inequality, indicate an underlying failure to grapple with the structural reality of white supremacy. But the prominence accorded the arguments at the time speaks to a very different constitutional climate, one in which segregationist legal claims were taken seriously.

But even if segregationists saw themselves as defenders of the Constitution, the terms of the debate—particularly after *Brown*—cast a different shadow within the national conversation. To begin with, the *Brown* decision produced a political backlash among whites in the South that brought racial conservatives to local and state office, and more generally emboldened die-hard white supremacists.[54] Thus, defenses of segregation increasingly repudiated creedal egalitarianism as such—even the old Wilsonian depiction of Jim Crow as tutelary and implicitly transitional—with Alabama Governor George Wallace notoriously proclaiming in 1963, "segregation now...segregation tomorrow...segregation forever."[55] This meant that, to the extent that pro-segregation politics were constitutionalist, they appeared fundamentally at odds with the specifically creedal constitutionalism that provided the organizing principles of American power abroad and the Cold War compact at home.

As Southern whites resisted federal government efforts to implement Supreme Court decisions such as *Brown*, through organizations like the Klan or the White Citizens' Councils, the constitutionalist credentials of segregationists appeared to collapse. White national policymakers found themselves clashing with local Southern politicians and officials who refused to abide by federal laws and constitutional mandates. Such intransigence, reinforced by extralegal violence and white supremacist lawlessness, had always been part of white rule in the former Confederacy. But in this Cold War moment, white officials and publics at the national level increasingly came to see Southern legal obstructionism and racial brutality as a growing threat to constitutionalism itself. It was the George Wallaces and Bull Connors (Birmingham commissioner of public safety) of the world—rather than moderate Black reformers like those in the NAACP—who undermined the Constitution, whatever the segregationist claims to textual fidelity. And this view spread nationally, in part due to the nightly scenes of violence against peaceful Black protesters that, by the early 1960s, arrived through television screens in homes across the country.[56]

Since the World War I era, segregationists had played a central role in promoting a politics of Constitution worship. But now, to many white officials in Washington, they appeared both un-American *and* lawlessly anti-constitutional. Indeed, just as Cold War commentators and politicians had recast the entire global and domestic history of socialist constitutionalism as inherently a contradiction in terms, they did something similar with Southern segregationism: the latter became branded as never, in truth, an American constitutional tradition.

This cultural turn against segregationism by white national elites validated the Cold War era's Black defenders of the creedal Constitution. For individuals like Roy Wilkins or especially Thurgood Marshall, it vindicated their claim to be the country's authentic defenders of the Constitution and, indeed, the country's "true" Americans. It thus reinforced an emerging and deep-seated post-war nationalism within a substantial segment of Black leadership. For someone like Marshall, African Americans had been the historic champions of the creed. And this meant that in the present they were perhaps more deeply American than anyone—more fully an embodiment of nationalist ideals.

SETTLERS NO MORE: REIMAGINING THE PAST FOR A NEW MULTIRACIAL AMERICA

A further reaffirmation of this Black embrace of the Constitution came in the fact that white national figures did not simply proclaim the anti-Americanism of open white supremacy. In addition, such figures fundamentally reframed their own sense of personal and political identity in the context of civil rights activism at home and decolonization abroad.

The United States' preeminent global position forced a reconsideration of how Americans related to the rest of the world. The classic settler view, expressed as recently as 1942 by General Douglas MacArthur in Australia, was that the United States was essentially a white outpost in the non-white world. Yet, given developments in which such a construction became ever more untenable—both domestically and overseas—white national elites began forging very different accounts of the nation's historical meaning and thus of white American self-understanding.

Perhaps the clearest example of this comes from the spread of a new phrase in the late 1950s—the now widespread idea of the country as a "nation of immigrants." As the historian Donna Gabaccia notes, the phrase itself first appeared in the late nineteenth century, but it was used quite sparingly. During that era, the most common term used to describe overseas migrants was the word "emigrant," often applied broadly to anyone moving from one jurisdiction to another—whether from a different state or from another country. Indeed, the loose usage of "emigrant" underscored how, throughout the nineteenth century, the border remained very much a port of entry for Europeans rather than a closed and highly restrictive barrier. In fact, the phrase "nation of immigrants" did not take hold during the late nineteenth century in part because it was mostly nativist writers and politicians who used "immigrant," creating popular associations between the term and a xenophobic politics of restriction.[57]

But during the Cold War, the phrase "nation of immigrants" aggressively reemerged in political discourse. And it did so with the word "immigrant" now shorn of any earlier negative connotations. In particular, it became closely connected with John F. Kennedy, whose 1958 book *A Nation of Immigrants*, published by the Anti-Defamation League (ADL), both highlighted his aspirations for the presidency and became—especially after his assassination—a significant touchstone in popular discussions about the meaning of American identity.[58]

It was not a coincidence that Kennedy, eventually the country's first Catholic president, popularized the phrase and the presentation of the country in these terms—nor that the ADL published the book. In many ways, the concept tied directly to tri-faith and Judeo-Christian notions of creedal inclusion that had circulated among pro-immigrant groups, especially Jewish and Catholic, going back to the 1930s and 1940s.

But Kennedy's arguments went much further. They attempted to retell the history of open movement for Europeans not just as a story of European inclusion as American settlers. Kennedy also told a story of long-standing universal acceptance in the United States of all peoples. In a decolonizing world, the settler—long an embodiment of colonizing power—increasingly became a figure of suspicion across Asia and Africa. As such, Kennedy's reframing was noteworthy. It reimagined the past in keeping with the global cultural changes of the era.

In conceiving of who counted as an American, Kennedy may have highlighted various European migrations across the centuries. But, importantly, he gave no particular religious or ethno-racial group pride of place as preeminent in directing the national ethos. In this way, the account provided a twentieth-century culmination of Frederick Douglass's "composite nation," discussed in chapter 2 with its earlier idea of the US as a home equally for all. For Kennedy too, everyone in the country was at root an immigrant, whether European, Asian, Black, or even Native American. He wrote, "we cannot really speak of a particular 'immigrant contribution,' to America because all Americans have been immigrants or the descendants of immigrants; even the Indians . . . migrated to the American continent." Some may have come earlier and some later, but all groups—regardless of race, religion, or even past experience of slavery—were motivated by the same two impulses: "the hope of personal freedom and the hope for economic opportunity." This meant that despite nativist attacks, every successive wave of immigrants—whether English, Irish, or Chinese—had in truth enriched and furthered the promise embedded in both the Declaration and the Constitution, "confirm[ing] the impulses in American life demanding more political liberty and more economic growth."[59]

This idea of the United States as a nation of immigrants, drawn to the country by ideals of capitalist democracy and liberal constitutionalism, offered a dramatic revisioning of how the country engaged with the world. For starters, simply calling the United States a universal "nation of immigrants" in the 1950s required some suspension of disbelief. Racially restrictive quotas remained on the books and, just as significant, dramatically suppressed the country's actual foreign-born population—"only 5 percent" of the overall population at the time.[60] Given these incredibly low numbers, numerous countries overseas had far greater claim to being a "nation of immigrants" than did the United States. In a sense, the phrase was far more an assertion of how those like Kennedy wished their country to be perceived, at home and abroad, than of concrete policies and statistical reality.

At an even deeper level, Kennedy also presented a revisioning of the very history of settlement, one that largely did away with the now complicated figure of the settler. For those like Teddy Roosevelt, American identity was forged through confrontation between the "English speaking races" and Native inhabitants, with the "winning of the west" — settlers wresting territorial and political control from Indigenous peoples — the "epic feat" of American history. But to Cold War politicians like Kennedy, one could not claim global leadership in an overwhelmingly non-white world and still define the country's origins through a story of racial struggle and conquest. Instead, he described Native peoples, enslaved African workers, Catholic immigrants, and early Puritans as all simply embodying different episodes in the same historical movement. This meant that the American nation was forged not through a constitutive settler-Native contest. Rather, the great national crucible was the steady and essentially non-conflictual peopling of what amounted to empty land, with heirs gathered from across the globe.

Indeed, Kennedy crucially refused to present even Puritan settlers as distinctively Anglo-European or as early participants in any project of territorial expansion. Rather, in the wake of the Nazi genocide of European Jewish people, Kennedy presented Puritans as essentially predecessors to the twentieth century's persecuted refugees. They came to the United States out of a "search for freedom of worship," just as in "our own day . . . anti-Semitic and anti-Christian persecution in Hitler's Germany and the Communist empire had driven people from their homes to seek refuge in America."[61]

This presentation of the Puritan was significant, suggesting a key alteration in certain historical understandings of the earliest days of settlement. When the prominent academic and diplomat David Jayne Hill wrote glowingly about the Mayflower Compact in the lead-up to World War I, he highlighted how the Constitution was the culmination of a long-standing Anglo-Protestant cultural commitment to self-government. The implication was that this commitment was a distinctively *settler* value — brought to North America by Puritans and their descendants rather than by Native inhabitants, enslaved Africans, or even later southern and eastern Europeans. The principles of self-government were ultimately of universal application — available to all regardless of race. But for Hill as well as for Woodrow Wilson, their Anglo-Protestant roots spoke to which groups were the cultural repositories of American freedom and so should enjoy domestic and global leadership.

Now, however, Puritans served a different end for those like Kennedy. In Kennedy's anti-totalitarian Cold War reading, Puritans had moral standing within the American experience because they highlighted the country's birth as a land of refuge from tyrannical oppression. This reimagining of the Puritan thus worked to alter the relevant cultural meaning of various communities. Seventeenth- and eighteenth-century Anglo-Americans were not Teddy Roosevelt's conquering pioneers, engaged in dispossession and racial combat. Instead, they were persecuted immigrants, part of one wave of a movement to North America of which Native peoples simply embodied another and earlier wave. In this way, settlers were recast as refugees, and all groups, Indigenous communities included, were migrants—sharing the land together and in search of the same creedal constitutional ends: namely, political liberty and economic opportunity.

This narrative consciously repudiated any connection between American national identity and the settler projects that defined other Anglo-European outposts in the decolonizing world. Rather than being bound culturally or by the "consanguinity of race" to white Australia or apartheid South Africa, the American "immigrant" had no specific racial background and was no morally blameworthy conqueror. If anything, the Puritan migration to the United States had an elevated moral standing precisely due to its foundation in histories of oppression and in a treacherous journey in search of freedom.

Kennedy's retelling suggested a remarkable development within white American historical memory and political consciousness. On the one hand, it spoke to a profound internalization, among a growing number of white political elites, of the idea that the country should not, now or ever, be conceived of as a white republic. On the other hand, the ground for this internalization was simply the erasure, from popular historical memory, of key elements and conditions in American political development—and with it, the seeming erasure of any deep need to tackle this history's potential ongoing legacies of racial and economic hierarchy.

THE FIRST POSTCOLONIAL NATION

If these Cold War arguments disconnected American identity from settler identity, they also provided the backdrop for an even more dramatic set of claims. National elites and policymakers began to conceive of early white Americans not as colonizers, but as anti-colonial resisters akin to non-white groups in the Global South. Kennedy himself became a key articulator of this view, especially during his time as chair of the Subcommittee on African Affairs in the Senate Foreign Relations Committee.[62] In one indicative speech from the late 1950s, Kennedy used language not unlike that of Indonesian President Sukarno at the 1956 Bandung Conference, discussed in chapter 10. In particular, Kennedy drew a direct line between the eighteenth-century Anglo-American colonists' revolt against the British Empire and independence movements across Africa: "From a small spark kindled in America, a flame has arisen not to be extinguished. . . . [T]hat very flame is today lighting what was once called 'the Dark Continent.'"[63]

If Kennedy and other US officials had begun drawing the connection, Seymour Martin Lipset's seminal 1963 book, *The First New Nation*, quickly became the most influential expression of this account of the US's historic relation to the world. It was in this book, a finalist for the National Book Award, that Lipset so forcefully presented the federal Constitution as the United States' "supreme symbol of authority," promoting much-needed "democratic stability." But his linkage of the Constitution to the exceptionalism of the American project was nonetheless critically distinct from that offered earlier by people like Woodrow Wilson. Rather than connecting American settlers to a shared European world, Lipset tied the country to non-European experiences. He contended that the very essence of American exceptionalism could be found in the country's status as the first truly *postcolonial* society: "The first new nation. . . . The first major colony successfully to break away from colonial rule through revolution." To the extent that the United States bore any meaningful relationship to European histories of empire, it was not as Teddy Roosevelt's white outpost in non-white surroundings. Precisely because the country from its birth had been anti-imperial, it had more in common with the independence projects of Indigenous societies than it did with English settler experiments in Australia or South Africa.[64]

Lipset's reframing of US exceptionalism fit naturally with the "nation of immigrants" rhetoric, underscoring why Kennedy himself had been a key progenitor of both perspectives. If all Americans were simply migrants in search of freedom and economic opportunity, then they were not European colonizers on Native land. Instead, they were best understood as colonized subjects of a British imperial crown—and subjects who in fact struck the first great historic blow against European empire.

There was obvious truth to the point that the American revolution had indeed been an anti-imperial break from England, as Nehru and Sukarno had themselves had emphasized. However, the anti-imperial narrative of Lipset and Kennedy ignored the equally central fact that independence and constitutional founding did not entail the end of colonization. Rather, it explicitly empowered local settler populations, and thus spurred a new phase of both expansion and political control over outsider groups. This meant that the United States offered more than simply one history of empire; instead, it had been marked by a double history of first British and then locally led expropriation.[65]

Despite that reality, the political utility of the emerging position was evident, given the Cold War battle for hearts and minds. In fact, under Lipset's brand of modernization theory, the American anti-imperial past cut against the idea that the Soviet Union offered a more congruent developmental model — no matter the latter country's rapid industrialization. He argued instead that American history offered recently independent states in Asia and Africa profound "clues as to how revolutionary equalitarianism and populist values may eventually be incorporated into a stable nonauthoritarian polity."[66] In other words, the United States was worthy of emulation because of how Americans had essentially traveled the same path as non-white and previously colonized societies, only at an earlier moment in time.

Without question, Lipset's anti-imperial reading of the country served the actual end of defending Cold War American imperium, including a tutelary project in the Global South with its own echoes of the old Wilsonian logic. Still, Lipset's account highlighted a dramatic break from the long-standing politics of white solidarity. And it thus had real implications for domestic political culture.

To begin with, Lipset and others believed deeply in this postcolonial story of the United States. Thus, many white Americans — including those at the highest level — now explicitly identified the American project with historically marginalized non-white communities. For these commentators and politicians, the country had more in common with a new nation-state like India than it did with apartheid South Africa.

The fact that Lipset essentially repeated, as his own self-understanding, arguments made earlier by Nehru was significant. When Nehru spoke to the US Congress in 1949, he fully recognized the durability and pervasiveness of white racism in the United States. He hoped that his analogy between the American and Indian independence movements would press US politicians to internalize their stated ideals — to appre-

ciate more completely the shared humanity of all peoples regardless
of race. But he was also aware that, in that moment, such an analogy
might surprise his white listeners, who would need to look beyond
what "appear[s] somewhat alien" to recognize those parallels across
the globe.[67] Now, however, Lipset asserted these propositions as simple
truths about the American condition. And he found a hospitable white
policy-making audience, fully ready to embrace them as their own.

BLACK COLD WARRIORS: RALPH BUNCHE, THURGOOD MARSHALL, AND THE AMERICAN MODEL

For a range of Black elites, these developments suggested the transformative effects of Cold War nationalism on American society. Not only
were white judges and politicians on the national stage adopting racial
reforms; they were explicitly rejecting notions of shared white solidarity, and instead identifying culturally with non-white communities. In
this context, more and more Black leaders also began to identify with
the essential promise of American institutions. They increasingly accepted the Myrdallian premise that the problem in collective life was
not the underlying nature of the economic and constitutional order.
Instead, it was the as yet incomplete fulfillment of the country's liberal
tradition—a tradition that Black activists, as true patriots, had a particular role in safeguarding and carrying into the future.

This narrative indicated that the goal of reform in Cold War America
was to fulfill this national project. And this aim would be achieved by
ensuring that everyone, regardless of race, enjoyed formal legal protections and had an equal opportunity to enjoy professional and middle-
class respectability. As a related implication, these Black elites tended to
downplay more systematic and structural critiques; nothing about the
deep social infrastructure of Cold War America or its engagement with
the world actually needed fundamental alteration.

This framing not only rejected long-standing Black radical assertions
about the inherently anti-democratic and racially subordinating structure of the constitutional system. It also acceded to a brand of creedal
constitutionalism far more preservationist in character than earlier varieties. In other words, Black leaders like Marshall or Roy Wilkins, while
deeply committed to a domestic reform agenda, more or less accepted
the governing Cold War rhetoric of basic class harmony, steady racial
progress, market legitimacy, and American exceptionalism.

One can see these developments in Martin Luther King Jr.'s early speeches, which display a real consistency with the broader Cold War discourse. His famous commencement address at Lincoln University in 1961, titled "The American Dream," is infused with creedal rhetoric. King begins by quoting from the Declaration of Independence, referring to its universal language as the heart of the American "dream." He then reads the US constitutional system through the principles of the Declaration, arguing that the American commitment to equality and individual rights is what "distinguishes democracy and our form of government from all of the totalitarian regimes that have emerged in history." King spends the bulk of the speech engaging with how through "slavery and segregation" the country has been "tragically divided against herself." But he nonetheless distinguishes fundamentally between American freedom and totalitarian tyranny, and presents the eighteenth-century "Founding Fathers of our nation" as heroic figures that "dreamed this noble dream"—effectively bequeathing it to future generations.[68]

Over the course of the 1960s, King, along with many African Americans activists and citizens, would come to question these venerative presumptions. And even during the 1950s there remained voices of explicit Black dissent from the Cold War narrative—including Du Bois and Malcolm X, the charismatic young minister and orator who began building a following within the Nation of Islam. But, far more systematically than in earlier periods, Black leaders tended to speak about national identity and to imagine the relevant field of political dispute primarily through the era's rigid politics of Constitution and nation.

This did not mean that mainstream African American institutions and leaders abandoned their strong identification with anti-colonialism. They continued to view domestic struggles against racism as joined to the overcoming of European empire. But they also increasingly saw no irreconcilable conflict between promoting the independence of polities across the globe and backing the basic contours of the US Cold War project, whether through new multilateral institutions or in foreign constitution-building exercises.

At the international level, for instance, Ralph Bunche became deeply identified with UN-led decolonization efforts. As a member of the US delegation during debates over the UN Charter, he pressed for a much more comprehensive UN-administered trustee system for colonial territories, one that would, as Carol Anderson writes, "include independence as the ultimate goal."[69] And upon receiving the Nobel Peace Prize, Bunche made clear his vision for how global institutions could shape a world of free and equal states, collectively pursuing peace and prosperity. This vision was grounded in the American post-war project of multilateral decision-making and rule-following as the centerpiece of the international order, with the UN at the heart of the system. He declared that the UN was "engaged in an historic effort to underwrite the rights of man," was "opposed to imperialism of any kind," and sought "to give reassurance to the colonial peoples that their aspirations for freedom can be realized, if only gradually, by peaceful processes."[70]

Bunche's own experiences in the State Department brought home that white American officials often failed to push as comprehensively in the directions he desired, either for decolonization or for multilateral, inclusive, and collaborative decision-making. Yet, critically, he and others rejected the need for any properly independent Black foreign policy—separate from and potentially in conflict with the US security state. At the end of the day, US Cold War aims, properly channeled, could fulfill a shared white and Black American aspiration for the world.

Indeed, when Martin Luther King Jr. publicly opposed the Vietnam War, Bunche was among the most forceful Black defenders of the US government—akin to his 1951 role with *We Charge Genocide*, the petition presented by William Patterson and Paul Robeson to the UN. In a 1967 interview disseminated in the *New York Times*, Bunche declared that King should give up his leadership role in either the civil rights movement or the anti-war movement, as "the two efforts have too little in common." He also told the press that he had been the one to push the NAACP to issue a statement more critical of King and to call King's linkage of civil rights and anti-war politics a "serious tactical mistake." Above all, Bunche maintained that he spoke out not as a UN official, but as a "United States citizen."[71]

Taken as a whole, Bunche's career in American government and the UN system perhaps best embodied the implications of Black investment in promoting the American-led international order. This investment entailed a forthright commitment to spreading anti-racist values everywhere. But it also meant rallying, in key moments of ideological pushback, to the Cold War state's security objectives—even if that involved denouncing other African American activists.

As for Thurgood Marshall, his Cold War politics spoke to a parallel development—namely, that of Black elite participation, whether as a private citizen or under US auspices, in foreign constitution-building. One can see this in his involvement with Kenya's first post-independence constitution. Certainly the Kenyan independence leader

Oginga Odinga, mentioned in chapter 10, interpreted Marshall's participation as a defense of US goals for the country.

The final years of British rule in Kenya had witnessed a mass anticolonial revolt known as the Mau Mau uprising and led by dispossessed Black Africans, "squatters," contesting imperial land policy. The revolt highlighted to the British the difficulty of permanent colonial authority in Kenya and helped to press those in London to accept, albeit hesitantly, local independence. But when colonial administrators gathered various Kenyan and British constituencies together in 1960 for extensive constitutional talks at London's Lancaster House, they still wanted assurances that the property rights of white settlers on the ground would be protected.[72]

The British government was wary of any new constitutional order that might allow the post-independence Kenyan state to meaningfully redistribute land, despite the fact that this had been the driving impetus behind the Mau Mau uprising and remained a central demand shaping the independence movement. As the legal scholar Makau Mutua writes, during the Lancaster negotiations "more conservative elements, including white settler interests, pushed for a federal system of government with a strong bill of rights that would protect private property interests, particularly land."[73] Initially, British colonial administrators were suspicious of Marshall's status as an advisor to the most significant African party, the Kenyan African National Union (KANU). Odinga and future president Jomo Kenyatta were key leaders of the party at the time. British officials feared how a Black American civil rights leader and litigator might approach the question of white interests in the country.[74]

But much to the relief of the British, Marshall strongly backed property safeguards for white settlers.[75] For Odinga, none of this was a surprise. Marshall's presence at the talks owed to his close ties with Tom Mboya, another Kenyan leader within KANU. Not without good reason, Odinga viewed Mboya as someone being "groomed" by American officials for "leadership."[76] According to the historian Penny Von Eschen, Mboya was being "overtly and covertly aid[ed]" by the US during this period.[77] And in Odinga's mind, Mboya was likely more committed to friendly relations with the US on pro-market terms than to systematically addressing the problem of African landlessness and dispossession.[78] Thus, despite Marshall's being a Black person and involved in the proceedings purely as a private citizen, Odinga considered him to be a servant of the American state's interests. According to Odinga,

Marshall's involvement "gave United States' circles a foot in the door of the conference and I was not happy about it."[79] This belief would only be further confirmed when Marshall toured Kenya in 1963 under the sponsorship of the US State Department.[80]

As for Marshall, he saw himself as genuinely committed to the interests of Kenya and no servant of US ends. Moreover, Marshall's suggestions for Kenya's constitution did not unthinkingly replicate the 1787 document. A committed New Dealer, he embraced FDR's more expansive socioeconomic vision of rights; the legal historian Mary Dudziak notes that at Lancaster House Marshall defended constitutional protections for "education, health, and welfare" along with union rights and "what would now be called a living wage." Even the property rights protections he promoted were actually modeled on the Nigerian constitution rather than the American one.[81]

Still, he brought to the Lancaster negotiations a background idea of the American model as the definitive embodiment of how to combine rights and democracy. Dudziak writes: "Marshall said that to prepare for this work, he 'looked over just about every constitution in the world just to see what was good.' Pounding his fist on the desk, he explained, 'And there's nothing that comes close to comparing with this one in the U. S. This one is the best I've ever seen.'"[82] A key consequence was that in practice he assumed that any legitimate constitutional government foundationally included respect for capitalist property relations.

Thus, in the context of these deliberations, his basic understanding of what a constitutional regime should look like often dovetailed more with the counter-majoritarian and property-protecting vision of the British than with that of the African nationalists he was advising. Indeed, one can more broadly read how American and British perspectives on appropriate governance in Kenya shared common threads in the way the Lancaster Constitution mirrored US language and design elements. Along with a bill of rights, it included an independent judiciary and a bicameral legislature named a Senate and a House of Representatives.[83]

Marshall was absolutely right to worry that without adequate property protections newly independent governments would engage in discriminatory confiscations of minority racial and ethnic communities — a real issue in the post-independence era.[84] But what he failed to appreciate was the extent to which the constitutional model he embraced fundamentally ignored the basic dynamics shaping the independence movement. For Odinga and many Kenyan Africans, colonization was principally about the theft of African land, and independence would not be meaningful without genuine property return. In a sense, one could argue that to the extent that the land question was not properly addressed, this created a destructive context in which empowered leaders would be likely to turn, cynically, to racially discriminatory confiscations, as occurred against Kenyan Asians. Such scapegoating provided a xenophobic way of tamping down popular discontent without providing a real remedy.

In any case, by enshrining detailed property protections, the ultimate 1963 Lancaster Constitution made it incredibly difficult to resolve the independence movement's constitutive grievance. As Odinga wrote, "our government's land policy was hobbled from the start by . . . the Constitution," including property compensation requirements that even specified that payment had to be made "in cash and not by bond." This meant that in order to resettle dispossessed Africans on land that had been stolen, the Kenyan government effectively would have to take out massive loans from Britain, its colonizer. "It is one thing to borrow and repay for productive assets," wrote Odinga, "but quite another to borrow huge sums which are promptly lost to our country when they are paid to the settler-sellers at the source of the loan, Great Britain."[85]

Of course, missing from this conversation was Britain's own decolonial and reparative responsibilities to provide—without strings—systematic economic restitution to the mass of Africans it had dispossessed, including the funding for any resettlement plan involving white-owned land. For Odinga, the constitutional model defended by the British as well as by Marshall essentially legitimated colonial theft and amounted to a basic nullification of the independence struggle. Indeed, it re-presented such theft, through carefully elaborated court-based procedures and payment schemes (overwhelmingly supervised by European lawyers and judges), as a victory for individual rights and the rule of law. All this occurred regardless of how new legal and financial practices might impoverish the country or still leave destitute those whose land was stolen. It led Odinga to warn fellow independence activists across Africa to be on guard against "giv[ing] themselves up to deceptive constitutional facades while imagining that they have truly attained complete freedom."[86]

Ultimately, the fact that the Lancaster Constitution was experienced by Kenyan Africans as a colonial imposition meant that, according to Makau Mutua, it "lacked a deep social base."[87] And on gaining the presidency, Kenyatta took advantage of this fact to implement new amendments—amendments that did not genuinely respond to the land question but that manipulated popular discontent to expand his institutional power. Step by step, these changes transformed the constitutional system into a brutal and personalized despotism. Soon Odinga found himself imprisoned and Tom Mboya was assassinated, likely by Kenyatta. But through it all, Kenyatta skillfully retained US support, by embracing American Cold War prerogatives and accepting pro-market frameworks that more or less turned the page on real land redress while massively enriching his family and his internal allies.

These developments highlighted for Odinga the particular challenges facing decolonizing societies that were aiming, as Nehru too had hoped, to combine political freedom with economic transformation for those most marginalized. In a world largely governed—even after formal independence—by Europe and the United States, he concluded: "The stage following on independence is the most dangerous. This is the point after which many national revolutions in Africa have suffered a setback, for . . . national governments have left too much in their countries unchanged, have not built for effective independence by transferring power and control to the authentic forces . . . and have forgotten that internal elements of exploitation are closely related to reactionary external pressures."[88]

As for Marshall, unfortunately he became emblematic of a type of US foreign policymaker who would drop in on African settings. Like such State Department officials, he also took for granted a Manichaean Cold War framing, which saw Kenyatta as a "modernizing" ally and avoided too close an assessment of the disconnect between the rhetoric and the reality of American constitution-promotion. He remembered with real pride his involvement with the Lancaster negotiations. To the end, he considered Kenyatta, as Dudziak writes, "a treasured friend,"[89] and refused to believe he had killed his other friend Tom Mboya.[90] In 1978, Marshall even traveled to Kenyatta's funeral as an official member of the American delegation. While there, at a time when the country had fully descended into a repressive brand of capitalist authoritarianism, he declared that he was "happy to find that the Schedule of Rights I drew for the Kenyan Government was working very well."[91]

Conclusion: Who Tells the Movement Story

In the decade plus following World War II, governing elites succeeded in entrenching at home ideological support for the basic terms of American power and Cold War dominance. This project had long-lasting transformative impacts within social movements themselves—with African American politics offering a key illustrative example. Between the 1930s and the 1950s, the driving institutions of Black movement politics shifted permanently. During the early 1930s, the Communist Party, led by Black activists at the local level, vied with the NAACP for a mass African American base in the South. Even after World War II, Black socialists—who combined their anti-colonialism with an internationalist opposition to American imperium—still enjoyed a significant voice in Black political life. W. E. B. Du Bois and Paul Robeson were among the most famous and esteemed Black figures in American society, and institutions like the Council on African Affairs and the Civil Rights Congress (although the latter never had more than 10,000 official members) retained real cultural influence.

But the post-war period's systematic suppression of Black radicalism— the state's destruction of its institutions as well as the prosecution, blacklisting, and exiling of its leadership—profoundly limited its political presence. Such ideas did not disappear entirely, of course. The historian John Munro details how they persisted in pockets of Black life as an alternative, if often subterranean, "anti-colonial front." He notes, for instance, the influence C. L. R. James continued to have on evolving Black radical thinking through his writings and through various study groups, especially in cities like Detroit, even after his deportation. Indeed, someone like James Boggs, the seminal Detroit-based Black socialist who had been a colleague of James, carried into 1960s struggles the pre–Cold War critiques of racial capitalism, American empire, and the federal Constitution, as I discuss in part IV of this book.[92]

But for many figures from pre–Cold War Black life, the break with the past could feel extreme. Someone like Du Bois was politically but also culturally isolated from erstwhile allies. He continued to personify a radical Black internationalism even under Cold War strictures, combining socialism, anti-colonialism, and opposition to American primacy. Yet, hounded by the security state—and with his US passport again revoked—he grew even more embittered about the American project and spent the final years of his life as an exile in Kwame Nkrumah's Ghana. His last act of defiance on US soil was to formally join the CPUSA in 1961, immediately before leaving.[93]

As for the renowned actor and activist Paul Robeson, he spent his final years largely in seclusion in the United States before dying in 1976. Although he lived to see renewed Black socialist and radical energy, the earlier Red Scare militancy meant that younger generations of African Americans did not grow up with him as part of their political identity. As the biographer Martin Duberman writes of Robeson, by the late 1960s he was "a faded memory to one generation and an unknown name to another. People over forty wondered what had ever become of him (the rumor spread that he had gone into self-exile in Russia), and many people under forty had no idea he had ever existed."[94]

By contrast, the NAACP's Thurgood Marshall became an increasingly powerful figure within the American state. He was appointed to a federal circuit court judgeship under Kennedy, made solicitor general under Lyndon Johnson, and finally appointed to the Supreme Court as the first Black American justice in 1967—taking over the seat previously held by none other than Tom Clark, who as attorney general had been so central in marshaling support for the Freedom Train. In a sense, the American state found a place for Black anti-racist and anti-colonial politics. But those voices that survived, like Marshall or Bunche, often found themselves operating as state intermediaries, negotiating white and non-white interactions on the global stage as part of the unfolding American Cold War project or engaged in similar negotiations in the context of domestic race relations.

These post-war years witnessed clear institutional success for traditional civil rights organizations and leadership, in terms of both practical ameliorative reforms and the growing incorporation of Cold War Black elites into positions of authority. This meant that, over time, the NAACP—as well as aligned activists and groups—enjoyed a central role in shaping not only the terms of reform efforts but also the memory of the preceding decades' movement struggles. This often elided the role of African American dissidents and their activities even in pervasive Black cultural accounts—given the degree to which these accounts too were filtered through the restrictions and narratives of the Cold War itself.

Indeed, one could make a very similar set of claims about the labor movement and working-class politics generally. The terms of the post-war settlement profoundly affected which leaders—past and present— gained moral and political authority going forward and which leaders were increasingly forgotten. Cold War strictures also influenced which institutions enjoyed representative status vis-à-vis social bases and therefore had the capacity to articulate demands and even to define communal identity.

Eventually, Cold War politics entailed the development of a fundamentally new American constitutional memory. In academic and even popular understandings of the Constitution and its meaning, scholars and commentators began to erase past radical traditions from the long history of constitutional struggle and debate.

CHAPTER 13

Constitutional Myths and the Victory of the Court

In 1955, Richard Hofstadter, the seminal historian and post-war intellectual of the American experience, famously declared, "it has been our fate as a nation not to have ideologies but to be one."[1] The occasion was a glowing *New York Times* review of Louis Hartz's recently published and soon-to-be landmark work, *The Liberal Tradition in America*.[2] In the review, Hofstadter reflected on what he considered a bedrock truth about American political identity—namely, the abiding cultural unity around the value of liberal constitutionalism. Echoing the basic thesis of Hartz's book, Hofstadter wrote that unlike Europe, the United States, "having no feudal traditions," also had "no socialist traditions" nor "deeply rooted and ardent class conflicts." And this American class exceptionalism helped to explain the ubiquitous love, from the founding, of "legalism" and the Constitution.[3]

Hofstadter's claims underscored the cultural and political cementing of a Cold War domestic compact. By the mid- to late 1950s, politicians, academics, and commentators had more or less all come to view the contemporary United States as defined by comprehensive liberal agreement—and in particular, by agreement around the official version of the creedal Constitution. As early as 1948, Richard Hofstadter himself had contended, in his seminal book, *The American Political Tradition*, that whatever the differences between Democrats and Republicans, the US maintained "a common ground, a unity of cultural and political tradition."[4]

But Hofstadter did not simply define the post-war moment as marked by a broad-ranging settlement. He appeared to claim that—from the very earliest days of colonization—the United States had *never* faced genuine ideological conflict or extensive class struggle. And remarkably, more and more scholars and government officials followed suit: they began to transcribe a historically contingent early Cold War settlement back across the entire American experience. In fact, during the 1950s and early 1960s, this "consensus" school of American history, associated with Hofstadter, came to dominate studies of US politics. And it often drove how politicians and commentators presented the national project.

Stepping back, the fact that these arguments became so pervasive, and so quickly, is especially striking. Twenty years earlier, the country had been engulfed in momentous strike waves, which in 1934 and 1936 seemed to raise the genuine possibility of social revolution. During the first four decades of the twentieth century, many scholars, politicians, and commentators would have been taken aback by the idea of the US as exceptional for the *absence* of class-based struggle. After all, near open class warfare appeared to define the country from the 1890s to the 1930s. In fact, precisely the opposite implication featured prominently in a common Progressive-era question in studies of American politics: Why had the United States—a country steeped in republican ideas of citizenship—found itself overcome by class conflict and institutional paralysis? Rather than presuming that the United States was a land "Without Feudalism," as the title to Hofstadter's 1955 review announced, earlier scholarly and political answers to this question often focused on the preservation of aristocratic privilege in the constitutional structure and in the economic relations shaping the factory and the farm.

As for socialist traditions, Hofstadter essentially mirrored the title of the German sociologist Werner Sombart's 1906 work, *Why Is There No Socialism in the United States?* But in the years since Sombart's analysis—which was translated domestically by the Left socialist journal the *International Socialist Review*—the country had witnessed robust labor radicalism, an electorally viable Socialist Party of America (SPA) under the leadership of Eugene V. Debs, and the substantial mass appeal in the 1930s of the Communist Party, especially among Black Americans in the South and immigrant workers in the North. As discussed in several previous chapters, a combination of reform and repression had contained these efforts. But suggesting, as Hofstadter did, that the country never had "socialist traditions" was a remarkable rereading of the recent past.

This presentation indicated that the political conversation had shifted to such a degree that elite conventional wisdom essentially erased earlier struggles from American history. And this transformation in elite understanding went hand in hand with a related and equally fundamental transformation in constitutional memory. As I discuss in chapters 10–12, Cold War officials and commentators elevated support for a fairly rigid account of the creedal Constitution into a pre-political article of faith. According to the historian Hans Kohn's own 1957 book on American nationalism (deeply resonant with the arguments of Hofstadter, Gunnar Myrdal, and Seymour Martin Lipset), the Constitution "represent[ed] the lifeblood of the American nation, its supreme symbol and manifestation," and was "so intimately welded with the national existence itself that the two [had] become inseparable."[5]

These voices went even further. They depicted American political culture as always marked not only by an absence of class struggle, but also by near unanimous veneration of the 1787 Constitution—from the founding to their own mid-twentieth-century moment. Looking over the past, Hartz saw only an abiding "cult of constitution worship." He characterized this as a distinctively US "cultural phenomenon" and the product of a "fixed, dogmatic liberalism" in the American "way of life."[6] Over the course of the 1950s, the earlier policy-making and scholarly fears of institutional and ideological fragility and breakdown vanished. And the age's key interpreters felt secure in suggesting that the preceding eras' central ideological conflicts—including over the basic legitimacy of the Constitution—had never happened at all.

It is one thing to overcome radical activism through repression and accommodation. But how did these Cold War interpreters effectively eliminate even the *awareness* of past radical traditions—including traditions of constitutional skepticism—from their accounts? And what were the long-term effects of this narrative erasure for American constitutional memory and politics?

In this chapter, I argue that the establishment response to the rise and fall of Joseph McCarthy and especially to the specter of "McCarthyism" played a decisive role in this narrative shift. It framed how officials, intellectuals, and academics retroactively defined the social struggles that had shaped American life from the Gilded Age to World War II—and thus how they interpreted their present and looked toward the future.

I begin with how Cold War framings reconceived past struggles— as well as ideological challenges from both the Right and the Left—as variants of the same threatening "populism." Such narratives asserted that any populist impulses existing within the public were not actually contrary to Hartz's "dogmatic liberalism." Instead they were, at root, pathological forms of the country's basic cultural and ideological unity. In this way, even political opponents of the Cold War settlement found their beliefs twisted to fit within a flattened history of American consensus.

In addition, this intellectual fixation with populism revealed a deep-seated suspicion among governing political and intellectual elites of mass democratic politics. Such distrust promoted a dramatic embrace not just of the 1787 Constitution generally, but especially of those counter-majoritarian and anti-democratic elements so critiqued by earlier constitutional opponents.

The chapter then explores how these fears of unchecked majorities produced a dramatic elevation, among political and legal elites, of the Supreme Court in particular as the premiere institution for safeguarding liberal constitutionalism. Indeed, these years saw the Court itself become increasingly synonymous with the Constitution as such. At the same time, the legal profession—rather than movement activists or even politicians—became more and more decisively identified as the essential articulators of constitutional meaning. Relatedly, the main scholarly repository of knowledge about broader American constitutional traditions moved from history and political science departments to law schools.

This shift in what it meant to engage with the Constitution had profound implications for constitutional politics going forward. In particular, it transferred energy and attention away from questions of institutional design and basic legal-political order, which had been so central to decades of Progressive-era debate. Instead, American constitutionalism became a matter almost exclusively of textual interpretation—overseen by lawyers and overwhelmingly concerned with court-based debate and resolution. Under the consolidating view, constitutionalism was best understood as the intergenerational and distinctively American language for working out, through reasoned deliberation, the basic meaning of the existing document. And in this process, the Supreme Court—as the guardian of the constitutional language—achieved an exalted status: an esteem that would have been stunning twenty-five years earlier.

Of course, this refurbished intellectual history of constitutional thought completely ignored earlier radical figures who had reflected deeply on the American constitutional system, but not through a narrowly legalist lens. And the retelling created a fundamental rupture in the constitutional memory of the Left, in keeping with broader trends spurred by the Red Scare. As discussed in chapter 11, Cold War repression had quelled radical politics, which by the early 1960s moved to the edges of cultural life. Just as importantly, mainstream academic and popular writing started to reinterpret the very meaning of past Left institutions and movements, and especially the history and traditions of American socialism—including its constitutionalist dimensions. The Cold War reinterpretation thus entirely omitted competing visions of constitutional design and constitutional politics from the historical record. Such reinterpretation enabled the Cold War model to stand alone: the sole American expression of how to combine constitutionalism and democracy.

This dramatic diminution in constitutional memory and imagination directly impacted future politics. Social struggle, especially over racial justice and Cold War violence, such as in Vietnam, returned to center stage in the 1960s. And yet, new generations of radicals—even when they maintained contact with pre–Cold War socialist influences like C. L. R. James—often operated without a memory of how American constitutionalism need not be Cold War constitutionalism. Many activists attempted to restitch a cross-generational Left cultural fabric, but they did so in a setting in which the richness of earlier traditions of constitutional experimentation had significantly disappeared down a Cold War rabbit-hole.

Looking at how 1950s and early 1960s politics altered constitutional memory points to a virtually unremarked-upon element of most American scholarship on the Constitution: today's field of constitutional law is, to a large extent, the product of a Cold War convergence in which virtually all constitutional debate narrowed to a discussion of the dynamics and discursive practices of the federal judiciary.[7] Given this, the key figures with the expertise to understand and comment on how judges operated tended to be law professors, who themselves—due to a combination of background, training, and professional acculturation—came to believe deeply in the document and in the Cold War terms of creedal constitutionalism.

This means that responsibility for the broader cultural memory of the Constitution has rested with a scholarly field that itself was shaped by and effectively enclosed within Cold War judgments about the country and its past. Scholars certainly acknowledged that political life faced extensive dissensus, including over matters of constitutional interpretation—such as which rights the Court should protect and what meaning it should give to particular textual language. But the assumption became that any dissensus took place against the backdrop of shared, continuous, and near unanimous fidelity to the constitutional system as a whole.

When legal scholars today celebrate a version of constitutionalism—especially court-centered reason-giving and intergenerational interpretive traditions—as central to liberal political ethics and practice, they also inadvertently commemorate related Cold War developments. And what Americans mean when they talk about the Constitution today connects to ideas that became entrenched during that era, at times through violence. These ideas rested on a deep suspicion of mass popular capacities. And they also, historically, followed a systematic oppression and erasure of other horizons of democratic constitutionalist possibility.

The Populist Threat to Constitutionalism

This Cold War constitutional politics and memory emerged from an anti-populist sensibility that spread across academic and governing elites. The political phenomenon of Joseph McCarthy—including his spectacular rise and fall—promoted an elite conventional wisdom about the most significant dangers facing the post-war American project: above all, the central domestic threat came from pathologies inherent in the very ideological consensus that defined the country's liberal-democratic essence. These pathologies, associated especially with conformity, fed a potential tyranny of the majority—which in turn emphasized the need to hem in majority rule through institutional checks, and to promote a public culture grounded in ethics of moderation, pluralism, and political responsibility.

COLD WARRIORS MAKE SENSE OF JOSEPH MCCARTHY

In the early 1950s, Wisconsin Republican Senator Joseph McCarthy orchestrated Senate hearings in which he lodged false accusations of rampant Soviet infiltration, including throughout the State Department and the military. If McCarthy's actions were decidedly "illiberal," for all their extremism they did not radically deviate from the overall politics of the Cold War state. Instead, his hearings were of a piece with the state's mass investigations and constant invocations of subversive threat to an American way of life, all of which sowed profound public anxiety and distrust.

If anything, McCarthy's tactics once more exposed basic tensions within Cold War constitutionalism. As discussed in chapter 11, what distinguished this era's Second Red Scare from the World War I–era First Red Scare was the extent to which President Truman, Attorney General Tom Clark, and others emphasized the centrality in the United States of values like free speech and religious toleration. Motivated by an anti-totalitarian framework, they distinguished American respect for dissent from Nazi and Soviet opposition to it. And yet, those like Truman and Clark preserved the constitutional state—and thus the presumptive protections of the First Amendment—through infringing on the rights of individuals and groups targeted as enemies. These measures also went hand in hand with promoting an overall climate in which many Americans understood that they would avoid personal and professional damage by acquiescing to top-down political obedience. Thus, for all the invocations of the Bill of Rights and of a bedrock American civil libertarianism, nothing about Second Red Scare practices expressed an especially strong culture of toleration and dissent. In a sense, McCarthy simply embodied a blunter authoritarian version of the era's intertwining of aggressive security measures with devotion to the constitutional state.

Yet many Cold Warriors, in government and in the academy, did not consider McCarthy a true Cold War ally or an extension of the official establishment framework. Nor did they see in his approach a more extreme mirror of their own policies. Instead, they conceived of McCarthyism's downfall as proof of the abiding liberalism and constitutional commitment—including civil libertarian commitment—of Americans and their legal-political order, even during the Cold War.

Above all, McCarthy and the idea of McCarthyism played this role by allowing politicians and scholars to reimagine all the diverse ideological strains of opposition to liberal constitutionalism as sharing the same core "populist" impulse. Left-wing socialists, right-wing fascists, and Southern segregationists—across American history—were combined under a single conceptual rubric. In the process, these ideological traditions were significantly cleansed, in popular construction, of their very distinct and often opposed principles and goals.

Furthermore, given who McCarthy targeted and how he presented the relevant dangers to the nation, Cold Warriors tended to look upon him as a profound menace to anti-communism itself. McCarthy notably focused his ire on an educated and overwhelmingly Anglo-Protestant elite, rather than on more conventional targets such as the white immigrant working class or even Black and other minority constituents.[8]

That historic elite, by and large, continued to hold institutional power across government, business, and the universities. But McCarthy's accusations suggested a natural endpoint of the Red Scare climate, in redirecting charges of treason back upon the very officials and institutions that had set the trajectory of the Cold War state.

In the 1950 Wheeling, West Virginia speech that helped to make him a household name, McCarthy made explicit who he viewed as the nation's enemy: "It has not been the less fortunate or members of minority groups who have been selling this Nation out, but rather those who have had all the benefits that the wealthiest nation on earth has had to offer—the finest homes, the finest college education, and the finest jobs in Government we can give. This is glaringly true in the State Department. There the bright young men who are born with silver spoons in their mouths are the ones who have been worst."[9] McCarthy found Truman's secretary of state, Dean Acheson, a particularly distasteful figure—which was one reason for his special obsession with imagined Soviet conspiracies in the State Department. As the historian Gary Gerstle details, McCarthy saw in Acheson every vice of the Anglo-Protestant elite: Acheson's mother was English and he had a British speaking style and demeanor, as well as all the benefits of education at "Groton, Harvard College, and Harvard Law School."[10]

In McCarthy's homophobic and misogynistic terms, all of this suggested that Acheson and those like him were not truly manly; out of cowardice or a weak will, they would easily fall prey to Soviet corruption.[11] Thus, rather than the sturdy American middle class, it was the educated elite—marked by aristocratic pretensions—that constituted the country's real "fifth column."[12] Of course, from the perspective of Acheson as well as many policy-making voices within and outside Washington, McCarthy's charges were delusions, motivated by resentment and status anxiety. Even worse, his accusations amounted to a direct assault on the Cold War institutions necessary to ensure global primacy and to counteract the real sources of Soviet subversion.

When McCarthy's political fortunes eventually collapsed, officials and academics breathed a sigh of relief, but they also began assessing what the McCarthyite phenomenon had meant for the country. And this assessment generated a number of striking—and often counterintuitive—conclusions, which would have long-term effects on public conversation. To begin with, as the political theorist Anton Jäger notes, commentators at the time focused on the fact that McCarthy himself was from Wisconsin—once such an epicenter of American socialism that the World War I–era National Security League speaker Robert McNutt McElroy infamously declared the whole state trea- sonous. More broadly, McCarthy's support seemed strongest on the Midwest plains, which previously had been associated with the Popu- list movement.[13] This commentary held even though McCarthy's poli- tics had none of the typical class-based economic appeals historically linked to Populism, Progressivism, or the SPA. Instead, his politics of denouncing Washington elites seemed all about scapegoating, para- noia, and conspiracy.

At a Cold War moment in which even labor leaders appeared to be re- treating from class-conscious politics, McCarthy's appeal—supposedly just where class politics had once been so strong—led scholars and commentators to make a further claim. Perhaps, as both Hofstadter and Hartz began to argue, socialist class politics had *never* truly taken hold in the United States. Rather, those past movements shared the same basic impulse as modern-day McCarthyism: namely, a general revolt of the masses against those perceived as their cultural "betters," rather than of a specific, class-conscious, and European-styled labor constituency.

Such a revolt was less about economic transformation and far more about resentment toward those with status. In Hofstadter's reframing of both the Populist movement and broader agrarian socialism in Kan- sas and Wisconsin, ultimately this politics emerged from small prop- erty owners' fears about their own slipping position within society. Such anxieties often devolved into an anti-intellectual, nostalgic, and xenophobic worldview, in which the masses or the plain people of real America understood themselves to be the "innocent pastoral victims of a conspiracy hatched in the distance."[14]

Of course, this analysis had a basic flaw. Close electoral studies indi- cated that McCarthy pulled from different pockets of support than had past agrarian reformers, like the Wisconsin Progressive Robert La Fol- lette Sr. As the political scientist Michael Rogin detailed in 1967, Mc- Carthy and La Follette both may have spoken to rural discontent. But this did not mean that earlier Populist, Progressive, and Socialist move- ments were *not* shaped by a specific class character. For instance, Mc- Carthy generally did well in rural parts of the state, regardless of class composition. However, "La Follette had been consistently rejected in the rich, southern countryside." Whatever the claims of Hofstadter and others, "support for agrarian radicals [had] rested," Rogin concluded, "on groups with clear-cut common economic interests."[15]

Indeed, opposition to McCarthy suggested the continuing persistence of such economic awareness. McCarthy's support came not from specifically working-class constituents, but instead from what Rogin called "the traditional sources of Republican strength." Furthermore, McCarthy did especially poorly with the urban working class, who understood him—for all the anti-elitist demagoguery—as a figure of business conservatism and an opponent of the New Deal.[16] Underscoring just this point, the historian of American socialism David Shannon remarked as early as 1961, "La Follette's most important opponents, powerful businessmen, were, for the most part, supporters of McCarthy." And there was notable irony in linking the two, since "the very forces that branded the elder La Follette as a seditious demagogue were helping to promote McCarthy; the avenues to power were open to McCarthy as they never were to 'Fighting Bob' La Follette."[17]

Yet, for Hofstadter and others, the sharper picture provided by county-level voting data receded in importance. Instead, the dominant analysis of McCarthyism was shaped by arguments about how the political masses in general shared certain psychological dispositions. These dispositions, infused with status anxiety, had potentially deleterious implications even during a time of growing American affluence like the 1950s. If anything, such affluence could even have a counterintuitive effect: newly enriched Americans were especially conscious of potential status reversals, and resentful of those who seemed more secure, cultured, and educated. The sociologists David Reisman and Nathan Glazer captured this perspective in what would become a seminal 1955 edited volume on the meaning of McCarthyism, *The New American Right*: "A great many Americans, newly risen from poverty or the catastrophe of the Depression, are much more fearful of losing their wealth than the scions of more established families already accustomed to paying taxes, to giving to charity, and to the practice of *noblesse oblige*." At the end of the nineteenth century, the masses had presumably fallen prey to Left excesses. But now they were especially susceptible to McCarthy, with his "gruff charm and his Populist roots," as well as to "prophets and politicians" of all varieties who "specializ[ed] in the bogeys of adults."[18]

This analysis was deeply influenced by the massive 1950 multiauthor study led by Theodor Adorno on what had made individuals embrace fascist appeals, *The Authoritarian Personality*. American policymakers and social scientists interpreted the McCarthy phenomenon as disproving older class-based analyses of American life by people like Charles Beard. And they took from Adorno a causal focus on how modern mass society exacerbated just those psychological tendencies that promoted extremist movements.[19]

This line of analysis no doubt became so compelling to officials and scholars in part because it amounted to a Cold War updating of the old Madisonian version of tyranny of the majority. It also dovetailed with the rediscovery of the nineteenth-century French author and politician Alexis de Tocqueville. Although Tocqueville's two-volume *Democracy in America* (1835 and 1840) had initially been treated as a significant work, it largely disappeared from public discussion "from the late 1860s until the late 1930s." But in the post-war era, writes the sociologist Robert Nesbit, the text became a phenomenon: "Tocqueville's name began slowly to rival Marx's," and *Democracy in America* was transformed into a critical work on totalitarianism — on why the US had remained free and what internal weaknesses nonetheless existed.[20] In particular, as Hartz himself detailed in *The Liberal Tradition in America*, Tocqueville became closely associated with the notion that, as an essentially liberal-egalitarian society without "social distinctions," the US left itself open to a "tyranny of opinion" that could sweep over mass publics.[21]

Effectively taking their lead from Madison and Tocqueville, prominent scholars such as Seymour Martin Lipset contended that individuals with "low status" — less educational and cultural attainment — were especially vulnerable to this tyranny of opinion and thus to authoritarian appeals.[22] Of course, Shannon had noted the substantial evidence for just the opposite contention: McCarthy and McCarthyism drew significantly from an educated business elite within the Republican Party. Shannon even quoted a 1954 *Fortune* magazine article to this effect: "'An aura of big business, or at least Big Money, has enveloped' Senator McCarthy. . . . A poll of 253 top business executives in the nation indicated considerable McCarthy strength."[23]

Regardless, Lipset focused his concerns on working-class constituents, pointedly concluding: "Acceptance of the norms of democracy requires a high level of sophistication and ego security. The less sophisticated and stable an individual, the more likely he is to favor a simplified and demonological view of politics, to fail to understand the rationale underlying the tolerance of those with whom he disagrees, and to find difficulty in grasping or tolerating a gradualist image of political change."[24] Madison had contended that the primary threats to liberty came from those less economically advantaged, who were particularly susceptible to demagoguery. Now Lipset and others gave a psychological and social scientific sheen to those eighteenth-century arguments.

CONSENSUS HISTORY AND PSYCHOLOGIZING
THE LONG AMERICAN EXPERIENCE

This status anxiety–focused analysis justified a very specific scholarly and political assessment of the American experience. If the McCarthy phenomenon disproved a class reading of past social movements, what background conditions explained the pattern of "mass" revolts of both Left and Right? Commentators began to contend that McCarthyite episodes reappeared in various eras of US history precisely because American life was so deeply rooted in egalitarianism and democracy, rather than in feudalism and aristocracy. In other words, the comprehensiveness of the country's creedal foundations, which Hartz called its "compulsive power," fed equalizing impulses. Although these impulses were overwhelmingly positive, they contained a "hidden conformitarian germ."[25] In certain contexts, Americans—especially those with specific personality types—could be pushed by demagogues like McCarthy to attack anyone and everyone who seemed different from themselves or who threatened their perceived status.

As the public intellectual, historian, and poet Peter Viereck explained in that same 1955 volume, *The New American Right*, McCarthyism spoke to how the very "spread of democratic equal rights facilitates . . . the equal violation of rights."[26] As a mobilization of majority tyranny, McCarthyism fed mass anxieties of being treated as "less-than," and then used those anxieties to turn violently against scapegoats. "The McCarthyites threaten liberty precisely because they are so egalitarian," concluded Viereck, "ruling foreign policy by mass telegrams to the Executive Branch and by radio speeches and Gallup Poll."[27]

Taken together, such arguments buttressed the idea of American history as marked, from the founding, by a unitary, egalitarian, and liberal political culture—though one prone to occasionally angry insistence on status equality. This explanatory framework also often coincided with a totalizing approach to all ideas that fell outside the terms of Cold War liberalism. It did not leave distinct conceptual spaces for different political ideologies with competing implications for collective life— some oppressive, some potentially emancipatory—and instead treated all excluded views as extremist threats. Whether socialist, fascist, Stalinist, or even Jim Crow segregationist, each alternative tended to be reduced to a "populist" attack on the American way of life and connected to psychological pathologies in mass democratic society.

In this view, one thing that every such movement shared was a politics of scapegoating: of capitalists, cultural elites, foreigners, ethnic minorities, or Black Americans. Thus, when past labor radicals attacked business elites as having class interests fundamentally opposed to the well-being of the democratic majority, that position was best understood *not* as a structural claim about actually existing conflicts within society, but as a populistic and demagogic form of scapegoating—an illiberal "class warfare" in which particular persons were intolerantly targeted.

Further underscoring the point, Viereck even concluded that McCarthyism constituted a "sublimated Jim Crow: against 'wrong' thinkers, not 'wrong' races."[28] Viereck may have admitted[29] that, in the words of a more recent scholar, McCarthy was "not a defender of segregation."[30] But through the reductionist lens of populism, McCarthy was lumped together with the un-American Ku Klux Klan. After all, he and his backers singled out specific social constituencies—such as Anglo-Protestant elites at the State Department—for particular conspiratorial abuse and violence.

In a sense, under the rubric of "populism," the era's consensus historians, social scientists, and commentators engaged domestically in the same collapsing of all threats that modernization theory participated in abroad. As discussed in chapter 10, under the terms of modernization theory, Soviet state socialism and anti-colonial radicalism both tended to be read as pathological detours from the ideal-typical end of American-style capitalist democracy and liberal constitutionalism. For all practical purposes, each embodied a threat to the unfettered promotion of an American-led global market order. Similarly, scholars and politicians at home now, definitionally and retroactively, interpreted the United States from its earliest beginnings in Cold War creedal terms. Any ideological deviation from these terms was recast as a brand of extremism—motivated at least in part by irrational but deep-seated psychological impulses—and an illiberal danger to the essential American model.

This recasting was especially significant because—just as with modernization theorists' assessments of much of Left politics abroad—it basically ignored the actual rights commitments of the remaining American radicals. In practice, Left activists facing Cold War crackdowns were the period's most vocal defenders of civil liberties—just as they had been during and after World War I. And, as the Second Red Scare intensified, the establishment legal community fell in lockstep line with the national security framework's combination of Constitution worship and state repression. The legal scholar Geoffrey Stone notes that, akin to how the ABA behaved during the First Red Scare, "the American Bar Association called in 1951 for the expulsion of all members of the Communist Party and urged state and local bar associations to disbar such individuals. Many state and local bar associations adopted loyalty tests and denied admission to the bar to would-be lawyers who refused to answer questions about their political beliefs and affiliations." As for the ACLU, it had by now abandoned whatever remained of its founder Crystal Eastman's radical internationalism. Instead the organization, in keeping with its equivocation in the context of Japanese internment, more or less embraced the Cold War compact alongside labor and African American leadership. Under ACLU policy, no staff would be hired or board members added if their "devotion to civil liberties [was] qualified by adherence to . . . totalitarian doctrine."[31]

By contrast, the socialist lawyer and politician Vito Marcantonio spent the final years of his life representing various individuals accused of subversion, from labor and other left-wing activists to W. E. B. Du Bois. Du Bois viewed Marcantonio as a "courageous" and "remarkable man," willing to risk personal attacks and political repression to defend him at a time when the ACLU refused and when Harvard law professor Zechariah Chafee—perhaps the country's most famous First Amendment scholar and legal academic critic of the Red Scare—never even replied to Du Bois's request for advice.[32]

In keeping with long-standing American socialist constitutional ideas, Marcantonio contended that socialist democracy required a foundational commitment to basic rights—from socioeconomic rights to those safeguarding political dissent. In a trial involving a labor leader, charged by the government with falsely signing a Taft-Hartley anticommunist affidavit while still being a Communist, Marcantonio used the closing argument to highlight the divide between "true democracy" and "dictatorship of the proletariat." In the case, government prosecutors sought in Cold War terms to maintain that the defendant believed these terms were equivalent. Marcontonio's response rejected the Manichaean binary that reduced politics to a divide between capitalist democracy and socialist tyranny. He maintained that socialist and communist trade unionists talked about "democracy because their struggle is part of the democratic struggle . . . of all people . . . who work for a living in this country." He argued that when the defendant used "true democracy," this entailed meaningful rights guarantees—including the "right of minorities to speak up." And rather than being "un-American,"

Marcantonio noted with a flourish how the accused often invoked Lincoln's own language in the Gettysburg Address to describe democracy: "Government of the people, by the people, and for the people." The aim was not dictatorship, but the genuine economic and political instantiation of self-rule.[33]

Commentators essentially treated this use of Lincolnian rhetoric as strategic, akin to CPUSA chairman Earl Browder's claims that "Communism is Twentieth-century Americanism." As for Marcantonio's deeper point about the long socialist and labor radical tradition of rights protection, this was more or less read out of the collective record—and indeed increasingly out of Cold War public consciousness. Whether socialist or fascist, all alternatives to Cold War liberalism allegedly carried with them the tyrannical dangers of populism. Just as policymakers asserted when describing social movements abroad, they characterized any embrace by domestic radicals of civil liberties as ultimately purely instrumental: whenever these forces actually gained power, "true democracy" would likely devolve into a "dictatorship of the proletariat." Such a vision depicted an American liberal society facing essentially equivalent and totalitarian pressures from both Left and Right; the moderate and gradualist Cold War order thus offered the only true protection of constitutional freedom, including of civil liberties such as free speech and dissent.

This last claim was of course particularly remarkable, given the security state's Cold War violence. But in a sense, the idea of McCarthyism absolved the broader legal-political order of responsibility for the climate of pervasive fear and conformity. Commentators such as Viereck rejected out of hand any notion of continuity between Joseph McCarthy and the overall Cold War culture. Indeed, Viereck argued that one of the many ways McCarthy undermined the Cold War project was that he could be used for propaganda purposes by Soviet sympathizers at home and abroad. For just this reason, it was critical for "Asians and Europeans . . . never to confuse genuine American anti-Communism, a necessary shield for peace and freedom against aggression, with the pseudo-anti-Communism of the demagogues, which is not anti-Communism at all but a racket."[34]

Such a reading—common during the period—did not treat McCarthy as an expression of the excesses that came with the security state's underlying ideology. Rather, the trajectory of McCarthyism provided a sign of that state's liberal constitutionalist core. The Senate eventually censured McCarthy, showing the government's success in standing

up to populist demagoguery. In addition, and at a deeper level, all of
the Red Scare's rights abuses became framed and blamed as populist
violations of the underlying order. These violations of civil libertarian
principle were not the responsibility of governing elites or the eventual
extension of their basic political objectives and ideological trajectory.
Instead, they resulted from wayward demagogues preying on the irra-
tionality of the masses.

In this way, commentators began to routinely characterize Red Scare
violations as fundamentally out of step with the real character of American liberal culture. Moreover, such perceived illiberalism was also presented as out of step with the genuine values of the Cold War, and of
the true government leaders who directed the American state overseas
and at home, like Truman and Eisenhower. As Viereck wrote, "American anti-Communism, in the proper sense of the term, usually turns
out to be a surprisingly sober and reasonable movement, fair-minded
and sincerely dedicated to civil liberties."[35] In a sense, just as Du Bois
and Marcantonio were reimagined as part of an all-encompassing and
extremist camp, many of the most militant enforcers of Cold War security politics were themselves reconceived as the core protectors of constitutional liberty.

MAJORITY TYRANNY AND THE ELEVATION
OF COUNTER-MAJORITARIANISM

By the end of the 1950s, fears among government officials and influential academics that McCarthyite populism would overwhelm the
legal-political order had abated. And commentators increasingly saw a
flourishing within the post–World War II United States of the liberal-
democratic ideal, moving beyond the social conflicts of 1945–1946 and
the excesses of the Red Scare.

In particular, they hailed the legal, political, and economic settlement of the post-war years as suppressing psychological tendencies
toward authoritarianism. As the renowned Harvard sociologist Samuel Stouffer concluded after a massive survey of public opinion in 1955's
Communism, Conformity, and Civil Liberties, the country faced no real
"national anxiety neurosis"[36] of the kind that made McCarthyism a potentially fatal threat to liberal constitutionalism. This was because the
basic institutional and ideological compact in the United States not
only facilitated affluence, but also broadened the educational and cultural attainment in the American public writ large.[37] For this reason, as

Seymour Martin Lipset contended, more and more Americans had a psychological grounding in "the rich associations which provide a basis for critical evaluation of experience."[38] They were, therefore, less susceptible to populist demagoguery.

Indeed, for many scholars evidence of such cultural maturity could be found in the growing apathy of citizens toward the political process itself. "American society," scholars like the political scientist Sidney Verba believed, was "operat[ing] on a lower level of intensity."[39] As another public opinion study concluded, reduced partisanship and political zeal indicated that "the resolution of many political problems"[40] had already been achieved in the United States. Although less mature decolonizing societies in the Global South were still subject to political passions and thus to extremism, the US largely evinced a moderation in psychological disposition and thus also in political ideology.[41]

Of course, this apathy might have resulted not only from Cold War affluence but also from the political climate generated by a decade of ideological suppression. But these scholars essentially ignored the immoderate means by which "moderation" had been encouraged. Instead, they depicted the depoliticization of collective life as merely a positive effect of the thriving liberalism in American society.

This official and academic agreement on the moderate nature of Cold War America did not mean that citizens should relax their vigilance. Stouffer may have maintained that the US as a whole would not likely collapse into authoritarianism. Still, given that McCarthy personified recurrent tendencies in collective life, the threats posed by a populist majority—which might inappropriately see threats everywhere, including among their "betters"—required ongoing attention. Stouffer's polling analysis concluded that although most Americans were generally respectful of civil liberties, those least respectful tended to be everyday citizens rather than "civic leaders": "The findings to be presented here will show that community leaders of all types—including businessmen—are *more likely* than the cross-section to accord a Socialist the right to express his views freely."[42]

In reaching this determination about the average citizen, Stouffer's approach ignored the larger political context. Americans had faced a decade of top-down state repression and mass loyalty campaigns, in which arguing for a socialist's right to speak—or implying that one might listen to socialists—might carry real personal costs. Unsurprisingly, a not insignificant proportion of respondents, generally outside positions of political power, now repeated elite propaganda and security judgments. Similarly, as the state contained actual Left radicalism, it was not wholly unexpected that the elites who had run Freedom Train events, or even participated in state crackdowns, would feel more secure about the ideological status of the Cold War state.

Nevertheless, such survey findings reinforced the basic anti-populist assessments circulating at the time. For Stouffer and others, this meant that the principal danger to American freedom came from majority tyranny. Thus, the key question of the age was: "*How can the sober second thought of the people be maintained in a state of readiness to resist external and internal threats to our heritage of liberties?*"[43]

The reference to "the sober second thought" invoked the late nineteenth-century Republican Senator George Frisbee Hoar's famous defense of why Americans needed a Senate.[44] As discussed in chapter 5, Hoar had been an outspoken congressional critic of the atrocities committed during the war in the Philippines. He was also an old Radical Republican ally of Charles Sumner. At the same time, Hoar was the scion of a prominent New England family and a defender of aristocratic constraints on mass democracy. In the context of growing Gilded Age frustration with the indirectly elected Senate, he rejected the need for direct election and argued that the body "was created that the deliberate will, the sober second thought of the people might find expression. It was intended that it should resist the hasty, intemperate, passionate desire of the people."[45] During those years, this argument marked Hoar out in class terms, for labor activists and reformers, as a conservative defender of the economic status quo.

Eventually, during the social struggles of the 1930s, New Dealers made their peace with institutions like the Senate, as well as the other counter-majoritarian roadblocks thrown up by the constitutional system. Massive electoral supermajorities provided by working-class constituencies overwhelmed the veto points that had long undermined socioeconomic reform. And with the capitulation of the Supreme Court, lawyers and politicians largely embraced FDR's brand of presidentialism, eventually seeing less need for more far-reaching reforms to the representative system.

But even during the World War II–era Bill of Rights celebrations, discussed in chapter 9, there remained real suspicions about whether the framers' political design truly deserved veneration rather than ultimate accommodation. Notably, speakers at the time had not always read Madisonian counter-majoritarianism and Bill of Rights guarantees as working together. Recall that Orville Poland, head of the Mas-

sachusetts Civil Liberties Commission, had framed his sesquicentennial speech around a view that the 1787 structure was cumbersome and
misshapen, but that the Bill of Rights gave moral value to the constitutional project as a whole.

Through the Cold War, however, the mood among many officials
and intellectuals—including many who still thought of themselves as
New Dealers—had changed dramatically. Commentators asserted the
fundamental importance of Hoar's "sober second thought," and even
seemingly embraced its aristocratic implications. Madison became a
touchstone, beyond simply the view that popular majorities were the
central threat to key liberties. Cold War scholars and politicians also
unapologetically embraced Madison's vision of institutional design as
essential to the preservation of post-war liberal democracy: by placing
fundamental constraints on the capacities of majorities to assert their
unconstrained democratic will, the overall system's checks and balances
operated hand in glove with the protections of the Bill of Rights.

In part, this newfound faith in counter-majoritarianism itself tied
back to the scholarly focus on psychological explanations of authoritarianism. That psychological turn had encouraged a related move
to explain politics through invocations of human nature. Arthur
Schlesinger Jr., the Pulitzer Prize–winning historian, political speech-
writer, and future John F. Kennedy advisor, offered perhaps the pithiest
distillation of emerging Cold War conventional wisdom about the connections between human nature and practical politics. In his own seminal 1949 defense of Cold War liberalism against the extremes of Right
and Left, Schlesinger wrote in *The Vital Center*, "consistent pessimism
about man, far from promoting authoritarianism, alone can inoculate
the democratic faith against it."[46] Those like the sociologist Edward
Shils had defended the value of promoting the "antipolitical" Madisonian tradition in overseas setting, out of a wariness that utopian ideologies could generate mass violence and descend into totalitarianism. At
home, commentators such as Schlesinger argued in parallel terms that,
given human nature, mass society was subject to irrational and destructive impulses, and that these had to be contained by institutional arrangements that slowed down and depoliticized collective life.

Indeed, Madison's remark about human nature in the *Federalist No.
51* became almost an official mantra during the Cold War: "But what is
government itself, but the greatest of all reflections on human nature?
If men were angels, no government would be necessary. If angels were
to govern men, neither external nor internal controls on government

would be necessary."[47] For those like Schlesinger, the quote encapsulated the particular genius of Madison and the framers, who had devised a system of government especially attuned to human frailty and
limitation. Indeed, this made the 1787 constitutional structure both
uniquely worthy of serving as the preeminent global model and essential for safeguarding against those domestic threats that remained even
within a culturally moderate and mature society. As Schlesinger concluded, it was precisely through "the more sober language of the Constitution" that Americans "wove individual freedom into our democratic fabric."[48]

For many Cold War officials and academics, events since the 1930s
fed this renewed and expanded worship not just of the Bill of Rights
but also of the framers' institutional design vision. Whereas states in Europe had collapsed into fascist or Stalinist tyranny, the US had avoided
that trap. Perhaps more importantly, the country had also generated a
new liberal compact: finding common ground across labor-business divides, and even across racial ones.

The Constitution was thus presented as a key element in navigating
treacherous political waters, in that it ensured gradualist but meaningful change while avoiding dangerous extremes. According to this conventional wisdom, the very counter-majoritarian features decried by
Progressive-era activists had warded off populist tyranny: these mechanisms reduced the necessity of a society of "angels," because they allowed power to counteract power in ways that preserved liberal democracy. Equally important, the system's persistent roadblocks and endless
veto points demobilized potentially threatening majorities, fostering
what Shils called a "moderation of political involvement"[49]—the type
of productive apathy that Cold War scholars now championed.

ALTERNATIVE LESSONS FROM THE AMERICAN
CONSTITUTIONAL EXPERIENCE

Yet this conventional wisdom again tended to flatten the country's history, significantly misreading the preceding decades, up to and including
the McCarthy phenomenon. In many ways, the Madisonian design—
ostensibly built for "men" rather than for "angels"—did not economize
on political virtue. It actually required a massive amount of social cohesion among empowered elites, if not actual agreement on political ends,
to avoid unproductive paralysis in the face of real collective problems
and crises.

For many pre–Cold War socialist and Progressive reformers, the basic fact of the long Gilded Age was the high degree of social conflict marking collective life. This meant that elites—for instance, labor and business leaders—fundamentally diverged on how to organize society. Under those circumstances, the proliferation of veto points across legal-political institutions actually intensified polarization and instability by making it virtually impossible for the existing system to address basic social dilemmas.

The point, of course, was not that there should be no checks on political power. Instead, reformers like the SPA presidential candidate Norman Thomas or W. E. B. Du Bois maintained that unless the system was structured to better fulfill popular needs—especially by promoting greater democratic agency—the legal-political order would be marked by continual cycles of crisis and disaffection. And, as emphasized by Du Bois, there existed no principled reason for any needed political checks to be foundationally rooted in existing state-based electoral systems, which wildly overrepresented the effective voting power of people in some geographic areas over others.

Likewise, various anti-colonial independence leaders believed that Cold War officials often misunderstood the innovative strengths of their own 1787 constitutional design—and thus misapplied lessons from the US founding. Figures like Kwame Nkrumah, Ghana's independence leader and first president, and Eric Williams, Prime Minister of Trinidad and Tobago, considered the US federalist system a reference point for the postcolonial twentieth-century world. But they drew fundamentally different conclusions about which aspects of American federalism were worthy of engagement.[50]

In particular, Nkrumah and Williams emphasized the idea of interstate federation, embedded in the notion of thirteen colonies forming a new and stronger United States. They hoped that pan-African or pan-Caribbean federation could similarly solve problems of neocolonialism by creating economic and political units strong enough to achieve genuine self-determination in a world still dominated by former imperial powers. But Cold War US commentators and policymakers often viewed these objectives with deep suspicion, even if they derived inspiration from the American example. After all, such new formations might become non-aligned and threatening alternatives to an American-led order. Instead, when US officials referenced and promoted federalism, they wanted above all to replicate more *internal* constraints within the nation-state, which would check presumably tyrannical majorities.

Yet if American policy-making elites featured the internal institutional dynamics of the 1787 model in overseas discussions, key independence leaders hardly considered this approach the most germane lesson for the moment. They contended that it entirely ignored the question of neocolonialism and, at its worst, further fractured the already limited power of poor constituencies to have their material needs met. As the Kenyan independence leader Oginga Odinga wrote of what frameworks like the Lancaster Constitution—discussed in chapter 12 and sharing extensive similarities with the American model—meant in practice for Kenyans: "It has been called a constitution of checks and balances, but I would say there were more checks than anything else."[51]

Above all, Cold War commentators failed to perceive the extent to which the post–World War II period was historically anomalous within the long American experience—let alone with respect to foreign polities. The country emerged from the war as the dominant global player, which fostered an unusual amount of cohesion among political elites: Washington converged around the necessity of both American primacy and fighting the Cold War, bringing in government officials as well as business, labor, and even Black American leaders. The existence of a clear ideological competitor in the form of the Soviet Union, along with the drive to entrench an American Century, created unique external conditions that were highly conducive to an internal politics of compromise. Despite the plethora of veto points, all of this helped to facilitate the post-war settlement, reduce the intensity of party polarization, and allow governing elites to manage economic and political decision-making.

Yet Cold War politicians and academics essentially began reading *all* of American history through these contingent developments of the 1940s and 1950s. They thus projected social cohesion and compromise back into the past, as the very essence of the country from its founding. And such commentators therefore failed to appreciate the extent to which the post-war settlement emerged *in spite of*—and not because of—constitutional counter-majoritarianism.

Just as important, explaining totalitarianism as a product of unconstrained populist energy—the tyranny of the majority—similarly misread the role of mass democratic politics in recent American history. Alongside the rise of American imperium, the other key factor that facilitated post-war domestic settlement was the strength, during the 1930s, of an organized working class. This mass base delivered the supermajorities needed to implement the New Deal, and then continued, in the interceding two decades, to muster enough electoral strength to maintain the social safety net their efforts had secured. In other words, without an overwhelming political majority able to override various institutional checks—including from the Supreme Court—the social stability and shared economic prosperity of the post-war order would have been far harder to establish.

None of this suggests that Peter Viereck, for instance, was completely wrong when he said that the "spread of democratic equal rights facilitates . . . the equal violation of rights." Yet his simple formula belied a far more complex relationship between American representative institutions and authoritarian tendencies. For starters, Norman Thomas had noted in the 1930s that mass publics became most amenable to dictatorial turns precisely in contexts where the legal-political system was paralyzed, thus inhibiting a forthright response to endemic social problems. As Thomas contended during the court-packing debates, the anti-democratic constraints built into the American constitutional order tended to "invite a strong man to step in as Dictator."[52]

Just as significantly, for both Thomas and Du Bois, it simply was not the case that the country was just as liable to proceed toward socialist transformation as toward right-wing authoritarianism. The malapportionment of the constitutional system, complete with overrepresentation of Southern white conservatives, made it especially difficult for left-wing popular mobilizations to claim political control. For this reason, the partial successes of the New Deal offered a profound testament to how much mass power labor activists and other reformers needed to enjoy to meaningfully influence the national state.

At the same time, business's material resources, combined with the structure of veto points and malapportionment, significantly elevated the potential power of conservative mobilization. It made the political center stage far easier to capture through mobilization around reactionary ends—from Southern white supremacy to McCarthyite pro-business and anti-communist zealotry—whether or not these views enjoyed genuine majority appeal. The historian David Shannon implied as much in his comparative assessments of La Follette and McCarthy. Both may have become Wisconsin senators, but they represented different constituencies and agendas. Early-twentieth-century Progressive and Socialist politicians like La Follette always had to swim upstream against a combination of institutional political structure and material strength. By contrast, far fewer roadblocks lay in the path of someone like McCarthy, who could proceed with the "avenues of power ... open" to him.

In effect, the Cold War discourse around the Constitution engaged in a double move. While corporate and state actors—whom C. L. R. James had derisively called the "American oligarchs"—were the primary source of coercive violence during the Red Scare, that violence was narratively displaced onto those with "lower status." And the country's democratic and civil libertarian achievements since the 1930s, key products of contentious mobilizations, were instead presented as the inevitable working out of near perfect and counter-majoritarian American institutions, overseen by moderating and culturally liberal elites. This latter move ignored the centrality of popular majorities—labor, feminist, immigrant, and Black constituencies operating inside and outside the legislative process—to the spread of essential protections, whether civil rights and voting laws or civil libertarian and socioeconomic guarantees. And it obscured the actual historical relationships between US political masses, especially working-class communities, and business and government elites.

This double move also exposed the extent to which a Cold War constitutional imagination was bound not only to defenses of market capitalism and American primacy, but also increasingly to a remarkably anti-democratic ethos about ordinary people and especially about mass mobilization. The era's textual veneration at times mirrored the sensibility of conservatives whom the 1920s journalist Norman Hapgood had mockingly called "professional patriots."[53] For key 1950s scholars and politicians, efforts to alter the Constitution through mass mobilization, such as by amendment packages, amounted to an embodiment of the simmering populist threat, which could violate the very sanctity and stability of the constitutional system. They maintained this view even though mobilizations around amendments had buttressed multiracial democracy during Reconstruction and then extended the vote to white women in recent decades.

As Hofstadter suggested in his own contribution to *The New American Right* volume, one should be wary of attempts to revise the Constitution's text, because they were often connected to a tyrannical drive within mass politics to overturn liberal constitutionalism itself. Hofstadter appreciated that "every dissenting movement brings its demands for Constitutional changes." In a sense, calls for change were embedded in the dynamics of American political contestation. Nonetheless, one of the ways that "latent hostility toward American institutions" expressed itself was through "a flood of proposals to write drastic changes into the body of our fundamental law." In particular, Hofstadter castigated what he called the "pseudo-conservative" move by the 1950s right wing to seek various constitutional amendments to reverse the New Deal order, including through limits on federal taxing power.[54] But more broadly, he indicated that radical efforts, whether from the Right or the Left, to rewrite the Constitution should together be read as potential threats to the very ideal of constitutionalism. Like McCarthy himself, they all carried with them a populistic and thus at its root anti-constitutional impulse.

The Emergence of Cold War Constitutional Law

This emerging intellectual distrust of the mass of citizens, among both government officials and their scholarly interlocutors, reinforced the overall defense of counter-majoritarianism. And this defense was connected in large part to *whom* commentators believed would likely occupy positions of power within the counter-majoritarian institutions—namely cultural and educated elites. As Lipset had implied, these elites were exactly the types of citizens who tended to have the psychological disposition and self-reflective capacities to safeguard liberal constitutionalism.

Over time, Cold War intellectuals came especially to associate these critical capacities with one specific institution: the federal judiciary, and, at its apex, the US Supreme Court. This embrace of the Court had the long-run effect of transforming the very *idea* of constitutionalism. It overwhelmingly became understood as an elite and relatively narrow conversation presided over by lawyers and judges. This shift therefore elevated the legal profession and the constitutional law expert into the defining custodians of constitutional meaning and memory, with significant ramifications for American political culture.

THE ERA'S SUPREME COURT REVERENCE

Although senators may have claimed to offer the country a "sober second thought," that body was now directly elected. It remained counter-majoritarian in the sense that it overrepresented particular geographic population centers—an issue long raised by the Socialist Party and other Progressive reformers. But for Cold War voices, merely giving rural Midwesterners or Southern white conservatives extra political power in Congress compared to urban centers on the coasts did not actually solve the problem of populism. Indeed, McCarthy stood as proof that voters anywhere, if left unchecked, were susceptible to demagogic appeals.

Ultimately, the courts seemed to best exemplify the ethic of deliberation, reason-giving, and critical self-reflection. If Stouffer had wondered who would maintain the people's "sober second thought" under Cold War conditions, the answer, increasingly, was judges. If anything, the phrase itself became ever more associated with them—a fact that legal academics and judges themselves embraced. As early as 1936, Supreme Court justice and New Deal ally Harlan F. Stone had claimed the phrase for the bench, famously writing in the *Harvard Law Review* that the role of the judge was precisely "to represent the sober second thought of the community."[55]

The era's defining account of judicial review elaborated on Justice Stone's underlying thought. In his 1962 classic of constitutional theory, *The Least Dangerous Branch*, the Yale Law School professor Alexander Bickel accepted the old Progressive critique: with a small number of unelected judges serving for life and able to wield massive influence on the country's direction, American-style judicial review was "a deviant institution in the American democracy." Bickel straightforwardly conceded that "when the Supreme Court declares unconstitutional a legislative act . . . it thwarts the will of representatives of the actual people . . . it exercises control, not on behalf of the prevailing majority, but against it. That, without mystic overtones, is what actually happens." But for Bickel, this undemocratic element in collective life was justified: a federal judiciary, armed with the powers of review, was uniquely suited within the constellations of American institutions to preserve "the enduring values of a society."[56]

Bickel, a former law clerk of the famed Harvard law professor, FDR confidant, and Supreme Court justice Felix Frankfurter, was a central voice in the post-war era's most prominent school of legal thought, known as the legal process school.[57] Shaped by the events of the New Deal, legal process scholars viewed the *Lochner*-era Supreme Court, which had struck down economic regulations in favor of strong private property and contract rights, as woefully misguided.[58] But unlike radical 1930s critics of judicial power, they opposed the idea that judges were simply class ideologues and that review should be abolished or structurally curtailed—for instance, through a legislative override. Bickel associated those latter views with a pre-war intellectual school known as legal realism, and specifically attacked none other than the former FDR antitrust champion, DC circuit court judge, and legal scholar Thurman Arnold for rejecting any divide between law and politics and effectively championing "nihilism." He decried Arnold's view—that judges dressed up their "personal preference and personal power" in "judicial dialectic"—as ultimately "cynicism pure and simple."[59]

According to Bickel, the problem during the 1930s was not the *role* of the judiciary in collective life. Rather, it was that the *Lochner* Court misunderstood that role. According to legal process scholars, the *Lochner* justices had set themselves up as a policy-making body or "superlegislature."[60] But that was not the appropriate judicial responsibility in a complex liberal-democratic order. Such an order was marked by many overlapping institutions, each with their own "special competence and special procedures tailored to its institutional functions."[61] The judicial role was instead bound specifically to its foundation "in reason,"[62] which meant that courts operated within this complex political framework as "the forum of principle."[63]

For those like Bickel, this legal process approach both restrained and unleashed the judiciary. It suggested leaving matters to other institutions when judges could not ground their rulings "in reason," such as by treating all similar cases alike or by basing a decision on the underlying principle of a given statute.[64] But it also suggested that the courts were the institutional site most functionally equipped to understand the totality of the legal-political system—those "enduring values," according to Bickel, that motivated a polity. Judges also best perceived which institutions—and thus which set of processes—were most appropriate for resolving specific questions. The court emerged as the place where, in the words of the historian Laura Kalman, "process and precedent were taken seriously, legal craft coveted, and cases decided according to law, regardless of who got what, when, and how."[65]

All of this indicated that while legislatures and courts both served the public interest through their own distinct processes, the federal bench offered a space free from the problems endemic to elected branches. Popular institutions were susceptible to the frenzy of mass political anxieties, which could lead publics to engage in destructive infringements on civil liberties or on the basic institutions of capitalist democracy. But Bickel declared that rather than being swept up "in the moment's hue and cry," courts were uniquely equipped to reduce these political passions. As unelected officials serving for life, they were "insulat[ed]" from the ordinary political process—significantly more so than even senators and presidents—and therefore far less beholden to populist demands.

Moreover, the court system was necessarily a slow-moving one, in which "the marvelous mystery of time" gave judges the opportunity to let passions cool and "to appeal to men's better natures." And to the extent that education was essential for avoiding the psychological tendencies associated with an authoritarian personality, perhaps no institutional figure in collective life had a more comprehensive education in the liberal mindset—at school and on the job—than the judge. As Bickel wrote, "judges have . . . the leisure, training, and the insulation to follow the ways of the scholar in pursuing the ends of government."[66]

All of this spoke to the special status of the Supreme Court, the peak of the judicial craft, in American life. For Bickel, the institution of the Court provided a central and liberalizing site of public education for the rest of society. It embodied nothing less than the American "spirit of moderation," with the justices, quoting his Yale law dean Eugene Rostow, "'inevitably teachers in a vital national seminar.'"[67]

Throughout the first half of the twentieth century, the federal judiciary and the power of judicial review had been on the defensive. But Bickel's arguments—and the fact that they captured a sensibility that pervaded the governing elite (even among some old New Dealers)—marked a profound move in the other direction. As Peter Viereck caustically noted about the political shifts within both the academy and the 1950s Northern Democratic Party,

> The intellectual liberals who twenty years ago wanted to pack the
> Supreme Court as frustrating the will of the masses (which is exactly
> what it ought to frustrate) and who were quoting Charles Beard to
> show that the Constitution is a mere rationalization of economic
> loot—those same liberals today are hugging for dear life that same
> court and that same Constitution. . . . They are hugging those two
> most conservative of "outdated" institutions as their last life pre-
> servers against the McCarthyite version of what their Henry Wal-
> laces used to call "the century of the common man."[68]

Viereck's remarks again conflated mass mobilizations of all varieties under the totalizing banner of populism. And he inaccurately characterized New Deal–era social democracy as drawing from the same "common man" base of support as the pro-business and anti-communist

McCarthy. Nonetheless, he had captured a remarkable political truth of the broader post-war period. As late as the 1930s, Bickel's claims would have been rejected by a wide swathe of scholars and reformers as essentially class-inflected justifications for minority rule. Many would have characterized him as dressing up the socioeconomic and cultural interests of a legal elite as expressions of political virtue. Yet, by the 1950s, figures like Thurman Arnold found themselves outside the intellectual currents of the times. Not only did academics and politicians largely take positions akin to Bickel's defense of judicial review; they also systematically rejected the need for any kind of judicial reform.

As discussed in chapter 3, the American federal bench presented one of the most extreme sites of judicial review globally. It was incredibly difficult for publics to overturn Supreme Court judgments, given the lack of a legislative veto and the massive impediments to formal constitutional amendment. Moreover, due to both the small size of the Supreme Court (only nine justices) and their lifetime tenure, a tiny coterie of empowered officials enjoyed truly outsized political power—regardless of whether their views actually corresponded to mass democratic sentiment, or even to broader elite views of the country's "enduring values." This extremism had not only fueled Progressive and Socialist efforts to curtail or even abolish judicial review. It had also fueled broader reformist desires, such as to limit how long federal judges (including Supreme Court justices) served, to expand the number of Supreme Court justices, and to introduce clear mechanisms of accountability for judicial misconduct.

Now, however, all those past debates, about virtually any kind of judicial reform, appeared definitively over. Indeed, in a context in which the Senate seemed not counter-majoritarian *enough*, the very extremism of the Supreme Court's power became repackaged as part of the genius of the framers' vision—and even as a critical component of what officials promoted abroad under the American model.

The reason for this turn again had to do with how commentators interpreted contingent Cold War dynamics as instead essential truths about American society. For instance, the famed political scientist Robert Dahl responded to worries that the intensity of American-style judicial review transformed an already counter-majoritarian institution into an effectively aristocratic one. Dahl argued that while a check on democracy, ultimately the Supreme Court was best seen as fulfilling rather than compromising democratic ideals. In an influential 1957 article, he argued that "the policy views dominant on the Court are never for long out of line with the policy views dominant among the lawmaking majorities of the United States. Consequently it would be most unrealistic to suppose that the Court would, for more than a few years at most, stand against any major alternatives sought by a lawmaking majority."[69] Dahl's analysis, and the broader academic conventional wisdom of the time, assumed that American life had always been and likely would always be marked by relative ideological agreement and depolarization. This meant that, whatever their differences, the parties largely converged; therefore, presidential nominees to the Supreme Court would tend to have views more or less consistent with those of the public writ large.

As a result, there was no need truly to worry, as Progressives and Socialists had, about an economically and politically empowered minority coalition—enjoying limited mass democratic appeal—using the counter-majoritarian institutions of the Electoral College, the Senate, and the Supreme Court to make permanent their ideological positions. In this way, Dahl paralleled the optimistic conclusions that union organizations such as Labor's Non-Partisan League (LNPL) reached in the late 1930s about why basic structural alterations to the judicial appointments process were ultimately unnecessary. As discussed in chapter 8, the LNPL at that time suggested that a focus on further structural reforms—beyond one-time court-packing—was not needed. Such a focus unreasonably assumed that labor would, in the future, become less capable of ensuring political majorities, and that a substantial segment of white working-class voters would somehow start supporting reactionary presidents and senators.

Similarly, Dahl concluded that, at worst, judges would simply hold up popular political programs for a contained period of time. In doing so, they would give society more of an opportunity to assess whether such initiatives actually coincided with the country's enduring constitutional values—thus offering that sober second thought. In this way, the courts, and particularly the Supreme Court, protected constitutional liberty. And they did so without compromising the basic democratic responsiveness of the legal-political system.[70]

A remarkable feature of these arguments regarding the court's sober second thought was the extent to which they diverged from the actual history of judicial behavior during periods of government crackdown. The Supreme Court—along with the federal courts more generally— had largely deferred to the state's security judgments, instead of serving as that voice of enduring constitutional values. During World War I, the Supreme Court upheld the constitutionality of the Espionage Act, including prison convictions for Eugene Debs and others whose only crime consisted in anti-war speech.[71] During World War II, the Court similarly justified mass Japanese internment as constitutional.[72]

As for the high tide of the Red Scare and McCarthyism, the Court again was hardly a champion of dissident rights, largely working alongside the state to suppress perceived threats to the Cold War order. In *Dennis v. United States* (1951), the Court gave constitutional cover to Truman's and FBI Director J. Edgar Hoover's mass arrests of the Communist Party leadership, on grounds that simply organizing such a party and promoting it through speeches and publications amounted to an illegal criminal conspiracy.[73] The next year, the Court similarly concluded that noncitizens could be deported just for being members of the CPUSA, even if such membership was lawful at the time the individual joined.[74]

Indeed, the Supreme Court only moved to shut down ideological prosecutions of the CPUSA once the Red Scare project had already succeeded in repressing dissent, breaking up left-wing organizations (like the Civil Rights Congress), and cementing Cold War agreement. The Court's 1957 *Yates v. United States* decision narrowly interpreted the Smith Act, the law at stake in *Dennis* and which had made it a crime to advocate violent government overthrow. *Yates* held that if such advocacy was only "as an abstract principle" without "any effort to instigate action to that end," the Act would not reach it.[75] The case was a major civil liberties victory, after which, Geoffrey Stone writes, "the government filed no further prosecutions under the Smith Act." But he also reminds us to "note all the changes that had taken place between 1951 and 1957."[76] The Court had stepped in only after McCarthy's downfall and significant easing of the Red Scare climate.

Ultimately, what drove this new Cold War–era defense of the courts seemed less connected with courts' (very mixed) actual record in upholding those values, including civil libertarian commitments, later determined to be enduring. Instead, it again revolved far more systematically around an assessment of *who* would likely end up on the Supreme Court or in the federal judiciary. For officials and scholars, McCarthy's demise generated a sigh of relief because it underscored that, at the end of the day, the most important institutions of the state—like the presidency—would not fall to populist demagogues. This meant that

Viereck's "sober and reasonable" anti-communists would largely direct the state, and thus would nominate and confirm those on the bench. As a result, the courts would overwhelmingly be composed of the same educational, cultural, and socioeconomic group as the officials who were broadly governing the Cold War project at home and abroad.

All of this deemphasized the need to focus on the actual outcomes of judicial decision-making. Justices might get certain cases right and others wrong, but overall one could count on their basic judgment to sustain the American model, with its distinctive combination of capitalist democracy and liberal constitutionalism. Moreover, the process of judicial decision-making—its slow unfolding, its emphasis on reason-giving, its references to past precedent—indicated that, over the long run, even outcomes should end up more right than wrong.

Underscoring this point, some of the most significant Cold War defenders of the Supreme Court and of American-style judicial review criticized much of the actual judicial thinking of the Court under Chief Justice Earl Warren. As discussed in chapter 12, Herbert Wechsler, a leading Northern constitutional scholar of the age, notoriously rejected the legal reasoning behind *Brown v. Board of Education*. Like Bickel, he was a significant proponent of legal process, and on those grounds he found the opinion lacking a neutral principle independent of the justices' preferred outcome. The case was clearly important in promoting Black elite buy-in to the Cold War creedal compact. But within the white legal academic establishment—and even if those figures backed desegregation as a necessary policy outcome—real debates circulated about whether the decision amounted to good judicial reasoning.[77]

Indeed, legal process concerns about the Warren Court became a perennial feature of the era's legal academic analysis. As Bickel and his coauthor Harry Wellington wrote in 1957, the Court seemed to reach decisions "accompanied by little or no effort to support them in reason."[78] Bickel spent much of the period arguing—as one 1971 review of his scholarship summarized—that most Warren Court rulings were "sloppy in reasoning . . . and mistaken in result." That same review even contended that this was the broadly shared perspective of elite "professional commentary on the Court" during the 1950s and 1960s.[79] As chapter 15 will explore, it was not really until the 1970s that Warren Court decisions—chief among them *Brown v. Board of Education*—became central for legal academics in their justifications of judicial review, and thus gained hallowed status as legal reasoning.

LAWYERS AND THE OWNERSHIP
OF THE CONSTITUTION

Still, in this earlier Cold War period, what Wechsler, Bickel, and others embraced—regardless of their disagreements with specific rulings—was the Supreme Court itself. They considered the institution of the Court, its membership and its process, as the defining embodiment of the American constitutional tradition. And this elevation of the Supreme Court, along with the judiciary more generally, went hand in hand with a profound alteration in how governing elites, across both parties, had come to view constitutional politics. In particular, all this entailed transforming constitutional politics into constitutional *law*.

Throughout the early twentieth century, when Progressives and Socialists engaged in constitutional debate, they certainly had disagreements with specific judicial decisions and presented competing theories of constitutional interpretation. But these activists and politicians often focused just as much on issues related to underlying accounts of governmental design, including by critiquing structural elements of the legal-political system as counter to mass democracy. Thus, much of their political energy was spent on institutional reforms—whether addressing state-based representation, constraining American-style judicial review, unleashing the presidency and the administrative state, altering the Senate, or revising the amendment process.

As for rights, many Socialists, Progressives, and even 1930s New Dealers argued for a broad expansion of constitutionally grounded protections. But crucially, they did not view the federal courts as the central champions of rights—whether free speech guarantees, the right to strike, or other socioeconomic protections. Indeed, the long arc of American history suggested to them that the courts far more often safeguarded the interests of those with economic and political power, whether enslavers or later business elites. Thus, SPA activists emphasized mass mobilizations as the privileged mechanism for instantiating rights commitments, whether to enact landmark legislation or constitutional amendments.

In a sense, FDR's Second Bill of Rights, discussed in chapter 10, remained consistent with this earlier Progressive-era politics, in that its rights framework was pointedly not judicially managed. FDR's approach treated rights, to an important extent, as the implementation by legislative majorities of popular demands. His anti-totalitarianism did not rest primarily on the courts or on counter-majoritarian checks and balances. Instead, it was grounded in presidential initiative and in legislative dynamism and action. As with the court-packing effort, the Second Bill of Rights therefore suggested a mode of constitutional politics that did not treat the judiciary reverentially or view it as necessarily the most important institutional space for constitutional decision-making.

But now, as Cold War orthodoxy dominated intellectual life and public policy, the courts truly gained primacy in the constitutional imagination. To begin with, the governing convergence around a rigid version of creedal constitutionalism meant that the American state's legal and political institutions were themselves sanctified as near perfect realizations of liberal democracy. Any interest in economic and legal-political design experimentation was often rejected out of hand, as evincing what Hofstadter suggested was that "latent hostility" to constitutionalism itself. In this way, the arena of constitutional conversation increasingly deemphasized questions of basic structure; instead it focused far more on matters of rights. This area, after all, was where McCarthyite populism could potentially overrun liberal constitutionalism.

Moreover, officials and scholars framed such rights as properly the purview of the judiciary. In fact, this focus on the judicial management of rights was another critical reason why FDR's Second Bill of Rights receded politically and culturally—along, of course, with how it muddied distinctions between American capitalist democracy and Soviet socialist tyranny. The 1944 initiative still had too much in common with the Progressive-era idea of rights as popular demands implemented and safeguarded by democratic majorities. Such a view was out of step with the anti-populist politics of the Cold War, in which democratic majorities were posited as the gravest threats to rights themselves. For these later commentators, the dangers posed by mass publics meant that the primary responsibility for preserving and elaborating rights had to be placed in an insulated judiciary.

All of this made for a clear shift during these years in what elites—and even publics—imagined when they discussed the Constitution. Constitutional debate had less and less to do with the basic organization of the state and the economy. These elements of collective life were now treated as largely outside the domain of contestation; they became permanent, almost natural artifacts of collective life.

Instead, constitutional debate revolved around the cases before the federal judiciary, and especially before the Supreme Court, with a particular emphasis on questions of rights. Consequently, what counted as the substance of constitutional analysis similarly narrowed to a focus on judicial opinions themselves: How did judges reference past precedents? To what degree did they display internal rational coherence in their writings? Did they have a consistent theory of constitutional interpretation?

Reflecting on this convergence of the judiciary with the Constitution, Louis Hartz noted the Supreme Court's culturally distinctive and "unusual power"[80] in the United States. In essence, the pervasive Cold War politics appeared to treat what the Supreme Court debated as the main expression of constitutional politics. Indeed, judicial discourse seemed to embody the sum total of constitutionalism itself.

This increasing focus on the exercise of judicial review as the near exclusive domain of constitutional conversation mirrored steady transformations occurring in the academy. As discussed in chapter 1, law schools traditionally did not present constitutional education—whether state or federal[81]—as key to their curriculum or larger mission. Harvard Law School Dean Christopher Columbus Langdell's model for legal education had spread in the late nineteenth century, and it became the standard across elite law schools. This traditional model emphasized private common law matters—subjects like contracts, torts, and property—and employed a case method analysis of appellate judicial decisions to study them.[82] Unlike those required courses, constitutional law principally resided in what the legal historian Robert Gordon calls the "third-year-elective outland."[83]

The founding of Cornell University's Department of Law, whose first year of operation coincided with the centennial anniversary of 1887–1888, serves as an illustrative example of this relative deemphasis on constitutional law. Structured as an undergraduate bachelor of laws (LL.B.) program, the department's offerings aligned with general legal instruction at the time. Thus, despite the Constitution's centennial, constitutional law was still relegated to the final year of study.[84] Indeed, in a way that would likely have frustrated members of the Centennial Commission, the university report on the organization of the new department made little mention of the subject beyond saying that such study could be pursued in greater depth in the history and political science departments, its traditional home.[85]

It was only in the late 1920s and 1930s that constitutional law became mandatory at most law schools. This move was part of a general recognition of the centrality of the modern administrative state to legal practice, and so went along with a growth in public law offerings as a whole, particularly administrative law.[86] Even so, given law schools' primary focus, "legal luminaries during the first half of the twentieth century, Roscoe Pound... Karl Llewellyn... and others," as the legal scholar and historian Mark Graber notes, were "best known for their writings" on private common law subjects. Furthermore, "the most celebrated work of legal scholarship during the decades before the Second World War, Benjamin Cardozo's *The Nature of the Judicial Process* (1921), [was] devoted almost entirely to how justices make decisions in nonconstitutional cases."[87]

By contrast, as suggested by Cornell's administrators, constitutional law—as a subject of higher education in the early twentieth century—was most commonly studied in undergraduate courses in history and political science, in keeping with the Progressive-era focus on institutional design. For this reason, as late as the 1950s, many of the scholars still most identified with the US Constitution, including Edward Corwin, Carl Friedrich, and Charles Beard himself, had often taught in humanities and social science departments, rather than at law schools.

Yet, through the Cold War period, as constitutionalism became almost definitionally associated with the courts, its scholarly identity similarly migrated to the legal academy. In fact, this period initiated the rise of the constitutional scholar as nothing less than the law school's preeminent public face. As Graber notes of the contrast before and after World War II, "legal luminaries during the second half of the twentieth century [were] best known for their constitutional analysis," with "virtually all law professors with any name recognition outside of law . . . scholars of" the Constitution.[88]

The shift was clearly enhanced by the transformation in what counted as constitutionalism. In an earlier period, it would have been hard for legal scholars like Bickel and Wechsler to claim ownership over constitutional study. In keeping with the case method approach, these scholars engaged in what Graber calls "grand constitutional theory"[89]—focused overwhelmingly on how judges should make decisions about constitutional interpretation.

But such a legalistic mode of analysis would have been viewed by earlier preeminent scholars of the American constitutional system, such as Charles Beard, as far too narrow to fully encompass constitutionalism. After all, this focus on judges tended to deemphasize close study of the broader legal-political structure or of the shifting economic and social context. For the same reason, teaching the Constitution only through a Langdellian case method would have been treated as deeply limited.

Such exclusive attention to appellate case law effectively removed from examination all the other, equally central sites of historic constitutional struggle—including the many matters related to institutional design, concerning everything from whether to have a Senate to how to restructure the courts themselves.

But the Cold War version of creedal constitutionalism aided the step-by-step reimagining of the constitutional domain as, properly, the domain of legal experts. And to the extent that constitutional practice was largely confined to court-based dispute, the people with true knowledge about such dispute were legal professionals. The elevation of the Supreme Court created a growing political presumption within government, the academy broadly, and ultimately the public that constitutional politics was in large measure a conversation conducted and overseen by lawyers and judges.

THE SUPREME COURT REPORTER
AND THE NATIONAL SEMINAR

One significant indicator of the times was the parallel development of a new journalistic figure—the Supreme Court reporter. At the forefront of this development was Anthony Lewis, who covered the institution for the *New York Times* from 1957 to 1964—momentous years in the history of the Warren Court. In the mid-1950s, the *Times* Washington bureau chief, James Reston, concluded that an expanding interest in the Supreme Court meant that the paper needed a reporter that properly focused on its intricacies.[90] As the journalist and current *Times* Supreme Court correspondent Adam Liptak notes, newspapers had long had "press reports on [Supreme Court] decisions." But these "were apt to be pedestrian recitations by journalists without legal training, rarely examining the court's reasoning or grappling with the context and consequences of particular rulings."[91] For Liptak, Lewis "created modern legal journalism,"[92] because he pioneered a new type of reporter, one that spread across pressrooms and even to the nightly news. This reporter focused on all internal developments within the Supreme Court—its personalities, legal debates, and rulings—and disseminated that information to a wide reading and viewing public.

Notably, in preparation for the job, the *Times* sent Lewis, then in his late twenties, to Harvard Law School for a year, where he attended classes, including in constitutional law, taught by some of the most significant legal process scholars in the country—Henry Hart, Paul

Freund, and even visiting professor Herbert Wechsler.[93] That training certainly prepared him to better understand judicial decision-making. But it also implicitly took for granted the growing identity between the Supreme Court and the Constitution, in which constitutional study became coterminous with study of the judiciary's practices and customs.

In many ways, the type of writing Lewis engaged in—as well as the brand of legal journalism he embodied—broadly promoted this cultural connection. It also set the template for a basic orientation to the Supreme Court that major newspapers replicated. Like Lewis, the new journalists too imbibed significant features of Cold War constitutional culture, including the almost unreflective identification of "constitutional" with what happened on the Supreme Court and in the federal judiciary. Just as significantly, it also meant that even if journalists disagreed with specific decisions, they deeply internalized a post-McCarthy-era belief in the Court's inherent value for promoting a liberal constitutional public ethos. In ways explicit and implicit, Rostow's and Bickel's invocation of the Supreme Court as a "vital national seminar" thus traveled the country by way of newspapers and television.

For Lewis, and especially for the younger journalists who followed, it helped profoundly that he agreed with the direction the Warren Court was moving the country—whatever the legal process concerns raised by his past professors. Indeed, it made him "a romantic about the Supreme Court," as he called himself in later years.[94] Perhaps above all, such romanticism came through in his famed 1964 book about *Gideon v. Wainright* (1963), the Warren Court decision commanding that states must provide criminal defendants, if they cannot afford one, with legal counsel as a constitutionally protected right. *Gideon's Trumpet*, a "bestseller . . . [that] has never been out of print for the past half century,"[95] and which became a TV movie starring Henry Fonda, expressed the full culmination of a liberal belief in the distinctive civil libertarian role of the courts. As he wrote for the *New York Times Magazine* in 1962, "slowly but perceptibly, with occasional retreats but with the over-all direction clear, the Court is taking up the role of conscience to the country."[96]

Thus, by the early 1960s, the old SPA concern about who owns the Constitution practically evaporated from public life. As noted in chapter 4, many Socialists had long been wary of moving reform primarily into channels of constitutional interpretation in the courts. They worried that a dominant focus on this path would empower a small number of political and legal elites to assert status as privileged intermediaries.

Such elites could then control the acceptable language of constitutional argument and fundamentally shape the terms under which any change occurred. Thus one critical reason for the focus on legislative efforts and amendment packages was to sustain mass democratic ownership over constitutional politics.

Yet Cold War officials, scholars, and journalists found little to worry about in these shifts. For figures like Bickel, depoliticizing collective life—including with respect to the Constitution—was precisely the goal. Therefore, greater constitutional control by a legal professional class should similarly be viewed as a positive outcome. As for younger Cold War liberals like Lewis, they may have been less anti-populist, but they still accepted both a post-McCarthy suspicion of the people and the linkage of rights protection with judging. And, in a way that would truly spread in the 1970s, they found in the Warren Court story proof that the judiciary could be a healthy steward of the nation, supervising steady and gradual reform. Still, regardless of one's specific verdict on the Warren Court, by the 1950s and early 1960s, as "a staple of modern liberalism," elite public culture was now becoming deeply infused with what the legal historian L. A. Powe Jr. has called the "cult of the Court."[97]

All of these developments—chief among them the ever more lofty status of the judiciary—had rippling effects well beyond the courtroom. In the academy, they further moved knowledge production about the Constitution to law schools. And as Graber suggests, they particularly enhanced the position and social standing of the constitutional law professor. This emerging professoriate became the increasingly esteemed translators of the Supreme Court to the public. And just as with Lewis's relationship to Harvard Law School, that role was often facilitated by the court reporter as an intermediary who sought out the constitutional law professor as expert and definer of the relevant boundaries of debate and concern.

Alongside the journalists they engaged with in the press, these professors also interacted directly and indirectly with judges and their opinions. And they certainly continued to disagree, at times strenuously, with federal judicial decisions—mirroring the likes of Bickel and Wechsler before them. But the elite of the legal academic profession maintained a deeply reverential attachment to the bench and especially to the Supreme Court as an institution; they too became effectively "romantic[s] about the Supreme Court." This affection often extended to the actual justices themselves—individuals whom elite law professors may have worked for, taught in class, or been colleagues with in the academy. By ideological inclination, professional training, and cultural identity, the professoriate thus became a central propagator—almost as a matter of course—of the vision of the Constitution, and of US constitutionalism, as an overwhelmingly successful and judicially managed American enterprise, marked above all by intergenerational interpretive discourse.

Given the substance of what legal scholars studied and wrote, this perspective obviously further reaffirmed the value of the constitutional law field itself, just as it expanded in law schools. It meant that, from the perspective of constitutional law professors—as elucidators of constitutional theory—*they* were the figures that truly engaged in an intellectual back-and-forth with the esteemed bench. Even more so than other lawyers, politicians, or journalists, the conversations supposedly linking the country's elite law schools to Washington, DC, and to courts beyond played a central role: they facilitated gradualist adaptation when necessary, and they aided judges in adjusting their own analyses in light of the country's enduring legal ideals.

Conclusion: Hartz's Lonely Dissent

Ultimately, this collapsing of the Constitution into the concerns of the Court had profound ramifications for constitutional memory. Above all, the growing centrality of the legal academy to constitutional study and knowledge production has influenced what we collectively remember, and what has been increasingly forgotten. In particular, it meant that the history of past struggles over the basic legitimacy of the Constitution receded from scholarly discussion, journalistic dissemination, and eventually from the broader political consciousness. Even when not the intentional choice of legal academics, future professors and attorneys were trained in a constitutional case method far removed from the late-nineteenth- and early-twentieth-century mass conflicts over the basic design of state and economy.

In this way, the general thrust of legal scholarship on the Constitution fit with the overarching consensus historiography and climate of the Cold War. Just as officials and commentators embraced an account of the United States as liberal from the founding, the main scholarly repository of constitutional history—and therefore of constitutional memory—now consisted of individuals shaped by very specific disciplinary boundaries. Their primary mode of study meant that, as legal scholars, they either deemphasized, or even were unaware of, those past popular constitutional projects that had once driven Gilded Age struggle.

Louis Hartz himself offers an interesting example of the evolving cultural changes around the memory of the Constitution. Although he was closely identified with Cold War consensus historiography, Hartz strongly expressed his political wariness about the narrowing of ideologically acceptable opinion in the United States. Hartz believed that the Constitution, complete with judicial review, could be understood as an American "rock of aristocracy": a consciously counterrevolutionary act pursued by framers like Alexander Hamilton to hamstring democracy. As Hartz declared of the unelected federal bench in particular, "Hamilton erected on the fixity of the fundamental law the judicial review of a set of life term judges who were very human indeed and who came as close to being a House of Lords as a purely liberal society could produce."

For Hartz, the resulting combination of liberal consensus and Constitution worship did not warrant national self-congratulation. He worried that the country's "irrational Lockianism" and unreflective acceptance of the Constitution as near ideal did more than leave it open to McCarthyite demagoguery. It framed as a threatening collectivism oftentimes necessary changes to state and economy, tarring anyone who deviated from capitalist faith or questioned domestic practices as un-American.[98]

Very little of Hartz's critique would have surprised early-twentieth-century Socialists or many Progressives. Indeed, it mirrored a long-standing view: in Europe, aristocracy was entrenched through the symbols of church and crown; in the United States, aristocracy was comparably entrenched through the symbols and concrete mechanisms of the Constitution.

Strikingly, Hartz did not see his own more critical positions as part of long-established and thoroughly American political traditions. Instead, given the Cold War climate, he quite understandably conceived of himself as a lonely voice of caution—not even of full-throated dissent—in the face of that totalizing "cult of constitution worship." Not only had those past Socialists and fellow travelers been erased from historical consciousness for Hartz; so too, in effect, had all their arguments about constitutional politics.

In addition to the long shadow of the Red Scare, this erasure ultimately had much to do with the prevailing narratives about McCarthy and McCarthyism, which often recast dissident views—left and right—as simply populist and anti-constitutional pathologies. These narratives conceived of such pathologies when expressed in the United States as either archaic holdovers or extremist deviations emerging from within American liberal egalitarianism. Over time, this erasure became even more deeply tied to elite sites of the legal profession and academy, which generated knowledge about the Constitution. Such sites imbibed Cold War politics, and they were largely disconnected from the dissenting political cultures that had sustained competing constitutional visions.

All of this spoke to how the mid-century Cold War intellectual and political climate projected into the future a basic cleavage of constitutional memory. In earlier eras, even if radical agendas did not enjoy majority or near-majority support, they nonetheless often had a substantial influence on the terms of legal-political debate. Such critiques provided a language of public opposition that governing elites and voices across the ideological spectrum had to engage with. Now, however, radical agendas played little role, even in the political and scholarly analysis of the late nineteenth and early twentieth centuries that had been their heyday.

As I explore in part IV of the book, this effective removal of past dissenting constitutional traditions from the public record would have real consequences. And these consequences existed both for Left strategy and for lasting cultural evaluations of radicalism in American politics, especially when open social conflict returned in the 1960s and early 1970s. In the face of violent American militarism overseas and entrenched racial subordination at home, worries about the anti-democratic features of the constitutional order and about creedalism's national mythmaking finally rose to the surface. But they did so against the backdrop of a far different political climate and cultural conversation about the Constitution, especially among white constituencies. The outcomes of those 1960s and 1970s struggles would come to define the horizon of constitutional meaning and American political possibility into the late twentieth century. And these outcomes involved real and enduring limitations, which have reverberated down to the present.

PART IV

Alternative Paths and Constitutional Erasure, 1965–1987

We cannot afford not to rewrite this document! We must attempt this last straw at National Salvation under this present system, for we must exhaust all legal means. We know that there can be no peace until there is land, bread, housing, education, clothing, justice and blessed liberty!

AFENI SHAKUR, "WE WILL HAVE A NEW
CONSTITUTION AND LIBERTY OR REVOLUTIONARY
SUICIDE AND LIBERATION" (1970)

My faith in the Constitution is whole; it is complete; it is total. And I am not going to sit here and be an idle spectator to the diminution, the subversion, the destruction, of the Constitution.

BARBARA JORDAN, "STATEMENT TO THE HOUSE
JUDICIARY COMMITTEE REGARDING THE
IMPEACHMENT OF RICHARD NIXON" (1974)

CHAPTER 14

Left Resurgence and the Decolonial Project

In late August 1968, Americans watched on their television screens as protesters faced an intense crackdown from police in the streets of downtown Chicago. The setting was the Democratic National Convention, and the conflict was over what to do about the war in Vietnam. Outside the convention hall, officers "lined up platoon style, shouting 'Kill, Kill, Kill' with clubs raised." In the end, "more than 1000 people, including 192 police, were injured and 662 were arrested. One young man was shot to death by the police."[1]

Inside the convention, the Democratic Party leadership was closing ranks to suppress opposition to the war. Americans had by then turned against the conflict, with opinion polls showing a majority opposed to having troops remain in Vietnam. As for the presidential election, 80 percent of Democratic primary voters supported candidates "critical" of the war, and a large majority backed Robert Kennedy or Eugene McCarthy, both anti-war figures. But through the arcane nomination system, party bosses used their control over non-primary delegates to push through Vice President Hubert Humphrey, who had not even participated in the primaries, as the party's nominee. The platform committee similarly ensured that the party maintained a pro-war position.[2]

For those in the streets, the events both inside and outside the Convention appeared of a piece. It did not seem a coincidence that just as Chicago Mayor Richard Daley was brutally disrupting protests — unleashing what anti-war Democratic Senator Abraham Ribicoff called "the Gestapo in the streets of Chicago"[3] — he also took advantage of his role as party boss to push delegates to Humphrey's side, regardless of whom voters had actually selected. All of this suggested a breakdown in the representative capacity and democratic legitimacy of American legal-political institutions. No matter who won the November presiden-

tial election, Humphrey or Richard Nixon, both parties—irrespective
of mass discontent—had seemingly signed on to the conflict along with
the broader Cold War security project. Reflecting on the moment, Eldridge Cleaver, the Black Panther Party for Self-Defense's (BPP) Minister of Information, declared in a statement, issued in conjunction with
one by white anti-war activists Abbie Hoffman, Jerry Rubin, and Stewart Albert, "it is very clear that there is no way left for us to offer any opposition through the traditional political machinery."[4]

The Cold War may have consolidated and firmly entrenched an official politics of constitutional veneration. But in many ways it also gave
rise to perhaps the last significant moment—at least before our own—
of sustained constitutional skepticism. For a short window in the late
1960s and early 1970s, the Vietnam War shattered the collective cer-
tainty that an American liberal constitutionalist compact was either
successfully proliferating abroad or resolving social disputes at home.

In particular, the war made hollow the underlying claims of the post-
war American project, especially the assumption of a basic antithesis
between old-style European empire and US leadership in the world's interest. The Pentagon Papers, published by the *New York Times* in 1971,
highlighted the false pretenses under which US officials had initiated
and then systematically extended the war, including through secret
bombing campaigns in Cambodia and Laos. And such practices were
hardly exceptional during the period. In 1975, the Senate Church Committee, named after Idaho Democrat Frank Church, investigated assassination plots and coup attempts against various foreign leaders—in
Latin America, Asia, and Africa—not to mention numerous covert operations aimed at destabilizing governments abroad. American troops
had ostensibly entered places like Vietnam to halt the spread of Soviet-
style authoritarianism and promote free self-government. But US actions appeared to do just the opposite: they resulted in mass death and
directly conflicted with anti-colonial self-determination.

Within the US, the war also raised profound questions about the
democratic legitimacy of American leaders and institutions. In the late
1960s, over 225,000 young men were drafted each year to fight in an increasingly unpopular conflict. Yet the governing class continued to invest in a security politics impervious to growing opposition. Or, as with
the Democratic Convention in Chicago, they explicitly ignored what
actual voters preferred. Further underscoring this broadening sense of
disenfranchisement among young people, many of those drafted had
not yet reached the age of twenty-one, a common voting age at the time.

This meant that large numbers were often sent to fight and die even as they were denied the ballot.

And if those young people engaged in mass protest—seemingly the only tool left available—fierce state violence resulted. Through programs like the FBI's COINTELPRO and the CIA's "Operation Chaos," security personnel systematically spied on, infiltrated, and sabotaged anti-war and civil rights organizations. Black political groups, such as the Black Panther Party, faced the most extreme acts of repression. As the scholar Nikhil Pal Singh writes, "by the end of [the 1960s] at least twenty-four Panthers had been killed by police, with untold numbers dead from internecine violence stoked by the FBI's covert operations, and hundreds jailed in the nationwide campaign to destroy the Party."[5]

All of these actions radicalized an expanding base of young people, especially students, and regardless of race. In the context of events in Chicago, membership in the anti-war student group, Students for a Democratic Society (SDS), more than doubled in just six months, up to eighty thousand people by the November 1968 general elections. One 1970 John D. Rockefeller Foundation "survey of U.S. college students" found "79 percent of respondents strongly or partially agreed that 'the war in Vietnam is pure imperialism.'"[6] For many flooding into groups like the SDS, the Cold War idea of the US as a near perfect distillation of liberal democracy—with a legal-political model that should be replicated everywhere—had become fundamentally untenable.

Critically, this wider radicalization occurred at precisely the moment when a Black Left internationalism experienced a profound revival within African American life. By the mid-1960s, Congress had passed landmark bills in keeping with long-standing civil rights movement aspirations: the Civil Rights Act (1964) and the Voting Rights Act (1965), as well as the Hart-Cellar Act (1965), which, in line with Kennedy's "nation of immigrants" language, finally abolished explicit racial restrictions in immigration policy. These bills were all steeped in creedal constitutional rhetoric and heralded a new era in American life, which now banned legal segregation and formal Jim Crow practices. Recall that, twenty years earlier, the sociologist and economist Gunnar Myrdal had seen just these potential civil rights victories as the country's "greatest opportunity for the future."[7] By committing itself to equality under the law, the United States would fulfill its own liberal promise and truly have the moral authority to guide a largely non-white world.

Yet such historic achievements did not, in the short term, alleviate domestic conflicts over race. Rather, the disconnect between the end of legally enforced segregation and the ongoing and patent injustice of Black life, especially in urban centers, only fed young Black discontent. Beginning in 1964, American cities were convulsed by waves of civic unrest and rebellion. These peaked in the wake of Martin Luther King Jr.'s assassination, also in 1968, which, according to the political theorist Brandon Terry, "unleashed the most widespread explosion of domestic violence in any day since the Civil War."[8] This unrest constituted a spontaneous response to a daily Black reality of poverty and police brutality, all of which persisted regardless of the new bills passed.

Although marginalized and repressed during the Red Scare, Black socialist and internationalist ideas returned to center stage among a new generation of African American activists increasingly skeptical of the Cold War civil rights bargain. Like earlier generations including Hubert Harrison, W. E. B. Du Bois, Harry Haywood, and Claudia Jones, these younger activists too rejected the Cold War creedal view of the country as intrinsically—if incompletely—liberal. And they argued that ideas of the US as the "first new nation" or as simply a nation of immigrants undermined the ability of most Americans—including Black people themselves—to appreciate the extent to which their society was a continuation of European projects of empire.

New movement voices thus contended that the mainstream politics of civic inclusion truncated the dilemma of race in the United States, deemphasizing both the links to global structures of inequality and the need for more thoroughgoing socioeconomic changes. The activist goal was not just US civil rights, but *decolonization*. Among those who gravitated to the Black Panthers, this colonial framing entailed skepticism too about the Constitution itself, given the document's cultural centrality in sustaining narratives of American exceptionalism. And just as in the Global South, genuine transformation might require the overcoming of existing constitutional structures, and even the wholesale rewriting of governing texts.

During this window of time, the BPP enjoyed a striking popular appeal and cultural salience. The political scientist Michael Dawson reminds us that, in one 1969 Harris Poll, Black respondents identified the Panthers as "being likely the most important black organization of the future."[9] Joshua Bloom and Waldo Martin Jr., in their essential history of the group, *Black Against Empire*, further write that "by 1970, [the party] had opened offices in sixty-eight cities. That year, the *New York Times* published 1217 articles on [them]. . . . The Party's annual budget reached 1.2 million dollars (in 1970 dollars). And circulation of the Party's newspaper, the *Black Panther*, reached 150,000."[10]

Perhaps most significantly, the war context made the Panthers' colonial reading of US domestic institutions and global primacy compelling to many of the era's non-Black Left organizations, like the SDS. These organizations increasingly looked to Black radicalism and to the Panthers specifically for direction and leadership. When Eldridge Cleaver contended that the electoral mechanisms of American institutions had failed, his words resonated with a multiracial, anti-war, and activist base. As an SDS resolution declared on the 1969 anniversary of Martin Luther King Jr.'s assassination, "the Black Panther Party is not fighting black people's struggles only, but is in fact the vanguard in our common struggles against capitalism and imperialism."[11] Such Black politics had become the movement home for a broad collection of groups that embraced its anti-colonial and socialist internationalism.

As I detail in the following pages, this political radicalization revived in public conversation—for the first time truly since the Great Depression—calls for revolutionary change, and with them calls for a new constitution. The chapter focuses especially on the BPP and its effort—through the Revolutionary People's Constitutional Convention (RPCC)—to replace the federal Constitution with a properly decolonial legal-political order. In many ways, that project was the last twentieth-century coalitional and mass political attempt to break explicitly from the established constitutional system. The Convention therefore also provides a window for assessing the political alliances and tensions among the vast array of burgeoning Left groups—anti-war, feminist, Indigenous, and Black freedom activists—as well as the specific challenges Left organizations faced in building cross-racial political support.

In exploring the Convention, this chapter seeks to fill a genuine lacuna in constitutional scholarship and memory. That entire episode is almost completely ignored today in the public recollection of the period. One reason directly concerns how Cold War dynamics transformed the nature of constitutional study, focusing teaching and writing around court-based jurisprudence and politics, as discussed in chapter 13. Given that "constitutionalism" narrowed to a concern with judicially managed debates about legal reform or textual interpretation, these radical activists disappeared from view. Indeed, despite their searching interrogation of the overarching constitutional system, such actors by and large are treated by mainstream scholarship as *not* having a meaningful constitutional vision or politics.

This connects to the second key reason why Black radical constitutional thinking from the era has been essentially written out of the legal scholarship. As establishment elites systematically contained socialist and internationalist activism in the 1970s, a caricature of the era's Left politics took hold in much of mainstream discussion. For those like the famed philosopher Richard Rorty, Black radicals—along with the white students they convinced—simply refused to "share in a national hope" and instead embraced a violent and rejectionist worldview that courted marginality and veered between "self-disgust" and "self-mockery."[12] According to this framing, the Black decolonial agenda was best thought of as sloganeering, and their militant posture best conceived of as emblematic of the destructiveness of the period.

By contrast, I argue that such an approach flattens the complexities of the Left, especially Black Left internationalist engagements with the legal-political order. It ignores these activists' efforts to build broad coalitional alliances—across gender and racial divides—behind a concrete and transformative agenda relevant for all. And it erases the actual constitutional vision embraced by some of the era's most significant voices and groups.

The Panthers in particular, in ways that mirrored earlier Socialist Party and Industrial Workers of the World (IWW) activists, invested deeply in the language of constitutional rights. They considered constitutionalism, broadly understood, a means to hold an armed state publicly accountable *and* to imagine a liberatory horizon beyond the limited terms of the 1787 text. If anything, engaging with their constitutional politics suggests pathways that were not pursued, but that remain relevant for today's debates about ongoing hierarchy and social crisis. Furthermore, reflecting on what actually produced the collapse of BPP multiracial coalitional efforts, including the Revolutionary People's Constitutional Convention, helps to make better sense of the post-1960s containment of Left activism. It also sheds light on the persistent challenges that racial minorities continue to face in convincing a broader majority of the need for structural change.

From Civil Rights to Decolonization

As the 1960s progressed, Black political debate became defined by a growing activist sentiment that the traditional civil rights frame—

focused on ending formalized inequality—was insufficient for providing substantive freedom. Against a backdrop of global independence movements, the growing watchword became decolonization, rather than just civil rights. Yet, if the idea of decolonization began to resonate, especially among young Black people, deep questions persisted of both means and ends: What, concretely, did such a project entail in the United States—rather than in an Asian or African context? And how could a subordinated Black minority spearhead change in this direction, given the permanent reality of majority white control?

KING TRANSCENDS THE CREEDAL CONSTITUTION

Perhaps more than anyone else, Martin Luther King Jr. underscored these shifting tides and wrestled seriously with the promise and peril embedded in pushing beyond the boundaries of American nationalist assumptions. King had been a preeminent articulator of the creedal Constitution, including the Cold War Manichaean divide between totalitarianism and an exceptional American liberalism. But in the overlapping contexts of Black urban immiseration and extreme US violence in Vietnam, King began to contend that simply completing the creedal national project would not be enough to generate liberation for Black and oppressed people, both within the country and across the world.

Domestically, he argued that the African American condition was one of "educational castration and economic exploitation": experiences rooted in how institutions had been organized and power structured since the earliest days of collective life. The result was a sustained non-white reality of "poverty amid plenty," which fundamentally contradicted the national mythology of an essentially liberal polity only requiring racial ameliorism. Instead, King declared that the country needed nothing less than "a radical restructuring of the architecture of American society."[13]

As for the world stage, he abandoned that established "Cold War civil rights" approach, which attempted to leverage Black support for American global primacy to achieve steady internal progress on race. At the NAACP's 1966 convention, Whitney Young, the head of the more moderate Urban League, had warned activists that the League would denounce any African American groups that tied issues of "domestic civil rights with the Vietnam Conflict."[14] Despite these admonitions, as well as the blowback from establishment Black figures like Ralph Bunche, King felt he could no longer refrain from voicing opposition to the war effort. He famously declared in 1967 that the time had come to "break the silence," and stated that the Vietnamese "must see Americans as strange liberators." The US had "vigorously supported the French in their abortive effort to recolonize Vietnam," and now was brutally imposing its own economic and security ends on a local population seeking its independence.[15]

What was most striking about King's evolving position is that he refused to argue against the war from within the terms of Cold War nationalism. The standard anti-war position was to critique the conflict as inconsistent with the country's moral fabric—as the isolated folly of an otherwise just creedal nation. By contrast, over the last year of his life, King repeatedly asserted that Vietnam was emblematic of the general structure of US institutions—institutions that reproduced everywhere "the giant triplets of racism, materialism, and militarism."[16]

As a result, the security prerogatives that the state projected abroad could be understood as extensions of domestic racial and class hierarchies. For that reason, not only was the war in Vietnam unjust. It was also now no longer acceptable for Americans, including Black people, to accede to the "smooth patriotism" of such Cold War imperatives and to avoid the "mandates of conscience."[17] At a time when "all over the globe men are revolting against old systems of exploitation and oppression,"[18] Cold War anti-communism placed this "smooth patriotism" ahead of meaningful solidarities between poor and excluded peoples.

In this way, King constructed his own brand of Black internationalism, which had clear historical resonances with the pre–Cold War radical tradition. He called on Black and poor communities within the United States to reject nationalist strictures, and instead to support solidaristic alliances of shared interest and commitment among oppressed peoples everywhere—regardless of one's location in Cold War rivalries. He saw this anti-nationalist shift in identification as part of "a genuine revolution of values" that would make political "loyalties...ecumenical rather than sectional."[19]

At home, this required reimagining the civil rights movement as a Poor People's Campaign—incorporating Black people, working-class and impoverished whites, Indigenous groups, and immigrant communities—with the goal of abolishing poverty and overcoming capitalism. And with respect to Vietnam, it led King to embrace the growing anti-war focus on opposing the draft. He argued that no one of good conscience could participate in the conflict, and that individuals drafted should explicitly seek conscientious objector status—even if they might be able to claim other exemptions.[20]

King's approach thus increasingly challenged all the basic Cold War assumptions of American politics, and it did not leave the Constitution untouched. The need to move beyond classic civil rights demands raised real questions about the extent to which the constitutional system would be an aid or a hindrance going forward. On the one hand, in speaking about desegregation victories, with the *Brown* decision clearly front and center, King noted the role of the Supreme Court. He wrote in 1967, "so far, we have had constitutional backing for most of our demands for change, and this has made our work easier, since we could be sure of legal support from the federal courts."[21]

Still, King doubted that the "radical restructuring" he had in mind could be achieved on the existing terms of Cold War constitutional politics. He continued, "the Constitution assured the right to vote, but there is no such assurance of the right to adequate housing, or the right to an adequate income." Even if the 1787 text could be interpreted to include these commitments, King's broader worry was that the legal-political infrastructure was built to contain the transformative power of those most oppressed in society—or, at the very least, that genuine freedom required "approaching areas where the voice of the Constitution is not clear."[22]

THE RISE OF BLACK POWER AND
THE DECOLONIAL PROJECT

In many ways, King's substantive critique of American society began to dovetail with the era's Black Power politics, even as he disagreed strenuously with aspects of that developing perspective. The term "Black Power" itself emerged from a dramatic 1966 Mississippi speech given by Stokely Carmichael, then chairman of the Student Nonviolent Coordinating Committee (SNCC), in which he decried police brutality and harassment: "This is the 27th time I have been arrested—I ain't going to jail no more!... We want Black Power!... That's right.... It's time we stand up and take over."[23] Not unlike the latter-day King, Carmichael too contended that the traditional civil rights narrative, grounded in nationalist rhetoric about the American creed, concealed more than it illuminated.

But if he and King both underscored the persistence of structural racial injustice, Carmichael gave this reality a specific name: internal colonialism. In his seminal book *Black Power* (1967), coauthored with Charles Hamilton, Carmichael explicitly rejected Gunnar Myrdal's famous vision of an internal American contest between its grand national principles and local prejudices: "There is no 'American dilemma' because black people in this country form a colony, and it is not in the interest of the colonial power to liberate them. Black people are legal citizens of the United States with, for the most part, the same *legal* rights as other citizens. Yet they stand as colonial subjects in relation to the white society. This institutional racism has another name: colonialism."[24]

For Carmichael and Hamilton, race relations in the United States mirrored those in colonized societies across Asia and Africa. The United States too was divided between racially privileged insiders and non-white peoples, whose land and labor served as the basis for elite wealth and power. Carmichael and Hamilton argued that, akin to "South Africa and Rhodesia," this created a lived experience of "black and white inhabit[ing] the same land [but] blacks subordinated to whites."[25] It also meant that Black liberation would require more than civil rights and inclusion in the existing social order. It would require decolonization: a full-scale transformation of the country, on terms of real material equality for those subordinated.

As discussed through previous chapters, some version of anti-colonialism had long been a defining political commitment across the Black ideological spectrum. This held for figures critical of the Cold War project, like W. E. B. Du Bois, and those more supportive, like Ralph Bunche and Thurgood Marshall. Furthermore, the specific framing of the United States as a colonial enterprise, thus analogizing the Black condition to that of colonized peoples abroad, had been commonplace on the African American Left for decades. Du Bois—in language virtually equivalent to that of Carmichael and Hamilton—remarked to an audience in Haiti in 1944 that colonial circumstances were not only those in which one "country belong[ed] to another country." They also encompassed "groups, like the Negros of the United States, who do not form a separate nation and yet who resemble in their economic and political condition a distinctly colonial status."[26]

All of this meant that the discourse of decolonization tapped into an established wellspring of Black sentiment. But it enjoyed a special prominence during these years because of the global historical moment—one of rippling non-white victories over oppressive European rule, in which new independent nations called for basic changes to the international economic and political order. These dynamics instilled within more and more African American activists a sense of globally shared non-white political destiny, as well as a belief that an anti-imperial and anti-capitalist future genuinely might be within reach.

The times thus promoted a Black interest in looking overseas for guidance on both political means and ends. Eldridge Cleaver began referring to the psychoanalyst and anti-colonial revolutionary Frantz Fanon's *The Wretched of the Earth* (1960) as "the Black Bible,"[27] due to its exploration of the violent structures shaping relations between colonizer and colonized. And Carmichael and Hamilton presented African Americans as above all members of the "Third World" rather than primarily US citizens: "Black Power means that black people see themselves as part of a new force, sometimes called the 'Third World': that we see our struggle as closely related to liberation struggles around the world."[28]

Black Power activists asserted the need for this alternative political identity in part because of the sense that the interests of the Black community—as an oppressed population within the United States—critically opposed those of the country's security apparatus. As such, in opposition to Black Cold Warriors, they called for a truly independent Black foreign policy, one committed to resisting the security state.

Nothing spoke more directly to the importance of an independent approach to international affairs than the US's active role in supporting the white apartheid government in South Africa. When the American foreign policy establishment faced a tension between egalitarian values and economic investments, they seemed to readily sacrifice the former. Focusing on the apartheid example, Carmichael and Hamilton wrote, "it seems inevitable that this nation would move to protect its financial interests in South Africa, which means protecting white rule in South Africa. Black people in this country then have the responsibility to oppose, at least to neutralize, that effort by white America."[29]

In keeping with their oppositional and internationalist stance, the Black Panther Party famously used organizational leadership titles that mirrored the government offices of the nation-state, including by designating party co-founder Huey Newton the Minister of Defense. The Party also engaged in direct outreach with overseas national liberation movements, newly independent governments in Asia and Africa, and even North Vietnam.[30] As a whole, the BPP offered a clear alternative to the accommodationist and domestically focused politics of Cold War civil rights—an alternative that became increasingly compelling to a broader range of left and anti-war activists.

CHALLENGES FOR THE COLONIAL METAPHOR

Still, if such Black activists conceived of themselves as part of the Third World rather than an American "we the people," this emerging politics of decolonization faced a twofold challenge. First, what concrete political agenda did it entail? In Asia and Africa, decolonization invoked a relatively clear set of objectives. These included the connected goals of overthrowing imperial political rulers, asserting local economic and political self-determination, and ensuring genuine formal and substantive nation-state equality on the international stage. But, as Du Bois had noted, African Americans did not form a "separate nation"—a fact that underscored the need to adapt the colonial metaphor for the particularities of the American condition.

In addition, there existed a second basic predicament: how to push past the terms of the American Cold War compact to this decolonized future? Huey Newton famously argued that the defining feature of American life had been "majority freedom and minority oppression": "While the majority group achieved their basic rights, the minorities achieved alienation from the lands of their fathers and slavery."[31] Implicit in these words was the unavoidable reality that African Americans, unlike Black people in South Africa, constituted only a small percentage of the overall US population. The country was a majority white society in which it had taken truly heroic struggle to end slavery in the nineteenth century and to generate civil rights achievements in the twentieth. To the extent that decolonization required something akin to King's "radical restructuring," what pathway existed for such a change?

Much of King's critique of Black Power politics had to do with this latter question of a viable strategic pathway. In particular, he was deeply suspicious of how one strain of Black Power activism romanticized armed struggle by making a connection between anti-colonial resistance abroad and potentially similar resistance at home.

One key impetus behind the creation of the BPP had been profound outrage at the impunity with which state officials and private white citizens were able to perpetrate daily acts of violence against African Americans. Party founders like Newton argued that, under conditions in which the state refused to protect Black people from threat—and indeed behaved lawlessly to sustain white rule—it was appropriate for African Americans to arm themselves as a matter of self-defense (hence the original full name of the party, the Black Panther Party for Self-

Defense). But over time, some members also began to argue that a guerrilla uprising could be an instrument for either overcoming the American state or establishing local autonomous and self-determining Black political zones. Such ideas were spurred by the success of guerrilla tactics in anti-colonial struggles abroad, especially in Cuba and Algeria.

Recognizing that in the United States there existed extreme asymmetries in power between the Cold War security apparatus and small bands of dissidents, Newton referred to this uprising as "revolutionary suicide."[32] As Brandon Terry notes, the driving argument was a version of "mutually assured destruction."[33] Such Black Power activists appreciated that armed struggle would produce extreme and indiscriminate violence from a US state already engaged in brutal crackdowns against any Black activist perceived to be radical. But defenders of guerrilla tactics imagined that white national elites would ultimately reach a détente with insurgents, given likely global pressure, creating the conditions for Black self-determination in their communities. These activists also hoped that some whites, particularly in the anti-war movement, might become sufficiently radicalized to participate in armed struggle, strengthening the overall prospects. Barring that, newly independent Third World states perhaps could also be brought in as military and political allies against the American security state.

None of these strategic defenses of armed struggle seemed remotely plausible for King.[34] For starters, he argued that the likely effect of Black guerrilla violence would be to galvanize white support behind even more extreme state repression. Precisely because of the American history of white supremacy, and the ever-lurking framing of Black political agency as a threatening fifth column, the resort to arms would end in brutal one-sided defeat and spur reactionary tendencies within white society. Underscoring the difference between the US and Third World Cuba or Algeria, King wrote, "it is perfectly clear that a violent revolution on the part of American blacks would find no sympathy and support from the white population and very little from the majority of the Negroes themselves."[35]

The hope that newly independent states in Asia and Africa might assist local activists in armed struggle ignored the power disparities that existed on the global stage—not to mention the likely unwillingness of Third World nations to be dragged into a losing fight with the world's preeminent superpower. Ultimately, King concluded that assistance from abroad offered no viable solution. Instead, the best way to truly achieve substantive self-determination for Asian, African, and Latin

American countries—along with Black freedom—involved changes internal to the American state: "The hard cold facts today indicate that the hope of the people of color in the world may rest on the American Negro and his ability to reform the structure of racist imperialism from within."[36]

These concerns, voiced by King and others, also suggested pitfalls with the Panthers' promotion of a "UN-supervised plebiscite," a non-violent alternative pathway to decolonization, added to their ten-point program in 1968.[37] This plebiscite amounted to a democratic vote "held throughout the black colony in which only black colonial subjects will be allowed to participate, for the purpose of determining the will of black people as to their national destiny."[38] Such a proposal offered a direct repudiation of any nationalist attachment to an American "we the people," let alone to the creedal Constitution, and also clearly invoked the CPUSA's earlier "Black belt" thesis.

As discussed in chapter 7, in the 1930s and 1940s Black Communist activists like Harry Haywood had worked imaginatively to craft an account of what Black self-determination might mean as a matter of concrete governance within the inevitable context of a dominant American polity. Haywood had argued for the breaking up of states in the South to create new constitutional structures that did not facilitate white minority rule and that ensured Black voting power and political authority. Of course, one clear effect of the intervening decades' Cold War suppression was that younger and radicalized Black activists may have taken on the overarching Black radical sentiment. But they were often disconnected from the details of how those earlier discussions concretely conceived of reshaping domestic constitutional structures.

As exemplified by the plebiscite call, the BPP's relevant imaginative model tended to be the post-war process by which African colonies abroad gained formal independence, including through the use of local referenda. But the problem of transposing such referenda to the American context was, as Terry summarizes, that "there was never . . . a careful working through of the democratic dilemmas that come from designing such a plebiscite and the legitimacy of its various possible outcomes (who would participate, whether such a vote entails territorial separatism, what happens to blacks who want to stay, and so on)."[39]

Indeed, these issues were apparent in the most sustained effort to pursue territorial separation as a method of decolonization: the creation of the Republic of New Afrika (RNA) by some of Malcolm X's supporters after his assassination. Founded in Detroit and then relocated to Mississippi, the RNA sought to decolonize Black people by creating a territorial nation-state in the South through an internationally backed plebiscite. Such independence would also go hand in hand with a push in international forums to impose reparations on the American state for slavery and coerced Black labor. This was to be paid to the RNA as part of its efforts to develop internal economic self-sufficiency.[40] "The main job of the Black government," RNA leader Imari Obadele declared of the focus on territorial control, "is to free the land."[41]

The RNA took very seriously this desire to gain formal recognition as a sovereign state. Members wrote their own constitution, known as the Code of Umoja ("unity" in Swahili). This code laid out the terms of citizenship, created a governing legislative body in the People's Center Council, and established a court system along with a related criminal law. When faced with FBI raids and local police repression, the RNA leaders persistently invoked their status as officials of a foreign government, and they sought formal recognition for the state from countries in the Third World.[42]

From the start, the effort to entrench the RNA faced a variety of internal conceptual dilemmas alongside the broader political implausibility. Territorial independence, even if one day achievable, appeared to replicate on American soil the profound imbalance in wealth and power between postcolonial states and their past imperial rulers. The RNA emphasis on territoriality effectively ignored the neocolonial dynamics that troubled Third World figures like Kwame Nkrumah and Oginga Odinga. As the historian Sam Klug writes of the disconnect between RNA arguments and the developing Third World analysis, the postcolonial reality was one in which formal territorial sovereignty did *not* necessarily entail substantive economic and political self-determination. After all, the "imperial power no longer depended as much on the control of physical space."[43]

Furthermore, the focus on land itself embodied a significant political limitation with respect to Indigenous peoples. Indeed, this limitation had existed in earlier invocations of African American separatism or colonization plans, whether in the Black belt, Kansas, or Liberia. As such, while those in the RNA, alongside other Black Power activists, may have strongly invoked Native expropriation as a foundational aspect of American colonialism, their own relationship to this expropriated territory could often fall prey to settlerist assumptions.

In general, the era's Indigenous activists—who gravitated to the framework of Red Power and to organizations like the American Indian

Movement (AIM)—viewed positively the shift in Black political emphasis from civil rights to decolonization. For the scholar and activist Vine Deloria Jr., a central intellectual figure in Red Power politics, the problem of the traditional civil rights movement was that the creedal and constitutional language of inclusion for African Americans seemed premised on the erasure of the country's settler past. It implicitly rejected the right of distinct peoples subject to the US state's sovereign control—including Indigenous nations—to be autonomous and self-determining polities. As Deloria wrote in his seminal 1969 book, *Custer Died for Your Sins*, "conflicts are created when Indians feel they are being defined out of existence by the other groups."[44] In this way, the embrace of decolonization by the period's Black radicals embodied a rubric within which Indigenous self-determination could be fully articulated.

At the same time, projects like the RNA never properly confronted what it meant that the territory they claimed for a new Black nation was still expropriated Indigenous land. Their territorial focus thus unwittingly reproduced the Euro-American drive for settlement. This version of Black decolonization, Klug explains, ignored "the possibility that [Indigenous peoples] might have a continuing interest in the land."[45]

Ultimately, though, the goal of a separate Black territorial nation-state—including through the RNA—foundered on two realities: the intensity of sustained federal and local police crackdowns against proponents, and the general lack of meaningful Black political support. This lack of support meant that territoriality failed both as the substantive agenda for decolonization and as an organizing strategy for the African American community. And the broader problems with either armed struggle or an internationally approved plebiscite challenged the basic utility of the colonial metaphor for the Black experience in the United States.

Decolonization through Constitutional Transformation

In the face of these profound dilemmas, radical African American activists could have simply abandoned the colonial conceptual framework. But by the end of the 1960s, activists in the Black Panther Party began to conceive of decolonization in a way that addressed their distinctly American conditions, and that accepted the inevitability of Black political embeddedness within the US project.

In particular, Party voices imagined decolonization as involving a refounding of the American polity, but on terms that distributed sovereign authority to communities long denied real material and political power. And they focused strategically on building a genuinely multiracial coalition committed to such change—not unlike that which King had sought to organize into a Poor People's Campaign before his assassination. As part of this coalition-building, the BPP even imagined collaboratively developing, alongside non-Black Left allies, a new constitutional document that could pave the way to a truly liberated society.

THE POLITICS OF BLACK LIBERATION AND AMERICAN REVOLUTION

Within the BPP, there had certainly been an awareness of how transforming the Black condition would necessarily involve accompanying changes in the larger society. In 1968, Eldridge Cleaver had evocatively summarized this linkage in his call for "Revolution in the White Mother Country and National Liberation in the Black Colony."[46] But at that time, Cleaver's framing centered on a fairly conventional version of the colonial analogy, which more or less directly grafted Third World politics onto the United States. In invoking Black liberation and American revolution, he referred to the "Black Plebiscite" as the party's "major political objective,"[47] especially given plans that July for a push on behalf of the initiative in the United Nations, alongside SNCC leaders.[48]

Yet as the plebiscite idea lost steam and activists connected to the party moved beyond it, they focused more explicitly on how Black liberation might fit within a vision of dramatic American political and economic transformation. James Boggs, once a colleague of C. L. R. James, was one key Black socialist voice. A longtime worker in the Detroit Chrysler plant and an influential figure for 1960s Black radical labor organizing, such as the Dodge Revolutionary Union Movement (DRUM), Boggs played a central role in sustaining Black socialist and internationalist politics even under Cold War strictures. On the relationship between Black people and the broader society, Boggs wrote in 1970, "the Black Power movement must recognize that if this society is ever going to be changed to meet the needs of black people, then Black Power will have to resolve the problems of the society as a whole and not just those of black people."[49]

In a sense, Boggs critiqued both a conventional internal colonialism narrative and a traditional civil rights one. The standard grafting of Third Worldism tended to treat the projects of Black freedom and of change in majority white society as on related but separate tracks. In Boggs's view, this continued to miss King's essential insight: that Black and white society were permanently and mutually entangled.

At the same time, formal equality clearly had failed to provide an adequate emancipatory horizon for African Americans, let alone for the society generally. This was demonstrated by the failures of the traditional civil rights frame to address the interpenetration of racial subordination with structural class domination. For Blacks to be free in the United States, all the existing corporate and governmental hierarchies would have to be dislodged. This was because such hierarchies denied most individuals—regardless of race—economic independence and daily control over their lives. As Boggs concluded, with clear echoes of King's call for a "radical restructuring," "Black Power cannot evade tackling all the problems of this society, because at the root of all the problems of black people is the same structure and the same system which is at the root of all the problems of all people."[50]

As the decade closed, the Black Panther Party systematically engaged with the implications of these arguments. Indeed, Bloom and Martin note that, from the party's founding, it had always diverged from "many black nationalists" in "ma[king] common cause" with non-Black entities on shared anti-war, anti-capitalist, and anti-imperialist grounds.[51] This had already involved work alongside the SDS in organizing around draft resistance.[52] It also included the party's close ties to San Francisco State University's Third World Liberation Front (TWLF), which brought Black, Latinx, and Asian American students together under the banner of "educational self-determination." The TWLF call for new ethnic studies programs reflective of non-European experiences and infused with anti-imperial values reverberated across California, leading to numerous student strikes and protest actions.[53]

As non-Black Left groups increasingly looked to the Panthers for leadership, including in the wake of the Chicago Democratic Convention, the Panthers turned even more aggressively to stitching together a broad-based social movement—one grounded in viewing Black freedom and American transformation as a unified project. New Left formations proliferated during the era, alongside the SDS and TWLF, including everything from Puerto Rican, Native American, Asian American, and Mexican American groups to emergent radical feminist, gay rights, and poor white collectives. The BPP thus reached out to these activists to create shared institutions and organizational homes for jointly developing insurgent projects.

By 1969, these movement-building efforts in Chicago developed into a "Rainbow Coalition," pursued by the Illinois party chairman, Fred Hampton, as an internationalist and multiracial political movement.[54] Figures like Hampton sought to develop solidarities with white communities despite racial divides by focusing on class-based and socialist organizing, which emphasized shared identities as fellow workers and as individuals economically exploited by capitalist elites. The goal was to build institutional power among oppressed groups outside the established sites of economic and political authority. Such coalitional alliance would create something akin to what various radical organizers in the first half of the twentieth century had sought: a permanently mobilized base of support that could effectively embody a government behind the government. This mass entity could continuously intervene in labor or political disputes, whenever the interests of the underlying communities were at stake.

Hampton and other Panther leaders believed the BPP was perhaps uniquely situated to serve as the connective tissue binding a new transformative alliance. This was the case even though the Panthers were always a relatively small organization, certainly by comparison with something like the 1930s CIO—a previous insurgent and class-conscious movement. As noted in chapters 8 and 11, the CIO's presence across the industrial economy meant that it had the ability—through strike actions at the point of production—to essentially shut down critical economic infrastructure, not to mention to bring out countless workers on election day. Any practical power the Panthers enjoyed paled before such past labor radicalism, let alone relative to the extreme might of the American state. As Nikhil Pal Singh writes, "with only a few shotguns and only a handful of members in many Party chapters across the country, the Panthers were not a 'real' threat to the organized violence of the state."[55] But the war in Vietnam had created a cultural opening for their vision of a unified global and domestic struggle against empire, and an American Left political environment in which the BPP enjoyed elevated status.

The Panthers' largest and most sustained national attempt to expand on projects like Chicago's "Rainbow Coalition" was its summer of 1969 "Revolutionary Conference for a United Front against Fascism." As the party declared in its conference announcement, this event aimed to bring together all the relevant formations on the political Left, so as to develop in common a full political agenda for "poor, black, oppressed workers and people of America." That conference led to the creation across the country of various National Committees to Combat Fascism (NCCFs): multiracial groups that would work in parallel with Panther chapters. "By April 1970," Bloom and Martin tell us, "NCCFs were opened and operating in at least eighteen cities around the country."[56] Thus, through the NCCF project and beyond, the party continued to experiment with multiracial and radical coalition-building with a view to broader national transformation.

DEVELOPING A PANTHER CONSTITUTIONAL POLITICS

Most significantly for the purposes of this book, Panther activists attempted to write — collaboratively with non-Black Left organizations — a comprehensive policy framework for a revolutionary society, beyond the BPP's own specific ten-point program. In 1970 this joint undertaking took the form of the party's drafting of a new constitution for the United States.

The Panthers' interest in constitutional politics as a register for presenting the combined objectives of Black liberation and American revolution did not materialize out of nowhere. Not unlike the Socialist Party or the IWW before them, party members often held together two arguments about the existing constitutional system. On the one hand, activists rejected any identification with a creedal nationalist project and instead asserted their own primary and internationalist political affiliation with oppressed peoples everywhere. For this reason, the ten-point program, initially distributed in 1967, had gone even further than King's call for individuals to declare conscientious objector status when drafted for Vietnam. The platform contended that all African Americans, as a colonized people, should be exempted permanently from any military service: "We will not fight and kill other people of color in the world who, like black people, are victimized by the white racist government of America."[57]

As the governing document of this colonial order, the Constitution was therefore often depicted as a symbolic and institutional embodiment of an unjust system. As one Panther member, James Mott, explained: "The Constitution is the ideological foundation of the American way of life." The text perpetuated a myth of liberal equality, while in practice facilitating a legal-political order that subordinated Black people. Referencing the presumptive creedal connection between the Declaration of Independence and the federal Constitution, Mott continued, "it is supposed to stand for life, liberty and the pursuit of happiness," but has instead "become a symbol of political oppression, economic exploitation and social degradation of a people who have suffered 400 years of humility."[58]

On the other hand, from their very genesis the Panthers had invoked their rights under the Constitution as a way of highlighting their own lawfulness as well as the violent impunity with which the state and private white vigilantes oppressed Black people. The initial ten-point program included repeated calls for American officials simply to make good on the constitutional rights they presumptively guaranteed to all, especially with respect to the carceral and security apparatus of the state.[59]

Focusing especially on police brutality in Black neighborhoods, Panthers also maintained that they had the Second Amendment constitutional right to carry weapons in community patrols of the police, so as to protect individuals against the everyday violation of Black rights. Reminiscent of early-twentieth-century socialists defending their speech rights against the police, Panthers who took part in such patrols even brought with them copies of the Bill of Rights. Like those past radical activists, Panthers too would reference the text in hand when collecting information about inappropriate police behavior.[60]

In keeping with a long history of dissident constitutional argument, activists invoked the text to undermine official narratives around the government's fidelity to the law. Community patrols of the police had been not Black extremism and violence but instead self-defense: a lawabiding and constitutionally protected method of ensuring that the actual source of collective violence, the armed state, could be held to public account. Underscoring this point, the legal scholar Bridgette Baldwin writes that Panther activists "required" those on community patrol "to stay within legal bounds—refrain from cursing, keep guns always visible, and read the law."[61]

This focus on lawfulness even extended to armed confrontations. If police employed violence against Black people and party members in their communities, the BPP's constitutional discourse suggested that defensive responses were legally grounded. As one BPP member contended, "the Constitution"—with the Bill of Rights front and center— was "based upon the idea of the power of the people to enjoy certain 'inalienable rights.'" Given that the existing government systematically denied such rights to Black people, in violation of its own Constitution, "the police . . . as arms of this type of government have no right in our communities." By implication, Panthers asserted an embedded right of resistance within the text when police initiated these attacks. Lawless state security personnel failed to "liv[e] up to . . . the Constitution, and . . . [were] therefore illegitimate bodies in our society." Under those circumstances, Black self-defense was consistent with the Declaration of Independence and even the Constitution.[62]

In this way, constitutional discourse served two connected functions for the Panther activists—it allowed them to articulate *both* a project of radical institutional rupture *and* one of respect for legality. Constitutional claims could even potentially extend to legal defenses of armed struggle. Still, one should note that, for various Panther activists, an additional benefit of constitutional argument was that it offered a potential off-ramp from violent confrontation with the state.[63] There were voices within the Party that were more skeptical of armed struggle's viability as a genuine pathway to change, for many of the reasons King had highlighted. Moreover, unlike groups such as the RNA, leading Panther members wanted to develop a project capable of including all oppressed Americans. Thus, they sought to imagine nonviolent mechanisms for building movement power and for transforming existing institutions.

As a consequence, constitution-writing in particular became a way to potentially reach a broader multiracial audience: the language of constitutionalism maintained contact with the norms and traditions of the majority white society, while still suggesting an irruptive politics. As a shared enterprise in re-founding, constitution-writing was culturally American. And yet, such writing nonetheless provided space for radical activists to proclaim a revolutionary agenda that reconceived prevailing arrangements root and branch.

Perhaps no one better articulated these interconnected qualities of Panther constitutionalism than the party member Afeni Shakur. Writing in the *Black Panther*, the party's newspaper, she asserted that it was long past time to replace "the outdated document of two centuries ago" and to forge genuinely equal and effective freedom for all, regardless of race. She emphasized the extent to which constitution-writing, though a fundamentally transformative enterprise, should be understood as a nonviolent alternative to armed struggle and "revolutionary suicide." As she concluded, "we cannot afford not to rewrite this document! We must attempt this last straw at National Salvation under this present system, for we must exhaust all legal means. We know that there can be no peace until there is land, bread, housing, education, clothing, justice and blessed liberty!"[64]

In addition to being both nonviolent and revolutionary, the constitution-writing exercise also emphasized the decolonial and coalitional nature of the Panther project. For starters, the symbolic action of writing a new governing document to replace the 1787 Constitution offered a concrete way of thinking through the specific meaning of decolonization in the American context. Alongside lowering old European flags and raising new Asian and African ones, the writing of new constitutions abroad had become a defining act of colonial rupture and Third World independence. It expressed the extent to which sovereign power was now transferred from imperial rulers to a local and self-determining people. By engaging in a similar form of symbolic break, the Panthers emphasized their own decolonial ambition: they aimed to move sovereign power from wealthy white governing elites—effectively the ideological descendants of the 1787 framers—to a broad coalition of those historically oppressed.

Since this document was meant to be written in collaboration with various non-Black political formations, the exercise also underscored the differences between national liberation in parts of Asia and Africa and Black liberation in the United States. Pushing beyond the idea of a plebiscite, the new document would re-found American society in ways that transcended its colonial infrastructure, while respecting the mutually entangled nature of white and Black communities, among many others. Moreover, such a collaboratively generated text could also articulate demands that had no direct relation to race and colonialism, thus expressing the will of all marginalized Americans regardless of background or identity.

Therefore, the Panther desire to write a new constitution also implicitly served an interest in movement-building activity for this united front. Working together on a common agenda embodied a concrete way of developing solidarity across constituencies, and of seeing how one's own freedom connected to overcoming the oppression faced by other communities. Thus, members like Afeni Shakur spent a significant amount of time in 1970 going to meetings, protests, and events organized by other Left groups, and also personally inviting them to participate in the Panthers' constitutional convening.

In line with the era's radicalized climate, these years witnessed a rebirth in feminist politics as well as the emergence of a self-assertive new gay rights movement. Such organizations often felt alienated by how various male Panther members embraced a militaristic and traditionalist posturing around gender norms and roles. Given these dynamics, Shakur in particular reached out to organizations like the Radicalesbians and the Gay Liberation Front to ask that they take part in planning meetings for the Panthers' constitutional convening, to ensure that their agendas would be adequately represented.[65] In a sense, Shakur and others, as with earlier BPP efforts around draft resistance or student strikes, explicitly sought a politics that could integrate Black liberation with the struggles facing other subordinated groups—without losing the distinctiveness or particularity of each community's history and experience.

THE REVOLUTIONARY PEOPLE'S CONSTITUTIONAL CONVENTION

The Panther experiment in constitution-writing culminated with the September 1970 staging in Philadelphia of a Revolutionary People's Constitutional Convention, perhaps the country's last culturally resonant moment of mass constitutional rejectionism. Indeed, the location and date embodied a large-scale counter-convention, in opposition to the by then routine anniversary celebrations of the 1787 text and its framers.[66]

As summarized in the *Black Panther* newspaper, keynote speeches like those by the party member Cetawayo (Michael) Tabor aimed to demonstrate how the existing constitutional order had, from the beginning, been designed to subordinate "240,000 [white] indentured servants, 800,000 black slaves, 300,000 Indians, and all women, to say nothing of sexual minorities."[67] This counter-convention therefore aspired to reclaim sovereign power for everyone oppressed—regardless of race, gender, or sexual orientation—who would now finally articulate, in their own terms, the substance of their liberation.

In the lead-up to the event, organizers faced intense police repression. Frank Rizzo, the Philadelphia police commissioner at the time and the city's future Democratic mayor, was a well-known opponent of desegregation and was absolutely committed to using the full force of the police against any and all Black activism. In 1971 Rizzo would infamously declare that all Panther members should be "strung up" and that combating them should be viewed as "actual warfare."[68] In the lead-up to the Convention, Rizzo's police department systematically attempted to shut down Panther offices and arrest Panther members. This came to a head the week before the actual event, when Rizzo used the pretense of an unrelated police killing to raid three BPP offices, arresting and stripping members naked at gunpoint—images captured in photographs that circulated across the country and overseas.[69]

But despite the police violence, the event itself went off peacefully and with strikingly large numbers given the climate of ever-present state repression. Participant estimates ranged from 12,000 to 15,000 people, with 5,000 to 6,000 attending the plenary sessions at Temple University as well as Huey Newton's opening speech (his first major event since his own release from prison). Thousands more stood outside the doors but could not get seats.

The actual delegates to the Convention, as one participant, George Katsiaficas, recalled later, came "from an array of organizations" besides the Panthers, speaking to the success of coalition-building efforts. Alongside the already mentioned Gay Liberation Front and Radicalesbians, these entities included "the American Indian Movement" and the Chicano activist group the Brown Berets, as well as "the Young Lords, I wor Keun (an Asian-American group), Students for a Democratic Society . . . and many feminist groups." Katsiaficas added that mingling in the crowds were also "representatives from African liberation movements, Palestine, Germany, Colombia, and Brazil."[70] Magazine reports at the time noted the presence of high-profile activists and celebrities, from Abbie Hoffman, Jerry Rubin, Tom Hayden, and William Kunstler to Muhammad Ali himself.[71]

Ultimately, the most remarkable aspect of the Convention was neither the collection of keynote speeches nor the general pageantry. Instead, what stood out was the actual substantive text the delegates produced.

Alongside plenary sessions, participants broke out into specific workshops in which delegates from across the various organizations developed constitutional reports framed around issue areas. These included (1) "internationalism and relations with liberation struggles around the world"; (2) "self-determination of street people"; (3) "self-determination of women"; (4) "demands from the male representatives of national gay liberation"; (5) "the family and the rights of children"; (6) "control and use of the legal system and political prisoners of war"; (7) "control and use of the educational system"; (8) "control and use of the military and police"; (9) "health"; and (10) "revolutionary art."[72]

Furthermore, the medium-term Panther ambition was for a "continuance committee" that would distribute these reports nationally to party chapters and coalitional partners. The reports would form the basis for further discussion in advance of a second conference. That subsequent conference would then ratify a new single constitutional document, fusing together the reports, and would also strategize how to pursue its political implementation.[73]

Taken together, these reports clearly constituted a continuation of the socialist and internationalist politics already expressed in the initial BPP ten-point program, with its earlier calls for a basic right to food, health, housing, clothing, and education as well as military exemption, full employment, and a guaranteed income.[74] Yet, as George Katsiaficas has noted,[75] the documents went significantly further than the spring 1967 platform in spelling out the details of a transformative agenda.

For starters, the substance of this agenda pushed away from a simplistic analogy between the United States and many newly independent Third World states, in which decolonization could partly revolve around simply eliminating a relatively thin layer of imperial administrators. Although the documents never used the phrase *settler* colonial, they nonetheless grappled with the reality that European colonists—in wresting political supremacy and land from Native peoples—had built a majority white society in a corner of the non-white world. Moreover, the different social position of groups such as African Americans (with their history of enslavement), Native peoples (with their experience of expropriation and extermination), Mexican Americans (given a related history of conquest and ongoing discrimination and dependent labor status), or Puerto Ricans (legal subjects of an imperial state) spoke to the real complexities of overcoming the American brand of colonialism. Each of these oppressed groups, while all caught up in the same overarching structures of colonial power, was located in collective life in profoundly distinct ways, with necessarily different implications for the meaning of freedom.

Thus, under the rubric of writing a new constitution, participants across the workshops stitched together a variety of proposals aimed at a specifically American, rather than Asian or African, decolonization. First, this meant constitutionally entrenching the sovereign right of all colonized peoples, including Puerto Ricans and Indigenous nations, to determine—once and for all—their future political status, as well as what legal relationship (if any) they wished to have with a reconstructed United States.[76]

Second, the reports called for material restitution for "any oppressed people throughout the world" harmed by American imperial power. Participants essentially took the idea of reparations, more commonly invoked for Black enslavement or Native expropriation, and transformed it into a global platform to contest all the extractive and violent effects of US statecraft. Such activists contended that the country's wealth had been built on colonial expropriation, at home and abroad.

Consequently, the United States had a responsibility to "take the wealth of the country and make it available as reparations" for Black Americans, Indigenous peoples, and colonized territories like Puerto Rico, as well as for nations including Vietnam that had been subjected to mass Cold War violence.[77] Rather than linking assistance to Cold War alignments or to accounts of American moral largesse—such as the Marshall Plan and other existing aid efforts—participants imagined a genuinely global and inclusive project of economic solidarity.

Third, within the country, the state had to engage in systematic resource redistribution. This was in part because some colonized groups, such as Black and Mexican American communities, would inevitably remain bound to a majority white society. Resource redistribution ensured that any such persons, along with poor whites, would nonetheless enjoy economic security, as well as control over the basic decisions shaping their material and workplace lives. The reports thus repeated many of the ten-point program's earlier material demands, and called for "full, equal, and non-exploitative employment," a "guaranteed adequate income for all," and the right to "health care, housing, food, clothing, transportation and education."[78]

Fourth, participants demanded basic changes to the representative scheme of the federal government, such that all communities gained equal participation in political decision-making. According to activists, the long history of extreme disenfranchisement meant that the governing class continued to be composed almost exclusively of the same gendered and racial elite. For this reason, "Black and third world people," as well as "women," had to be "guaranteed proportional representation in the administration of [governing] institutions."[79]

Fifth, decolonization required a basic shift in the cultural self-understanding of the overall society. In response, Convention participants called not just for a constitutional right to universal education, from preschool to higher education or "advanced study."[80] They also declared the need for what the earlier ten-point program described as "education that teaches us our true history and our role in the present-day society."[81]

For BPP activists, creedal nationalism was only the latest iteration of long-standing national mythologies grounded in white innocence and political heroism. In contrast to all these mythologies, Convention participants argued that many Black and brown communities experienced living in the United States as a form of internal exile. This meant that accepting the dominant cultural accounts forced oppressed groups to essentially celebrate their exile and to suppress their own deep estrangement. Tales of white frontier valor told Native peoples that, as a requirement for gaining minimal respect (not even actual sovereignty and political autonomy), they must first agree to their own expropriation as the natural order of things. Similarly, reading the 1787 framers as proto-liberal egalitarians required Black communities to deny that their sustained experience of enslavement and subordination embodied an essential truth about the nation's character.

At root, then, was the goal of reconstructing the country's shared historical memory, and of creating a broader public consciousness in which marginalized groups could speak the existential truths of their lives and articulate grievances in their own language. This was also why the Convention included an entire workshop on "revolutionary art." In anti-colonial struggles abroad, such art had been central to marking cultural breaks with the imperial past and to shifting collective accounts of community, including through new flags, symbols, institutional names, and iconography, as well as literary and other art forms.

The last decolonial demand involved the abolition of the existing security apparatus of the state. It was perhaps the most extensively articulated element in the reports, and clearly resonated with independence politics in Asia and Africa, where military and police personnel were long used to repress anti-colonial activism. With respect to the US military, the documents therefore asserted an end to the draft and a constitutional mandate constraining "U. S. aggression and interference in the internal affairs of [foreign] nations."[82] They also called for a demobilization of the standing army, "since historically a standing army has been used for offensive actions against the people of the United States and around the world."[83]

The reports demanded a similar demobilization with respect to both policing and the prison system. Given the inherent racial and class injustice of the prison system, all incarcerated individuals were entitled to new trials.[84] And for those convicted in these new trials, "jails would be replaced by a community rehabilitation program."[85] As for existing police forces, the reports detailed the creation of new civilian agencies, in which there was "no distinction between the people and the police because of their function." In other words, rather than armed, often white security personnel patrolling streets, new civilian entities would consist of community members skilled in resolving local social problems. Such agencies would replace not only municipal and state police departments, but also the FBI and its "national body of police." They would be organized through locally and democratically controlled oversight boards and would ban outright the ubiquitous use of "secret" security officials, informants, and "un-uniformed police."[86]

These reports did not include every decolonial element that circulated in the mid-twentieth century, some of which have since gained global currency. For starters, the reports may have mirrored Congressperson Vito Marcantonio's 1930s call to combine the end of colonial rule in Puerto Rico and elsewhere with genuine material restitution. But unlike Marcantonio, they did not really explore how post-independence migration policy could be a mode of decolonization.[87] They also did not specifically mention land return to Native American communities. Nor did they discuss truth commissions to create an established public record of past colonial crimes, or actual judicial proceedings to hold state officials accountable. And, of course, the BPP calls had their own internal complexities and clear challenges for implementation.

Nonetheless, the reports constituted a remarkable effort to address the specific dynamics of the American experience, rather than merely impose a Third World frame. One illustration of this was the extent to which many of these demands were universal in application. Whether concerning wealth redistribution or an end to the security state, these proposals may have addressed racial domination. But they did so in ways, following arguments from James Boggs or Martin Luther King Jr., that transformed the social experience for all, regardless of race, including for marginalized and poor white communities.

The workshops on gay and women's liberation perhaps best reflected the Convention's desire to create a comprehensive agenda. Rather than forcing all claims into a single narrative register—and thus reproducing one of the cultural critiques Black radicals made of mainstream white creedalist society—the Convention aimed to ensure that LGBTQ+ and feminist activists could articulate their agenda in their own language, which might not be decolonial. Thus, reports included the constitutional "right to be gay anytime, anyplace," guarantees that "all modes of human sexual self-expression deserve protection of the law and social sanction," and full LGBTQ+ "represent[ation] in all governmental and community institutions." They also demanded extensive rights for transgender persons, from "the right to free physiological change and modification of sex" to greater linguistic respect for all gender-nonconforming individuals, for instance by ensuring that "language be modified so that no gender takes priority."[88]

Finally, "The Workshop on the Self-Determination of Women,"

facilitated by Afeni Shakur, articulated a striking synthesis of Black and socialist feminism. It argued that "women in a class society have been continuously exploited, through their work, both in their home and outside their home." This was because the functioning of existing capitalist relations rested fundamentally on the often unpaid, privatized, and hidden provision of reproductive and caring work, structurally consigned to women. Within this context, women of color often found themselves doubly exploited. Their care work within their own families enjoyed limited support and recognition from state and public resources; and they were also routinely the poorly paid caregivers for other middle-class and affluent families.

For this reason, the report highlighted the specific intersection of race and class within this gendered division of labor. It called for "an end to the sexism which forces women into the lowest paying service jobs and the racism that insures that third world women will be the lowest paid of all." It then detailed specific policies that should be established as emancipatory alternatives to the "patriarchal family." These included— alongside a restatement of the need for universal full employment, a guaranteed income, and other basic socioeconomic protections—the "socialization of housework and child care with the sharing of work by men and women," extensive reproductive rights ("there should be free and safe birth control, including abortion, available on demand"), and constitutionally "guaranteed paid maternity leave."[89]

Unfortunately, these reports embodied the high-water mark for the Panthers' efforts at collaboratively articulating a concrete vision of a decolonial and revolutionary alternative. Plans for participants to reconvene in Washington, DC, in November 1970 to hold a massive ratification of the new constitution more or less collapsed. Thousands of activists arrived in DC on the appointed dates—Katsiaficas reports the number as 7,500 people—but no second convention was actually held. Instead, Newton told an assembled audience that they would have a "rain check" for another constitution-writing exercise, once the actual revolution came.[90]

Blocked Pathways and Systematic Political Defeat

By late 1970, the Black Panther Party was already being consumed by problems that, over the next year, would lead to a profound splintering of the movement. Following the analysis of the Panther scholars Bloom and Martin, I describe how a combination of state repression and state accommodation steadily isolated the BPP from a broader base of support, and also helped to sow deep internal divisions. The constitutional project, along with the wider organizing around a united front, ultimately fell victim to these developments. At the same time, party activists were never able to connect means and ends—including with respect to their constitutional vision—in ways that effectively imagined a step-by-step process for structural transformation.

THE COMBINED CHALLENGE OF STATE REPRESSION AND STATE ACCOMMODATION

While in August 1968 Eldridge Cleaver contended (and many Americans concurred) that the existing legal-political system could not address collective demands, just three years later fewer white and even Black Americans would have agreed. The war may have radicalized a striking number of young people, but much of this radicalization was pegged to the particular dynamics of the conflict. Bloom and Martin note how a variety of "concessions" sapped anti-war and activist interest in more wholesale structural changes.[91] As both major political parties moved to contain the war after the 1968 election, this dampened revolutionary energy and also reaffirmed faith in the ameliorative potential of the wider system.

President Richard Nixon's "Vietnamization" approach meant a steady decline in US troops on the ground in Vietnam, from 540,000 at the start of his first term to 160,000 at the end of 1971. Just as significant as the reduction in troops and related casualty numbers, fewer Americans found themselves drafted—down to less than 95,000 by 1971.[92] That same year, Congress proposed (with a unanimous vote in the Senate) the Twenty-Sixth Amendment, reducing the voting age to eighteen, and the states ratified it soon after. The constitutional amendment responded to anti-war and student activist claims about youth disenfranchisement. And it even suggested that—despite the massive supermajorities needed for formal textual alteration—the process could, in exceptional circumstances, still function. After his 1972 reelection, Nixon finally ended the draft entirely.

In this context, with Democratic leadership shifting gears and defending an end to the war, and with even Nixon pursuing a drawdown, anti-war sentiment became thoroughly mainstreamed. Yet, crucially, it also became disconnected from the larger anti-imperial and anti-capitalist vision the Panthers espoused. One could, with far less internal

tension, oppose the war *and* be a resolute Cold Warrior—and someone who believed deeply in the American liberal constitutional model.
For many white Americans, including more and more young people,
whereas the war once suggested the limits of US institutions, by 1972 it
could be treated as a deviation from national principle. Reinforcing this
sense was the fact that the existing governing framework seemed able, in
the final analysis, to incorporate anti-war demands.

Within Black life, insurgent energy similarly declined. This was due
not only to the US drawdown in Vietnam, but also to a slow but meaningful incorporation of Black Americans into economic and political
life. Lyndon Johnson's "Great Society" social programs began to alleviate some of the worst extremes of immiseration. At the same time, another key response of the Democratic Party to the 1968 Convention—
besides shifting positions on the war—was to become a far more racially
diverse elected body. Bloom and Martin write that between 1969 and
1975, "the number" of "Black people" in "political offices across the
United States" "more than tripled to 3,499."[93]

These officeholders overwhelmingly espoused views that aligned far
more with traditional civil rights positions than with Black radical internationalism. But for many African Americans, the dramatic rise in electoral representation—especially in cities with large Black populations—
could be concretely experienced as a victory for the idea of Black Power.
And these state accommodations cooled the pressure cooker that had
become American politics, and that fed the mass appeal of groups like
the Black Panthers.

The carrot of accommodations also went hand in hand with the stick
of a sustained state assault on the Panthers' organizational infrastructure and leadership.[94] During these years, Nixon made good on his 1968
"law and order" campaign, initiating an intense crackdown on Left entities, especially those with any Black leadership. Indeed, groups such as
the Panthers did not simply recede in the face of a moderating anti-war
and activist base. White officials confronted them by force, through systematic infiltration and intense violence, leaving their movements deci-
mated and engulfed in internal recrimination.

The constitution-writing project was a clear victim of these secret federal police efforts at sabotage. Huey Newton had been personally disappointed with the lack of enthusiasm that greeted his keynote speech
at the Revolutionary People's Constitutional Convention and, in part
for that reason, seemed to have soured on the drafting experiment. He
began associating it with Eldridge Cleaver, whom he viewed as a threat

to his position in the party, and so did not mind when the overall effort began to fade. Critically, these interpersonal conflicts had been stoked by the state. The FBI worked assiduously to sow discord, for instance by circulating disinformation to pit Newton and Cleaver against one another. In fact, after the September 1970 Convention's success as a mass event, the bureau's Los Angeles office recommended the following to various covert operatives and informants within the Panthers: "Each division which had individuals attend [the RPCC] write numerous letters to Cleaver criticizing Newton for his lack of leadership ... [in order to] create dissension that later could be more fully exploited."[95]

Such secret police actions went much further than psychological operations. Even before the RPCC, Fred Hampton—a central figure in developing the united front strategy—had been assassinated by a Cook County tactical unit in a raid coordinated with the FBI and the Chicago Police Department.[96] Then, just two days after the end of the Convention, which Afeni Shakur played such a pivotal role in promoting and organizing, she too stood trial in New York with a number of New York BPP members on bombing conspiracy charges. The group became known as the New York 21 and included RPCC plenary speaker Cetawayo Tabor among those indicted.

Shakur would eventually be acquitted, in part due to extensive evidence of the role that three paid police informants played in generating various plots in order to subvert the organization and jail its leaders.[97] Nonetheless, Shakur would spend substantial time, over a year, in prison. And, like many Black people subjected to the carceral state, she would then face real personal hardship and poverty on release. Indeed, today she is far better remembered as the mother of the late musician and actor Tupac Shakur—with her post-prison difficulties memorialized in his lyrics—than as a leading young Black activist in the 1960s. That history, when she was almost identical in age to Fred Hampton and, not unlike him, brutalized by the state, has been largely forgotten. Under circumstances like these, with members murdered, imprisoned, or forced into exile, it was nearly impossible for the Panthers to sustain mass mobilization.

The crackdowns also exacerbated a fissure in the movement over the near-term viability of armed struggle. Perhaps unsurprisingly, given their experience of extreme government repression, the New York 21 argued in 1971, in an open letter drafted by nine of Shakur's codefendants, that any gradualist approach to change had become untenable. The letter contended that activists had to take up arms immediately against the US state. But for the national leadership, the coalitional inroads the party had made—along with the increasingly de-radicalized dynamics of American politics—meant that such armed struggle was doomed. And this ideological debate occurred in the cauldron of systemic state sabotage, pitting party members against each other, and promoted distrust and paranoia. It ultimately led to the expulsion from the party of most of the New York 21 Panthers, along with Eldridge Cleaver.[98]

All of this spoke to the success of the government's two-pronged strategy of repression and accommodation. State violence pushed elements within the party toward championing ever more extreme means and rhetoric, just as ameliorative reforms made that rhetoric appear increasingly irresponsible and dangerous to potentially sympathetic white and even Black citizens. The split that resulted effectively ended the era of the BPP as the epicenter of a truly national and multiracial mass political movement. Indeed, by the end of 1972, the party had largely retrenched back to its early base in Oakland, California, with most nationwide chapters shuttered.[99]

THE COLD WAR LIMITS OF THE PANTHERS' CONSTITUTIONAL IMAGINATION

If external factors drove the decline of the BPP, the collapse of united front efforts like the Revolutionary People's Constitutional Convention also spoke to internal limitations and tensions that activists were never able to resolve. For starters, the September 1970 RPCC had not been without its own interorganizational conflicts, especially over gender politics. Some feminist activists at the event continued to experience the Black Panther Party as deeply infused with a destructive masculinist sensibility. Although one of the Convention keynote speakers, Audrea Jones, was an African American woman and a Panther member, her talk did not specifically focus on women's oppression. In fact, much to the chagrin of many feminists attending, beyond general references to sexism none of the keynote speeches engaged meaningfully with issues of patriarchy.

As for the workshop on women's self-determination, the document no doubt distilled key aspects of Black and socialist feminism. But it excluded some of the more radical lesbian feminist demands, such as, according to the historian Alice Echols, "an end to the sexual programming of children, the destruction of the nuclear family ... the establishment of communal child-care facilities under the control of 'woman-identified women,'"[100] and an affirmative commitment to strengthening same-sex female relationships instead of simply protecting "homosexual" or "bisexual" identity.[101]

Moreover, dynamics in the workshop again reinforced concerns about Panther gender politics. Some women delegates believed that male Panther members were attempting to delay or even cancel the workshop, given their uneasiness with potential demands. When the workshop finally took place, these feminist participants were uncomfortable with the presence, supposedly as protection, of male Panther guards in the room. All of this led to a partial walkout of the Convention by members of the group Radicalesbians, and to their writing a separate unofficial report. Such actions dramatized, in miniature, the profound difficulties of bridging coalitional divides.[102]

Beyond these difficulties, the Panthers' constitutional vision was strikingly limited in thinking concretely about the relationship between institutional process and transformative outcome. With the steady incorporation of Black people into electoral politics in the late 1960s and early 1970s, BPP activists never fully articulated why the Black achievement of the formal right to vote—in the context of an unaltered representative framework—did not complete American democracy.

For instance, unlike earlier Black socialists, BPP voices did not systematically engage with how poor and minority voting strength was profoundly diluted across gerrymandered single-member districts and state units in ways that constrained the radical potential of the ballot. Their main electoral constitutional suggestion entailed a general defense of proportional representation on race and gender grounds. Such an idea was no doubt innovative, seeking the meaningful political inclusion of women and minorities into traditionally exclusionary institutions and spaces. It certainly presaged future global trends, as today 120 countries have some version specifically of legislative gender quotas— with African polities leading the way.[103] And it may have helped, given that governing bodies remained disproportionately dominated by historically empowered elites—though, in the American context, legislative and other institutional quotas ultimately proved a bridge too far for white national politicians.

Still, from the beginning of the 1970s, more women and minorities were clearly being elected, appointed, and broadly incorporated into positions of power. To the extent that the principal RPCC demand regarding the electoral process was for increased racial and gender diversity in officeholders, the existing system appeared capable of meeting these goals. Just as significantly, if Panther activists sought an anti-capitalist and anti-imperial future, diversifying the composition of the political class over the 1970s actually seemed to have the opposite effect—only buttressing the legitimacy of Cold War creedalism.

Tellingly, the Panther constitutional framework entailed very few of the types of procedural demands Socialist Party activists had pressed for half a century earlier. The 1912 SPA platform included a comprehensive set of institutional reforms to the operation of government that could be implemented through popular codification, either by congressional legislation or by formal amendments. These reforms spoke to how the existing representative system failed as an embodiment of mass democracy. And they reconstructed the actual mechanisms of the 1787 Constitution, imagining that, by creating a broad enough working-class popular base, majoritarian voting could overcome—and eventually replace—the established legal-political order.

By contrast, the Panther Convention documents largely avoided the intricacies of what mode of government would concretely substitute for the 1787 Madisonian framework. In fact, the reports as a whole do not look like what we traditionally associate with a written constitution—organized as articles elaborating the specific powers of various branches of government. Although the documents offer some discussion of constitutional structure and constitutional rights, they far more closely resemble an expansive party agenda.

Part of the reason for this disconnect from conventional constitutionalism has to do with the distinct goals party activists associated with their brand of constitutional politics, and with their desire to frame the demands of their liberation agenda as a new American constitution. Again, the use of the word "constitution" was meant to underscore the symbolic importance of claiming sovereign authority for peoples historically marginalized—groups who had been able to gain partial inclusion only by first acceding to the ideological narratives and reform horizons governing elites deemed acceptable. Referring to their agenda as *constitutional* highlighted the fact that Black people and other oppressed groups had never been able to impose, within the United States, an actual conscious moment of decolonial rupture and accounting, in which they too could claim genuine self-determination and power.

Still, the lack of specificity about what exactly should replace the 1787 institutions implicitly left unchallenged the federal model as the defining account of representative democracy. And it indicated the degree to which many movement activists were on the other side of a Cold

War historical divide: one that truly separated them from Debs, Du Bois, or Harry Haywood. The intervening Cold War years may not have been enough to extinguish Black revolutionary politics, especially against the backdrop of Third World liberation struggles. But those preceding decades had largely erased from public consciousness, including within the Black counter-public, the extensive early-twentieth-century debates directly on constitutional structure. Those discussions—what to do with the states, whether or not to have a Senate, how to organize the federal judiciary—had been part of the drinking water of pre–Cold War Left politics. But limited memory of them existed to inform and sustain a subsequent generation.

THE BOGGSES AND THE POSSIBILITIES OF THE CITY

It was revealing that the Black socialist figure during these years that maintained an interest in the intricacies of constitutional design was none other than James Boggs, a person who spanned the Cold War divide and offered a Left intellectual link between distinct eras. Boggs thought seriously about how to update Communist Black belt ideas of self-determination for 1960s and 1970s American life. In particular, he argued that urban centers—rather than the rural South—had become the heart of Black cultural and political experience. As he and his spouse, Grace Lee Boggs, the Chinese American socialist author and activist, announced in their coauthored 1966 essay for the *Monthly Review*, "The City Is the Black Man's Land."

The Boggses hoped to mobilize poor and working-class African American constituents to claim power over key cities, with the aim of reorganizing local economies and institutions "around the concrete grievances of the masses."[104] Their ideas actually connect to recent 2010s efforts in Jackson, Mississippi by mayors Chokwe Lumumba (once himself a member of the Republic of New Afrika) and his son Chokwe Antar Lumumba to create, in the words of the latter, the "most radical city on the planet."[105]

But notably, the Boggses argued that the transformative capacity of Black city control—its potential to serve as revolutionary "beachheads"—would be hamstrung without structural changes to the federal constitutional system. In ways that followed 1930s and 1940s analyses by Du Bois and Haywood, they noted how state-based representation was the holdover of "an agricultural era."[106] And, in the present, it gave disproportionate power to demographically white and geographically rural and suburban spaces. The result was that national policy—a product of these institutional mechanisms—deemphasized the needs of Black poor and working classes living in cities, including by undermining their access to the broad provision of necessary goods as a basic public right.

In fact, starting in the 1970s, just these background realities would feed the electoral viability of establishment figures—including an emerging generation of Black politicians—who could work with business and national white elites to divide a limited municipal pie, on terms often dictated by corporate interests. Rather than promoting cities as radical beachheads, these politicians would largely replace one party machine with another.

Partially foreseeing these developments, the Boggses contended that it was essential for a "black revolutionary organization . . . to formulate a new Constitution that establishes a new relationship of government to people and to property, as well as new relationships between the national government, the states, and the cities." Four years before the RPCC, they too argued that radical groups should write a new constitution, which—as movement energy expanded—could become a galvanizing basis for a broad "call to a Constitutional Convention." For the Boggses, any such initiative would require activists to establish a clear account of institutional design—one that they could then promote in public debate. This way, as Black electoral coalitions gained control over cities, urban mass movements had a practical agenda for "defend[ing] themselves against the counterrevolutionary forces of the national power structure."[107]

Significantly, the Panthers in their constitutional thinking never meaningfully took up the Boggses' invitation to conceive of "new relationships" between national, state, and city governments. In arguing for proper federal electoral representation for cities—where large Black majorities actually lived—the Boggses imagined how aims of Black self-determination and genuine American democracy could reinforce one another.

These potential changes could have taken many forms. They might have included giving senators to major cities in a reconceived upper house—thus better representing the actual demographic and geographical diversity of the country. A place like New York City (the country's largest, with a population now nearing 8.5 million) could then have a voice in the Senate more comparable to that enjoyed by Wyoming (the country's smallest state by population, with fewer than 600,000 individuals). Or, perhaps more simply, they might have included assigning additional senators based on actual state population to reduce the malapportionment of the body. Other ideas might have entailed eliminating the Senate entirely (or making it largely ceremonial) and reconstructing the House on grounds of proportional representation, as SPA activists had long wanted. Such a House could be organized around multimember districts more likely to map the voting power of Black majorities. Indeed, related institutional reforms could have run the gamut from narrower alterations, like statehood or senators for cities such as Washington, DC, to a sweeping reimagination of federalism and the electoral system writ large.

Whatever the specific proposal, the Boggses' interest in city-based activism and representation indicated a practical concern with the deep impact of national and state dynamics. When left unaddressed, these dynamics imposed real constraints all the way down to the municipal level, with rippling racial and class effects rarely acknowledged in collective life. Indeed, the difficulties today facing radical efforts in places like Jackson, Mississippi are intricately tied to a hostile and white conservative-run state-level context, marked by top-down austerity and the denial of basic resources.[108]

RADICAL BLACK ORGANIZING AND THE MATTER OF INSTITUTIONAL DESIGN

The Boggses' basic idea of reconfiguring the role of the city in the legal-political infrastructure was absolutely of a piece with creative experiments in American decolonization. In this way it was consistent with Panther ambitions, as well as with some of the motivations that led RPCC participants to call for race- and gender-based representation.

None of this is to deemphasize the real creativity embedded in the RPCC's decolonial agenda and vision for a new American political community. However, the Panthers' lack of a thick institutional analysis ceded the debate over the procedural and electoral structures of democracy to white and African American mainstream voices. As more establishment Black politicians claimed control of city machinery, groups like the Panthers more or less had no argument to offer about why this failed to prove that American institutions worked effectively after all. In reality, the mere existence of African American mayors or even congressional representatives did not uproot the combination of racial and class hierarchy that many poor Black constituents experienced.

To a meaningful extent, the misallocations and blockages of the institutional system made it very difficult for those historically marginalized to drive national and state agendas, even if there were now more minority elected officials. But without any developed account of how American legal-political design contained transformative changes, Panther activists essentially acceded to a status quo in which democratic design was considered consonant with the existing electoral and representative arrangements. And for those increasingly suspicious of revolutionary talk, if American frameworks were imperfect, perhaps that simply meant that no system of government could be ideal. As Cold Warriors like Arthur Schlesinger contended, aspiring to more simply demonstrated a refusal to be sufficiently mature and realistic about the limits of politics. In the past, Du Bois had opposed the US model on *behalf* of democracy itself. But now Panther activists offered little sense of how design experimentation could transcend a constricted Cold War democratic imagination.

At the end of the day, the BPP's lack of structural remedies also spoke to activists' uncertainty about their level of support in the wider population. The party may have been at the forefront of a radicalizing movement politics for a short period. But could an actual majority of Americans—overwhelmingly white—be convinced of its ends?

The earlier SPA's interest in formal structural adaptations to the 1787 Constitution was linked to faith, especially in the years before World War I, that Socialists would one day claim a real electoral majority. This belief was underscored by those electoral victories the party did achieve, which then fed an investment in electorally grounded transformative change. SPA leaders like Eugene Debs or Allan Benson believed they could use victories at the ballot box as a springboard to implementing constitutional reforms on the road to socialism. Reforms would then open up the governing order for more and more radical alterations. As a result, Socialists would be able to improvise, from within the existing status quo, a whole new legal, political, and economic system.

Black radical organizing—even at moments of heightened non-Black Left support—faced a basic predicament in pursuing a broader transformative and decolonial agenda: the lack of a plausible pathway for implementation. As a substantive matter, in many ways the Panthers in the late 1960s had converged on an overarching approach that had much in common with Martin Luther King Jr.'s own policy commitments at the end of his life. King too had hoped to create a permanently mobilized and increasingly radical multiracial, class-conscious united front. His primary strategy for change—the Poor People's Campaign—revolved around what Brandon Terry calls "mass civil disobedience," the "discipline[d]" use of large-scale protests and labor strikes to demonstrate coalitional "power" and to achieve specific demands.[109]

In many ways, King's vision connected to Du Bois's earlier account for mass insurgent action on behalf of democracy and against racial capitalism. As King declared, "if one hundred thousand Negroes [repeatedly] march in a major city to a strategic location, they will make municipal operations difficult; they will exceed the capacity of even the most reckless local government to use force against them."[110] Unfortunately, his assassination undercut the Campaign's energy and reach; without King the Campaign (and the movement) faced greater difficulties in building the national networks and mobilizing the necessary numbers for such directed and large-scale actions. And declining radicalism, within white anti-war and Black political spaces, sapped the ability of other movement organizations, like the Panthers, to fulfill the same ambitions.

As for an electoral strategy, Black politicians may have started winning elections, but this more establishment version of Black Power diverged markedly from the Left internationalism the Boggses or the BPP embraced. Unfortunately, even during periods of peak cultural resonance, more radical Black activists had real trouble actually winning at the ballot box. Take for instance the limited ability of DRUM and other related Revolutionary Union Movements (RUMs) to succeed in union elections. These Left labor efforts emphasized class consciousness and shared cross-racial worker solidarity, but they made little headway with rank-and-file white workers. Even worse, as the historian Jefferson Cowie tells us, such alternative unions "found it impossible to win . . . even in locals with black majorities." Their "uncompromising language" may have energized young radicals, white and Black. But it largely "alienated the older generation of black workers," whose own long experience with violent white business and state crackdowns made them deeply risk-averse when it came to new revolutionary calls for Black liberation.[111]

Thus, unlike early-twentieth-century Left formations, whether the SPA or New Deal–era activists, groups like the Panthers operated in a political context in which their potential to claim an actual popular majority seemed increasingly off the table. Neither King's mass "militant non-violence"[112] nor the old Socialist hope of building a revolutionary voting majority appeared viable as pathways.

All of this left movement activists in a precarious position, in which finding solutions to the dilemma of how to get from here to there could feel increasingly out of reach. And this fact limited substantive interest in transitional adaptations, intermediate institutional reforms to the prevailing constitutional framework. Such adaptations, including those implied by the Boggses, may have provided a bridge between the present and the utopian future. They would also have assisted in conceiving of change as not simply an either-or choice between armed struggle and gradualist accommodation. Yet, the dilemma of how to meaningfully achieve such intermediate institutional steps deflated interest in thinking concretely about ways to alter, piece by piece, the landscape of American legal-political institutions.

Alongside external state action, this central gulf between the present and the future also ultimately contributed to the Panther split and the tensions within Black radicalism more generally. In a context of blocked pathways, the only two options seemed to be focusing at the local level on basic services for those in need or further committing, against all odds, to a single great revolutionary break. The vast majority of Panther members chose the former. In late November 1970, Newton began referring to community efforts as "survival programs." These included a variety of free services for poor Black neighborhoods, from children's breakfasts (an already established backbone of the party) to healthcare clinics, ambulances, clothing, busing (including to prisons for family members), and educational centers.[113]

Although the survival programs reached thousands of poor families and had a massive impact on their well-being, the very name of the effort underscored the party's defensive posture. Meanwhile, a "small cadre," to use Brandon Terry's term, embraced armed overthrow, no matter the total implausibility of recreating a Cuban Revolution in the United States.[114] And both approaches effectively signaled a retreat from constitutional engagement and an acceptance that the party was blocked in its aim of genuinely establishing a mobilized and transformative American majority.

Conclusion: The Victory of Law and Order

In truth, the Panthers' ambitions for a multiracial united front faced something like a historical impossibility in the early 1970s. Moved by anti-colonial politics in Asia and Africa, Black radicals had embraced their own version of Third World internationalism. And while the

Vietnam War escalated, more and more white students were open to linking foreign and domestic politics through critiques of empire. But radical activists operated in a context at home almost totally devoid of that early-twentieth-century white working-class culture of Left internationalism. In fact, the degree to which white anti-war radicalism dissipated in response to policy shifts in Vietnam indicated both the depth of Cold War nationalist attachment and the broader societal constraints on transformative change.

Groups like the Panthers, through their outreach to foreign liberation movements—not to mention the titles ("Minister of Defense") they gave party members—consciously challenged the basic legitimacy of the Cold War state. As late as the 1930s, there were social bases within white working-class society for comparable brands of anti-nationalist politics. But the Black radical focus on class solidarity now proved less effective, given the post-war cultural rise of "middle class" as a dominant white identity and the steady decline of worker self-consciousness and militancy. Many now-middle-class white constituents, including union members, fully identified politically and psychically with the nation-state and its larger security objectives. The country had been shaped by World War II, the Manichaean Cold War struggle with the Soviet Union, and of course post-war material prosperity. And after three decades of the American Century, a large swathe of the country had deeply imbibed exceptionalist narratives and faith in US primacy.

In fact, the limited appeal of BPP united front efforts to traditional labor—including with the Revolutionary People's Constitutional Convention and throughout the 1968–1970 heyday—was telling. All these projects aimed to bring together poor and working people regardless of race, not dissimilar to the insurgent democratic organizing of the CIO in the 1930s. But persistent skepticism from the traditional labor movement, a key space for reaching white New Deal constituents, spoke to an ongoing structural roadblock. Radical activists certainly viewed labor mobilization as critical. But established and white-led unions were downright hostile, and organizations like DRUM remained contained in their practical reach. Thus, even at its peak, the united front movement always amounted to the mobilization of a political minority, even if it enjoyed outsized cultural salience for a short time.

This meant that Left activists sought to build a white working-class base just as more and more white Americans rejected socialist class rhetoric. Members of this latter group increasingly conceived of themselves in Cold War nationalist terms, even when they shared the same economic complaints as poorer Black people. The Panthers may never have been a credible threat to the US state's actual monopoly on violence; still, most white citizens absolutely rejected the right of the BPP and other Left groups even to challenge what Nikhil Pal Singh calls the US's "monopoly on legitimate symbolic violence"[115]—or the security state's claim that it alone served and protected the nation.

Especially as national politicians implemented ameliorative reforms, the very idea of Black radical contestation became anathema to mainstream white American politics. Many white voters—New Deal liberals among them—viewed the overturning of legal segregation, alongside the de-escalation of the war, as rightly altering perceptions about Left politics, including Black activism. African American communities may have continued to face intense and intertwined racial and class hierarchies. And mainstream white sentiment certainly found some of the government's actions heavy-handed. But civil rights successes seemed to indicate that the main creedal ends had more or less been achieved, and that it was time to turn the page on protest and rebellion.

As part of this shift, mainstream views largely came to accept the state's presentation of socialist and internationalist activism, particularly among Black radicals, as a genuine collective threat. Indeed, at the national level, Nixon's 1968 election and then landslide 1972 reelection—not to mention the political rise of the former actor Ronald Reagan in California—cemented the reality of a white majority moving decisively in a rightward political direction. At a more local level, the trajectory of Philadelphia police chief and eventual Mayor Frank Rizzo offered another bellwether. Rizzo's treatment of the Panthers in advance of the 1970 convention—not to mention his generally brutal approach to policing Black communities—never became a damaging political scandal. Instead, it proved an asset with many white voters, who had previously formed a core part of the New Deal coalition.

Perhaps the final ingredient fueling white conservatism revolved around economic changes. The early 1970s witnessed the definitive end of the American Cold War boom and the beginning of what Jefferson Cowie calls "a global restructuring of work itself," including deindustrialization, plant closings, and permanently stagnating wages.[116] This resulted in an economic and cultural context in which politicians like Rizzo could play on classic racist solidarities—even going so far as to urge Philadelphians in 1978 to "vote white"[117]—and present busing programs in the North or Lyndon Johnson's social spending programs as zero-sum attacks on white middle-class status and opportunity.

Ultimately, these dynamics recalibrated white public assessments of legality and illegality in ways that fundamentally shifted the viability of further structural change. As discussed in chapter 12, during the height of the traditional civil rights movement one remarkable feature of mainstream white national politics involved the racial inversion of who appeared to be properly American. A significant number of white national politicians treated Black protesters engaged in civil disobedience as lawful citizens asserting their constitutional rights. White supremacists in the South, meanwhile, were presented as un-American.

In a sense, though, the formal overcoming of segregation and the drawing down of the Vietnam War—alongside growing white public wariness of additional change—accelerated a reversion to established accounts of Black political danger. And for mainstream white audiences, such racial fears were further reinforced by the very different and often militarized self-presentation of groups like the Panthers by comparison with traditional civil rights protesters. The appeal to many white citizens of Nixonian "law and order" rhetoric powerfully embodied this reversion. Such rhetoric gave both a language and a voice to a growing white cultural focus on continuing Black and student activism as the preeminent and lawless threats to "the great silent majority"[118] of white middle-class Americans.

In fact, one striking feature of the state's crackdown on Black Left activism is how the intensity of white official responses bore little correlation to whether activists had actually used violence. Afeni Shakur eventually became associated with the New York 21's call in 1971 for immediate armed struggle, in the context of indictments on false charges and imprisonments. Before then, she had explicitly stated that her goal with the 1970 Convention was to "exhaust all legal means": to pursue a version of King's "militant non-violence." Yet, as with Fred Hampton, national white politicians and security personnel responded just as brutally as if either had actually taken up arms.

Indeed, even when the state clearly perpetrated violence against individuals, as in the case of Fred Hampton's assassination, the very fact of being killed or arrested often served as proof that activists—especially Black activists—had engaged in criminality. All of this underscored the profound propaganda victory the FBI and other government bodies achieved during these years: they had not only subverted Black organizations; they had also succeeded in depicting all Black radical thinking and organizing as violent extremism.

Most significantly, as chapter 15 details, Nixon's particular law-and-order rhetoric increasingly became part of a wider cultural concern, across the ideological spectrum, with addressing the previous years' perceived social disorder. Such an emphasis nullified whatever remained of mainstream interest in large-scale debates about the basic terms of state and economy. And this broadening anxiety about law and order pushed to the center a deeply nostalgic reinvestment in a narrowed conception of American values, traditions, and institutions.

CHAPTER 15

The Rise of Originalist America

A June 17, 1972, break-in of the Democratic Party headquarters at the Watergate complex in Washington, DC, gave rise to perhaps the most famous political scandal in American history. The revelation that President Richard Nixon had been involved in the burglary's cover-up reverberated throughout the nation, as did the discovery of a much wider White House–run intelligence and spying operation against Nixon's perceived enemies. The scandal eventually resulted in high-profile prosecutions of presidential aides and Nixon's own resignation in the face of an impeachment process.[1]

For the broader public consciousness, Watergate offered the era's defining illustration of a state out of control. It dramatically heightened the atmosphere of governmental impropriety, alongside Senate hearings and newspaper exposés covering everything from the lies in Vietnam to FBI and CIA violence at home.[2] And, of course, this was layered over the sense of chaos and threat embedded in Nixon's own law-and-order arguments, which tended to blame societal disarray, in racialized terms, on Black activists and their allies.

As the historian Philip Jenkins highlights, all of this created a dramatic and popular "zeal" to "root out . . . misconduct in public life."[3] This zeal went hand in hand with a political discourse that treated the preceding decade as marked by pervasive lawlessness on all sides—by radicals and by the state. Whatever Nixon's own claims to upholding the law, many political elites, even beyond the liberal Left, considered the president and those around him just as complicit in creating the overall climate of disorder.

Thus, by the mid-1970s, American politics became increasingly consumed by the questions of why chaos had taken hold since the mid-1960s civil rights victories, and what might be done to prevent such tumult in the future. Critically, this concern with lawlessness had profound effects on constitutional culture. To the extent that politicians and publics were worried about anarchy and violence—whether from the state or from groups on the ground—they began to gravitate to the idea that adherence to a fundamental law was central to reining in threats to liberal order. In fact, a lack of fidelity to the federal Constitution—on the part of both government officials and young radicals—emerged as a key explanation for why the country had gone so far astray during the post-1965 period.

In this general atmosphere, more and more voices, including even those strongly identified with 1960s civil rights and anti-war activism, began to embrace the Constitution in near-religious terms. They believed that championing the document would prove critical to overcoming the destructiveness of the recent and even the longer-term past. This developing perspective eventually silenced those doubts that still circulated in mainstream politics about the constitutional order itself. Even today, this understanding of the period between the Voting Rights Act and Nixon's resignation—and of its key lessons—maintains a powerful popular presence.

But, as I argue in the following pages, this conventional view fails in key critical respects. As chapter 14 detailed, such an account disserves the actual constitutional politics of Left activists at the time, as well as the tensions and the repression they faced in attempting to build a transformative popular majority. In addition, this perspective misses how the narrative, and the political lessons implicitly embedded within it, have helped to build a collective ideological framework with profound and long-term effects for constitutional life.

In particular, this account obscures the extent to which the mainstream schools of political thought that emerged from this period—post-1960s liberalism and conservatism—were founded on shared basic assumptions about the appropriate contours of political and constitutional debate. For all the very real ideological disagreements across the partisan divide, both perspectives accepted a set of narrowed boundaries for this debate, resulting in a far more constrained imaginative horizon than had existed in earlier periods of American history: dispute across the relevant political spectrum now almost universally assumed Cold War notions about global primacy, market capitalism, and the genius of the American constitutional model.

In the following pages, I explore this political closure more fully, along with its deep and persistent ramifications. I begin by considering the remaining sites of political radicalism that existed in the 1970s, especially connected to feminist and Indigenous activism. I then chart the shift in public life from radical 1960s critique to a climate of constitutional rededication, including by examining the cultural meaning of two bicentennials—1976's Independence Day events and 1987's constitutional bicentennial festivities. The nature of these celebrations highlights the effects of a growing conservative political movement within white constituencies, already launched through the 1970s social and economic transformations.

Above all, the emerging cross-party climate of constitutional rededication—which differed drastically from the Progressive and New Deal periods—proved especially conducive to the consolidation and spread of a specific conservative legal culture. This culture actively embraced and then amplified the era's constitutional devotion, and especially emphasized the need to return to the framers' own vision. It harnessed the call for constitutional fidelity and restoration to expand public support for an end to the racial and gender transformations that had been unleashed in the preceding years. By the dawn of the twenty-first century, the cultural and institutional power of such ideas would drive political and legal argument.

Much legal scholarship focuses on the differences between the two opposed legal frameworks in current constitutional discourse—living constitutionalism versus originalism. But I argue that understanding their real continuities remains just as critical for making sense of our current moment. Living constitutionalism is the approach most associated with Left-liberal constitutional interpretation, built on the idea of the document as an unfolding project, evolving with the cultural norms of the society. This connects back to FDR and Charles Beard (discussed in chapters 8 and 9), who embraced a vision of appropriate constitutional meaning that required attentiveness to the problems of the time. Originalism, by contrast, is identified with the political Right, and emphasizes the importance of judges abiding by how the Constitution would have been understood at the time the specific portion of the text was written and adopted.

But the dominant versions of both approaches, whether liberal or conservative, code the document in highly salutary terms. And both believe that the Constitution expresses a special national character and destiny. Indeed, one of the defining features of emerging 1970s constitutional reverence was the extent to which minority and women public figures—more present on the political stage than ever before—

themselves accepted the genius of the eighteenth-century framers. This
was so even as they often noted, in "living" terms, the centuries required
to fulfill the initial promise, and even though the framers would almost
surely not have allowed them on that political stage.

To a profound extent, this has meant that while major divisions exist
between the two interpretive approaches—including over basic issues
of inclusion and rights—both swim in the same currents of constitutional veneration. Today, of course, more Americans, especially outside
the political Right, have become deeply concerned with the implications of originalist thinking on the courts. More also seem increasingly
dissatisfied with a political and constitutional system that dispropor-
tionally appoints judges whose views on major issues counter those of
most Americans. But a background atmosphere that has long venerated
the text and the founders creates yet another obstacle to truly reconsider-
ing the system, and to altering the structures that produce these results.

All of this raises real questions about the overall cultural politics of
post-1960s constitutional rededication, of which living constitutionalism itself was a central piece. That cultural politics helped to build an
ideological home conducive to the spread and entrenchment of conservative legal ideas—one in which many of its more liberal adherents
now seem constrained. As I turn to in the book's conclusion, any genuine effort today to grapple with the resulting constitutional reality requires a serious engagement with the costs of that broader venerative
framework.

The Declining Possibility of Remaining Left Spaces

To fully appreciate the conservative turn in constitutional politics, it
helps to first engage with those key ongoing reformist sites in 1970s
American life. The defeat of the Black Panther Party (BPP) as a national
organization with mass political strength did not necessarily eliminate
ideas like those expressed at the Revolutionary People's Constitutional
Convention. In particular, the 1970s saw the flourishing of women's activism, including among working-class minority women. Such activism
proceeded both within and outside of explicitly feminist formations,
from the numerous Left feminist collectives that emerged during the
time to Black women-led entities aimed at movement-building among
the poor. At the same time, radical Indigenous politics also claimed a
significant cultural space, deepening arguments around the meaning of
American decolonization.

But for distinct reasons, these various movements were ultimately unable to redirect the dominant American constitutional culture away from its ever more restorationist bent. And this reality reinforced a sense that Cold War creedal constitutionalism offered the only politically and historically relevant American constitutional model—and the tendency for alternative visions to sink even more deeply into the hidden recesses of collective memory.

FEMINISM, WELFARE RIGHTS, AND CONSTITUTIONAL ENGAGEMENT

As the women's movement gained center stage, a remarkable constellation of new organizations emerged across the country that directly contested the established relationship between family, state, and economy. Many of these groups were explicitly feminist women's collectives. And even when the organizations were cross-gender, radicalized women activists played a central role in shaping their goals and strategic choices.

One embodiment of this spirit was the National Welfare Rights Organization (NWRO), which fought tirelessly during these years to dramatically expand the economic and political power of the poor. As the historian Felicia Kornbluh writes, the NWRO would become "the largest national organization of poor people in the history of the United States," with "twenty thousand to thirty thousand card-carrying members and 540 local chapters."[4]

The NWRO was multiracial and cross-gender, with the African American professor and activist George Riley as its founder. But Black women, many of whom were on public assistance, overwhelmingly composed the group's membership. And its most charismatic leaders where Black women like Beulah Sanders and Johnnie Tillmon, who would eventually become the group's executive director. These activists very much understood their work as bringing together feminist aspirations with the Black freedom objectives of the 1960s, as expressed by projects like Martin Luther King Jr.'s Poor People's Campaign. Indeed, the main national reform goal of the NWRO was the establishment of a substantial and adequate guaranteed income, as both King and the Panthers demanded.

This call for a guaranteed income went hand in hand with the idea that welfare protections—health, housing, education—should be understood as basic universal rights rather than as government largesse. While this agenda was universal in scope, Sanders and Tillmon—not unlike Afeni Shakur in the BPP—saw it as especially critical for over-coming the specific domination experienced by poor minority women. The push for a guaranteed income, for instance, was grounded in a cri-tique of the post-war domestic settlement's focus on wage-earning as the precondition both for freedom from poverty and for general social standing. By contrast, NWRO activists saw such a bargain—including in welfare-for-work programs—as often imposing deeply coercive work relations as a condition simply of avoiding extreme immiseration.[5]

Furthermore, they viewed poor minority women as most likely to get the worst end of the bargain, given their particular structural lo-cation within a racist and sexist social order. Such women were often consigned to the lowest-paid work in private labor markets, and lacked the solidaristic connections across gender and race that might help to improve pay and working conditions. Or they were subject to absolute financial dependence if outside the labor market: they often had no choice but to raise children and rely on male breadwinners, especially given gender relations and the lack of access to reproductive health care or child care.

For all these reasons, Sanders, Tillmon, and others rejected the tra-ditional terms of Cold War welfare programs, based as they were on judgments about the "deserving poor" and the necessity of work. In-stead embracing the idea of welfare as a right, they sought to reconsti-tute the conditions under which the poor were integrated into family and economic structures. They argued that only if the most margin-alized women enjoyed economic security—without being forced to depend on male partners or take whatever the labor market offered—could they gain meaningful independence and power over their lives.

Significantly, those like Beulah Sanders rejected thinking of wel-fare rights as a single-issue matter. Indeed, Sanders consciously linked American violence abroad during the Cold War to the everyday do-mestic harms experienced by the most marginalized within the coun-try. Sanders had run in New York for state senate on the Freedom and Peace Party ticket in 1968, and was also centrally involved in the anti-war movement. She had been the only Black speaker at the national rally following the 1970 shootings at Kent State University. When Sanders and other NWRO activists occupied the federal Department of Health, Education, and Welfare that same year, she called for an end to the Vietnam War and a drastic shift in Cold War security spending in general: such wasted dollars, she contended, were a direct threat to economic freedom and well-being at home.[6]

Indeed, the NWRO operated in a context in which smaller Left feminist collectives increasingly explored the mutually constitutive relationships between patriarchy, racial capitalism, and empire.[7] Take for instance the theorizing and activities of the Chicago Women's Liberation Union (CWLU), perhaps the preeminent socialist feminist group during these years. Their 1972 manifesto called for a truly emancipatory society "in direct opposition to the present one which is based on the domination of the few over the many through sex, race, and class."[8] The CWLU threw itself into ground-level organizing, in service of the concrete needs of marginalized women. The legal scholar Cynthia Bowman writes that, throughout the decade, the group "ran a Liberation School, helped develop women's studies programs in the Chicago area, and operated a prison project that offered courses at the women's prison in Dwight, Illinois. A lesbian chapter worked for a municipal ordinance to protect gay and lesbian rights, and CWLU worked with other organizations to support cases about sex discrimination in employment and to promote reproductive rights."[9] These activities were understood both as ways to improve the immediate conditions of those most subordinated and as ways to further radicalize such women.

At the same time, Barbara Smith, along with her sister Beverly Smith and Demita Frazier among others, founded the Combahee River Collective (named after Harriet Tubman's successful military raid during the Civil War). An organization of Black lesbian and socialist feminists, the group aimed to further elaborate and confront the particular interlocking modes of oppression facing Black women specifically. Their 1977 statement became a touchstone for both Black feminist politics and what would remain of the American Left.[10] For all their insurgent energy, the NWRO had been largely focused on pressure campaigns vis-à-vis legislatures, courts, and government agencies. Even when linking the domestic and the foreign, their critique avoided directly repudiating American capitalism (rather than traditional labor markets) or the basic American right to exercise an international police power (as opposed to particular wars like Vietnam). By contrast, the Combahee River Collective explicitly embraced an anti-capitalist and internationalist opposition to post-war American national narratives, maintaining that "we realize that the liberation of all oppressed peoples necessitates the destruction of the political-economic systems of capitalism and imperialism as well as patriarchy."[11]

Unsurprisingly, these various groups both overlapped and diverged with respect to the Constitution. The NWRO embraced a politics of fidelity, arguing for the illegality of governmental infringements on benefits and for constitutional rights to welfare. Not unlike Paul Robeson in the 1930s and 1940s (discussed in chapters 9 and 11), they attempted to develop as capacious a version of creedal constitutionalism as possible—in contrast to the dominant Cold War variant. As the historian Felicia Kornbluh writes, this encompassed arguments like the idea that "to realize the promise of equality [in the Fourteenth Amendment] . . . the U. S. government must grant citizens" a set of substantive socioeconomic protections or "'a right to life' that could not be vitiated by a tightfisted legislature." In the apt and stirring words of Dorothy Parker, the twelve-year-old daughter of one organizer, "one thing I can truely [*sic*] say is that while I am on welfare my mother is learning her rights and believe me she is getting them."[12]

Socialist and radical feminist organizations, further to the left, also often articulated an expansive rights agenda as something that could be promoted in the here and now, against the backdrop of the existing legal-political order. In this way, such formations found common ground with groups like the NWRO, or even with mainstream liberal feminists, around everything from expanding welfare rights, social insurance, and child care funding to guaranteeing abortion rights and improving health services generally.[13] But akin to how the early-twentieth-century ACLU founder and socialist activist Crystal Eastman backed women's suffrage or the Equal Rights Amendment (ERA), these more radical collectives also emphasized the ultimate constraints on genuine rights achievements under the prevailing system. In the end, there would have to be a fundamental overcoming of the broader institutional order—since that order rested on interlocked class, racial, and patriarchal relations for its operation. For members of the Combahee River Collective or the CWLU, women's liberation was a necessarily internationalist and revolutionary project, inherently incompatible with the American state and economy.

Such a perspective certainly implied that freedom would require a clear break from the 1787 Constitution. Even so, after the collapse of projects like the Panther Convention, Left organizations—including feminist ones—increasingly paid little attention to explicitly articulating this constitutional break or the terms of an alternative constitutional system.

There were numerous reasons why feminist groups and women activists, even those who were consciously revolutionary, tended not to politically elaborate anti-Constitution arguments. One issue tied to the question of organizing. Many poorer women, whom activists sought to incorporate into their movements, were most interested in material improvements and meaningful respect from society. The historian Premilla Nadasen's reflections on welfare rights organizing are indicative of a broader reality. As she writes, poor women drawn to that movement did not seek "a different kind of economic system, but wanted to share in the prosperity that had come to define post-war America."[14] For even radical activists, this often meant that maintaining contact with their social base required pursuing legal and political strategies that emphasized constitutional inclusion rather than social and institutional rupture. One sees this in the practical political efforts of entities like the Chicago Women's Liberation Union or the Combahee River Collective.

Just as significant, the partial success of reform efforts may have defused the need to elaborate an explicit analysis of why the constitutional system inhibited change. While male officials may have rejected genuinely replacing governing structures of family and economy, such elites did seem willing to accommodate some actual shifts. Against the backdrop of intense feminist mobilizing, politicians across the country appeared to accept that the status quo could not be preserved in its entirety. Along with funneling constitutional politics away from explicit debates about rejectionism, reform victories also reinforced those tendencies within social constituencies—across racial and class lines—more conciliatory toward and even supportive of the existing constitutional framework.

Litigation successes in the federal courts suggested that key rights could be claimed under the prevailing order, through shifts in judicial interpretation. In 1970, the Supreme Court held in *Goldberg v. Kelly* that the due process clause of the Fourteenth Amendment required that certain welfare recipients receive a fair hearing before they could be denied their benefits.[15] While the case only concerned the process for terminating benefits, it suggested that the Court might one day actually agree with the NWRO that welfare could be thought of as a substantive and guaranteed right. Most notably, in 1973 the Court read into the same Fourteenth Amendment a constitutionally protected right to abortion in *Roe v. Wade*, embodying a profound achievement for feminist politics.

Ultimately, the intensifying conservatism of the 1970s would limit many of these aspirations. Nixon's 1971 veto of universal child care on anti-communist grounds was a bellwether. It signaled that the electoral and political will to pursue significant alterations to the structure of reproductive labor, or to expand socioeconomic rights, had perhaps definitively passed. In a context of economic stagnation and white middle-class status anxiety, debate over social provisions became dominated by a racist targeting of Black women as undeserving and a waste of scarce resources. Nadasen writes that "journalistic accounts, government reports, political rhetoric, and academic studies highlighted cases of welfare fraud, portrayed recipients as lazy and dishonest, and characterized the welfare bureaucracy as inefficient."[16]

In some ways, this climate fed those pockets of revolutionary sentiment arguing that the existing social order had to be replaced. However, it was not conducive to linking such politics to debates about constitutional overhaul. Groups with the most revolutionary orientations were very small islands within the society at large. The times when labor, socialist, and even Black radicals invested most attention in the practical details of constitutional transformation and design were periods—like in the early to mid-twentieth century—when it seemed plausible to build a majority Left electoral coalition on behalf of revolutionary reforms to state and economy. But in Nixon's America those Left electoral pathways were decidedly blocked. Therefore, one could imagine some revolutionary feminists viewing a focus on the structure of representative and legal institutions as liberal ameliorism, tinkering with process in a way that seemed unlikely to uproot patriarchy. Even worse, it may be an irrelevant distraction from immediately addressing the everyday and ongoing harms facing oppressed communities. In this way, a general deemphasis on structural constitutional specifics echoed the turn away, by the Black Panthers and other Black radical groups, from projects that pushed constitutional rewriting and reconstruction.

Further complicating any neat categorization of the era's feminist constitutional politics, organizational efforts proclaiming opposition to the system as a whole, including the Constitution, did not necessarily connect to more radical concrete demands than did those that were constitutionally faithful. Take, for instance, the move to establish a wage for housework, echoing Crystal Eastman's arguments from a half century earlier. Such organizing emerged as one of many experiments during the era to transform the gendered division of labor, along with the economic and political bargaining power of women within the family unit.

As the legal historian Deborah Dinner has detailed, proponents contended that "childrearing was necessary to replenish the workforce—

the fundamental commodity in capitalism."[17] As articulated by Selma James and her coauthor Mariarosa Dalla Costa in their seminal 1972 book, *The Power of Women and the Subversion of the Community*, capitalist society treated the household work of women—essential for the economy to function—as an expression of feminine identity rather than as the expropriated labor that it was. By requiring payment for such work, feminist advocates aimed to do more than just spotlight this reality. They also hoped to challenge the very capacity of the existing order to survive.[18] And these arguments touched a real nerve, with activists like Margaret Prescod—once a Black Panther breakfast volunteer—co-founding an aligned New York City group, Black Women for Wages for Housework.[19]

Selma James's involvement spoke to the socialist and internationalist revolutionary aims at the heart of the project. She had been a long-time anti-capitalist and anti-imperialist voice and was also the partner of C. L. R. James, moving with him to England when he was detained and then deported from the US.[20] Yet, just as in the 1920s, some feminists saw paying for housework as potentially further naturalizing the idea that reproductive labor was best understood as work carried out by women in the home. According to critics, the actual proposal may have shifted the terms under which women carried out gendered labor, but it did not go far enough in confronting patriarchal family structures—despite the claims about generating a crisis in capitalism. In this way, it remained an open question whether, for example, a housework wage or a guaranteed income entailed the more revolutionary reform proposal. A group like the NWRO may have asserted their constitutional fidelity, and avoided explicitly anti-capitalist rhetoric, but its agenda could have just as far-reaching disruptive effects for existing gender and market relations.

Ultimately, the driving dilemma was that both pressure groups like the NWRO and smaller radical formations faced an unavoidable political constraint, even by comparison with the Panthers in the late 1960s. For a period, however brief, the Black Panther Party had gained the cultural and institutional presence to conceive of itself as the leadership for a truly national and multi-coalitional mass popular base. At various points, Left feminist groups may have been able to drive aspects of the discussion about how gender, family, race, and capitalism intersected. But they were never organizationally situated to operate as the linchpin for the type of united front that Martin Luther King Jr., Fred Hampton, or Afeni Shakur once imagined. Their calls—whether for an expansive

broadening of creedal constitutional meaning or for a revolutionary
overcoming of the status quo—were swimming against the tide.

THE WOMEN'S STRIKE AND THE MAINSTREAM
FEMINIST MONOPOLY ON CONSTITUTIONAL POLITICS

One clear effect was that, over time, constitutional politics within modern feminism became increasingly associated with a fairly conventional
Cold War creedal variant. Mainstream groups like the National Organization for Women (NOW), co-founded by Betty Freidan, Pauli Murray, Shirley Chisholm, and others, or the Women's Rights Project at the
ACLU, co-founded by future Supreme Court justice Ruth Bader Ginsburg, tended to combat gender discrimination by invoking a creedal
rhetoric familiar from 1950s and 1960s legal debates around race and racial inclusion. Indeed, when NOW revived the push for the ERA, this
push primarily followed Alice Paul's rather than Crystal Eastman's discursive model: it presented the constitutional amendment as fulfilling
the overall constitutional spirit, rather than as part of a transformative
reform package to reconceive state and economy.

During this period, mainstream strategies may have avoided anti-
capitalist, let alone anti-imperialist, analyses. Still, at least initially—
and against the backdrop of the Vietnam War, the NWRO, and even
the Panthers—such groups included as demands significant changes to
the gendered division of labor, in ways that would have been transformative for marginalized women. Alongside the end to sex-based legal
barriers, NOW backed the call for a guaranteed income and sought
dramatic extensions to the social welfare state.

In fact, NOW's efforts—not dissimilar to the NWRO—also aimed
to expand the boundaries of creedal constitutionalism. The group's
Women's Strike for Peace and Equality offers a telling illustration. On
August 26, 1970, to commemorate the fiftieth anniversary of the cer-
tification of the Nineteenth Amendment constitutionalizing women's
suffrage, the group organized protests and demonstrations throughout the country, including in New York City, where as many as 50,000
women participated. The day went hand in hand with a strike against
both paid and unpaid work, seeking to show the gendered inequalities
that shaped labor both at home and in formal workplaces. All in all, it
was a mass event on behalf of women's rights unlike anything the country had previously seen.[21]

The overall framework for the events was nonetheless markedly different from the Panthers' Revolutionary People's Constitutional Convention (RPCC), which would occur just ten days later in Philadelphia. If the RPCC's September date acted as a counter–Constitution Day exercise to proclaim a new sovereign and revolutionary people, the Women's Strike's anniversary timing instead embraced ideas of constitutional continuity and completion. Still, the strike absolutely pressed, in its own way, against the terms of the "Cold War civil rights" script. The invocation of "peace" as part of the day's rallies underscored mainstream feminist opposition to the Vietnam War, suggesting a willingness to link the domestic and foreign. The organizers also focused attention on three main demands: "free abortions" on demand, "24-hour day care . . . and equal educational and employment opportunities."[22] The achievement of these demands would, of course, have had profound implications for women's status and power in society, across class and racial backgrounds.

Unfortunately, as a rightward-drifting state blocked child care funding and other modes of social provision, only parts of these feminist efforts would succeed—those primarily involving the end of formal legal barriers. This meant that the elimination of these barriers became detached from meaningful changes to underlying economic structures—structures that tightly shaped the lives of poor women in particular. The federal courts, for instance, never moved beyond procedural protections when it came to welfare, rejecting efforts to constitutionalize substantive socioeconomic rights. As a result, marginalized women may have had the benefit of pre-termination benefits hearings, but that did little good if the state rolled back essential programs altogether. As for foreign policy, with the end of the Vietnam War the dominant drift of feminist politics was also away from engaging with US Cold War security practices.

Not unlike with the post-war labor movement, for mainstream leaders in the women's movement all of this could seem like an unavoidable, unfortunate, but ultimately acceptable compromise. After all, throughout the decade, those at NOW or the Women's Rights Project could feel real achievement in how legal regimes that had once forced women into gender-specific roles were being uprooted one after another. Indeed, for liberal litigators like Ginsburg, deeply attached to a version of the Cold War creed, the existing constitutional compact was proving compatible with real social change—even if there remained some limits.

But this trend would have profound implications for feminist and broader reform politics in the United States going forward. Above all, those like Ginsburg increasingly monopolized culturally what it meant to have any kind of constitutional politics within modern feminism. The NWRO, with its more expansive idea of rights, collapsed in 1975, under the weight of funding issues intensified by public hostility and conservative backlash. And its more flexible and capacious creedal constitutionalism receded with it. As for more revolutionary feminist collectives, they had always enjoyed a type of dissident status. And even when they had greater cultural resonance, they never fully developed—for understandable reasons—a detailed agenda of constitutional opposition.

Over time, more or less the only articulated feminist constitutional framework left standing was an adaptation of that old Cold War civil rights script. The idea that feminism *required* contesting Cold War foreign policy largely disappeared from the mainstream movement after Vietnam. Similarly, the idea that transformative economic demands— like the right to a guaranteed income or free and universal health care—were essential to a properly *feminist* constitutional politics also vanished from the predominant discussion. All of this created a context in which achievements like abortion rights were lauded, even as a class-based lack of access defined the experience for many poor women.

In a sense, mainstream feminism's potential willingness to separate issues of women's formal inclusion and formal reproductive rights from an agenda aimed at transforming race, economy, and security structures had been an issue from the beginning. Even during the 1970 Women's Strike, Bayard Rustin, the great Black activist, organizer, and writer, pointedly declared of the day's events, "what is wrong with [feminists'] demands . . . is that they don't go far enough." Although the strike's three agenda items had real teeth, Rustin questioned the unwillingness of NOW organizers to explicitly call for further structural changes, including transformations in the basic provision of health, education, and employment. NOW's failure to do so, at a moment of real Left energy and political radicalization among women activists, made Rustin wonder if the group would eventually "become just another middle class foray into limited social reform."[23]

When buoyed by a broader Left climate, mainstream feminist organizations embraced the larger structural aspirations of the time. But when that climate receded, the ambitions and cultural horizon of the dominant feminist politics became more constrained. In effect, as the decade progressed, the venerative side of staging the Women's Strike on the fiftieth anniversary of the Nineteenth Amendment would be reinforced, while its most unruly and critical were edges increasingly pushed to the margins.

INDIGENOUS OPPOSITION TO CREEDAL NATIONALISM

As for the specifically anti-colonial dimensions of Left radicalism, Native American activists during the 1970s did the most to sustain this counternarrative of the country. Perhaps most visibly, in 1972's Trail of Broken Treaties, a caravan of Indigenous organizations traveled from the US West Coast to the Washington, DC, office of the Bureau of Indian Affairs. This caravan raised general awareness about the ongoing oppression of Native peoples, as well as the demands for actual self-determination. These demands were partially drafted by the Sioux-Assiniboine activist Hank Adams, who in 1968 had also been a member of the national steering committee of the Poor People's Campaign.

Organized as a twenty-point position paper, the caravan's political agenda embodied a fundamental reimagining of the relationship between the US federal state and Native communities. Its preamble articulated the hope of a truly post-settler and postcolonial relationship between the US and Native American nations, grounded in a basic change in how American officials and citizens engaged with Indigenous peoples: "We seek a new American majority—a majority that is not content merely to confirm itself by superiority in numbers, but which by conscience is committed toward prevailing upon the public will in ceasing wrongs and in doing right."[24]

The paper then laid out what US acceptance of the basic sovereignty of Native American nations entailed, beginning with the internal right of Indigenous peoples to control their territory and govern their members. It further contended that US federal action with respect to such polities would only be legitimate if based on treaty obligations. Therefore, it held that all existing treaties should be enforced, with Indigenous peoples enjoying the ability to seek restitution before an appropriate arbiter for the violation of legal rights.

Moreover, the document called for the "Restoration of the Native American Land Base," the 110 million acres expropriated through the 1887 Dawes Act and other practices of settler theft. It also declared that the US government should provide extensive "health, housing, employment, economic development, and education[al]" assistance to all Indigenous peoples, as effective reparations for the history of dispossession and subordination. In order to facilitate this basic settler-Native reordering, the paper demanded the dismantling of the Bureau of Indian Affairs and the creation of new committees and structures to implement treaty responsibilities and facilitate resource redistribution.[25]

Crucially, such a project fundamentally rejected the creedal constitutional frame as an appropriate basis for US relations with Indigenous peoples. As the political scientist Kevin Bruyneel writes, "unlike the redemptive discourse of the civil rights movement" or mainstream feminism, its "principles were not drawn from the rights-based language of the US Constitution and the Declaration of Independence."[26] This approach extracted real reforms from the American federal government, highlighted by the 1975 passage of the Indian Self-Determination and Education Assistance Act, which "devolve[d] power to the tribes to contract for health, education, and welfare services . . . and ced[ed] tribes more control over the education of indigenous children in public schools."[27]

Despite these achievements, the sheer dominance of creedal narratives of nationhood—especially with Black radicalism contained—reinforced a telling disjunction in American public consciousness. On the one hand, Indigenous efforts during the 1970s sustained some degree of broader cultural awareness of colonialism as a framework for thinking about US history and governing arrangements. It also embodied a real site of Left alliance-building, as illustrated by Hank Adams's earlier connections to the Poor People's Campaign and the American Indian Movement's own participation in the Panthers' RPCC.

On the other hand, national political elites—along with most Americans—could largely compartmentalize the question of Native American status, as well as associated critiques of US colonialism, from the rest of popular conversation. In a context of wider Left decline, Indigenous activism often found itself operating on a track separate from the prevalent discussions about internal US identity, politics, and reform. As non-Indigenous movements that had rejected creedal mythmaking and engaged in anti-colonial critique became less politically relevant, decolonization retreated as a resonant analysis for thinking about how to reform the general orientation of American society.

Political discourse could thus proceed along two distinct paths. The first and dominant one embraced creedal constitutionalism and the Cold War compact as the established language for debate. The second path could invoke a colonial relationship when engaged in targeted discussions of Native American policy or policy toward overseas territories such as Puerto Rico.

But that second path had limited power in shaping the terms of the first. Dominant national narratives, even when able to recognize the evils of Indigenous expropriation and removal, inevitably treated that process as peripheral to the overall collective story. At a deep level, American national mythmaking—whether creedal or explicitly white supremacist—had long been premised on the erasure of Indigenous peoples. So, unsurprisingly, Native American colonial analysis—even during a period when US society was open to ameliorative change—faced profound hurdles in overcoming that pervasive mythmaking within internal American politics.

Under the dominant political framing, Indigenous dispossession may have been an isolated wrong. But it offered no broader insight into the structuring terms of the internal state and economy. Nor did it raise questions about the need for a parallel decolonial transformation within the country, operating in tandem with changes to Indigenous-US relations. For most Americans, whether politicians or ordinary citizens, Indigenous critiques were tangential to their prevailing electoral and cultural debates. And then, as the Red Power movement itself abated—due to partial reform successes, and yet more state repression—even this secondary discourse around colonialism often faded from public awareness.

Creedal Constitutional Rededication in the 1970s

All of this spoke to an undeniable development. The defeat of Black Power as a significant Left formation, alongside Left decline more broadly, went hand in hand with even more thoroughgoing investments in Cold War constitutionalism across the mainstream American political spectrum. Even many Left-liberal politicians and commentators, including those who had previously been anti-war and civil rights activists, came to interpret both the revolutionary agenda of the late 1960s and the state's violent response to it through this narrative frame.

Such commentators struggled to make sense of growing white conservatism, and of the popular success of the government's larger campaign to discredit virtually all Left activists as dangerously un-American. These were years, embodied by the 1976 Independence Day bicentennial celebrations, in which there existed widespread public desire to close the book on the recent past and on critical interrogations of the actual national experience. During this era, a conservative language around constitutional origins gained broad cultural standing. In response, Left-liberal voices increasingly concluded that constitutional rededication ultimately offered the only viable pathway for preserving hard-won victories, let alone for pursuing change in the future.

THE CONVERGING LIBERAL ACCOUNT
OF 1960S SUCCESS AND FAILURE

In accounting for the country' conservative drift, Left-liberal commentators often returned to cultural explanations reminiscent in their own way of post-war consensus historiography. Take for example how Todd Gitlin, the former president of Students for a Democratic Society (SDS), explained the collapse of the Panthers and other allied Left organizations in his seminal book, *The Sixties: Years of Hope, Days of Rage*. Although published in 1987, the book nonetheless distilled the types of arguments that had begun to crystallize a decade earlier. Gitlin wrote of Left defeat in these terms: "The odds have been against the Left in laissez-fair-loving, race-divided, history-burying America from the start. The two-party system, solidified by law, militates against the ideological margins—even as the parties lose their hold on the voters."[28]

Unlike the general orientation of mid-century consensus history, Gitlin—along with many of the post-1960s Left-liberal voices—refused to elide the country's history of racial subordination and ethnic cleansing. But in line with someone like Louis Hartz, as discussed in chapter 13, he nonetheless suggested that the US was deeply culturally committed, perhaps even from the founding, to a relatively conservative brand of liberalism. Such embedded values linked individualistic capitalism to a self-congratulatory belief in national greatness and exceptionalism.

Gitlin thus chided radical organizations of the late 1960s and early 1970s—organizations within which he himself had once been a leader— for embracing a "millennial, all or nothing" approach that lacked political maturity. This Left activist approach ignored the underlying nature of American society. It therefore imagined utopian alternatives that were naïve and unfeasible, at times falling into destructive fantasies of violent rupture. Instead, the only option for the country, Gitlin now argued, was an "honorable Left"—one mature enough to seek change on terms that tapped into the ameliorative, redemptive, and creedal commitments of American civic culture.[29]

With the country's rightward electoral shift, highlighted again by Nixon's landslide win over George McGovern, there was real validity to these critiques of the Left. Despite the Left desire to build a coalitional, popular majority behind ideas like Black liberation, more and more white Americans instead seemingly identified with the Cold War state. And this identification took place even as that state failed to address real economic grievances, lied to its citizens, and violently suppressed dissidents.

Moreover, the path of steady reform through means that embraced both the creed and the Constitution had met with actual success. This was evidenced by past civil rights victories, not to mention the ongoing legal and legislative achievements of the women's movement. Of course, as with both Progressive-era constitutional amendments and New Deal–era social programs, it could be hard to disentangle exactly which entities deserved credit for political successes and which deserved blame for failures. As Gitlin himself recognized, one could argue that a background context of radical energy during all of these periods played an important role: it created space for movement, making more moderate reforms appear reasonable and worth implementing—if at least in part to stave off more dramatic calls for change.

Still, analysis like Gitlin's tended to replicate a basic problem, one comparable to early Cold War liberal thinking. Such thinking had understood all of American history through the contingent historical processes that shaped the mid-twentieth century, from the New Deal and World War II to the Cold War. These processes created a governing class committed to particular ideological elements: market capitalism with a small welfare state, legal racial reform, and American global primacy. They had also facilitated a Democratic Party supermajority able, for a short period, to overcome—albeit only partially—the major constitutional roadblocks to social change. However, many early Cold Warriors, as chapter 13 detailed, then proceeded to read these specific and contingent facts as enduring truths. And it led them to conclude that the constitutional order was a near perfect mechanism for liberal democracy, rather than a hindrance to meaningful reform.

In the wake of radical defeat, Left-liberals like Gitlin perceived the post-1960s climate as similarly indicative of near fixed features of American life such as the supposed "moderating genius" of "the political system."[30] The implication of such a perspective was that 1960s and even 1970s liberal reforms on race and gender, preserved despite the country's increasing move rightward, were evidence of a permanent and moderate middle course that governing arrangements by and large promoted. Unlike various early Cold Warriors, Gitlin himself chafed against this political reality; his use of "moderating genius" had a critical undertone. He may have strongly believed that the resulting changes were profound achievements, in which movement activists should take deep pride. But the overall post-1960s American state and economy— "solidified by law"—did not amount to a proper instantiation of justice. Yet Gitlin concluded that the existing arrangements enjoyed a general degree of social legitimacy. Furthermore, partial reform possibilities appeared more or less all that was available as a non-destructive political horizon.

Taking a step back, such a view often fell prey to two difficulties with long-term ramifications. First, its politics of pragmatism could accede to the era's narrowing political terrain. Gitlin castigated a "total Left" for its "all-or-nothing" demands, which failed to appreciate how the US was "a society crisscrossed by divisions" and "not poised on the edge of radical change." But taken too far, that rejection of a "millennial" Left could treat virtually all efforts at structural transformation as unserious evasions of "practical politics." Again, Gitlin certainly agreed that— even if "some . . . demands had been institutionalized"—marginalized communities still lacked equal and effective freedom.[31] Especially in other hands, the invocation of pragmatism could devolve into settling permanently for that middle course, and then justifying the indefinite accommodation to injustice as all that could be done.

In addition, conceiving of American institutions as enduringly moderate suggested that, at the end of the day, the center could likely be counted on to hold. But those institutions had hardly played a moderating function during the Gilded Age preceding the New Deal, a century prior. That age, lasting decades, was one in which the legal-political system only intensified polarized and extreme class and racial struggle, often by operating to block reform agendas and deepen social conflict. What if the institutions again reverted back to that earlier role? Or what if a new Right, on gaining political dominance, refused to abide by the terms of the domestic Cold War settlement? There seemed no guarantee that the country would not return to a version of the previous cultural and institutional status quo.

Elected officials and movement activists that gravitated to the new liberalism certainly worried about the rise of an unconstrained Right, one uninterested in the prevailing compact on race, gender, and social welfare. Yet they tended to see an embrace of the creed and the Constitution as the best way to contain conservative forces.[32] Still, by sharing this language—in order to preserve recent gains or even to justify the middle course—they also relinquished a key element of the country's longtime leftward anchor.

THE IMPERIAL PRESIDENCY AND THE CONSTITUTION AS SOLUTION

In attaching center and Left-liberal politics to a near sanctified account of the Constitution, perhaps the single most significant event of those years was the Watergate scandal. For liberals of various stripes—who now also occupied much of the space left vacant by the suppression of radical activists—the Watergate break-in stood for a larger and violent lawlessness represented by the emergent Right. Indeed, Nixon's willingness to use discretionary force against all he deemed enemies hearkened back to McCarthyite "populism."

In this context, among the most politically resonant assessments of "Watergate's significance even before Richard Nixon had left office"[33] came from Arthur Schlesinger in his 1973 book, *The Imperial Presidency*. In a sense, this was unsurprising. A quarter century earlier, Schlesinger had been a key architect of Cold War liberalism. And now Schlesinger again turned to arguments about American exceptionalism and constitutional genius as a solution to the problems of the day.

For Schlesinger, Nixon signified the subversion of the constitutional order in favor of an "imperial" and discretionary security state, one located primarily in the presidency and operating both at home and abroad in ways that violated basic American principles. Like Left radicals, Schlesinger fully accepted the illegality and illegitimacy of many American Cold War actions. But he suggested that this did not delegitimize the US's global project or speak to a deep-rooted and inherently imperialist foundation to national identity. Rather, these destructive actions were the product of a country that had lost touch with its original ideals—especially during the preceding decade of war in Vietnam and social unrest at home.

Schlesinger reminded readers that the framers of the federal Constitution, the nation's "Founding Fathers," had designed a system of government "new to the world in the eighteenth century and still uncommon in the twentieth." This was a system premised on checks and balances, which safeguarded the liberty of all because power was "dispers[ed] . . . among three independent branches." In a full-throated embrace of the Constitution, Schlesinger contended that the 1787 creation

was an "extraordinary document," one that established a genuinely preeminent form of representative democracy.[34]

For Schlesinger, the problem was that in recent decades some governing elites, individuals like Nixon, had treated the security apparatus
as their own playground, increasingly abandoning that original vision.
The solution to the imperial presidency was thus a "reinvigoration of
the written checks of the Constitution." And this would only be possible if "the spirit of the American people" became infused, once more,
with the values of the Constitution itself.[35]

Schlesinger's diagnosis is especially striking because the period in
which he viewed the Constitution as coming under new assault—the
Cold War decades culminating with the bombing of Laos and Cambodia and with Watergate—had witnessed increasingly reverential language around the Constitution. Political elites, including Nixon himself, had consolidated around a rigid account of creedal constitutional
faith. In other words, the rise of a broad Cold War constitutional discourse and of the "imperial presidency" coincided very neatly.

This fact spoke to how a brand of constitutional politics had played
a significant role in justifying American primacy and international police power in the first place. As discussed in chapters 10 and 11, the overarching Cold War climate tended to treat global interventionism and
domestic containment of radical dissenters as central to the very preservation and promotion of a fundamentally imperial American constitutionalism. Thus, the invocation of constitutional veneration proved to
have a Janus-like, double-sided, quality: it could serve to critique Nixonian excess while still validating the larger Cold War project, which
gave seemingly inexhaustible fuel to further security state overreach.

It was no surprise, then, that the federal judiciary, as in the context of
the Vietnam War, steadfastly avoided genuinely constraining unilateral
presidential war-making or security-based grabs for power. Schlesinger
may have hoped that the courts, along with Congress, would "reclaim
their own dignity"[36] and rein in the presidency. But judges were themselves often deeply invested in a constitutional discourse that took for
granted the need for an aggressive American global presence. When
asked to confront Cold War prerogatives, judges often instead went out
of their way to legalize security practices.

Take for instance *Orlando v. Laird* (1971), in which army enlistees,
backed by anti-war and civil liberties groups, challenged the constitutionality of the Vietnam War. Congress had never explicitly authorized
Lyndon Johnson's actions, in plain violation of Article I of the Con-

stitution, as well as of classic republican assumptions that legislative preapproval was essential to avoid presidents descending into military despotism. Regardless, the Second Circuit treated congressional appropriations bills and conscription measures as an implied authorization, enough after the fact to rubber-stamp extreme executive adventurism. The degree to which the courts transformed into faithful servants of the national security state did not speak to a failure of willpower, as Schlesinger suggested. Instead, it illustrated how the American Cold War brand of constitutionalism was itself deeply intertwined with assumptions about the necessity of existing security frameworks.

Ultimately, the problem was that individuals with Schlesinger's views — strong commitments to judicially imposed constitutional limits on executive overreach in national security — were a clear minority in institutions like the federal bench. And the rhetoric Schlesinger used around constitutional greatness was incredibly malleable. In a context in which Cold War dynamics and official commitments to global primacy exerted ongoing pressure to assert discretionary power overseas, it could be easily disconnected from Schlesinger's specific goals of presidential restraint. In this way, his assessment of the document as "extraordinary" could simply become part of the broader reverential chorus, even as that chorus quietly abandoned the critique of the "imperial presidency."

CONSTITUTIONAL REDEDICATION AND INTERPRETIVE EVOLUTION

Regardless of the potential uses of constitutional commitment for "imperial presidential" ends, the call to constitutional rededication became a persistent feature of emerging post-1960s Left-liberal politics, perhaps most powerfully expressed by Barbara Jordan at Nixon's Watergate impeachment hearings. Jordan was the first Black person elected to Congress from Texas after Reconstruction[37] and the first African American congresswoman to serve from the South. Her opening statement to the House Judiciary Committee during the impeachment process was heard by millions across the country. Jordan, known for always having "a copy of the Constitution in her purse,"[38] declared before rapt television audiences that "my faith in the Constitution is whole; it is complete; it is total. And I am not going to sit here and be an idle spectator to the diminution, the subversion, the destruction, of the Constitution."[39] Quoting from Madison and Hamilton, she contended that either Congress would hold Nixon accountable for his lawlessness or it would abandon the nation's founding ideals.

The fact that it was Jordan, an African American woman, who declared her devotion before the country had a particular resonance. Her sitting in judgment of a white male president embodied the success of the civil rights and women's movements: the real inclusion of previously marginalized persons into positions of institutional power. In this way, moments like Jordan's speech to Congress served as touchstone cultural events, further burnishing creedal constitutional politics after a period of radical attack.

Her words also offered a version of the New Deal living Constitution appropriate for the new post–civil rights age. Jordan began her remarks by highlighting the profound exclusions that had shaped American experience: "Earlier today, we heard the beginning of the Preamble to the Constitution of the United States: 'We, the people.' It's a very eloquent beginning. But when that document was completed on the seventeenth of September in 1787, I was not included in that 'We, the people.' I felt somehow for many years that George Washington and Alexander Hamilton just left me out by mistake. But through the process of amendment, interpretation, and court decision, I have finally been included in 'We, the people.'"[40] FDR had presented the federal Constitution as "living" because it was properly understood as an outline aimed at addressing social problems as they emerged; it was meant to adjust to the dilemmas of the day. Alongside that idea, Jordan—herself a lawyer—indicated a second, critical meaning: the Constitution was also living in that it was incompletely inclusive at the founding.

But for Jordan, that incompleteness did not suggest a basic illegitimacy, as Panthers like Cetawayo Tabor or Afeni Shakur had contended. Instead, the framers had devised a system whose underlying spirit and text made it open to the steady incorporation of outsider groups over time—with the result that the United States had moved from a "we the people" restricted by gender and race in the eighteenth century to a truly universal understanding of who "the people" encompassed.

This idea of constitutional evolution, grounded in an incomplete yet fundamentally liberal promise, became central during these years to the new theorizing that shaped constitutional study in the legal academy. As discussed in chapter 13, in the early Cold War law schools and law professors had become the key institutional repositories for constitutional memory and ongoing constitutional discussion—with a particular focus on the Supreme Court. However, many of the most esteemed constitutional scholars of the 1950s and 1960s, such as Alexander Bickel and Herbert Wechsler, questioned whether Warren Court civil rights decisions were sufficiently grounded in objective legal reasoning, as opposed to just normative aspirations.

Now, however, many of the professors who had entered the legal academy in the 1970s were themselves former clerks of Warren Court justices.[41] An early indicator of this generational shift, and of how it might alter legal academic discourse, came from the student editors of the *Harvard Law Review*. They "respectfully dedicate[ed]" one 1969 issue "to Chief Justice Earl Warren, who with courage and compassion led a reform of the law while the other branches of government delayed."[42]

This resulting crop of 1970s law professors—admirers of the Warren Court or even former employees of its justices—did more than simply treat decisions like *Brown v. Board of Education* as morally well-meaning. They elevated various Warren Court cases, with *Brown* as the centerpiece, to the status of exalted texts within the legal academy. And they developed sophisticated grand theories of constitutional interpretation that incorporated notions of liberal evolutionary change—especially on matters of race, gender, and equality—into the basic meaning of the federal Constitution.[43]

These arguments, whether from Barbara Jordan in the political realm or law professors in the academy, reinforced one another in public life. In the process, they set the terms for a new Left-liberal constitutional culture. To understand this culture's development and eventual effects, it is useful to remember how the historical rise of the constitutional law professoriate had two related implications. As discussed in chapter 13, it first meant that what became conventionally understood as a "constitutional matter" revolved around textual interpretation and legal cases—topics addressed by lawyers and in law schools. Left on the outside were the issues of basic institutional design, which had been the bread and butter of Progressive-era constitutional study by historians and political scientists at a time when law schools tended to treat the topic as a third-year elective.

Second, constitutional change therefore also became presented in public discourse as a subject supervised by the courts and concerned above all with debates about judicial doctrine, especially over the meaning of rights. Indeed, by the late 1960s, this shift to an almost exclusive identification of the Constitution with the courts was apparent even in the period's Black radical opposition to the document. As we have seen, that opposition largely bypassed pre–Cold War conversations about how to reconfigure the actual structures of the existing constitutional system.

Both Jordan and the new law professoriate took more or less as given this court-centric and Cold War constitutional politics. Unlike the Bickels of the past, they rallied behind theories of interpretation that placed creedal inclusion at the constitutional center, and with it the achievements of the traditional civil rights movement and of liberal feminism. Yet they did so on terms that nonetheless accepted the Cold War compact's limitations on what counted as a relevant constitutional topic or project. This meant that both a Black radical anti-colonial vision and Progressives' and Socialists' earlier structural accounts of mass democratic design remained totally absent.

Of course, it was to be expected that a legal academy oriented to the judiciary—and deeply attached personally and professionally to Supreme Court justices—would be uninterested in the constitutional politics of Progressive-era reformers or Panther Convention participants. But given that the legal profession, and especially the legal academy, increasingly enjoyed a monopoly on what counted in the public realm as constitutional expertise, the result nonetheless proved dramatic.

For a broadly Left-liberal person coming of age politically after the heyday of the civil rights movement and after the collapse of radical activism, this brand of creedal constitutionalism became simply how one talked about the Constitution. It was the language of the post-1960s liberal elected politician—regardless of race or gender—and its terms shaped the historical, legal, and political knowledge about the document produced by scholars and commentators and consumed by the public.

In a sense, the creed and the Constitution gained an ever more sanctified status within the liberal Left. And it did so not only because it had generated real ameliorative reforms, evident in changes all around and reflected in who now attended professional schools, held elected office, or sat in boardrooms. For a Left-liberal person—with no direct connection to the preceding years' actual radical movements—embracing a shared redemptive project about the document also amounted to perhaps the only way one could imagine invoking constitutionalism to rebut the politics of white backlash, let alone conservative claims more generally.

THE 1976 BICENTENNIAL AND THE
SEARCH FOR THE PAST

This Left-liberal call for rededication to the Constitution, including to its framers, may have responded to the era's conservative political drift. But it also echoed that larger climate. One can see this in the ubiquitous 1976 nationwide bicentennial events celebrating US independence from the British Empire. As the historian Richard B. Morris—then president of the American Historical Association—remarked at the time, such events were notable for the extent to which local and national dignitaries, conservative and liberal, celebrated an armed revolt as instead a moment for the restoration of shared bonds: "The two words most muted during the two hundredth year of American independence . . . have been 'people' and 'revolution.'"[44]

According to the official planners in the American Revolution Bicentennial Administration (ARBA), the group established by Nixon and Congress to oversee and coordinate local, state, and national commemorations, the country was exiting "some of the bitterest times in our history."[45] In this context, a common pride in the eighteenth-century founders and their achievements—with the Constitution chief among them—became a key way to close the door on recent struggles.[46]

Of course, not everyone agreed with papering over the past. In Philadelphia, much to Mayor Frank Rizzo's displeasure, a coalition of Left activists staged counterprotests to the official celebrations. Rizzo had wanted the federal government to send 15,000 troops to squash the protests, but no such troops arrived. The counter-events went off peacefully, drawing around 30,000 people, and the *New York Times* called them an "echo of the protest days of the 1960s." They included calls for Indigenous self-determination, Puerto Rican independence ("a Bicentennial without colonies"), and women's rights. Black Panther Party Chairwoman Elaine Brown pointedly rejected the hero worship of the founders, declaring the nation's history to be one "of murder and plunder."[47]

Still, such anti-nationalist and Left gatherings were essentially drowned out in a sea of patriotic spectacles, celebrations that the *Washington Post* viewed as embodying "a moment of deep and moving reconciliation." Countless citizens took part in local events or visited key nationalist attractions—whether in DC, Boston, Philadelphia, or New York City, where millions toured Operation Sail '76 (a collection of 224 historic ships in the city's harbor). Many more watched celebrations on television from the comfort of their homes.[48]

Moreover, in contrast to Elaine Brown or Puerto Rican independence activists, even the dominant Left-liberal critique of these events embraced a version of the prevailing "return to origins" sentiment. Take for example the *Nation*'s response to the 1976 bicentennial. On the one hand, the editors attacked the ARBA and many of the ongoing festivities for the extent to which corporate elites — following a now established template familiar from the post–World War II Freedom Train — tended to drive event content and themes. They decried the conservative and business tendency to "splash" the American history of racial and gender discrimination "with a heavy coat of whitewash." Invoking Progressive-era dissent, the magazine called on citizens to read Beard's *Economic Interpretation of the Constitution of the United States* alongside the *Federalist Papers* as part of a "balanced approach" that would "demystify once and for all this nation's revolutionary past."[49]

On the other hand, the editors asserted that such demystification did not mean a radical break with the Constitution or its framers. They referenced Beard not to repudiate the constitutional system or to claim that it was grounded, from the founding, in an oppressive class rule. Rather, appreciating the potential economic interests of competing framers allowed citizens to recognize the human frailties and historical limitations of even revolutionary leaders, thus avoiding a destructive brand of idolatry.

In fact, in keeping with Cold War creedal nationalism, the *Nation* reaffirmed the deep ethical relationship between recent civil rights victories and the nation's guiding and connected documents, the Declaration and the Constitution. With a more open-eyed gaze, the editors also extolled the genuine achievements of the founders and echoed the broader public discourse about the need, in a fractured political moment, for an embrace of origins. The magazine argued for bicentennial celebrations less focused on jingoistic pageantry and more driven by civic education, in which "the Declaration would be widely published and read — not just respectfully invoked. Copies of the Constitution and the Bill of Rights would be as plentiful as Gideon Bibles."[50]

CONSERVATIVES DEFINE THE ASCENDING CONSTITUTIONAL LANGUAGE

This wider culture of reinvestment in national origins provided a perfect climate for the elevation of a consolidating conservative legal-political discourse. By the late 1970s, conservative activists, lawyers, and politicians had been fighting a decades-long battle to contain the scope of racial and gender transformations in American society, as well as to chip away at the social welfarist elements of the Cold War domestic settlement. Given shifts in white middle-class politics, these efforts continued to build in momentum, culminating with the 1980 presidential victory of Ronald Reagan.

Conservative figures championed and extended the worshipful popular culture that swirled around the revolutionary generation. In particular, politicians and commentators emphasized that many of the preceding decades' social changes were illegitimate because they violated what, by the 1980s, conservatives were increasingly calling "originalism." This was broadly understood as the meaning that would have been ascribed to the Constitution at the time a specific part of the text was ratified. For Edwin Meese—Reagan's attorney general and a key popularizer of the new approach—abiding by the framers' "Original Intention" was the only true way to construct a "jurisprudence that seeks to be faithful to our Constitution."[51]

The political scientist Calvin TerBeek highlights that this conservative rebuttal to liberal constitutionalism initially gained prominence after *Brown v. Board of Education*, as an account of why that case was wrongly decided. In the 1950s, the *National Review*, through its "in-house authority on the Constitution and civil rights," James Kilpatrick (a committed segregationist), became "central to diffusing the idea of constitutional text properly interpreted only through a fixed, historical lens."[52] This approach then migrated, during the Warren Court years, across right-wing political and legal circles.

By the time the New Right solidified its political power under Reagan, such a mode of interpretation had become a central way that conservative politicians, journalists, and lawyers talked to each other about the Constitution. One key space for developing and promoting these ideas was the Federalist Society, which became especially associated with advancing originalism inside and outside the legal academy and with cultivating a new potential class of future conservative judges.[53] Founded in 1982, the Society's name invoked the *Federalist Papers* and the essays Madison, Hamilton, and others had published to defend the proposed 1787 document during ratification debates. And not unlike pro-business and pro-Constitution advocacy during and after World War I, it received a strong funding push from wealthy donors. As the political scientist Steven Teles writes, "conservative foundations were especially vital in the Society's early years." This ensured a financial war chest that allowed the group to avoid time-consuming "direct mail and corporate" fundraising drives. Instead it could focus on building its membership and influence across law schools and the legal profession, and on broadly disseminating its constitutional arguments.[54]

Originalism's success as the new conservative legal-political language did not result primarily from its inherent academic or analytical qualities.[55] To begin with, originalism would come to refer to a variety of competing theories, each with their own potential flaws, not unlike any other interpretive approach. In the legal academy, eventually these debates often concerned whether to prioritize the intentions of the Constitution's drafters and ratifiers, or to largely ignore those intentions in favor of what the text's public meaning at the time of ratification had been. The former approach raised questions about how to divine the single true intention of large groups and about why those views should matter given that they were not ratified as part of the written document. In addition, it left unaddressed the issue of how to handle the numerous modern questions for which eighteenth- or nineteenth-century actors had no conception. The latter fell prey to Thurman Arnold's and Charles Beard's points about the open-endedness and profound indeterminacy of the text, and the document's ability to fit a number of competing perspectives.

Moreover, broad aims of either abiding by the framers' intentions or the text alone had a long history within judicial interpretation, well before *Brown*. Such interpretive sensibilities had been associated, in different eras, with wildly divergent political ideologies and Supreme Court justices—from the pro-slavery Jacksonian Roger Taney to the New Dealer Hugo Black. This ideological divergence again spoke to the text's indeterminacy and to the fact that it was hardly self-evident that something like "originalism" necessarily had a single political valence. Conservative politicians often invoked the term to suggest that there existed an objectively valid answer to most constitutional puzzles, and that this answer also tended to coincide with their own political preferences.[56] But, simply put, there was no guarantee that a genuinely consistent originalist could reach a single objectively valid outcome, let alone reliably end up supporting the political goals of the New Right.[57]

But by the 1980s, the approach increasingly formed "the bedrock of constitutional conservatism"[58] and also enjoyed growing public resonance, for reasons independent of its academic bona fides. For starters, calling oneself an originalist provided conservative political elites and their constituents a clear ground for denouncing Warren Court opinions as "activism"—liberal policy preferences dressed up as law. During the preceding years, the Warren Court in particular had played a leading role in expanding rights, especially for racial minorities and women. This was partly due to the ideological temperament and policy preferences of those who served on the bench, which in turn resulted from how the mid-century Cold War settlement reshaped both political parties and thus the nature of presidential nominations to the judiciary. It was also filtered through a recognition of the very real counter-majoritarian constraints on formal constitutional amendment.

Even if there might have been supermajority support for new rights provisions, a skewed legal-political structure made any such provisions near impossible to add through an alteration of the actual language of the document. This had been clear to many generations of critics and activists, and it was again dramatized by the ultimate collapse of the ERA. All of this further pushed debates into the federal bench. Against this background, the Warren and early Burger Courts elaborated new constitutional guarantees within the existing text—as with *Roe v. Wade*'s right to abortion—even if these guarantees were not explicitly enumerated in the written document. Such an approach was more in line with a living constitutionalist tradition, which conceived of the text as responsive to an evolving constitutional culture and able to encompass legal principles and rights commitments not bound to the particularities of the ratifying era.

But in response, conservative claims that constitutional rights should only entail what was strictly stipulated in the text or intended by framers of the 1787 document or the later Fourteenth Amendment became a powerful way of asserting the supposed lack of legal objectivity in the previous period's judicially managed reforms. In the past, of course, there had been many different interpretive methods for criticizing judicial "activism," as exemplified in chapter 13 by the legal process ideas of Bickel or Wechsler. So beyond the question of activism alone, originalism's strength connected to how it marshaled the authority of the framers, just as enthusiasm for them was cresting and they were being extolled even by liberals and minority groups.

Originalism thus amounted to a compelling way for conservatives to question the transformations wrought by both feminist and Black freedom struggles while still operating within the general terms of creedal constitutionalism. Given how the framers had been folded into creedal stories, originalism—in a post–Civil Rights era—helped to defuse the argument that conservative resistance was effectively white supremacist or supportive of gender hierarchy.

This originalist success depended significantly on how Cold War constitutional politics had fundamentally reshaped the popular relationship with the founding generation and with the document. After all, in a sense, early-twentieth-century Socialists and even various Progressives were "originalists" too: they looked to the framers in their attempts to understand the document, and especially in developing their accounts of why the existing constitutional system was so fundamentally undemocratic. And they found their answer in the intentions of individuals like Madison and Hamilton, whom they depicted as primarily interested in preserving class rule in a post-revolutionary context.

Yet, the combination of World War II and the early Cold War popularized a very different notion of both the framers and the 1787 structure. The rediscovery of the Bill of Rights transformed Madison into the architect of the country's anti-totalitarian charter of individual liberty. And the system's intricate arrangement of checks and balances was instead presented as the paramount expression of liberal democracy, with the framers praised as geniuses of political construction. All this resulted in a lavish rehabilitation of the basic reputation of the late-eighteenth-century political class.

The other great critique of the framers was the old Garrisonian and radical abolitionist argument, mirrored by the Black Panther Elaine Brown at the bicentennial counter-event and protest, that the Constitution was a pro-slavery document that operated to sustain racial subordination and to facilitate the theft of Indigenous land. Creedal constitutionalists, going all the way back to Frederick Douglass and Abraham Lincoln, had rejected this view. And during the 1941 Bill of Rights anniversary, commentators had attempted to read enslavers like Madison as effectively proto-abolitionists, creators of a constitutional system inherently opposed to racism. Still, despite those efforts, proto-abolitionist interpretations had an air of absurdity as long as Jim Crow remained the law of the land. Indeed, in the 1950s, originalism's associations with pro-segregation politics—and its use of a historical lens to challenge *Brown*—meant that its full creedal credentials were very much in doubt.

But by the 1970s and 1980s, conservatives had made their peace with *Brown*, even as they sought to limit its reach and to redirect it against continuing racial reforms like desegregation remedies and affirmative action. In effect, a mainstream American sense that the Jim Crow era had definitively ended provided originalists with a cultural opening. It meant that invoking the eighteenth- and nineteenth-century past to answer present-day questions could proceed more or less without fear about what the *actual* historical reality of that broader society might have been. Politically relevant conservatives were no longer explicitly rejecting racial equality, as Kilpatrick had. Thus, an embrace of the textual drafters did not require interrogating too deeply whether those founders were in fact creedalists at all.

THE FLATTENING OF CONSTITUTIONAL HISTORY AND ITS RAMIFICATIONS

In this context, Americans could just focus on earlier generations' exceptional contributions—especially at the founding—and gloss over unwholesome truths. With the end of legal segregation, it became more plausible to interpret someone like Madison as perhaps himself embodying the values of later, more enlightened Americans. To the extent that liberal defenders of a living Constitution suggested that decisions like *Brown* accorded with the overall animating spirit of the Constitution (beyond even just the Fourteenth Amendment), did this not imply that the 1787 framers were in fact partly responsible for current improvements? Had they not initiated a collective project with the resources to overcome whatever deficiencies—racial or otherwise—may have existed at the start?

All of this underscored how, by the dawn of the Reagan era, public discourse increasingly flattened the distinct periods of constitutional development into one primary moment of founding. Through this process, virtually any constitutional improvement—no matter how remote from the eighteenth-century genesis—could be seen as proof of the wisdom of that initial generation. It became increasingly commonplace, rather than an absurdity, to treat Madison and Hamilton as incipient creedal constitutionalists, regardless of their actual views.

A careful reading of the *Nation* or close consideration of Barbara Jordan's words made clear that their versions of constitutional commitment opposed this unthinking flattening of all constitutional meaning. The federal Constitution had gone through numerous and profound alterations that shaped late-twentieth-century American society—from the practical re-founding of the Civil War and Reconstruction, to women's suffrage under the Nineteenth Amendment, to the New Deal judicial entrenchment of the modern administrative state. These key developments had shaped the inclusive creedal Constitution that they celebrated.

As left-of-center scholars in the academy began to argue in the 1980s, the United States should be understood as having multiple founding generations.[59] Indeed, when someone like Jordan embraced the Constitution, a large part of what she embraced was the egalitarian potential of the Reconstruction Amendments and thus the values of Radical Republicans — individuals like Thaddeus Stevens, Frederick Douglass, and Charles Sumner — who attempted to confront a white supremacist society. She certainly did not embrace the constitutional world of the original framers or even the broader one of the 1860s — still deeply exclusionary on race and gender grounds. For her, some Reconstruction figures, alongside twentieth-century movement activists like King, were just as significant as Madison and Hamilton — if not more so — in shaping the elements worth celebrating in the constitutional system.

However, for the wider public, the idea of multiple and ongoing refoundings within a formally unbroken — but substantially reconceived — constitutional project had little cultural resonance. Americans did not think of themselves as existing under a second, third, or even fourth republic, in which the Constitution and the country had been fundamentally transformed following the Civil War, the New Deal, and then the 1960s civil rights era. Even the journalist E. L. Godkin's more simplified idea, voiced in 1887 — that future generations would remember the political leaders of 1865 as the country's true founders, given the post–Civil War reconstitution of society and the explicit formal changes to the text — seemed entirely absent from the popular constitutional imagination.[60]

Indeed, adopting an alternative framework would have required Americans, at a time of general desire to rally around a shared past, to confront historical discontinuities and complexities and to engage more deeply with the organizing values of pre–Civil War America. That earlier society had cast aside an imperial ruler with worldwide reverberations, but to what degree had it also been diametrically opposed to twentieth-century creedal values? The increasingly dominant, simplified historical narrative did not reopen those old wounds. Instead, Hamilton and Madison gained a reflected glory from the achievements and struggles of later figures: individuals — like Frederick Douglass and Martin Luther King Jr. — whose ideological commitments may have directly contradicted those of founding-era elites.

As a result, the view became pervasive that the long, uncertain road to judicial and legislative civil rights victories in the 1950s and 1960s was virtually inevitable. This historical vision did not include any significant roadblocks that the 1787 structure may have placed in the way of meaningful reform. Political discussion focused on what had now been achieved, rather than on the multigenerational delay and continuing impediments. Furthermore, these achievements increasingly validated faith in the constitutional system's overall justness—and in its putative eighteenth-century authors.

This flattened and venerative climate fit perfectly with the spread of originalism as an intuitive way to think about the Constitution, even outside conservative spaces. It is true that over time, especially by the end of the twentieth century, some "originalist" legal scholars in the academy presented themselves as uninterested in founders' worship and simply committed to a methodology that emphasized the textual meaning of the constitutional document when particular pieces of text (whether in 1789, 1791, 1868, or 1920) were ratified.

But that eventual scholarly assertion does not capture the call to originalism's broader cultural import, particularly as it took off in public life. Rather, this import was associated with how Meese, along with various lawyers and politicians connected to the Federalist Society (which used Madison's image as the logo of the organization), wrapped the national project in upholding the constitutional world of the founding. Given the currents of the 1980s, this was a call that many—including those who did not think of themselves as conservatives—saw as patriotic common sense. If the framers were best understood as having created an ideal system of liberal-democratic governance—and even as incipient defenders of a universalist and egalitarian creed—then why not simply follow their dictates across a range of sociopolitical questions?

In this way, the American Right maintained contact with creedal constitutional rhetoric, while pushing back against the implications civil rights and women's rights activists derived from it. Returning to the framers might not always provide a clear political resolution—let alone a conservative one—to modern questions. But a legal and political culture that worshipped eighteenth-century settler founders certainly promoted a politics far removed from the insurgent and radical demands of the 1960s or the 1930s.

This constitutional culture also placed on the intellectual defensive those Left and liberal voices arguing for creative judicial interpretations in favor of socioeconomic, reproductive, or welfare rights. And this was so even though such voices' support for and participation in creedal constitutional rhetoric had been central to its eventual cultural dominance.

Again, courts had elaborated new guarantees in the 1960s and early 1970s in part because of the basic democratic deficiency of the larger constitutional system, in which new amendments might have mass support but the process of approving them was almost impossibly difficult. Yet, to the extent that all sides—whether living constitutionalist or originalist—accepted the wisdom of the founding design, its underlying structural flaws could be excised from public debate. The question of the constitutional system's democratic legitimacy could then be drastically reduced to a singular focus on what conservatives viewed as the new liberal judicial activism: court-managed reform that deviated from the clear guidance of the written text.

In this way, collective debate ignored the institutional contexts that funneled constitutional change into specific pathways, let alone the wider matter of whether the Madisonian design actually warranted deification.[61] Precisely because all the relevant sides seemingly accepted a Cold War constitutional framing, it was far easier for originalist assumptions to drive constitutional conversation, both inside and outside the legal profession. Thus, Attorney General Meese could castigate liberals for not using the amendment process if they sought constitutional reforms, say on abortion rights—even though everyone knew that the mechanism was essentially foreclosed because of the constitutional structure itself.[62]

The Constitution's Bicentennial and Marshall's Sober Second Thought

By the late 1980s, this Cold War constitutional framing had become well entrenched. Americans had moved far from the politics of national self-examination that existed in the 1960s and early 1970s. Instead, conservative political ascendancy now buttressed an even more self-congratulatory climate, which praised American exceptionalism and raised to seemingly mythic status the eighteenth-century framers. Against this background, just over a decade after celebrating the nation's bicentennial, Americans shifted their focus to celebrating that of the Constitution in 1987.

At its outset, the constitutional bicentennial looked as if it might end up facing many of the same pitfalls that shaped the 1887 anniversary.

Initially, celebration efforts received limited support from Congress—the first appropriation in 1983 was only for $331,000—and there were fears that the events would face "widespread public indifference."[63] But as the date approached, these concerns proved premature. Millions in congressional funding poured in, and the celebrations became a defining part of the cultural moment.

None other than Chief Justice Burger chaired the commission established by Congress to oversee the nationwide festivities. Indeed, he retired from the Supreme Court to lead an effort he viewed as essential to deepening a common American ethos within the country's citizens. On discussing his decision to step down from the bench, he declared it "more important that we have an adequate celebration in terms of a lesson in civics, in history, than for me to remain on the Supreme Court another few years."[64]

The original document was placed on continuous display for eighty-seven hours in the rotunda of the National Archives as September 17, Constitution Day, approached. During those three-plus days alone—what Archives staff called a constitutional "vigil"—almost 40,000 people waited in line to view the manuscript. On the 17, the *CBS Evening News* with Dan Rather "opened and closed in the Rotunda."[65] In Philadelphia, festivities on September 17 embodied what the *New York Times* called "the climax of a yearlong celebration,"[66] complete with "a four-hour nationally televised parade" and concluding with another televised "nighttime entertainment gala."[67] On the steps of Independence Hall, President Reagan declared that "it was then—in 1787—that the revolution truly began."[68] His proclamation underscored a now commonplace view: the total identification of nationhood and the Declaration of Independence with fidelity to the Constitution.

Along with parade festivities, perhaps the most noteworthy activity of the bicentennial year involved the repeated request from various organizers to have citizens sign their name to the text, just as the drafters did two hundred years earlier. The National Conference of Christians and Jews (NCCJ), with its roots in the pre–World War II tri-faith project of creedal toleration, "collected signatures from six million Americans on copies of the Constitution, reaffirming their allegiance to the document."[69] Visitors to the National Archive's "vigil" were similarly asked "to affix their names to a document that [would] be preserved permanently at the Archives."[70] As for the central bicentennial exhibit in Philadelphia—housed at the Second Bank of the United States and tellingly titled "Miracle at Philadelphia"—visitors were also invited to add their signature.[71] Writing at the time, the legal scholar Sanford Levinson saw the persistent invocation of religious language alongside these requests as part of a pervasive treatment of the Constitution as a "sacred object": the document and its traditions embodied nothing less than the country's "civil religion."[72]

For individuals like Attorney General Meese, these were all positive developments. Indeed, he had seen the approaching constitutional bicentennial as another opportunity to spread the true "meaning of constitutional fidelity."[73] But establishment voices of skepticism did exist. For Thurgood Marshall, now long entrenched as a justice on the Supreme Court, the bicentennial constitutional culture appeared little more than an exercise in idolatry, complete with the "blind pilgrimage to the shrine" on the part of the faithful.

Marshall saw all of this as serving a broader politics, but not one of constitutional rededication—as Barbara Jordan may have wanted. Instead he saw merely conservative restoration and national triumphalism. In response, he declared that he did not "find the wisdom, foresight, and sense of justice exhibited by the framers particularly profound. To the contrary, the government they devised was defective from the start, requiring several amendments, a civil war, and momentous social transformation to attain the system of constitutional government, and its respect for the individual freedoms and human rights, that we hold as fundamental today. When contemporary Americans cite 'The Constitution,' they invoke a concept that is vastly different from what the framers barely began to construct two centuries ago." For Marshall, whatever was worth defending about the constitutional system resulted from the arduous effort and toil of many individuals who had initially been excluded from its purview. Thus, he planned to spend September 17 "quietly commemorat[ing] the suffering, struggle, and sacrifice that has triumphed over much of what was wrong with the original document, and observ[ing] the anniversary with hopes not realized and promises not fulfilled."[74]

Marshall's words were a striking commentary from a central Black proponent of the mid-century Cold War creed. As discussed in chapter 12, he had once referred to the overall American constitutional model as the "best I've ever seen."[75] The fact that he—a constitutional believer and committed Cold Warrior—openly rejected the bicentennial celebration spoke to his perception of how decisively the dominant constitutional politics appeared to shut the door on further social change.

Unlike during the post–World War II years, this closure against continuing reform proceeded even if one embraced all the terms of the Cold War compact. After all, Marshall himself had engaged in this full embrace: backing everything from anti-communism to market capitalism, global primacy to the basic justness of American statecraft. In the 1950s and 1960s, Marshall had championed the American model, at home and abroad, because of a genuine faith that it offered a mechanism for inclusion and material prosperity. Now most aspects of that economic and racial agenda were foreclosed, even in its more moderate and ameliorate versions. As such, bicentennial encomiums to the genius of the framers left a bitter taste in his mouth.

The fact that Marshall, hardly a radical figure during earlier decades, stood out as a lonely public voice of bicentennial skepticism offered yet another indicator of the times. It spoke to the degree to which the "Left" had become "conspicuous by its absence," as Todd Gitlin remarked that same constitutional bicentennial year.[76] As late as 1976, Panther activists like Elaine Brown could still bring thousands of people into the streets for counterprotests that directly challenged the basic legitimacy the American nation-state and its founders. But those days were long gone. Now the only notes of dissent seemed to come from well within the Center-Left establishment.

Crucially, this dissent only appeared through a register of living constitutionalism, as with Marshall's comments. It was certainly true that over the following years, Marshall's basic view—veneration of the living Constitution, but with a healthy dose of skepticism about the eighteenth-century founders—did become a type of Left-liberal conventional wisdom within the legal professoriate.[77] This was especially the case as conservative originalism gained even greater power on the federal bench and in the culture at large. Yet, perhaps for that very reason, even when liberal academics engaged with the public, they tended to package their accounts of constitutional change in ways that avoided Marshall's bluntness.

Take as a small indicator the original name of the most established liberal legal organization present today on law campuses, pushing back against the Federalist Society. Founded in 2001, the group is now known as the American Constitution Society. But as an initial pilot program at Georgetown University Law Center, it started as the Madison Society for Law and Policy—not to be outdone by the Federalist Society. Whatever liberal law professors—shaped by the civil rights and women's movements—may have actually thought about Madison, an enslaver, this was a telling first choice. It suggested the sense of political unease involved in publicly disavowing the founding generation, even in the way that Marshall did. Any explicit skepticism seemed a way to consign oneself to the political margins—even if the skepticism was ultimately constitutionally faithful, and a far cry from earlier Socialist and Black radical critiques.

Conclusion: Mythmaking and Founders Worship after the Cold War

One final factor played a key role in shaping American constitutional culture at the end of the twentieth century and the beginning of the twenty-first: the disintegration of the Soviet Union. That disintegration became all the confirmation one needed of the country's exceptionalism and constitutional greatness. For Democrats and Republicans alike, Soviet collapse effectively closed debates about alternatives to the American model.

This meant that victory did not cause the old Cold War orthodoxy to wither away. Instead, it supercharged a late-twentieth-century version of that orthodoxy. Soviet breakdown seemed to further bolster the legitimacy of capitalism and, beyond that, of the unregulated variety that increasingly defined American life. On race, it was true that extensive structural disparities persisted between white and Black society. But the integration of elite institutions, and the growth of the Black middle and professional classes, reinforced the idea that the page had indeed been turned on past struggles. As for international power, the notion of American indispensability gained yet more currency. Perhaps American interventionism or state violence had proved excessive in the past. But now the fall of communism offered the only proof one seemed to need for the basic goodness of the national project, at home and abroad.

With respect to the Constitution, that sense of near perfection became ever more ubiquitous in collective life. As the legal scholar Mark Tushnet wrote in 2005 of the mood of the times, Americans overwhelmingly took for granted that "the existing Constitution" was "entirely adequate to meet the needs of contemporary society."[78] This idealization of the governing system went hand in hand with a particular nonfiction literary culture. For decades, the most widespread and acclaimed historical works—consumed by Americans across the political spectrum— were panegyrics to the great statesmen of the past. And these panegyrics focused especially on the eighteenth-century founders,[79] returning time and again to their wisdom and subtlety.

Indeed, one such biography provided the basis for one of the most popular (and, indeed, artistically remarkable) creations of the early twenty-first century—a musical in honor of none other than Alexander Hamilton. A national sensation, it was distinctive for starring a largely minority cast in the roles of the Anglo-American revolutionary elites. Emblematically, this presentation of the settler founding replicated the broader constitutional flattening that had become so pervasive. In the musical, Hamilton is anachronistically depicted as a proto-creedalist and proto-abolitionist. Just as disconcertingly, he also becomes the avatar for a meritocratic and racially inclusive twentieth-century nation of immigrants (even declaring, "Immigrants: we get the job done").[80]

In effect, Americans, almost regardless of race, had reconstructed the meaning of their own past such that, most of the time, the actual settler history no longer resonated with the country's self-perception. In all this historical mythmaking and hagiography, much was clearly lost. Certainly, memories of the SPA's constitutional politics of mass democracy and the Black radical vision of decolonization had faded away. But so had the questions—raised by King in those months before his murder—of whether Americans would be willing to confront the structural hierarchies of their own society or the forms of power that they projected abroad.

Simply turning the page on such matters suppressed, for a time, real social conflicts. But as our present confirms, without confronting these questions it is impossible to suppress them permanently or to entirely erase them from collective life.

Constitutional Accounting

At the close of the twentieth century, the dominant American mood may have been marked by pervasive faith in the American model. But the convulsive events since, touching virtually every aspect of American society, fundamentally punctured such faith. The country has experienced endless military overreach in places like Afghanistan and Iraq, launched in part on false premises and punctuated by rights violations abroad as well as security excesses at home. It has faced a near economic collapse in the context of the 2007–2008 global financial meltdown and then a combined health and economic crisis in the form of the COVID-19 pandemic. As the country reeled from these socioeconomic disasters, exacerbated by extreme class inequalities, the carceral state's generational effects on poor and Black communities led to mass protest and social rebellion unlike anything Americans had witnessed since the 1960s. On top of everything else, Donald Trump's presidency seemed to expose the hollowness of any invocation of national exceptionalism, particularly given his misogyny, racism, and open willingness to subvert elections.

Such events may seem unrelated. But each of these crises emerged from policies based in core assumptions about the American model and its global project: commitment to the moral value of US interventionism, faith in the market and in a capitalist economic system, and the presumption that domestic legal-political institutions were basically just—bending toward racial equality and inclusion and simply needing small-scale reforms. The policies that launched the nation down these paths fit neatly within the official Cold War creedal constitutional frame. And, as political elites responded, the dominance of that frame led them back to the same old toolkit: more intervention, more marketized social services, more minor racial and economic adjustments.

The size of these crises would have made them difficult to contain under any circumstances. But they were further exacerbated by the unremedied flaws of the constitutional system, particularly by how it paralyzed popular majorities while facilitating minority rule. Starting in the years immediately after the breakup of the Soviet Union, then accelerating with the election of the first Black president in 2008, American political decision-making became defined by an intensifying divergence between what many Americans wanted and what their legal-political institutions generated. Indeed, even if political elites had the creative imagination to pursue large-scale change, it became seemingly impossible—given the need for overwhelming supermajorities—for popularly backed reforms to make their way through governing arrangements.

In a sense, we have witnessed the completion of a political cycle. The internal limitations of the country's political, economic, and cultural path in the half century since the Left's systematic defeat in the 1970s have been laid bare. Not only have social problems proven too endemic to remedy through that old Cold War compact, with its official version of the creedal constitution. In addition, the Right has so thoroughly chipped away at the welfarist constraints on corporate power that key socially legitimating elements of the mid-century settlement no longer exist. This results in a modern politics—complete with socialists *and* white nationalists—less beholden to the conventional terms of Cold War politics than at any time since the 1960s, or perhaps even since the social struggles preceding the Cold War. The US continues to wield outsized global power. But, in effect, Americans collectively seem to have come unmoored from the sureties and ideological premises that had for so long dictated political life.

All this points back to the same dilemma that left-leaning movements struggled with in the 1970s, not to mention in the early twentieth century. The question returns of how to create a truly transformative majority, at once cross-racial and class conscious. And, echoing those historical moments, neither this dilemma nor the country's broader crises can be seriously confronted without overcoming the fundamental weaknesses of the American constitutional system.

How We Teach (and Learn) the Constitution

These developments carry a particular professional meaning for me as a law professor, in which capacity I teach constitutional law each fall to first-year students. Over the last decade, I have come to find something about my own field especially concerning. The course I oversee, modeled after other classes long taught at American law schools, had remarkably little to say about virtually any of these dilemmas as they unfolded. And this disconnect was reflected back to me by the students themselves. Even if they did not identify as part of the Left, more and more of them were dismayed by everything from the Supreme Court and its growing divergence—on issues like abortion rights—from public sentiment to the dysfunctional realities of representation in the Senate and of presidential candidates winning the popular vote but losing elections. I felt confronted by questions, whether stated or unstated, that had never been part of my training: Why had the American model broken down? Why was the constitutional system intensifying both social crises and white authoritarianism? And how could Americans build the type of movement politics capable of transforming their legal-institutional landscape?

This is because constitutional law in the United States—as described in earlier chapters—focuses primarily on the internal analysis of judicial, particularly Supreme Court, decision-making. More or less the entire scope of a constitutional law class consists in examining how judges resolved legal professional disputes about the textual interpretation of key clauses.

For this reason, course topics generally revolve around those matters that past Supreme Court justices considered worthy of deliberation. The only significant reform conversation that typically occurs in the class centers on the kind of reform that the Court deemed important to address through its doctrine or that ultimately could be implemented through shifts in judicial interpretation. The result has been a course that sometimes appears to exist in an alternate universe. And teaching it seems to require first bracketing out the prevailing realities, and then proceeding as if we still live in the comforting days of the Constitution's bicentennial.

These tendencies were just as pronounced in the legal scholarship. Most traditional constitutional writing produced by law professors has involved doctrinal explication or engagement with big-picture theories about how judges should interpret the Constitution. Indeed, until very recently this general atmosphere permeated most law schools. Even the name the liberal founders of the Madison Society eventually settled on, the American Constitution Society, spoke to this disconnect. No Progressive-era reformist group would have given itself such a moniker.

This name, in the early twentieth century, would have immediately re-verberated with the "professional patriotism" of the business Right. Of course, times have changed, and such a name represented a rhetorical ef-fort to claim the Constitution for reformist ends by left-leaning lawyers who, after *Brown*, embraced a living constitutionalist approach.

Yet, as the Trump presidency proceeded, there seemed something deeply antiquated about holding on to a politics of constitutional re-dedication as the primary language for reform. In a sense, past left-of-center strategic choices, from the 1930s to the fallout of student and civil rights protest, were clearly compelling in their time—and they bore undeniable fruit for politicians and reformers. But each defensible choice was a step further down a path that, along with numerous ex-ogenous factors, left the country adrift without the political resources and institutional arrangements to address deep-seated problems in the present. And despite it all, it was as if legal training, and much of the legal professional elite, remained in a Cold War cultural moment, even as none of those terms continued to make sense of the structural reality confronting Americans.

Thus, over these last few years I confronted a central dilemma in my own teaching: namely, the extent to which I felt ill-equipped to answer increasingly present (and pressing) questions about the overarching constitutional system: Where did this pervasive constitutional venera-tion come from? How did it intersect with the main ideological battles of collective life? What were the alternative visions of constitutional possibility?

I suspected that the constitutional law field—which might reason-ably be asked these questions—was itself a key product of the very de-velopments that warranted explanation. As I wrote this book, I began to see it as a belated, and in some sense personal, constitutional educa-tion. I wanted to resolve for myself important questions that I felt un-able to answer and that I therefore too rarely presented to my students. Indeed, this project has at least partly been something of an origin story for my field—a field that has deeply shaped the nation's understanding of its political structures, and yet is seemingly disconnected at just the moment when Americans require serious interrogation of their consti-tutional system.

In completing the book, I have increasingly come to believe that to make our way out of the general American fog, the broader public needs to fully reclaim cultural and political ownership of both con-stitutional memory and constitutional politics from a small coterie of judges and lawyers. Such a reclamation would, I hope, place transformative agendas—like those that once circulated broadly—at the heart of collective conversations going forward.

Should Lawyers Own the Constitution?

Understandably, given the extreme power of the Supreme Court and the federal bench, most people concerned with constitutional politics today follow court cases. They may even echo some of the discursive norms of judges and professional lawyers. But what would it mean for the broader public to develop a separate identity and to take control of constitutional memory and constitutional politics?

REJECTING THE CONSTITUTIONAL ARBITERS

It is perfectly comprehensible for lawyers at law schools to focus their study and teaching of the Constitution on court cases and on judicial practices. These schools are in the business of training future members of a particular profession, and our educational responsibility rests in preparing them for practice in the law. Furthermore, any real reckoning with the modern American state requires a proper understanding of the logics of the judiciary. Given the constraints of the amendment process, the US has a system that channels constitutional change into the courts, further expanding their power and emphasizing the importance of legal debates over textual interpretation. All of this underscores the obvious and clear value of the profession's work, as well as the importance of the internal debates that have consumed the study of constitutional law.

The problem, however, concerns the effects of this focus on the broader political culture. A very particular professionalized space seems to dominate American knowledge production and cultural memory around the meaning of the constitutional system as a whole. Due to specific mid-twentieth-century dynamics, the constitutional law field today remains defined by its professional and cultural investment in the existing legal-political infrastructure and by its distinctive relationship with powerful state actors, especially members of the federal bench. But such federal judges, whatever their virtues, are not structurally unbiased actors. They are governing elites forged by a very specific vision of the Constitution. And, as embodiments of the American state, they are also institutional players whose activity involves an imposition of that state's will. By training, they have limited experience in how to think of large-scale alternatives to the contemporary organization of state and economy.

By contrast, the more expansive questions underpinning today's controversies—over basic constitutional design, imperial power, structural hierarchies, or capitalist market relations—do not routinely appear in the courtroom. And even if they *did* appear in a courtroom, many federal judges—both center-left and conservative—would be unmoved. Given their ideological commitments and professional acculturation, most are among the political actors who have drunk deeply from the well of constitutional veneration, complete with a belief in the majesty of the Supreme Court and faith generally in the ideological terms of the American project.

Just as critically, and as unsurprisingly, many in the constitutional law professoriate have shared much the same romance around the Constitution and its related national narrative. This romance implicitly underpins a defense of the elite bar's professional work and embedded relationships. For the better part of a century now, most constitutional law professors have been trained by legal academics with deep personal connections to members of the bench. They then worked as clerks for those federal judges and Supreme Court justices and, in fact, often understand their function as precisely participating in a common conversation with the judiciary and on the judiciary's terms. This conversation, including the scholarship that results, provides conceptual framing and synthesis to court decisions and may gently move judges in more fruitful directions. Naturally, constitutional scholars have been opposed to particular decisions and even to the overall interpretative approach of specific justices. But the American legal academic elite has for decades acculturated to the norms and ends of the judiciary; it thus operates in some ways as an effective extension of the bench.

Most problematically, it was not only constitutional law courses that appeared trapped in an alternate universe, seemingly detached from the country's broader structural problems and discussions. More or less the entirety of popular American constitutional awareness seemed similarly entangled, given the centrality of judge-centered scholarship and commentary to general collective understandings. Over the previous hundred years, the legal expert, as a distinctive type of constitutional believer, had emerged to direct the overall conversation about the Constitution. And the general political culture seemed to simply assume the positionality of that constitutional law expert—instead of maintaining a separate existence as a constituency *outside* of and distinct from the professional field. Even "popular constitutionalism" often proceeded through movement actors engaging in lawyerly interpretation and rhetorical invocations for the imagined or real judge.

The problem, of course, is that judges—and the legal professionals who have revered and venerated them—are embodiments of a constitutional order that now appears broken, and that has never truly worked for those at the bottom. At a time of rolling national crises and institutional dysfunction, perhaps we should not grant such actors virtually exclusive power to define what counts as a constitutional matter and what must stay outside the bounds of constitutional discussion. And yet our shared political inheritance hands the reins of constitutional authorship, memory, and knowledge to such officials and lawyers, to the exclusion of nearly everyone else.

THE LIMITATION AND PROMISE OF LEGAL-ELITE ACTIVITY

Given the undeniable legal-political realities of the contemporary era, more constitutional scholars are now thinking creatively about basic institutional redesign. This is a very welcome development. But many likely share the same limitations I have faced in teaching introductory constitutional law courses: we have been granted expert status with respect to this document, but our expertise has little to say about how the existing Constitution became so intertwined with the very definition of the American project, or about what that means for a present in which both seem to be under siege. Thus, for all the real positives of current legal scholarly attention to matters of design, this attention can tend to reproduce the general problems with the elite bar's long-term constitutional ownership.

Indeed, new cross-partisan academic exercises in fixing broken elements of the constitutional order often treat the issue as an almost scientific matter of technical management. Take the National Constitution Center's Constitutional Drafting Project, completed in 2020, which had teams of "libertarian," "progressive," and "conservative" legal experts construct alternative design remedies, in the process seeking to find common ground across the aisle. Similarly, President Joe Biden's commission on the Supreme Court, launched in April 2021, proceeded on the assumption that a lawyerly elite, ranging from George Bush Jr.–appointed federal judges to liberal constitutional law professors, could devise a workable, nonpartisan fix for what ails the courts.

For starters, such initiatives implicitly reinforce the idea that a legal professional class should enjoy authorial status over constitutional politics writ large, even when this politics has little to do with the actual courtroom expertise claimed by lawyers. Moreover, reform projects framed in this way can fall prey to the old Cold War constitutional parameters: they aspire to a consensual middle course, with jointly agreed upon policy adjustments—and this can once more paper over the fundamental conflicts of interest exposed in recent years. Such an orientation also can reproduce a version of mid-twentieth-century founders worship, again presenting past framers as apolitical architects and hoping that a legal elite may step into those familiar shoes and play a similar drafting or reform function. Thus, even if the 1787 text is less glorified, the Cold War and anti-populist ideal of elite statesmanship, exemplified by the framers, often circulates.

Still, legal-elite exercises in drafting new constitutions should not be totally dismissed. Some embody real institutional experimentation, and they indicate the present moment's greater ideological openness. Furthermore, particular proposals can be valuable points of contact and conversation between the law professoriate and movement activists. Indeed, lawyers will inevitably have an important role to play in any collective project of constitutional reform, given the continuing power of the courts and the overarching role of the legal profession as key intermediaries between individuals and institutions. Legal experts remain essential for navigating everyday personal encounters with state and corporate entities; they also have insight into how those entities can subvert constitutional and legal structures for their own ends. The profession as a whole therefore offers a significant site of advice and knowledge about the transformative implications of various constitutional adjustments, as well as the trade-offs involved in specific strategic choices. Lawyers also have real value in defending activists and marginalized persons from public and private violence, as well as in helping to develop arguments legally cognizable within the prevailing terms of judicial doctrine and government practice.

But, again, none of this means that the current legal professional class should direct the constitutional reform agenda. Indeed, twentieth-century history suggests that the elite bar's control will tend to promote a narrower technocratic approach,[1] focusing change on the legal-political questions and institutions most related to scholarly expertise in the Constitution. Even despite the best and most expansive intentions, this may rein in ideas of constitutional possibility—of what can be included in a constitutional system in the first place.

Thus, while the legal profession has a clear function going forward, in my view this role should diverge fundamentally from the mid-twentieth-century vision of the litigator as a driving social change agent—not to mention the mythic depiction of the constitutional framers as apolitical statesmen. Instead, lawyers are better conceived of as simply one of the various social constituencies with views about institutional reform: at decisive moments, legal activists may mobilize in concert with other groups to press for particular changes. Such lawyers may operate in conjunction with movements, or (in certain contexts) even become movement constituents themselves. Their constitutional legal work can also provide one of the many vital services required by organized bases and vulnerable groups. And at least part of the value of such work would rest on its implications for movement-building, with lawyerly efforts impacting the relative material and political strength of those at the margins.[2]

Claiming Control of the Constitution

These last decades' clear ideological limitations make evident the problems with handing over the reins of change to a professional class shaped by the Cold War creedal constitutional sensibility of the twentieth century. But any repositioning (or demoting) of the constitutional lawyer underscores that this moment requires genuine popular ownership of the memory, terms, and ambitions of constitutional politics.

EXPANDING WHERE CONSTITUTIONAL POLITICS TAKES PLACE

All of this speaks broadly to a key reform objective: moving the locus of constitutional politics from the insulated spaces of the judiciary to arenas, including legislatures, that are more open to the demands and language of mass movements and mobilized publics. Although written constitutions are commonly imagined as embodying the polity's fundamental principles, that presentation is a poor match for the US situation, where the hurdles of the amendment process push any debate over these principles back into the courts, with all their democratic weaknesses.

These pervasive constraints on textual alteration indicate that, at least for the time being, focusing on rewriting a constitutional text may not be markedly productive. And especially when formal revision is foreclosed, popular constitutional control entails rejecting a culturally originalist and textualist fixation with only the Constitution's words, let alone with how they are interpreted by empowered judges.

As such, conversation should appreciate how legislative settings can be sites of constitutional overhaul, similar to how FDR conceived of the Second Bill of Rights.[3] That project sought to expand, both in law and in the broader discourse, what counted as enduring values and institutional commitments—and it was understood to be an exercise primarily in legislative constitutionalism. Worship of the 1787 text, alongside an originalist constitutional culture, has meant that Americans rarely think of legislation as how basic commitments routinely become entrenched. Yet a range of twentieth-century bills—such as the Civil Rights and Voting Rights Acts—provided the legal basis for Cold War creedal constitutionalism, well beyond the written words of long-deceased framers.

Such a change in collective orientation would direct attention to the question of *where* mass movements and organized majorities can best exercise sustained control. It would also further underscore the need to clear away the obstacles that today block avenues for popular lawmaking, from the constraints on legislation all the way to those on textual amendments.

CONSTITUTIONAL VISIONS BEYOND
THE COLD WAR MYTHS

But constitutionalism cannot simply move to different legal-political spaces. Instead, its content and even its heroes require significant rethinking. And such rethinking entails the arduous project of reshaping a collective memory fundamentally constructed by cultural life during the Cold War.

This means, in part, reviving the constitutional visions of pre- and anti–Cold War activists, whose reform imaginations extended well beyond what Supreme Court justices condoned or even conceived of as a constitutional subject. When Americans look to their constitutional history for inspiration and community-building, they need struggles and figures besides the often deified eighteenth-century framers, and the later presidents and judges who have soaked up so much of the conversation.

In fact, an implication of Black internationalist politics is that inspiration, or a sense of shared constitutional imagination, need not assume co-nationality. A broad array of such activists saw a common and global anti-colonial project as highlighting how their relevant interlocutors were often in the Third World: individuals like Jawaharlal Nehru or the Kenyan independence leader Oginga Odinga. Today, even when Americans think in comparative terms about constitutionalism, they seek engagement from the same internationally circulating community of legally trained experts and jurists. But someone like Odinga, given his own politically grounded analysis of the limits of a model for Kenya mirroring the US federal Constitution, may have more productive insights for movement constituents than those typically stamped as the experts one learns from. In this way, reshaping constitutional memory implicitly entails profoundly reconceiving, including in internationalist terms, our intellectual and political inheritances.

Relatedly, constitutional rethinking should claim the imaginative space to dramatically alter what types of rights and institutional arrangements may be written into the text of a document, and what is understood as *constitutional*. As mentioned in the preceding chapters, the federal Constitution is an outlier, compared to other countries and to US state constitutions—not only for the incredible difficulty of amending it, but also for its brevity and overwhelming focus on property and negative rights. Americans often imagine that a national text can only deal with those elements included in the basic outlines of the 1787 model. Yet there is no reason why a constitution could not move beyond tinkering with electoral and judicial structures to include the kinds of sociopolitical demands that galvanized past movements and that link to various global examples today.

The great Left traditions of alternative American constitutionalism, especially tied to socialist democracy and anti-colonial politics, point to these basic reconsiderations. Their historic critiques of the governing order—grounded in the claim that the US has never been a true democracy—remain just as apt. And taken together, their institutional and ideological vision for a reconceived country combine an expansive project of domestic liberation with that of a non-imperial future.

With respect to analysis of the infrastructure of the federal government, one can do worse than some of the insights of the 1912 Socialist Party of America (SPA) platform. Socialists argued that a legal-political system empowering the many, rather than the few, should base constitutionalism in legislative and popular majorities. As such, their platform sought to eliminate the Senate and the Electoral College, break up the system of state-based representation, dramatically extend voting rights, systematically implement proportional representation across government (for instance, by having multimember House districts), constrain presidential power, simplify the amendment process, and impose fundamental reforms on the bench.

All of these proposals have either direct relevance to the present or clear twenty-first-century analogues.[4] With respect to the Senate, one could imagine (alongside disbandment) defusing the intensity of its malapportionment through the addition of population-based senators as well as by moving toward something akin to Britain's House of Lords—with a far more limited ability in the upper house to block legislation.

As for the courts, this may mean personnel shifts—mentioned in chapter 1—such as relatively short term limits and dramatic expansions of the number of judges on the Supreme Court, in the process deemphasizing the significance of any one judge. Such a project could also include checks on the extreme power of American-style judicial review, through everything from supermajority requirements for court decisions to allowing congressional override of rulings through legislative action. Along with a simplified amendment process, these institutional alterations would ensure that court-based interpretation was no longer the core of actual constitutional decision-making. The resulting design vision would bring constitutional and regular lawmaking closer together, allowing popular majorities to renegotiate the existing order in ways more responsive to public need.

At the same time, the insights of Black and Indigenous radicals also remain critical. They contended that, in the end, real changes to the basic terms of state and economy would not endure unless Americans also examined and revised the society's colonial infrastructure. Take, for example, the Panthers' constitution-writing exercise, which hoped to formally incorporate a set of explicitly decolonial commitments into a new document. While aiming now to draft new constitutional language may be premature, these underlying ideas nonetheless offer a valuable jumping-off point.

Along comparable lines, one could call for a serious commitment to real self-determination for Indigenous nations and for territories such as Puerto Rico and Guam. This might involve new institutions, grounded in respect for treaties, to negotiate policy with sovereign Native nations; versions of monetary and land-based reparations, at home but also for communities abroad that have faced security state intervention; universally guaranteed socioeconomic rights, income, and job provisions alongside other forms of resource redistribution to historically subordinated populations; and even the extensive demobilization and reimagining of the military, security, and policing frameworks.

During the Revolutionary People's Constitutional Convention, key Black Panther Party activists also made common cause with feminist groups. Following the work of Afeni Shakur, Beulah Sanders, and many others, such ideas in the present can similarly treat basic changes to the gendered division of labor, along with strong reproductive rights, as vital to any vision of constitutional change. Linking race, gender, class, and empire emphasizes the interlocked nature of hierarchy and thus of freedom. It also connects to the further Panther aim of viewing concrete legal-political changes as bound to symbolic and cultural changes in national self-understanding and identity.

Even if many of these ideas are currently outside mainstream political debate, they suggest a vision of constitutionalism very different from that traditionally offered by legal-political elites. They bring to the foreground analytical frameworks that circulated in past movement politics, but that were overwhelmingly treated by constitutional decision-makers as irrelevant or incompatible with the country's governing projects. Explicitly recovering these alternative understandings can highlight the value, today, of mobilized groups reclaiming authorial control and developing their own rich accounts of constitutional meaning and history.

Perhaps above all, this rethinking of constitutionalism requires us to grapple with a key observation: that what *counts* as a constitutional matter can become a stand-in for essential debates about who has power in society, and on what terms. The Socialist and Panther parties focused attention on the federal Constitution in part because they saw it as a decisive symbolic representation of the overarching social order. In the United States, they believed that in practice this order gave sovereign power to a racial and class elite. At exceptional moments of social ferment, it nonetheless may have been the case that partial reforms became achievable. But the basic operation of existing institutions systematically strengthened the hand of socially dominant groups—groups whose interests opposed those of most in society.

Socialist and Panther activists thought of constitutional change not just as a matter of finding fixes for particular institutional dysfunctions. Their efforts sprang from a guiding commitment to altering the prevailing distribution of power as such. They thus sought a legal, political, and economic system that invested sovereign authority in all constituencies, including those at the margins. They cared about the Constitution because their driving political concerns centered on the foundational matter of who actually exercised power across the landscape of institutional life.

This way of thinking about constitutionalism fundamentally rejects a common presentation, which depicts courts—and the text more generally—as sites where policymakers can tinker with interpretation or procedural arrangements, largely independent of underlying social cleavages and struggles. In opposition to that classic frame, these earlier activists believed that constitutional politics should place those struggles front and center—always questioning where sovereign authority actually and dynamically resides across governing arrangements in any given moment.

This does not mean that such an approach is only zero-sum. Both Crystal Eastman and Martin Luther King Jr. recognized that, in a structurally hierarchical society like the United States, meaningful change would have to produce winners and losers. Yet they also maintained that claiming power for those most marginalized was the necessary condition for creating a social order that truly belonged to everyone. Shifts in sovereign power would not only address ongoing structural injustices; ensuring equal and effective freedom for oppressed communities would also make such freedom broadly accessible and meaningful for all.

The Role of Constitutional Politics in Building a Transformative Majority

Although support for real transformation remains, for now, a decidedly minority position, the moment nonetheless fundamentally differs from that of a half century ago. Generational and demographic shifts— alongside the acknowledged problems of the American model and of connected presumptions about global primacy—have produced a contemporary Left more self-assertive and widely resonant than at any time since perhaps the 1930s and 1940s. This results in real intellectual and political space for the articulation of new horizons, and in a plausible (if not necessarily probable) institutional path forward. But this path would require a new constitutional politics—one engaged with the Constitution but well outside the creedal constitutional myths of the last century—to support that long-standing effort to build a transformative majority in American society.

Today, just as a century ago, some activists express real skepticism about engaging with the constitutional domain at all—often out of opposition to the domination of the domain by legal experts and technocratic policy approaches. Ultimately, coalitional movements themselves must develop the ends and strategic means of any emerging politics, including by addressing the issues of whether to focus on, and how to pursue, interventions in the existing constitutional system.

But groups like the SPA and earlier Black and Third World radicals like W. E. B. Du Bois, Harry Haywood, and James and Grace Lee Boggs cautioned against such disavowal of constitutional politics altogether. These older socialist traditions—whether connected to labor, Black, or feminist politics—offer more than just expansive reform ideas that can be picked up or adapted. They highlight the value for movements of having a constitutional *politics* while refusing to fall prey to the fetishizing of constitutional law.

In ways deeply relevant for the present, they underscored that courts, for instance, remained an extraordinarily powerful site for the application of state power. And the design of legal institutions has produced deeply distorting effects on our politics, fundamentally constraining the capacity of transformative majorities to pursue liberating change. Constitutional arrangements establish the rules of the game, so to speak, and any effort to seek extensive change without struggle over these rules would result in a profound disadvantage.

Indeed, even if one wanted to create a social order that dramatically decentered the importance of any constitutional text and its privileged interpreters in the judiciary, movements and activists nonetheless require an account of how their political struggles intersect with the constitutional domain. They need an understanding of when and how to use the courts, even if only to hold those in power to rules they themselves have accepted or to provide marginalized communities with a reprieve from everyday violence. Movements also need an approach as to which institutional reforms in the constitutional landscape could have transformative implications—and which means to use, as between elections, litigation, and mass strikes, for example. Otherwise, whether or not activists explicitly foreground proceduralist questions—such as what to do with the Senate or the Supreme Court—their efforts will inevitably bump up against the structural limitations of the legal-political framework broadly understood.

A GOVERNMENT BEHIND THE GOVERNMENT

Still, the SPA and other voices agreed that movements must not imagine the end goal in terms akin to Left-liberal constitutional lawyers. Such legal experts generally frame their proposals—which often suggest valuable policy reforms—in ways that ultimately reaffirm the existing order, with all its structural and symbolic limitations. And even when more mainstream reformers explicitly call for something different, these calls are usually conceived of in deeply apolitical terms—they are about finding a new, idealized constitutional alternative that would stand above ordinary politics.

By contrast, earlier generations of socialists and fellow activists were often deeply suspicious of any vision of constitutionalism premised on the sanctification of a fundamental law—even with respect to their own constitutional achievements. Given the profound disparities in power and resources, existing processes were *always* susceptible to manipulation by those who enjoyed economic and political dominance within the status quo. These Left voices worried that, if new arrangements were idealized—with constitutions and constitution-making again placed beyond meaningful popular engagement—the result might well preserve oppressive power imbalances, even as it rearranged their terms. This emphasized the importance of allowing marginalized and working people to operate within institutional spaces that permanently provided them the room to push for further change, including by reimagining the basic parameters of the legal-political system.

For all these reasons, figures from Eugene Debs, Allan Benson, and Eastman to Du Bois, Haywood, and the Boggses did not think of constitutionalism as a constraint on democracy. Rather, they viewed it as one site for ongoing experimentation in response to emerging hierarchies as well as to new political horizons. In fact, they saw such constitutional flexibility as facilitating both democracy *and* rights protection, instead of considering these two goals as inherently in tension. This was because activists like Eastman considered racial and economic elites the primary threats to everything from civil rights and civil liberties to reproductive and labor protections. Even if some degree of counter-majoritarianism might be necessary, too much counter-majoritarianism would liberate these elites to trample on the rights of the oppressed and poor.

Instead, the best way to promote a generally rights-respecting culture was to develop the type of organized majority that could serve as a permanently active "government behind the government." Far more than deeply insulated elites, such a majority would be likely to embrace rights guarantees as in its own interests and thus to defend such guarantees in public life. And this collective entity would most clearly express itself in the legal-political arena through mobilization, legislation, and amendment. Thus, the best long-term means of safeguarding vulnerable groups from danger involved the promotion of a society in which expansive guarantees were conceived of as popular rights, won through mass commitment.

CONSTITUTIONAL POLITICS, POWER-BUILDING, AND POLITICAL ECONOMY

Because of their focus on long-term political struggle and improvement, socialist traditions tended to view all the elements of their agenda as critically about power-building. These activists avoided fixating on any single procedural solution or pathway—even as they may have backed proportional representation, judicial reforms, simplifying the amendment process, or abolishing the Senate. Importantly, they did not even distinguish fundamentally between demands traditionally framed as economic, political, or constitutional. Instead, socialists argued that capitalism and the legal-political system worked hand in glove—by simultaneously undermining labor power at work and poor people's vote in the electoral process—to strengthen the few and weaken the many.

Therefore, a key lesson for the present from earlier radicals involves how they viewed the need for things like labor strength in *constitutional* terms, and how they concomitantly engaged in constitutional politics to strengthen labor's hand. Without systematic unionization and working-class power at the point of production, it would be incredibly difficult to match the cultural and material resources that business elites wielded throughout the legal-political system. Achieving and deepening structural changes, including to the Constitution, could not occur without a dramatic expansion in the actual social power of Left constituencies.

Indeed, that connection between constitutionalism and political economy speaks to the great and continuing challenge to any contemporary reform politics: labor's relative cultural and political weakness today is a major hurdle for any genuinely class-conscious popular majority, even with more favorable generational, demographic, and ideological shifts. Simply put, there remains no replacement for the old labor movement as a politicizing force, especially within white society. For all the flaws and exclusivities of pre–Cold War labor solidarity, its galvanizing worldview nonetheless played a significant role among many Americans—pushing multiracial, and even global, class alliances above an appeal to white racial identity or to the nation-state's security objectives.

This suggests that, just as was true a century ago, activists should understand constitutional change as inherently joined to the legal terrain within which workers organize. Just as the voting power of poor people is decidedly compromised by the political process, labor organizes at a severe disadvantage given a deeply unfriendly legal backdrop.[5] That legal environment must be altered in ways that make it far easier for workers to unionize and to strike. Moreover, these workplace transformations are themselves properly understood as profoundly democratizing reforms. They make the institutions people inhabit on a daily basis far more amenable to collective self-rule, and they promote a continuous exercise in shared decision-making. Indeed, as socialists long argued, greater worker authority and representational power in the economy must be viewed as a foundational building block for reshaping—as a *constitutional matter*—who actually enjoys sovereign power in the country.

More generally, a broader set of reforms in the economic, social, and legal-political context can operate in tandem to expand the capacity of marginalized people to have their voices heard and their interests met. These include mechanisms that initially may seem outside the constitutional struggle—like socializing child care, a universal income, a guaranteed non-exploitative job, or the institutional entrenchment of unions. But each would increase the relative power of working people within society, perhaps just as much as various procedural and electoral alterations to the legal-political system.

Thus, by shifting the basic distribution of authority in the society, individual reforms could have what might be considered a constitutional effect: making it harder for business and racial elites to dominate collective life. Moreover, the greater the strength mobilized bases develop in one setting—for instance, in the economic realm—the more likely that they will have the organizational capacity to protect their essential rights and pursue their interests in other domains. As a consequence, earlier Left activists viewed socialism, democracy, and rights as all bound together, and as linked to jointly overcoming what Martin Luther King Jr. called "the giant triplets of racism, materialism, and militarism"—to which we should add sexism and patriarchy. Political actors thus formulated a plethora of specific demands that could be pursued both separately and simultaneously, each of which would be self-reinforcing and would increase the power of those traditionally on the outside.

IMMIGRATION AT THE INTERSECTION OF THE DOMESTIC AND THE FOREIGN

For the anti-colonial tradition broadly understood, whether through the Panthers or the Combahee River Collective, a focus on power-building underscored the need to strengthen those communities whose position in society combined domestic racial, gender, and class oppression with imperial structures. Spotlighting these groups not only brought Americans face to face with the imperial dimensions of their society. It also directed movement efforts toward linking the internal and external dimensions of US elite power—including in constitutional politics—and in the process contesting both dimensions.

Following this thread would, I argue, entail placing issues of immigrant rights front and center. This connection may not be immediately intuitive. But today, immigrant status is perhaps the matter that sits most explicitly at that foreign/domestic intersection. It constitutes an essential component of the struggle over equal and effective freedom for all. Such an effort would involve asking what immigrant freedom requires, particularly when American interventionism and economic power have often shaped the conditions under which people leave their homes for the United States. John F. Kennedy's "nation of immigrants" story presented the country as an exceptional polity that had, out of moral beneficence, been kind enough to admit those in need. But the historical reality is far more complex. From the very earliest days of North American colonization, the United States has controlled the movement, both within and outside its formal borders, of various outsider communities—including Black people, Mexicans, Asians, and Indigenous nations—whose labor or land may have been required but whose status was fundamentally contested.

Formal racial restrictions may no longer be in effect today. Yet the

application of a flawed quota system to Latin America reaffirms the old
settler hierarchies, especially by treating Mexican migrants as more or
less equivalent to migrants from any country in Europe or Asia, despite
the much deeper economic ties across the border. It means that the US
relationship to non-white, especially Latin American, immigrant workers within its borders continues to be one of economic extraction and
discretionary power. Indeed, the current treatment of such migrant labor reproduces many of the classic practices of the settler and Jim Crow
past. Undocumented individuals in particular often find themselves engaged in hard and exploitative work, the result of long-standing and
state-sponsored capitalist patterns of production, and under the continuous threat of legally sanctioned intimidation and violence. Just as
in the nineteenth century, such migrants constitute a racially subordinated class further denied meaningful protections—including ordinary legal recourse for harms and political rights like voting—as a result of their dependent status.

In this way, migration embodies a critical site in which one can see the
lasting effects of American empire: as a project of both settlerism and
global primacy. Whatever may be the theoretical legitimacy of closed
borders for a small, postcolonial state in the Global South, such arguments do not apply very easily to the United States, as an imperial hegemon that has used control over movement to extract wealth and project
dominance. A natural extension of the goal of decolonization therefore
might be the embrace of presumptive admission for all—the policy that
long defined the approach for European immigrants alone—and the
basic decriminalization of entry.[6] In the 1930s, this view of decolonization was precisely what led Vito Marcantonio to contend that genuine
independence for Puerto Rico had to go hand in hand with presumptive admission policies. Similarly, Indigenous activists today, organizing
through ten-point programs like the Red Deal, have explicitly attacked
restrictive border policies. They responded to the Trump Muslim Ban
by declaring "No Ban on Stolen Land."[7] The implication was that the
US's colonial foundations undermine its legal, political, and moral authority in the present to systematically exclude and criminalize people
for residing within an expropriated border.[8]

Furthermore, the everyday reality for millions of essential workers
in the United States, whose agricultural and domestic labor upholds
the reproduction of collective life but who have no representative voice,
invokes those basic constitutional and democratic ambitions of past

Socialists, feminists, and African American activists. Debs, Eastman, and Du Bois all pressed Americans to think beyond the limited terms of nineteenth-century membership and its narrow electorate. Today's voting rights struggle could similarly attend to what true universal suffrage requires. In addition to ending felony disenfranchisement and eliminating pretextual voting barriers, an essential expression of that broader commitment could include basing the franchise on residence rather than citizenship—as existed at points in American history.

Indeed, immigrant freedom embodies a central way of reimagining how economic opportunity can spread in American life. Whether on the nineteenth-century frontier or in the post–World War II era of US global dominance, external authority and control have tended to be the precondition for providing to some insiders a degree of social-democratic experience. Yet our present moment highlights what has always also been true: the long-term effect of American empire has been to enrich empowered elites in ways that sustain class and racial hierarchies. Thus, centering immigration is a critical means of both enhancing the power of those at the margins and wedding a politics of anti-imperialism to that of economic possibility for all.

This centering pushes back against some of the exclusionary and preservationist elements that have long resided within traditional American labor politics specifically. It reinforces the idea that the full protection of immigrant status should be understood as a paramount objective of labor activism itself—a necessary element of building the strength of working people generally, across the border and regardless of race or gender. In fact, it mirrors the arguments of those like Hubert Harrison who a century ago emphasized within Socialist Party debates the centrality of Black labor to labor freedom writ large. As he contended, so long as Black workers—a significant part of the working class—remained systematically subordinated under Jim Crow (including through the denial of political and legal rights), labor success at the ballot box or in the workplace would remain precarious at best. Similarly, by directly attacking immigrant workers, today's harsh border policies undermine labor's overall mobilizing power and fracture worker alliances at home and abroad.

Thus, linking labor and immigrant freedom rejects a closed vision of in-group solidarity and pushes movement constituencies toward more transformative accounts of shared class, social concern, and institutional arrangement. And again, whether or not particular policies—

like resident voting—are formally incorporated into a written constitution, their pursuit involves a revision of the basic terms and narratives of membership and thus of constitutional community.

My invocation of these past agendas, and my reflections on their potential contemporary extensions, does not derive from any technical legal expertise. Nor is every suggestion above necessitated by the historical arguments in this book. Instead, this discussion expresses my own partial attempt to think alongside movements today about the long traditions of insurgent democratic activism, and about how to strategically pursue a democratic and non-imperial order—an emancipatory constitutionalism—drawn from those same traditions. Indeed, a common theme in this book has been how key activists in past moments thought broadly and flexibly, in ways that far exceeded what twentieth-century American politics eventually allowed. They appreciated the profound constraints of their own society but refused to let those constraints dictate their political imagination.

The Question of Means

As it was for those historical figures, the question of how to get from here to there remains a similarly driving force in the contemporary era. And their ideas about bridging that divide are also deeply instructive. Past socialist and anti-colonial Left traditions not only oriented around broader constitutional politics (rather than constitutional law); they also often embraced an adaptable approach to means, whether electoral or non-electoral. This flexibility, perhaps best expressed in Du Bois's 1930s writing on Reconstruction, involved among other things a refusal to privilege in advance specific pathways as to what defines constitutional change.

A SECOND CONVENTION?

There is a very understandable American tendency to associate constitutional change with a new drafting exercise, seen recently in percolating discussions about a second constitutional convention. The US history of constitutional conventions—whether in 1787 or when transforming Indigenous land into settler states in the American union—has imprinted on the national psyche a sense that constitution-writing is *the* way to instantiate popular sovereignty. Indeed, this formal devotion to constitution-drafting has become part of what the US promoted abroad as a distinctive element of its global project. And there certainly are times when mass publics embrace writing new constitutions as genuinely central to their collective struggles for popular sovereignty.

But, as many past activists well understood, there are also times when other levers are better suited to shift the collective terrain in a democratic direction. Norman Thomas in the 1930s may have wanted a convention eventually. But he worried that pursuing one in the short term could prove counterproductive: such a convention could just as easily reproduce or even strengthen the dysfunctions and hierarchies of the moment, given the continuing power of reactionary forces in society.

It is telling that the most significant convention push today comes from the American Right. A growing number of Republicans contend that for originalism's restorationist project to succeed, conservatives will need more than multigenerational control over federal judges. Precisely because of the party's deepening minority status, they are calling for a second convention to further strengthen the stranglehold of states and state-based representation over the entire legal-political system. Alongside election interference (through everything from laws that restrict the vote to direct subversion of election results), one can see the convention call as another conservative mechanism for eroding actual popular representation.

Groups like the organization Convention of States (whose supporters include Sean Hannity, James Dobson, Marco Rubio, Ron DeSantis, Mark Meadows, and Sarah Palin, among others) have so far succeeded in getting nineteen of the thirty-four states required under Article V of the Constitution to agree to such a call.[9] Their package of wide-ranging constitutional changes would further undermine national government as a site of democratic lawmaking. It would allow state-level institutions, which disproportionately empower the Right, to effectively nullify policies that conservative officials oppose. Potential amendments include "a balanced budget, term limits for congress, repealing the federal income tax," and—most significantly, in light of the unrepresentative allocation of control across states—"giving states the power to veto any federal law, supreme court decision or executive order with a three-fifths vote from the states."[10]

This second convention call is very much a product of today's social conflicts and the fracturing of the old Cold War creedal constitutional compact. If elements of the American Left are ever more vocal in their skepticism of the Cold War terms, some voices on the Right have also begun to proclaim that even originalist arguments abide by too much of an anti-traditionalist mid-twentieth-century compact.[11] But even in this environment, it is telling that the convention call is still explicitly framed by proponents in terms of originalist veneration, both by employing Article V and in supposedly returning the country more fully to the ideological and institutional vision of the founders.[12] Critically, this speaks to the very real advantages conservatives believe Article V provides to them—regardless of the unpopularity of their views—given the centrality of the states in any formal changes and their decisive advantages at that governmental level.

All of this underscores why, for Left movements, pressing for a new constitutional convention under the terms of Article V would not be a productive choice. This is due to both the current array of political forces and the likely outcome of such an effort, as well as to the state-based distortions of the Article V convention process itself as a mechanism for expressing popular sentiment. This does not mean that writing new constitutions wholesale or holding conventions should be avoided in all contexts and at all times. But the wisdom of such a choice is an open political question, and any answer must be informed by how best to achieve actual emancipatory ends, given the structural constraints that exist within society.

REFORM PRIORITIZATION AND THE
SPECTER OF THE RIGHT

In keeping with this instrumentalist orientation, activists today could prioritize reforms based on a combined assessment: feasibility in the moment, utility for movement-building, and the relative material and political power it extends to underlying communities. This would mean formulating shorter-term ambitions alongside a longer-term agenda. For example, one might press for DC statehood or reforms to gerrymandering because of how they aid democratic self-governance and expand the voting strength of particular blocs. These changes may also have immediate majority support and so be achievable in the near term, even as they potentially open up political space for yet farther-reaching shifts. In all these efforts, the goal would involve strategically using tools available within the existing legal-political system, while linking these with a political vision that remains committed to transcending that system.

Unfortunately, intense conservative resistance has blocked all efforts at even the most seemingly small-bore interventions, like DC state-hood. There is no doubt that today's Right—shaped in part by existing constitutional incentives—views any attempt to implement even minor democratic reforms as an attack on its ability to wield power. Those of-ficials and activists will likely recirculate racist claims of "voter fraud," itself a long-standing Jim Crow argument. And they will take advantage of whatever minoritarian tools continue to be at their disposal, while potentially fomenting more open violence.

Such realities place any project of basic democratization in a pro-found catch-22, creating among the country's most daunting political difficulties. The very anti-democratic features of today's governing rules fundamentally impede the capacity of the existing process to achieve even limited reforms that have wide backing. And the growing divide between demographics—where people live—and state-based represen-tation may only make matters worse. It creates the need for ever larger supermajorities for much-needed federal legislation. This is before con-templating the even greater popular percentages required—given state-based hurdles—to use the Article V constitutional amendment process on behalf of these efforts.

This structural context also further emphasizes the need for precisely the kind of movement-building that could unblock the political system, including by spurring party realignment. In the year before his murder, King had hoped to create just this organized base, capable of exercis-ing what he called "militant non-violence"—or the ability to operate as that government behind the government, engaging in permanent mo-bilization at sites of conflict, whether in the workplace or in relation to the state. The same objective, connecting extra-electoral mass action with an ability to wield real electoral influence, continues to be vital at present. It may not rebuild something fully equivalent to the 1930s la-bor movement—either at the ballot box or at the point of production. But the goal persists of developing a mass base broad enough to claim popular authorization, to move from large-scale and spontaneous pro-tests to holding actual institutional power in the face of an entrenched conservative minority.

RULES AND RUPTURE

This centrality of movement power for any systemic change ultimately speaks to how, at the end of the day, reshaping the constitutional or-der and redistributing sovereign power could require significant acts of institutional rupture. Because of the deep procedural constraints on democratic lawmaking, Americans may end up contemplating practices that have, understandably, received little support thus far. For example, one could imagine a movement-aligned president signing bills passed in the House regardless of the Senate's approval, perhaps aimed at systematically reforming the courts or the electoral system. Or, if the courts continue to strip essential rights and to entrench deeply unpopular social and economic policies, local and federal officials may refuse to enforce those decisions.

Such actions raise the very fears that undergird a liberal embrace of the Constitution's longevity. The understandable worry is that any political elite defection from procedural rules—even to expand democracy—would open the door to other defections, especially by the Right and in decidedly authoritarian directions. Such actions also have a whiff of the 1950s segregationist "massive resistance" campaign, which ultimately backfired for them, delegitimizing the explicitly white supremacist Right among a broader white audience and political elite.

Furthermore, given the Right's institutional and material power today, liberal defenders of constitutional fidelity reasonably argue that, whatever the Constitution's flaws, fidelity to the document imposes some restraint on white authoritarianism. Any cabining function grounded in the Constitution's long standing in American life—however limited—disappears once a ruptural path is pursued.

These very valid worries emphasize the political stakes of employing extra-procedural means, and they underscore that such choices cannot be taken lightly. But they also ignore a driving lesson from Du Bois on the politics around everything from Civil War and abolition to Reconstruction and the New Deal. Many of the decisive moments of democratic expansion in the United States did not follow constitutional niceties. For example, the actual historical process that generated the Fourteenth Amendment included, among other things, military rule in the former Confederacy and the refusal of Republicans to seat in Congress officials from those ex-Confederate states—elected as they were by white-only votes. And democratic expansions have often required both sustained and mass collective pressure—not unlike the intensive strikes that asserted profound power over the economy during the New Deal—as well as the willingness of political actors to deviate from procedural norms, albeit on behalf of democracy.

Furthermore, not unlike today, these past developments also took place in a context of significant *right-wing* norm-breaking—from open secession and civil war to the violent subversion of Black rights and fair elections. As with Crystal Eastman's reflections in the context of brutal labor suppression in the 1910s and 1920s, the modern Right does not impartially play by a rulebook that advantages its ends. It today actively erodes electoral institutions through everything from voter disenfranchisement to partisan interference with elections and electoral results. Effectively, this is an attack on *democratic* norms, but often through disruptive tools that a flawed constitutional system makes easy to manipulate—especially at the state level and in the courts.

This context underscores that overcoming deepening cycles of paralysis and disaffection may not be possible without a sober evaluation of the timing and necessity of breaking from established constitutional practice. In fact, if there were truly a transformative majority able to call for a second convention in the United States, the terms of such a convention would almost certainly jettison the Article V process. This is due not only to its profoundly anti-democratic features, but also to the likelihood that an organized mass public—one that appreciates the need for a new constitution—would almost inevitably understand that abiding by the old rules would maintain the same cultural and political vise-grip of that system's limitations.

Therefore, any new text's authority would not derive from fidelity to an eighteenth-century state-based framework already widely discredited in the eyes of movement constituents. Instead, a popular front committed to a different constitutional order would find legitimacy in the power of its popular mobilizing and strength. In this way, such politics would actually mirror the 1787 framers themselves, who rejected the amendment process of the preceding Articles of Confederation to write and ratify their own document.[13]

In line with these implications, Du Bois in particular emphasized that the success or failure of legal-political rupture ultimately rested on whether reformers had the approval of a galvanized popular majority. This majority's support for new arrangements would give them meaningful legitimacy, even if the process diverged from the previous written text. This fact underscores the deeply intertwined relationship between movement-building and constitutional transformation. The latter is only possible, and democratically authorized, with a mass political base committed to such change and able to exercise real power over state and economy—including through all those "militant nonviolent" means King suggested, like large-scale sustained protests and strike actions.

But without such movement capacity, liberal constitutionalists rightly express concern about breaking established rules to pursue one-off adaptations, like passing a law without Senate approval. This may well reinforce a vicious cycle of tit-for-tat political reprisals, as government control passes from one party to another.[14] In other words, if "norm-breaking" on behalf of democracy occurred absent meaningful popular authorization, it would very likely fail as an instrument for positive constitutional reconstruction.

That does not suggest that no deviations from long-standing institutional practice should take place in the meantime. But it does emphasize the need, in every political moment, for careful judgment: Which deviations currently have real popular backing and so may be worth pursuing, all things considered, despite the tit-for-tat consequence? For instance, in the present, one clear case would be to jettison the Senate filibuster—itself a sub-constitutional norm of the upper house—including to pass much-needed measures like various voting rights bills. The harder question arises when even such partial reforms require more intensive breaks from the rules that shape lawmaking and intergovernmental reciprocity. But these are precisely the political choices Americans may have to confront. Failing to do so will mean simply acceding to the worst defects of the existing system and political culture.

These dilemmas—tied in various ways to today's entrenched right wing—again reinforce the driving centrality of creating the type of united popular front that earlier activists sought. The simple truth is that there is no way to genuinely alter the terms of American life—including the constitutional order—without specifically confronting and overcoming the Right's disproportionate political power.

Indeed, as this book's retelling of US constitutional history reveals, democratization and constitutional rupture have tended to go hand in hand because significant moments of democratic struggle faced violent resistance from the Right, buttressed by the existing legal-political structure. This includes Civil War secession; white mob attacks and killings of Black people during and after Reconstruction; anti-labor suppression in the early twentieth century; and state and private violence against civil rights and Black Power activists during the 1960s and 1970s.

These were all periods of intense political conflict. And they suggest that one cannot count on institutional change to occur primarily through moral suasion and apolitical consensus-building—even when dutifully following existing processes. Many election speeches feature platitudinous language about reaching across the aisle. But, despite such talk, the prevailing state of American conservatism means that to-day as in the past, real change will likely require both breaking the Right in its current form and repudiating the institutional mechanisms it employs to project unrepresentative power.

One should note that within mainstream constitutional scholarship the role of extra-procedural action in constitutional change—whether at the founding or during Reconstruction and the New Deal—has been detailed.[15] Thus, it is hardly a radical position to appreciate that given the constraints of constitutional process, including of Article V, rup-tural means may well be necessary in the future too for significant struc-tural change. The problem is that many of today's liberal political voices, who pledge their fidelity to the document, seem paralyzed by the depth of the predicament. There may be an intellectual recognition of the bind on democracy imposed by the existing constitutional system. But there is a deep-seated wish, no doubt understandable, that somehow change can proceed without the hard forms of organizing and politi-cal struggle required to generate popular legitimacy for ruptural means.

Yet, despite this wish, the country faces a fairly stark choice: to persist on its present course or to collectively press ahead for genuine change with all the real risks that may entail. We should be clear-eyed in assessing these risks, and only pursue ruptural strategies when mass politics can validate and deepen specific efforts. Even so, merely holding on to the currently dissolving Cold War constitutional compact offers no meaningful alternative. Instead, such stasis would keep the country trapped inside the same revolving door of social crises—now against a global backdrop marked by extreme inequality; food, energy, and health insecurity; and pending ecological disaster.

ONE NARRATIVE OR MANY?

In the final analysis, any talk of constitutional reform is ultimately far less about legal-political adjustments than about coalition-building. How can we expand and empower the social bases open to transforma-tive change? What projects, and what narratives, might garner broad support and encourage solidarity?

Any coalition-building undertaking needs to appreciate that, what-ever the flaws of creedalism—and especially of Cold War creedal con-stitutionalism—a significant bloc of potential Left-liberal allies con-tinues to embrace this romance of American nationalism. Despite our more open political moment, it remains hard to dislodge a faith that the idealized creedal nationalist project can be redeemed. This remains the case even though the specific conditions that made this story compelling after the 1960s—as the only way to achieve even minor reforms—have become less relevant. My own view is that the long twentieth century underlines how such narratives can too easily devolve into a destructive and preservationist politics. Nonetheless, the ongoing power of these interconnected visions cannot be wished away.

That reality only reiterates the importance of a specific political strategy—namely, the central goal of building a majority, which must be achieved *before* emphasizing first-order debates about the inherent truth of American nationalist narratives. Center-left Americans drew a conventional wisdom from the 1960s: the need for individuals to embrace a common civic nationalist frame as a precondition for social cohesion and ameliorative change. This lesson was based on an underlying account of why the civil rights movement succeeded—namely because Americans rallied to the creedal story of the country's inherent, historically unfolding moral goodness.

But the truth, as we have seen, is far more complicated. For one thing, Cold War conditions and global decolonization created external pressures on national elites to find a shared reformist ground. Perhaps even more relevantly, many of the Left activists that were central to the civil rights project—from King to Du Bois—were themselves deeply ambivalent about, or even opposed to, either creedal constitutionalism or any brand of American nationalism.

This speaks to how perspectives overflowing the boundaries of the most restrictive Cold War creedal constitutional variant should *all* be appreciated as part of the American experience. Some thinkers and activists, like Paul Robeson, gave voice to the disruptive potential in creedal constitutionalism; some were creedalist but *anti*-constitutional; others anti-creedal, anti-constitutional, and anti-nationalist. They express rich collective traditions that have, at moments in the past, been aligned despite their ideological divergence.

In my view, there is no need to require Americans to adopt a single civic precommitment. Instead, organizers should aim to develop, in concert with existing social bases, a common political program. And they should do so whether different constituencies would view these changes as fulfilling or transcending either the creed or the Constitution.

Such a majority-first approach draws from a basic awareness of the need to meet people where they are, culturally and politically. The focus therefore would be on joint political efforts, like those aimed at democratizing governing arrangements or the economy, or contesting the state's security apparatus. So long as programmatic goals respond to cross-coalitional need, distinct groups can develop shared political commitments, despite fundamentally different philosophical or identitarian grounds. Constituencies with competing narratives of nation and Constitution need not fight in the abstract over their affective attachments. Instead, they can build productive cooperation through ongoing projects. In so doing—by seeking majority first, and deemphasizing the desire for consensus around one story of peoplehood—progress can be achieved on some of the most expansive elements of even a transformative decolonial agenda.

In some ways, Left-liberals in the United States often seem trapped in a broader set of nationalist assumptions, of which constitutional genuflection is only the most extreme example. There is the sense that unless everyone speaks of the country through a redemptive language, as typified by Barack Obama's civic appeals, the nation will come apart at the seams. But one piece of Obama's legacy is the demonstration that even the most charismatic version of that creedal nationalist faith was not enough. It failed to reconcile the country, and to overcome fundamental cleavages between haves and have-nots. Thus, a focus on civic agreement may be misplaced. In a deeply plural society—and regardless of the many competing accounts of belonging and identity—actually addressing underlying problems may be a far better way to bind Americans together under a common aspiration for the future.

The Hope of a Democratic and Non-Imperial Society

In the end, all these dilemmas are ultimately the present-day embodiments of the perennial challenge facing emancipatory politics in the United States. The country's settler structure meant that the definition of who counts as worthy of full membership was historically narrowly drawn. And each era has struggled with how to convince the polity's majority—including insiders who have enjoyed benefits derived from subordinating others—to expand the membership terms of their community and to participate, effectively, in the reconstruction of their own society. Yet, despite these difficulties, during all the great US transformations, some segment of perceived insiders confronted the extent to which the social order actually reproduced unfreedom for themselves as well, whether through economic or political dependence. And these individuals came to see their interests as better aligned with outsider groups, and to believe that the only way to overcome their own oppressive experience involved the expansion of freedom for all.

Encouraging such shifts and building these solidarities remains the struggle of the day. And no magic discursive frame exists—creedal nationalist or socialist internationalist—that will somehow alleviate these challenges.

Moreover, these difficulties must be thought through against a distinctive cultural-political context. As this book has argued, the story of the rise of the US Constitution is at one and the same time the story of the rise of American global power. The current-day dysfunctions of the constitutional system are ideologically and institutionally connected to growing uncertainties about the legitimacy and future of the American Century, both at home and abroad. And a common fate of great empires has been slow decline, marked by the failure of governing elites to address pervasive social problems and—not unrelatedly—to abandon materially and ethically corrosive imperial ambitions.

The most likely collective outcome in the United States suggests a similar path. Such decline was presaged a century ago by the great Jamaican-American writer and Harlem Renaissance figure Claude McKay in the *Liberator*, the magazine he coedited at the time alongside its founders, Max and Crystal Eastman. In his poem "America," McKay wrote of his own conflicted feelings about the country—a country to whose energy and political potential he felt deeply attached, despite all the ways in which it also dehumanized him. In language that evokes various strands of Black politics, he begins,

> Although she feeds me bread of bitterness,
> And sinks into my throat her tiger's tooth,
> Stealing my breath of life, I will confess
> I love this cultured hell that tests my youth.
> Her vigor flows like tides into my blood,
> Giving me strength erect against her hate.
> Her bigness sweeps my being like a flood.

But the poem then takes an unexpected path. McKay invokes his status as an outsider to the American project, derived from both his Black identity and his identification with what would later be called the Third World. As an intimate stranger reflecting on the dynamics of a great empire, he ends with a note of caution against hubris and a premonition of what the future holds. In words tinged by a sense of loss, he foresees the same fate that befalls all such powers:

> Yet, as a rebel fronts a king in state,
> I stand within her walls with not a shred
> Of terror, malice, not a word of jeer.
> Darkly I gaze into the days ahead,
> And see her might and granite wonders there,
> Beneath the touch of Time's unerring hand,
> Like priceless treasures sinking in the sand.

The twentieth-century story of creedal constitutionalism speaks, in part, to the enduring ideological appeal of notions of American exceptionalism. And McKay's poem—in its melancholic recognition of both the allure of the American story and the inevitability of its breakdown—comprehends creedal constitutionalism's appeal.

It also, perhaps, raises a question that follows from the historical narrative of this book: Can members of a dominant imperial power truly choose to abandon the pillars of that power in favor of a transformed society? Such a society would extend meaningful freedom to all at home and embrace actual self-determination for all abroad. It would also embody the type of change—aspiring to a democratic and non-imperial future—that suggests true exceptionalism.

In this way, a project undertaken by Americans today to engage, finally, in a proper constitutional accounting and to transcend their own legal-political order can be thought of as an effort to arrest "time's unerring hand." It would be part of a broader aim to confront the perennial obstacles to revising the country's internal political identity and external practices.

This alternative society remains far in the distance. But such an alternative is nonetheless the project of our times, much as it constituted the central aspiration for many that came before us. Paralleling those earlier moments, today's efforts require a clear understanding of profound constraints and of the narratives that entrench them. They also necessitate holding firm to the vision of a country different and new, but rooted still in the solidarities and shared possibilities of this one.

ACKNOWLEDGMENTS

In many ways, this book is a reflection on my experience teaching constitutional law over the last decade plus. Thus, my first acknowledgment must be of the wonderful students I have had the privilege of interacting with in the classroom, who have pushed me to think more critically about the nature of the American project. Each summer, I also have benefited from working with law student research assistants on various projects, which ultimately informed this book. I would especially like to thank Madelaine Horn for her work finding New Deal sources, Matthew Tinker for similar work on Black Panther sources, Preston Bruno for locating Bill of Rights celebration sources, and Leslie Irwin for assisting with final footnote corrections. I also thank Julia Canzoneri, Connor Grant-Knight, Charlene Hong, Lauren Kloss, Ahin Lee, Ryan Madden, Tessa Morland, John Ra, Mario Roque, Sergio Rudin, Sarah Sloane, Taylor Stoneman, Haochen Sun, and Madeline Weiss.

Throughout most of the time I worked on this manuscript I was a member of the Cornell University community. I am incredibly grateful for the support and advice of many people across the campus. I would like to thank Michael Kammen, whom I feel very fortunate to have had the opportunity to spend time with as I was beginning this project. His scholarship and enthusiasm were deeply meaningful as I found my footing with the research. Sid Tarrow and Mike Dorf were model colleagues and friends, willing to read pages whenever necessary and to serve as essential sounding boards. They embodied the very best of the spirit of collegiality and intellectual generosity that marked the whole community. And they were hardly alone in making a profound impact on this book. I would also like to thank Liz Anker, David Bateman, Cynthia Bowman, Josh Chafetz, Kevin Clermont, Sherry Colb, Deborah Dinner, Matt Evangelista, Jason Frank, Jill Frank, Kevin Gaines, Larry

Glickman, Bob Hillman, Sital Kalantry, Mary Katzenstein, Jonathan Kirshner, Julilly Kohler-Hausmann, Mitchel Lasser, Rachel Liseno, Alex Livingston, Joe Margulies, Patchen Markell, Jamila Michener, Saule Omarova, Eduardo Peñalver, Aimée Plukker, Jeff Rachlinski, Russell Rickford, Stewart Schwab, Steve Shiffrin, Jed Stiglitz, Nelson Tebbe, Chantal Thomas, Gerald Torres, and Penny Von Eschen.

This book would never have been possible without the dedicated engagement of my colleagues at the Cornell Law Library. From tracking down hard-to-find sources to providing creative ways to answer discrete research questions, I am extremely indebted to everyone there, especially Alison Shea, Jane Sutton Drumheller, Amy Emerson, Kathy Hartman, Cynthia Lange, and Matt Morrison. The essential financial assistance provided by the Law School's Walter T. Southworth Faculty Research Fund also ensured that I could devote the time necessary to completing the project. In addition, I feel privileged to be joining the Boston College community and would like to thank my new colleagues at the Law School and across campus for their support and encouragement during the last stages of this process.

I am very appreciative of all the work done by the editors at the University of Chicago Press. I would like to thank Christopher Rhodes for his excitement about this project, even when it only existed as the germ of an idea. I would also like to thank Charles Myers and Sara Doskow for their continued faith and unwavering support, as well as the rest of the excellent editorial team — including Evan Young, Lindsy Rice, Erika Barrios, Michaela Rae Luckey, and Ben Pettis (who prepared the index). I am further appreciative of two anonymous reviewers for their careful comments and incredibly instructive suggestions. Ben Platt also served as an invaluable editing voice as I revised the manuscript for publication. His superb work on the initial draft made an enormous difference in helping me to clarify and, hopefully, strengthen these arguments.

I should note that pieces of the book have appeared in earlier forms in various articles, essays, and chapter contributions, such as "Constitutionalism and the Foundations of the Security State," *California Law Review* 103 (2015); "Colonialism and Constitutional Memory," *UC Irvine Law Review* 5 (2015); "Progressivism and the Disenchanted Constitution," in *The Progressives' Century: Democratic Reform and Constitutional Government in the United States*, ed. Stephen Skowronek, Stephen Engel, and Bruce Ackerman (New Haven, CT: Yale University Press, 2016); "Constitutionalism and the American Imperial Imagination," coauthored with Aslı Bâli, *The University of Chicago Law Re-*

view 85 (2018); "Goodbye, Cold War," *n+1* 30 (Winter 2018); "How We Study the Constitution: Rethinking the *Insular Cases* and Modern American Empire," *Yale Law Journal Forum*, November 2, 2020; "Why Americans Worship the Constitution," *Public Seminar*, October 11, 2021; "Anti-'CRT', A Century Old Tradition," *Harvard Civil Rights-Civil Liberties Law Review* 58 (2023); and "The Cold War's Continuing Power: U. S. Constitutional Law and Historical Memory," in *Routledge Research Handbook on the Politics of Constitutional Law*, ed. Mark Tushnet and Dimitry Kochenov (New York: Routledge Publishing, forthcoming 2024).

Over the years I have presented chapters and drafts at numerous workshops and conferences, and this book has greatly benefited from the feedback of attending colleagues and friends. I would like to acknowledge the specific advice of Hussein Agrama, Talal Asad, Wendy Brown, Susan Buck-Morss, Joshua Cohen, Omar Dajani, Stephen Engel, Owen Fiss, Megan Ming Francis, Paul Frymer, Adom Getachew, Jonathan Gould, Desmond Jagmohan, Maryam Jamshidi, Jeremy Kessler, Ben Levin, Saba Mahmood, John McCormick, Matthew Meyer, Christopher Muller, Vlad Perju, Charles Petersen, Jennifer Pitts, Claire Priest, Kim Lane Scheppele, Jed Shugerman, Josh Simon, Stephen Skowronek, Marc Spindelman, Jordan Steiker, Milo Ward, and Lisa Wedeen. I also would like to thank all those who read draft material, suggested fruitful paths for research, or provided moral support, including Ashraf Ahmed, Kate Andrias, Anthony Barnett, Paulo Barrozo, Monica Bell, Nolan Bennett, Nikolas Bowie, Abel Bradshaw, Wade Bradshaw, Pedro Cabán, Sergio Campos, Ken Chen, Youmna Chlala, Adrienne Clay, Daniel Denvir, Ryan Doerfler, Veena Dubal, Daniel Farbman, Gustavo Flores-Macías, Nick Frayn, Eli Friedman, Aaron Gavin, Jeffrey Green, Jamal Greene, David Grewal, Lani Guinier, Brian Highsmith, Betsy Hillman, Anton Jäger, Amy Kapczynski, Ramzi Kassem, Daniel Kato, Madhav Khosla, Issa Kohler-Hausmann, Sarah Kreps, Jedidiah Kroncke, Genevieve Lakier, Daniel Markovits, Shannon McSurely, James Miller, Anne Norton, K-Sue Park, Victor Pickard, Ed Quish, Jessica Ratliff, Danya Reda, Daphna Renan, Corey Robin, Wadie Said, Esty Schachter, George Shulman, Reva Siegel, Nico Silins, Rogers Smith, Brandon Terry, Mark Tushnet, Ntina Tzouvala, George Van Cleve, Tim Vasko, Gabriel Winant, Patrick Wolfe, and Taisu Zhang.

Furthermore, my special thanks go out to numerous people across the country—some of whom I did not previously know—who took the time to read either all of the manuscript or portions of it as I completed my revisions for publication. This was a remarkable act of generosity and willingness to carve out time from incredibly busy schedules. It means a great deal to me and I am truly indebted. These readers include Bruce Ackerman, Amna Akbar, Joshua Bloom, Kevin Bruyneel, Ted Fertik, Joseph Fishkin, Willy Forbath, Simon Gilhooley, Daragh Grant, Paul Kahn, Sam Klug, Paul Kramer, Sanford Levinson, Karuna Mantena, Samuel Moyn, David Pozen, and Laura Weinrib. Aslı Bâli, Jedediah Britton-Purdy, Alex Gourevitch, and Darryl Li deserve particular thanks as key interlocutors and readers for now more than a decade. Their friendship, insight, and inspiration have had an enormous impact on the book and on my thinking generally.

Finally, this project would not have been possible without my family. My parents, Phyllis Safiya Gabriel and Kipkorir Aly Azad Rana, continue to be essential teachers to whom I am forever indebted. Part of the motivation for this book emerged from deep respect for the political lives they have led and the sense that the commitments and actions of those like them have rarely been presented as part of the American story, let alone constitutional memory. I hope that these pages provide, in one small way, a record of their values and efforts. I also thank my Kenyan and American relatives for their kindness and great warmth, as well as my wonderful second family, Denny Lienau, Sri Lienau, Denette Lienau, Annette Lienau, Ava Azizgolshani, Hesham Azizgolshani, and Najib Younis (who, with real affection and care, proofread the manuscript). I am most indebted to Odette Lienau, my best friend and closest intellectual partner, for her love and boundless support. Not only has she had to hear more than anyone should reasonably be expected to about this book; Odette also has offered essential guidance and feedback, over many years, that has immeasurably improved this text. This includes spending a tremendous amount of time painstakingly reading and editing the entire manuscript with truly incredible thoughtfulness and skill. The book itself is dedicated to our two amazing children, Navaz and Taleb. They have been an endless source of joy, love, and hope for the future, and I am so grateful to be sharing this life with them.

NOTES

Preface

1. See Philip Taft, "Violence in American Labor Disputes," *Annals of American Academy of Political and Social Science* 364 (1966): 127–40, especially 128; and Bruce Laurie, *Artisans into Workers: Labor in Nineteenth-Century America* (New York: Hill and Wang, 1989), 208–10.

Chapter 1

1. Throughout the book I capitalize the word "Constitution" when referring to the US Federal Constitution operative since 1789. Given the number of constitutions discussed in the following pages—in the states, in foreign countries, and proposed by contesting social movements—this capitalization clarifies when I am talking about the US federal document.

2. Republican members of the House of Representatives started this practice in 2011, with notable Democrats such as Nancy Pelosi participating. Two years later, the desire to participate in the reading was so strong that Congress "ran out of Constitution before they ran out of readers." "66 Minutes to Read the U.S. Constitution," *ABC News*, January 15, 2013, https://abcnews.go.com/blogs/politics/2013/01/66-minutes-to-read-the-constitution/.

3. As just one illustration, President Barack Obama began his second inaugural address by maintaining that the inauguration itself "bear[s] witness to the enduring strength of our Constitution." Barack Obama, "Second Inaugural Address," transcript of speech delivered at the United States Capitol, Washington, DC, January 21, 2013, https://obamawhitehouse.archives.gov/the-press-office/2013/01/21/inauguraladdress-president-barack-obama.

4. Congress formally established the holiday in 2005 against the backdrop of the Iraq War. The move was spearheaded by Democratic Senator Robert Byrd from West Virginia, who pressed through an amendment to an appropriations bill that made September 17, the date of the text's 1787 Convention signing in Philadelphia, a special day of commemoration. The bill mandated that every educational institution "receiving Federal funds," regardless of whether the institution was private or public, grade school or university level, "shall hold an educational program on the United States Constitution on September 17." Consolidated Appropriations Act, 2005, Pub. L. No. 108-447, div. J, tit. I, § 111(b), 118 Stat. 2809, 3344 (codified at

36 U.S.C. §106 [2006]). Although Byrd was a sharp administration critic and opponent of the war, the Bush White House strongly backed the law. In fact, for years,
Bush had been issuing executive proclamations declaring the week of September 17
to be "Constitution Week." For more on political circumstance around the 2005 bill,
see Jason Frank, "Constitution Day" (unpublished manuscript, September 2012), on
file with author.

5. See as just a small sampling of the extensive liberal and left popular commentary, Ryan Doerfler and Samuel Moyn, "The Constitution Is Broken and Should Not
Be Reclaimed," *New York Times*, August 19, 2022, https://www.nytimes.com/2022
/08/19/opinion/liberals-constitution.html; Louis Menand, "American Democracy
Was Never Designed to Be Democratic," *New Yorker*, August 22, 2022, https://www
.newyorker.com/magazine/2022/08/22/american-democracy-was-never-designed
-to-be-democratic-eric-holder-our-unfinished-march-nick-seabrook-one-person
-one-vote-jacob-grumbach-laboratories-against-democracy; Ian Millhiser, "Democracy in America Is a Rigged Game," *Vox*, June 15, 2022, https://www.vox.com
/the-highlight/23066920/democracy-juneteenth-in-america-is-a-rigged-game;
Zach Beauchamp, "Call It Authoritarianism," *Vox*, June 15, 2021, https://www.vox
.com/policy-and-politics/2021/6/15/22522504/republicans-authoritarianism
-trump-competitive; Corey Robin, "Trump and the Trapped Country," *New Yorker*,
March 13, 2021, https://www.newyorker.com/news/our-columnists/trump-and
-the-trapped-country; Jedediah Purdy's "The Republican Party Is Succeeding Because We Are Not a True Democracy," *New York Times*, January 3, 2022, https://
www.nytimes.com/2022/01/03/opinion/us-democracy-constitution.html as
well as "The Constitutional Flaw That's Killing American Democracy," *Atlantic
Monthly*, August 28, 2022, https://www.theatlantic.com/ideas/archive/2022/08
/framers-constitution-democracy/671155/; Osita Nwanevu, "The Constitution
Is the Crisis," *New Republic*, October 19, 2020, https://newrepublic.com/article
/159823/constitution-crisis-supreme-court; Robert Ovetz, *We the Elites: Why the
U.S. Constitution Serves the Few* (London: Pluto Press, 2022); and George William
Van Cleve, *Making a New American Constitution* (Denver, CO: Maroon Bells Press,
2020). At the edges of this debate, there have even been percolating questions about
whether "blue" states, like New York or California, should remain faithful to undemocratic national directives. See Richard Kreitner, *Break It Up: Secession, Division, and the Secret History of America's Imperfect Union* (New York: Little, Brown
and Co., 2020).

6. See for example Michael Kammen's *A Machine That Would Go of Itself: The
Constitution in American Culture* (New York: Alfred A. Knopf, Inc., 1986), with its
seminal contention that from the founding, "the basic pattern of American constitutionalism [has been] one of *conflict within consensus*" (p. 29). See also Jonathan
Gienapp, *The Second Creation: Fixing the American Constitution in the Founding Era*
(Cambridge, MA: Harvard University Press, 2018) and Larry Kramer, *The People
Themselves: Popular Constitutionalism and Judicial Review* (New York: Oxford University Press, 2004) for key accounts of the solidification of constitutional support
and meaning during the early republic.

7. See Mila Versteeg and Emily Zackin, "American Constitutional Exceptionalism Revisited," *University of Chicago Law Review* 81 (2014): 1670; and Richard

Albert, "The World's Most Difficult Constitution to Amend?" *California Law Review* 110 (2022): 2005–22.

8. For more on how constitutional arrangements are "structurally biased" against left-of-center political factions, see generally Jonathan Gould and David Pozen, "Structural Biases in Structural Constitutional Law," *NYU Law Review* 97 (2022): 59–136.

9. For sustained examination of the role of constitutional structure in promoting a "tyranny of the minority" antithetical to multiracial democracy, see especially Steven Levitsky and Daniel Ziblatt, *Tyranny of the Minority: Why American Democracy Reached the Breaking Point* (New York: Penguin Random House, 2023). See also the following important recent and forthcoming contributions: Michael Klarman, "Foreword: The Degradation of American Democracy—and the Court," *Harvard Law Review* 134 (2020): 1264; Jedediah Purdy, *Two Cheers for Politics: Why Democracy Is Flawed, Frightening—and Our Best Hope* (New York: Basic Books, 2022); Osita Nwanevu, *The Right of the People: Democracy and the Case for a New American Founding* (New York: Random House, forthcoming 2024); and Nikolas Bowie and Daphna Renan, *Supremacy: How Rule by the Court Replaced Government by the People* (New York: Liveright, forthcoming 2024).

10. For an excellent account of these debates, see especially Ryan Doerfler and Samuel Moyn, "Democratizing the Supreme Court," *California Law Review* 109 (2021): 1703–72.

11. Waleed Shahid and Nelini Stamp, "Only Democracy Reform Can Stop Trump," *Crooked*, January 11, 2021, https://crooked.com/articles/democracy-reform-trumpism/.

12. One notable site of political exception is the Democratic Socialists of America (DSA). Their political platform, from their 2021 convention, calls for a host of systematic structural reforms to the electoral and legal system, aimed at "end[ing] minority rule," as well as "a second constitutional convention to write the founding documents of a new socialist democracy." DSA Political Platform, https://www.dsausa.org/dsa-political-platform-from-2021-convention/. As for the academy, a long-standing and important voice calling for large-scale overhaul has been the legal scholar Sanford Levinson. For decades, through books and various projects, Levinson has attempted to push the public to think seriously about the anti-democratic nature of the existing order and how else to organize a constitutional system. See Sanford Levinson, *Our Undemocratic Constitution: Where the Constitution Goes Wrong (and How We the People Can Correct It)* (New York: Oxford University Press, 2006); Sanford Levinson and Jack Balkin, *Democracy and Dysfunction* (Chicago: University of Chicago Press, 2019). See also the recent constitution drafting exercise he spearheaded: The Delegates of the Democracy Constitution, "A New Constitution for the United States," *Democracy: A Journal of Ideas*, Summer 2021, https://democracyjournal.org/magazine/61/a-new-constitution-for-the-united-states/.

13. Timothy Shenk, *Realigners: Partisan Hacks, Political Visionaries, and the Struggle to Rule American Democracy* (New York: Farrar, Straus and Giroux, 2022), 338–39 (quotations on 338).

14. Quoted in Jeff Zeleny and Dan Merica, "Obama to Deliver DNC address from Philadelphia to Underscore American Democracy," *CNN.com*, August 19,

2020, https://www.cnn.com/2020/08/19/politics/obama-dnc-speech-location/index.html.

15. Barack Obama, "2020 Democratic National Convention Speech," transcript of speech delivered in Philadelphia, PA, August 20, 2020, https://www.cnn.com/2020/08/19/politics/barack-obama-speech-transcript/index.html; also quoted in Shenk, *Realigners*, 338.

16. Maggie Astor, "Trump's Call for 'Termination' of Constitution Draws Rebukes," *New York Times*, December 4, 2022, https://www.nytimes.com/2022/12/04/us/politics/trump-constitution-republicans.html.

17. Karoun Demirjian and Toluse Olorunnipa, "White House Rebukes Trump's Suggestion to Suspend Constitution over 2020 election," *Washington Post*, December 3, 2022, https://www.washingtonpost.com/politics/2022/12/03/trump-constitution-truth-social/.

18. As Jared Goldstein contends in *Real Americans: National Identity, Violence, and the Constitution* (Lawrence: University Press of Kansas, 2021), American brands of nationalism today are noteworthy for the extent to which they are often wrapped up with a politics of what he calls "constitutional nationalism."

19. The Declaration of Independence (U.S. 1776), para. 3.

20. Gunnar Myrdal, *An American Dilemma: The Negro Problem and Modern Democracy*, vol. 2 (New York: Harper & Row, 1944), 1021.

21. For a recent scholarly and critical analysis of the idea of the "American Creed," see Joseph Margulies, *What Changed When Everything Changed: 9/11 and the Making of National Identity* (New Haven, CT: Yale University Press, 2013), especially 17–61.

22. Barack Obama, "A More Perfect Union," transcript of speech delivered in Philadelphia, PA, March 18, 2008, https://www.americanrhetoric.com/speeches/barackobamaperfectunion.htm.

23. Such a story is an account of identity and common purpose that provides individuals a framework for making sense of what it means to be a member of one's political community. For more generally on ideas of both peoplehood and constitutive stories see especially Rogers Smith, *Stories of Peoplehood: The Politics and Moral of Political Membership* (New York: Cambridge University Press, 2003), 98. As Ken Kersch remarks, "these stories are typically historical and interpretative: they are rooted in interpretations of the group's (or nation's) past and offer a shared understanding of the group's mores, understood in light of where they have been and where they are going." Ken Kersch, "Constitutive Stories about the Common Law in Modern American Conservatism," in *NOMOS: American Conservatism*, ed. Sanford Levinson (New York: New York University Press, 2016), 211–55 (quotation on 241).

24. Laurence Tribe, "America's Constitutional Narrative," *Daedalus* 141 (2012): 18–42 (quotation on 23). Similarly, for Akhil Amar, another noted constitutional scholar writing in 1997, the document was what "we Americans have in common, one of the things that *constitute* us as Americans." Akhil Reed Amar, "A Few Thoughts on Constitutionalism, Textualism, and Populism," *Fordham Law Review* 65 (1997): 1657–62 (quotation on 1658).

25. For more on the settler foundations of American political institutions and identity, see especially Aziz Rana, *The Two Faces of American Freedom* (Cambridge, MA: Harvard University Press, 2010).

26. Gienapp, *Second Creation*, 164–201 (quotations on 189).

27. Gienapp, 189.

28. See Simon Gilhooley, "The Textuality of the Constitution and the Origins of Original Intent" (PhD diss., Cornell University, 2014), 142–97.

29. Robert Wiebe, *The Search for Order, 1877–1920* (New York: Hill and Wang, 1967), xiii.

30. The dominant curricular and pedagogical models focused especially on private common law—subjects like contracts, torts, and property. Richard K. Neumann Jr., "Osler, Langdell, and the Atelier: Three Tales of Creation in Professional Education," *Legal Communication and Rhetoric* 10 (2013): 172.

31. Mark Graber, "Constitutional Politics and Constitutional Theory: A Misunderstood and Neglected Relationship," *Law & Social Inquiry* 27 (2002): 318.

32. See Theodore Roosevelt, *The Winning of the West: From the Alleghanies to the Mississippi, 1769–1776*, vol. 1 (New York: G. P. Putnam's Sons, 1889).

33. Daniel Webster, "Exclusion of Slavery from the Territories, August 12, 1848," in *The Writings and Speeches of Daniel Webster*, vol. 10 (New York: Little, Brown and Co., 1903), 37.

34. Stephen Douglas, "Third Lincoln-Douglas Debate, September 15, 1858," in *Lincoln: Speeches and Writings*, vol. 1, ed. Don Fehrenbacher (New York: Library of America, 1989), 586–634 (quotation on 598).

35. See Simon Gilhooley, *The Antebellum Origins of the Modern Constitution: Slavery and the Spirit of the American Founding* (New York: Cambridge University Press, 2020), 116–24 for more on how the idea of the Constitution as fostering union through a "spirit of compromise" (p. 118) shaped the era's political judgments. In this context, Webster's analysis of the specifics of that compromise embodied only one version, for instance alongside those articulated by Northern and Southern Democrats (p. 117).

36. See James Oakes, *Freedom National: The Destruction of Slavery in the United States, 1861–1865* (New York: W. W. Norton, 2013); Jack Balkin, *Constitutional Redemption: Political Faith in an Unjust World* (Cambridge, MA: Harvard University Press, 2011); and Garry Wills, *Lincoln at Gettysburg: The Words That Remade America* (New York: Simon & Schuster, 1992).

37. Wills, *Lincoln at Gettysburg*, 146, 147.

38. My analysis resonates with Peter Gourevitch's classic article, "The Second Image Reversed: The International Sources of Domestic Politics," *International Organization* 32 (1978): 881–912. In the law, the most significant exception to the tendency to focus, almost exclusively, on the domestic is Derrick Bell's classic analysis of "interest convergence." See Derrick Bell, "*Brown v. Board of Education* and the Interest Convergence Dilemma," *Harvard Law Review* 93 (1980): 518–33. See also Mary Dudziak's essential engagement with the Cold War backdrop of racial reform, *Cold War Civil Rights: Race and the Image of American Democracy* (Princeton, NJ: Princeton University Press, 2001).

39. W. E. B. Du Bois, *The Souls of Black Folk: Essays and Sketches* (New York: Fawcett Publishing Co., 1961), 23.

40. See Michael Ignatieff, *Blood and Belonging: Journeys in the New Nationalism* (New York: Farrar, Straus and Giroux, 1993), 6.

41. See generally Rana, *Two Faces*.

42. Quoted in Marilyn Lake and Henry Reynolds, *Drawing the Global Colour Line: White Men's Countries and the International Challenge of Racial Equality* (New York: Cambridge University Press, 2008), 197.

43. Zachary Elkins, Tom Ginsburg, and James Melton, *The Endurance of National Constitutions* (New York: Cambridge University Press, 2009), 42.

44. Elkins, Ginsburg, and Melton write, "by the second year of life a full 85 percent of post-1789 states had adopted their first constitution, and by five years, almost 95 percent of them had such instruments" (*Endurance of National Constitutions*, 42). Linda Colley in *The Gun, the Ship, and the Pen: Warfare, Constitutions, and the Making of the Modern World* (New York: W. W. Norton, 2021), 3–12, offers a compelling argument about the relationship between war-making and constitution writing over the "long nineteenth century." Technological changes dramatically raised war's human and material costs. When regimes broke down, or even if they "avoided collapse," political elites "found themselves needing to reorder domestic government." In the process, constitutions emerged as a valuable instrument for "rally[ing] wider support and justify[ing] expanding fiscal and manpower demands" (p. 7).

45. Tom Ginsburg, "Written Constitutions around the World," *Insights on Law and Society* 15 (2015): 4–7, 5.

46. For a critical reading of the problems with the spread of the constitutional form, see Martin Loughlin, *Against Constitutionalism* (Cambridge, MA: Harvard University Press, 2022).

47. See David Law and Mila Versteeg, "The Declining Influence of the United States Constitution," *NYU Law Review* 87 (2012): 762–858 (quotations on 850).

48. Nonetheless, I do see this book as in the direct lineage of Michael Kammen's foundational 1986 text, *A Machine That Would Go of Itself.* Despite my own disagreements in interpretation, hinted at earlier, as well as differences in intention, Kammen's work remains the most important sustained attempt in recent decades to assess the Constitution's role as a cultural force shaping broader public discourse.

49. For more on social criticism and my approach to history, see Rana, *Two Faces*, 17–19.

50. Indeed, the ideological consolidation around creedal constitutionalism that I am concerned with in this book is above all an *elite* one—entailing near unanimity among politically represented views in the public arena—and so this reconstruction of the constitutional past is by and large an elite reconstruction. This is not to say that mass beliefs play no role in the following account; certainly, the judgments of organized elites about underlying public opinion vitally shape those elites' approach to constitutional politics, be it venerative or skeptical. But, for my purposes, this does mean that the significance of mass sentiment is almost always mediated by elite political agents, broadly understood. One of the key differences between this project and a traditional book on the US Constitution is thus my choice of *which* elites to emphasize. Relatedly, it is worth stating up front that my use of the term "elite" is not pejorative. I include within it a fairly capacious set of political actors, given that they range from politicians to social movement activists and enjoy varying social, economic, and political standing. In other words, this category of politically engaged and relevant actors is not reducible merely to what C. Wright Mills famously referred to as the "power elite," i.e., exclusively those interconnected corporate,

military, and political groups that wield dominant authority in American life. See C. Wright Mills, *The Power Elite* (New York: Oxford University Press, 1956).

51. Ginsburg, "Written Constitutions," 4.

52. Note that such enduring values are often (although not always) written down in a single governing constitutional text. England's "ancient constitution" is the example of an unwritten constitution—referencing the underlying laws and customs of the society—most widely explored by scholars. See for instance Daniel Hulsebosch, "The Ancient Constitution and the Expanding Empire: Sir Edward Coke's British Jurisprudence," *Law and History Review* 21 (2003): 439–82.

Chapter 2

1. See Michael Kammen, *A Machine That Would Go of Itself: The Constitution in American Culture* (New York: Alfred A. Knopf, Inc., 1986), 127–55 for an excellent overview of the circumstances surrounding the centennial celebrations. This discussion draws from his work.

2. See Walter Nugent, "The American People and the Centennial of 1876," *Indiana Magazine of History* 75 (1979): 53–69 (statistics on 63 and quotation on 60).

3. Dorothy Gondos Beers, "The Centennial City, 1865–1876," in *Philadelphia: A Three Hundred Year History*, ed. Russell F. Weigley (New York: W. W. Norton, 1982), 464.

4. Nugent, "The American People," 59.

5. Kammen, *A Machine That Would Go of Itself*, 139–40.

6. Nugent, "The American People," 55.

7. Kammen, *A Machine That Would Go of Itself*, 128–31.

8. Kammen, 134, 136, 131.

9. Kammen, 138–40.

10. Kammen, 131, 144.

11. Kammen, 151.

12. Quoted in Kammen, 143.

13. An indicator of this shift in focus was the *Century*'s (which Kammen describes as "the most popular middle-class magazine of that era") centennial special issue. Rather than emphasizing the Constitution, its celebratory articles concerned "The Inauguration of Washington," "Washington in New York in 1789," and "Washington at Mt. Vernon after the Revolution." Kammen, 152.

14. Quotations in Kammen, 128, 129.

15. Kammen, 130.

16. See generally Duncan Bell's terrific scholarship for more on the late-nineteenth-century pervasiveness of ideas of "racial kinship" across Anglo-America and the notion specifically of the US and England as the two pillars of global "civilization," especially *Dreamworlds of Race: Empire and the Utopian Destiny of Anglo-America* (Princeton, NJ: Princeton University Press, 2020), quotation on 14.

17. See Theodore Roosevelt, *The Winning of the West: From the Alleghanies to the Mississippi, 1769–1776*, vol. 1 (New York: G. P. Putnam's Sons, 1889), 1.

18. Quoted in Marilyn Lake and Henry Reynolds's essential book, *Drawing the Global Colour Line: White Men's Countries and the International Challenge of Racial Equality* (New York: Cambridge University Press, 2008), 197. The book's subtitle,

which I draw from in titling this section, highlights the centrality of this phrase for Roosevelt's thinking.

19. See, for example, Thomas Jefferson's depiction of the uniqueness of the new United States, marked above all by an "immensity of land" and a "lovely equality." As the historian Brian Steele notes, this was a polity Jefferson routinely depicted as "essentially a classless society, with no 'paupers,' and very few rich." Brian Steele, "Inventing Un-America," *Journal of American Studies* 47 (2013): 881–902 (quotations on 891).

20. See Aziz Rana, *The Two Faces of American Freedom* (Cambridge, MA: Harvard University Press, 2010), for a fuller account of American settler empire, its ideologies, and its constitutional practices (pp. 12–14) and for an exploration of the idea of republican freedom (pp. 50–55). See also Patrick Wolfe's seminal *Traces of History: Elementary Structures of Race* (New York: Verso, 2016) for an excellent comparative analysis of the relationship between land, labor, and race in various polities marked by colonial settlement.

21. Frederick Jackson Turner, "The Significance of the Frontier in American History," in *The Frontier in American History* (New York: Henry Holt and Co., 1920), 1–38 (quotation on 37).

22. Theodore Roosevelt, "Manhood and Statehood," in *The Strenuous Life: Essays and Addresses* (New York: The Century Co., 1902), 245–59 (quotation on 254).

23. For more on immigration policies in the nineteenth century, see Rana, *Two Faces*, 114–20.

24. Turner, "Significance of the Frontier," quotations on 22, 23.

25. Roosevelt, *The Winning of the West*, 108.

26. For more on nativism and the Know Nothing Party, see Eric Foner, *Free Soil, Free Labor, Free Men: The Ideology of the Republican Party before the Civil War* (New York: Oxford University Press, 1970), 226–60; and Tyler Anbinder, *Nativism and Slavery: The Northern Know Nothing Party and the Politics of the 1850s* (New York: Oxford University Press, 1992).

27. J. Hector St. John de Crèvecoeur, *Letters from an American Farmer* (New York: Fox, Duffield, and Co., 1904), 54.

28. Caroline Elkins and Susan Pederson, "Settler Colonialism: A Concept and Its Uses," in *Settler Colonialism in the Twentieth Century*, ed. Caroline Elkins and Susan Pedersen (New York: Routledge, 2005), 4. See also Lorenzo Veracini, *Settler Colonialism: A Theoretical Overview* (New York: Palgrave Macmillan, 2010).

29. Theodore Roosevelt, "National Life and Character," *Sewanee Review* 2 (1894): 353–76 (quotation on 366).

30. Rogers Smith, *Civic Ideals: Conflicting Visions of Citizenship in U.S. History* (New Haven, CT: Yale University Press, 1997), 6.

31. Gary Gerstle, *American Crucible: Race and Nation in the Twentieth Century* (Princeton, NJ: Princeton University Press, 2017), 5, 4, 45.

32. Resonant with this critique, the historian Barbara Welke has also argued that over the "long nineteenth century" "privilege and subordination" in the United States were best understood as "interlocked and interdependent." See Barbara Young Welke, *Law and the Borders of Belonging in the Long Nineteenth Century United States* (New York: Cambridge University Press, 2010), 5.

33. See Simon Gilhooley, "The Textuality of the Constitution and the Origins of Original Intent" (PhD diss., Cornell University, 2014), for an excellent overview of the culture of constitutional veneration in the antebellum period, especially 142–97 (quotation on 177).

34. One representative address described the Constitution as "a stupendous monument of man's last, and greatest efforts for the preservation of liberty." Quoted in Gilhooley, "Textuality of the Constitution," 177.

35. On the rise of the toasts to the Constitution, see Gilhooley, 187–96.

36. See Samuel Danforth, "Brief Recognition of New England's Errand into the Wilderness," in *The Wall and the Garden: Selected Massachusetts Election Sermons*, ed. A. William Plumstead (Minneapolis: University of Minnesota Press, 1968), 53–77.

37. Sacvan Bercovitch, *Rites of Assent: Transformations in the Symbolic Construction of America* (New York: Routledge, 1993), 11; also quoted in Sam Haselby, *The Origins of American Religious Nationalism* (New York: Oxford University Press, 2015), 202.

38. Quoted in Haselby, *Origins of American Religious Nationalism*, 202.

39. See Jonathan Gienapp, *The Second Creation: Fixing the American Constitution in the Founding Era* (Cambridge, MA: Harvard University Press, 2018), 9–11, 164–201 (quotation on 189).

40. Abraham Lincoln, "Address to the Young Men's Lyceum of Springfield, Illinois," in *The Writings of Abraham Lincoln*, ed. Steven Smith (New Haven, CT: Yale University Press, 2012), 7–14 (quotations on 7, 11).

41. See Kammen, *A Machine That Would Go of Itself*, 75–92.

42. Kammen, 79 (quotation from Story on the same page).

43. Speaking of the first half-century-plus of the Constitution's existence, one scholar in the 1930s remarked that there was "little in the way of an effort to reach the masses with some knowledge of the Constitution." Daniel Knowlton, "The United States Constitution in the Schoolbooks of the Past," in *Social Studies* 29 (1938): 7–14 (quotation on 8).

44. H. Arnold Bennett, *The Constitution in School and College* (New York: G. P. Putnam's Sons, 1935), 103.

45. Milton Klein, "Mythologizing the U.S. Constitution," *Soundings* 78 (1995): 180.

46. Kammen, *A Machine That Would Go of Itself*, 81.

47. Knowlton, "Constitution in the Schoolbooks," 12.

48. Klein, "Mythologizing the U.S. Constitution," 182.

49. Kammen, *A Machine That Would Go of Itself*, 90–92 (quotation on 91).

50. For scholarship on how "judicial supremacy"—the idea of the Supreme Court as the ultimate arbiter of constitutional meaning—is a twentieth-century phenomenon, see generally Keith Whittington, *Political Foundations of Judicial Supremacy: The Presidency, the Supreme Court, and Constitutional Leadership in U.S. History* (Princeton, NJ: Princeton University Press, 2007). See also Nikolas Bowie's and Daphna Renan's powerful exploration of how racist reaction by white national elites against Reconstruction promoted a politics of disempowering Congress and emphasizing the constitutional centrality of the Court in *Supremacy: How Rule by the Court Replaced Government by the People* (New York: Liveright, forthcoming 2024).

51. Irving Brant, "John Marshall and the Lawyers and Politicians," in *Chief Justice John Marshall: A Reappraisal*, ed. W. Melville Jones (Ithaca, NY: Cornell University Press, 1956), 41–60 (quotation on 55).

52. Justin Crowe, *Building the Judiciary: Law, Courts, and the Politics of Institutional Development* (Princeton, NJ: Princeton University Press, 2012), 2.

53. Brant, "John Marshall," 54.

54. Rana, *Two Faces*, 109, 142–48.

55. See generally Christopher Tomlins's excellent *Freedom Bound: Law, Labor, and Civic Identity in Colonizing English America, 1580–1865* (Cambridge, UK: Cambridge University Press, 2010) for a systematic account of the "manning," "planting," and "keeping" involved in American colonial control and territorial transformation.

56. See generally John Dinan, *The American State Constitutional Tradition* (Lawrence: University Press of Kansas, 2006).

57. See Bethel Saler, *The Settlers' Empire: Colonialism and State Formation in America's Old Northwest* (Philadelphia: University of Pennsylvania Press, 2015), 78–79, 249–51; Mila Versteeg and Emily Zackin, "American Constitutional Exceptionalism Revisited," *University of Chicago Law Review* 81 (2014): 1648–49; and Dinan, *American State Constitutional Tradition*, 42.

58. Versteeg and Zackin, "American Constitutional Exceptionalism Revisited," 1649.

59. Dinan, *American State Constitutional Tradition*, 272.

60. Samuel Bryan, "Centinel Letter I, October 5, 1787," in *The Anti-Federalists*, ed. Cecilia Kenyon (Indianapolis, IN: Bobbs-Merrill, 1966), 2–14 (quotation on 4–5).

61. Quoted in Rana, *Two Faces*, 150.

62. One should note that even today, state constitutional practices, as Versteeg and Zackin highlight, often deviate from the federal model when it comes to rights provision, the detailed elaboration of policy choices, and the frequency of revision. See generally Versteeg and Zackin, "American Constitutional Exceptionalism Revisited." Yet I would argue that there is a meaningful difference between the present and the nineteenth century. Today, the reach of the federal government and the dominance of the US Constitution alters the terrain on which state constitutional politics occurs. My conjecture is that some of the present-day willingness to diverge from the federal model and engage in constitutional experimentation is due to the sense that the US Constitution—and its supremacy—exists as a backstop constraining potential abuse or excess. Such sentiment no doubt circulated in the nineteenth century too. However, the more limited reach of the federal government underscored the primacy of state and local decisions, including constitutional ones, over collective life. In this "society of island communities" one could not presume necessarily that the federal government would serve as that backstop. In addition, as the book will explore, by the late nineteenth century a significant piece of reformist state constitutional energy was prompted by explicit farmer and worker discontent with the terms of the federal model and a desire to create local conditions free from such expanding federal constitutional control. Thus, nineteenth-century state constitutional design likely hinted at real—if often submerged—tensions over settler identification with the concrete federal system.

63. See especially the historian Garry Wills's book on the Gettysburg Address, its

genesis, meaning, and legacy. There he writes, "The Gettysburg Address has become an authoritative expression of the American spirit—as authoritative as the Declaration itself, and perhaps even more influential, since it determines how we read the Declaration. For most people now, the Declaration means what Lincoln told us it means, as a way of correcting the Constitution without overthrowing it." Garry Wills, *Lincoln at Gettysburg: The Words That Remade America* (New York: Simon & Schuster, 1992), 146–47.

64. The Declaration of Independence (U.S. 1776), para. 2.

65. See Abraham Lincoln, "Address Delivered at the Dedication of the Cemetery at Gettysburg, November 19, 1863," in *Selected Writings of Abraham Lincoln*, ed. Albert Bushnell Hart (New York: Gregg Publishing Co., 1920), 280–81 (quotations on 280).

66. See Abraham Lincoln, "Fragment on the Constitution and Union," in *The Collected Works of Abraham Lincoln*, vol. 4, ed. Roy P. Basler (New Brunswick, NJ: Rutgers University Press, 1953), 168–69 (quotation on 169).

67. "A word fitly spoken is like apples of gold in pictures of silver." Proverbs 25:11 (King James Version). For more on the role of this biblical metaphor in Lincoln's constitutional thought, see Jack Balkin, *Constitutional Redemption: Political Faith in an Unjust World* (Cambridge, MA: Harvard University Press, 2011), 18–23.

68. Lincoln, "Fragment," 169.

69. See Dorothy Roberts, "Foreword: Abolition Constitutionalism," *Harvard Law Review* 133 (2019): 55.

70. Stephen Douglas, "Third Lincoln-Douglas Debate, September 15, 1858," in *Lincoln: Speeches and Writings*, vol. 1, ed. Don Fehrenbacher (New York: Library of America, 1989), 586–634 (quotation on 598).

71. The Declaration of Independence (U.S. 1776), para. 29.

72. For an extended reinterpretation of the American Revolution as best understood as a revolt by settlers "to defend their long-granted privileges and thus their cultural and political supremacy" against both the London administrators and other imperial subjects, see Rana, *Two Faces*, 20–98, 22.

73. Description and quotation in Wendell Phillips Garrison and Francis Jackson Garrison, *William Lloyd Garrison, 1805–1879: The Story of His Life Told by His Children*, vol. 3 (New York: Century Co., 1889), 412. As early as 1843, Garrison introduced a resolution before the Massachusetts Anti-Slavery Society, using the same language and calling for the repudiation of the Constitution as well as the repeal of the union with enslavers: "That the compact which exists between the North and the South is 'a covenant with death, and an agreement with hell,'—involving both parties in atrocious criminality; and should be immediately annulled." Quoted in Balkin, *Constitutional Redemption*, 253n7.

74. Wendell Phillips, *The Constitution, A Pro-Slavery Compact*, 3rd ed. (New York: Anti-Slavery Society, 1856), 9.

75. See Roberts, "Abolition Constitutionalism," 56.

76. Abraham Lincoln, "Speech at Peoria, Illinois, October 18, 1854," in *Lincoln on Race and Slavery*, ed. Henry Louis Gates Jr. (Princeton, NJ: Princeton University Press, 2009), 56–68 (quotation on 67).

77. Wills, *Lincoln at Gettysburg*, 101.

78. Lincoln, "Gettysburg Address," 281.

79. Lincoln, "Speech at Peoria," 68.

80. Abraham Lincoln, "Address on Colonization to a Deputation of Negroes, August 14, 1862," in *Lincoln on Race and Slavery*, ed. Henry Louis Gates Jr. (Princeton, NJ: Princeton University Press, 2009), 235–41 (quotations on 236, 237).

81. Abraham Lincoln, "Fourth Debate with Stephen A. Douglas, September 18, 1858," in *Lincoln on Race and Slavery*, ed. Henry Louis Gates Jr. (Princeton, NJ: Princeton University Press, 2009), 156–59 (discussion of African American rights on 157).

82. Abraham Lincoln, "Last Public Address, April 11, 1865," in *Lincoln on Race and Slavery*, ed. Henry Louis Gates Jr. (Princeton, NJ: Princeton University Press, 2009), 316–20 (quotation on 318).

83. Charles Sumner, "Are We a Nation? November 19, 1867," in *Charles Sumner: His Complete Works*, ed. George Frisbie Hoar (Boston: Lee and Shepard, 1900), 3–65 (quotations on 63, 62).

84. Quoted in Hans L. Trefousse, *Thaddeus Stevens: Nineteenth Century Egalitarian* (Chapel Hill: University of North Carolina Press, 1997), xi.

85. "Thaddeus Stevens," *New York Times*, August 13, 1868, 4.

86. Lincoln, "Address on Colonization," 238.

87. "Majority Government," *Nation*, April 26, 1877, 245.

88. The historian Michael Dennis describes Wilson as personifying the emerging white middle-class sensibilities in the urban South, especially the commitment to "regional progress through national reconciliation, industrial growth, agricultural diversification, and racial control." See Michael Dennis, "Looking Backward: Woodrow Wilson, the New South, and the Question of Race," *American Nineteenth Century History* 3 (2002): 77–104 (quotation on 77).

89. Woodrow Wilson, "Reconstruction of the Southern States," *Atlantic Monthly* 87 (1901): 1–14 (quotations on 11), also quoted in Dennis, "Looking Backward," 82.

90. Wilson, "Reconstruction of the Southern States," 6, 11. Wilson decried Reconstruction practices for producing a "vast 'laboring, landless, homeless class' once slaves, now free; unpracticed in liberty, unschooled in self-control; never sobered by the discipline of self-support, never established in any habit of prudence; excited by a freedom they did not understand, exalted by false hopes; bewildered and without leaders, and yet insolent and aggressive, sick of work, covetous of pleasure, a host of dusky children untimely put out of school" (p. 6).

91. Quoted in Hugh Tulloch, *The Debate on the American Civil War Era* (New York: Manchester University Press, 1999), 214.

92. Quoted in Lake and Reynolds, *Drawing the Global Colour Line*, 70.

93. The Progressive politician and author Frederick Howe recalled in his memoir that in American universities at the turn of the century, "Mr. Bryce's *American Commonwealth* was at the time a work of Biblical authority." Quoted in Hugh Tulloch, *James Bryce's American Commonwealth: The Anglo-American Background* (Wolfeboro, NH: Boydell Press, 1988), 10.

94. Quoted in Matthew Frye Jacobson, *Barbarian Virtues: The United States Encounters Foreign Peoples at Home and Abroad, 1876–1917* (New York: Hill and Wang, 2000), 182.

95. James Bryce, *The American Commonwealth* (New York: Macmillan, 1888), 92; also quoted in Lake and Reynolds, *Drawing the Global Colour Line*, 49.

96. Quoted in Mark Pittenger, *American Socialists and Evolutionary Thought, 1870–1920* (Madison: University of Wisconsin Press, 1993), 181.

97. See Tulloch, *Debate on the American Civil War*, 218–20.

98. David Blight, *Race and Reunion: The Civil War in American Memory* (Cambridge, MA: The Belknap Press of Harvard University Press, 2001), 9.

99. "Gettysburg: A Common Ideal," *Outlook*, July 12, 1913, 554–55 (quotation on 554).

100. See Plessy v. Ferguson, 163 U.S. 537 (1896).

101. *Plessy*, 551.

102. Quotations in Stephen Hahn, *A Nation under Our Feet: Black Political Struggles in the Rural South from Slavery to the Great Migration* (Cambridge, MA: The Belknap Press of Harvard University Press, 2003), 119, 122.

103. Dorothy Roberts writes that Douglass may have been the most "well known" figure, but that his arguments were part of robust Black "antebellum abolitionist constitutionalism." Various non-enslaved African Americans employed universal language found in the Constitution to assert in court cases and legal disputes their right to equal citizenship. Roberts, "Abolition Constitutionalism," 57–58 (quotation on 57).

104. Roberts, 56.

105. US Const. amend. V.

106. US Const. art. IV, sect. 4.

107. Frederick Douglass, "The Constitution of the United States: Is It Pro-Slavery or Anti-Slavery," in *Frederick Douglass: Selected Speeches and Writings*, ed. Philip S. Foner and Yuval Taylor (Chicago: Chicago Review Press, 2000), 380–90 (quotation on 388).

108. Frederick Douglass, "Our Composite Nationality (1869)," in *The Speeches of Frederick Douglass*, ed. John McKivigan, Julie Husband, and Heather Kaufman (New Haven, CT: Yale University Press, 2018), 278–303 (quotations on 295, 294).

109. The historian Mason Lowance writes that Douglass chose the date for the speech because, as with other African Americans, he "did not wish to participate in the celebration of hypocrisy and could not join the festivities recalling the Declaration of Independence." Mason Lowance, "Frederick Douglass (1818–1895)," in *Against Slavery: An Abolitionist Reader*, ed. Mason Lowance (New York: Penguin Classics, 2000), 38.

110. For more on Douglass's rhetoric of egalitarian redemption, see generally George Shulman's seminal account, *American Prophecy: Race and Redemption in American Political Culture* (Minneapolis: University of Minnesota Press, 2008), 1–88.

111. See James Redpath, "The Three Oligarchies," *National Anti-Slavery Standard*, January 26, 1867, Cornell University, Kroc Rare Manuscripts Collection.

112. See Richard Taylor, *Destruction and Reconstruction: Personal Experiences of the Late War*, ed. Richard B. Harwell (1879; London: Longmans, Green & Co., 1955), 299. This quote comes from a meeting between Stevens and Richard Taylor, a Confederate general during the war and the son of President Zachary Taylor. In keeping with the accusations that Stevens was a wild-eyed extremist, Taylor may well have sought to smear Stevens as lawless. Still, if Stevens uttered such a statement it would not have surprised either his political friends or his enemies.

113. Frederick Douglass, "Sources of Danger to the Republic (1867)," in *The Speeches of Frederick Douglass*, ed. John McKivigan, Julie Husband, and Heather Kaufman (New Haven, CT: Yale University Press, 2018), 217–46 (quotations on 224, 229).

114. Quoted in Christopher Robert Reed, *All the World Is Here! The Black Presence at White City* (Bloomington: Indiana University Press, 2000), 135.

115. Quotations in Blight, *Race and Reunion*, 311.

116. This juxtaposition between Turner and Sampson over the *Civil Rights Cases* draws from David Blight's powerful exploration in *Race and Reunion*, 310–11.

117. Henry McNeal Turner, "Communications," *The Christian Recorder*, December 13, 1883.

118. See generally LeeAnna Keith, *The Colfax Massacre: The Untold Story of Black Power, White Terror, and the Death of Reconstruction* (New York: Oxford University Press, 2008).

119. Turner, "Communications."

120. According to the legal historian John Witt, "only slightly more than 3,100 emigrated to Liberia in the ten years after the end of the war. Almost two-thirds of those emigrants left the United States in the first three years following Lee's surrender at Appomattox." John Fabian Witt, *Patriots and Cosmopolitans: Hidden Histories of American Law* (Cambridge, MA: Harvard University Press, 2007), 137.

121. See Cedric Robinson, *Black Movements in America* (New York: Routledge, 1997), 89–90 (statistics on 90).

122. See generally William Collins, "The Great Migration of Black Americans from the US South: A Guide and Interpretation," *Explorations in Economic History* 80 (2021): 1–17.

123. "Progress of the Anarchists," *New York Times*, January 25, 1867, 4.

124. John McKivigan, Julie Husband, and Heather Kaufman, "Introduction to 'Self-Made Men' (1893)," in *The Speeches of Frederick Douglass*, ed. John McKivigan, Julie Husband, and Heather Kaufman (New Haven, CT: Yale University Press, 2018), 414.

125. Frederick Douglass, "Self-Made Men (1893)," in *The Speeches of Frederick Douglass*, ed. John McKivigan, Julie Husband, and Heather Kaufman (New Haven, CT: Yale University Press, 2018), 414–53 (quotation on 431). The phrases echo language from another key Reconstruction-era lecture, "Let the Negro Alone (1869)," in *The Speeches of Frederick Douglass*, ed. John McKivigan, Julie Husband, and Heather Kaufman (New Haven, CT: Yale University Press, 2018), 247–66.

126. Douglass, "Self-Made Men," 431.

127. Douglass, 431.

128. Dred Scott v. Sandford, 60 U.S. 393, 407 (1857).

129. For more on the meaning of Douglass's speech, "Self-Made Men," in the post-Reconstruction period, see David Blight, *Frederick Douglass: Prophet of Freedom* (New York: Simon & Schuster, 2018), 566–68.

130. As James Oakes details, Republicans argued that while private property was both legal and just, slavery was not ordinary property but only "a servile status—'persons held in service.'" See James Oakes, *Freedom National: The Destruction of Slavery in the United States, 1861–1865* (New York: W. W. Norton & Co., 2013), 8–14 (quotation on 9).

131. See Benjamin Lynerd, "Republican Ideology and the Black Labor Movement, 1869-1872," *Phylon* 56 (2019): 19–36, especially 28–29, on the importance for Douglass and other figures within Black labor politics of the "homestead agenda" for republican "economic independence" (p. 28).

132. See Hahn, *A Nation under Our Feet*, 139–40 (quotation on 136).

133. Quoted in Hahn, 135.

134. Hahn, 135–42 (quotations on 141, 140).

135. Hahn, 135–42 (quotations on 141).

136. As one example of the general hostility enslaved peoples felt for the hypocrisy of Independence Day festivities, Nat Turner planned his slave revolt to begin on July 4, 1831. Matthew Dennis, *Red, White, and Blue Letter Days: An American Calendar* (Ithaca, NY: Cornell University Press, 2002), 287n18.

137. Eric Foner, *Reconstruction: America's Unfinished Revolution, 1863–1877* (New York: Harper & Row, 1988), 289.

138. Foner, *Reconstruction.*

139. Kammen, *A Machine That Would Go of Itself,* 133.

140. Abraham Lincoln, "Annual Address before the Wisconsin State Agricultural Society, September 30, 1859," in *Complete Works*, vol. 1, ed. John G. Nicholay and John Hay (New York: The Century Co., 1907), 576–84 (quotation on 581).

141. See Walter Licht, *Industrializing America: The Nineteenth Century* (Baltimore, MD: Johns Hopkins University Press, 1995), 183.

142. Lincoln, "Annual Address," 582.

143. This and some of the following language draws from Rana, *Two Faces*, 185. See also Licht, *Industrializing America*, 183.

144. See Rana, *Two Faces*, 185. See generally Alan Trachtenberg, *The Incorporation of America: Culture and Society in the Gilded Age* (New York: Hill and Wang, 2007); Jack Beatty, *Age of Betrayal: The Triumph of Money in America* (New York: Vintage, 2008).

145. See generally Rana, *Two Faces*, 162–64, 228–29.

146. For instance, the pages of the *American Journal of Sociology* took as axiomatic that European-style class divisions were growing in America and debated whether a deepening class war had become "inevitable." See for example the roundtable discussion, "Is Class Conflict in America Growing and Is It Inevitable?" *American Journal of Sociology* 13 (1908): 756–83. It includes an introductory piece by John Commons, responses from Graham Taylor, Jane Addams, Alvin Johnson, Henry Raymond Mussey, Robert Hoxie, and C. P. Gilman, and a final reply from Commons.

147. See Alex Gourevitch, *From Slavery to Cooperative Commonwealth: Labor and Republican Liberty in the Nineteenth Century* (New York: Cambridge University Press, 2015), 1–7, 174 (quotation on 5).

148. See Jeffrey E. Mirel, *Patriotic Pluralism: Americanization Education and European Immigrants* (Cambridge, MA: Harvard University Press, 2010), statistic and quotation on 13.

149. Rana, *Two Faces*, 237.

150. Quotations in Jacobson, *Barbarian Virtues*, 72.

151. Jacobson, 89.

152. Bennett, *Constitution in School and College*, 104.

153. See Simon Gilhooley, *The Antebellum Origins of the Modern Constitution: Slavery and the Spirit of the American Founding* (New York: Cambridge University Press, 2020), 116–24.

154. Woodrow Wilson, *Congressional Government: A Study in American Politics* (Boston: Houghton, Mifflin, and Co., 1885), quotations on 5.

155. E. L. Godkin, "Some Things Overlooked at the Centennial," *The Nation*, September 22, 1887, 226; see also Kammen, *A Machine That Would Go of Itself*, 141.

156. Godkin, "Some Things Overlooked," 226.

157. Godkin, 226.

158. See generally Douglass, "Sources of Danger to the Republic."

159. Henry Cabot Lodge, "The Constitution and Its Makers," in *The Democracy of the Constitution: And Other Addresses and Essays* (New York: Charles Scribner's Sons, 1915), quotations on 37, 35–36, also partially quoted in Kammen, *A Machine That Would Go of Itself*, 154.

Chapter 3

1. Matthew Frye Jacobson, *Barbarian Virtues: The United States Encounters Foreign Peoples at Home and Abroad, 1876–1917* (New York: Hill and Wang, 2000), 88. For more on the Haymarket affair, see Paul Avrich, *The Haymarket Tragedy* (Princeton, NJ: Princeton University Press, 1984).

2. Avrich, *The Haymarket Tragedy*, 221.

3. Quoted in Jacobson, *Barbarian Virtues*, 62; and see also Alexander Sexton, *The Rise and Fall of the White Republic: Class Politics and Mass Culture in Nineteenth Century America* (New York: Verso, 2003), 344.

4. Herbert Croly, *Progressive Democracy* (New York: Macmillan, 1914), 379, 380.

5. The term comes from a speech by George Wickersham, the Republican President William Howard Taft's attorney general. Wickersham decried such "tinkering," arguing of dangers promoted by "a modern school of political thought which finds little in the Constitution to praise, much to criticize, and a great deal to alter." For more on conservative anxieties over "Constitution tinkering," see Kammen, *A Machine That Would Go of Itself: The Constitution in American Culture* (New York: Alfred A. Knopf, Inc., 1986), 204–8, 226–31 (quotation on 205).

6. See especially Daniel Rodgers, *Atlantic Crossings: Social Politics in a Progressive Age* (Cambridge: The Belknap Press of Harvard University Press, 1998); and James Kloppenberg, *Uncertain Victory: Social Democracy and Progressivism in European and American Thought, 1870–1920* (New York: Oxford University Press, 1986).

7. See Noam Maggor, "To Coddle and Caress These Great Capitalists: Eastern Money, Frontier Populism, and the Politics of Market-Making in the American West," *American Historical Review* 122 (2017): 55–84, 68.

8. See John Dinan, *The American State Constitutional Tradition* (Lawrence: University Press of Kansas, 2006), 187.

9. Andrea Katz, "The Lost Promise of Progressive Formalism," *Texas Law Review* 99 (2021): 679–742, 707.

10. See Cyril Brickfield, *Problems Relating to a Federal Constitutional Convention* (Washington, DC: US Government Printing Office, 1957), appendix table 2, 89–91.

11. Katz, "Lost Promise of Progressive Formalism," 707.

12. See John Kowal and Wilfred Codrington, *The People's Constitution: 200 Years, 27 Amendments, and the Promise of a More Perfect Union* (New York: The New Press, 2021), 138. Indeed, Kowal and Codrington note that since thirty-one states participated in a convention call, this number satisfied—if "barely"—the two-thirds "threshold required to summon a convention" (p. 137). Given these numbers, doing nothing on the question of direct election of Senators may have intensified pressure on Congress to respond to such convention petitions.

13. Brickfield, *Problems Relating to a Federal Constitutional Convention*, 90.

14. Aziz Rana, *The Two Faces of American Freedom* (Cambridge, MA: Harvard University Press, 2010), 176–77. For more on the history of the Populist movement, see especially Lawrence Goodwyn, *Democratic Promise: The Populist Moment in America* (New York: Oxford University Press, 1976), and Charles Postel, *The Populist Vision* (New York: Oxford University Press, 2009).

15. See especially William Forbath, "The Ambiguities of Free Labor: Labor and the Law in the Gilded Age," *Wisconsin Law Review* (1985): 767–817, on the era's legal and ideological debates, and "Politics, State-Building, and the Courts, 1870–1920," in *The Cambridge History of Law in America*, vol. 2, ed. Michael Grossberg and Christopher Tomlins (New York: Cambridge University Press, 2008), 643–96, on the courts' role in nineteenth-century administration.

16. See generally Howard Gilman, *The Constitution Besieged: The Rise and Demise of Lochner Era Police Powers Jurisprudence* (Durham, NC: Duke University Press, 1993).

17. James Weaver, *A Call to Action: An Interpretation of the Great Uprising, Its Sources ad Causes* (Des Moines: Iowa Printing Co., 1892), 74–75.

18. Sylvester Pennoyer, "The Case of *Marbury v. Madison*," *American Law Review* 30 (1896): 188–202 (quotation on 202).

19. Letter from Samuel Gompers, President, American Federation of Labor, to Charles Warren, April 18, 1924, unpublished material on file with the Library of Congress, Manuscripts Division, Charles Warren Papers.

20. See William Ross, *A Muted Fury: Populists, Progressives, and Labor Unions Confront the Courts, 1890–1937* (Princeton, NJ: Princeton University Press, 1994), 110–54.

21. "Progressive Platform of 1912," *National Party Platforms: 1840–1956*, ed. Kirk Porter and Donald Bruce Johnson (Urbana: University of Illinois Press, 1956), 175–83 (quotation on 176); also quoted in Ross, *A Muted Fury*, 148.

22. Weaver, *A Call to Action*, 73.

23. Quoted in Leon Fink, "Labor, Liberty, and the Law: Trade Unionism and the Problem of the American Constitutional Order," *Journal of American History* 74 (1987): 904–25, 913–15.

24. Walter Clark, "The Revision of the Constitution of the United States," *American Law Review* 32 (1898): 5.

25. Clark, 7.

26. See generally John James Kaiser, "Judicial Knight Errant: Walter Clark and the Long Progressive Era in North Carolina" (Ph.D. diss., University of North Carolina Greensboro, 2015).

27. Woodrow Wilson, *Congressional Government: A Study in American Politics* (New York: Houghton Mifflin Co., 1885), 5.

28. August Spies, *August Spies' Auto-Biography: His Speech in Court, and General Notes* (Chicago: Niña van Zandt, 1887), 1.

29. Spies, *Auto-Biography*, 6.

30. Spies, 6.

31. J. Hector St. John de Crèvecoeur, *Letters from an American Farmer* (New York: Fox, Duffield, and Co., 1904), 54.

32. Spies, *Auto-Biography*, 3–4.

33. Spies, 12.

34. Spies, 12.

35. J. Allen Smith, *The Spirit of American Government* (New York: Macmillan Co., 1907), 27.

36. For a reading of Smith as a "Pacific Northwest Progressive" interested in municipal and constitutional reform, see Thomas McClintock, "J. Allen Smith, A Pacific Northwest Progressive," *Pacific Northwest Quarterly* 53 (1962): 49–59.

37. Charles Edward Russell, "The Invisible Government," *International Socialist Review* 14 (August 1913): 71–75 (quotation on 71).

38. For examples of these arguments about American "plutocracy," see William Brown, "Plutocracy or Democracy," *International Socialist Review* 1 (July 1900): 1–16, and William Noyes, "The Implications of Democracy," *International Socialist Review* 1 (October 1900): 193–203.

39. Smith, *Spirit of American Government*, 29, 30.

40. Werner Sombart, *Why Is There No Socialism in the United States?*, trans. Patricia Hocking and C. T. Husbands (New York: Macmillan Press, 1976). The pieces that became the book were written at a time when Sombart's politics were broadly socialist, although by the 1930s he would infamously accommodate himself to the Nazi regime. See C. T. Husbands, "Editor's Introductory Essay," in *Why Is There No Socialism in the United States?*, trans. Patricia Hocking and C. T. Husbands (New York: Macmillan Press, 1976), xvi.

41. Werner Sombart, "Studies in the History of the Development of the North American Proletariat," *International Socialist Review* 6 (1905): 358–67 (quotations on 365).

42. Along with the work by J. Allen Smith already cited, for a sense of literature see also Sydney George Fisher, *True History of the American Revolution* (Philadelphia: J. B. Lippincott, 1902); Allan Benson, *Our Dishonest Constitution* (New York: B. W. Huebsch, 1914); Gustavus Myers, *History of the Supreme Court of the United States* (Chicago: Charles H. Kerr & Co., 1912); Gilbert Roe, *Our Judicial Oligarchy* (New York: B. W. Huebsch, 1912); and most prominently Charles Beard, *An Economic Interpretation of the Constitution of the United States* (New York: Macmillan Co., 1913).

43. Vernon Louis Parrington, "Introduction," in J. Allen Smith, *The Growth and Decadence of Constitutional Government* (New York: Henry Holt & Co., 1930), xiv. For a seminal account—and critique—of "Progressive historiography," see William Novak, "The Legal Origins of the Modern American State," in *Looking Back at Law's Century*, ed. Austin Sarat, Bryant Garth, and Robert Kagan (Ithaca, NY: Cornell University Press, 2002), 249–83.

44. Sidney Pearson, "Herbert Croly and Liberal Democracy," *Society* 35 (1998): 62–71 (quotation on 67).

45. Croly, *Progressive Democracy*, 47.

46. Croly, 49.

47. Croly describes the "friends of the new Constitution" as "possess[ing] the prestige of comparative wealth and social position, the habit of leadership, usually a sufficient command of the existing machinery of government, and the determination to succeed at any cost." Croly, 48, 49.

48. Croly, 49.

49. "Go east you hear them laugh at Kansas; go west and they sneer at her; go south and they 'cuss' her; go north and they have forgotten her. Go into any crowd of intelligent people gathered anywhere in the globe, and you will find the Kansas man on the defensive." William Allen White, "What's the Matter with Kansas?" in *A Populist Reader: Selections from the Works of American Populist Leaders*, ed. George Brown Tindall (New York: Harper and Row, 1966), 192–99 (quotation on 197).

50. William Allen White, *The Old Order Changeth: A View of American Democracy* (New York: Macmillan, 1910), 22.

51. Woodrow Wilson, *Division and Reunion: 1829–1889* (New York: Longmans, Green, and Co., 1893), 13, 12.

52. According to Forrest McDonald, Beard's account was nothing less than the "generally accepted" academic "view of the founding" during the Progressive era as a whole. See Forrest McDonald, "A New Introduction," in Charles Beard, *An Economic Interpretation of the Constitution of the United States* (New York: Free Press, 1986), xxi.

53. Croly, *Progressive Democracy*, 49.

54. Charles Beard, "Introduction to the 1935 Edition," in Beard, *Economic Interpretation*, xlii, xli.

55. According to the historian Forrest McDonald, Charles Beard was central to the scholarly "discover[y]" of *Federalist No. 10* as an important account of Madisonian political thought: "[Beard] had doubtless read *The Federalist* as a graduate student and perhaps earlier, but the emphasis in those days was upon the later essays, which are concerned with the structure of government and the formal distribution of powers; number 10 had been generally neglected by scholars." McDonald, "A New Introduction," xii. By contrast with existing approaches, Beard read the structural discussion in documents like *No. 51* through *No. 10* and placed them collectively at the center of his theory of the Constitution.

56. Beard, *Economic Interpretation*, 156.

57. Alexander Hamilton, John Jay, and James Madison, *The Federalist Papers*, ed. Isaac Kramnick (New York: Penguin Books, 1987), no. 10 (Madison).

58. See Beard, *Economic Interpretation*, 157 for his discussion of Madison's belief in the "supreme danger" of "an overbearing majority."

59. *Federalist Papers*, no. 51 (Madison).

60. See generally Beard, *Economic Interpretation*, 156–61.

61. For more on how the framers combined a defense of settler egalitarianism with deep suspicion of the poor, see Rana, *Two Faces*, 121–25, 135–42.

62. Quoted in Beard, *Economic Interpretation*, 158n1.

63. Beard, 161.

64. Quoted in Noyes, "The Implications of Democracy," 199.

65. Beard, *Economic Interpretation*, 61.

66. Clark, "Revision of the Constitution of the United States," 1.

67. Elizabeth Cady Stanton, "Address to Anniversary of American Equal Rights Association, May 12, 1869, New York City," in *Elizabeth Cady Stanton, Feminist as Thinker: A Reader in Documents and Essays*, ed. Ellen Carol DuBois and Richard Cándida Smith (New York: New York University Press, 2007), 187–205 (quotation on 189).

68. See Mari Jo Buhle, *Women and American Socialism, 1870–1920* (Urbana: University of Illinois Press, 1981), 68.

69. Quoted in Angela Davis, *Women, Race, and Class* (New York: Vintage Books, 1981), 70.

70. Quoted in Aileen S. Kraditor, *The Ideas of the Woman Suffrage Movement, 1890–1920* (New York: Columbia University Press, 1965), 197.

71. Michael David Cohen, "School for Suffrage: The American Woman's Republic," *The Good Society* 25 (2016): 209–30 (quotation on 221).

72. Quoted in Cohen, 222.

73. Emma Goldman, "The Tragedy of Woman's Emancipation," in *Anarchism and Other Essays* (New York: Dover, 1969), 213–25 (quotation on 217).

74. See Ellen Carol DuBois, "Working Women, Class Relations, and Suffrage Militance: Harriot Stanton Blatch and the New York Woman Suffrage Movement, 1894–1909," in *Woman Suffrage and Women's Rights* (New York: New York University Press), 176–209, especially 183–85.

75. See Charlotte Perkins Gilman, *Women and Economics: A Study of the Economic Relation between Men and Women as a Factor in Social Evolution* (Berkeley: University of California Press, 1998), 144.

76. Buhle, *Women and American Socialism*, 68.

77. Mary Livermore, "Cooperative Womanhood in the State," *North American Review* 153 (September 1891): 283–95 (quotations on 295).

78. For more generally on the AWR, see Cohen, "School for Suffrage" (quotation on 223).

79. Herbert Croly, *The Promise of American Life* (New York: Macmillan, 1909), 212.

80. Croly, *Progressive Democracy*, 51, 44.

81. Croly, 45.

82. Croly, 245.

83. James Morone, *Democratic Wish: Popular Participation and the Limits of American Government* (New York: Basic Books, 1990), 112.

84. "Progressive Platform of 1912," 176.

85. See generally Katz's excellent article, "The Lost Promise of Progressive Formalism."

86. See generally Rana, *Two Faces*, 245–47.

87. Croly, *Progressive Democracy*, 226.

88. Croly, 232.

89. Quoted in Ross, *A Muted Fury*, 119.

90. Croly, *Progressive Democracy*, 97, 304.

91. Pearson, "Herbert Croly and Liberal Democracy," 67.

92. Theodore Roosevelt, *The Rough Riders: An Autobiography*, ed. Louis Auchincloss (New York: Library of America, 2004), 721.

93. Quoted in Niels Aage Thorsen, *The Political Thought of Woodrow Wilson*,

1875–1910 (Princeton, NJ: Princeton University Press, 1988), 13; also partially quoted in Katz, "Lost Promise of Progressive Formalism," 723.

94. See Nikolas Bowie and Dapha Renan, "The Separation-of-Powers Counter-revolution," *Yale Law Journal* 131 (2022): 2020–2125 (quotation on 2065).

95. See generally Bowie and Renan, 2047–77.

96. Woodrow Wilson, *Constitutional Government in the United States* (New York: Columbia University Press, 1908), 60.

97. Croly, *Progressive Democracy*, 154.

98. Wilson, *Constitutional Government*, 60; also quoted in Katz, "Lost Promise of Progressive Formalism," 705.

99. "Extremes Meet," *Outlook*, May 13, 1911, 54.

100. For more on this concept see Bruce Ackerman, "Transformative Appointments," *Harvard Law Review* 110 (1988): 1164–84.

101. Frederick Douglass, "Sources of Danger to the Republic (1867)," in *The Speeches of Frederick Douglass*, ed. John McKivigan, Julie Husband, and Heather Kaufman (New Haven, CT: Yale University Press, 2018), 217–46 (quotation on 230).

102. Woodrow Wilson, "The Place of the United States in Constitutional Development," in W. Cameron Forbes, *The Philippine Islands*, vol. 2 (New York: Houghton Mifflin Co., 1928), 511–12 (quotation on 511).

103. See Ross, *A Muted Fury*, 91.

Chapter 4

1. For the remainder of the book, sometimes the word "Socialist" will be capitalized. I will do so when referring to the Socialist Party of America—its supporters and ideological commitments. Other times, I will leave the word "socialist" uncapitalized when discussing more generally socialist values and beliefs as well as political actors who conceived of themselves as socialists, even if they were not members of the party, had broken from it, or even actually actively opposed the party politically.

2. See James Weinstein, *The Decline of Socialism in America* (New York: Monthly Review Press, 1967), 116–18; and Joseph Conlin, "The I. W. W. and the Socialist Party," *Science and Society* 31 (1967): 22–36 (numbers on 22). For more on the regional diversity and truly national dimensions of the Socialist Party of America at the beginning of the century, see especially David Shannon's excellent and still essential volume, *The Socialist Party of America: A History* (New York: Macmillan, 1955), 1–42.

3. Eugene V. Debs, "Why We Have Outgrown the United States Constitution," *Progressive Woman* 5 (September 1911): 5, https://www.marxists.org/archive/debs/works/1911/110900-debs-outgrowntheconstitution.pdf.

4. *Appeal to Reason*, March 2, 1912, 2.

5. One advertisement for Gustavus Myers's *History of the Supreme Court* declared it "beyond a doubt the book of the year for Socialists," and even included a blurb from Debs referring to it as "an invaluable work. . . . The service you [Myers] have rendered the American people, and especially to the workers of the nation, can scarcely be overestimated." See "Gustavus Myers' *History of the Supreme Court*," *International Socialist Review* 13 (1912): 94. As for examples of popular education,

another advertisement, this time for Ruskin University, "[a] combination of eleven hitherto independent colleges offer[ing] instruction in technical, literary, and scientific branches," publicized lectures in "American Economic History," including "Class Struggle on the Adoption of the Constitution." See "Ruskin University," *International Socialist Review* 3 (March 1903).

6. Shannon, *Socialist Party of America*, 9.

7. Shannon, 26–27.

8. For more on the idea of "fundamental law" and its relation to conventional notions of constitutionalism, see Ryan Doerfler and Samuel Moyn, "Imagining a Post-Constitutional Political Culture," *Public Seminar*, October 12, 2021, https:// publicseminar.org/essays/post-constitutional-political-culture/.

9. See "Socialist Platform of 1912," in *National Party Platforms: 1840–1956*, ed. Kirk Porter and Donald Bruce Johnson (Urbana: University of Illinois Press, 1956), 188–91, 189.

10. Quoted in Ira Kipnis, *The American Socialist Movement* (New York: Columbia University Press, 1952), 111.

11. "Socialist Platform of 1912," 189.

12. "Socialist Platform of 1912," 189.

13. For an excellent and still defining account of SPA thinking about the Constitution, especially free speech issues, see John Wertheimer's dissertation, "Free Speech Fights: The Roots of Modern Free-Expression Litigation in the United States" (PhD diss., Princeton University, 1992), 129–237. There Wertheimer notes how "the Socialist perception of the American legal system as a whole was overwhelmingly negative. Their rhetorical bashing of courts, constitutions, and judges knew few bounds" (p. 216).

However, Wertheimer tends to treat Socialists as falling into two camps. On the one hand, there were anti-constitutionalists who called for "abolishing the Constitution altogether" (p. 220). On the other, there were "Constitutional Socialists" who pressed for free speech commitments, including in the courts, and "refused to abandon the founding document" (p. 221). Part of why Wertheimer makes this claim is because his analysis does not always disaggregate the various constellations of socialist and socialist-leaning parties and papers across the late nineteenth and early twentieth centuries. More significantly, his focus on constitutional rights, rather than constitutional structure, means that he tends to lump all brands of constitutionalism in with support for the US Constitution specifically. This approach then deemphasizes the extent to which activists often combined a genuine commitment to constitutional rights with the belief in the need for thoroughgoing structural transformations—including to instantiate those rights.

As we will see, there were indeed conservative SPA politicians who came to adopt an anti-formalist reading of the Constitution in line with many Progressive reformers. This even entailed a focus on changing how the text was interpreted rather than rewriting the text. But such politicians on the party's right wing were making arguments that contradicted the spirit and letter of SPA platforms throughout its existence as a serious electoral force. See *National Party Platforms: 1840–1956* for repeated demands for the abolition of judicial review, the calling of a constitutional convention, the simplification of the amendment process, and basic changes to the executive and legislative branches (pp. 166, 190–91, 210, 241, 293, 353, 371).

Thus, although there were certainly competing constitutional positions and sensibilities within the party, I see views like that of Eugene Debs—combining free speech commitments *and* a belief that the Constitution would have to be fundamentally altered—as the SPA's ideological center of gravity, especially during its 1910s heyday.

14. Lochner v. U.S., 198 U.S. 45, 75 (1905) (J. Holmes, dissenting).

15. Allan Benson, *Our Dishonest Constitution* (New York: B. W. Huebsch, 1914), 54.

16. Debs, "Why We Have Outgrown the United States Constitution," 5.

17. Benson, 72.

18. Benson, 75, 86.

19. Crystal Eastman, "The Socialist Party Convention (1920)," in *Toward the Great Change: Crystal Eastman and Max Eastman on Feminism, Antimilitarism, and Revolution*, ed. Blanche Wiesen Cook (New York: Garland Publishing, Inc., 1976), 436–44 (quotation on 437).

20. Debs, "Why We Have Outgrown the United States Constitution," 5.

21. Benson, *Our Dishonest Constitution*, 75.

22. See *National Party Platforms*, 166, 190, 210, 241, 353, 371.

23. This was a term popularized by Gilbert Roe, a reformist lawyer and advisor to Wisconsin Progressive Robert La Follette Sr., in his book *Our Judicial Oligarchy* (New York: B. W. Huebsch, 1912).

24. See for example "Shall We Elect Social-Democratic Judges?" *Social-Democratic Herald*, January 29, 1910, and "Law! Law! Law! Who Makes the Law!" *Social-Democratic Herald*, February 12, 1910.

25. Debs, "Why We Have Outgrown the United States Constitution," 5.

26. On the destructive implications of the Electoral College specifically, Benson declared, "Conceivably the time may come when this inaccurate system of registering the people's will may result in giving a majority of the electoral vote to a man whom the great majority of the people distrust and have reason to distrust. At a critical time, such an 'election' may precipitate a revolution. At any time such an election is an assault upon the fundamental principles of popular government." Benson, *Our Dishonest Constitution*, 66.

27. Benson, 66.

28. "Socialist Platform of 1912," 190.

29. For more on Crystal Eastman and her combination of civil libertarian ideals and radical constitutional critique, see John Witt's excellent biographical sketch in *Patriots and Cosmopolitans: Hidden Histories of American Law* (Cambridge, MA: Harvard University Press, 2007), 157–208.

30. See Amy Aronson's essential new biography, *Crystal Eastman: A Revolutionary Life* (New York: Oxford University Press, 2020), 9.

31. Crystal Eastman, "The Socialist Vote," *Liberator*, December 1918, 33, also quoted in Aronson, *Crystal Eastman*, 202.

32. Aronson, *Crystal Eastman*, 9.

33. See Sylvia Law, "Crystal Eastman: NYU Law Graduate," *NYU Law Review* 66 (1991): 1983–84.

34. Aronson, *Crystal Eastman*, 9.

35. Eastman, "The Socialist Party Convention," 437.

36. Eastman, 437.

37. Quoted in Melvyn Dubofsky, *We Shall Be All: A History of the Industrial Workers of the World* (Urbana: University of Illinois Press, 2000), 89.

38. Benson, *Our Dishonest Constitution*, 77, 75.

39. See Ira Kipnis, *The American Socialist Movement* (New York: Columbia University Press, 1952), 388–89.

40. Quoted in Dubofsky, *We Shall Be All*, 90.

41. Helen Marot, *American Labor Unions: By a Member* (New York: Henry Holt and Co., 1914), 52.

42. When describing the ultimate cooperative commonwealth to come, Debs nonetheless imagined the replacement of the state as it was understood by a non-coercive "administration of national industries." This was because "[w]ith the end of class rule political government will cease to exist. Its functions, which are essentially coercive, will no longer be required." Debs, "Why We Have Outgrown the United States Constitution," 5.

43. Quoted in Kipnis, *American Socialist Movement*, 389.

44. Quoted in Laura Weinrib's foundational account of the shifting politics of civil liberties in the first half of the twentieth century, *The Taming of Free Speech* (Cambridge, MA: Harvard University Press, 2016), 27.

45. Weinrib, 27.

46. See generally Joseph Conlin, "The IWW and the Question of Violence," *Wisconsin Magazine of History* 51 (1968): 316–26 (quotations on 316, 321). This violent perception of Haywood became fixed in the public imagination due to his murder trial in the bombing death of Idaho Governor Frank Steunenberg. Yet, far less noted in the mainstream press was that Haywood and the other WFM leaders were ultimately acquitted given the lack of evidence. Indeed, Conlin writes of the IWW years specifically, "[I]t bears repeating that despite dozens of prosecutions and the investigative powers of a dozen states, the Bureau of Investigation, the Immigration Bureau, and the Justice Department, *no Wobbly was ever proved to have committed an act of violence*" (p. 325).

47. Conlin, 321.

48. Quoted in Dubofsky, *We Shall Be All*, 92.

49. Quoted in Dubofsky, 92; and for more on such IWW tactics, see Dubofsky, 84–113.

50. Conlin, "IWW and the Question of Violence," 321. Conlin further details that while the evidence of actual IWW violence was virtually nonexistent, business owners routinely employed agents provocateurs to undermine the union: "A reporter for the *New York Post* wrote that lumber millowners frankly admitted to him that 'the peculiar reputation for violence and lawlessness which has been fixed upon the I.W.W. was largely the work of their own ingenious publicity agents'" (p. 324).

51. See Wertheimer, "Free Speech Fights," 192.

52. August Spies, *August Spies' Auto-Biography: His Speech in Court, and General Notes* (Chicago: Niña van Zandt, 1887), 66.

53. "Socialist Platform of 1912," 188–91 (quotation on 189).

54. "Socialist Platform of 1912," quotations on 190–91.

55. Benson, *Our Dishonest Constitution*, 85.

56. Quoted in "Wants House Abolished: Berger of the House May Be Disciplined for Criticism in Resolution," *New York Times*, April 28, 1911.

57. See generally "Socialist Platform of 1912," 188–91 (quotations on 189, 190).

58. See Dubofsky, *We Shall Be All*, 89.

59. Quoted in Marot, *American Labor Unions*, 56–57.

60. Joe Hill, "Mr. Block," in *Rebel Voices: An I. W. W. Anthology*, ed. Joyce Kornbluh (Ann Arbor: University of Michigan Press, 1964), 135–36.

61. Charles Edward Russell, "The Invisible Government," *International Socialist Review* 14 (August 1913): 71–75 (quotation on 75).

62. "When They Ask You," *International Socialist Review* 16 (1916): 650–51 (quotation on 651).

63. See "The World of Labor," *International Socialist Review* 1 (1900): 114–20.

64. Quoted in Dubofsky, *We Shall Be All*, 90.

65. Justus Ebert, *The I. W. W. in Theory and Practice* (Chicago: Industrial Workers of the World, 1918), 64.

66. Benson, *Our Dishonest Constitution*, 174.

67. Benson, 173, 175–76.

68. Allan L. Benson, "What's Wrong with the Socialist Party?" *New Appeal*, whole no. 1,176 (June 15, 1918): 1–7 (quotation on 7).

69. Indicative of this desire to avoid anything with a whiff of lawlessness, Benson begins his 1918 critique of the SPA by declaring "anarchists" to be the root cause of all the party's problems. According to him, they were undermining the party from within through their commitment to "sabotage" under the guise of direct action. Benson, 2.

70. "The Interpretation of the Constitution," *Social-Democratic Herald*, January 4, 1913, also partially quoted in Wertheimer, "Free Speech Fights," 225.

71. For a volume demonstrating how groups across society incorporated the Declaration, as well as the idea of writing one's own Declaration, into the politics of nineteenth- and early twentieth-century reform, see *We, the Other People: Alternative Declarations of Independence by Labor Groups, Farmers, Women's Rights Advocates, Socialists, and Blacks, 1829–1975*, ed. Philip S. Foner (Urbana: University of Illinois Press, 1976).

72. Quoted in Dubofsky, *We Shall Be All*, 91. For more on the rise of the discourse of "wage slavery," see Alex Gourevitch, *From Slavery to the Cooperative Commonwealth: Labor and Republican Liberty in the Nineteenth Century* (New York: Cambridge University Press, 2015), 97–137.

73. See Aronson, *Crystal Eastman*, 196.

74. In fact, the Eastmans had a family association with abolitionism, as their mother, Annis Ford Eastman, had a close working relationship with "the abolitionist Thomas Beecher," even "succeed[ing]" him as "pastor of the prominent Park Church" in Elmire, New York. Aronson, 2.

75. See James Redpath, "The Three Oligarchies," *The National Anti-Slavery Standard*, January 26, 1867, on file with Cornell University, Kroc Rare Manuscripts Collection.

76. Redpath. Here Redpath very consciously inverts the Old Testament story in the Book of Genesis about Noah cursing Canaan for Ham's supposed transgression of "seeing the nakedness of his father." Noah declares, since Ham in turn is the father of Canaan, that "Cursed be Canaan; a servant of servants shall he be unto his brethren"—Genesis 9:22, 25 (King James Version). In the years before the Civil

War, enslavers commonly invoked these passages as a religious justification for why persons of African descent could be held in bondage. Redpath, by contrast, places Reconstruction-era Americans—white and Black—in the role of Ham and highlights instead the virtues of Ham and the moral and political failures of Noah.

77. See Redpath, "The Three Oligarchies."

78. See A. M. Simons, "Economic Aspects of Chattel Slavery (pt. 3)," *International Socialist Review* 4 (September 1903): 167–68.

79. This discussion draws on Andrew Zimmerman's terrific article, "From the Second American Revolution to the First International and Back Again: Marxism, the Popular Front, and the American Civil War," in *The World the Civil War Made*, ed. Gregory P. Downs and Kate Masur (Chapel Hill: University of North Carolina Press, 2015), 306. On the statistical percentage of German-born soldiers in the Union army, see Walter Kamphoefner and Wolfgang Helbich, "Introduction," in *Germans in the Civil War: The Letters They Wrote Home*, ed. Walter Kamphoefner and Wolfgang Helbich, trans. Susan Carter Vogel (Chapel Hill: University of North Carolina Press, 2006), 20.

80. Germans that made up the senior Union officer corps included men such as "Carl Schurz, Franz Sigel, Alexander Schimmelpfennig, August Willich, and Ludwig Blenker," among others. See Zimmerman, 307. Although in the following decades some German radicals would become increasingly conservative, Zimmerman tells us that during the war these soldiers were a continuous thorn in the side of more moderate Republicans.

81. Indeed, the paper's editor, Charles A. Dana, told Marx that he was "not only one of the most highly valued, but one of the best paid contributors attached to the journal." Quoted in Zimmerman, 310.

82. Karl Marx, "Address of the International Workingmen's Association to Abraham Lincoln, President of the United States of America," November 1864, https://www.marxists.org/archive/marx/iwma/documents/1864/lincoln-letter.htm.

83. Ebert, *I. W. W. in Theory and Practice*, 67.

84. Jeffery Perry, *Hubert Harrison: The Voice of Harlem Radicalism, 1883–1918* (New York: Columbia University Press, 2009), 144.

85. See generally Mark Pettinger, *American Socialists and Evolutionary Thought, 1870–1920* (Madison: University of Wisconsin Press, 1993), 173–86.

86. Quoted in Pettinger, 180.

87. Quoted in Pettinger, 145.

88. Quoted in Michael Dawson, *Blacks In and Out of the Left* (Cambridge, MA: Harvard University Press, 2013), 27.

89. Hubert Harrison, "Socialism and the Negro," *International Socialist Review* 13 (1912): 65–68 (quotations on 66, 65).

90. Harrison, 67.

91. Eric Arensen, "Specter of the Black Strikebreaker: Race, Employment, and Labor Activism in the Industrial Era," *Labor History* 44 (2003): 319–35 (quotations on 320).

92. Quoted in Arensen, 323.

93. Harrison, "Socialism and the Negro," 66.

NOTES TO PAGES 162–174

94. See Benjamin Lynerd, "Republican Ideology and the Black Labor Movement, 1869–1872," *Phylon* 56 (2019): 19–36, especially 29–30 (quotation on 30).

95. David Blight, *Frederick Douglass: Prophet of Freedom* (New York: Simon & Schuster, 2018), 560.

96. See generally Joseph Conlin, "The I. W. W. and the Socialist Party," *Science and Society* 31 (1967): 22–36.

97. For more on the class cohesiveness and explicit feudal pretensions of the rich during the Gilded Age, see Michael McGerr, "Progressivism, Liberalism, and the Rich," in *The Progressives' Century: Political Reform, Constitutional Government, and the Modern American State*, ed. Stephen Skowronek, Stephen Engel, and Bruce Ackerman (New Haven, CT: Yale University Press, 2016), 243–63.

Chapter 5

1. See Sarah Cleveland, "Powers Inherent in Sovereignty: Indians, Aliens, Territories, and the Nineteenth Century Origins of Plenary Power over Foreign Affairs," *Texas Law Review* 81 (2003): 207, 208; Juan Torruella, *The Supreme Court and Puerto Rico: The Doctrine of Separate and Unequal* (Rìo Piedras: University of Puerto Rico, 1985), 23; and Aziz Rana, *The Two Faces of American Freedom* (Cambridge, MA: Harvard University Press, 2010), 272.

2. Paul Kramer, *The Blood of Government: Race, Empire, the United States, and the Philippines* (Chapel Hill: University of North Carolina Press, 2006), 157, 146 (quotations on 152, 157). See also Paul Kramer, "The Water Cure," *New Yorker*, February 17, 2008, https://www.newyorker.com/magazine/2008/02/25/the-water-cure.

3. Mark Twain, "Mark Twain Says He's Discouraged," *New York World*, June 17, 1900, in *Life as I Find It: A Treasury of Mark Twain Rarities*, ed. Charles Neider (New York: Cooper Square Press, 2000), 325–32 (quotation on 331).

4. Kramer, *Blood of Government*, 154.

5. See generally Duncan Bell, *Dreamworlds of Race: Empire and the Utopian Destiny of Anglo-America* (Princeton, NJ: Princeton University Press, 2020).

6. See Theodore Roosevelt, "Expansion and Peace," in *The Strenuous Life: Essays and Addresses* (New York: P. F. Collier and Son, 1911), 23–36 (quotation on 29).

7. Marilyn Lake and Henry Reynolds, *Drawing the Global Colour Line: White Men's Countries and the International Challenge of Racial Equality* (New York: Cambridge University Press, 2008), 105.

8. For more generally on the centrality of China in the American expansionist imagination, see Jedidiah Kroncke, *The Futility of Law and Development: China and the Dangers of Exporting American Law* (New York: Oxford University Press, 2015). Kroncke's terrific book explores how American missionaries and elite policymakers in the late nineteenth and early twentieth centuries came to see the transformation of China as central to their projects of legal, economic, and cultural export.

9. Theodore Roosevelt, "The Strenuous Life," in *The Strenuous Life: Essays and Addresses* (New York: P. F. Collier and Son, 1911), 3–22 (quotations on 9, 8).

10. Roosevelt, 3.

11. See Frederick Jackson Turner, *The Frontier in American History* (Tucson: University of Arizona Press, 1986), 37.

12. See Roosevelt, "Expansion and Peace," 36.

13. Quoted in Sam Erman, *Almost Citizens: Puerto Rico, the U.S. Constitution, and Empire* (Cambridge, UK: Cambridge University Press, 2019), 38.

14. See Lanny Thompson, "The Imperial Republic: A Comparison of the Insular Territories under U.S. Dominion after 1898," *Pacific Historical Review* 71 (2002): 561–63 (quotation on 563).

15. Sam Erman, "Puerto Rico and the Promise of United States Citizenship: Struggles around Status in a New Empire, 1898–1917" (PhD diss., University of Michigan, 2010), 32.

16. Erman, 29–39.

17. Quotations in Rafael Rojas, "*Otro gallo cantaría*: Essay on the First Cuban Republicanism," in *The Cuban Republic and José Martí: Reception and Use of a National Symbol*, ed. Mauricio A. Font and Alfonso W. Quiroz (New York: Lexington Books, 2006), 7–17 (quotations on 15).

18. See Louis Peréz, *Cuba between Empires: 1878–1902* (Pittsburg, PA: University of Pittsburgh Press, 1983), 315–28 (quotation on 321).

19. See "Cuban Universal Suffrage. Constitutional Convention Votes for Unrestricted Ballot," *New York Times*, January 11, 1901, 6.

20. See Alejandro De La Fuente, *A Nation for All: Race, Inequality, and Politics in Twentieth Century Cuba* (Chapel Hill: University of North Carolina Press, 2001), 12–13.

21. See Peréz, *Cuba between Empires*, 313–14.

22. Peréz, 323–24.

23. Quoted in Peréz, 318.

24. Quoted in Lance Banning, *The Jeffersonian Persuasion: Evolution of a Party Ideology* (Ithaca, NY: Cornell University Press, 1978), 262n43.

25. Alexander Hamilton, John Jay, and James Madison, *The Federalist Papers*, ed. Isaac Kramnick (New York: Penguin Books, 1987), no. 8 (Hamilton).

26. Gene Clanton, *Congressional Populism and the Crisis of the 1890s* (Lawrence: University Press of Kansas, 1998), 139.

27. Clanton, 152.

28. Downes v. Bidwell, 182 U.S. 245, 380 (1901) (J. Harlan, dissenting).

29. Quoted in Gerard Magliocca, *The Heart of the Constitution: How the Bill of Rights Became the Bill of Rights* (New York: Oxford University Press, 2018), 79.

30. See generally Magliocca, 76–81.

31. See Akhil Reed Amar, *The Bill of Rights: Creation and Reconstruction* (New Haven, CT: Yale University Press, 1998), 284–87.

32. Amar, 286–87.

33. Magliocca, *Heart of the Constitution*, 66–70.

34. *Downes*, 182 U.S. 245.

35. Quoted in Mark Sullivan, *Our Times: The United States, 1900–1925*, vol. 1 (New York: Charles Scribner's Sons, 1934), 552.

36. William Neville, "Speech on Imperialism," transcript of speech delivered at the United States Capitol Building, Washington, DC, February 6, 1900, http://courses.missouristate.edu/bobmiller/populism/texts/documents/speech_on_imperialism.htm.

37. See J. L. Franz, "History of the United States (Concluded)," *International Socialist Review* 3 (1902): 42.

38. J. Neal Steere, "Professor against Annexation, August 27, 1898," in *The Anti-Imperialist Reader: From the Mexican War to the Election of 1900*, vol. 1, ed. Philip S. Foner and Richard C. Winchester (New York: Holmes & Meier, 1984), 241.

39. See Kramer, *Blood of Government*, 146–51 (quotations on 149, 148).

40. The phrase was coined by the journalist John L. O'Sullivan in his editorial for the July and August *Democratic Review* on the issue of Texas's admission to the Union. For more on the concept in American political thought, see generally Frederick Merk, *Manifest Destiny and Mission in American History: A Reinterpretation* (Cambridge, MA: Harvard University Press, 1995).

41. For more on the law and practice of North American settlement, see generally Aziz Rana, *The Two Faces of American Freedom* (Cambridge, MA: Harvard University Press, 2010), 99–175.

42. "The Population of Hawai'i by Race / Ethnicity: U.S. Census 1900-2010," Native Hawaiian Data Book, accessed April 23, 2018, www.ohadatabook.com/T01 -03-11u.pdf.

43. For more on Hawaii and territorial governance, see Thompson, "The Imperial Republic," 542–45.

44. On the protectionist claims of some anti-annexationists, including Samuel Gompers in the AFL, see Pedro Cabán, *Constructing a Colonial People: Puerto Rico and the United States, 1898–1932* (Boulder, CO: Westview Press, 1999), 38.

45. Carman F. Randolph, "Constitutional Aspects of Annexation," *Harvard Law Review* 12 (1898): 291–315 (quotation on 304).

46. Quotations in Erman, *Almost Citizens*, 4, 8.

47. Dred Scott v. Sandford, 60 U.S. 393, 407 (1857).

48. For more on *Dred Scott* as the culmination of a settler legal imagination with respect to expansion and membership see Rana, *Two Faces*, 167–72.

49. *Downes*, 182 U.S. at 360–61 (C.J. Fuller, dissenting).

50. Kramer, *The Blood of Government*, 165.

51. Quoted in Kramer, 295.

52. See generally Mona Francesca Katigbak, "Historical Transcendence: The Significance of the Bill of Rights of the Malolos Constitution," *Philippine Law Journal* 73 (1998): 309–50, especially 313–21; and also George Malcolm, "The Malolos Constitution," *Political Science Quarterly* 36 (1921): 91–103.

53. This discussion of LeRoy's growing wariness of the initial race-based imperial justifications relies on Kramer's essential account. See especially Kramer, *Blood of Government*, 191–98, 289–99. I then argue that this wariness was part of the process by which Republican officials turned toward both creed and Constitution as alternative bases for American global authority.

54. James LeRoy, "Race Prejudice in the Philippines," *Atlantic Monthly*, July 1902, 100–112 (quotations on 108–9, 100); also partially quoted in Kramer, *The Blood of Government*, 195.

55. James LeRoy, *Philippine Life in Town and Country* (Manila: Limited Editions, 1968), 55, 56; also partially quoted in Kramer, *The Blood of Government*, 192.

56. Quoted in Lake and Reynolds, *Drawing the Global Colour Line*, 168.

57. Quotations in Kramer, *Blood of Government*, 296.

58. See Lake and Reynolds, *Drawing the Global Colour Line*, 190–97.

59. W. E. B. Du Bois, *The Souls of Black Folk: Essays and Sketches* (New York: Fawcett Publishing Co., 1961), 23.

60. LeRoy, "Race Prejudice in the Philippines," 106, 109.

61. The following discussion of how new notions of American international authority connected to earlier ideas expressed by the Monroe Doctrine draws from Rana, *Two Faces*, 284–87.

62. See James Tully, *Public Philosophy in a New Key: Imperialism and Civic Freedom*, vol. 2 (New York: Cambridge University Press, 2008), 133.

63. See Jeffrey Keith, "Civilization, Race, and the Japan Expedition's Cultural Diplomacy," *Diplomatic History* 35 (2001): 179–202; and Gerard Magliocca, *American Founding Son: John Bingham and the Invention of the Fourteenth Amendment* (New York: New York University Press, 2013), 171.

64. Magliocca, *American Founding Son*, 171–77; Jack Hammersmith, "Ohio's John A. Bingham in Meiji Japan: The Politician as Diplomat," *Ohio History* 126 (2019): 58–71.

65. Theodore Roosevelt, "National Duties," in *The Strenuous Life: Essays and Addresses* (New York: P. F. Collier and Son, 1911), 228–44 (quotations on 244, 236).

66. Theodore Roosevelt, "State of the Union, December 6, 1904," in *America as a World Power, 1872–1945*, ed. Robert H. Ferrell (Columbia: University of South Carolina Press, 1971), 105–7 (quotation on 105–6).

67. See Kramer, *Blood of Government*, 356–57 (quotation on 356).

68. LeRoy, "Race Prejudice in the Philippines," 111.

69. LeRoy, 100, 112.

70. This implication builds from Sam Erman's account of how debates about extending citizenship to Puerto Rico were interwoven with the emerging domestic resolutions around Reconstruction and the Reconstruction Amendments. See generally Erman, *Almost Citizens*.

71. See Magliocca, *Heart of the Constitution*, 81, 193n23.

72. David Jayne Hill, *Americanism: What It Is* (New York: D. Appleton & Co., 1916), viii, 27.

73. Hill, 28.

74. Hill, 13–14, 15, 29.

75. Hill, 66.

76. Hill, vii.

77. See Nikhil Pal Singh, *Black Is a Country: Race and the Unfinished Struggle for Democracy* (Cambridge, MA: Harvard University Press, 2004), 17–18: "'American universalism,' historian John Higham summarizes, is 'our egalitarian ideology . . . molded by the Enlightenment and forged in the revolution . . . simultaneously a civic credo, a social vision and a definition of nationhood'" (ellipses in original).

78. Hill, *Americanism*, 134.

79. See Hill, 177–79.

80. Hill, 177.

81. See Erman, *Almost Citizens*, 12 for how debates about annexing the Dominican Republic rehearsed later concerns, including over what the Reconstruction Amendments would mean for non-white overseas inclusion.

82. Frederick Douglass, *The Life and Times of Frederick Douglass, from 1817 to 1882, Written by Himself* (Hartford, CT: Park Publishing, 1882), 496.

83. See Millery Polyné, "Expansion Now! Haiti, 'Santo Domingo,' and Frederick Douglass at the Intersection of U.S. and Caribbean Pan-Americanism," *Caribbean Studies* 34 (July-December 2006): 3–45 (quotation on 6).

84. See Vince Schleitwiler, *Strange Fruit of the Black Pacific: Imperialism's Racial Justice and Its Fugitives* (New York: NYU Press, 2017), 41.

85. W. E. B. Du Bois, "The Present Outlook for the Dark Races of Mankind," *A. M. E. Church Review* 17 (October 1900): 95–110 (quotation on 106).

86. David Levering Lewis, *W. E. B. Du Bois: A Biography* (New York: Henry Holt, 2009), 227.

87. DuBois, "The Present Outlook," quotations on 102.

88. Douglass, *Life and Times*, 496.

89. Vince Schleitwiler employs the phrase as a way of presenting Du Bois's initial combination of critique and acceptance with respect to American imperial ambitions. Schleitwiler, *Strange Fruit*, 42.

90. See Robert Tsai, *America's Forgotten Constitutions: Defiant Visions of Power and Community* (Cambridge, MA: Harvard University Press, 2014), 152–84 for an excellent overview of the Sequoyah statehood project (statistics on 176).

91. See generally *Constitution of the State of Sequoyah* (Muskogee, I.T.: Phoenix Printing Co., 1905).

92. With respect to Sequoyah, Republicans were also swayed by the worry that the territory would be a Democratic Party stronghold—given the emergent Populist and rural political alliances on the ground—and they had no interest in effectively ceding four Senate votes to their political opponents. If Sequoyah were to have entered the Union it would have done so alongside rather than instead of Oklahoma. Tsai, *America's Forgotten Constitutions*, 177–78.

93. *Constitution of the State of Sequoyah*, 26.

94. See for example Tiya Miles, *Ties That Bind: The Story of an Afro-Cherokee Family in Slavery and Freedom* (Berkeley: University of California Press, 2005).

95. Tsai, *America's Forgotten Constitutions*, 160–63.

96. Tsai, 168.

97. Quoted in Tsai, 158.

98. See Rana, *Two Faces*, 229–30.

99. For more on the implications of this distinction for settler legal frameworks and modes of racial management, see Patrick Wolfe's essential book, *Traces of History: Elementary Structures of Race* (New York: Verso, 2016), 141–201.

100. For a sustained critique of the idea of inclusion as a meaningful path to Indigenous freedom, see Jodi Byrd's seminal contribution, *Transit of Empire: Indigenous Critiques of Colonialism* (Minneapolis: University of Minnesota Press, 2011). On the constitutional implications, see Maggie Blackhawk, "Foreword: The Constitution of American Colonialism," *Harvard Law Review* (forthcoming 2023).

101. Quotations in David Nichols, *Lincoln and the Indians: Civil War Policy and Politics* (Urbana: University of Illinois Press, 2000), 196. For more on the history of forced Indigenous assimilation during these years, see Frederick Hoxie, *A Final Promise: The Campaign to Assimilate the Indians, 1880–1920* (Lincoln: University of Nebraska Press, 1984).

102. Frederick Douglass, "The Future of the Negro People of the Slave States," in *Frederick Douglass: Selected Speeches and Writings*, ed. Philip S. Foner and Yuval Taylor (Chicago: Lawrence Hill Books, 1999), 474–85 (quotation on 485).

103. Douglass, 485.

104. Quoted in William B. Gatewood Jr., *"Smoked Yankees" and the Struggle for Empire: Letters from Negro Soldiers, 1898–1902* (Urbana: University of Illinois Press, 1971), 13.

105. Quoted in Kramer, *Blood of Government*, 120.

106. "Ida Wells-Barnett Against Expansion," in *The Black Press Views American Imperialism, 1898-1900*, ed. George P. Marks (New York: Arno Press, Inc., 1971), 109.

107. See Merline Pitre, "Frederick Douglass and the Annexation of Santo Domingo," *Journal of Negro History* 62 (October 1977): 390–400 (quotation on 397).

108. Quoted in Gatewood, *"Smoked Yankees,"* 15.

109. For more on Fagen's role in the Filipino independence movement, the uncertainty around whether he was ever killed, and his larger mythology, see generally Michael Morey, *Fagen: An African American Renegade in the Philippine-American War* (Madison: University of Wisconsin Press, 2019); and Michael Robinson and Frank Schubert, "David Fagen: An Afro-American Rebel in the Philippines, 1899–1901," *Pacific Historical Review* 44 (1975): 68–83.

110. Lewis, *W. E. B. Du Bois*, 227.

111. William Howard Taft, *Four Aspects of Civic Duty* (New York: Charles Scribner's Sons, 1906), 81, 82, 83.

112. Woodrow Wilson, "The Place of the United States in Constitutional Development," in W. Cameron Forbes, *The Philippine Islands*, vol. 2 (New York: Houghton Mifflin Co., 1928), 511–12 (quotation on 511).

113. Wilson, 512.

114. See Aziz Rana, "Constitutionalism and the Predicament of Postcolonial Independence," in *Revolutionary Constitutionalism: Law, Legitimacy, Power*, ed. Richard Albert (New York: Hart, 2020), 71–90, and especially 84–86 for more on the connections between Wilson's views of Reconstruction and global international order.

115. Wilson, "Place of the United States in Constitutional Development," 511.

116. Quoted in Niels Aage Thorsen, *The Political Thought of Woodrow Wilson, 1875-1910* (Princeton, NJ: Princeton University Press, 1988), 13.

117. Wilson, "Place of the United States in Constitutional Development," 511.

118. Anna Su, *Exporting Freedom: Religious Liberty and American Power* (Cambridge, MA: Harvard University Press, 2015), 50.

119. See Katigbak, "Historical Transcendence," 321.

120. Autonomy Act (Jones Act (Philippine Government)), Pub. L. No. 64-240, 39 Stat. 545 (1916); Puerto Rican Federal Relations Act (Jones Act (Puerto Rico)), Pub. L. No. 64-368, 39 Stat. 951 (1917).

121. See Linda Colley, "Empires of Writing: Britain, America, and Constitutions, 1776–1848," *Law and History Review* 32 (2014): 237–66, especially 261–64. As Colley writes, "In the case of Britain, advocating, sponsoring, and writing constitutions for others—of the 'right' sort—increasingly became a persistent aspect of imperial policy, and a strategy that was often deployed in continental European and in other areas of influence outside the empire" (pp. 263–64). See generally Linda Colley, *The Gun, the Ship, and the Pen: Warfare, Constitutions, and the Making of the Modern World* (New York: Liveright, 2021).

122. Woodrow Wilson, "The Fourteen Points," in *Woodrow Wilson: Essential Writings and Speeches of the Scholar-President*, ed. Mario R. DiNunzio (New York: New York University Press, 2006), 403–7 (quotation on 407).

123. For more on American interventionism during the Wilson years in the Dominican Republic, see especially Rana, *Two Faces*, 287–89.

124. Quoted in Su, *Exporting Freedom*, 50. Su writes that "The United States in the Philippines was his model for the rest of the world," and, in particular, "guided . . . his views on the mandate system." For more specifically on the idea of the mandate system in shepherding colonized peoples toward sovereign independence, see Antony Anghie, *Imperialism, Sovereignty, and the Making of International Law* (New York: Cambridge University Press, 2004), 115–95.

125. Wilson, "The Place of the United States in Constitutional Development," 512.

Chapter 6

1. Michael Kammen, *A Machine That Would Go of Itself: The Constitution in American Culture* (New York: Alfred A. Knopf, Inc., 1986), 208.

2. "The National Association for Constitutional Government," *Constitutional Review* 1 (1917): 35–37 (quotations on 36).

3. Norman Hapgood, *Professional Patriots* (New York: Albert & Charles Boni, 1927), 8.

4. See "Calls for Strict Ban on German Language: American Defense Society Also Urges Vigorous Steps to Put an End to Plots," *New York Times*, February 25, 1918, 4.

5. See "Assails Navy Plan as Far Too Slow: Security League's President Also Denounces It as Weak and Insufficient," *New York Times*, January 21, 1916, 5.

6. For more on the history of both groups, especially the larger and more influential National Security League, see Mark R. Shulman, "The Progressive Era Origins of the National Security Act," *Dickinson Law Review* 104 (2000): 289–330; Robert D. Ward, "The Origins and Activities of the National Security League, 1914–1919," *Mississippi Valley Historical Review* 47 (1960): 51–65; and John Carver Edwards, *Patriots in Pinstripes: Men of the National Security League* (Lanham, MD: University Press of America, 1982).

7. See Edwards, *Patriots in Pinstripes*, 53.

8. See James M. Beck, "Preface," in *America at War: A Handbook of Patriotic Education References*, ed. Albert Bushnell Hart (New York: George H. Doran Co., 1918), iii, iv, arguing that such books produced by the National Security League "render a special service . . . in again bringing to the attention of the American people the continuing importance of preparedness."

9. See Kammen, *A Machine That Would Go of Itself*, 252.

10. Referring to one of Warren's pamphlets on the virtues of the Supreme Court, the executive secretary of the NSL wrote to him in 1924 that they had printed 15,000 copies and sent them "into practically every State in the Union." Letter from E. L. Harvey, Executive Secretary National Security League, to Charles Warren, February 16, 1924, Library of Congress, Manuscripts Division, Charles Warren Papers.

11. Kammen, *A Machine that Would Go of Itself*, 225.

12. See Ward, "Origins and Activities of the National Security League," 52, 54.

13. Quotation in Sven Beckert, *The Monied Metropolis: New York City and the Consolidation of the American Bourgeoisie, 1850–1896* (New York: Cambridge University Press, 2001), 4.

14. Robert Lee Bullard, Personal Diary, June 29, 1928 (unpublished list of benefactors), Library of Congress, Manuscripts Division, Robert Lee Bullard Papers. In the note, Bullard lists the twenty men, all New York City residents, "who upon my retirement raised (among themselves) and gave me twenty thousand dollars."

15. Kammen, *A Machine That Would Go of Itself*, 225.

16. See George Washington, *Farewell Address to the People of the United States* (New York: Houghton Mifflin Company, 1913); Alexander Hamilton, "Federalist No. 8: Consequences of Hostilities Between States," in *The Federalist: A Commentary on the Constitution of the United States*, ed. Paul L. Ford (New York: H. Holt and Company, 1898), 46.

17. "Says We Face Revolution: National Security League Calls on Public to Awake," *New York Times*, October 17, 1919, 7.

18. David Jayne Hill, *Americanism: What It Is* (New York: D. Appleton & Co., 1916), 171, 172, 173.

19. Hill, 179, 176.

20. Alexander Livingston, *Damn Great Empires! William James and the Politics of Pragmatism* (New York: Oxford University Press, 2016), 44.

21. Ralph Barton Perry, *The Free Man and the Soldier: Essays on the Reconciliation of Liberty and Discipline* (New York: Charles Scribner's Sons, 1916), 7, 44, 61. For more on Perry's critique of German authoritarianism, embodied in the figure of Friedrich Nietzsche, see especially Livingston, *Damn Great Empires*, 42–52.

22. Hill, *Americanism*, 176, 178.

23. As the historian Thomas Pegram describes, this term became common during the 1910s and 1920s to refer to the project of creating a culturally homogenous national identity built around Anglo-Protestant religious and political values. See generally Thomas Pegram, *One Hundred Percent American: The Rebirth and Decline of the Ku Klux Klan in the 1920s* (Chicago: Ivan R. Dee, 2011).

24. Shulman, "Progressive Era Origins of the National Security Act," 305.

25. See Pegram, *One Hundred Percent American*, 95–96.

26. Roland G. Fryer Jr. and Steven D. Levitt, "Hatred and Profits: Under the Hood of the Ku Klux Klan," *The Quarterly Journal of Economics* 127 (2012): 1883.

27. See Kathleen M. Blee, *Women of the Klan: Racism and Gender in the 1920s* (Berkeley: University of California Press, 1991), 38; and Jared A. Goldstein, "The Klan's Constitution," *Alabama Civil Rights and Civil Liberties Law Review* 9 (2018): 285–377.

28. See "Popularizing the Federal Constitution," *Constitutional Review* 4 (1920): 235–39 (quotation on 235).

29. Kammen, *A Machine That Would Go of Itself*, 73.

30. "Popularizing the Federal Constitution," 235.

31. Quoted in "Popularizing the Federal Constitution," 235.

32. See "The American's Creed," 65th Cong., 2nd sess., *Congressional Record* 56 (April 6, 1918): H 4720–21; and Myrtle Cheney Murdock, *The American's Creed and William Tyler Page* (Washington, DC: Monumental Press, 1958), 20.

33. Quoted in Murdock.

34. Page quoted in Murdock, 17, 18.

35. Abraham Lincoln, "Address to the Young Men's Lyceum of Springfield, Illinois," in *The Writings of Abraham Lincoln*, ed. Steven Smith (New Haven, CT: Yale University Press, 2012), 7–14 (quotations on 11).

36. "Constitution Day, September Seventeenth," *Constitutional Review* 3 (1919): 181–84 (quotation on 181).

37. Kammen, *A Machine That Would Go of Itself*, 220–23.

38. "Says We Face Revolution," 7.

39. "The Observance of Constitution Day," *Constitutional Review* 4 (1920): 46–48 (quotation on 47).

40. "Observance of Constitution Day," 48.

41. Kammen, *A Machine That Would Go of Itself*, 222.

42. See Jill Lepore, *The Story of America: Essays on Origins* (Princeton, NJ: Princeton University Press, 2012), 81.

43. Blee, *Women of the Klan*, 39.

44. Kammen, *A Machine That Would Go of Itself*, 235.

45. "American Lawyers Support the Constitution," *Constitutional Review* 10 (1926): 185–89 (quotation and information about the contest on 186).

46. Kammen, *A Machine That Would Go of Itself*, 233. To give a flavor of the speeches, that year's winning oration, after describing the Constitution as "the most finished, polished, and balanced relation between a people and their government that human mind has ever conceived," concluded by proclaiming that "Our Constitution has brought into being a new sun. It is the sun of individual freedom, and as long as there are Americans, God willing, it shall never sink into the sea of forgotten destinies." Don Tyler, quoted in "The National Oratorical Contest," *Constitutional Review* 8 (1924): 245–48 (quotations on 247, 248).

47. Samuel Weaver, "The Constitution in Our Public Schools," *Constitutional Review* 11 (1927): 105–12 (quotation on 107).

48. Lepore, *Story of America*, 81.

49. See Pegram, *One Hundred Percent American*, 96. In fact, according to Pegram, of the Indiana Klan's state legislative agenda, what it called the "Americanization and Education" program, the only element that was actually enacted into law was a requirement for Indiana students to study the Constitution (p. 202).

50. Weaver, "Constitution in Our Public Schools," 107.

51. See for example Etta V. Leighton, *Our Constitution in My Town and My Life: With 115 Questions and Answers* (New York: Institute for Public Service, 1924).

52. Leighton, 21–22.

53. *An Act to Establish an Uniform Rule of Naturalization*, ch. 3, 1 Stat. 103 (1790).

54. Dorothee Schneider, "Naturalization and United States Citizenship in Two Periods of Mass Migration, 1894–1930, 1965–2000," *Journal of American Ethnic History* 21 (2001): 50–82 (quotations on 54).

55. Rogers Smith, *Civil Ideals: Conflicting Visions of Citizenship in U. S. History* (New Haven, CT: Yale University Press, 1997), 446.

56. Act of 1906, Pub. L. No. 59-338, §§ 4(4), 8, 34 Stat. 596, 598–99.

57. See generally Kammen, *A Machine That Would Go of Itself*, 235–48.

58. Quoted in Kammen, 238.

59. Quoted in Kammen, 238.

60. "Education and 'The Faith of the Fathers,'" *Constitutional Review* 5 (1921): 181 (quotation on 182–83).

61. "American Bar Association to Promote American Ideals," *Constitutional Review* 7 (1923): 55–60 (quotation on 58).

62. "American Bar Association," 56.

63. Robert Lee Bullard, "The Meaning of Citizenship" (undated), unpublished speech on file with the Library of Congress, Manuscripts Division, Robert Lee Bullard Papers, 2–3.

64. See Henry Litchfield West, "Universal Military Training," *National Service* 3 (1918): 305.

65. Henry Litchfield West, *Universal Military Training: As a Permanent Principle of National Defense* (New York: National Security League, 1918), 1.

66. Quoted in "Assails Navy Plan."

67. Leslie M. Shaw, "A Republic, Not a Democracy," *Constitutional Review* 9 (1925): 140–43 (quotation on 141).

68. Charles Warren, *The Trumpeters of the Constitution* (Rochester, NY: University of Rochester, 1927), 20.

69. James Beck, "A Rising or a Setting Sun?" *Constitutional Review* 8 (1924): 3–15 (quotation on 5).

70. Warren, *Trumpeters of the Constitution*, 65.

71. Warren, 69.

72. See Cass Gilbert, "Division of Pictorial Publicity," in United States Committee on Public Information, Division of Pictorial Publicity, *Victory Dinner and Dance of the Division of Pictorial Publicity* (New York: printed in the shop of William Edwin Rudge, 1919), Library of Congress, Manuscripts Division, Cass Gilbert Papers. His unpublished correspondences are filled with letters to and from these above organizations as well as influential pro-war and pro-Constitution figures like Nicholas Murray Butler and James Beck, among others. See for example letter from Cass Gilbert to Nicholas Murray Butler, December 7, 1933; letter from Elon H. Hooker, Chairman of the American Defense Society, to Cass Gilbert, February 16, 1931; letter from Cass Gilbert to Robert Lee Bullard, March 26, 1931, Library of Congress, Manuscripts Division, Cass Gilbert Papers.

73. Quoted in Paul Spencer Byard, "Representing American Justice: The United States Supreme Court," in *Cass Gilbert, Life and Work: Architect of the Public Domain*, ed. Barbara Christen and Steve Flanders (New York: W. W. Norton & Co., 2001), 272–88, 285.

74. After his personal audience, he further gushed:

He is making Italy proud of itself. He is restoring her ancient glory.... He is not forgetting the army and navy, they are both ready, well equipped, up to date, well disciplined, well armed. They are forces to be reckoned with, especially now, since Italy is so well worth fighting for.

Cass Gilbert, Mussolini 15, June 6, 1933 (unpublished manuscript), Library of Congress, Manuscripts Division, Cass Gilbert Papers; also quoted in Kammen, *A Machine That Would Go of Itself*, 268.

75. Letter from Cass Gilbert to Nobile Giacomo de Martino, Italian Ambassador

to the US, October 11, 1932, Library of Congress, Manuscripts Division, Cass Gilbert Papers.

76. Letter from J. Alfred Pisani to Giulio C. Pisani Jr., April 26, 1933, Library of Congress, Manuscripts Division, Cass Gilbert Papers. For more on Gilbert's trip to Italy as part of the construction of the Supreme Court building, see Kammen, *A Machine That Would Go of Itself*, 266–69.

77. For an excellent introduction to the complicated reception of Mussolini and fascism in the United States during the 1920s, see John Diggins, *Mussolini and Fascism: The View from America* (Princeton, NJ: Princeton University Press, 1972).

78. "The Constitution Anniversary Association," *Constitutional Review* 7 (1923): 191–93 (quotation on 192).

79. See generally Alfred Brooks, *Converted and Secret Americans* (New York: National Security League, 1918).

80. Brooks.

81. James A. Van Osdol, "Future Organization and Defense of the Constitution," *Constitutional Review* 13 (1929): 121–25 (quotation on 122).

82. "Constitution Anniversary Association," 191.

83. "Constitution Anniversary Association," 191.

84. "Teaching Constitutional Government," *Constitutional Review* 5 (1921): 120–24 (quotation on 121).

85. "Calls for Strict Ban on German Language," 4.

86. "Calls for Strict Ban on German Language," 4.

87. See Sally Miller, *Victor Berger and the Promise of Constructive Socialism* (Westport, CT: Greenwood Press, 1973), 191–226.

88. See Louis Waldman, *Albany: The Crisis in Government: The History of the Suspension, Trial and Expulsion from the New York State Legislature in 1920 of the Five Socialist Assemblymen by Their Political Opponents* (New York: Boni & Liveright, 1920), 2–7.

89. See generally Geoffrey Stone, *Perilous Times: Free Speech in Wartime* (New York: W. W. Norton, 2004), 135–233.

90. George Sutherland, *Constitutional Power and World Affairs* (New York: Columbia University Press, 1918), 102.

91. Warren was a close personal friend and a political advisor to fellow pro-war and pro-Constitution advocate John W. Davis, US Solicitor General and conservative Democratic nominee for president in 1924. See for example Western Union telegram from John W. Davis to Charles Warren, August 6, 1924, Library of Congress, Manuscripts Division, Charles Warren Papers, asking Warren to prepare a critical "survey" of the "Republican record" for use during the presidential campaign. His collected papers on file with the Library of Congress also include glowing correspondence from everyone from Louis Brandeis and Franklin Delano Roosevelt to Oliver Wendell Holmes Jr., Calvin Coolidge, Herbert Hoover, and countless others.

92. Espionage Act of 1917, Pub. L. No. 65-24, 40 Stat. 217.

93. Trading with the Enemy Act of 1917, Pub. L. No. 65-91, 40 Stat. 411.

94. Sedition Act of 1918, Pub. L. No 65-150, 40 Stat. 553. On Warren's role as primary author, see Letter from Charles Warren to "Gard," April 22, 1918, Library of Congress, Manuscripts Division, Charles Warren Papers.

95. See Miller, *Victor Berger*, 193.

96. Robert Goldstein, *Political Repression in Modern America* (Urbana: University of Illinois Press, 1978), 108.

97. See Goldstein, 108; see also Charles Warren, "Arrest and Internment of Alien Enemies," (undated), 535–44, unpublished "War Notes," Library of Congress, Manuscripts Division, Charles Warren Papers.

98. See Warren, "Arrest and Internment of Alien Enemies," 544.

99. Geoffrey R. Stone et al., *The First Amendment*, 2nd ed. (Blue Springs, MO: Aspen Publishers, 2003), 20.

100. See Warren, "Arrest and Internment of Alien Enemies," 544.

101. See Letter from Warren to "Gard," 2. As he told one friend, "It has been an arduous but exciting and eventful four years, and I feel I have given my very best efforts to the United States. I leave on the books at least four permanent records of my work.".

102. Letter from Warren to "Gard," 2.

103. See Charles Warren, "What Is Giving Aid and Comfort to the Enemy," *Yale Law Journal* 27 (1917): 331–47 (quotation on 331).

104. See Letter from Warren to "Gard," 2.

105. The proposed bill would have established military commissions for such speech crimes as "causing or attempting to cause insubordination or refusal of duty by any member" of the armed forces; "delivering or transmitting, or causing to be delivered or transmitted" to any member of the military "any written or printed matter which shall support or favor the cause of the enemy country or of its allies in the war, or which shall oppose the cause of the United States"; and "printing or publishing any such printed matter." See S. 4364, 65 Cong. (1918).

106. S. 4364, 65 Cong. (1918).

107. Letter from Charles Warren to Lee Slater Overman, April 8, 1918, Library of Congress, Manuscripts Division, Charles Warren Papers.

108. Warren received dozens of letters of support for his position. See for example Letter from W. E. D. Stokes to Charles Warren, April 20, 1918, Library of Congress, Manuscripts Division, Charles Warren Papers, stating "Don't, for Heaven's Sake, resign. I have, for 6 months written to the President and told him that the War cannot be run by the Criminal Courts,—that we got to try these cases by Court Martial; you know how I have worked over this question."

109. Theodore Roosevelt, "The Children of the Crucible," in *America at War: A Handbook of Patriotic Education References*, ed. Albert Bushnell Hart (New York: George H. Doran Co., 1918), 314, 316. For many pro-Constitution activists in groups like the NSL and the American Defense Society, Teddy Roosevelt was both an intense pro-war advocate and an embodiment of the pre-war failure of Progressives to embrace sufficiently the Constitution.

110. See Jerold Auerbach, *Unequal Justice: Law and Social Change in Modern America* (New York: Oxford University Press, 1976), 104.

111. Auerbach, 102.

112. Ellen Nore, *Charles A. Beard: An Intellectual Biography* (Carbondale: Southern Illinois University Press, 1983), 80, quoting Nicholas Murray Butler, President of Columbia University, Commencement Address, June 6, 1917.

113. "West Is Crowded with Pro-Germans, Dr. McElroy Says: Government

Should Investigate University of Wisconsin, He Declares," *New York Tribune*, April 17, 1918, in John Bradley Winslow et al., *Report upon the Statements of Professor Robert McNutt McElroy and the Executive Committee of the National Security League Relating to the University of Wisconsin* (Madison: University of Wisconsin, 1919), 16–19 (quotation on 18).

114. "West Is Crowded with Pro-Germans," 18.

115. As one FBI special agent explained government support for the organization, "The Legion as a body are watching during the day and night so that nothing may start and no trouble may occur." Regin Schmidt, *Red Scare: The FBI and the Origins of Anticommunism in the United States, 1919–1943* (Copenhagen, Denmark: Museum Tusculanum Press, 2000), 109, quoting Report, M. J. Fraser, Special Agent, March 4, 1920.

116. See Hapgood, *Professional Patriots*, 57.

117. For instance, Geoffrey Stone writes that "the United States has made substantial progress" in the last century in balancing security with civil liberties, in large part because of "the development of a national culture" grounded in constitutional attachment and "more attuned" to those values. Stone, *Perilous Times*, 533.

118. "National Association for Constitutional Government," 37.

119. Gerard Magliocca, *The Heart of the Constitution: How the Bill of Rights Became the Bill of Rights* (New York: Oxford University Press, 2018), 87. Still, this does not mean that today's more commonplace civil libertarian discourses, connected in principle to the Bill of Rights, were totally absent from constitutional conversation. As the legal historian Jeremy Kessler discusses, the wartime draft became a significant space for some Progressive lawyers to begin innovating civil libertarian notions of free expression as grounds for conscientious objection. In this way, they imagined that civil libertarianism and administrative state-building could sustain each other. See generally Jeremy Kessler's terrific article, "The Administrative Origins of Modern Civil Liberties Law," *Columbia Law Review* 114 (2014): 1083–1166. Nonetheless, such ideas played a limited role in World War I's mass project of constitutional celebration. The era's central pro-war and pro-Constitution advocates tended to be deeply suspicious of such defenses of dissent.

120. See more generally Robert Wiebe's *The Search for Order, 1877–1920* (New York: Hill and Wang, 1967) on the rise and fall of the Progressive era.

Chapter 7

1. See Michael Ignatieff, *Blood and Belonging: Journeys in the New Nationalism* (New York: Farrar, Straus and Giroux, 1993), 7–8 ("Ethnic nationalism claims . . . that an individual's deepest attachments are inherited, not chosen. It is the national community that defines the individual, not the individuals who define the national community"). With respect to the United States, Jared Goldstein's *Real Americans: National Identity, Violence, and the Constitution* (Lawrence: University Press of Kansas, 2021) offers a powerful recent account of how American ethno-nationalist politics has historically invested deeply in constitutional veneration.

2. See Lara Jakes, "Pompeo's Parting Message as Secretary of State: Multiculturalism Is 'Not Who America Is,'" *New York Times*, January 19, 2021, https://www.nytimes.com/2021/01/19/us/politics/pompeo-multiculturalism.html.

3. See Jennifer Schuessler, "The Ideas Behind Trump's 1776 Commission Report," *New York Times*, January 19, 2021, https://www.nytimes.com/2021/01/19/arts/1776-commission-claims-trump.html.

4. An Act Relating to the Social Studies Curriculum in Public School, Texas House Bill No. 3979 (June 15, 2021), h-3, 4(b)(x).

5. On American business anxieties about the 1917 Mexican Constitution, see John A. Britton, *Revolution and Ideology: Images of the Mexican Revolution in the United States* (Lexington: University Press of Kentucky, 1995), 40–42.

6. See generally Roberto Gargarella, *Latin American Constitutionalism, 1810–2010* (New York: Oxford University Press, 2013), 98–104 (quotation on 101).

7. See Roberto Gargarella, "Equality," in *Comparative Constitutional Law in Latin America*, ed. Rosalind Dixon and Tom Ginsburg (Northampton, MA: Edward Elgar Publishing, 2017), 176–97, especially 186.

8. Burton Alva Konkle, "Americanizing Americans," *Constitutional Review* 8 (1924): 97–103 (quotation on 97).

9. David Jayne Hill, *Americanism: What It Is* (New York: D. Appleton & Co., 1916), viii.

10. Hill, viii.

11. Quoted in Adam Tooze, *The Deluge: The Great War and the Remaking of the Global Order, 1916–1931* (New York: Penguin, 2014), 60.

12. See generally David Jayne Hill, *Present Problems in Foreign Policy* (New York: D. Appleton, 1919).

13. See Aziz Rana, *The Two Faces of American Freedom* (Cambridge, MA: Harvard University Press, 2010), 291.

14. "Constitution Day," *American Standard* 2 (1925): 420. Emphasizing the Klan's commitment to the Constitution, the journal was itself named after George Washington's words at the start of the Federal Constitutional Convention: "Let us raise a standard to which the wise and the honest can repair; the event is in the hands of God." These words appeared on the cover of every issue of the *Standard*.

15. "Calls for Strict Ban on German Language: American Defense Society Also Urges Vigorous Steps to Put an End to Plots," *New York Times*, February 25, 1918.

16. "League Starts War on German Press: National Campaign Organized to Limit Papers to English Language," *New York Times*, June 3, 1918, 5.

17. "League Starts War," 5. According to its Committee on Foreign Language and Foreign Press: "The animosity, clannishness, and the propaganda of undemocratic ideas are sources of injury to the community, and the substitution of other languages for our own clearly fosters them." "Aim to Make America a Land of One Tongue," *New York Times*, July 22, 1918, 7.

18. Thomas Pegram, *One Hundred Percent American: The Rebirth and Decline of the Ku Klux Klan in the 1920s* (Chicago: Ivan R. Dee, 2011), 96.

19. Mark R. Shulman, "The Progressive Era Origins of the National Security Act," *Dickinson Law Review* 104 (2000): 289–330 (quotation on 319).

20. Shulman, 306.

21. For more on the era's academic embrace of tutelage—how white scholars, including Hart, routinely contended that "self-government proved to be an art that few races had mastered, one that required training"—see Robert Vitalis, *White*

World Order, Black Power Politics: The Birth of American International Relations (Ithaca, NY: Cornell University Press, 2015), 29–58, 40.

22. See Hiroshi Motomura, *Americans in Waiting: The Lost Story of American Immigration and Citizenship in the United States* (New York: Oxford University Press, 2006), 126–28 (quotations on 126, 128).

23. The preceding discussion of the 1917, 1921, and 1924 laws draws from Rana, *Two Faces*, 236–41.

24. Leslie M. Shaw, "A Republic, Not a Democracy," *Constitutional Review* 9 (1925): 140–43 (quotation on 141).

25. Quotations in Kevin M. Schultz, *Tri-Faith America: How Catholics and Jews Held Postwar America to Its Protestant Promise* (New York: Oxford University Press, 2011), 17.

26. Schultz, 17.

27. See K. Healan Gaston, *Imagining Judeo-Christian America: Religion, Secularism, and the Redefinition of Democracy* (Chicago: University of Chicago Press, 2019), quotations on 72.

28. See Meyer v. Nebraska, 262 U.S. 390 (1923) and Pierce v. Society of Sisters, 268 U.S. 510 (1925).

29. *Meyer*, 399.

30. For more on John Collier and the Pueblo Indian dance controversy of the 1920s, see generally Tisa Wenger's excellent book, *We Have a Religion: The 1920s Pueblo Indian Dance Controversy and American Religious Freedom* (Chapel Hill: University of North Carolina Press, 2009), quotations on 120.

31. Wenger, 222–36 (quotation on 224).

32. Gaston, *Imagining Judeo-Christian America*, 71, 153.

33. See Jonathan Zimmerman, *Whose America? Culture Wars in the Public Schools* (Cambridge, MA: Harvard University Press, 2002), 13–31 (quotation on 26).

34. Zimmerman, 20, 21.

35. Quoted in Zimmerman, 26. On specifically Irish American participation in banning textbooks, see Albert Kerr Heckel, "Pure History and Patriotism," *Historical Outlook* 16 (1925): 106. Such ethnic societies saw a Beardian critical historiography as perhaps sullying the achievements of revolutionary actors, of which Irish Americans were one. As Heckel notes, these groups wanted textbooks "to make clear that" national victories or achievements like "the Battle of Bunker Hill [were] won by Irish volunteers."

36. See especially Gaston, *Imagining Judeo-Christian America*, 230–55, for more on the late-twentieth-century identification of Judeo-Christian with conservative "family values" and suspicion of "multicultural, multi-religious" America (quotation on 232).

37. Quoted in Wenger, *We Have a Religion*, 117.

38. Clinton Rickard, *Fighting Tuscarora: The Autobiography of Chief Clinton Rickard* (Syracuse, NY: Syracuse University Press, 1973), 53.

39. For a terrific account of Kellogg's political project, see David Temin, "Our Democracy: Laura Cornelius Kellogg's Decolonial-Democracy," *Perspectives on Politics* 19 (2021): 1082–97.

40. Temin, 1087.

41. Laura Cornelius Kellogg, *Our Democracy and the American Indian and Other*

Works, ed. Kristina Ackley and Cristina Stanciu (Syracuse, NY: Syracuse University Press, 2015), 71, 73.

42. Kellogg, 80, 81, 91, 89.

43. Kellogg, 97, 91.

44. Temin, "Our Democracy," quotation on 1091.

45. Temin, 1082.

46. See Theodore Kornweibel Jr., *No Crystal Stair: Black Life and the Messenger, 1917–1928* (Westport, CT: Greenwood Press, 1975) for an excellent overview of the magazine and its influence during the era (circulation information on 54).

47. See W. E. B. Du Bois, "Close Ranks," *Crisis* 16 (1918): 111.

48. "Americanism," *Messenger*, September 1920, 80.

49. As one example, see the editorial in the Chicago-based black weekly *Broad Ax* defending the Constitution Day celebrations and contending that "each individual daily enjoys advantages which would not be his but for the wisdom of the pioneers who gave a Constitution to a united country." "Constitution Day, September 17," *Broad Ax*, September 17, 1921, 1.

50. "Our Reason for Being," *Messenger*, August 1919, 11–12 (quotation on 12).

51. For more on the *Messenger*'s views of the IWW and the AFL as well as its broader approach to Black labor organizing, see Cornelius Bynum, *A. Philip Randolph and the Struggle for Civil Rights* (Chicago: University of Illinois Press, 2010), 110–14.

52. "Our Reason for Being," 12.

53. See "Constitution Day—September 17," *Messenger*, September 1919, 10–11 (quotation on 10).

54. "Constitution Day—September 17," 10.

55. Kornweibel, *No Crystal Stair*, 3.

56. "Constitution Day—September 17," 11.

57. "American Lawlessness," *Messenger*, July 1918, 9.

58. Quoted in Elizabeth Cobbs, "Fighting on Two Fronts: World War One, Women's Suffrage, and John Pershing's 'Hello Girls,'" *South Central Review* 34 (2017): 31.

59. Quoted in Johanna Neumann, "Who Won Women's Suffrage? A Case for 'Mere Men,'" *Journal of the Gilded Age and the Progressive Era* 16 (2017): 347–67 (quotation on 357).

60. Quoted in Cobbs, "Fighting on Two Fronts," 32.

61. Holly J. McCammon, Karen E. Campbell, Ellen M. Granberg, and Christine Mowery, "How Movements Win: Gendered Opportunity Structures and U.S. Women's Suffrage Movements, 1866 to 1919," *American Sociological Review* 66 (2001): 49–70 (quotation on 49).

62. See generally McCammon et. al., "How Movements Win," for a discussion of the "gendered opportunity structures" that eventually led to suffrage.

63. Quoted in Kornweibel, *No Crystal Stair*, 11.

64. Quoted in Kornweibel, 22.

65. Quoted in Kornweibel, 23.

66. See Kornweibel, 220–61 (quotation on 261 and circulation information on 54).

67. Just as with the word "socialist," throughout the book the word "Communist" will sometimes be capitalized. I will do so when referring to the CPUSA—

established in 1919 following a split with the Socialist Party over the Russian Revolution. But other times, I will use "communist" without capitalizing it when discussing more generally political actors that conceived of themselves as communists or were accused of having communist ideological commitments, even if they were not members of the American political party, had broken from the party, or actually actively opposed it. Without wading into ideological debates over the differences between socialism and communism, I will also by and large treat communist activism as within the broader family of revolutionary socialist efforts.

68. See generally Jeffery Perry, *Hubert Harrison: The Voice of Harlem Radicalism, 1883–1918* (New York: Columbia University Press, 2009) and *Hubert Harrison: The Struggle for Equality, 1918–1927* (New York: Columbia University Press, 2020) for a compelling account of his life and politics.

69. See generally Hubert Harrison, "Wanted—A Colored International," in *A Hubert Harrison Reader*, ed. Jeffrey Perry (Middletown, CT: Wesleyan University Press, 2001), 223–28.

70. Harrison, 223, 225, 224.

71. See generally Marilyn Lake and Henry Reynolds, *Drawing the Global Colour Line: White Men's Countries and the International Challenge of Racial Equality* (New York: Cambridge University Press, 2008), 284–309.

72. See Seok-Won Lee's excellent essay on Du Bois's views of race, colonialism, and Japanese empire, "The Paradox of Racial Liberation: W. E. B. Du Bois and Pan-Asianism in Wartime Japan, 1931–1945," *Inter-Cultural Studies* 16 (2015): 513–30 (quotation on 522).

73. "Americanism," 80.

74. See Manning Marable, *W. E. B. Du Bois: Black Radical Democrat* (Boulder, CO: Paradigm Publishers, 1986), 205–6 for Du Bois's effusive praise of the People's Republic of China.

75. See generally Adom Getachew's excellent account of anti-colonial visions of a post-imperial order, *Worldmaking after Empire: The Rise and Fall of Self-Determination* (Princeton, NJ: Princeton University Press, 2019).

76. For more on the Council on African Affairs (CAA), its rise in the 1930s, its combination of Black left and liberal activism, and its collapse in the context of Cold War repression, see Penny Von Eschen's essential book, *Race Against Empire: Black Americans and Anti-Colonialism* (Ithaca, NY: Cornell University Press, 1997).

77. Quoted in Robin Kelley, *Freedom Dreams: The Black Radical Imagination* (Boston: Beacon Press, 2002), 49.

78. Kelley, 49.

79. See Beverley Tomek, "The Communist International and the Dilemma of the American 'Negro Problem': Limitations of the Black Belt Self-Determination Thesis," *WorkingUSA: The Journal of Labor and Society* 15 (2012): 549–76 (quotation on 570).

80. Kelley, *Freedom Dreams*, 49.

81. Kelley, 49.

82. Harry Haywood, *Negro Liberation* (New York: International Publishers Co., 1948), 11, 116.

83. Haywood, 164.

84. Haywood, 165.

85. Haywood, 164.

86. Haywood, 140.

87. See Harry Haywood, *Black Bolshevik: Autobiography of an Afro-American Communist* (Chicago: Liberator Press, 1978), 230.

88. Haywood, *Negro Liberation*, 164.

89. Haywood, *Negro Liberation*, 165.

90. For a sense in the post–World War II moment of the internal CPUSA debates over the viability and wisdom of the Black belt thesis, see Francis Franklin, "The Status of the Negro People in the Black Belt and How to Fight for the Right to Self-Determination," *Political Affairs* 25 (1946): 438–56; and Max Weiss, "Toward Clarity on the Negro Question," *Political Affairs* 25 (1946): 457–78.

91. Robin Kelley, *Hammer and Hoe: Alabama Communists during the Great Depression* (Chapel Hill: University of North Carolina Press, 1990), 23.

92. On the centrality of an anti-imperial internationalism to Eastman's vision of politics and solidary, see Aronson, *Crystal Eastman*, 120–82.

93. Crystal Eastman, "The Socialist Party Convention," in *Toward the Great Change: Crystal Eastman and Max Eastman on Feminism, Antimilitarism, and Revolution*, ed. Blanche Wiesen Cook (New York: Garland Publishing, Inc., 1976), 436–44 (quotation on 437); also quoted in John Witt, *Patriots and Cosmopolitans: Hidden Histories of American Law* (Cambridge, MA: Harvard University Press, 2007), 208.

94. See Crystal Eastman and Roger Baldwin, "Letter to All American Union Locals, Affiliated Organizations, Correspondents and Members" (August 31, 1917), in *Toward the Great Change: Crystal Eastman and Max Eastman on Feminism, Antimilitarism, and Revolution*, ed. Blanche Wiesen Cook (New York: Garland Publishing, Inc., 1976), 295–96 (quotation on 295).

95. Eastman, "Socialist Party Convention," 440.

96. See for example "Pacifists Arrested in Stormy Meeting," *New York Times*, September 17, 1917.

97. Eastman, "Socialist Party Convention," quotations on 438, 437.

98. Eastman, quotation on 436.

99. Eastman and Baldwin, "Letter to All American Union Locals," 295.

100. Quoted in Witt, *Patriots and Cosmopolitans*, 202.

101. Aronson, *Crystal Eastman*, 182.

102. See generally Laura Weinrib, "Untangling the Radical Roots of America's Civil Liberties Settlement: Causation, Compromise, and the Taming of Free Speech," *Jerusalem Journal of Legal Studies* 18 (2018): 135–58 (quotations on 146, 147).

103. Quoted in Gary Gerstle, *American Crucible: Race and Nation in the Twentieth Century* (Princeton, NJ: Princeton University Press, 2017), 145.

104. Kelley, *Hammer and Hoe*, 159–60.

105. "Campaign of 1936: Election Platform of the Communist Party," *National Party Platforms: 1840–1956*, ed. Kirk Porter and Donald Bruce Johnson (Urbana: University of Illinois Press, 1956), 356–60 (quotation on 360).

106. "Checks, Constitution Browder's Claim against Vagrancy Charge," *Cornell Daily Sun*, October 20, 1936, 5.

107. Quoted in Michael Kammen, *A Machine That Would Go of Itself: The Constitution in American Culture* (New York: Alfred A. Knopf, Inc., 1986), 280.

108. See generally Nancy F. Cott, *The Grounding of Modern Feminism* (New Haven, CT: Yale University Press, 1987), 53–81, especially 59–61, for an excellent account of the National Woman's Party.

109. H.R.J. Res. 75, 68th Cong. (1923).

110. See Cott, *Grounding of Modern Feminism*, 66–81.

111. See Adkins v. Children's Hospital, 261 U.S. 525 (1923).

112. Quoted in Cott, *Grounding of Modern Feminism*, 76.

113. Crystal Eastman, "Now We Can Begin," in *Crystal Eastman on Women and Revolution*, ed. Blanche Wiesen Cook (New York: Oxford University Press, 2020), 52–57, 53.

114. Eastman, 54.

115. Nancy F. Cott, "Feminist Politics in the 1920s: The National Woman's Party," *Journal of American History* 71 (1984): 43–68 (quotation on 48).

116. Amy Aronson, *Crystal Eastman: A Revolutionary Life* (New York: Oxford University Press, 2020), 253.

117. Eastman, "Now We Can Begin," 54, 57.

118. Aronson, *Crystal Eastman*, 253.

119. See Aronson, 253–56.

120. Eastman, "Now We Can Begin," 56.

Chapter 8

1. See Bruce Ackerman, *Revolutionary Constitutions: Charismatic Leadership and the Rule of Law* (Cambridge, MA: Harvard University Press, 2019), 389–91; and Ira Katznelson, *Fear Itself: The New Deal and the Origins of Our Time* (New York: W. W. Norton, 2013), 264–66.

2. These two paragraphs are drawn from the discussion in Aziz Rana, *The Two Faces of American Freedom* (Cambridge, MA: Harvard University Press, 2010), 311–12.

3. Quoted in Laura Weinrib, *The Taming of Free Speech: America's Civil Liberties Compromise* (Cambridge, MA: Harvard University Press, 2016), 224. See also Joseph Fishkin and William Forbath, *The Anti-Oligarchy Constitution: Reconstructing the Economic Foundations of American Democracy* (Cambridge, MA: Harvard University Press, 2022), 253 on Corwin's professional standing and his views of the judicial turn.

4. See Bruce Ackerman, *We the People: Transformations*, vol. 2 (Cambridge, MA: The Belknap Press of Harvard University Press, 1998), 255–420; Fishkin and Forbath, in *The Anti-Oligarchy Constitution*, 251–318, also offer an excellent interpretation of New Deal constitutionalism as inscribing within the existing legal-political order a social democratic vision of political economy, which they associate with Roosevelt's phrase "democracy of opportunity."

5. These paragraphs also draw from Rana, *Two Faces*, 312–13.

6. Paul Brest et al., *Processes of Constitutional Decisionmaking: Cases and Materials*, 6th ed. (New York: Wolters Kluwer, 2015), 563.

7. Brest, 626.

8. Quoted in Eric Schickler, *Racial Realignment: The Transformation of American Liberalism, 1932–1965* (Princeton, NJ: Princeton University Press, 2016), 57.

9. Quoted in Schickler, 57.

10. Steven Lawson, "Progressives and the Supreme Court: A Case for Judicial Reform in the 1920s," *Historian* 42 (1980): 419–36 (quotation on 423).

11. Quotations in Schickler, *Racial Realignment*, 54–55.

12. Labor's Non-Partisan League, *Packing the Court, or Petting the Sweatshop* (1937), Kheel Center for Labor-Management Documentation and Archives, Cornell University Library, ILGWU, David Dubinsky, President's Records.

13. See James Grey Pope, "The Thirteenth Amendment versus the Commerce Clause: Labor and the Shaping of American Constitutional Law, 1921–1957," *Columbia Law Review* 102 (2002): 1–122, especially 15–25.

14. Thurman Arnold, *The Symbols of Government* (New Haven, CT: Yale University Press, 1935), 231.

15. See David Williams, "The Bureau of Investigations and Its Critics, 1919–1921: The Origins of Federal Political Surveillance," *Journal of American History* 68 (1981): 563.

16. National Popular Government League, "Bulletin No. 177," March 3, 1937, quotation on 7, *Proquest History Vault*, Zechariah Chafee Jr. Papers.

17. Norman Thomas, "A Socialist Looks at the Constitution," *Annals of the American Academy of Political and Social Science* 185 (1936): 92–101 (quotation on 94).

18. National Popular Government League, "Bulletin No. 177," quotations on 1, 7.

19. National Popular Government League, 2.

20. See Salvatore John LaGumina, *Vito Marcantonio: The People's Politician* (Dubuque, IA: Kendall/Hunt Publishing Co., 1969), 28–29.

21. "Decisions of the Supreme Court in Recent Cases," 74th Cong., 1st sess., *Congressional Record* 79 (May 29, 1935): S 8372.

22. Thomas, "A Socialist Looks at the Constitution," 100.

23. LaGumina, *Vito Marcantonio*, 29.

24. See Pope, "Thirteenth Amendment versus the Commerce Clause," especially 62–64.

25. Thomas, "A Socialist Looks at the Constitution," 99.

26. See Pope, "Thirteenth Amendment versus the Commerce Clause," 62–63n301.

27. For a sustained academic argument that these were in fact the long-term effects of the system generated by the NLRA, see Christopher Tomlins, *The State and the Unions: Labor Relations, Law, and the Organized Labor Movement in America, 1880–1960* (New York: Cambridge University Press, 1985).

28. National Popular Government League, "Bulletin No. 177," 7.

29. Thurman Arnold, *The Folklore of Capitalism* (New Haven, CT: Yale University Press, 1937), quotations on 29.

30. Arnold, 29.

31. See Fishkin and Forbath, *Anti-Oligarchy Constitution*, 322.

32. Charles Beard, "The Living Constitution," *Annals of the American Academy of Political and Social Science* 185 (1936): 29–34 (quotation on 30).

33. Quotations in Beard, 30.

34. Beard, 30, 31, 34.

35. Beard, 32.

36. For more specifically on Beard's 1930s ideas of constitutional reform to generate a "workers' republic," as well as his excitement about aspects of the German Weimar Constitution, see Clyde Barrow, "Building a Workers' Republic: Charles A. Beard's Critique of Liberalism in the 1930s," *Polity* 30 (1997): 51–52.

37. Quotation in Beard, 30, 29.

38. Beard, 29.

39. At the time, unsurprisingly, "the *American Historical Review* did not even review *Black Reconstruction*" on publication, as Manning Marable notes. Manning Marable, *W. E. B. Du Bois: Black Radical Democrat* (Boulder, CO: Paradigm Publishers, 2005), 147.

40. Quoted in Marable, 147.

41. W. E. B. Du Bois, *Black Reconstruction in America, 1860–1880* (New York: Atheneum, 1992), 728.

42. Du Bois, 336.

43. Quotations in Du Bois, 336.

44. Quotations in Du Bois, 336.

45. W. E. B. Du Bois, *The World and Africa and Color and Democracy* (New York: Oxford University Press, 2007), 296.

46. Quotations in Du Bois, *Color and Democracy*, 297, 294. See Rebecca Zietlow, *Enforcing Equality: Congress, the Constitution, and the Protection of Individual Rights* (New York: New York University Press, 2006), 94, on race and the Wagner Act, as well as generally Katznelson's seminal *Fear Itself*, especially 257–60, for an account of how white supremacy undermined even the era's most radical achievements.

47. Quotations in Du Bois, *Color and Democracy*, 295.

48. Quotation in Timothy Shenk, *Realigners: Partisan Hacks, Political Visionaries, and the Struggle to Rule American Democracy* (New York: Farrar, Straus and Giroux, 2022), 196.

49. Du Bois, *Color and Democracy*, 296.

50. Barry Cushman, "Court-Packing and Compromise," *Constitutional Commentary* 29 (2013): 2.

51. W. E. B. Du Bois, letter to Jesse Sterling, March 10, 1937, University of Massachusetts Amherst Libraries' Department of Special Collections and University Archives, W. E. B. Du Bois Papers.

52. See Thurman Arnold, "A Reply," *American Bar Association Journal* 23 (1937): 364–94, where, in his own inimitable way, Arnold declared, "The reasons for urging the plan are practical. The reasons for opposing it are mystical" (p. 367). As a side note, *Harper's* columnist Louis Cassels would later contend that one of the things that most "endeared" Arnold to FDR was his willingness to write publicly and forcefully on behalf of the plan. Quoted in Wilson Miscamble, "Thurman Arnold Goes to Washington: A Look at Antitrust Policy in the later New Deal," *Business History Review* 56 (1982): 1–15 (quotation on 8).

53. National Popular Government League, "Bulletin No. 177," 1.

54. Quoted in Weinrib, *Taming of Free Speech*, 211.

55. See LaGumina, *Vito Marcantonio*, 29.

56. Speech by Rep. Vito Marcantonio, 74th Cong., 2nd sess., *Congressional Record* 80 (February 11, 1936): H 1850.

57. Labor's Non-Partisan League, *Packing the Court.*

58. George Berry, letter to Executive Board Members, March 29, 1937. Kheel Center, ILGWU, David Dubinsky, President's Records.

59. David Dubinsky, President-General Secretary IGLWU, letter to Affiliated Local Unions and Joint Board Members, February 19, 1937, Kheel Center, ILGWU, David Dubinsky, President's Records.

60. Raymond Pace Alexander, "Alexander O.K.'s President's Plan," *Chicago Defender*, February 13, 1937, 1.

61. "Hot Debate Marks Court Plan O.K.," *New York Amsterdam News*, March 20, 1937, 15.

62. See generally Laura Kalman, *FDR's Gambit: The Court Packing Fight and the Rise of Legal Liberalism* (New York: Oxford University Press, 2022), for an excellent overview of political back and forth in Congress and the FDR administration over the court-packing plan.

63. Herbert Lehman, "Gov. Lehman's Letter," *New York Times*, July 20, 1937.

64. See Weinrib, *Taming of the Free Speech*, 213.

65. Franklin Roosevelt, "Fireside Chat on Reorganization of the Judiciary, March 9, 1937," in *The Public Papers and Addresses of Franklin D. Roosevelt: 1937 Volume*, ed. Samuel I. Rosenman (New York: The Macmillan Company, 1941), 122–33 (quotations on 132).

66. Pope, "Thirteenth Amendment versus the Commerce Clause," quotation on 97; see also Rana, *Two Faces*, 299, 389n100, 313.

67. Kalman, *FDR's Gambit*, 198–99, 208–52.

68. See Neil Devins, "Government Lawyers and the New Deal," *Columbia Law Review* 96 (1996): 237–67 (discussion on 250–54). For more on Roberts's motivations and the continued scholarly uncertainty about what led to his shift, see Kalman, *FDR's Gambit*, 260–62.

69. Kalman suggests that at least with respect to Van Devanter's retirement, the decision could well have been a "strategic move" given that it was "preceded by multiple consultations with congressional critics of the court bill." Kalman, *FDR's Gambit*, 199.

70. "Public Opinion on America's Greatest Issues," *American Institute of Public Opinion*, June 20, 1937. See also Kalman, *FDR's Gambit*, for a careful account of how even before these developments the era's public opinion data were significantly more divided on the matter than other New Deal legislative initiatives (pp. 90–94).

71. See Ackerman, *We the People*, vol. 2, 25–27 (quotation on 26).

72. Keith Whittington, *Political Foundations of Judicial Supremacy: The Presidency, the Supreme Court, and Constitutional Leadership in U.S. History* (Princeton, NJ: Princeton University Press, 2007), 267, also quoted in Kalman, *FDR's Gambit*, 132.

73. Fishkin and Forbath, *Anti-Oligarchy Constitution*, 251.

74. Franklin Roosevelt, "Fireside Chat," quotations on 127–28.

75. Franklin Roosevelt, "Address on Constitution Day, September 17, 1937," in *The Public Papers and Addresses of Franklin D. Roosevelt: 1937 Volume*, ed. Samuel I. Rosenman (New York: The Macmillan Company, 1941), 359–67 (quotation on 363).

76. Roosevelt, "Fireside Chat," 124.

77. Roosevelt, "Address on Constitution Day," 362.

78. Fishkin and Forbath, *Anti-Oligarchy Constitution*, 284.

79. Roosevelt, "Address on Constitution Day," 361.

80. Of such reactionary intentions, FDR proclaimed, "I do not think you will be able long to fool the American people as to your purposes." Roosevelt, "Fireside Chat," 132.

81. Roosevelt, "Address on Constitution Day," 361.

82. See generally Fishkin and Forbath, *Anti-Oligarchy Constitution*, 308–11 (quotation 309).

83. Kate Andrias discusses how the AFL in particular was wary of these arrangements due to a "longstanding opposition to state involvement in labor relations." Kate Andrias, "An American Approach to Social Democracy: The Forgotten Promise of the Fair Labor Standards Act," *Yale Law Journal* 128 (2019): 684.

84. Andrias, 689.

85. Quoted in Fishkin and Forbath, *Anti-Oligarchy Constitution*, 311. The language can be found in Kate Andrias, "An American Approach to Social Democracy," 682.

86. Katznelson, *Fear Itself*, 270–72 (quotation on 271).

87. Andrias, "American Approach to Social Democracy," 682–83.

88. Andrias, 684.

89. Fishkin and Forbath, *Anti-Oligarchy Constitution*, 327.

90. Katznelson, *Fear Itself*, 175.

91. Katznelson, 169, 170, 172.

92. Quotations in Du Bois, *The World and Africa* and *Color and Democracy*, 295, 296, 297.

93. Andrias, "American Approach to Social Democracy," 688.

94. Arnold, *Symbols of Government*, 236.

95. See generally Rexford Tugwell, *The Emerging Constitution* (New York: Harper's Magazine Press, 1974).

96. "Social Control vs. the Constitution," *New Republic*, June 12, 1935, 116–18 (quotation on 118).

97. Berry, "Letter to Executive Board Members."

98. United States Congressional Senate Committee on the Judiciary, Hearing on 75 S.1392: A Bill to Reorganize the Judicial Branch of Government, Statement of William Green, President of the AFL, March 16, 1937, 97–127 (quotations on 98, 110).

99. Sidney Hillman, Speech, March 5, 1937, Kheel Center, ILGWU, David Dubinsky, President's Records.

100. Labor's Non-Partisan League, "The Supreme Court v. The People," April 1, 1937, 25, 28, Kheel Center, ILGWU, David Dubinsky, President's Records.

101. See generally Barbara Griffith for the late 1940s story of Operation Dixie, *The Crisis of American Labor: Operation Dixie and the Defeat of the CIO* (Philadelphia: Temple University Press, 1988), quotation on 147.

102. See generally Schickler, *Racial Realignment*, for more on the mid-century role of the labor movement in pushing the Democratic Party toward racial liberalism.

103. Labor's Non-Partisan League, "The Supreme Court vs. the People," 29.

104. Quoted in Weinrib, *Taming of Free Speech*, 211.

105. See Weinrib, 211 for a short but powerful encapsulation of Thomas's worries about the approach taken by labor.

106. "The Court Dictatorship Must Be Ended by Labor," *Socialist Call*, July 10,

1937, Seeley G. Mudd Manuscript Library, Princeton University, ACLU Records, Roger Baldwin Years.

107. "A Fight for the Welfare of Millions," *New York City Daily Worker,* July 8, 1937, Seeley G. Mudd Library, ACLU Records, Roger Baldwin Years.

108. "The Court Dictatorship," *Socialist Call.*

109. "Public Opinion on America's Greatest Issues," *American Institute of Public Opinion.*

Chapter 9

1. *Fortune* Magazine and The Roper Organization, "Roper Fortune #13: Special American: Tenth Anniversary, Question 1" (December 1939), distributed by the Roper Center for Public Opinion Research, https://doi.org/10.25940/ROPER-31097163.

2. David Ciepley, *Liberalism in the Shadow of Totalitarianism* (Cambridge, MA: Harvard University Press, 2006), 237.

3. See Gerard Magliocca, *The Heart of the Constitution: How the Bill of Rights Became the Bill of Rights* (New York: Oxford University Press, 2018), 91–92 (quotation on 92).

4. Magliocca, 100.

5. See Geoffrey Stone, *Perilous Times: Free Speech in Wartime* (New York: W. W. Norton & Co., 2004), 33–73.

6. See Magliocca, *Heart of the Constitution,* 52–53 (quotation on 52).

7. Abrams v. United States, 250 U.S. 616 (1919).

8. Buck v. Bell, 274 U.S. 200, 207 (J. Holmes, majority opinion).

9. Minersville School District v. Gobitis, 310 U.S. 586 (1940).

10. For more on FDR's liberalism, see Aziz Rana, *The Two Faces of American Freedom* (Cambridge, MA: Harvard University Press, 2010), 301–3.

11. Franklin Roosevelt, "Commonwealth Club Speech Campaign, September 23, 1932," in *The Roosevelt Reader: Selected Speeches, Messages, Press Conferences, and Letters of Franklin D. Roosevelt,* ed. Basil Rauch (New York: Rineheart, 1957), 77.

12. See John Wertheimer, "A 'Switch in Time' beyond the Nine: Historical Memory and the Constitutional Revolution of the 1930s," in *Studies in Law, Politics, and Society,* vol. 53, ed. Austin Sarat (Bingley, UK: Emerald Group Publishing, 2010), 3–34, 19.

13. See generally Wertheimer, 3–34.

14. Wertheimer, quotation on 19.

15. Wertheimer, 20.

16. "The Bill of Rights," *New York Times,* December 15, 1941, 22.

17. Wertheimer, "A 'Switch in Time' beyond the Nine," 20.

18. Orville Poland, "Address on the Bill of Rights, February 2, 1939," in *Addresses on the Bill of Rights* (Boston: Civil Liberties Commission, 1939), 5, 7.

19. Franklin Roosevelt, "Address on Bill of Rights Anniversary, December 15, 1941," in *The Public Papers and Addresses of Franklin D. Roosevelt: 1941 Volume,* ed. Samuel I. Rosenman (New York: Harper & Brothers Publishers, 1950), 554–57 (quotation on 554).

20. Roosevelt, 555.

21. "'Anti-isms' Week Set Up in Schools," *New York Times*, April 25, 1940, 11.

22. Roosevelt, "Address on Bill of Rights Anniversary," 555.

23. "Council against Intolerance Plans Sesquicentennial Celebration of Bill of Rights," *Jewish Telegraphic Agency*, September 17, 1941.

24. Franklin Roosevelt, "Bill of Rights Day Proclamation No. 2524, November 27, 1941," in *The Public Papers and Addresses of Franklin D. Roosevelt: 1941 Volume*, ed. Samuel I. Rosenman (New York: Harper & Brothers Publishers, 1950), 497–99 (quotation on 498).

25. "'Civil Rights Year' to Begin March 4," *New York Times*, January 29, 1939, 5.

26. Howard Mumford Jones, "Address on the Bill of Rights, February 2, 1939," in *Addresses on the Bill of Rights* (Boston: Civil Liberties Commission, 1939), 9, 20.

27. Gary Gerstle, *American Crucible: Race and Nation in the Twentieth Century* (Princeton, NJ: Princeton University Press, 2017), 211.

28. See Penny Von Eschen, *Race Against Empire: Black Americans and Anti-Colonialism, 1937–1957* (Ithaca, NY: Cornell University Press, 1997), 32–35. For more on the Black response to and experience of World War II, see generally Matthew Delmont, *Half American: The Epic Story of African Americans Fighting World War II at Home and Abroad* (New York: Viking, 2022).

29. Quotations in Von Eschen, *Race Against Empire*, 33.

30. Wertheimer, "A 'Switch in Time' beyond the Nine," 27, 22.

31. Eleanor Roosevelt, "My Day, February 27, 1939," in *Eleanor Roosevelt's My Day: Her Acclaimed Columns, 1936–1945*, ed. Rochelle Chadakoff (New York: Pharos Books, 1989), 113.

32. See generally Allida M. Black, "Championing a Champion: Eleanor Roosevelt and the Marian Anderson 'Freedom Concert,'" *Presidential Studies Quarterly* 20 (1990): 719–36; see also Susan Stamberg, "Denied a Stage, She Sang for a Nation," *Morning Edition*, NPR, April 9, 2014, https://www.npr.org/2014/04/09/298760473/denied-a-stage-she-sang-for-a-nation.

33. Wertheimer, "A 'Switch in Time' beyond the Nine," 22, 20.

34. Quoted in Michael Denning, *The Cultural Front: The Laboring of American Culture in the Twentieth Century* (New York: Verso, 1997), 128.

35. See "'Civil Rights Year' to Begin March 4."

36. William Allen White, *The Old Order Changeth: A View of American Democracy* (New York: Macmillan, 1910), 22.

37. Quoted in Cornelius Bynum, *A. Philip Randolph and the Struggle for Civil Rights* (Chicago, IL: University of Illinois Press, 2010), 151, 150.

38. See Thomas Sugrue, *Sweet Land of Liberty: The Forgotten Struggle for Civil Rights in the North* (New York: Random House, 2008), 33–39 (quotation on 34).

39. See Glenda Gilmore, *Defying Dixie: The Radical Roots of Civil Rights, 1919–1950* (New York: W. W. Norton, 2008), 307–11 (quotations on 310, 310–11).

40. Quotations in Bynum, 151.

41. Clyde W. Barrow, "Introduction to the Transaction Edition," in *The Republic: Conversations on Fundamentals* (New York: Routledge, 2017), ix.

42. Carl Friedrich, "Review: The Republic: Conversations on Fundamentals," *Yale Law Journal* 53 (1944): 370–73, reference to *Fortune* viewing it as a "classic" and other quotations on 370.

43. Clyde Barrow, a Beard scholar, argues that the focus on the wartime con-

text has been overstated in analyses of *The Republic*, and that Beard had long been uncomfortable with the reduction of his arguments to those of pre–World War I Progressives and Populists. See generally Barrow, "Introduction to the Transaction Edition," in *The Republic: Conversations on Fundamentals* (New York: Routledge, 2017), as well as his other scholarship: "Beyond Progressivism: Charles A. Beard's Social Democratic Theory of American Political Development," *Studies in American Political Development* 8 (1994): 231–81; and *More Than a Historian: The Political and Economic Thought of Charles A. Beard* (New Brunswick, NJ: Transaction Publishers, 2000), 112–28. Still, Beard's clear invocations of the European context as well as juxtapositions of European thinking and the American founders suggests that this context should not be ignored.

44. Charles Beard, *The Republic: Conversations on Fundamentals* (New York: Viking Press, 1945), 316, 24, 22.

45. Beard, 21.

46. Beard, 252.

47. Beard, 23, 253, 252, 301.

48. Richard Hofstadter, "Beard and the Constitution: The History of an Idea," *American Quarterly* 2 (1950): 195–213 (quotation of Beard on 213).

49. See Missouri ex rel Gaines v. Canada, 305 U.S. 337 (1938).

50. West Virginia State Board of Education v. Barnette, 319 U.S. 624, 642 (1943) (J. Jackson, majority opinion).

51. Schneiderman v. United States, 119 F.2d 500, 503, 504 (9th Cir. 1941).

52. Schneiderman v. United States, 320 U.S. 118, 119, 122, 138 (1943).

53. "County Plans Unity Example," *Los Angeles Times*, November 30, 1941, A2.

54. John Lechner, "The Inner Ramparts," An Address Delivered before the Los Angeles City Council on Americanism Day, February 18, 1941, Americanism Education League documents, Bancroft Library, University of California, Berkeley, Japanese American Evacuation and Resettlement Records.

55. Stone, *Perilous Times*, 287.

56. Korematsu v. United States, 323 U.S. 214 (1944).

57. For more on Norman Thomas and the ACLU during the fight over Japanese internment, see Greg Robinson, "Norman Thomas and the Struggle against Internment," *Prospects* 29 (2005): 419–34 (quotations on 424, 427).

58. *Korematsu*, 242 (J. Murphy, dissenting).

59. Quoted in Robinson, "Norman Thomas and the Struggle against Internment," 420.

60. Gerstle, *American Crucible*, 210–20 (quotation on 215).

61. See Stone, *Perilous Times*, 296.

62. For a discussion of the settler immigration policy toward Asian migrants, see Rana, *Two Faces*, 189–93, 215–16.

63. Stone, *Perilous Times*, 283–86.

64. For more generally on the story of Japanese internment, see Stone, 283–309.

65. Quoted in Manning Marable, *W. E. B. Du Bois: Black Radical Democrat* (Boulder, CO: Paradigm Publishers, 2005), 158–59.

66. Robinson, "Norman Thomas and the Struggle against Internment," 425–26 (quotation on 426).

67. Quoted in Marable, *W. E. B. Du Bois*, 159.

68. Studs Terkel's Pulitzer Prize–winning oral history of World War II famously used the phrase as its title, *The Good War: An Oral History of World War II* (New York: New Press, 1984).

Chapter 10

1. Quotations in Franklin Roosevelt, "The Annual Message to the Congress, January 6, 1941," in *The Public Papers and Addresses of Franklin D. Roosevelt: 1940 Volume*, ed. Samuel I. Rosenman (New York: The Macmillan Company, 1941), 663–78 (quotation on 666).

2. Laurence Tribe, "America's Constitutional Narrative," *Daedalus* 141 (2012): 18–42, 19.

3. Seymour Martin Lipset, *The First New Nation: The United States in Historical and Comparative Perspective* (New York: Basic Books, 1963), 314.

4. Henry Luce, "The American Century," *Diplomatic History* 23 (1999): 159–71 (quotation on 171).

5. See generally Stephen Wertheim's excellent *Tomorrow, the World: The Birth of U.S. Global Supremacy* (Cambridge, MA: The Belknap Press of Harvard University Press, 2020), 80–114, especially on how the "idea of an American century became a mainstream proposition in 1941" (p. 83).

6. Quotations in Roosevelt, "The Annual Message to the Congress," 672.

7. See Thomas Borstelmann, *The Cold War and the Color Line: American Race Relations in the Global Arena* (Cambridge, MA: Harvard University Press, 2001), 28–29, 44.

8. See generally Borstelmann, 46.

9. Quoted in Frenise Logan, "Racism and Indian–U.S. Relations, 1947–1953: Views in the Indian Press," *Pacific Historical Review* 54 (1985): 73.

10. See for example Priyamvada Gopal, *Insurgent Empire: Anticolonial Resistance and British Dissent* (New York: Verso, 219), 211–14.

11. See especially Robin Kelley, *Hammer and Hoe: Alabama Communists during the Great Depression* (Chapel Hill: University of North Carolina Press, 1990), 13–116.

12. *Constitution of the Union of Soviet Socialist Republics*, art. 123 (1936).

13. Quoted in Martin Duberman, *Paul Robeson* (New York: Random House, 1989), 211.

14. See Disha Karnad Jani, "The League against Imperialism, National Liberation, and the Economic Question," *Journal of Global History* 17 (2022): 216.

15. Gopal, *Insurgent Empire*, 266.

16. Quoted in Borstelmann, *Cold War and the Color Line*, 76.

17. For an excellent recent account of the book's ideas and legacy, along with the role of the Carnegie Corporation in shaping the text, see Maribel Morey, *White Philanthropy: Carnegie Corporation's* An American Dilemma *and the Making of a White World Order* (Chapel Hill: University of North Carolina Press, 2021).

18. See David Southern, *Gunnar Myrdal and Black-White Relations: The Use and Abuse of* An American Dilemma, *1944–1969* (Baton Rouge: Louisiana State University Press, 1987), quotations on xiii, xiv.

19. See Gunnar Myrdal, *An American Dilemma: The Negro Problem and Modern Democracy*, vol. 1 (New York: Harper & Row, 1944), lxix.

20. Myrdal, lxix.

21. See Gunnar Myrdal, *An American Dilemma: The Negro Problem and Modern Democracy*, vol. 2 (New York: Harper & Row, 1944), 1021.

22. Myrdal, *American Dilemma*, vol. 1, lxix.

23. Myrdal, *American Dilemma*, vol. 2, 1021.

24. Myrdal, *American Dilemma*, vol. 1, lxix.

25. Myrdal, *American Dilemma*, vol. 2, 1021.

26. Southern, *Gunnar Myrdal and Black-White Relations*, 212.

27. Myrdal, *American Dilemma*, vol. 1, 7.

28. Myrdal, 13.

29. See generally G. John Ikenberry, *After Victory: Institutions, Strategic Restraint, and the Rebuilding of Order after Major War* (Princeton, NJ: Princeton University Press, 2001), 163–214.

30. See Wertheim, *Tomorrow, the World*, 115–44, for what he describes as the "instrumental internationalism" of wartime policymakers, who saw in new potential global frameworks mechanisms for the projection of American power.

31. See Ikenberry, *After Victory*, 203–5.

32. Quotations in Franklin Roosevelt, "Address to Congress on Yalta," March 1, 1945, in *The Public Papers and Addresses of Franklin D. Roosevelt: 1944-45 Volume*, ed. Samuel I. Rosenman (New York: Harper & Brothers Publishers, 1950), 570–86 (quotation on 586).

33. UN Charter, preamble (1945), https://www.un.org/en/about-us/un-charter/full-text.

34. Stephen E. Schlesinger, *Act of Creation: The Founding of the United Nations* (Boulder, CO: Westview Press, 2003), 237.

35. GA Res. 217 (III), International Bill of Human Rights (December 10, 1948), https://documents-dds-ny.un.org/doc/RESOLUTION/GEN/NR0/043/88/PDF/NR004388.pdf?OpenElement. Today the International Bill of Human Rights also consists of the International Covenant on Economic, Social and Cultural Rights and the International Covenant on Civil and Political Rights, which were jointly adopted by the UN General Assembly in 1966. See GA Res. 2200 (XXI), International Covenant on Economic, Social and Cultural Rights, International Covenant on Civil and Political Rights (December 16, 1966), https://documents-dds-ny.un.org/doc/RESOLUTION/GEN/NR0/005/03/IMG/NR000503.pdf?OpenElement.

36. Quoted in Kirsten Sellars, *The Rise and Rise of Human Rights* (Glouchestershire, UK: Sutton Publishing, 2002), 23.

37. See Carol Anderson, *Eyes Off the Prize: The United Nations and the African American Struggle for Human Rights, 1944–1955* (New York: Cambridge University Press, 2003), 131–33.

38. See generally GA Res. 217 (III) A, Universal Declaration of Human Rights (December 10, 1948), https://documents-dds-ny.un.org/doc/RESOLUTION/GEN/NR0/043/88/PDF/NR004388.pdf?OpenElement.

39. Quoted in Sellars, *Rise and Rise*, 23; see also Anderson, *Eyes Off the Prize*, 133.

40. Bill Ong Hing, *Making and Remaking Asian America through Immigration Policy, 1850–1990* (Stanford, CA: Stanford University Press, 1993), 33–36.

41. Hing, 35.

42. See generally Leia Castañeda Anastacio, *The Foundations of the Modern Phil-*

ippine State: Imperial Rule and the American Constitutional Tradition in the Philippine Islands, 1898–1935 (New York: Cambridge University Press, 2016), 241–58 (quotation on 248, 256).

43. Kevin Bruyneel, The Third Space of Sovereignty: The Postcolonial Politics of U.S.–Indigenous Relations (Minneapolis: University of Minnesota Press, 2007), 125.

44. Bruyneel, 125.

45. Bruyneel, 125.

46. Vine Deloria Jr. and Clifford Lytle, The Nations Within: The Past and Future of American Indian Sovereignty (New York: Pantheon Books, 1984), 174.

47. Quoted in David Wilkins, "Introduction," in On the Drafting of Tribal Constitutions (Norman: University of Oklahoma Press, 2007), xxi.

48. Deloria and Lytle, The Nations Within, 173.

49. Appendix A, "Model Constitution," in On the Drafting of Tribal Constitutions (Norman: University of Oklahoma Press, 2007), 173.

50. Wilkins, "Introduction," in On the Drafting of Tribal Constitutions, xxiii.

51. Harold Zink, The United States in Germany, 1944–1955 (New York: D. Van Nostrand Co., 1957), 179.

52. Quoted in Zink, 179n5.

53. Constitution of Japan, art. 9 (1947), https://japan.kantei.go.jp/constitution _and_government_of_japan/constitution_e.html.

54. Quoted in Kenneth Pyle, Japan in the American Century (Cambridge, MA: The Belknap Press of Harvard University Press, 2018), 134.

55. Constitution of Japan, preamble.

56. Constitution of Japan, art. 14.

57. Pyle, Japan in the American Century, 137.

58. Douglas MacArthur, "We Shall Win, or We Shall Die," in Sally Warhaft, ed., Well May We Say: The Speeches That Made Australia (Melbourne, Australia: Black, Inc., 2004), 107–8 (quotation on 107); also quoted in Nikhil Pal Singh, "The Problem of Color and Democracy," in The Short American Century: A Postmortem, ed. Andrew J. Bacevich (Cambridge, MA: Harvard University Press, 2012), 59–81 (quotation on 64).

59. See Tom O'Lincoln, Australia's Pacific War: Challenging a National Myth (Brunswick, Victoria (Australia): Interventions, 2011), 53, 65–67.

60. Quoted in Pyle, Japan in the American Century, 121.

61. See Paul Ham, Hiroshima Nagasaki: The Real Story of the Atomic Bombings and Their Aftermath (New York: St. Martin's Press, 2011), 147–65, on the indifference to Japanese civilian life displayed by the "Target Committee," or group of military officials and scientists tasked with determining the cities that would be subjected to atomic bombs.

62. For more on the particularly extreme violence of the American war effort against the Japanese, see Gary Gerstle, American Crucible: Race and Nation in the Twentieth Century (Princeton, NJ: Princeton University Press, 2017), 201–3.

63. See Nils Gilman, Mandarins of the Future: Modernization Theory in Cold War America (Baltimore, MD: Johns Hopkins University Press, 2003), 43.

64. Kwame Nkrumah, Neo-Colonialism: The Last Stage of Imperialism (New York: International Publishers, 1969), quotations on xi.

65. See Oginga Odinga, Not Yet Uhuru (Nairobi, Kenya: Heineman, 1967).

66. For an excellent recent distillation of the complexities around "economic self-determination" in a postcolonial setting, see Odette Lienau, "The Multiple Selves of Economic Self-Determination," *Yale Law Journal Forum* 129 (2020): 674–89.

67. Odinga, *Not Yet Uhuru*, 260–69 (quotations on 268, 267). The quoted language comes from excerpts Odinga includes of writing by his close political ally at the time, Bildad Kaggia. These excerpts lay out the cooperative land redistribution plan they both embraced.

68. Odinga, 256.

69. For a quick account of the idea of "commercial peace" in US foreign policy see Aziz Rana, *The Two Faces of American Freedom* (Cambridge, MA: Harvard University Press, 2010), 284–87. See also James Tully, *Public Philosophy in a New Key: Imperialism and Civic Freedom*, vol. 2 (New York: Cambridge University Press, 2008), 133, 143–49.

70. See Neil Smith, *American Empire: Roosevelt's Geographer and the Prelude to Globalization* (Berkeley: University of California Press, 2004), 373. Smith incisively develops this argument by focusing in particular on the ideas of Isaiah Bowman, a Johns Hopkins University president, State Department advisor to FDR, and significant voice in the UN's founding.

71. Smith, 374–415 (quotation on 375).

72. Franklin Roosevelt, "Message on the State of Union, January 11, 1944," in *The Public Papers and Addresses of Franklin D. Roosevelt: 1944–45 Volume*, 32–44 (quotation on 41).

73. Quotations in Roosevelt, 41.

74. For a powerful theoretical reconstruction of a socialist critique of work under capitalism, see Alex Gourevitch, "The Right to Strike: A Radical View," *American Political Science Review* 112 (2018): 905–17.

75. For more generally on the preservationist dimensions of the Second Bill of Rights, see Samuel Moyn, *Not Enough: Human Rights in an Unequal World* (Cambridge, MA: The Belknap Press of Harvard University Press, 2018), 68–88.

76. Roosevelt, "Message on the State of Union," 41.

77. Harry S. Truman, "Special Message to the Congress on Greece and Turkey: The Truman Doctrine, March 12, 1947," in *Public Papers of the Presidents of the United States: Harry S. Truman, 1947* (Washington, DC: United States Government Printing Office, 1963), 176–80 (quotation on 178–79).

78. Truman, 178.

79. For a terrific account of how post-war democratic theory was shaped by what Kyong-Min Son calls Truman's "starkly dichotomous worldview," see Son's *The Eclipse of the Demos: The Cold War and the Crisis of Democracy before Neoliberalism* (Lawrence: University Press of Kansas, 2020), 37–70 (quotation on 38).

80. Gerard Magliocca, *The Heart of the Constitution: How the Bill of Rights Became the Bill of Rights* (New York: Oxford University Press, 2018), 135.

81. See Magliocca, 135–36.

82. See Joshua Cherniss, *A Mind and Its Time: The Development of Isaiah Berlin's Political Thought* (Oxford, UK: Oxford University Press, 2013), 188–233 (quotation on 225).

83. Isaiah Berlin, "Two Concepts of Liberty," in *Four Essays on Liberty* (Oxford: Oxford University Press, 1969), 134, 157.

84. See Aaron Gavin's excellent analysis of Berlin's view of anti-colonial movements in "Militant Liberalism and Its Discontents: On the Decolonial Origins of Endless War" (PhD diss., Cornell University, 2017), 59–72 (quotation on 61).

85. Berlin, "Two Concepts of Liberty," 134, 157.

86. "I Guardiani Della Libertà Americane," *Nuovo Mondo*, July 23, 1945, 9–13 (quotation on 9), Emeroteca Archivio Storico Capitolina, Rome, PER.1706 (M.155). All translations of *Nuovo Mondo* from the Italian are by Aimée Plukker, whom I thank immensely for discovering these articles during her archival research.

87. "I Guardiani Della Costituzione," *Nuovo Mondo*, October 15, 1945, 40–44 (quotations on 40, 44), Emeroteca Archivio Storico Capitolina, Rome, PER.1706 (M.155).

88. See Edward Shils, *The Torment of Secrecy: The Background and Consequences of American Security Policies* (Glencoe, IL: The Free Press, 1956), quotations on 14, 154.

89. Quoted in Gilman, *Mandarins of the Future*, 43.

90. See Begüm Adalet, *Hotels and Highways: The Construction of Modernization Theory in Cold War Turkey* (Stanford, CA: Stanford University Press, 2018), 1–54.

91. Quotations in Gilman, *Mandarins of the Future*, 1–2.

92. Quotations in Gilman, 1–2.

93. Quoted in Gilman, 71.

94. Quoted in Ikenberry, *After Victory*, 174.

95. See generally Ikenberry, 172–75.

96. For a comprehensive account of the role of the Marshall Plan, intended and unintended, in entrenching the Cold War, see generally Benn Steil, *The Marshall Plan: Dawn of the Cold War* (New York: Simon & Schuster, 2018).

97. Quoted in Ikenberry, *After Victory*, 202.

98. For more on the American desire for willing foreign investment in the US-led global order, see G. John Ikenberry, *Liberal Leviathan: The Origins, Crisis, and Transformation of the American World Order* (Princeton, NJ: Princeton University Press, 2011), 159–219.

99. See generally Adalet, *Hotels and Highways*, for an invaluable and extended account of how Turkish elites, for instance, internalized related judgments, but even more significantly actively participated in the construction of modernization ideas and practices for their country.

100. For the quotations and description of the day, see Ricardo T. Jose, "July 4, 1946: The Philippines Gained Independence from the United States," National World War II Museum, July 2, 2021, https://www.nationalww2museum.org/war/articles/july-4-1946-philippines-independence.

101. See Daniel Immerwahr, *How to Hide an Empire: A History of the Greater United States* (New York: Picador, 2019), 230–38 (quotation on 237).

102. Jawaharlal Nehru, "A Voyage of Discovery: Address to the U.S. House of Representatives," October 13, 1949, in *Selected Works of Jawaharlal Nehru*, vol. 13, ed. S. Gopal (New Delhi: Jawaharlal Nehru Memorial Fund, 1992), 301–4 (quotations on 302, 301).

103. Nehru, 302.

104. See Madhav Khosla, *India's Founding Moment: The Constitution of a Most Surprising Democracy* (Cambridge, MA: Harvard University Press, 2020), 44–55.

105. Nehru, "Voyage of Discovery," 302.

106. See Robert Vitalis, "The Midnight Ride of Kwame Nkrumah and Other Fables of Bandung," *Humanity* 4 (2013): 281n18.

107. Sukarno, "Address Given by Sukarno (Bandung, 18 April 1955)," in *Asia-Africa speak from Bandung* (Jakarta, Indonesia: Ministry of Foreign Affairs, 1955), 19–29, https://www.cvce.eu/en/obj/opening_address_given_by_sukarno _bandung_18_april_1955-en-88d3f71c-c9f9-415a-b397-b27b8581a4f5.html.

108. Nehru, "Voyage of Discovery," 303.

109. On the centrality of the state to Indian political imagination, see Sudipta Kaviraj, "On the Enchantment of the State: Indian Thought on the Role of the State in the Narrative of Modernity," *European Journal of Sociology* 46 (2005): 263–96.

110. Nehru, "Voyage of Discovery," 303.

111. Khosla, *India's Founding Moment*, 47.

112. One can see this cosmopolitan aspiration to a new global universalism that learns from both East and West at the center of India's constitution-writing project. See especially Sujit Choudhry, Madhav Khosla, and Pratap Bhanu Mehta, "Locating Indian Constitutionalism," in *The Oxford Handbook of the Indian Constitution*, ed. Choudhry, Khosa, and Mehta (New York: Oxford University Press, 2016), 1–13, 4–7; and Sandipto Dasgupta, *Legalizing the Revolution: India and the Constitution of the Postcolonial World* (New York: Cambridge University Press, 2023).

113. Geoffrey Robinson, *The Killing Season: A History of the Indonesian Massacre, 1965–1966* (Princeton, NJ: Princeton University Press, 2018), 177–85.

114. Robinson, 183–85.

115. Stuart Schrader, "The Murderous Legacy of Cold War Anticommunism," *The Boston Review*, May 19, 2020, https://www.bostonreview.net/articles/stuart -schrader-murderous-legacy-anticommunism/.

116. Quoted in Pedro Cabán, "The End of the Commonwealth of Puerto Rico," *Dissent*, April 30, 2021, https://www.dissentmagazine.org/online_articles/the-end -of-the-commonwealth-of-puerto-rico.

117. Quoted in Franklin Roosevelt, "Message to the Congress Recommending Self-Government for Puerto Rico, September 28, 1943," in *The Public Papers and Addresses of Franklin D. Roosevelt: 1943 Volume*, ed. Samuel I. Rosenman (New York: Harper & Brothers Publishers, 1950), 412–17 (quotation on 413); see also David Rezvani, "The Basis of Puerto Rico's Constitutional Status: Colony, Compact, or 'Federacy'?" *Political Science Quarterly* 122 (2007): 121.

118. "Puerto to Be Our Gibraltar in Caribbean, Says Admiral Leahy," *New York Times*, May 25, 1940, 6.

119. Cabán, "End of the Commonwealth."

120. Puerto Rican Federal Relations Act, Pub. L. No. 81-600, 64 Stat. 319 (1950) (codified as amended at 48 U.S.C. §§ 731b–731e).

121. *Constitution of the Commonwealth of Puerto Rico*, https://www.refworld.org /docid/3e9a9dba4.html.

122. For more on the severity of US colonial repression during this era, see generally Nelson Denis, *War against All Puerto Ricans: Revolution and Terror in America's Colony* (New York: Nation Books, 2015).

123. Cabán, "End of the Commonwealth."

124. See Gerald Meyer, *Vito Marcantonio: Radical Politician, 1902–1954* (Albany: State University of New York Press, 1989), 154.

125. Meyer, quotations on 152.

126. Mark Neocleous, *Critique of Security* (Montreal: McGill-Queen's University Press, 2008), 102–3.

127. See Benedict Kerkvliet, *The Huk Rebellion: A Study of Peasant Revolt in the Philippines* (Berkeley: University of California Press, 1977), quotation on 243.

128. Luce, "The American Century," 170.

129. For more on the persistence of these links all the way to the twenty-first-century "war on terror," see Antony Anghie, *Imperialism, Sovereignty, and the Making of International Law* (New York: Cambridge University Press, 2004), 279–91.

130. See especially Robert Vitalis's essential account of the American academic ties between earlier studies of racial development and new post-war social scientific frameworks in *White World Order, Black Power Politics: The Birth of American International Relations* (Ithaca, NY: Cornell University Press, 2015), 22, 129–81.

131. See Gilman, *Mandarins of the Future*, 1–3.

132. Quotations in Gilman, 5.

133. Quoted in Wertheim, *Tomorrow, the World*, 167.

134. See Borstelmann, *Cold War and the Color Line*, 129–30, on how some Eisenhower administration officials read Congolese Prime Minister Patrice Lumumba's fierce anti-colonial statements as suggesting that he "might not even be mentally competent" (p. 130).

135. See Fredrick Logevall's essential *Embers of War: The Fall of an Empire and the Making of America's Vietnam* (New York: Random House, 2012), especially 334–52, for a powerful account of how American policymakers waded deeper and deeper into what would become the Vietnam War through a series of faulty interpretations about local political dynamics and popular desires.

136. For a comprehensive account of how American officials, perceiving existential threat, used guerrilla tactics and fought terror with "counter-terror," see generally Michael McClintock, *Instruments of Statecraft: U.S. Guerrilla Warfare, Counter-Insurgency, and Counter-Terrorism, 1940–1990* (New York: Pantheon, 1992).

137. It was just this tendency of Cold War elites to engage in self-absolution—by focusing on the perceived justice of the country's ends—that so worried the theologian and commentator Reinhold Niebuhr about the direction of American foreign policy in the 1950s. Despite being a "Cold Warrior" himself and an ardent critic of the Soviet Union, Niebuhr in 1952's *The Irony of American History* emphasized the messianic consistencies between Soviet and American ideologies. American identity may have been grounded in the idea that it "knew nothing of sin or guilt," but its actions—like using nuclear weapons against Japan and potentially using them again—could be morally grave. Reinhold Niebuhr, *The Irony of American History* (New York: Charles Scribner's Sons, 1954), 39. Under these circumstances, for the United States to continue to "believe itself to be peculiarly innocent" was at best a dangerous illusion and at worst a threat to the world (p. 39).

138. Gilman, *Mandarins of the Future*, 14.

139. Robinson, *Killing Season*, 184.

140. See as an example again Borstelmann, *Cold War and the Color Line*, 128–32,

for the role of racist judgments about Lumumba and the Congolese people in justifying deposing him from power.

141. For instance, Suharto's authoritarian regime, marked by spasms of mass violence in the mid-1960s, was largely justified by local Indonesian elites both internally and to the international community on developmental grounds—as what "accelerated modernization" required politically. See generally Brad Simpson, "Indonesia's 'Accelerated Modernization' and the Global Discourse of Development, 1960–1975," *Diplomatic History* 33 (2009): 467–86. As for Turkey, see especially Adalet, *Hotels and Highways.*

142. See Tom Ginsburg, Aziz Z. Huq, and Mila Versteeg, "The Coming Demise of Liberal Constitutionalism?" *University of Chicago Law Review* 85 (2018): 239.

143. Barbara A. Perry, "Constitutional Johnny Appleseeds: American Consultants and the Drafting of Foreign Constitutions," *Albany Law Review* 55 (1992): 767–91 (quotations on 775).

144. Perry singles out the law professor Albert Blaustein as among the Cold War period's most prolific American constitutional consultants, providing drafting advice in South Vietnam as well as "Bangladesh (1972), Cambodia (1974), Zimbabwe (1978–1980), Peru (1979), Liberia (1982–1983), Niger (1983–1988), Brazil (1985, 1988), Namibia (1987), Uganda (1988–1989), Mozambique (1988–1989), and Fiji (1989)." Perry, 778. In recent years, with both the collapse of the Soviet Union and post-9/11 American interventions in Iraq and Afghanistan, these ventures only proliferated further across eastern and central Europe as well as the Middle East. For more on the figure of the US-sponsored constitutional consultant, see also Tom Ginsburg, "Constitutional Advice and Transnational Legal Order," *UC Irvine Journal of International, Transnational, and Comparative Law* 2 (2017): 13–15.

145. Quotations in Lipset, *First New Nation*, 314, 313.

146. See Lipset, 313–17 (quotation on 316).

147. Patricia Sullivan, "Political Scientist Seymour Lipset, 84," *Washington Post*, January 4, 2007, https://www.washingtonpost.com/archive/local/2007/01/04/political-scientist-seymour-lipset-84/9734c1e1-ebeb-4a43-ba8a-4faa88e5be7b/.

Chapter 11

1. George Lipsitz, *Rainbow at Midnight: Labor and Culture in the 1940s* (Urbana: University of Illinois Press, 1994), 99.

2. See generally Tejasvi Nagaraja, "Soldiers of the American Dream: The Second World War, Race and Freedom in the Shadow of U.S. Power" (unpublished manuscript, Microsoft Word document on file with author, 2022), for a powerful account of the ideological radicalism unleashed by the war and its immediate aftermath, as well as state and business efforts to contain it.

3. Quoted in Wendy Wall's essential book *Inventing the "American Way": The Politics of Consensus from the New Deal to the Civil Rights Movement* (New York: Oxford University Press, 2008), 172, and see 169 for how such figures were "haunted by the 'spectres of 1919.'"

4. See for example Geoffrey Stone, *Perilous Times: Free Speech in Wartime* (New York: W. W. Norton, 2004), 528–58.

5. Lipsitz, *Rainbow at Midnight*, 99.

6. *Fortune* Magazine and The Roper Organization, "Roper Fortune # 56: Update on 10th Anniversary Survey Questions, Question 2," (September 27–October 10, 1946), distributed by the Roper Center for Public Opinion Research, https://doi .org/10.25940/ROPER-31097205.

7. Lipsitz, *Rainbow at Midnight*, 136.

8. Gary Gerstle, *American Crucible: Race and Nation in the Twentieth Century* (Princeton, NJ: Princeton University Press, 2017), 235–36 (quotation on 235).

9. Wall, *Inventing the "American Way,"* 170.

10. See generally Wall, 165–72 (quotation on 171).

11. As one indicative example, Read Lewis, co-founder of *Common Ground* magazine and a central figure in the Common Council for American Unity (CCAU), a tri-faith and pro-immigrant organization, declared in 1950 to members of the CCAU that communists were attempting to "confuse and divide the American people mak[ing] doubly important . . . unit[ing] Americans"—Wall, 263.

12. Quotations and statistics from *Fortune* Magazine and The Roper Organization, "Roper Fortune # 56: Update on 10th Anniversary Survey Questions, Questions 16 and 24" (September 27–October 10, 1946), distributed by the Roper Center for Public Opinion Research, https://doi.org/10.25940/ROPER-31097205.

13. The tendency over the post–New Deal decades, at least until very recently, has been for a solid majority to support constitutional fidelity, with some ebb and flow. Still, surveys often found a quarter to a third of respondents—not an insignificant number—declaring the Constitution to be either "outmoded" or "outdated" and needing to be "modernized." In 1991, in response to the *Los Angeles Times*'s question "Do you think [the Constitution and the Bill of Rights] have proven flexible enough to remain the basis of American law . . . or are they outmoded and in need of revision?" 31 percent answered "outmoded." *Los Angeles Times*, "Los Angeles Times Poll #263: Presidential Politics and the Economy, Question 30" (November 21–24, 1991), distributed by the Roper Center for Public Opinion Research, https://doi.org /10.25940/ROPER-31092963. Twenty years later, in response to a near identical question from the Associated Press and National Constitution Center, 28 percent rejected the view that the "United States Constitution is an enduring document that remains relevant" and instead described it as "outdated." Associated Press and Gfk Roper Public Affairs & Corporate Communications, "Associated Press Poll: August 2012, Question 61" (August 16–20, 2012), distributed by the Roper Center for Public Opinion Research, https://doi.org/10.25940/ROPER-31112898.

Perhaps most noteworthy, in the context of the Trump presidency, the overturning of *Roe v. Wade*, and growing concerns about the dysfunctions of the electoral system, is that support for constitutional change appears to be increasing. One 2017 Rasmussen Poll had only 48 percent agreeing that the Constitution should be "left as written," with 46 percent supporting changes, either minor or major. "Support for Current Constitution Hits 10-Year Low," *Rasmussen Reports*, October 11, 2017, https://www.rasmussenreports.com/public_content/politics/general _politics/october_2017/support_for_current_constitution_hits_10_year_low. A 2022 Rasmussen poll further highlights these trends, along with the general complexity of popular sentiment. Rasmussen reports that "82 percent of likely U.S. voters have a favorable opinion of the Constitution," but 49 percent of "Democrats believe the Constitution 'should be mostly or completely rewritten.'" Among Democrats, those numbers jump to 57 percent who think the text is "rooted in racism," and 64 percent who agree it is a "sexist document." "U.S. Constitution 'Racist' and 'Sexist' Most Democrats Believe," *Rasmussen Reports*, July 13, 2022, https://www.rasmussenreports.com/public_content/politics/partner_surveys/july_2022/u_s_constitution_racist_and_sexist_most_democrats_believe.

14. For an excellent overview of post-war efforts to establish a world constitution, see Robert Tsai, *America's Forgotten Constitutions* (Cambridge, MA: Harvard University Press, 2014), 185–217 (book sales statistics on 206). This discussion draws especially from Tsai's account.

15. Quoted in Tsai, 207.

16. See Gilbert Jonas, *One Shining Moment: A Short History of the American Student World Federalist Movement, 1942–1953* (New York: iUniverse.com, Inc., 2001), 42–43.

17. Jonas, 9.

18. Jonas, 159, Appendix 6.

19. Quoted in Jonas, 159, Appendix 6.

20. Jonas, 35.

21. Jonas, 42–43.

22. Jonas, 135, Appendix 1.

23. For more from Gilbert Jonas, a student world federalist leader and author of a key book on the movement, on how past activists carried their "multilateralism" and "internationalism" into their future political lives, see Jonas, 133.

24. Jonas, 128–31.

25. See Jonas, 42–43, 196; and Tsai, *America's Forgotten Constitutions*, 206.

26. *An Appeal to the World: A Statement on the Denial of Human Rights to Minorities in the Case of Citizens of Negro Descent in the United States of America and an Appeal to the United Nations for Redress*, ed. W. E. B. Du Bois (New York: NAACP, 1947).

27. Penny Von Eschen, *Race Against Empire: Black Americans and Anticolonialism, 1937–1957* (Ithaca, NY: Cornell University Press, 1997), 17.

28. Von Eschen, 17–21, 196n54.

29. W. E. B. Du Bois, "Introduction," in *An Appeal to the World*, 1–14 (quotations on 13, 12).

30. Du Bois, 11, 10.

31. Du Bois, 9, 11.

32. Quoted in Lipsitz, *Rainbow at Midnight*, 340.

33. Lipsitz, 340.

34. Douglas Stuart, *Creating the National Security State: A History of the Law That Transformed America* (Princeton, NJ: Princeton University Press, 2008), 8.

35. See especially Stone, *Perilous Times*, 348–49.

36. Stone, 372.

37. See Stone, 372–73.

38. Quotations in Lipsitz, *Rainbow at Midnight*, 193.

39. See Reuel Schiller, *Forging Rivals: Race, Class, Law, and the Collapse of Postwar Liberalism* (New York: Cambridge University Press, 2015), 26.

40. See Schiller, 29; and Salvatore John LaGumina, *Vito Marcantonio: The People's Politician* (Dubuque, IA: Kendall/Hunt Publishing Co., 1969), 96–97.

41. See generally Lipsitz, *Rainbow at Midnight*, 182–203 (polling data on 191).

42. Quoted in Lipsitz, 192.

43. See Manfred Berg, "Black Civil Rights and Liberal Anticommunism: The NAACP in the Early Years of the Cold War," *Journal of American History* 94 (2007): 75–96, especially 88–92.

44. Martin Duberman, *Paul Robeson* (New York: Random House, 1989), 395.

45. Duberman, 25.

46. Quoted in Duberman, 55.

47. See Duberman, quoting Robeson as saying that over time his youthful embrace of the American project became infused with a "questioning of accepted values" (p. 29).

48. See generally Carol Anderson, *Eyes Off the Prize: The United Nations and the African American Struggle for Human Rights, 1944–1955* (New York: Cambridge University Press, 2003), 101–12; and Kirsten Sellars, *The Rise and Rise of Human Rights* (Gloucestershire, UK: Sutton Publishing, 2002), 20.

49. See Berg, "Black Civil Rights and Liberal Anticommunism," 83–84; and Manning Marable, *W. E. B. Du Bois: Black Radical Democrat* (Boulder, CO: Paradigm Publishers, 1986), 174–75.

50. Anderson, *Eyes Off the Prize*, 92.

51. Glenda Gilmore, *Defying Dixie: The Radical Roots of Civil Rights, 1919–1950* (New York: W. W. Norton, 2008), 435.

52. Quoted in *We Charge Genocide: The Historic Petition to the United Nations for Relief from a Crime of the United States Government against the Negro People* (New York: Civil Rights Congress, 1951), 5.

53. See Anderson, *Eyes Off the Prize*, 184–95 (quotation on 192).

54. Chip Gibbons, "The Repression Lists," *Jacobin*, August 5, 2016, https://jacobinmag.com/2016/08/no-fly-list-terror-watch-list.

55. See generally Duberman, *Paul Robeson*, 381–445.

56. See Denise Lynn, "The Deportation of Claudia Jones," *Black Perspectives*, October 5, 2018, https://www.aaihs.org/the-deportation-of-claudia-jones/; and see generally Carole Boyce Davies, *Left of Karl Marx: The Political Life of Black Communist Claudia Jones* (Durham, NC: Duke University Press, 2008), 198–200.

57. Andrew Lanham, "When W. E. B. Du Bois Was Un-American," *Boston Review*, January 13, 2017, http://bostonreview.net/race-politics/andrew-lanham-when-w-e-b-du-bois-was-un-american.

58. See Charisse Burden-Stelly, "Black Cold War Liberalism as an Agency Reduction Formation during the Late 1940s and the Early 1950s," *International journal of Africana Studies* 19 (2018): 77–112 (quotation on 111).

59. See Gerald Horne, "Civil Rights Congress," in *Encyclopedia of the American Left*, ed. Mari Jo Buhle, Paul Buhle, and Dan Georgakas (New York: Garland Publishing, 1990), 134–35.

60. See Von Eschen, *Race Against Empire*, 134–37, 141–44 (quotation on 142).

61. American Bar Association, *Law Day USA Planning Guide* (Chicago: ABA, 1962), 3.

62. This discussion of the Freedom train draws from Wendy Wall's excellent account in *Inventing the "American Way,"* 201–40 (quotation on 3).

63. Wall, quotations on 219.

64. See Wall, 202–9.

65. Wall, 201, 214–16.

66. Quoted in Wall, 212.

67. Wall, 212–16.

68. Wall, 219–20.

69. Wall, 216.

70. Wall, 221, 222.

71. C. L. R. James [under the pseudonym G. F. Eckstein], "Price of Imperialism to the People: The Iron Heel," *Fourth International* 10 (1949): 208–14, https://www.marxists.org/archive/james-clr/works/1949/08/price-imperialism.htm.

72. Quoted in Wall, *Inventing the "American Way,"* 217.

73. Wall notes how in Brooklyn so many people (upwards of one hundred thousand) besieged the train that the numbers of those waiting were "five to ten times as many as could be allowed on board during the twelve-hour stop," while in Boston the line to get in "stretched, four abreast, for half a mile"—Wall, 220.

74. Wall, 3.

75. Wall, 217.

76. See Robin Kelley, *Hammer and Hoe: Alabama Communists during the Great Depression* (Chapel Hill: University of North Carolina Press, 1990), 13–56 on the organizing campaigns, replete with intense personal risk, that helped to build the party's base among the Black poor in Alabama.

77. Stone, *Perilous Times*, 528–58.

Chapter 12

1. Editors of *Fortune* and Russell W. Davenport, *U.S.A.: The Permanent Revolution* (New York: Prentice Hall, 1951), 90–91, 95.

2. John Ruggie's seminal account of the post-war era's "embedded liberalism" describes these practices as efforts by governing elites to "fuse power with legitimate social purpose." See John Ruggie, "International Regimes, Transactions, and Change: Embedded Liberalism in the Postwar Economic Order," *International Organization* 36 (1982): 382.

3. Reuel Schiller, *Forging Rivals: Race, Class, Law, and the Collapse of Postwar Liberalism* (New York: Cambridge University Press, 2015), 24.

4. Schiller, 22.

5. See generally Frederick Harbison, "The General Motors–United Auto Workers Agreement of 1950," *Journal of Political Economy* 58 (1950): 397–411 (quotation on 399).

6. Schiller, *Forging Rivals*, 22–23 (quotation on 22).

7. Davenport, *U.S.A., the Permanent Revolution*, 66–67, also quoted in Wendy Wall, *Inventing the "American Way": The Politics of Consensus from the New Deal to the Civil Rights Movement* (New York: Oxford University Press, 2008), 197.

8. Quoted in Alan Brinkley, *The End of Reform: New Deal Liberalism in Recession and War* (New York: Vintage Books, 1995), 224.

9. Quoted in Jefferson Cowie, *Stayin' Alive: The 1970s and the Last Days of the Working Class* (New York: The New Press, 2010), 28.

10. See Schiller, *Forging Rivals*, 228.

11. See Beth Sims, *Workers of the World Undermined: American Labor's Role in U.S. Foreign Policy* (Boston: South End Press, 1992).

12. See Nelson Lichtenstein, *Walter Reuther: The Most Dangerous Man in Detroit* (Urbana: University of Illinois Press, 1995), 404.

13. As a young man Reuther had spent time working in an auto plant in the Soviet Union, and during the 1930s he had close connections with CPUSA activists. But as Lichtenstein writes of "Reuther and other political engaged activists, the break with the Communists" in the context of the Nazi-Soviet Pact "was not merely a question of foreign policy but," as with Randolph or Bunche, "a profoundly ideological and moral issue." See generally Lichtenstein, 25–73, quotation on 155.

14. See Jefferson Cowie, *The Great Exception: The New Deal and the Limits of American Politics* (Princeton, NJ: Princeton University Press, 2016), 160.

15. See generally Cowie, *The Great Exception*, 160–63.

16. See, for instance, Schiller, *Forging Rivals*, 138–40, on the late 1950s conflicts between Randolph and then AFL-CIO President George Meany over the organization's failure to address adequately segregation and discrimination within local unions.

17. George Lipsitz, *Rainbow at Midnight: Labor and Culture in the 1940s* (Urbana: University of Illinois Press, 1994), 194.

18. See generally Nancy Fraser, "Feminism, Capitalism, and the Cunning of History," *New Left Review* 56 (2009): 97–117.

19. See generally Leila J. Rupp and Verta Taylor, *Surviving in the Doldrums: The American Women's Rights Movements, 1945 to the 1960s* (New York: Oxford University Press, 1987).

20. Hoyt v. Florida, 368 U.S. 57, 62 (1961)

21. Rupp and Taylor, *Surviving in the Doldrums*, 26.

22. Quoted in Rupp and Taylor, 136.

23. Rupp and Taylor, 50.

24. For more on male union officials' discomfort with challenges to sex discrimination and gendered hierarchies within labor, see Dennis Deslippe's post-war story of the United Packinghouse Workers of America (UPWA) in *"Rights, Not Roses": Unions and the Rise of Working-Class Feminism, 1945–80* (Urbana: University of Illinois Press, 2000), 67–88.

25. See generally Matthew Lassiter, *The Silent Majority: Suburban Politics in the Sunbelt South* (Princeton, NJ: Princeton University Press, 2007).

26. Quoted in David Southern, *Gunnar Myrdal and Black–White Relations: The Use and Abuse of an American Dilemma, 1944–1969* (Baton Rouge: Louisiana State University Press, 1987), 123.

27. See Manfred Berg, "Black Civil Rights and Liberal Anticommunism: The NAACP in the Early Years of the Cold War," *Journal of American History* 94 (2007): 84–86.

28. Berg, 85.

29. Quoted in Wall, *Inventing the "American Way,"* 231.

30. See Wall, 230, 238, quotation on 239.

31. See Lipsitz, *Rainbow at Midnight*, 340.

32. Walter White, *A Man Called White: The Autobiography of Walter White* (Athens: University of Georgia Press, 1995), 347, also quoted in Penny Von Eschen, *Race*

Against Empire: Black Americans and Anticolonialism, 1937–1957 (Ithaca, NY: Cornell University Press, 1997), 112.

33. See Berg, "Black Civil Rights and Liberal Anticommunism," 86–88.

34. Berg, 94, 93.

35. Berg, 87.

36. Gary A. Donaldson, *Truman Defeats Dewey* (Lexington: University Press of Kentucky, 1999), 206.

37. Sidney Tarrow, *Movements and Parties: Critical Connections in American Political Development* (New York: Cambridge University Press, 2021), 106–7 (quotation on 107). For more on the NAACP's shifting legislative and litigation strategies over the first half of the twentieth century, see Megan Ming Francis's essential *Civil Rights and the Making of the Modern American State* (New York: Cambridge University Press, 2014).

38. See Tarrow, *Movements and Parties*, 108; and Francis, *Civil Rights*, 6.

39. See generally Southern, *Gunnar Myrdal and Black-White Relations*, 127–50.

40. See generally Mary Dudziak, *Cold War Civil Rights: Race and the Image of American Democracy* (Princeton, NJ: Princeton University Press, 2001).

41. Brown v. Board of Education, 347 U.S. 483 (1954).

42. Quoted in Dudziak, *Cold War Civil Rights*, 100.

43. Quoted in Dudziak, 107.

44. See Edward White, "The Unacknowledged Lesson: Earl Warren and the Japanese Relocation Controversy," *Virginia Quarterly Review* 55 (1979): 613–29 (quotation on 615).

45. Quotations in "Edward Martin Is Dead at 87; Ex-Senator from Pennsylvania," *New York Times*, March 20, 1967, 33.

46. Quotations in Wall, *Inventing the "American Way,"* 219.

47. See Frank Lawrence Owsley, "The Pillars of Agrarianism," in *The South: Old and New Frontiers*, ed. Harriet Chappell Owsley (Athens: University of Georgia Press, 1969), 177–89 (quotation on 186). As Frank declared:

The federal government should have supreme control over war and peace, the army and navy, interregional or even interstate commerce, banking, currency, and foreign affairs. On the other hand, the sections should have equal representation in the federal legislative body and in the election of the president and the cabinet. The legislative body should be composed of a senate only and should be elected by the regional congresses. Finally . . . the several regions should have an equal share in making the tariff, which would be in the form of a treaty or agreement between all the sections, somewhat in the fashion of the late Austro-Hungarian tariff treaties. (p. 187)

48. U.S. v. Harris, 106 U.S. 629 (1883).

49. See generally Daniel Kato's essential *Liberalizing Lynching: Building a New Racialized State* (New York: Oxford University Press, 2016) for more on Supreme Court jurisprudence and racial violence from post-Reconstruction to the 1960s.

50. "The Decision of the Supreme Court in the School Cases—Declaration of Constitutional Principles," 84th Cong., 2nd sess., *Congressional Record* 102 (March 12, 1956): S 4459–64 (quotations on 4460).

51. *Brown v. Board of Education*, 494.

52. Herbert Wechsler, "Toward Neutral Principles of Constitutional Law," *Harvard Law Review* 73 (1959): 1–35 (quotations on 33, 17, 19).

53. See David Strauss, "Little Rock and the Legacy of *Brown*," *St. Louis University Law Journal* 52 (2008): 1065–86, 1071.

54. See generally Michael Klarman, "How *Brown* Changed Race Relations: The Backlash Thesis," *Journal of American History* 81 (1994): 81–118.

55. Quoted in Dan T. Carter, *The Politics of Rage: George Wallace, the Origins of the New Conservatism, and the Transformation of American Politics* (Baton Rouge: Louisiana State University Press, 2000), 109.

56. See generally Klarman, "How *Brown* Changed Race Relations."

57. See generally Donna Gabaccia, "Nations of Immigrants: Do Words Matter?" *Pluralist* 5 (2010): 5–31.

58. See Gabaccia, 23.

59. See John Kennedy, *A Nation of Immigrants* (New York: Harper and Row, 1964), 64.

60. Gabaccia, "Nations of Immigrants," 24.

61. Kennedy, *Nation of Immigrants*, 6.

62. See Sam Klug, "Making the Internal Colony: Black Internationalism, Development, and the Politics of Colonial Comparison in the United States, 1940–1975" (PhD diss., Harvard University, 2020) for an excellent analysis of Kennedy's views as well as the broader linkage US officials increasingly drew between American independence and anti-colonial revolutions across Asia and Africa, particularly in chapter 3.

63. Quoted in Klug, 139.

64. Seymour Martin Lipset, *The First New Nation: The United States in Historical and Comparative Perspective* (New York: Basic Books, 1963), 314, 313, 15.

65. See Aziz Rana, *The Two Faces of American Freedom* (Cambridge, MA: Harvard University Press, 2010), 1–175, on British colonization of North America and then how US independence unleashed new cycles of imperial expansion.

66. Lipset, *The First New Nation*, 15.

67. Jawaharlal Nehru, "A Voyage of Discovery: Address to the U.S. House of Representatives," October 13, 1949, in *Selected Works of Jawaharlal Nehru*, vol. 13, ed. S. Gopal (New Delhi: Jawaharlal Nehru Memorial Fund, 1992), 301–4, 302.

68. Martin Luther King Jr., "The American Dream," in *A Testament of Hope: The Essential Writings and Speeches of Martin Luther King, Jr.*, ed. James M. Washington (New York: Harper San Francisco, 1986), 208–16 (quotations on 208).

69. Carol Anderson, *Eyes Off the Prize: The United Nations and the African American Struggle for Human Rights, 1944–1955* (New York: Cambridge University Press, 2003), 53.

70. Ralph Bunche, "Nobel Lecture: Some Reflections on Peace in Our Time," *The Nobel Prize*, December 11, 1950, https://www.nobelprize.org/prizes/peace/1950/bunche/lecture/.

71. See "Bunche Disputes Dr. King on Peace: Sees Error in Fusing Rights and Antiwar Campaigns—His View Is Challenged," *New York Times*, April 13, 1967, 1, 32.

72. See generally Makau Mutua, *Kenya's Quest for Democracy: Taming Leviathan* (Boulder, CO: Lynne Rienner Publishers, Inc., 2008), 56–61. See also Aziz Rana,

"Constitutionalism and the Predicament of Postcolonial Independence," in *Revolutionary Constitutionalism: Law, Legitimacy, Power*, ed. Richard Albert (New York: Hart, 2020), 79–83, for an account of the Lancaster process and its ultimate demise post-independence in Kenya.

73. Mutua, *Kenya's Quest for Democracy*, 59.

74. See Mary Dudziak, *Exporting American Dreams: Thurgood Marshall's African Journey* (New York: Oxford University Press, 2008), 48–49.

75. Dudziak, *Exporting American Dreams*, 54.

76. Oginga Odinga, *Not Yet Uhuru* (Nairobi, Kenya: Heineman, 1967), quotation on 200.

77. Von Eschen, *Race Against Empire*, 166.

78. Odinga, *Not Yet Uhuru*, 296, 310–12.

79. Odinga, 177.

80. On Marshall's government-backed trip to Kenya, see Mary Dudziak, "Working toward Democracy: Thurgood Marshall and the Constitution of Kenya," *Duke Law Journal* 56 (2006): 773.

81. See Dudziak, *Exporting American Dreams*, 74–75 (quotations on 74).

82. Dudziak, 73.

83. See *Constitution of Kenya* (1963), http://kenyalaw.org/kl/fileadmin/pdfdownloads/1963_Constitution.pdf.

84. On Marshall's worries especially over the discriminatory evictions and expropriations of Kenyan Asians, see Dudziak, *Exporting American Dreams*, 121–24.

85. Odinga, *Not Yet Uhuru*, 259. See generally Odette Lienau for a powerful exploration of how twentieth-century debt practices shaped the conditions of postcolonial sovereignty, in *Rethinking Sovereign Debt: Politics, Reputation, and Legitimacy in Modern Finance* (Cambridge, MA: Harvard University Press, 2014), 1–56, 124–53.

86. Odinga, *Not Yet Uhuru*, 255.

87. Mutua, *Kenya's Quest for Democracy*, 65.

88. Odinga, *Not Yet Uhuru*, 255–56.

89. Dudziak, "Thurgood Marshall's Bill of Rights for Kenya," 308.

90. Dudziak, *Exporting American Dreams*, 154.

91. Dudziak, 170.

92. See John Munro, *The Anti-Colonial Front: The African American Freedom Struggle and Global Decolonization, 1945–1960* (New York: Cambridge University Press, 2017), 280–310, especially 287–88.

93. David Levering Lewis, *W. E. B. Du Bois: A Biography* (New York: Henry Holt, 2009). He wrote of his decision, "Today, I have reached a firm conclusion. Capitalism cannot reform itself; it is doomed to self-destruction" (p. 709).

94. Martin Duberman, *Paul Robeson* (New York: Random House, 1989), 543.

Chapter 13

1. Richard Hofstadter, "Without Feudalism," *New York Times*, February 27, 1955, BR7.

2. Hartz's book was hailed when it came out and today stands as "perhaps the most famous interpretation of American history of the second half of the twentieth

century." See *The American Liberal Tradition Reconsidered: The Contested Legacy of Louis Hartz*, ed. Mark Hulliung (Lawrence: University Press of Kansas, 2010), back cover.

3. Quotations in Hofstadter, "Without Feudalism," BR7, 34.

4. Richard Hofstadter, *The American Political Tradition: And the Men Who Made It* (New York: Alfred Knopf, Inc., 1948), xxxix.

5. Hans Kohn, *American Nationalism: An Interpretative Essay* (New York: Macmillan Co., 1957), 8. For more on the links between Kohn, Hofstadter, and Myrdal in particular, see Jared Goldstein, *Real Americans: National Identity, Violence, and the Constitution* (Lawrence: University Press of Kansas, 2021), 2, 19.

6. Louis Hartz, *The Liberal Tradition in America: An Interpretation of American Political Thought since the Revolution* (New York: Harcourt Brace Jovanovich Publishers, 1955), 9.

7. For an analogous exploration of the Cold War foundations of the American study of comparative law, see Ugo Mattei, "The Cold War and Comparative Law: A Reflection on the Politics of Intellectual Discipline," *American Journal of Comparative Law* 65 (2017): 567–607. There Mattei notes that "rather than" thinking of the conflict "as a historical time," it is "more productive to see the Cold War as a broader *regime of knowledge production*" (pp. 567–68). By this he means that the concrete geostrategic confrontation between the US and the Soviet Union had rippling effects on how generations of legal-political elites understood the world and the role of law within it. He pursues these points by focusing on how Cold War–era comparative law scholars in the US and Western Europe attempted to respond to Marxist ideas of non-comparability between socialist and bourgeois legal systems. In the process, they developed many of the taxonomic and conceptual hallmarks that are still associated with that field today.

8. See Gary Gerstle, *American Crucible: Race and Nation in the Twentieth Century* (Princeton, NJ: Princeton University Press, 2017), 252–53.

9. Senator McCarthy, speaking on "Communists in Government Service," 81st Cong., 2nd sess., *Congressional Record* 96 (February 20, 1950): S 1954; also partially quoted in Gerstle, *American Crucible*, 252.

10. Gerstle, 253.

11. See Gerstle, 253–54.

12. Gerstle, 252–54.

13. See Anton Jäger, "The Masses against the Classes; or, How to Talk About Populism Without Talking About Class," *Nonsite*, May 14, 2019, https://nonsite.org/article/the-masses-against-the-classes-or-how-to-talk-about-populism-without-talking-about-class#foot_src_30-11876.

14. For more on Hofstadter's critique of the Populist movement, see his *Age of Reform: From Bryan to FDR* (New York: Vintage Books, 1955), 3–93 (quotation on 35).

15. See Michael Rogin, *The Intellectuals and McCarthy: The Radical Specter* (Cambridge, MA: MIT Press, 1967), 91–95 (quotations on 91).

16. Rogin, 95, quotation on 100.

17. David Shannon, "Was McCarthy a Political Heir of La Follette?" *Wisconsin Magazine of History* 45 (1961): 3–9 (quotations on 6, 7).

18. David Reisman and Nathan Glazer, "The Intellectuals and the Discontented Classes—1955," in *The Radical Right*, ed. Daniel Bell (New York: Doubleday, 1963), 87–113 (quotations on 93).

19. See especially Kyong-Min Son, *The Eclipse of the Demos: The Cold War and the Crisis of Democracy before Neoliberalism* (Lawrence: University Press of Kansas, 2020), 55–58.

20. Robert Nisbet, "Many Tocquevilles," *American Scholar* 46 (1977): 59–75 (quotations on 60). For more on the role of Cold War anti-totalitarianism in the Tocqueville revival, see James Kloppenberg, "The Canvas and the Color: Tocqueville's 'Philosophical History' and Why It Matters Now," *Modern Intellectual History* 3 (2006): 498; and Michael Kammen, *Alexis de Tocqueville and Democracy in America* (Washington, DC: Library of Congress, 1998), 12.

21. Quoted in Hartz, *Liberal Tradition in America*, 11.

22. Seymour Martin Lipset, "Democracy and Working-Class Authoritarianism," *American Sociological Review* 24 (1959): 482.

23. David Shannon, "Was McCarthy a Political Heir of La Follette?" 6.

24. Lipset, "Democracy and Working-Class Authoritarianism," 492.

25. Hartz, *Liberal Tradition in America*, quotations on 11.

26. Peter Viereck, "The Revolt against the Elite—1955," in *The Radical Right*, ed. Daniel Bell (New York: Doubleday, 1963), 135–54 (quotation on 139).

27. Viereck, 139.

28. Viereck, 141.

29. Viereck, 140.

30. See William Hixson, *Search for the American Right: An Analysis of the Social Science Record, 1955–1987* (Princeton, NJ: Princeton University Press, 1992), 48.

31. Geoffrey Stone, *Perilous Times: Free Speech in Wartime* (New York: W. W. Norton, 2004), quotations on 420–21.

32. W. E. B. Du Bois, *In Battle for Peace: The Story of My 83rd Birthday* (New York: Oxford University Press, 2007), 64.

33. See Vito Marcantonio, "Closing Argument to the Jury on Behalf of the Defendant," in *I Vote My Conscience: Debates, Speeches and Writings*, ed. Annette T. Rubinstein (New York: The Vito Marcantonio Memorial, 1956), 453–76 (quotations on 467, 468). The case itself involved Ben Gold, the longtime president of the International Fur and Leather Workers Union of the United States and Canada (IFLWU). Gold would eventually be convicted, but then have that conviction overturned by the Supreme Court on grounds of government contact with jury members during the trial. Gold v. United States, 352 U.S. 985 (1957).

34. Viereck, "The Revolt against the Elite," 142.

35. Viereck, 142.

36. Samuel Stouffer, *Communism, Conformity, and Civil Liberties: A Cross-Section of the Nation Speaks Its Mind* (New York: Doubleday & Co., 1955), 58.

37. See Stouffer, 91, emphasizing how greater education was closely correlated with greater "tolera[tion]" of "nonconformists."

38. Lipset, "Democracy and Working-Class Authoritarianism," 492.

39. Quoted in Nils Gilman, *Mandarins of the Future: Modernization Theory in Cold War America* (Baltimore, MD: Johns Hopkins University Press, 2003), 55.

40. Quoted in Son, *Eclipse of the Demos*, 59.

41. See Gilman, *Mandarins of the Future*, 55–62.

42. Stouffer, *Communism, Conformity, and Civil Liberties*, 26.

43. Stouffer, 14.

44. See George Frisbee Hoar, "Has the Senate Degenerated?" *Forum* 23 (1897): 141.

45. Hoar, 141.

46. Arthur Schlesinger Jr., *The Vital Center: The Politics of Freedom* (Boston: Da Capo Press, 1949), 170.

47. James Madison, "Federalist No. 51: Method of Balancing the Departments of Government," in *The Federalist: A Commentary on the Constitution of the United States*, ed. Paul L. Ford (New York: H. Holt and Company, 1898), 342–48 (quotation on 344).

48. Schlesinger, *Vital Center*, 157–58, 158.

49. Edward Shils, *The Torment of Secrecy* (Glencoe, IL: The Free Press, 1956), 226.

50. For a discussion of US and postcolonial federalisms, see Adom Getachew, *Worldmaking after Empire: The Rise and Fall of Self-Determination* (Princeton, NJ: Princeton University Press, 2019), 110–21; and Sam Klug, "Making the Internal Colony: Black Internationalism, Development, and the Politics of Colonial Comparison in the United States, 1940–1975," 151–54 (PhD diss., Harvard University, 2020).

51. See Oginga Odinga, *Not Yet Uhuru* (Nairobi, Kenya: Heineman, 1967), 233, also quoted in Makau Mutua, *Kenya's Quest for Democracy: Taming Leviathan* (Boulder, CO: Lynne Rienner Publishers, Inc., 2008), 61.

52. Quoted in Laura Weinrib, *The Taming of Free Speech* (Cambridge, MA: Harvard University Press, 2016), 211.

53. See Norman Hapgood, *Professional Patriots* (New York: Albert & Charles Boni, 1927).

54. Richard Hofstadter, "The Pseudo-Conservative Revolt—1955," in *The Radical Right*, ed. Daniel Bell (New York: Doubleday, 1963), 66.

55. Harlan F. Stone, "The Common Law in the United States," *Harvard Law Review* 50 (1936): 25. See also Keith Whittington, "Sober Second Thoughts: Evaluating the History of Horizontal Judicial Review by the Supreme Court," *Constitutional Studies* 2 (2017): 99–101.

56. Alexander Bickel, *The Least Dangerous Branch: The Supreme Court at the Bar of Politics* (New Haven, CT: Yale University Press, 1962), 18, 16–17, 26.

57. See Neil Duxbury, *Patterns of American Jurisprudence* (New York: Oxford University Press, 1995), 238–41. The legal historian Morton Horwitz describes legal process thinking as enjoying a "virtual hegemony" on the legal academy between the late 1940s and the mid-1960s. See Morton Horwitz, *The Transformation of American Law, 1870–1960: The Crisis of Legal Orthodoxy* (New York: Oxford University Press, 1992), 269.

58. Laura Kalman, *The Strange Career of Legal Liberalism* (New Haven, CT: Yale University Press, 1996), 18–19.

59. Bickel, 80, 84; also quoted in Laura Kalman, *Legal Realism at Yale, 1927–1960* (Chapel Hill: University of North Carolina Press, 1986), 202.

60. Felix Frankfurter, quoted in Kalman, *Strange Career*, 20.

61. William Eskridge and Philip Frickey, "The Making of 'The Legal Process,'" *Harvard Law Review* 107 (1994): 2036.

62. Duxbury, *Patterns of American Jurisprudence*, 259.

63. Quoted in Kalman, *Strange Career*, 27.

64. Duxbury, *Patterns of American Jurisprudence*, 260.

65. Kalman, *Strange Career*, 27.

66. Bickel, *Least Dangerous Branch*, 26, 25.

67. Bickel, 26.

68. Viereck, "The Revolt against the Elite—1955," 142.

69. Robert Dahl, "Decision-Making in a Democracy: The Supreme Court as a National Policy-Maker," *Journal of Public Law* 6 (1957): 285.

70. For a recent critique of how mid-century figures like Bickel and Dahl misread the nature of federal constitutional design, see Pamela Karlan, "The New Countermajoritarian Difficulty," *California Law Review* 109 (2021): 2323–55.

71. Debs v. United States, 249 U.S. 211 (1919).

72. Korematsu v. United States, 323 U.S. 214 (1944).

73. Dennis v. United States, 341 U.S. 494 (1951).

74. Harisiades v. Shaughnessy, 342 U.S. 580 (1952).

75. Yates v. United States, 354 U.S. 298, 318 (1957).

76. Geoffrey Stone, *Perilous Times: Free Speech in Wartime* (New York: W. W. Norton, 2004), 415, 413.

77. See Kalman, *Strange Career*, 33–36.

78. Kalman, *Legal Realism at Yale*, 200–203 (quotation on 201).

79. J. Skelly Wright, "Professor Bickel, the Scholarly Tradition, and the Supreme Court," *Harvard Law Review* 84 (1971): 769–805 (quotations on 770).

80. Hartz, *Liberal Tradition in America*, 9.

81. For a reflective look back at the lack of state constitutional law instruction in the first half of the twentieth century by the 1950s and 1960s University of Pennsylvania Law School dean, see Jefferson B. Fordham, "On Legal Education," *Kentucky Law Journal* 54 (1966): 460–61.

82. Richard K. Neumann Jr., "Osler, Langdell, and the Atelier: Three Tales of Creation in Professional Education," *Legal Communication & Rhetoric* 10 (2013): 172.

83. Robert Gordon, "The Geologic Strata of the Law School Curriculum," *Vanderbilt Law School* 60 (2013): 350.

84. Cornell University, *Announcement of the School of Law for the Year 1887–1888* (Ithaca, NY: Cornell University, 1887), 9.

85. *Report of the Executive Committee on the Proper Organization of the Law Department of Cornell University*, October 27, 1886 (Ithaca, NY: Cornell University, 1886), 3–4.

86. Gordon, "Geologic Strata," 350.

87. Mark Graber, "Constitutional Politics and Constitutional Theory: A Misunderstood and Neglected Relationship," *Law & Social Inquiry* 27 (2002): 318.

88. Graber, 318.

89. Graber, 312.

90. Lincoln Caplan, "Anthony Lewis: What He Learned at Harvard Law School," *Missouri Law Review* 79 (2014): 875.

91. Adam Liptak, "Reporter Brought Law to Life, Elevating Supreme Court News," *New York Times*, March 26, 2013, A1, quotation on A24; also quoted in Dahlia Lithwick, "Anthony Lewis," *Missouri Law Review* 79 (2014): 971.

92. Adam Liptak, "Anthony Lewis and the First Amendment," *Missouri Law Review* 79 (2014): 863.

93. Caplan, "Anthony Lewis," 876–78.

94. Quoted in Linda Greenhouse, "The Rigorous Romantic: Anthony Lewis on the Supreme Court Beat," *Missouri Law Review* 79 (2014): 907.

95. Caplan, "Anthony Lewis," 892.

96. Quoted in Greenhouse, "The Rigorous Romantic," 913.

97. L. A. Powe Jr., "Writing the First Draft of History: Anthony Lewis as Supreme Court Correspondent," *Journal of Supreme Court History* 29 (2004): 187; also quoted in Greenhouse, "The Rigorous Romantic," 913.

98. Hartz, *Liberal Tradition in America*, quotations on 103, 11.

Chapter 14

1. See Joshua Bloom and Waldo E. Martin Jr., *Black Against Empire: The History and Politics of the Black Panther Party* (Berkeley: University of California Press, 2013), 209.

2. See Bloom and Martin, 205–8 (quotation on 208).

3. Quoted in Peggy McCarthy, "Ribicoff and Daley Head to Head," *New York Times*, August 25, 1996, CN 13, also partially quoted in Bloom and Martin, *Black Against Empire*, 209.

4. Eldridge Cleaver, "Opening Salvos from a Black/White Gun," *Black Panther*, October 5, 1968, 2.

5. Nikhil Pal Singh, *Black Is a Country: Race and the Unfinished Struggle for Democracy* (Cambridge, MA: Harvard University Press, 2004), 202.

6. Bloom and Martin, *Black Against Empire*, quotation on 264, statistics on 209.

7. See Gunnar Myrdal, *An American Dilemma: The Negro Problem and Modern Democracy*, vol. 2 (New York: Harper & Row, 1944), 1021.

8. Brandon Terry, "Requiem for a Dream: The Problem-Space of Black Power," in *To Shape a New World: Essays on the Political Philosophy of Martin Luther King, Jr.*, ed. Tommie Shelby and Brandon M. Terry (Cambridge, MA: The Belknap Press of Harvard University Press, 2018), 303.

9. Michael Dawson, *Blacks In and Out of the Left* (Cambridge, MA: Harvard University Press, 2013), 141.

10. Bloom and Martin, *Black Against Empire*, 392.

11. Quoted in Bloom and Martin, 299.

12. See Richard Rorty, *Achieving Our Country: Leftist Thought in Twentieth-Century America* (Cambridge, MA: Harvard University Press, 1998), 8, 6.

13. Martin Luther King Jr., *Where Do We Go From Here: Chaos or Community?* (Boston: Beacon Press, 1994), 119, 141.

14. Quoted in Manning Marable, *Race, Reform, and Rebellion: The Second Reconstruction in Black America, 1945–1982* (Jackson: University Press of Mississippi, 1984), 105.

15. Martin Luther King Jr., "A Time to Break Silence," in *A Testament of Hope: The Essential Writings and Speeches of Martin Luther King, Jr.*, ed. James Washington (New York: Harper Collins Publishers, 1986), 231–44 (quotations on 231, 235).

16. King, *Where Do We Go From Here*, 196–97.

17. King, "A Time to Break Silence," 231.

18. King, *Where Do We Go From Here*, 200.

19. King, 201.

20. King, "A Time to Break Silence," 239–40.

21. King, *Where Do We Go From Here*, 138.

22. King, 141, 138.

23. Quoted in Terry, "Requiem for a Dream," 291.

24. Stokely Carmichael and Charles Hamilton, *Black Power: The Politics of Liberation in America* (New York: Vintage Books, 1967), 5.

25. Carmichael and Hamilton, 5.

26. W. E. B. Du Bois, "The Colonial Groups in the Postwar World," in *Against Racism: Unpublished Essays, Papers, Addresses, 1887–1961*, ed. Herbert Aptheker (Amherst: University of Massachusetts Press, 1985), 229.

27. Quoted in Terry, "Requiem for a Dream," 309.

28. Carmichael and Hamilton, *Black Power*, xi.

29. Carmichael and Hamilton, xi.

30. Singh, *Black Is a Country*, 205.

31. Huey Newton, "To the People's Revolutionary Constitutional Convention," in *Off the Pigs! The History and Literature of the Black Panther Party*, ed. G. Louis Heath (Metuchen, NJ: Scarecrow Press, Inc., 1976), 378.

32. See generally Huey Newton, *Revolutionary Suicide* (New York: Penguin Books, 1973).

33. Terry, "Requiem for a Dream," 320.

34. This analysis draws from Brandon Terry's essential essay on the relationship between King and the Black Power movement, "Requiem for a Dream."

35. King, *Where Do We Go From Here*, 60.

36. King, 59.

37. "Black Panther Party Platform and Program," in *Off the Pigs!*, 250. Bloom and Martin note that the common presentation of the ten-point program as drafted in October 1966 is likely mistaken, with its initial writing probably in spring 1967, its mass dissemination in May 1967, and the plebiscite call included a year later. See Bloom and Martin, *Black Against Empire*, 71, 122–23, 417n8.

38. "Black Panther Party Platform and Program," 250.

39. Terry, "Requiem for a Dream," 321.

40. See Sam Klug, "'What, Then, of the Land'? Territoriality, International Law, and the Republic of New Afrika," *Journal of the History of International Law* 23 (2021): 184–205.

41. Quoted in Robert Tsai, *America's Forgotten Constitutions: Defiant Visions of Power and Community* (Cambridge, MA: Harvard University Press, 2014), 239.

42. See generally Tsai, 218–53.

43. See Klug, "'What, Then, of the Land'?," 200.

44. Vine Deloria Jr., *Custer Died for Your Sins: An Indian Manifesto* (Norman: University of Oklahoma Press, 1969), 193.

45. Klug, "'What, Then, of the Land'?," 196.

46. See Eldridge Cleaver, "Revolution in the White Mother Country and National Liberation in the Black Colony," *North American Review* 253 (1968): 13–15.

47. Cleaver, 14.

48. Bloom and Martin, *Black Against Empire*, 122–23.

49. James Boggs, *Racism and Class Struggle: Further Pages from a Black Worker's Notebook* (New York: Monthly Review Press, 1970), 173; also quoted in Michael Dawson, *Blacks In and Out of the Left* (Cambridge, MA: Harvard University Press, 2013), 160.

50. Boggs, *Racism and Class Struggle*, 173; also quoted in Dawson, *Blacks In and Out of the Left*, 160.

51. Bloom and Martin, *Black Against Empire*, 12.

52. See Bloom and Martin, 126–33.

53. For more on the TWLF and the student strikes, see Bloom and Martin, 271–87 (quotation on 272).

54. See Bloom and Martin, 292–93.

55. Singh, *Black Is a Country*, 202.

56. See Bloom and Martin, *Black Against Empire*, announcement quotation on 299, and NCCF office information on 302.

57. "Black Panther Platform and Program," 249.

58. James Mott, "The Death of an Ideology of the Constitution of the United States," *Black Panther*, August 15, 1970, 10.

59. See generally "Black Panther Party Platform," 248–51.

60. For more on the Panthers' use of constitutional rights in political debate, see generally Bridgette Baldwin, "In the Shadow of the Gun: The Black Panther Party, the Ninth Amendment, and Discourses of Self Defense," in *In Search of the Black Panther Party*, ed. Jama Lazarow and Yohuru Williams (Durham, NC: Duke University Press, 2006), 67–93, and 69 on the carrying of the Bill of Rights.

61. Baldwin, "In the Shadow of the Gun," 82.

62. The party member developed these arguments under the name "Candy" for the *Black Panther*. See Candy, "Pigs—Panthers," *Black Panther*, November 22, 1969, 15. For an excellent elaboration of this Panther essay and how such ideas actually connect to language in the constitutional text, including the Ninth Amendment, see Baldwin, "In the Shadow of the Gun," 80–87.

63. In fact, "Candy," the Panther member quoted above, may have essentially developed a constitutional right to resistance, but nonetheless argued that Panther politics and commitments were nonviolent. "Candy" draws a "sharp contrast" between BPP efforts at feeding and caring for their communities and police methods of "terror, intimidation, brutality, and murder." Candy, "Pigs—Panthers," 15.

64. Afeni Shakur, "We Will Have a New Constitution and Liberty or Revolutionary Suicide and Liberation," *Black Panther*, August 15, 1970, 11.

65. See Marc Stein, *City of Sisterly and Brotherly Love: Lesbian and Gay Philadelphia, 1945–1972* (Philadelphia: Temple University Press, 2004), 335.

66. Panther chief of staff David Hilliard pointedly explained that Philadelphia was chosen for the convention because "it was 'the same place where the pigs had theirs.'" Quoted in Baldwin, "In the Shadow of the Gun," 84.

67. "Not to Believe in a New World after Philadelphia Is a Dereliction of the Human Spirit," *Black Panther*, September 26, 1970, 19–20 (quotation on 19); also quoted in George Katsiaficas, "Organization and Movement: The Case of the Black

Panther Party and the Revolutionary People's Constitutional Convention of 1970,"
in *Liberation, Imagination, and the Black Panther Party*, ed. Kathleen Cleaver and
George Katsiaficas (New York: Routledge, 2001), 147.

68. Quoted in Ray Holton, "Mayor Rizzo Is Entombed in Cold Print," *Washington Post*, October 26, 1977, https://www.washingtonpost.com/archive/politics
/1977/10/26/mayor-rizzo-is-entombed-in-cold-print/4791d7b6-cc02-4188-994a
-0f025d051b19/.

69. See Timothy J. Lombardo, *Blue-Collar Conservatism: Frank Rizzo's Philadelphia and Populist Politics* (Philadelphia: University of Pennsylvania Press, 2018), 143.

70. See Katsiaficas, "Organization and Movement," 146.

71. Trevor Wyatt Moore, "A Rumbling in Babylon: Panthers Host a Parley,"
Christian Century, October 28, 1970, 1296.

72. "Revolutionary Peoples' Constitutional Convention, Philadelphia Workshop Reports," in *Liberation, Imagination, and the Black Panther Party*, ed. Kathleen
Cleaver and George Katsiaficas (New York: Routledge, 2001), 289–300.

73. Katsiaficas, "Organization and Movement," 153–54 (quotation in 153).

74. See generally "Black Panther Party Platform," 248–51.

75. Katsiaficas, "Organization and Movement," 151.

76. See "Revolutionary Peoples' Constitutional Convention, Philadelphia Workshop Reports," 289, 297. Expressing a politics of both constitutional fidelity and
rupture, the Workshop on Internationalism strikingly referred to such commitments as grounding a new, genuinely emancipatory "international bill of rights"
(p. 289).

77. "Revolutionary Peoples' Constitutional Convention," 290.

78. "Revolutionary Peoples' Constitutional Convention," 292, 293.

79. "The People and the People Alone Were the Motive Force in the Making of
History of the People's Revolutionary Constitutional Convention Plenary Session!"
Black Panther, September 12, 1970, 3.

80. "Revolutionary Peoples' Constitutional Convention, Philadelphia Workshop
Reports," 297.

81. "Black Panther Party Platform," 247.

82. "The People and the People Alone," 3.

83. "Revolutionary Peoples' Constitutional Convention," 298.

84. See "Revolutionary Peoples' Constitutional Convention," 295–97.

85. "The People and the People Alone," 3.

86. "Revolutionary Peoples' Constitutional Convention," 299.

87. The reports include language rejecting the US's right to "nationhood" and
asserting protections of "all people to travel," but do not engage more systematically
with the question of borders and migration. "Revolutionary Peoples' Constitutional
Convention," 289–90.

88. Quoted in "Revolutionary Peoples' Constitutional Convention," 294.

89. Quotations in "Revolutionary Peoples' Constitutional Convention," 292, 293.

90. Katsiaficas, "Organization and Movement," 154.

91. This subsection's analysis of BPP decline draws heavily from Bloom and Martin, *Black Against Empire*, especially 346–49, 364–71(quotation on 346), as well
as from Katsiaficas's specific discussion of the fallout of the Revolutionary People's
Constitutional Convention, "Organization and Movement," 154–55.

92. Bloom and Martin, *Black Against Empire*, 347–48.

93. Bloom and Martin, 348.

94. Bloom and Martin, 366.

95. Katsiaficas, "Organization and Movement," 153–54 (quotation on 153).

96. See Bloom and Martin, *Black Against Empire*, 237–46.

97. Bloom and Martin, 213–14.

98. See Bloom and Martin, 358–71.

99. See Bloom and Martin, 379–81.

100. Alice Echols, *Daring to Be Bad: Radical Feminism in America, 1967–1975* (Minneapolis: University of Minnesota Press, 1989), 223.

101. "Revolutionary Peoples' Constitutional Convention, Philadelphia Workshop Reports," 292.

102. For more on the tensions at the Convention between male Panther members and feminist activists, see Echols, *Daring to Be Bad*, 222–23, and Stein, *City of Sisterly and Brotherly Loves*, 334–39.

103. See Marie Berry, Yolande Bouka, and Marilyn Muthoni Kamuru, "Implementing Inclusion: Gender Quotas, Inequality, and Backlash in Kenya," *Politics and Gender* 17 (2021): 640–64 (statistics on 641), for a thoughtful assessment of the strengths and limitations of legislative gender quotas. In particular, the authors explore the difficulties of translating, without additional structural economic and political alterations, gains for "individual women" into "increases in women's power more broadly" (p. 642).

104. See James Boggs and Grace Lee Boggs, "The City Is the Black Man's Land (1966)," in *Pages from a Black Radical's Notebook: A James Boggs Reader*, ed. Stephen Ward (Detroit, MI: Wayne State University Press, 2011), 162–70, quotations on 162, 168.

105. Quoted in Makani Themba, "The Most Radical City on the Planet," *Boston Review*, April 29, 2019, https://bostonreview.net/articles/makani-themba-most-radical-city-planet/.

106. Boggs and Boggs, "City Is the Black Man's Land," quotations on 168.

107. Boggs and Boggs, 168.

108. See Ryan Zickgraf, "The Jackson Water Crisis is a Disaster Created by Austerity," *Jacobin*, September 9, 2022, https://jacobin.com/2022/09/jackson-water-crisis-austerity-climate-change-flood-infrastructure.

109. Terry, "Requiem for a Dream," 306.

110. Quoted in Terry, 306.

111. See Jefferson Cowie, *Stayin' Alive: The 1970s and the Last Days of the Working Class* (New York: The New Press, 2010), quotations on 60.

112. Quoted in Terry, "Requiem for a Dream," 306.

113. See Bloom and Martin, *Black Against Empire*, 380–86, 354–55 quotation on 354.

114. For more on the two post-1970 directions in the party, see Terry, "Requiem for a Dream," 413n166.

115. Singh, *Black Is a Country*, 204.

116. See Jefferson Cowie, *The Great Exception: The New Deal and the Limits of American Politics* (Princeton, NJ: Princeton University Press, 2016), 179–83 (quotation on 182).

117. Karen Heller, "He Once Told Philadelphia to 'Vote White.' Now the Protests Have Brought His Statue Down," *Washington Post*, June 4, 2020, https://www.washingtonpost.com/lifestyle/style/statue-frank-rizzo-philadelphia-confederate-protests/2020/06/03/f948ce5c-a5a6-11ea-bb20-ebf0921f3bbd_story.html.

118. The latter phrase was invoked by Nixon in a November 1969 televised address: Richard Nixon, "Address to the Nation on the War in Vietnam, November 3, 1969," in *Public Papers of the Presidents of the United States: Richard Nixon, 1969* (Washington, DC: United States Government Printing Office, 1971), 901–9 (quotation on 909).

Chapter 15

1. See generally Garrett Graff, *Watergate: A New History* (New York: Simon & Schuster, 2022).

2. Philip Jenkins, *Decade of Nightmares: The End of the Sixties and the Making of Eighties America* (New York: Oxford University Press, 2006), 48–54.

3. Quoted in Jenkins, 49, 48.

4. See generally Felicia Kornbluh, *The Battle for Welfare Rights: Politics and Poverty in Modern America* (Philadelphia: University of Pennsylvania Press, 2007), quotation on 2.

5. See especially Premilla Nadasen, *Welfare Warriors: The Welfare Rights Movement in the United States* (New York: Routledge, 2005), 136.

6. See Kornbluh, *Battle for Welfare Rights*, 154–56, 2–3, and also generally Nadasen, *Welfare Warriors*.

7. See generally Alice Echol's essential *Daring to Be Bad: Radical Feminism in America, 1967-1975*, 2nd ed. (Minneapolis: University of Minnesota Press, 2019) for an account of the variety of revolutionary feminist orientations during the era that sought to comprehensively overcome women's condition as a subordinated sex-class.

8. Quoted in Cynthia Bowman, "Recovering Socialism for Feminist Legal Theory in the 21st Century," *Connecticut Law Review* 49 (2016): 126. See Bowman's terrific article for an overview of feminist efforts during the 1970s to incorporate but also to critique socialist politics.

9. Bowman, "Recovering Socialism for Feminist Legal Theory," 127.

10. For more on the influence of the statement, see Keeanga-Yamahtta Taylor, "Introduction," in *How We Get Free: Black Feminism and the Combahee River Collective*, ed. Keeanga-Yamahtta Taylor (Chicago: Haymarket Books, 2017), 1–14.

11. "Combahee River Collective Statement," in Taylor, *How We Get Free*, 15–27, quotation on 19.

12. Kornbluh, *Battle for Welfare Rights*, quotations on 126, 127.

13. In discussing their political agenda, the CRC write, "We might . . . become involved in workplace organizing at a factory that employs Third World women or picket a hospital that is cutting back on already inadequate health care to a Third World community, or set up a rape crisis center in a Black neighborhood. Organizing around welfare and daycare concerns might also be a focus. . . . Issues and projects the collective members have actually worked on are sterilization abuse, abortion rights, battered women, rape, and health care." "Combahee River Collective Statement," in Taylor, *How We Get Free*, 26.

14. Nadasen, *Welfare Warriors*, 235.

15. See Goldberg v. Kelly, 397 U.S. 254 (1970).

16. Nadasen, *Welfare Warriors*, 198.

17. See generally Deborah Dinner, *The Sex Equality Dilemma: Work, Family, and Legal Change in Neoliberal America* (New York: Cambridge University Press, forthcoming 2024), for a terrific exploration of the 1970s feminist efforts to reconceive economic and familial relations, quotation on 98. This discussion is drawn from her analysis, especially 98–101.

18. Dinner, 99.

19. Dinner, 97.

20. Dinner, 99.

21. Catherine Gourley, *Ms. and the Material Girls: Perceptions of Women from the 1970s through the 1990s* (Minneapolis, MN: Twenty-First Century Books, 2008), 7, 9; Judy Klemesrud, "It Was a Great Day for Women on the March," *New York Times*, August 30, 1970, 128.

22. Serena Mayeri, *Reasoning from Race: Feminism, Law, and the Civil Rights Revolution* (Cambridge, MA: Harvard University Press, 2011), 44.

23. Quotations in Mayeri, 44.

24. "Trail of Broken Treaties Twenty-Point Position Paper," October 1972, http://www.aimovement.org/archives/index.html.

25. "Trail of Broken Treaties."

26. Kevin Bruyneel, *The Third Space of Sovereignty: The Postcolonial Politics of U.S.–Indigenous Relations* (Minneapolis: University of Minnesota Press, 2007), 164.

27. Bruyneel, 158.

28. Todd Gitlin, *The Sixties: Years of Hope, Days of Rage* (New York: Bantam Books, 1987), 436.

29. Gitlin, quotations on 437.

30. Gitlin, 437.

31. Gitlin, quotations on 437, 434.

32. Years later, during the 2004 presidential election, Gitlin would implore antiwar activists opposed to the US invasion of Iraq to focus on electing the Democratic presidential candidate, John Kerry. To those doubtful that the legal-political system could accommodate meaningful change, including around war-making, he declared, "That state can be defeated, and to say that we don't have the luxury of waiting to November 2 [election day] is to say we don't have the luxury of the U.S. Constitution. I beg to differ. We have the luxury of the U.S. Constitution." Quoted in "Naomi Klein v. Todd Gitlin: A Debate on Resistance and the RNC," *Democracy Now!* August 26, 2004, https://www.democracynow.org/2004/8/26/naomi_klein_vs_todd_gitlin_a.

33. See John Herbert, "Revisiting Arthur Schlesinger's *The Imperial Presidency*: Richard Nixon, George W. Bush, and Executive Power," in *Watergate Remembered: The Legacy for American Politics*, ed. Michael Genovese and Iwan W. Morgan (New York: Palgrave Macmillan, 2012), 29.

34. See generally Arthur Schlesinger, *The Imperial Presidency* (New York: Popular Library, 1974), quotations on 13, 9, 25.

35. Schlesinger, 397.

36. Schlesinger, 397.

37. Francis Clines, "Barbara Jordan Dies at 59; Her Voice Stirred the Nation," *New York Times*, January 18, 1996, 1.

38. Clines, 1.

39. Barbara Jordan, "Remarks on Impeachment During Watergate," University of Virginia, Miller Center, July 24, 1974, https://millercenter.org/the-presidency /impeachment/my-faith-constitution-whole-it-complete-it-total.

40. Jordan.

41. See David Fontana's excellent analysis of the new class of law professor that dominated the American legal academy beginning in the 1970s, "The Rise and Fall of Comparative Constitutional Law in the Postwar Era," *Yale Journal of International Law* 36 (2011): 25.

42. Quoted in Fontana, 26.

43. See generally Fontana, 23–26 (quotation on 26).

44. Quoted in Christopher Cappozzola, "'It Makes You Want to Believe in the Country': Celebrating the Bicentennial in an Age of Limits," in *America in the Seventies*, ed. Beth Bailey and David Farber (Lawrence: University Press of Kansas, 2004): 34.

45. Cappozzola, 34.

46. See Simon Gilhooley, *The Antebellum Origins of the Modern Constitution, Slavery and the Spirit of the American Founding* (New York: Cambridge University Press, 2020), 13–15.

47. John Kifner, "2 Counterrallies in Philadelphia," *New York Times*, July 5, 1976, 14.

48. Cappozzola, "'It Makes You Want to Believe in the Country,'" 39–44 (quotation on 44).

49. "No Sale," *Nation*, January 10, 1976, 5.

50. "No Sale," 5.

51. Edwin Meese, "The Great Debate: Speech Before the Federalist Society Lawyers Division," transcript of speech delivered in Washington, DC, November 15, 1985, https://fedsoc.org/commentary/publications/the-great-debate-attorney -general-ed-meese-iii-november-15-1985.

52. Calvin TerBeek, "'Clocks Must Always Be Turned Back': Brown v. Board of Education and the Racial Origins of Constitutional Originalism," *American Political Science Review* 115 (2021): 826.

53. See especially Jamal Greene, "Selling Originalism," *Georgetown Law Journal* 97 (2009): 657–721; and generally Steven Teles, *The Rise of the Conservative Legal Movement: The Battle for Control of the Law* (Princeton, NJ: Princeton University Press, 2008), 135–80.

54. Teles, *Rise of the Conservative Legal Movement*, 151.

55. Jamal Greene is particularly thoughtful on how the rise of originalism is best understood as a political rather than a primarily academic development. See Greene, "Selling Originalism."

56. On the bending, by conservative judges in particular, of interpretative method to fit desired political outcomes, see Neil Buchanan and Michael Dorf, "A Tale of Two Formalisms: How Law and Economics Mirrors Originalism and Textualism," *Cornell Law Review* 106 (2021): 591–676.

57. Indeed, in the twenty-first century, it has become increasingly common for both center-left scholars and judges to lay out originalist defenses for liberal

accounts of rights, race-conscious remedies, and economic regulation, among other things. This development responds to a liberal sense that such arguments are on firmer ground given how today's conservative federal judiciary is replete with ostensibly originalist jurists. But it also speaks to the openness of the historical record and the extent to which a return to that record can provide support for various competing ideological positions. See for example Mark Joseph Stern, "Hear Ketanji Brown Jackson Use Progressive Originalism to Refute Alabama's Attack on the Voting Rights Act," *Slate*, October 4, 2022, https://slate.com/news-and-politics/2022 /10/ketanji-brown-jackson-voting-rights-originalism.html; and see generally Akhil Amar, *America's Constitution: A Biography* (New York: Random House, 2005) and "Rethinking Originalism," *Slate*, September 21, 2005, https://slate.com/news-and -politics/2005/09/original-intent-for-liberals.html.

58. TerBeek, "'Clocks Must Always Be Turned Back,'" 826.

59. See Bruce Ackerman, "The Storrs Lectures: Discovering the Constitution," *Yale Law Journal* 93 (1984): 1013–72, for an early elaboration of his idea of "constitutional moments"—with US history actually composed of three distinct constitutional republics under a single formal document. His foundational *We the People: Foundations*, vol. 1 (Cambridge, MA: The Belknap Press of Harvard University Press, 1991) would later develop this argument in depth. And in the 2000s, see also Reva Siegel, "She the People: The Nineteenth Amendment, Sex Equality, Federalism, and the Family," *Harvard Law Review* 115 (2002): 947–1046, for a seminal reading of how the Nineteenth Amendment's ratification should be understood as marking a profound shift in the constitutional meaning of women's citizenship, including by breaking from "traditional conceptions of the family" (p. 947), and thus reshaping Fourteenth Amendment equality jurisprudence as well.

60. Since the 2010s, rolling racial justice protests and a more searching scrutiny of the historical past have helped to give some popular salience to such ideas. With respect to current historical and legal scholarship, the work that engages with these themes includes Dorothy Roberts, "Foreword: Abolition Constitutionalism," *Harvard Law Review* 133 (2019): 1–122, especially 54–71; Eric Foner, *Second Founding: How the Civil War and Reconstruction Remade the Constitution* (New York: W. W. Norton, 2019); and Noah Feldman's *The Broken Constitution: Lincoln, Slavery, and the Refounding of America* (New York: Macmillan, 2021).

61. For more on how in recent decades both living constitutionalism and originalism buttressed Cold War faith in judicial power and existing structural arrangements, see David Singh Grewal and Jedediah Purdy, "The Original Theory of Constitutionalism," *Yale Law Journal* 127 (2018): 664–705 (reviewing Richard Tuck, *The Sleeping Sovereign: The Invention of Modern Democracy* [2016]).

62. In that same speech quoted earlier before the Federalist Society, Meese remarked, "If we want a change in our Constitution or in our laws we must seek it through the formal mechanisms presented in that organizing document of our government." Since the flaws of the process were no longer part of the broader constitutional discussion, he could simply focus on the democratic weaknesses of court-led interpretive change without being compelled to answer for the broader constitutional dysfunctions. Meese, "The Great Debate."

63. James Rubin, "Burger's Bicentennial Commission Troubled from Start," *AP News*, June 23, 1986, https://apnews.com/article/82073cc727d4c628bfe910c2161589f0.

64. Rubin.

65. *Celebrating the Constitution: A Bicentennial Retrospective* (Washington, DC: The National Archives and Records Administration, 1988), 25, 26.

66. William Stevens, "After 2 Centuries, Great Day for Constitution," *New York Times*, September 18, 1987.

67. William Stevens, "Philadelphia Gears Up for Bicentennial Party," *New York Times*, September 16, 1987.

68. Stevens, "After 2 Centuries."

69. Stevens.

70. *Celebrating the Constitution*, 44.

71. See Sanford Levinson, *Constitutional Faith* (Princeton, NJ: Princeton University Press, 1988), 13, 180.

72. Levinson, 9.

73. See Meese, "The Great Debate."

74. Thurgood Marshall, "Reflections on the Bicentennial of the United States Constitution," *Harvard Law Review* 101 (1987): 1–5 (quotations on 2, 5).

75. Mary Dudziak, *Exporting American Dreams: Thurgood Marshall's African Journey* (New York: Oxford University Press, 2008), 73.

76. Gitlin, *The Sixties*, 437.

77. The *Journal of American History*'s special volume for the bicentennial offered a striking academic encapsulation of where left-liberal scholarship was heading, in keeping with much of Thurgood Marshall's instincts. See generally "The Constitution and American Life: A Special issue," *Journal of American History* 74 (1987): 656–1178. The issue included essays from a range of historians and legal scholars on the Constitution's interplay with everything from race, gender, and labor to foreign affairs. Articulating a percolating sentiment in the essays, the historian Hendrik Hartog called for an approach to constitutional history that engaged with "the moral complexity of American constitutional experience" and that took seriously "the changing aspirations of diverse groups within the society." In this way, constitutional analysis could "interpret . . . a society that has been and remains structured by divisions of wealth, gender, and race, yet, at the same time, has been and remains committed to values of democracy, fairness, and respect." See Hendrik Hartog, "The Constitution of Aspiration and 'The Rights that Belong to Us All,'" *Journal of American History* 74 (1987): 1013–34 (quotations on 1034).

78. See Mark Tushnet, "'Our Perfect Constitution' Revisited," in *Terrorism, the Laws of War, and the Constitution: Debating the Enemy Combatant Cases*, ed. Peter Berkowitz (Stanford, CA: Hoover Institute Press, 2005), 131–58 (quotation 132).

79. See David Waldstreicher and Jeffrey Pasley, "*Hamilton* as Founders Chic: A Neo-Federalist, Antislavery Usable Past?" in *Historians on Hamilton: How a Blockbuster Musical is Restaging America's Past*, ed. Renee Romano and Claire Bond Potter (Newark, NJ: Rutgers University Press, 2018), 137–66, for an incisive account of the 1990s and 2000s phenomenon of "Founders Chic" and its brand of "literary flag waving" (p. 141).

80. On the historical evasion involved in presenting the Euro-Protestant settler Hamilton as similarly situated to today's non-white immigrant communities and as a proto-abolitionist, see William Hogeland's excellent essay, "From Ron Chernow's

Alexander Hamilton to Hamilton: An American Musical," in *Historians on Hamilton*, 17–41. See also Waldstreicher and Pasley, "*Hamilton* as Founders Chic," 156–60.

Conclusion

1. See generally David Pozen and Adam Samaha, "Anti-Modalities," *Michigan Law Review* 119 (2021): 729–96, for more on how the highly specialized language of constitutional lawyering produces disempowering popular effects, especially by treating as non-constitutional the most common forms of political argument.

2. See Scott Cummings, "Movement Lawyering," *University of Illinois Law Review* (2017): 1645–732; and Amna Akbar, Sameer Ashar, and Jocelyn Simonson, "Movement Law," *Stanford Law Review* 73 (2021): 821–84 for powerful accounts of precisely how lawyers and legal scholars can participate in such movement building.

3. See Joseph Fishkin and William Forbath, *The Anti-Oligarchy Constitution: Reconstructing the Economic Foundations of American Democracy* (Cambridge, MA: Harvard University Press, 2022), 419–87, for a detailed exploration of how to constitutionalize a more democratic political economy outside the direction of the courts.

4. Indeed, one can read the Democratic Socialists of America's platform, from 2021, as a conscious effort to update the 1912 SPA legal-political agenda for the present day. See DSA Political Platform, https://www.dsausa.org/dsa-political -platform-from-2021-convention/.

5. See Kate Andrias and Benjamin Sachs, "Constructing Countervailing Power: Law and Organizing in an Era of Political Inequality," *Yale Law Journal* 130 (2021): 546–635 for an excellent recent discussion of labor law as a mechanism for building worker power and organizing capacity.

6. For contemporary scholarship in international law engaging with the relationship between migration and anti-colonial transformation, see Chantal Thomas, "What Does the Emerging International Law of Migration Mean for Sovereignty?" *Melbourne Journal of International Law* 14 (2013): 392–450; and E. Tendayi Achiume, "Migration as Decolonization," *Stanford Law Review* 71 (2019): 1509–74.

7. The Red Nation, *The Red Deal: Indigenous Action to Save Our Earth* (Brooklyn, NY: Common Notions, 2021), 37.

8. For more on how today's Indigenous activism connects to a long tradition of Indigenous internationalism, see Nick Estes's essential *Our History Is the Future: Standing Rock versus the Dakota Access Pipeline and the Long Tradition of Indigenous Resistance* (New York: Verson, 2019), 201–45.

9. Ed Pilkington, "Inside Steve Bannon's 'Disturbing' Quest to Radically Rewrite the US Constitution," *Guardian*, October 19, 2022, https://www.theguardian.com /us-news/2022/oct/19/steve-bannon-us-constitution-tea-party-republican-state -legislatures.

10. Jamiles Lartey, "Conservatives Call for Constitutional Intervention Last Seen 230 Years Ago," *Guardian*, August 11, 2018, https://www.theguardian.com/us-news /2018/aug/11/conservatives-call-for-constitutional-convention-alec.

11. See Adrian Vermuele, "Beyond Originalism," *Atlantic Monthly*, March 31, 2020, https://www.theatlantic.com/ideas/archive/2020/03/common-good

-constitutionalism/609037/; and James Chappel, "Nudging Toward Theocracy: Adrian Vermuele's War on Liberalism," *Dissent*, Spring 2020, https://www.dissentmagazine.org/article/nudging-towards-theocracy.

12. See generally the Convention of States website, https://conventionofstates.com/.

13. See generally George William Van Cleve, *Making a New American Constitution* (Denver, CO: Maroon Bells Press, 2020); and Jedediah Purdy, *Two Cheers for Politics: Why Democracy Is Flawed, Frightening—and Our Best Hope* (New York: Basic Books, 2022), for contemporary defenses of a "popular convention" that avoids the Article V process, as well as more on the links between such an approach and the actual practices of the founders.

14. See Josh Chafetz and David Pozen, "How Constitutional Norms Break Down," *UCLA Law Review* 65 (2018): 1430–59 for an incisive account of how norms "decompose—dynamically interpreted and applied in ways that are held out as compliant but end up limiting their capacity to constrain the conduct of government officials" (p. 1430).

15. See especially Bruce Ackerman's *We the People: Foundations*, vol. 1 (Cambridge, MA: The Belknap Press of Harvard University Press, 1991) and *We the People: Transformations*, vol. 2 (Cambridge, MA: The Belknap Press of Harvard University Press, 1998). See also David Pozen and Thomas Schmidt, "The Puzzles and Possibilities of Article V," *Columbia Law Review* 121 (2021): 2317–96.

INDEX